THE BLACKWELL HANDBOOK OF PERSONNEL SELECTION

Handbooks in Management

Donald L. Sexton and Hans Landström
The Blackwell Handbook of Entrepreneurship

Edwin A. Locke
The Blackwell Handbook of Principles of Organizational Behavior

Martin J. Gannon and Karen L. Newman
The Blackwell Handbook of Cross-Cultural Management

Michael A. Hitt, R. Edward Freeman and Jeffrey S. Harrison
The Blackwell Handbook of Strategic Management

Mark Easterby-Smith and Marjorie A. Lyles
The Blackwell Handbook of Organizational Learning and Knowledge Management

Henry W. Lane, Martha L. Maznevski, Mark Mendenhall, and Jeanne McNett
The Blackwell Handbook of Global Management

Arne Evers, Neil Anderson, and Olga Voskuijl
The Blackwell Handbook of Personnel Selection

THE BLACKWELL HANDBOOK OF PERSONNEL SELECTION

Edited by

ARNE EVERS, NEIL ANDERSON, AND OLGA VOSKUIJL

Blackwell Publishing

BLACKWELL PUBLISHING
350 Main Street, Malden, MA 02148-5020, USA
9600 Garsington Road, Oxford OX4 2DQ, UK
550 Swanston Street, Carlton, Victoria 3053, Australia

First published 2005 by Blackwell Publishing Ltd

1 2005

Library of Congress Cataloging-in-Publication Data

The Blackwell handbook of personnel selection / edited by Arne Evers, Neil Anderson,
and Olga Voskuijl.
     p.   cm. — (Handbooks in management)
   Includes bibliographical references and index.
   ISBN-13: 978–1–4051–1702–9 (hard cover : alk. paper)
   ISBN-10: 1–4051–1702–8 (hard cover : alk. paper)
   1. Employee selection.   2. Employee screening.   3. Employment tests.   4. Employees—
Recruiting.   I. Evers, Arne.   II. Anderson, Neil, 1961–   III. Voskuijl, Olga.   IV.
Series.
   HF5549.5.S38B55   2005
   658.3′112—dc22

                                                                      2005006582

A catalogue record for this title is available from the British Library.

Set in 10 on 12 pt Baskerville
by SNP Best-set Typesetter Ltd, Hong Kong
Printed and bound in the United Kingdom
by TJ International, Padstow, Cornwall

The publisher's policy is to use permanent paper from mills that operate a sustainable forestry
policy, and which has been manufactured from pulp processed using acid-free and elementary
chlorine-free practices. Furthermore, the publisher ensures that the text paper and cover board
used have met acceptable environmental accreditation standards.

For further information on
Blackwell Publishing, visit our website:
www.blackwellpublishing.com

Contents

Contributors

Natalie J. Allen

Department of Psychology, The University of Western Ontario, London, Ontario, CANADA N6A 5C2

E-mail: nallen@uwo.ca

Neil Anderson

Department of Work and Organizational Psychology, University of Amsterdam, Roetersstraat 15, 1018 WB Amsterdam, THE NETHERLANDS

E-mail: N.R.Anderson@uva.nl

Dave Bartram

SHL Group plc, The Pavilion, 1 Atwell Place, Thames Ditton, Surrey KT7 0NE, UNITED KINGDOM

E-mail: dave.Bartram@shlgroup.com

Walter C. Borman

Personnel Decisions Research Institutes, Inc., 100 South Ashley Drive, Suite 375, Tampa FL 33602, USA

E-mail: wally.borman@pdri.com

Marise Ph. Born

Erasmus Universiteit Rotterdam, FSW, Instituut Psychologie, Postbus 1738 (kamer W J505), 3000 DR Rotterdam, THE NETHERLANDS

E-mail: born@fsw.eur.nl

Paula M. Caligiuri

Human Resource Management Department, Rutgers University, 94 Rockafeller Road, 200B Levin Building, Piscataway, New Jersey 08854, USA

Email: caligiuri@smlr.rutgers.edu

David Chan

Department of Social Work and Psychology, National University of Singapore, 10 Kent Ridge Crescent, Singapore 119260, REPUBLIC OF SINGAPORE

E-mail: davidchan@nus.edu.sg

Nicole Cunningham-Snell
Shell Centre, PSSL-LD, York Road, London SE1 7NA, UNITED KINGDOM
E-mail: N.Cunningham-Snell@shell-com

Filip de Fruyt
Ghent University, Henri Dunantlaan 2, Gent 9000, BELGIUM
E-mail: filip.defruyt@rug.ac.be

Irene E. de Pater
Department of Work and Organizational Psychology, University of Amsterdam, Roetersstraat 15, 1018 WB Amsterdam, THE NETHERLANDS
E-mail: I.E.dePater@uva.nl

Stephan Dilchert
University of Minnesota, Department of Psychology, 75 E River Road, Minneapolis MN 55455-0344, USA
E-mail: Dilc0002@umn.edu

Robert L. Dipboye
Rice University, PO Box 1892, Houston TX 77251-1892, USA
E-mail: dipboye@rice.edu

Arne Evers
Department of Work and Organizational Psychology, University of Amsterdam, Roetersstraat 15, 1018 WB Amsterdam, THE NETHERLANDS
E-mail: a.v.a.m.evers@uva.nl

Sacha Geerlings
Department of Work and Organizational Psychology, University of Amsterdam, Roetersstraat 15, 1018 WB Amsterdam, THE NETHERLANDS
E-mail: sacha.geerlings@xs4all.nl

Anna L. Imus
Department of Psychology, 340C Psychology Building, Michigan State University, East Lansing MI 48824-1116, USA
E-mail: schne248@msu.edu

Ute-Christine Klehe
Psychologisches Institut, Arbeits- und Organisationspsychologie, Universität Zürich, Rämistrasse 62, CH-8001 Zürich, SWITZERLAND
E-mail: u.klehe@psychologie.unizh.ch

Filip Lievens
Department of Personnel Management and Work and Organizational Psychology, Ghent University, Henri Dunantlaan 2, 9000 Ghent, BELGIUM
E-mail: filip.lievens@ugent.be

Deniz S. Ones

University of Minnesota, N218 Elliott Hall, 75 E River Road, Minneapolis MN 55455-0344, USA
E-mail: Deniz.S.Ones-1@tc.umn.edu

Lisa M. Penney

Department of Psychology, 126 Heyne Building, University of Houston, Houston TX 77204-5022, USA
E-mail: lisa.penney@mail.uh.edu

Robert E. Ployhart

Department of Management, Moore School of Business, University of South Carolina, Columbia SC 29208, USA
E-mail: ployhart@moore.sc.edu

Robert A. Roe

Universiteit Maastricht, PO Box 616, 6200 MD Maastricht, THE NETHERLANDS
E-mail: r.roe@os.unimaas.nl

Ann Marie Ryan

Department of Psychology, 333 Psychology Building, Michigan State University, East Lansing MI 48824-1116, USA
E-mail: ryanan@msu.edu

Alan M. Saks

Division of Management, Joseph L. Rotman School of Management, and Centre for Industrial Relations, University of Toronto, 105 St. George Street, Toronto, Ontario, CANADA M5S 3E6
E-mail: saks@utsc.utoronto.ca

Jesús F. Salgado

Departamento de Psicología Social, Universidad de Santiago de Compostela, 15782 Santiago de Compostela, SPAIN
E-mail: psjesal@usc.es

Neal Schmitt

Department of Psychology, Michigan State University, East Lansing MI 48824-1116, USA
E-mail: schmitt@msu.edu

Benjamin Schneider

Department of Psychology, University of Maryland, College Park MD 20742, USA
E-mail: ben@psyc.umd.edu

Dora Scholarios

Dept. of Human Resource Management, University of Strathclyde, 50 Richmond St. Glasgow G1 1XU, UNITED KINGDOM
E-mail: d.scholarios@strath.ac.uk

Jan te Nijenhuis
Open Universiteit, Postbus 2960, 6401 DL Heerlen, THE NETHERLANDS
E-mail: Jan.teNijenhuis@ou.nl

George C. Thornton III
Colorado State University, Department of Psychology, Fort Collins, Collorado 80523-52323, USA
E-mail: thornton@lamar.colostate.edu

Henk van der Flier
Vrije Universiteit, Van der Boechorststraat 1, 1081 BT Amsterdam, THE NETHERLANDS
E-mail: h.van.der.flier@psy.vu.nl

Annelies E. M. van Vianen
Department of Work and Organizational Psychology, University of Amsterdam, Roetersstraat 15, 1018 WB Amsterdam, THE NETHERLANDS
E-mail: A.E.M.vanVianen@uva.nl

Chockalingam Viswesvaran
Dep. of Psychology, Florida International University, University Park, Miami FL 33199, USA
E-mail: Vish@fiu.edu

Olga F. Voskuijl
Department of Work and Organizational Psychology, University of Amsterdam, Roetersstraat 15, 1018 WB Amsterdam, THE NETHERLANDS
E-mail: Ovoskuijl@fmg.uva.nl

Michael A. West
University of Aston, Birmingham B4 7ET, UNITED KINGDOM
E-mail: m.a.west@aston.ac.uk

David Wigfield
Shell Centre, PSSL-LD, York Road, London SE1 7NA, UNITED KINGDOM
E-mail: David.wigfield@shell.com

Charles Woodruffe
19 Dunraven Street, London W1Y 4JR, UNITED KINGDOM
E-mail: charles.woodruffe@humanassets.co.uk

Notes on the Editors

Arne Evers is Associate Professor in Work and Organizational Psychology at the University of Amsterdam. His research interests include personnel selection, discrimination in selection, test and scale construction, organizational diagnosis, and work stress. He has published chapters or articles on these issues in *Journal of Organizational Behavior*, *International Journal of Testing*, *European Journal of Psychological Assessment*, *Journal of Occupational and Organizational Psychology*, *Educational Psychology*, and the *Handbook of Work and Organizational Psychology* (Psychology Press, UK). Arne is a member of the Committee on Testing of the Dutch Association of Psychologists (COTAN) and of the standing Committee on Tests and Testing of the European Federation of Psychological Associations.

Neil Anderson is Professor of Organizational Psychology at the University of Amsterdam. His research interests include recruitment and selection, organizational and work group socialization, innovation at work, and organizational climate. Neil has relevant ongoing research projects, either collaboratively or alone, into interviewer and applicant decision making in assessment interviews, the structure and properties of popular "Big Five" measures of personality, and the practitioner–researcher divide in Work and Organizational Psychology. He has co-authored and edited a number of books, including the *Handbook of Industrial, Work and Organizational Psychology* (Sage, UK) and the *International Handbook of Selection* (Wiley, UK) and his work has appeared in several scholarly journals including *Journal of Applied Psychology*, *Human Relations*, *Journal of Organizational Behavior*, *Journal of Occupational and Organizational Psychology*, and *International Journal of Selection and Assessment*. Neil has been Visiting Professor to the University of Minnesota (USA) and the Free University of Amsterdam (The Netherlands). Neil is a Fellow of the British Psychological Society and the Society for Industrial and Organizational Psychology.

Olga Voskuijl is Assistant Professor in Work and Organizational Psychology at the University of Amsterdam. Her research interests concern personnel selection; theory, modeling, and measurement of job performance; job analysis; measurement and analysis of ability, personality, and vocational development. She has published on these topics in journals such as *International Journal of Selection and Assessment*, *International Journal of Human Resource Management*, and *European Journal of Psychological Assessment*.

Notes on the Contributors

Natalie J. Allen is a Professor in the Department of Psychology at The University of Western Ontario in Canada. Much of her research deals with the conceptualization and measurement of employee commitment to organizations, the development of employee commitment, and its behavioral consequences. She is the co-author, with John Meyer, of an award-winning book entitled *Commitment in the Workplace: Theory, Research and Application* (Sage, 1997). More recent research focuses on psychological issues associated with teams. Dr. Allen's work appears in various journals, including the *Journal of Applied Psychology*, *Journal of Organizational Behavior*, *Journal of Occupational and Organizational Psychology*, *Group Dynamics*, *Human Resource Management Review*, *Journal of Vocational Behavior*, and the *Academy of Management Journal*. Dr. Allen is a Fellow of the Canadian Psychological Association, an Associate Editor of the *Journal of Occupational and Organizational Psychology*, and has been a visiting scholar at universities in The Netherlands, Australia, and the UK.

Dave Bartram is Research Director of the SHL Group plc. Prior to joining SHL in 1998, he was Dean of the Faculty of Science and the Environment, and Professor of Psychology in the Department of Psychology at the University of Hull. He is a Chartered Occupational Psychologist, Fellow of the British Psychological Society (BPS), and a Fellow of the Ergonomics Society. He is Past-President and a Council member of the International Test Commission (ITC), a member of the British Psychological Society's Steering Committee on Test Standards and of the European Federation of Psychologists Association's Standing Committee on Tests and Testing. He is President-Elect of the International Association of Applied Psychology's Division 2 (Measurement and Assessment). He is the author of several hundred scientific journal articles, papers in conference proceedings, and book chapters in a range of areas relating to occupational assessment, especially in relation to computer-based testing.

Walter C. Borman is CEO of Personnel Decisions Research Institutes and is Professor of Industrial-Organizational Psychology at the University of South Florida. He is a Fellow of the Society for Industrial and Organizational Psychology, and in 1994–95 served as

President of the Society. Borman has written more than 300 books, book chapters, journal articles, and conference papers. He recently co-edited the I/O volume of the *Handbook of Psychology* (Borman, Ilgen, & Klimoski, 2003), and, with two PDRI colleagues, wrote the Personnel Selection chapter for the 1997 *Annual Review of Psychology*. He also has served on the editorial boards of several journals in the I/O field. He was the recipient of SIOP's Distinguished Scientific Contributions Award for 2003. Dr. Borman's main areas of interest are performance measurement, personnel selection, job analysis, and assessment centers.

Marise Ph. Born is Associate Professor in Industrial/Organizational Psychology at the Department of Psychology of the Erasmus University Rotterdam, The Netherlands. Marise's research interests are in the areas of personnel selection, job search and choice, personality and individual differences, cross-cultural research, and test development. She is currently on the editorial boards of the *International Journal of Selection and Assessment* and *European Journal of Personality*. She is also council member of the International Test Commission and serves on the Committee on Testing of the Dutch Association of Psychologists (COTAN).

Paula M. Caligiuri is the Director of the Center for Human Resource Strategy (CHRS) and she is Associate Professor of Human Resources Management at Rutgers University in the School of Management and Labor Relations. Paula is also a Visiting Professor at Università Bocconi business school in Milan, Italy. Paula researches, publishes, and consults in three primary areas: strategic human resource management in multinational organizations, global leadership development, and global assignee management. Her academic publications include several articles in the *International Journal of Human Resource Management*, *Journal of World Business*, *Journal of Applied Psychology*, *Personnel Psychology*, and *International Journal of Intercultural Relations*. Her book (with Allan Bird and Mark Mendenhall), *Global Dimensions of HRM: Managing the Global Workforce*, is due out in 2005. She is on several editorial boards and is an Associate Editor for *Human Resource Management Journal*.

David Chan is Associate Professor at the National University of Singapore and Scientific Advisor to the Center for Testing and Assessment in Singapore. His research includes areas in personnel selection, longitudinal modeling, and adaptation to changes at work. He has published numerous journal articles, authored several Handbook chapters, and co-authored a textbook in personnel selection. He has received several scholarly awards, including the Society for Industrial and Organizational Psychology's Distinguished Early Career Contributions Award, William Owens Scholarly Achievement Award, Edwin Ghiselli Award for Innovative Research Design, the American Psychological Association's Dissertation Research Award, and the Michigan State University Social Science College Award. He currently serves on six editorial boards and regularly reviews for over ten journals. He is currently a consultant to the Prime Minister's Office in Singapore, the Ministry of Community Development and Sports, the Singapore Police Force, and the Singapore Prison Service.

Nicole Cunningham-Snell is a Senior Consultant with Shell International's leadership development team and is based in London. She has worked as an Occupational Psychologist with Shell for seven years and currently manages the design and delivery of Shell's suite of leadership assessment and development programs globally. Nicole's work also involves competencies, appraisal systems, multi-rater feedback systems, selection methods, assessor training, team-building, and she has facilitated learning events globally. She obtained her Ph.D. in 1999 from Goldsmiths College, University of London, and is a member of the British Psychological Society.

Filip de Fruyt obtained a Master's in Biomedical Sciences and a Ph.D. in Psychology. He is appointed as Professor in Differential Psychology and Personality Assessment at the Ghent University in Belgium. His research spans a broad area, including adaptive and maladaptive individual differences, their structure and development, and applied personality psychology. He has been a member and secretary of the Executive Board of the European Association of Personality Psychology for six years, and is currently associate editor of the *European Journal of Personality* and consulting editor for the *International Journal of Selection and Assessment.*

Irene E. de Pater is a Ph.D. student in work and organizational psychology at the University of Amsterdam, The Netherlands. Her current research interests include career development, managerial development, personality, and gender and work. She has co-authored publications with Tim Judge, Erin Johnson, and Annelies van Vianen.

Stephan Dilchert is a doctoral student of industrial and organizational psychology at the University of Minnesota. His research interests lie in the domains of cognitive ability and personality as predictors in personnel decisions. He has published and presented over a dozen papers on the organizational consequences of using cognitive ability measures in personnel selection as well as on group differences on personality traits and their implications for adverse impact. He has also reviewed tests for the *Mental Measurements Yearbook.* He is currently investigating the merits of newly proposed intelligence constructs for personnel selection. He has recently completed a meta-analysis of the practical intelligence literature, assessing the utility of the construct in comparison to general mental ability and other specific cognitive abilities.

Robert L. Dipboye is chair of the psychology department at the University of Central Florida. Previous to this he was the Herbert S. Autrey Professor at Rice University. He has published widely on the topic of selection. He is a Fellow of the American Psychological Association, the Society of Industrial and Organizational Psychology (SIOP), and the American Psychological Society and a member of the Society of Organizational Behavior. He was on the editorial boards of the *Academy of Management Review*, the *Journal of Organizational Behavior*, and the SIOP Frontier Series and was Associate Editor of the *Journal of Applied Psychology.*

Sacha Geerlings is a graduate student in Work and Organizational Psychology at the University of Amsterdam. Her Master's thesis concerned the attitudes on ethical matters of selection psychologists. Furthermore, she compared the ethical guidelines of individual European countries with the European Meta-Code. Her research interests include fairness in selection and the ethics of selection.

Anna L. Imus is a graduate student in Industrial and Organizational Psychology at Michigan State University. She obtained her B.S. from George Mason University where she was given the Outstanding Undergraduate Researcher award. Her current research interests include understanding well-being as it relates to preferential selection, applicant perceptions of the hiring process, and other selection-related issues.

Ute-Christine Klehe is a junior faculty member at the Institute of Work- and Organizational Psychology at Zürich University, Switzerland. After obtaining her Master's degree in psychology at the University of Marburg, Germany, in fall 2000, she completed her Ph.D. with Gary Latham at the Rotman School of Management, University in Toronto, Canada, in 2003, followed by a one-year post-doctoral scholarship with Neil Anderson at the University of Amsterdam, The Netherlands.

Her main interests of research include typical versus maximum performance as well as selected areas from personnel selection, such as structured selection interviews and the adoption of selection procedures by organizations. So far her work has been chosen for the SIOP Flanagan award and has appeared in the *International Journal of Selection and Assessment*.

Filip Lievens is Associate Professor at the Department of Personnel Management and Work and Organizational Psychology at Ghent University, Belgium. His current research interests focus on alternative selection procedures (e.g., assessment centers, situational judgment tests, web-based assessment) and organizational attractiveness. He is the author of over 30 articles and has published in the *Journal of Applied Psychology*, *Personnel Psychology*, *Journal of Organizational Behavior*, *Journal of Occupational and Organizational Psychology*, *Applied Psychology: An international Review*, and *International Journal of Selection and Assessment*.

Deniz S. Ones is the Hellervik Professor of Industrial Psychology at the University of Minnesota. Her research focuses on personnel selection and on personality, integrity, and cognitive ability assessment for decision making. She received multiple awards for her work in these areas: the 1994 Wallace best dissertation and the 1998 McCormick early career distinguished scientific contributions awards from the Society for Industrial and Organizational Psychology (SIOP), and the 2003 Cattell early career award from the Society for Multivariate Experimental Psychology. She is a Fellow of both Divisions 5 (Evaluation, Measurement, and Statistics) and 14 (Industrial and Organizational Psychology) of the American Psychological Association. She has served or continues to serve on the editorial boards of six journals. She is the current editor in chief of the *International Journal of Selection and Assessment*. In 2001 and 2002, she co-edited the two-volume *Handbook of Industrial, Work and Organizational Psychology*, a special issue of the journal *Human Performance* on use of cognitive ability tests, and an issue of the *International Journal of Selection and Assessment* on counterproductive work behaviors.

Lisa M. Penney received her Ph.D. in Industrial/Organizational Psychology at the University of South Florida in November of 2003. She is currently a Research Associate at Personnel Decisions Research Institutes, Inc. Dr. Penney's research has been presented in several scholarly publications and conferences. Moreover, her work on the effects of incivility in the workplace and counterproductive work behavior has been the subject of numerous stories in media outlets, including *Newsweek Japan*, the *Orlando Sentinel*, and the *Arizona Republic*. Dr. Penney's primary areas of interest are counterproductive work behavior, job stress, and leadership.

Robert E. Ployhart is an Associate Professor at George Mason University. His primary program of research focuses on understanding staffing within the context of forces shaping contemporary Human Resources (e.g., developing multilevel staffing models, enhancing the effectiveness and acceptability of recruitment and staffing procedures, identifying cultural/subgroup influences on staffing processes, merging technology with assessment). His second program of research focuses on applied statistical/measurement models and research methods, such as structural equation modeling, multilevel modeling, and longitudinal modeling. Rob has published over 40 articles and chapters on these topics. He is an active member of both the Society for Industrial and Organizational Psychology and the Academy of Management, and has won awards from both organizations. Rob serves on several editorial boards and has consulted on a number of projects in the private and public sectors.

Robert A. Roe is Professor of Organization Theory and Organizational Behavior at the University of Maastricht. Previously, he taught at the universities of Amsterdam, Delft, Tilburg, and Nijmegen. Robert has been Director of the Netherlands Aeromedical Institute, and has worked with numerous companies and public organizations as a consultant. He was founding director of the Work & Organization Research Center (Tilburg), and founding president of the European Association of Work & Organizational Psychology. He received a special award for initiating the bi-annual European Congress of W&O Psychology and for promoting European integration in this field. Robert has served on several editorial boards. He has published over 300 journal articles and book chapters, as well as some books, covering personnel selection and appraisal, performance, motivation, competence, organizational assessment, and other issues. Robert has a strong interest in conceptual and methodological issues, including the application of design methodology.

Ann Marie Ryan is a Professor of Industrial-Organizational Psychology at Michigan State University. Her primary area of expertise is employee selection, with a particular focus on issues of fairness and hiring processes, applicant perceptions and recruiting, and diversity in organizations. She has co-authored numerous articles and book chapters. She recently served as president of the Society for Industrial and Organizational Psychology, and currently serves as editor of *Personnel Psychology*.

Alan M. Saks is a Professor of Organizational Behaviour and Human Resources Management at the University of Toronto where he holds a joint appointment and teaches in the Division of Management, the Joseph L. Rotman School of Management, and the Centre for Industrial Relations. His major research interests are in the areas of recruitment, job search, the transfer of training, and the socialization of new employees. He is the author of *Research, Measurement, and Evaluation of Human Resources*, and co-author of *Organizational Behaviour: Understanding and Managing Life at Work*, and *Managing Performance* *through Training & Development.* He currently serves on the editorial boards of the *Academy of Management Journal, Journal of Organizational Behavior*, and *Journal of Vocational Behavior*.

Jesús F. Salgado is Professor of Work and Organizational Psychology and Human Resources in the University of Santiago de Compostela, Spain. He has been visiting fellow at the Goldsmiths College of the University of London (1999, 2000). He has authored over 70 articles published in leading psychology and management journals, including *Academy of Management Journal, Journal of Applied Psychology, Personnel Psychology, Journal of Occupational and Organizational Psychology, Human Performance, International Journal of Selection and Assessment, Applied Psychology: An International Journal, Journal of Organizational Behavior, European Journal of Personality*, and *European Journal of Work and Organizational Psychology*. He also has authored two books and a number of chapters in international handbooks. His research is mainly on the criterion validity and the international validity generalization of personnel selection procedures. Currently, he is co-editor of the *International Journal of Selection and Assessment* and he is on the editorial board of six journals. Jesús is a fellow of the Society for Industrial and Organizational Psychology.

Neal Schmitt is University Distinguished Professor of Psychology and Management at Michigan State University. He was editor of the *Journal of Applied Psychology* from 1988–94 and has served on ten editorial boards. He has also been a Fulbright Scholar at the University of Manchester Institute of Science and Technology. He has received the Society for Industrial and Organizational Psychology's Distinguished Scientific Contributions Award (1999) and Distinguished Contributions Award (1998). He served as the Society's President in 1989–90. He has co-authored three textbooks, *Staffing Organizations* with Ben Schneider, *Research Methods in Human Resource Management* with Richard Klimoski, *Personnel Selection* with David Chan, co-edited *Personnel Selection in Organizations* with Walter Borman and *Measurement and Data Analysis* with Fritz Drasgow, and published approximately 150 articles. His current research centers on the effectiveness and outcomes of organizations' selection procedures, particularly as they relate to subgroup employment and applicant reactions and behavior.

Benjamin Schneider is Professor of Psychology at the University of Maryland and a Senior Research Fellow with Personnel Research Associates, Inc. In addition to Maryland, Ben has taught at Michigan State University and Yale University and for shorter periods of time at Dartmouth College (Tuck School), Bar-Ilan University (Israel, on a Fulbright), University of Aix-Marseilles (France), and Peking University (PRC). He has published more than 125 professional journal articles and book chapters, as well as eight books. Ben's interests concern service quality, organizational climate and culture, staffing issues, and the role of personality in organizational life. Ben was awarded the Year 2000 Distinguished Scientific Contributions Award by the Society for Industrial and Organizational Psychology. In addition to his academic work, Ben over the years has consulted with numerous companies including Citicorp, AT&T, Allstate, Sotheby's, the Metropolitan Opera, Prudential, GEICO, IBM, American Express, Giant Eagle, and MeadWestvaco.

Dora Scholarios is a Reader in Organizational Behaviour at the Department of Human Resource Management in the University of Strathclyde, Glasgow, Scotland. She received her Ph.D. in Industrial/Organizational Psychology from The George Washington University in Washington, DC (1990). Dora's research interests are in the areas of personnel selection and classification, social process perspectives of selection, and the effects of emerging forms of work on career patterns and employee well being. She has been involved in several large research projects funded by the US Army Research Institute for Behavioral and Social Sciences, the UK's Economic and Social Research Council, and the European Union.

Jan te Nijenhuis is employed at the Dutch Open University. Previously, he worked as Assistant Professor and Postdoc at the University of Amsterdam and Leiden University. He won a prize for talented young researchers for his Master's thesis on test training. His Ph.D. project at the Department of Work and Organizational Psychology of the Free University on the assessment of immigrants was carried out at and paid for by Dutch Railways and won a prize for the best dissertation on applied psychology. Jan is interested in applied and fundamental research into personality and individual differences, with a focus on personnel psychology, and has published many professional journal articles and book chapters. He is a member of the Society for Industrial and Organizational Psychology and the International Society for Intelligence Research.

George C. Thornton III is Professor of Industrial and Organizational Psychology in the Department of Psychology at Colorado State University. His current research interests include the effectiveness of developmental assessment centers for managers and students, the role of industrial psychology in employment discrimination litigation, and the cross-cultural study of achievement motivation to work. He is the author of three books, several chapters, and numerous articles and conference presentations on assessment center methods. He has helped both public and private organizations develop assessment centers. He has lectured on the assessment center method in numerous countries in Europe and Asia.

Henk van der Flier is Professor and Head of the Department of Work and Organizational Psychology at the Vrije Universiteit Amsterdam, The Netherlands. He was Head of the Department of Industrial Psychology of the Dutch Railways until 1990 and Manager Product Development and Quality of the Arbo Management Group until 1998. His research interests and publications are in the fields of working conditions, safety, personnel selection, psychometrics, and cross-cultural psychology.

Annelies E. M. van Vianen is Associate Professor in Work and Organizational Psychology at the University of Amsterdam, The Netherlands. Her research interests include person environment fit, expatriation, organizational culture, career development, personnel selection, and gender and work. She is the author of 50 Dutch and 30 international scientific journal articles, such as in the *Academy of Management Journal*, *International Journal of Human Resource Management*, *Personnel Psychology*, and *International Journal of Selection and Assessment*. For several years, she was the editor of the Dutch scientific journal *Gedrag en*

Organisatie [Behavior and Organization]. She is reviewer for over ten top journals in the field of I/O.

Chockalingam (Vish) Viswesvaran is an Associate Professor of Psychology at Florida International University, Miami. He has authored over 100 journal articles and book chapters on topics relating to personnel selection and performance. He serves on the editorial boards of three journals. He also serves as the associate editor of the *International Journal of Selection and Assessment*. He has received best dissertation and early career distinguished scientific contributions awards from the Society for Industrial and Organizational Psychology (SIOP). He is a fellow of SIOP, Divisions 14 (I/O) and 5 (Evaluation, Measurement, and Statistics) of the American Psychological Association. Recently, he co-edited the two-volume *Handbook of Industrial, Work and Organizational Psychology*, a special issue of the *International Journal of Selection and Assessment* on the role of technology on staffing, and a special issue of the journal *Human Performance* on use of cognitive ability tests.

Michael A. West is Professor of Organizational Psychology and Head of Research at Aston Business School. He has also been a member of the Centre for Economic Performance at the London School of Economics since 1991. After receiving his Ph.D. he spent a year working in the coalmines of South Wales before beginning his academic career. He has authored, edited, or co-edited 14 books, including *Effective Teamwork* (2004, Blackwell), the first edition of which has been translated into 12 languages, *The Secrets of Successful Team Management* (2003, Duncan Baird), *Developing Team Based Organisations* (2004, Blackwell), *The International Handbook of Organizational Teamwork and Cooperative Working* (2003, Wiley), *Effective Top Management Teams* (2001, Blackhall), *Developing Creativity in Organizations* (1997, BPS) and the *Handbook of Workgroup Psychology* (1996, Wiley).

David Wigfield is a Senior Consultant with Shell International's global leadership development team and is based in London. David's research interests are in the areas of leadership, personnel selection, cross-cultural psychology, and police culture. He has published several articles. He has worked as an occupational psychologist in both public and private organizations, developing and implementing a range of HR interventions including leadership development events, competencies, assessment centers, appraisal systems, and multi-rater feedback systems. David is an Associate Fellow of the British Psychological Society.

Charles Woodruffe has worked as a business psychologist for almost 20 years, having previously been a university lecturer in personality and social psychology. His company – Human Assets Limited – is based in London and specializes in designing and implementing systems for choosing, developing, and retaining the talented people his clients need now and in the future to fulfill their business strategies. His work ranges from specifying the HR strategy to the design of assessment centers to executive coaching. Charles and his colleagues are consultants to a range of organizations in the private and public sectors. Present and past clients include Shell, Ernst & Young, Exxon-Mobil, British Airways, Royal Bank of Scotland, Nomura International, Unisys, HSBC, the Department for Constitutional Affairs, the Bank of England, and the Security Service. Charles has published widely on his areas of expertise, including his books *Development and Assessment Centres* and *Winning the Talent War*. He is a Fellow of the CIPD and a Chartered Occupational Psychologist.

Preface

The *Handbook of Personnel Selection* presents a unique collection of state-of-the-science and practice chapters from internationally eminent authors in the field. It serves to update and extend the *International Handbook of Selection and Assessment* (edited by Anderson & Herriot) and published by John Wiley & Sons back in 1997. Over the intervening period the field of recruitment and selection has become more complex, more reactive to business imperatives, more technologically dependent, and more globalized in its methods, techniques, and operational conditions. Our new *Handbook of Personnel Selection* is therefore a timely reminder that as business organizations change, so too must their concomitant human resource management (HRM) methods and procedures. Significant advances and trends are evident over recent years, especially in the areas of applicant decision making and reactions, the use of Internet-based recruitment and testing methodologies, multilevel selection for person–team and person–organization fit, ethical issues including anti-discriminatory imperatives, developments in predictor methods and evidence as to their international efficacy, expatriate selection and placement, and debates over the interchange between research and practice in employee selection. We are confident that the 23 chapters comprising this Handbook both reflect these advances and hopefully contribute further to them as key emergent themes critical to the success of work organizations in the twenty-first century.

We have divided this Handbook into five parts to signify these major themes:

Part I   Preparing for selection
Part II   Developments in the use of different kinds of predictors
Part III Decisions and their context
Part IV   Criterion measures
Part V   Emerging trends and assessment for change

The 23 chapters have been contributed by 36 authors from 8 countries (the USA, The Netherlands, the UK, Belgium, Canada, Spain, Singapore, and Switzerland). A unique feature of this Handbook is, therefore, its "trans-Atlantic" perspective and grounding, with most of our authors originating from either Europe or North America. This was intentional on the part of the editors and reflects the cutting edge of science and practice in global employee selection that has emerged in very recent years in those countries, largely as a result of changing trends in HRM and use of human resources in work organizations in the USA and Europe.

Over the three-year period that it has taken to produce this Handbook, several people have provided us with significant help and support. First, we would acknowledge the professionalism, dedication, and vision of our contributing authors. They presented us with excellent first draft manuscripts, without exception they responded very courteously to our editorial suggestions for improvements and changes, and ultimately made our task as editors a smooth-running and pleasurable one to have undertaken. Their chapters, we believe, present some of the most thorough and thought-provoking reading in employee selection currently available. This Handbook would also not have been possible without the characteristically exemplary administrative support of Joke Vermeulen, our departmental secretary at the Department of Work and Organization Psychology at the University of Amsterdam. She has been a tower of strength throughout. Finally, we would like to thank both Rosemary Nixon and Joanna Pyke, respectively our commissioning editor and editorial controller at Blackwell Publishing, over the long haul to publication of this Handbook. They too have been a pleasure to work with.

Any collection of chapters purporting to provide such cutting-edge reviews may be criticized on certain grounds (variously, some lack of standardization, difference in level of coverage of different chapters, concentration of author country of origin, and so forth). As joint editors who took on this task partly as a contribution centered within our own department at the University of Amsterdam (six of the authors are based in the personnel psychology group here), we believe that this volume fulfills its purpose – to provide a unique state-of-the-science and practice overview of international trends in personnel selection.

ARNE EVERS
NEIL ANDERSON
OLGA VOSKUIJL
Amsterdam, January 2005

1

Relationships between Practice and Research in Personnel Selection: Does the Left Hand Know What the Right Is Doing?

NEIL ANDERSON

There has been growing concern, expressed by several authors internationally in Industrial, Work, and Organizational (IWO) psychology, of an increasing divide between research and practice in personnel selection. While many would recognize that selection psychology has flourished as a research-based professional practice, there have been unambiguous signs that the practitioner and scientific wings of the discipline have been moving away from each other over the past decade or so (e.g., Anderson, Herriot, & Hodgkinson, 2001; Dunnette, 1990; Hodgkinson, Herriot, & Anderson, 2001; Sackett, 1994). Indeed, the unhealthy development of a "practitioner–researcher divide" has been claimed, the effects of which are undoubtedly deleterious to the synergistic functioning of the combined profession of selection psychology within IWO psychology more generally (Anderson et al., 2001). The aims of this chapter are fourfold:

1. to establish the field of the science–practice interface in selection as a *"process domain"* topic area worthy of research in its own right;
2. to argue that the most pragmatic way forwards is where a *"natural distance"* between research and practice exists *combined with* sufficient and appropriate channels for exchange between the two;
3. to describe a typographical model of four types of research generated in selection psychology; and
4. to present four historic examples of the interface between science and practice in our field, drawing from them to illustrate possible future scenarios.

This chapter considers these vexed issues in relation to recruitment and selection psychology specifically and draws from several examples of functional and dysfunctional relationships between research and practice in personnel selection historically in order to illustrate possible scenarios of the interchange between research and practice. In so doing, this chapter aims to explore possible future relations between the researcher and practitioner wings of the discipline and thus to highlight several mechanisms through which the practice–research interface can be optimized. The argument presented assumes that robust research should be driving professional practice in one direction, while simultaneously, changes in professional practice should be stimulating new directions for research in the other. That is, that selection psychology should benefit from a bi-directional and synergistic network of relations between research and practice, with each wing of the discipline remaining in sufficiently close contact with each other to avoid isolation and division (Levy-Leboyer, 1988; see also, Rynes, Brown, & Colbert, 2002). While such an argument might seem axiomatic, in this chapter I argue perhaps more controversially for a "natural distance" between the research and practice wings of selection psychology. I argue furthermore that such a distance is not only healthy for the state of the combined profession but is necessary given the complexities of modern-day organizational science. Finally, and in counterbalance, I assert that it is not this distance or "divide" that should concern us unduly but the mechanisms and links for transfer of knowledge in both directions between the practitioner and researcher arms of employee selection psychology. Thus, that the benefits of natural distancing are partially dependent upon compensatory mechanisms for bi-directional knowledge transfer. Let me initially lay out the case for specialization of functions as the inevitable way forward for selection psychology.

FRAGMENTATION OR SPECIALIZATION: TOWARD A VIABLE SYSTEMS MODEL OF SELECTION PSYCHOLOGY

Although selection psychology has long been held to be a prototypical example of a highly successful area in IWO psychology precisely because of its science-based practice, there have been relatively few models proposed over the years to illustrate and encapsulate these relationships (Salgado, Viswesvaran, & Ones, 2001; Viswesvaran, Sinangil, Ones, & Anderson, 2001). This has been a regrettable shortcoming in the literature from both a researcher and practitioner perspective, as important questions over links between both interest groups, mechanisms to enhance practice–research interchange, competing reward pressures on researchers versus practitioners, and the transfer of key research findings into organizational practice have remained notably under-explored in selection psychology. Over the years a rather naïve, prescriptive, but unexamined set of assumptions has built up, in essence suggesting that the closer the linkages between research and practice, the better (Anderson et al., 2001). This may be the case, but then again, it may not. Indeed, I argue here that there is a natural distance necessary between research and practice for each to flourish independently and dependently of one another, similar to research and practice in the medical sciences (Rice, 1997). Undoubtedly, specialization of labor now occurs in selection psychology, with early career entrants to our profession deciding within the first few years of their careers whether a scientific track (doctoral research, postdoctoral fellowship, faculty position) or a practitioner career track (trainee consultant, junior consultant, senior consultant) is more to their calling. To switch tracks mid-career has become increasingly problematical and as science has become more methodologically and statistically complex we have witnessed an increasing specialization among younger researchers into one or perhaps at most two sub-areas of the discipline (see also Hyatt et al., 1997).

Is this specialization such a bad thing? Several arguments can be marshaled to present a sensible case that some degree of specialization is both positive and indeed an absolute necessity as selection psychology has become more complex in its scientific designs and efforts. First, consider the parallel with the medical sciences. The expectation that a medical student could go on both to perform successfully as a general practitioner and to engage in meaningful scientific research at the same time would clearly be untenable. Indeed, specialization into either career track would be seen to be absolutely necessary given the complex nature of medical research on the one hand and the demands on practicing doctors to be able to diagnose accurately patients' ailments on the other. Why should selection psychology be any different? Indeed, the complexities of research in modern IWO psychology are such that specialization is similarly necessary, and moreover, our field has grown so rapidly that simply to keep pace with a specific research area, specialization of research topics and interests is nowadays essential (Viswesvaran et al., 2001). Second, and again taking a somewhat wider vantage point, all modern-day professions to a greater or lesser extent exhibit elements of separation between research and practice. This is true in the management sciences (Hodgkinson et al., 2001), law, the medical and health sciences, the actuarial sciences and commercial insurance, industrial economics, and most pertinently, clinical and counseling psychology (Rice, 1997), to name just some possible examples of relevant comparator professions. Again, why should selection psychology be any different? Rather, the question is one of an appropriate degree of specialization coupled with sufficient mechanisms to integrate the scientist and practitioner sub-groups in order to guard against an irreparable divide between the two. Third, it can be argued that science should retain a degree of independence from commercial interests in personnel selection and that this degree of independence is therefore entirely appropriate (e.g., Dunnette, 1990). An excessively pragmatic agenda, or one determined solely by vested commercial interests, would stultify research and would critically limit the range and type of studies being undertaken and research questions being addressed in IWO psychology. Moreover, potentially controversial topics and research questions which may challenge present-day commercial practices may be in danger of never being explored should researchers be restricted to pursuing research agendas determined solely on the grounds of current commercial interests and passing consultancy fads. Fourth, and by inference, it would likewise be unhealthy for practitioners to be in some way confined to only being able to offer consultancy services in areas where scientific research offers overwhelming validation of particular methods or approaches in selection. Indeed, this would critically limit the ability of practitioners to explore new techniques and methods, to be capable of responding to emerging market demands where validatory evidence has yet to be published, and for practitioners to embrace quickly developments in organizational practices ahead of longer-term strategic research efforts (Levy-Leboyer, 1988). So equally, there is a natural distance for practice to inhabit away from the scientific research and this situation of a natural distancing is both healthy and functional for both wings of the profession of selection psychology. Fifth, and finally, there are valuable benefits to be gained on occasions from researchers pursuing lines of enquiry, whole topic areas, and commercially sensitive research away from the day-to-day milieu of demands for immediately applicable action research findings. Early research into the structure of personality and the development of exploratory factor analytical techniques are good examples of where early-phase, speculative research turned out (in this case decades later) to be highly valued practically and commercially. Even today a research proposal suggesting that personnel scientists wanted to undertake a multi-year project that involved culling thousands of trait descriptor words from dictionaries and other sources, then trying to cluster them using statistical methods which are highly controversial and unfinished, would be none too highly rated. In other instances a natural distance allows researchers to pursue studies that may go counter to current fads or transient commercial interests (e.g., critical research into emotional intelligence), but which may well turn out in the longer term to produce findings that overturn the *zeitgeist* (e.g., meta-analytic findings now indicate that even unstructured interviews have reasonable validity). Again, the question is crucially one of the degree of this distance and the existence of mechanisms to integrate and allow transfer of knowledge between science and practice in the longer term rather than the naïve presumption that science and practice must coexist in precisely the same professional space and be utterly mutually dependent on each other on a day-to-day basis.

MODELING SCIENCE–PRACTICE RELATIONS IN PERSONNEL SELECTION

Having argued the case for a natural disjuncture between the scientific and practice wings of selection psychology as a research-based discipline, it is apt to return to the issue of modeling relations between the two. Despite Dunnette's (1990) seminal chapter calling for greater discussion of this issue in IWO psychology, notably little attention has been given to these important relations. This has resulted in few models of these relations having been proposed in the literature let alone having been validated through empirical studies and field research. One exception to this is the model originally proposed by Anderson et al. (2001). In this model we formulated a simple 2 × 2 factorial along the dimensions of the *rigor* of research and its *relevance* to professional practice. This produced four "cells" of types of research – *Popularist, Pragmatic, Pedantic*, and *Puerile Science*. In an extension and application of this model to selection psychology, Anderson, Lievens, van Dam, and Ryan (in press) presented a number of examples of research occupying each cell together with cut-point indicators to suggest borderlines between high and low conditions on each of the dimensions of methodological rigor and practical relevance. Figure 1.1 illustrates this latter model.

In instances where methodological rigor is low but practical relevance is high, the model suggests that *Popularist Science* can be generated. Here, although the theme of research examined might indeed be a topical one, Popularist studies fail to examine the research question(s) with sufficient methodological rigor. Such studies might have been rushed to publication in an effort to address a "hot topic" theme within selection psychology, for example, or may have been unduly influenced by vested interests in "proving" the relevance of a present fad or favored psychometric tool. Without doubt this quadrant of research in selection psychology points up the importance of independent, expert reviews of manuscripts submitted for publication, but of course not all published sources in our field are refereed journals so Popularist findings do make it into the public domain. Poorly conceived or conducted studies falling into this category, it can be argued, represent

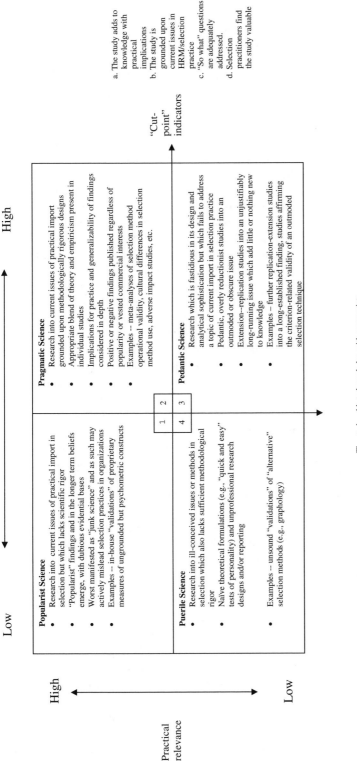

FIGURE 1.1 Types of research in selection psychology

Source: Based upon Anderson, Lievens, van Dam, & Ryan (2003), developed and extended from Anderson, Herriot, & Hodgkinson (2001).

perhaps the greatest current pitfall to science-based practice in selection psychology. For organizational practices in employee selection to be based upon such unreliable findings calls into question the veracity of our claim to be a science-based professional practice. Readers of this chapter will no doubt have encountered such beliefs among personnel and line managers, often where there is an unquestioning faith in a particularly dubious method lacking proper validation via methodologically robust applied studies. Critically, therefore, it beholds our field to demand robust research to lie behind each and every applied practice in employee selection and assessment, and for faddish techniques and bandwagon methods to be subjected to scrutiny even where these methods promise lucrative consultancy fees or selection product income.

In quadrant 2, which is comprised of studies high in both methodological rigor and practical relevance, we term the type of research generated as *Pragmatic Science*. In selection situations, as in others in IWO psychology more generally, this quadrant of research should dominate our field and should form the basis of professional practice wherever practicable. Several notable examples of such Pragmatic Science are cited in Figure 1.1, but are merely illustrative of a considerably more extensive scientific basis for the field. For instance, as will be discussed later in this chapter, considerable research now supports the widespread use of tests of cognitive ability and general mental ability (GMA) in selection and this evidence generalizes across job families, organizations, and even countries (Schmidt & Hunter, 1998; Salgado & Anderson, 2002, 2003). This is just one example of where selection psychology can justifiably claim the status of a science-based practice; others will be alluded to later in this chapter. The central point of import here is that only this quadrant of the four presented in our model truly serves the long-term interests of selection psychology, for its science, its practice, and for interdependencies between the two. Following logically from this, selection psychologists need to question (a) how can we maximize this quadrant in terms of the proportion of research efforts and outputs it occupies, (b) how can we optimize links and relations between research and practice to ensure that key findings are translated into organizational practices, and (c) simultaneously, how can we ensure feedback from practice to research to ensure that researchers are pursuing themes of enquiry that are relevant, topical, and priority concerns of clients and organizations internationally?

Where methodological rigor is high but practical relevance is low, what we term *Pedantic Science* is likely to emerge. In this case studies have been robustly based upon a fastidious design, or have been analyzed with considerable attention to detail, but unfortunately fail to address an issue of topical concern for organizational selection practices. Examples of this type of research include long-running themes of enquiry into research questions of marginal or peripheral import to present-day organizational practices or where replication–extension studies fail to add anything new to well-established findings in employee selection. In effect, this is the "safe heaven" quadrant wherein a minority of researchers may be continuing to pursue pet themes of personal interest using conventional methodologies in a scientific sub-field which has become outmoded by organizational change (see also Herriot & Anderson, 1997). Here, again, the review process is critical in screening out such Pedantic Science and this is especially the case given the opportunity costs to selection psychology of such ivory tower research continuing unabated and in spite of changes in the environment of applied selection practices and emergent trends in employee selection. Over some period of time the dangers of too great a proportion of Pedantic Science being undertaken become only too clear: science loses its relevance to professional practice and may take on a self-serving and highly dysfunctional character in increasing isolation from demands for practical relevance and as a founding basis for organizational selection practices.

Finally, quadrant 4 represents the worst-case situation of research of dubious practical relevance being undertaken using unacceptable methods and designs. This we term *Puerile Science*. Clearly, we should seek to minimize the scale and even the existence of this quadrant of research as it is of no value either scientifically or practically. Examples of this type of research do, unfortunately, exist; for instance, where basically unsound psychological assessment techniques have been "validated" through unsound methods and study designs (an invalid examination of the criterion-related validity of graphology, for example).

In our original formulation of this model, as in Figure 1.1, we present the four quadrants as being equal in size and scale. In actual fact Pragmatic Science has dominated the field of selection and assessment, perhaps with less beneficial incidents of Popularist and Pedantic Science being less evident but nonetheless present and exerting some impact upon our field. We (Anderson et al., 2001) argued on the grounds of several sources of evidence, however, that the latter two forms of science had been increasing because of dysfunctional reward pressures on researchers and practitioners in selection psychology. Such trends are certainly to be guarded against, since the former (Popularist Science) is likely to result in untheorized, unvalidated practices while the latter (Pedantic Science), as argued earlier, is liable to result in the isolation and discrediting of research from selection and assessment practices in organizations.

Science–Practice Relations: A New Area for Research in IWO Psychology

At the start of this chapter I stated that one of its aims is to establish science–practice relations as a topic for research in selection in its own right. As the situation too often stands internationally at present researchers continue to research what can best be called *"content domains"* in selection (e.g., criterion-related validity, adverse impact, applicant reactions, and so forth), whereas on the other side of the fence, practitioners continue to practice with commercially popular approaches, methods, and decision-making tools. That the findings from our research efforts may fail to influence practice should be a major concern to researchers (Dunnette, 1990; Rynes et al., 2002; Viswesvaran et al., 2001). We should perhaps approach this topic area as a challenge for micro-level organization development research – a new *"process domain"* for research studies. In other words, that the findings from studies in selection can form the basis of intervention programs in organizations, that the clients for such interventions are HRM specialists and selection practitioners in organizations who may well not be qualified psychologists, and where the overall aim of such research is to establish the efficacy of such interventions. As I argue subsequently in this chapter, a strictly scientific, rational-economic logic may not be the best approach to getting our findings translated into common practice by HR specialists. Before any of this can occur, however, researchers in selection themselves need to be persuaded that this topic area warrants being treated seriously as a scientific enterprise on its own merits. What arguments are there for this to happen?

First, applied psychologists involved in selection research would surely acknowledge that the psychological aspects of practitioners accepting, being influenced by, and acting upon our findings are relevant questions for research. Rather than the seminal scientist-practitioner model advocated so eloquently by Sackett (1994), this can perhaps be termed the "scientist-scientist model" whereby reflexivity is encouraged amongst researchers over the impact of their scientific outputs. Second, the psychological and economic costs of researchers not opening this up as a new area for research are simply too high (Rynes, Bartunek, & Daft, 2001; Rynes et al., 2002). The current situation internationally is at best that there is an imperfect synergy between research and practice in employee selection. Research fails to influence practice, practice fails to influence research, and so the cycle of isolationism is perpetuated. The crucial question is "why does robust research fail to influence practice (and, of course, vice versa)?" Of any area in selection psychology it could be argued that this is where our knowledge is most fragmented and incomplete – we know plenty about major *content domains*, far less about the *process domain* of why this knowledge fails to influence practice in organizations on occasions. True, it is not the responsibility of researchers to implement these findings in organizations on a day-to-day basis, but my argument here is that it is the responsibility of researchers to verify the impact of research findings. After all, should this not be the life-blood of organizational psychology research? Third, put bluntly, such relations are interesting in their own right. Why do organizations satisfice by not adopting the most valid and reliable predictor methods? Why are HR practitioners apparently unmoved by demonstrably huge utility gains from improving the criterion-related validity of their selection procedures? How can psychometric test development for employee selection be better grounded upon psychological theory and empirical research? Why do researchers dismiss trends in selection practices in organizations as being unscientific and therefore falling outside of the bounds for reputable enquiry? All are important questions and should stimulate further applied research and will help to build science–practice bridges by better understanding the reasons for the imperfect transfer of knowledge in our discipline. In opening up this so-called *process domain* for future research we can profitably begin by examining the lessons from the past. In the following section, I do precisely this by debating four historic scenarios of research–practice relations in selection psychology.

RESEARCH–PRACTICE SYNERGY: FOUR HISTORIC SCENARIOS IN SELECTION PSYCHOLOGY

As the title of the present chapter suggests, relations between science and practice in selection psychology are at their worst where each wing of the discipline is unaware of, or is purposely ignoring, what the other is presently working on (literally, "the left hand not knowing what the right is doing" as the popular saying goes). Note, I distinguish here between being unaware of current developments and consciously ignoring them or choosing not to take them into account, although it is difficult to attribute these two different scenarios precisely post hoc. The more problematic of the two is where either wing of our discipline is simply unaware of developments in the other. This is because such a lack of knowledge would indicate structural deficiencies in information exchange and transmission between researchers and practitioners, or vice versa, such that the one "hand" is literally unaware of what the other is doing (Dunnette, 1990; Hyatt et al., 1997). While information transmission between the two wings of selection psychology is some way from being perfect, it is reasonable to argue that owing to the extensive range of journals and newsletters now in existence, ongoing contacts between practitioners and scientists, regular conferences, and professional meetings, selection psychology benefits from well-established contacts and channels for information exchange generally. Additionally, research funding bodies in several countries (the USA, the UK, The Netherlands, Australia) have increasingly emphasized practical relevance as a criterion for research program grants, and so across selection psychology internationally the funding pressures have been toward applied relevance over more recent years. These mechanisms and funding pressures are likely, if anything, to have improved researcher–practitioner links at least in terms of the transfer of knowledge and the stakeholder pressures placed upon researchers to undertake practically relevant, applied research (i.e., Pragmatic Science).

Overviewing the history of selection psychology, it is possible to identify four main scenarios of relations between science and practice, the first three being highly functional and beneficial, the final one being counterproductive to the health of the profession. These are:

1. robust research informing professional practice;
2. unreliable research failing to influence professional practice;
3. trends in practice influencing empirical research efforts;
4. robust research failing to influence professional practice.

This section of this chapter considers each scenario in turn and gives key examples of how research appears historically to have influenced, or not, professional practice and vice versa across different countries internationally (see also Highhouse, 2002 for such an historical perspective). Unavoidably, these examples and the interpretation of whether research has appropriately influenced practice have relied upon judgments by the present author, but this overview is nevertheless useful and valid in illustrating the different scenarios identified above.

Scenario 1: Robust research informing professional practice

The default position in terms of research–practice relations that all IWO psychologists generally, and selection psychologists in particular, would like to think exists is that robust research appropriately informs professional practice. In this scenario Pragmatic Science routinely forms the basis for consultancy interventions, we all adhere to the strictures of being scientist-practitioners (Sackett, 1994), and all research findings are automatically translated into professional practice with little delay or tension between scientific and real-world demands. Needless to say, this is an idealized scenario. More realistically, selection practices will be influenced by some of the main research findings, there will be delays between scientific publication and their translation into professional practice, and there will be necessary compromises between the findings from pure and applied science in our area and the day-to-day demands of selection practitioners actually running employee selection procedures (Rynes et al., 2001, 2002).

One example of this scenario historically in selection psychology is the use of tests of cognitive ability, or general mental ability (GMA), across different countries. This example also nicely illustrates apparent tensions between scientific research methods, in this case the increasing use of meta-analysis techniques to establish generalized criterion-related validity, and the day-to-day demands of personnel practitioners to show validity in the specific situation of their particular organization and selection context. There is now an overwhelming body of evidence that tests of GMA represent the best "stand alone" predictors of job performance and training success in both the USA (e.g., Hunter & Hunter, 1984; Schmitt, Gooding, Noe, & Kirsh, 1984; Schmidt & Hunter, 1998) and Europe (e.g., Salgado & Anderson, 2002, 2003; Salgado, Anderson, Moscoso, Bertua, & De Fruyt, 2003a; Salgado et al., 2003b). Schmidt and Hunter, in their review of predictive validity studies into selection methods spanning 85 years in the USA, report average operational validities for GMA measures of .44 for predicting job performance and .58 for predicting training success. Salgado and Anderson (2002, 2003) found that in the context of European selection the magnitude of operational validities for GMA tests is somewhat higher than in the USA. Their meta-analysis across eleven countries in the European Union resulted in corrected observed validity coefficients (Rho's) of .62 for predicting job performance and .54 for predicting training success. Operational validity was not moderated by country culture, but as in the earlier US meta-analyses, was substantially moderated by job complexity, with operational validity being notably greater for high-complexity jobs. The authors also present summary evidence for the popularity of GMA tests across different countries in Europe. They report that tests of GMA are more widely used in European countries than in the USA, suggesting that this popularity in Europe had not been restricted by organizational concerns over possible employment discrimination cases being brought by applicants owing to the less stringent anti-discrimination legislation in most European countries compared with the USA. Rynes et al. (2002). in their survey of HR practitioners in the USA. found that a commonly held belief was that GMA tests were less valid predictors than the research findings indicate, leading perhaps to their lower popularity in America than in Europe. Interestingly, there is also evidence across the multiple surveys into GMA test use by European organizations that they have become more popular over time (see also Robertson & Smith, 2001). It is reasonable to argue that this increased popularity has been fundamentally influenced by the publication of such supportive and robust research findings. Of course, other factors influence the decisions of organizational recruiters over which methods to use, including cost-effectiveness, training requirements, commercial availability, adverse impact, and so forth, but it would be churlish to argue that such compelling evidence for criterion-related validity has not influenced the increasing use of cognitive ability measures in professional practice. Indeed, this example can be held up as an archetypal illustration of the benefits of pragmatic research influencing professional practice in our field internationally. There have been tensions, however, between the move by researchers toward using meta-analytical techniques to summarize criterion-related validity coefficients across multiple organizations and job types and the preferences of selection practitioners for direct, situational-specific evidence that GMA measures display validity and reliability for their particular situation (Chan, 1998; Goldstein, Zedeck, & Goldstein, 2002; Murphy, 1996). Regardless of these tensions, the increasing use of measures of GMA by organizations internationally can be attributed at least in part to the reassurance provided by this now voluminous body of evidence supporting their use in applied selection contexts. As Salgado and Anderson (2003) conclude: "The magnitude of the operational validities found suggests that GMA measures may be the best single predictor for personnel selection for all occupations" (p. 16).

Other less positive research findings have also influenced professional practice but in this case toward the non-use of certain so-called "alternative" methods of selection. Evidence failing to support the criterion-related validity of such methods as graphology and to some extent references or testimonials has limited their use or at least the reliance placed upon these methods by practitioners (Robertson & Smith, 2001). Another example of robust research informing professional practice can be drawn from research into gender and race sub-group differences and the potential adverse impact of selection methods (Arvey, 1979a; Borman, Hansen, & Hedge, 1997). Particularly in the USA, organizations have made extensive efforts as a result of the research findings in this area to ensure nondiscriminatory practices in selection, and there is evidence that organizations in Britain are following suit to be able to demonstrate the lack of adverse impact of their selection procedures (e.g., Ones & Anderson, 2002; Robertson & Smith, op. cit.). One other area that has received very recent research attention is that of applicant reactions and decision making (Ryan & Ployhart, 2000). Although it is early days, it is likely that this too will become an example of pragmatic research efforts influencing organizational practices. In summary, it can be argued across several areas of research in personnel selection that organizational practices have been fundamentally influenced by the key findings concerned. While there may be delays between publication of research findings and their translation into organizational practice, along with an imperfect alignment of the interests of scientific researchers and personnel practitioners, there is an overwhelming case that professional selection represents some of the best elements of research-based practice (Dunnette, 1990; Tenopyr, 2002).

To summarize, this first scenario represents in many ways the ideal of research–practice relations. Fortunately the field of selection psychology is replete with examples over its history of this scenario actually being the case; here I have chosen to illustrate the point with just some of the possible examples of stringent research having impacted beneficially upon professional practices in employee selection. This stated, there has been a rather naïve and unquestioned set of presumptions in our field that this scenario will automatically be the default of science–practice relations (see also Chapter 6 of Dipboye and Chapter 11 of Lievens & Thornton, this volume). However, there is no guarantee that this scenario will be the default option; quite the opposite. It behooves selection psychologists in both the research and practice wings of our discipline to ensure that a bi-directional and symbiotic relation exists between science and practice; we cannot merely take this for granted. To further highlight this point, the three other scenarios identified might just as likely typify science–practice relations in our field, as several examples throughout the history of selection psychology vividly illustrate.

Scenario 2: Unreliable research failing to influence professional practice

The second research–practice scenario identifiable is where less than reliable research findings have fortuitously failed to influence professional selection practices in organizations.

In this case, adopting an historical perspective is particularly informative (e.g., Salgado, 2001). By its very nature science develops over time, with the findings from earlier studies based upon less stringent research and analytical techniques being questioned and falsified by more recent research (Kuhn, 1970; Pfeffer, 1993). In choosing the term "unreliable" research, I should clarify that this may only turn out to be so with the benefit of hindsight and subsequent advances in research methods and analytical techniques (Ryan, personal correspondence). At the time the original studies were conducted researchers may well have used the most sophisticated approaches available to them; this is an inherent quality of advances in research across all fields (Kuhn, 1970). Indeed, falsification of prior empirical findings and proposed theoretical models is held to be a central tenet of scientific enquiry, with "normal" science in IWO psychology making progress precisely by this route (Anderson, 1998). We should not therefore be surprised if earlier findings in our field are questioned or even modified by subsequent research using more robust designs and analytical procedures. The interesting corollary to this point is that selection practices have not always historically followed research findings in our field. Of several examples perhaps the most immediately striking is the continued use of all types of interviews, even completely unstructured interviews, despite earlier narrative reviews which cast doubt incorrectly upon their likely value (chronologically: Wagner, 1949; Mayfield, 1964; Ulrich & Trumbo, 1965; Wright, 1969; Arvey, 1979b; Arvey & Campion, 1982). It was not until the mid-1980s onward that a series of published meta-analyses into interview predictive validity began to change this perception of its apparent inherent unreliability and invalidity (e.g., McDaniel, Whetzel, Schmidt, & Maurer, 1994; Huffcutt, Roth, & McDaniel, 1996; Salgado & Moscoso, 2002). In the Salgado and Moscoso (2002) meta-analysis, for instance, unstructured interviews were found to have a mean corrected operational validity of .20 whereas for highly structured interviews Rho was reported at a substantial .56 (i.e., close to the levels of operational validity reported for tests of GMA internationally, as above). McDaniel et al. (1994) reported average operational validities of .37 for all types of interviews, .44 for structured interviews, and .33 for unstructured interviews. This series of meta-analytic findings have essentially rehabilitated the credibility of interviews as an assessment device, and even in the case of unstructured interviews, some value is likely to be added to organizational selection procedures from their inclusion (e.g., Herriot, 1989). In terms of the scenario of relations between research and practice, it is abundantly clear that the popularity of interviews did not drop over the earlier period before these meta-analytic findings were known. If anything, the interview remained almost universally popular for all types of jobs regardless of the folklore knowledge among personnel practitioners that it may lack validity or reliability (Dipboye, 1997). This was a clear example of the research not influencing practice despite recruiters apparently knowing about these untowardly critical research findings. Yet, these beliefs among HR practitioners appear to persist over more recent years regardless of the publication of these important meta-analytical findings (Eder & Harris, 1999). That is, a proportion of practitioners seemingly still believe that all types of interview are inherently flawed. Here, it is likely that the more recent research findings have not been disseminated among HR practitioners perhaps as widely as they should have been in order to influence professional practice positively.

A further example of unreliable research failing to influence practice occurs in the area of personality testing, but with the twist that this research was hugely impactful in the USA but not so in Europe. In their retrospective review of personality research and personality testing for selection over the last millennium, Barrick, Mount, and Judge (2001) hint at this differential impact. Citing Guion and Gottier's (1965) influential review, these authors concluded: "There is no generalizable evidence that personality measures can be recommended as good or practical tools for employee selection" (p. 159). This damning conclusion had a huge impact on the popularity of personality testing in the USA, and as Barrick et al. suggest, this conclusion, which has subsequently been proven to be erroneous, largely went unchallenged for a period of around 25 years. Yet, in the European Union, Guion and Gottier's dismissal failed to have anywhere near the same level of impact on the professional practice of use of personality inventories for selection purposes (Salgado & de Fruyt, Chapter 8, this volume). In point of fact, the opposite can be argued to have occurred (see also, Herriot & Anderson, 1997). In successive surveys of the popularity of personality tests over this 25-year period, there is actually evidence of a considerable *growth* in organizational use of such measures for employee selection (e.g., Bartram, Lindley, Marshall, & Foster, 1995; Hodgkinson & Payne, 1998; Robertson & Makin, 1986; Shackleton & Newell, 1994). Why this striking difference between the USA and Europe? One explanation is that the Guion and Gottier (1965) review and its conclusion simply did not reach European researchers at that time. Some 40 years ago, journals were consulted far less internationally than they are today with the advent of electronic access and much stronger links between researchers in different countries. So, one plausible explanation is quite simply that European researchers were not so aware of Guion and Gottier's conclusion, or at least not so influenced by it. Certainly academic reviews of the value of personality testing in Europe at that time were far less accepting of this apocalyptic conclusion, and their message of effectively a moratorium on the use of personality inventories for personnel selection was not even quoted in key HR texts of that period in the UK (e.g., Barber, 1973; Torrington & Chapman, 1979). Another plausible explanation is that this review slightly predated a period of considerable growth in selection consultancy firms in Europe, especially throughout the boom years of the 1980s, where many of these consultancies included personality testing as part of their product-mix and advisory services. Whatever is the explanation, the continued growth in the popularity of personality testing for employment across Europe over this period stands in stark contrast to the American experience (Barrick et al., 2001). Ironically, this might be described as a clear case of the right hand [in Europe] not knowing what the left hand [in the USA] was doing, yet this ignorance brought unforeseen benefits with hindsight. Since then, of course, the series of meta-analyses into personality inventory predictive validity have proven beyond any reasonable doubt that well-developed personality tests are robust predictors in the cultural context of both the USA (e.g., Barrick & Mount, 1991) and Europe (Salgado, 1997).

What can be concluded from these examples of this second scenario whereby unreliable research fortuitously fails to influence professional practice? The first point must surely be to acknowledge that research is not an infallible panacea upon which to base every aspect of employee selection practice in organizations. Science continues to develop, its earlier findings and conclusions sometimes (although more rarely than might be expected) overturned, and its methods and analytical conventions continue to advance. We should not forget that personnel psychology is a relatively young science, and it has been the advent and popularization of meta-analysis techniques in particular that have advanced our understanding over the past two decades (Schmidt & Hunter, 1998). Second, we as researchers should be thankful that selection practitioners often receive our findings with a healthy degree of skepticism! By its very nature, again, research is specialized into one aspect of the wider picture, whereas the popularity of selection methods is determined by HR practitioners with imperfect knowledge of the scientific evidence and facing a plethora of different demand characteristics (Latham & Whyte, 1994). Third, this scenario provides support for my earlier assertion that there should be a natural distance between research and practice in selection psychology. It would be notably dysfunctional for every organization's selection procedure to slavishly follow the findings of every published study, or even to attempt to keep pace immediately with the sheer range of published findings in real time. Rather, a period for reflection, critical examination of the key findings, and a translation of the balance of scientific opinion into professional practice carries a much more intuitive and specious appeal. Finally, this second scenario highlights the importance of research being open to, and influenced by, developments in professional practice internationally. The question of why these findings failed to change practice is an intriguing one, and, it can be argued, one that has received too little attention by researchers in the past.

Scenario 3: Trends in practice influencing empirical research efforts

It would of course be wrong to suggest that there exists only a one-way relation between research and practice in selection. Several examples can be cited where recent trends in employee selection practices in organizations have stimulated new directions for applied research, meta-analyses, and theory building (e.g., Lievens, van Dam, & Anderson, 2002). Research into competency frameworks, multi-rater performance appraisal, emotional intelligence, computer-based testing, honesty and integrity testing, drug and alcohol testing, Internet-based recruitment, telephone-based interviews, and computer-adaptive testing are all examples of this happening. Of all of these areas, most attention recently has been directed at Internet-based recruitment and assessment. This flurry of research activity has been as a direct result of organizations moving with striking haste into web-based recruitment and selection procedures (see, for instance, Anderson, 2003, for a recent review). Especially in the USA, many large organizations have begun to rely on the Internet for both recruitment and screening purposes. Lievens and Harris (2003) quote the figure of 88 percent of Global 500 companies in the USA now using web-based recruitment procedures. This growth has been the principal factor in stimulating recent research in this area; a clear example of developments in practice influencing research efforts, it can be argued.

Unavoidably there may be a delay between changes in selection practices in organizations occurring and subsequent research being undertaken (Lievens, personal communication). Certainly in the case of Internet-based procedures this was due to the sheer speed with which organizations adopted the new technology. Should research be in such a reactive position or should we facilitate more speculative theory-building efforts and empirical studies in advance of such developments? I would argue for the latter. Especially in the case of this example it was foreseeable that some organizations would adopt web-based solutions given their inherent advantages of cost-effectiveness, immediacy of response, convenience to applicants, and so forth. Perhaps what was not foreseeable was the scale of the adoption of this new technology. This has resulted in there being a dearth of research into the effects of web-based recruitment and assessment contrasted with huge growth in their use by practitioners in organizations (Lievens & Harris, 2003). More research is now appearing, but the wider question remains as to how we can foster more speculative studies ahead of such developments in practice in future. Perhaps selection researchers had indeed become rather too conservative in their approach and we needed more visionary thinking some years previously for the knowledge base to stay ahead of these changes in practice.

For the future it would obviously be advantageous for selection research to lead such developments in practice, that is, to take a far more proactive stance than its traditionally reactive one. A prerequisite for this to happen, once again, is for there to be sufficient feedback contacts and information channels from practice back to research such that selection scholars are continually challenged by pragmatism. Perhaps it is now timely for a top-tier journal in personnel selection to commission a special issue on the science–practice *and* practice–science interface similar to AMJ's special research forum edited by Rynes, Bartunek, and Daft in 2001? We might also facilitate a few purely speculative workshops involving both practitioners and researchers to generate likely future scenarios and trends, and to stimulate a far more visionary stance and cutting-edge thinking (and if such a suggestion sounds ludicrous, surely this is in itself indicative of our field lacking vision!). To conclude, while there are examples of trends in practice influencing research, the field could benefit substantially from better links for practice-driven research.

Scenario 4: Robust research failing to influence professional practice

The fourth and final scenario, where robust research fails for whatever reasons to influence selection practice, is potentially the most troublesome for selection psychology as a profession. In this scenario we have borne all of the costs of producing Pragmatic Science and yet have not reaped any of the benefits from its practical application. As in the case of the second scenario outlined above, this fourth scenario is less common than where robust research has influenced professional practice (Scenario 1). However, there are clearly examples of where research has apparently exerted too little impact upon selection practices in organizations (see, for instance, Rynes et al., 2001, 2002); here I focus on two in particular – the Five Factor Model (FFM) of personality and occupational personality test development, and the impact of utility analysis on selection method choice by HR practitioners.

Over the past two decades a considerable body of evidence has built up supporting the taxonomic structure of the FFM or "Big Five" as a latent model of personality and individual differences (Digman, 1990). Most impressively, this body of research indicates the applicability of the FFM across many different countries (McCrae & Costa, 1997), for a substantial range of original personality measures (Costa & McCrae, 1988; Ferguson, Payne, & Anderson, 1994), and across different languages and cultures (Yang & Bond, 1990). In relation to selection, however, the most important finding across recent research studies has been that FFM-based personality inventories display greater criterion-related validity than personality measures based upon alternative models of personality (Salgado, 1997). This meta-analytical evidence, drawn from studies in Europe, not the USA, would lead one to expect that there should have been a quantum shift toward FFM-based personality inventories by commercial test publishers across Europe. Not only has this not been the case, but as Hough (2001) pithily observes: "I/O psychologists have been lax in attending to the taxonomic structure of their variables, perhaps due partly to excessive empiricism, and perhaps partly the result of pragmatic attention to an immediate, applied goal" (p. 21).

While this evidence for the superiority of FFM-based measures has been published relatively recently in Europe, seminal findings in the USA have been around for some years now (e.g., Barrick & Mount, 1991; Costa & McCrae, 1992). Given the now substantial body of evidence one might have expected commercially published measures of personality for occupational selection to have universally incorporated these findings into their design and underlying construct model. Yet, this has not been the case. Some proprietary tests do profess links to the FFM but relatively few measures have been developed psychometrically from their inception to be based upon this taxonomic structure (one exception is of course Costa & McCrae's, 1992, Revised NEO Personality Inventory; see also Anderson & Ones, 2003). Debate is ongoing as to whether the FFM represents the most comprehensive and parsimonious typology of normal adult personality, perhaps suggesting that commercial test publishers have merely exercised caution "while the jury is out" before becoming converts to this approach (Hough, 2001; Schmitt, personal correspondence). There is also an inevitable time-lag before research findings are disseminated into commercial practice, leaving open the possibility that commercially published personality inventories may move toward the FFM as a typological framework in years to come. For whatever reasons, the FFM, despite a considerable volume of evidence internationally having built up for its construct and criterion-related validity, does not appear to have influenced commercial test publishers as much as perhaps it should have done (Hogan & Roberts, 2001). It is true that for some proprietary personality tests second-order factors can be computed from summing raw scores on primary dimensions and that these second-order factors resemble the FFM (e.g., Hogan Personality Indicator, 16PF5, some versions of the OPQ family of measures), but for many other tests relations with the FFM are not described. This has led for calls for test publishers to fully document their model of personality underlying commercially published measures and to describe links to the FFM (Anderson & Ones, 2003). Further, HR practitioners appear to be attracted to personality measures that offer a more fine-grained level of analysis, that is, considerably more dimensions than just the five superordinate dimensions of the FFM (De Fruyt & Salgado, 2003). Regardless of these possible tensions between research and practice, or possibly even precisely because of them, it is apparent that the FFM has yet to have the impact on construct models of personality upon which proprietary tests of personality for selection are being currently based.

The second example of this final scenario, where again robust research findings do not appear to have exerted sufficient influence on professional practice, concerns the topic of utility analysis in personnel selection. In fact, this example is particularly apt as utility analysis models are founded upon the notion that HR practitioners choose between different selection methods largely on rational-economic criteria (Boudreau, Sturman, & Judge,

1997). These assumptions are a microcosm of assumptions that research generally should influence practitioner actions on the basis of objective and rational evidence in support of the added value of such interventions (Anderson et al., in press; Latham & Whyte, 1994). In the Latham and Whyte (1994) study, 143 experienced HR and line managers evaluated the persuasiveness of utility analysis outputs (dollar savings) compared with more general, narrative information on the benefits of different selection methods. Counter to some of the core assumptions of utility analysis, financially based cost-saving information influenced managers in a *negative* direction, leading the authors to conclude: "Those who rely on utility analysis and are successful in getting their recommendations accepted may be successful in spite of, rather than because of, reliance on this technique" (p. 43). Utility analysis appears to have been stultified in its usage to persuade selection practitioners as to the financial benefits of more valid predictors because of its apparent computation of huge financial savings which lack credibility among practitioners (Cascio, 1993). More problematic regarding the present chapter is whether the assumption that providing scientific evidence to practitioners is the most persuasive language in which to communicate realized benefits. Conversely, practitioners might be more swayed by the power-relations and politics of their current organization, often with HR practitioners not occupying particularly lofty positions in the organizational hierarchy. Certainly, utility analysis, as presently configured, does not compare like-for-like interventions at an organizational level of analysis, thereby perhaps leaving practitioners somewhat incredulous over the huge financial paybacks claimed. So, have our assumptions of persuasion by rational-economic evidence in selection been misplaced? And if so, could we ever expect that scientific evidence will impact upon practice as much as it should (on the grounds of rational-economic criteria) do? These are key questions and challenges that strike at the heart of research–practice relations in selection psychology; as Anderson et al. (in press) conclude:

> we have typically placed too much emphasis on selection practices as rational technical interventions and therefore often fail to have an impact in organizations . . . [rather] selection researchers should consider their interventions as organizational interventions that are subject to the same pressures as other organizational innovations. (p. 11; see also, Johns, 1993)

In conclusion, this fourth scenario presents the most troublesome and challenging scenario for selection psychologists. It undermines our self-identity as scientist-practitioners (Sackett, 1994) certainly but, more tellingly, where substantial bodies of evidence fail to influence practice this is unambiguous evidence for a practitioner–researcher divide in our field. While many would like to think idealistically that Scenario 1 always typifies research–practice relations in IWO psychology, the examples cited above cannot be swept away in a self-delusory attempt to persuade ourselves that all is always rosy in terms of these relations. Most troublesome of all are suggestions that rational-scientific logic *itself* fails to engage practitioner interests in research findings. Rather, we may need to explore ways of communicating the key findings of selection research that take account of political realities and practitioner mindsets in organizations; for too long perhaps a minority of researchers have clung onto the mindset that practitioners should be listening to these messages regardless of their medium (Rynes et al., 2001).

DIRECTIONS FOR FUTURE RESEARCH IN RESEARCH–PRACTICE RELATIONS

Having identified and described these four scenarios for research–practice relations in personnel selection internationally, the final section of this chapter goes on to consider several promising directions for future research into questions surrounding research–practice relations in IWO psychology. Of the four scenarios, the first three are clearly positive in terms of their effects and outcomes whereas the final one is negative, and potentially highly negative in the case where a substantial body of research is failing to influence selection practices in organizations. A series of important questions can be posed following from these scenarios:

1. How can we as a profession ensure that Scenarios 1 and 2 are predominant in science–practice relations, and simultaneously, that Scenario 3 is minimized or even eradicated?
2. Why has robust research failed to influence employee selection practices in some cases, whereas in others less reliable scientific evidence has been rightly overlooked by selection practitioners?
3. How can we engineer a situation where a "natural distance" exists between research and practice but also robust research findings still influence practitioner actions (i.e., Scenario 1) after being "translated" into pragmatic terminology?
4. How can we ensure the ongoing existence of strong researcher–practitioner links through structural features and channels of communication (journals, newsletters, conferences, interest groups, etc.)?
5. At an international level, how can we best ensure sharing of information and best practice experiences across national borders and cultures in personnel selection?

All five questions are central to advancements in *process domain* research into science–practice relations in selection. In the final section of this chapter I suggest two main directions for future research. Rather paradoxically, however, even a cursory review of the contributions to this important topic area in the literature reveals that research into research–practice relations is very sparse. With a few notable exceptions (e.g., Anderson et al., 2001; Dunnette, 1990; Rynes et al., 2001, 2002; Sackett, 1994), researchers have in general neglected these critically important issues, perhaps preferring instead to continue forth on their own research agendas rather than stopping to reflect upon whether their findings might be having as much impact upon professional practice as they might. This has not been a healthy situation for selection psychology specifically, or indeed for IWO psychology more widely (Viswesvaran et al., 2001). The impact of our research findings on practice is every bit as important as the contents of the findings per se, yet selection psychology has curiously and dysfunctionally neglected these issues of transfer over more recent years. Researchers may believe that their results are falling upon deaf ears, yet on the other hand, one hears embittered complaints from practitioners at conferences internationally that studies are written up in a style that engenders reactions of either non-comprehension, utter boredom, or derision of intricately designed studies that empirically confirm the blindingly obvious (i.e., Pedantic Science, see Figure 1.1). It is therefore timely to call for greater attention to be given to research–practice relations in selection psychology, the present chapter being one attempt to highlight the importance of these issues. Two directions for future research and major lines of enquiry seem particularly valuable at the present juncture – research into practitioner beliefs and strategies of persuasion, and validation research into the effectiveness of Continuing Professional Development (CPD) training interventions in IWO psychology internationally.

In comparison with the concentration of efforts by researchers into *content domain* issues of selection (i.e., predictive validity, construct validity, reliability, adverse impact, etc.), there has been precious little research into, firstly, practitioner beliefs over key research findings, and secondly, tactics through which to change practitioner beliefs and day-to-day practices. This is a severe shortcoming in our understanding of how science might and does influence practice. Standing in contrast to the now large number of surveys into selection method use in organizations (e.g., Bartram et al., 1995; Robertson & Makin, 1986; Shackleton & Newell, 1994), for instance, our knowledge of practitioner *beliefs* about method validity, reliability, and adverse impact is at best rudimentary (see also, Robertson & Smith, 2001). In fact, the whole area of practitioner beliefs about selection methods and processes is a gargantuan one into which research has made little or no inroads (Johns, 1993; Ryan, personal correspondence). Only in relation to the impact of utility analysis has this area been breached initially, specifically concerning the persuasion of practitioners toward the use of more valid predictor methods (Boudreau et al., 1997; Latham & Whyte, 1994). Fundamental questions remain basically unaddressed, however, including which selection methods HR practitioners believe to be more valid and why, how practitioners choose between different predictors and sources of evidence on applicants in real-life selection situations, and how best we can "frame" the key research findings when presenting them to practitioners in order to persuade them toward adopting more valid, reliable, and fair predictor techniques. This paucity of research interest is also at odds with the concentration of research over several decades upon recruiter decision making *within* selection procedures at each stage in the process. Selector decision making *over* different predictor techniques, in contrast, has received almost no research attention.

Second, future research should be directed at evaluating the efficacy of different methods of practitioner training as part of professional CPD events. In several countries now (the USA, UK, Australia, for instance) compulsory CPD is an integral part of remaining licensed or chartered as laid down by the relevant national professional psychology bodies (APA, BPS, and APS). In addition, in many other countries which do not yet have compulsory CPD training, events are run to update practitioners and to educate further practicing psychologists. Given that one of our areas of specialist expertise is the evaluation of training effectiveness (e.g., Goldstein, 1997), it would be sensible to examine the efficacy and transfer of such CPD events to practice, particularly in the field of selection and assessment. CPD represents a mainstream channel through which practitioner beliefs and actions can be directly influenced and it is therefore of considerable interest to evaluate the effectiveness of alternative training interventions in this regard. Compulsory CPD is a relatively new departure in most countries; surely IWO psychologists could be much more involved in validating these interventions in future? This is especially the case for CPD training events on employee selection practices. Many such events will have a professed pragmatic element to them, usually around the theme of updating practitioners on recent developments in research and how these can be applied in practice. The transfer of these points into subsequent practice by attending psychologists is one immediately obvious question area: Do CPD events result in genuine changes to practice, or are events merely attended and the information listened to politely by delegates in order to earn CPD credits? Clearly, such events offer a critical case site for the evaluation of research–practice relations, with the subject pool being IWO psychologists themselves. If such events are failing to persuade fellow IWO psychologists to develop and update their professional practices we should hardly be surprised if HR and line managers remain stubbornly unaffected by our collective research efforts and dissemination of key findings.

Concluding Comments

In this chapter I have argued for four main points and issues. First, that there exists a natural distance between the professional spaces occupied by the scientific and practitioner wings of selection psychology. However, as an absolutely essential corollary to this point, networking mechanisms, channels of information flow and communication, and structural means toward bi-directional influence between both wings need to be strong and healthy. Second, that there exist four types of science in selection psychology (Popularist, Pragmatic, Pedantic, and Puerile Science), and that in keeping with our original formulation of this four-quadrant model, the future of both wings of our discipline can only feasibly be served by Pragmatic Science (Anderson et al., 2001). Third, that it is possible to identify four types of scenarios over the history of selection psychology of relations between research and practice: Scenario 1 where robust research appropriately informs practice, Scenario 2 where unreliable research fortunately fails to affect practice, Scenario 3 where advances in practice stimulate new directions for research, and Scenario 4 where strong research regrettably fails to change selection practices. Examples to support the existence of these three scenarios were presented, but with the caveat that, on balance, the first scenario is most often represented over time in our field. I further argued that *content domain* research should be supplemented with *process domain* studies designed to shed light upon research–practice and practice–research relations. Fourth and finally, I argue for two key directions for future research into these neglected topics in personnel psychology: practitioner beliefs and tactics to persuade practitioners on the basis of research evidence, and validation research into the current rush toward CPD events internationally.

Note

I wish to thank David Chan, Gerard Hodgkinson, Filip Lievens, Rob Ployhart, Ann Marie Ryan, Sonja Schinkel, Neal Schmitt, and my fellow editors for their valuable comments on an earlier version of this chapter.

References

Anderson, N. (1998). The people make the paradigm. *Journal of Organizational Behavior, 19*, 323–328.
Anderson, N. (2003). Applicant and recruiter reactions to new technology in selection: A critical review and agenda for future research. *International Journal of Selection and Assessment, 11*, 121–136.

Anderson, N., Herriot, P., & Hodgkinson, G. P. (2001). The practitioner–researcher divide in Industrial, Work and Organizational (IWO) psychology: Where are we now, and where do we go from here? *Journal of Occupational and Organizational Psychology, 74*, 391–411.

Anderson, N., Lievens, F., van Dam, K., & Ryan, A. M. (2003, in press). Future perspectives on employee selection: Key directions for future research and practice. *Applied Psychology: An International Review*.

Anderson, N., & Ones, D.S. (2003). The construct validity of three entry level personality inventories used in the UK: Cautionary findings from a multiple-inventory investigation. *European Journal of Personality, 17*, S39–66.

Arvey, R. D. (1979a). *Fairness in selecting employees*. Reading, MA: Addison-Wesley.

Arvey, R. D. (1979b). Unfair discrimination in the employment interview: Legal and psychological aspects. *Psychological Bulletin, 86*, 736–765.

Arvey, R. D., & Campion, J. E. (1982). The employment interview: A summary and review of recent research. *Personnel Psychology, 35*, 281–322.

Barber, D. (1973). *Basic personnel procedures*. London: Institute of Personnel Management.

Barrick, M. R., & Mount, M. K. (1991). The big five personality dimensions and job performance: A meta-analysis. *Personnel Psychology, 44*, 1–26.

Barrick, M. R., Mount, M. K., & Judge, T. A. (2001). Personality and performance at the beginning of the new millennium: What do we know and where do we go next? *International Journal of Selection and Assessment, 9*, 9–29.

Bartram, D., Lindley, P. A., Marshall, L., & Foster, J. (1995). The recruitment and selection of young people by small businesses. *Journal of Occupational and Organizational Psychology, 68*, 339–358.

Borman, W. C., Hansen, M., & Hedge, J. W. (1997). Personnel selection. *Annual Review of Psychology, 48*, 299–337.

Boudreau, J. W., Sturman, M. C., & Judge, T. A. (1997). Utility analysis: What are the black boxes, and do they affect decisions? In N. Anderson & P. Herriot (Eds.), *International handbook of selection and assessment* (pp. 303–321). Chichester, UK: John Wiley & Sons.

Cascio, W. F. (1993). Assessing the utility of selection decisions: Theoretical and practical considerations. In N. Schmitt, W. C. Borman, & Associates (Eds.), *Personnel selection in organizations* (pp. 310–340). San Francisco: Jossey-Bass.

Chan, D. (1998). The conceptualization and analysis of change over time: An integrative approach incorporating longitudinal means and covariance structures analysis (LMACS) and multiple indicator latent growth modeling (MLGM). *Organizational Research Methods, 1*, 421–483.

Costa, P. T., Jr., & McCrae, R. R. (1988). From catalogue to classification: Murray's needs and the five factor model. *Journal of Personality and Social Psychology, 55*, 258–265.

Costa, P. T., Jr., & McCrae, R. R. (1992). *Revised NEO Personality Inventory (NEO-PI-R) and NEO Five-Factor Inventory (NEO-FFI) professional manual*. Odessa, FL: Psychological Assessment Resources.

De Fruyt, F., & Salgado, J. F. (2003). Applied personality psychology: Lessons learned from the IWO field. *European Journal of Personality, 17*, S123–131.

Digman, J. M. (1990). Personality structure: Emergence of the Five Factor Model. *Annual Review of Psychology, 41*, 417–440.

Dipboye, R. L. (1997). Structured selection interviews: Why do they work? Why are they underutilized? In N. Anderson & P. Herriot (Eds.), *International handbook of selection and assessment* (pp. 455–473). Chichester, UK: John Wiley & Sons.

Dunnette, M. D. (1990). Blending the science and practice of industrial and organizational psychology: Where are we now and where are we going? In M. D. Dunnette & L. M. Hough (Eds.), *Handbook of industrial and organizational psychology* (2nd ed., Vol. 1, pp. 1–37). Palo Alto, CA: Consulting Psychologists Press.

Eder, R. W., & Harris, M. M. (1999). Employment interview research: Historical update and introduction. In R. W. Eder & M. M. Harris (Eds.), *The employment interview handbook* (pp. 1–27). Thousand Oaks, CA: Sage.

Ferguson, E., Payne, T., & Anderson, N. (1994). Occupational personality assessment: An evaluation of the psychometric properties of the Occupational Personality Questionnnaire (OPQ). *Personality and Individual Differences, 17,* 217–225.

Goldstein, H. W., Zedeck, S., & Goldstein, I. L. (2002). *g*: Is this your final answer? *Human Performance, 15,* 123–142.

Goldstein, I. L. (1997). Interrelationships between the foundations for selection and training systems. In N. Anderson & P. Herriot (Eds.), *International handbook of selection and assessment* (pp. 529–542). Chichester, UK: John Wiley & Sons.

Guion, R. M., & Gottier, R. F. (1965). Validity of personality measures in personnel selection. *Personnel Psychology, 18,* 135–164.

Herriot, P. (1989). Selection as a social process. In M. Smith & I. T. Robertson (Eds.), *Advances in staff selection* (pp. 171–187). Chichester, UK: John Wiley & Sons.

Herriot, P., & Anderson, N. (1997). Selecting for change: How will personnel and selection psychology survive? In N. Anderson & P. Herriot (Eds.), *International handbook of selection and assessment* (pp. 1–34). Chichester, UK: John Wiley & Sons.

Highhouse, S. (2002). Assessing the candidate as a whole: A historical and critical analysis of individual psychological assessment for personnel decision making. *Personnel Psychology, 55,* 363–396.

Hodgkinson, G. P., Herriot, P., & Anderson, N. (2001). Re-aligning the stakeholders in management research: Lessons from Industrial, Work and Organizational Psychology. *British Journal of Management, 12,* 41–48.

Hodgkinson, G. P., & Payne, R. L. (1998). Graduate selection in three European countries. *Journal of Occupational and Organizational Psychology, 71,* 359–365.

Hogan, R. T., & Roberts, B. W. (2001). Introduction: Personality and industrial-organizational psychology. In B. W. Roberts & R. T. Hogan (Eds.), *Personality psychology in the workplace* (pp. 3–16). Washington, DC: American Psychological Association.

Hough, L. M. (2001). I/Owes its advances to personality. In B. W. Roberts & R. Hogan (Eds.), *Personality psychology in the workplace* (pp. 19–44). Washington, DC: American Psychological Association.

Huffcutt, A. I., Roth, P. L., & McDaniel, M. A. (1996). A meta-analytic investigation of cognitive ability in interview evaluations: Moderating characteristics and implications for incremental validity. *Journal of Applied Psychology, 81,* 459–473.

Hunter, J. E., & Hunter, R. F. (1984). Validity and utility of alternative predictors of job performance. *Psychological Bulletin, 96,* 72–98.

Hyatt, D., Cropanzano, R., Finder, L. A., Levy, P., Ruddy, T. M., Vandeveer, V., et al. (1997). Bridging the gap between academics and practice: Suggestions from the field. *The Industrial-Organizational Psychologist, 35* (1), 29–32.

Johns, G. (1993). Constraints on the adoption of psychology-based personnel practices: Lessons from organizational innovation. *Personnel Psychology, 46,* 569–592.

Kuhn, T. S. (1970). *The structure of scientific revolutions* (2nd ed.). Chicago: University of Chicago Press.

Latham, G. P., & Whyte, G. (1994). The futility of utility analysis. *Personnel Psychology, 47,* 31–46.

Levy-Leboyer, C. (1988). Success and failure in applying psychology. *American Psychologist, 43,* 779–785.

Lievens, F., & Harris, M. M. (2003). Research on Internet recruitment and testing: Current status and future directions. In C. L. Cooper & I. T. Robertson (Eds.), *International review of industrial and organizational psychology* (pp. 131–165). Chichester, UK: John Wiley & Sons.

Lievens, F., van Dam, K., & Anderson, N. (2002). Recent trends and challenges in personnel selection. *Personnel Review, 31*, 580–601.

Mayfield, E. C. (1964). The selection interview: A re-evaluation of published research. *Personnel Psychology, 17*, 239–260.

McCrae, R. R., & Costa, P. T., Jr. (1997). Personality trait structure as a human universal. *American Psychologist, 52*, 509–516.

McDaniel, M. A., Whetzel, D. L., Schmidt, F. L., & Maurer, S. D. (1994). The validity of employment interviews: A comprehensive review and meta-analysis. *Journal of Applied Psychology, 79*, 599–616.

Murphy, K. R. (1996). Individual differences and behavior in organizations: Much more than g. In K. R. Murphy (Ed.), *Individual differences and behavior in organizations* (pp. 3–30). San Francisco: Jossey-Bass.

Ones, D. S., & Anderson, N. (2002). Gender and ethnic group differences on personality scales in selection: Some British data. *Journal of Occupational and Organizational Psychology, 75*, 255–276.

Pfeffer, J. (1993). Barriers to the advancement of organizational science: Paradigm development as a dependent variable. *Academy of Management Review, 18*, 599–620.

Rice, E. E. (1997). Scenarios: The scientist–practitioner split and the future of psychology. *American Psychologist, 52*, 1173–1181.

Robertson, I. T., & Makin, P. J. (1986). Management selection in Britain: A survey and critique. *Journal of Occupational Psychology, 59*, 45–57.

Robertson, I. T., & Smith, M. (2001). Personnel selection. *Journal of Occupational and Organizational Psychology, 74*, 441–472.

Ryan, A. M., & Ployhart, R. E. (2000). Applicants' perceptions of selection procedures and decisions: A critical review and agenda for the future. *Journal of Management, 26*, 565–606.

Rynes, S. L., Bartunek, J. M., & Daft, R. L. (2001). Across the great divide: Knowledge creation and transfer between practitioners and academics. *Academy of Management Journal, 44*, 340–355.

Rynes, S. L., Brown, K. G., & Colbert, A. E. (2002). Seven common misconceptions about human resource practices: Research findings versus practitioner beliefs. *Academy of Management Executive, 16*, 92–102.

Sackett, P. R. (1994, April). *The content and process of the research enterprise within industrial and organizational psychology*. Presidential address to the Society for Industrial and Organizational Psychology conference, Nashville, TN.

Salgado, J. F. (1997). The five factor model of personality and job performance in the European Community. *Journal of Applied Psychology, 82*, 30–43.

Salgado, J. F. (2001). Some landmarks of 100 years of scientific personnel selection at the beginning of the new century. *International Journal of Selection and Assessment, 9*, 3–8.

Salgado, J. F., & Anderson, N. (2002). Cognitive and GMA testing in the European Community: Issues and evidence. *Human Performance, 15*, 75–96.

Salgado, J. F., & Anderson, N. (2003). Validity generalization of GMA tests across countries in the European Community. *European Journal of Work and Organizational Psychology, 12*, 1–17.

Salgado, J. F., Anderson, N., Moscoso, S., Bertua, C., & De Fruyt, F. (2003). International validity generalization of GMA and cognitive abilities as predictors of work behaviours: A European contribution and comparison with American findings. *Personnel Psychology, 56*, 573–605.

Salgado, J. F., Anderson, N., Moscoso, S., Bertua, C., De Fruyt, F., & Rolland, J. P. (2003). A meta-analytic study of general mental ability validity for different occupations in the European Community. *Journal of Applied Psychology, 88*, 1068–1081.

Salgado, J. F., & Moscoso, S. (2002). Comprehensive meta-analysis of the construct validity of the employment interview. *European Journal of Work and Organizational Psychology, 11*, 299–324.

Salgado, J. F., Viswesvaran, C., & Ones, D. S. (2001). Predictors used for personnel selection: An overview of constructs, methods and techniques. In N. Anderson, D. S. Ones, H. K. Sinangil, & C. Viswesvaran (Eds.), *Handbook of industrial, work and organizational psychology* (pp. 165–199). London: Sage.

Schmidt, F. L., & Hunter, J. E. (1998). The validity and utility of selection research methods in personnel psychology: Practical and theoretical implications of 85 years of research findings. *Psychological Bulletin, 124*, 262–274.

Schmitt, N, Gooding, R. Z., Noe, R. A., & Kirsch, M. (1984). Meta-analyses of validity studies published between 1964 and 1982 and the investigation of study characteristics. *Personnel Psychology, 37*, 402–422.

Shackleton, V. J., & Newell, S. (1994). European management selection methods: A comparison of five countries. *International Journal of Selection and Assessment, 2*, 91–102.

Tenopyr, M. L. (2002). Theory versus reality: Evaluation of *g* in the workplace. *Human Performance, 15*, 107–122.

Torrington, D., & Chapman, J. (1979). *Personnel management.* London: Prentice-Hall International.

Ulrich, L., & Trumbo, D. (1965). The selection interview since 1949. *Psychological Bulletin, 63*, 100–116.

Viswesvaran, C., & Ones, D. S. (2000). Perspectives on models of job performance. *International Journal of Selection and Assessment, 8*, 216–226.

Viswesvaran, C., Sinangil, H. K., Ones, D. S., & Anderson, N. (2001). Introduction to the Handbook and Volume 1 – Personnel psychology: Where we have been, where we are, (and where we could be). In N. Anderson, D. S. Ones, H. K. Sinangil, & C. Viswesvaran (Eds.), *Handbook of industrial, work and organizational psychology* (pp. 1–9). London: Sage.

Wagner, R. (1949). The employment interview: A critical review. *Personnel Psychology, 2*, 17–46.

Wright, O. R. (1969). Summary of research on the selection interview since 1964. *Personnel Psychology, 22*, 391–413.

Yang, K., & Bond, M. H. (1990). Exploring implicit personality theories with indigenous or imported constructs: The Chinese case. *Journal of Personality and Social Psychology, 58*, 1087–1095.

Part I

PREPARING FOR SELECTION

2

Job Analysis: Current and Future Perspectives

Olga F. Voskuijl

It no longer needs to be stressed that the nature of work is changing rapidly. In the past decade many authors (e.g., Cascio, 1995; Herriot & Anderson, 1997; Lawler, 1994) described developments in information technology, the global economy, economic competition, and the impact of those changes on the organization and nature of work. This would result in instability of jobs in terms of responsibilities and tasks. As a consequence the usefulness of detailed job analysis is questioned. Schmidt (1993) stated more than ten years ago that some methods of job analysis were only suited to disappearing stable bureaucratic organizations. Some authors describe job analysis as old-fashioned and inflexible and embrace the concept and practice of competency modeling (e.g., Schippmann, 1999). However, others (e.g., Sanchez & Levine, 2001) argue that with a shift of focus and principles traditional job analysis techniques can be broadened to work analysis and keep their relevance for organizations.

This chapter focuses on the role of "conventional" job or work analysis, now and in the future, and discusses the difference between these approaches of work and competency modeling. In the first section the characteristics of job analysis are described. The second section describes some of the most well-known instruments and methods of job analysis. The third section discusses future-oriented job analysis and a comparison between job analysis and competency modeling. The fourth section summarizes the consequences of past developments in work for job analysis and presents future research needs.

JOB ANALYSIS

Job analysis has been defined as "the collection and analysis of any type of job related information by any method for any purpose" (Ash, 1988, p. 1) or more specifically, according to Cascio (1991, p. 188): "The objective of job analysis is to define each job in terms of the behaviors necessary to perform it. Job analysis comprises of two major elements: job descriptions and job specifications." Job descriptions refer to defining the job in terms of its task requirements and include characteristics of the job such as the procedures, methods, and standards of performance. Job specifications refer to "people requirements," that is, what the job calls for in terms of behaviors, knowledge, abilities, skills and other personal characteristics. The latter definition reflects the well-known distinction of job-related behavior of McCormick and his associates (e.g., McCormick, Jeanneret, & Mecham, 1972) between generalized worker activities and attribute requirements. Most of the definitions of job analysis focus on the *type of work-related information* (or job descriptor) to be collected; the type of information is one of the choices to be made when applying job analysis. In relation to the purpose of job analysis in specific situations McCormick (1976) mentioned several other aspects that must be considered, for example: *the method of data collection* and *the agent or source of the information*. We describe these three aspects in more detail.

Type of work-related information

McCormick (1976) distinguished the following types of information: work activities; work performance (e.g., time taken and error analysis); job context (such as social context and physical working conditions); machines, tools, equipment, and work aids used; job-related tangibles and intangibles such as materials processed and services rendered; and personnel requirements. Work activities and personnel requirements in particular were the subject of research. Work activities are divided into job-oriented and worker-oriented activities; job-oriented activities are usually expressed in job terms and indicate what is accomplished. Worker-oriented activities refer, for example, to behaviors performed in work (e.g., decision making). Personnel requirements include Knowledge, Skills, Abilities, and Other characteristics, known as KSAOs. It must be noted, however, that Harvey (1991) and Harvey and Wilson (2000) excluded the process of inferring required worker traits or abilities, according to the American Uniform Guidelines on Employee Selection Procedures (1978). In their opinion job analysis methods should describe observable work behavior independently of the characteristics of the people who perform the job, and job analysis data should be verifiable and replicable. Required personal traits do not meet these characteristics. However, the development of a job analysis instrument for the identification of personality-related job requirements by Raymark, Schmit, and Guion (1997) illustrates the opposite position, which is seen as especially useful in the context of personnel selection. Another example of the use of work-related personality constructs in the description of jobs is the category of Worker Characteristics in the Occupational Information Network (O*NET; Peterson, Mumford, Borman, Jeanneret, & Fleishman, 1999). These worker characteristics include abilities, work styles, and occupational values and interests. O*NET is the new occupational information tool of the US Department of Labor that replaces the "old" Dictionary of Occupational Titles (DOT; Mumford & Peterson, 1999).

Method of data collection

Various methods exist for collecting job information: questionnaires, interviews with (groups of) incumbents, direct observation of job incumbents, diaries kept by incumbents, documentation such as instruction materials and maintenance records, recordings of job activities (e.g., video tapes, electronic records). Combinations of several methods are possible. Multi-method approaches result in more complete pictures of the jobs (Morgeson & Champion, 1997).

Agent or source of the information

Traditionally, job incumbents, supervisors, and professional job analysts were the most important sources of job information. As the boundaries of jobs become less clear-cut, job analysis demands a broader range of information agents; for example, customers or training experts. Besides people, devices also can be used as sources of job information; we mentioned as a method of data collection the use of videotapes and other electronic information: in those cases cameras and computers are the sources. Sanchez and Levine (2001) stress the importance of electronic records of performance (e.g., in call centers the number of calls handled) as reliable sources of work information. Each type of resource has its particular strengths and weaknesses; for example, incumbents might have the most information about the content of a job, but professional job analysts might be more familiar with job analysis methods.

Recently the reliability of job analysis data of incumbents has been questioned (Sanchez & Levine, 2000; Sanchez, 2000). Sanchez (2000) states that job analysts prefer incumbent ratings because these ratings have high face validity. He describes several disadvantages of the use of incumbent job analysis data: a) it takes up the valuable time of large numbers of incumbents, b) incumbents are not always motivated to rate their jobs conscientiously, c) rating instructions and the survey format are not always well understood, and d) there is no empirical evidence that incumbents are most qualified to ensure valid job information. Sanchez, Zamora, and Visweswaran (1997) found that incumbents of complex jobs and incumbents with lower levels of satisfaction produce higher ratings of job characteristics than non-incumbents. However, it is possible that the differences within incumbents and between incumbents and others reflect real differences; for example, employees in complex jobs may have more freedom to develop unique patterns or profiles of activities (Landy & Vasey, 1991), which are all "right." In general there are no "true" job analysis ratings. The meta-analyses of Voskuijl and Van Sliedregt (2002), and of Dierdorff and Wilson (2003), revealed that rater source did affect the reliability coefficients but there were other important moderators as well. This brings us to the psychometric properties of job analysis instruments.

Validity and reliability of job analysis data

Job analysis outcomes are often the result of subjective judgments and human judgment has proven to be fallible, thus leading to inaccuracy. Morgeson and Campion (1997) distinguished two broad categories of inaccuracy: social and cognitive. Both are divided in two subcategories of sources of inaccuracy: social in social influence processes (e.g., conformity pressures) and self-presentation processes (e.g., social desirability); cognitive in limitations in information processing systems (e.g., information overload) and biases in information processing systems (e.g., extraneous information). Morgeson and Campion mention six likely effects on job analysis data of those sources: interrater reliability, inter-rater agreement, discriminability between jobs, dimensionality of factor structures, mean ratings, and completeness of job information. These effects refer to different aspects of validity or, in the terms of Morgeson and Campion (1997, 2000), accuracy. However, most of the hypothesized effects have not yet been the subject of research; reliability is the best-documented aspect of the accuracy of job analysis instruments.

Reliability.   Almost every study on job analysis presents some measure of interrater relia-bility or intrarater reliability. Interrater reliability refers to consistency across raters, often expressed in intraclass correlations and means of pair-wise correlations; according to Rosenthal and Rosnov (1991) these measures are interchangeable. Intrarater reliability refers, for example, to a type of test–retest measurement. It is difficult to compare the results of the meta-analyses of Voskuijl and Van Sliedregt (2002) and Dierdorff and Wilson (2003), mentioned earlier, because the databases and the classification and treatment of job analysis data differ. For example, while Voskuijl and Van Sliedregt included human attributes in the meta-analysis, Dierdorff and Wilson followed Harvey in excluding attrib-utes from job analysis data. Besides, the database from Dierdorff and Wilson goes further back, which resulted in much more data, and especially data referring to tasks, while the Voskuijl and Van Sliedregt study showed a lack of task data. The study of Dierdorff and Wilson shows that tasks generally have higher interrater reliability than generalized worker activities. However, task data showed lower estimates of intrarater reliability. In both studies professional analysts display higher interrater reliabilities than other sources (e.g., incumbents, supervisors, trained students).

In Voskuijl and Van Sliedregt's meta-analysis, only rating strategy contributed to unique variance in interrater reliability coefficients. Although the literature on information pro-cessing in judgment tasks (e.g., Fiske & Neuberg, 1990; Harvey & Wilson, 2000) suggests that decomposed strategies (judging elements of the job) lead to more reliable results than holistic approaches (the rater judges the job as an undivided entity rather than the ele-ments or task of the job; Cornelius & Lyness, 1980), the meta-analysis shows that holistic judgment is as good or better than decomposed judgments. The decomposed strategies might cause information overload, or they might lead to careless ratings because they are often time-consuming and they might be experienced as rather dull. Another possible explanation is an interaction between job type and type of rating strategy; decomposed strategies might be less effective for jobs whose tasks are no less complex than the job as a whole (Sanchez & Levine, 1994).

Accuracy or validity.   Sanchez and Levine (2000) question the relevance of research on the accuracy (validity) of job analysis data in terms of reliability. They argue that measures of interrater reliability or interrater agreement ignore the impact of job analysis results on personnel decisions. They advocate employing consequential criteria as well. Job analysis results as worker attributes and work data are the basis of performance measures and orga-nizational programs such as selection and training. The authors state that the impact of job analysis on different personnel decisions varies along a continuum that is comparable to the continuum between immediate and ultimate criteria described by Thorndike (1949); "The ultimate criterion embodies everything that ultimately defines success on the job"

(Sanchez & Levine, 2000, p. 815). As ultimate criteria are practically unavailable, the consequences of job analysis data in the long term are unknown as well. So, Sanchez and Levine are concerned about the absence of "true" job scores to use as the standard for accuracy and they propose estimating consequential validity as an alternative. However, one must be aware that the immediately available consequences of job analysis data do not tell the whole story about the value of job analysis results. The same holds for reliability data. Both types of information are relevant indicators of validity.

In response to the arguments of Sanchez and Levine (2000) in favor of consequential validity, Harvey and Wilson (2000) stress the importance of the distinction made earlier by Harvey (1991) between job description and job/worker specification. They state that the arguments of Sanchez and Levine are correct for the "speculative" inferences of job specifications (e.g., required human attributes). However, because the description of work is or should be based on observable and verifiable behavior, they consider consequential validity "irrelevant for assessing properly conducted job analyses" (p. 829). In their opinion the accuracy of job descriptive data can and must be assessed directly. In another reaction to Sanchez and Levine, Morgeson and Campion (2000) reason that consequential validity reflects usefulness and that is something different than accuracy. Besides, the assessment of consequential validity has the same problems associated with judging job analysis data. Summarizing, it can be stated that the opponents of Sanchez and Levine's point of view about accuracy acknowledge the value of consequential validity for certain purposes (e.g., to become aware of the impact of job analysis data on personnel decisions). However, the concept of consequential validity cannot replace other aspects of validity.

Relevancy of job analysis

As mentioned above, it has been argued that "traditional" job analysis is not always relevant to the changing world of work (e.g., Schuler, 1989). By traditional is meant lists of tasks or very detailed descriptions of what an incumbent does. Those detailed methods have been accused of lots of things, for instance of being archaic, and of emphasizing the status quo and neglecting interpersonal processes (Schmidt, 1993; Sanchez & Levine, 2001). They inventory what is done and how it is done and they should indicate what could be the best way to reach certain goals (Offermann & Gowing, 1993). Furthermore, job analysis would suppose or create job boundaries that hinder innovation and flexible reactions to changing environments (Sanchez, 1994).

Another argument that could be used against the use of detailed job analysis is related to the "specificity–generality dilemma" regarding the relation between criteria and personality measures in personnel selection. That is, the question about the necessity of assessing applicants on fine-grained personality variables or on broad personality variables. Ones and Visweswaran (1996) state that general and complex criterion measures such as overall job performance need similarly complex and broad predictors (e.g., such as the Big Five). However, several authors have presented various arguments against this perspective (e.g., Ashton, 1998; Hogan & Roberts, 1996; Paunonen, Rothstein, & Jackson, 1999; Tett, Guterman, Bleier, & Murphy, 2000). Tett et al. (2000) summarized the main issues regarding the debate about the use of specific versus general measures in the prediction of job performance. They mention, as an argument in favor of prediction based on narrow personality traits, the fact that there is evidence that narrow trait scales can explain criterion variance that is concealed in more general measures. Further, they stress the importance of matching the content of the predictor and criterion variables. An issue that is especially important in the context of a discussion of the relevance of job analysis is their argument that the trade-off between narrow and broad-bandwidth measures with respect to time is not obvious. In their opinion job analysis can identify the relevant specific concepts, thus saving time by not measuring irrelevant content that is included in broad measures. Tett et al. conclude: "Thus specificity not only allows better use of testing time, it promotes it when guided by systematic job description" (p. 208). The use of narrow personality traits will rely more heavily on detailed job analysis than the use of more general personality variables.

In general, the arguments against job analysis are not strong enough to abolish one of the oldest human resource management tools. The descriptions of several methods and instruments presented in the next section show that job analysis could be more than the identification of lists of tasks as some opponents suggest. Of course, it is wise to look further than the often artificial boundaries of jobs; therefore Sanchez and Levine (1999) propagated the use of the term work analysis to indicate that the analysis is not limited to a fixed set of tasks. It is easy to apply most of the described job analysis instruments to a broader interpretation of the concept job. Besides, it is often difficult to avoid describing or thinking in terms of more or less delimited "portions" of work; even an ever-changing amoeba has boundaries and, in the case of work, job or work analysis can help to identify those boundaries and what they enclose.

SOME METHODS AND QUESTIONNAIRES TO COLLECT WORK-RELATED INFORMATION

Harvey (1991) developed a taxonomy of job analysis methods, based on two dimensions: a) specificity of job analysis information and b) the degree to which items are rated on a common metric. Specificity of information refers to the degree of behavioral and technological detail provided by the job descriptor items. The job- and worker-oriented activities described earlier are respectively highly and moderately specific. The degree of specificity has an effect on the possibility of cross-job comparisons. Job analysis data in terms of a high level of behavioral specificity (e.g., task statements) makes cross-job comparisons very difficult, if not impossible.

The possibility of cross-job comparisons refers to the other dimension in Harvey's taxonomy, the degree to which items are rated on a common metric. For this dimension Harvey distinguishes cross-job-relative, within-job-relative, and qualitative ratings. Cross-job-relative means that scales are rated relative to other jobs. Within-job-relative means that the items are rated relative to the other items. For example, in relative-time-spent scales or in relative importance scales, the other items are the standard. In qualitative ratings there is often no standard at all. Harvey advises against the use of instruments that do not allow cross-job comparisons because the use of those instruments is limited in job classification, career planning placement, and other personnel activities.

Combining the three levels of both dimensions leads to nine categories. Most of the standardized questionnaires belong to the category that combines the moderate level of both dimensions: moderate behavioral specificity and within-job-relative scales. The widely used Position Analysis Questionnaire (PAQ, discussed below) is an example of this category (McCormick et al., 1972). Although the PAQ manual in general cautions against it, the specific instruction for the use of the importance scales of this worker-oriented questionnaire directs job analysts to make job-within-relative ratings (Harvey, 1991). Some instruments incorporate several sections and cover more than one category of the taxonomy, for example Functional Job Analysis (FJA; Fine & Wiley, 1971). Next, some of the most well-known instruments and methods will be described. An exhaustive overview is presented in Gael's (1988) handbook.

Position Analysis Questionnaire (PAQ).   The PAQ, developed by McCormick and coworkers (1972, 1976, 1979), is based on the worker-oriented approach. This means that generalized worker behaviors are involved and that the instrument has a moderate level of behavioral specificity. The 187 items of the PAQ are job elements that describe behaviors that are involved in work activities (e.g., advising). McCormick et al. (1972, p. 349) describe a job element as: "a generalized class of behaviorally related job activities . . .". The term generalized refers to the fact that the elements are not job specific, in order to make it possible to compare different jobs. The items fall into the following divisions: information input, mental processes, work output, relationships with other persons, job context, and other job characteristics (e.g., job demands). Most items are rated on five-point importance scales (Importance to this job: 1 = very minor; 5 = extreme). Occupational psychologists established the linkage between job elements and 76 attributes. On an 11-point scale the relevance of each attribute to each element was rated (weighed). There are a variety of methods to produce different attribute profiles for different jobs, for example the additive method by simply adding the attribute weightings for each job element (Sparrow, Patrick, Spurgeon, & Barwell, 1982; Sparrow, 1989). The PAQ is considered to be the best established and most thoroughly researched of the standardized job analysis questionnaires (Cunningham, 1996). The research also resulted in some criticism. For example, Cornelius, DeNisi, and Blencoe (1984) stated that the PAQ might be more suited for blue-collar jobs than for managerial and professional jobs, while McCormick suggested that the instrument covered a broad range of jobs.

Functional Job Analysis (FJA).   Functional Job Analysis results from the development of the *Dictionary of Occupational Titles* (US Department of Labor, 1965), which describes the characteristics, methods, work requirements, and activities required to perform almost all jobs in the United States. Functional Job Analysis aims at generating task statements and identifies for each task what the worker does (behavior), why and how he or she does it, and what is accomplished by his or her work (Fine, 1988). Further, the job analyst describes for each task the orientation and level of involvement of the worker with data, people, and things, the well-known Worker Functions. Furthermore, required training time is operationalized as level of Reasoning, Mathematics, and Language in the General Educational Development (GED) scales and the Specific Vocational Preparation Scale (SVP). The method is a combination of the worker-oriented approach (e.g., the Worker Functions), the work-oriented approach (a task inventory), and the qualitative approach (the description of job-specific tasks). The worker-oriented scales do, but the job-specific task descriptions do not, allow cross-job comparisons. The Occupational Information Network (O*Net), the new replacement for the DOT (Peterson et al., 1999), is especially focused on cross-job descriptors. O*Net is described in the last section of this chapter.

Critical Incidents Technique (CIT). As the name indicates, the CIT is not a questionnaire but a technique (Flanagan, 1954). This approach generates critical behaviors observed by incumbents or others who have experience of the job being studied. These job experts describe anecdotes or incidents that illustrate effective and ineffective (and sometimes also average) job performance. Each incident must describe: a) what led up to the incident, b) what the individual did, c) what the consequences of the behavior of the employee were, and d) whether the consequences were within the control of the employee. The incidents are categorized in performance dimensions. The technique is especially suited for the development of behaviorally anchored rating scales (the incidents form the scale anchors) and the development of situational interviews. For example, Huffcutt, Weekley, Wiesner, Groot, and Jones (2001) used this technique to develop interview questions to illustrate the differential effectiveness of situational interviews and behavioral description interviews. However, the development of instruments by means of the CIT is time-consuming and the applicability is limited, according to Harvey's taxonomy. This approach can be considered as high on behavioral specificity, with very limited possibilities to compare jobs.

Ability Requirements Scales (ARS). The Ability Requirement Scales were developed by Fleishman and several coworkers (e.g., Fleishman & Mumford, 1988, 1991; Theologus, Romashko, & Fleishman, 1973). Through the abilities requirements approach, information about the characteristics of job incumbents are identified. Abilities are defined as "relatively enduring attributes of the individual that influence a broad range of task performance" (Fleishman & Mumford, 1988, p. 918). Examples of abilities are: verbal comprehension, inductive reasoning, mathematical reasoning, and knowledge. The results of this type of job analysis provide the information to guide selection or development of selection procedures. The scales are based on the development of a taxonomy of abilities that might describe work activities, based on factor analytic studies. The resulting Ability Requirement Scales eventually encompass 37 scales, with most of them having a cognitive (e.g., verbal comprehension) or physical (e.g., static strength) character; personality variables were not included. The scales have a seven-point behaviorally anchored rating format. Because the information is not directly tied to fluctuating tasks but to the relatively stable characteristics of individuals, this approach offers a taxonomic system that is likely to be stable in a changing environment. It is said to be generalizable to different jobs and different circumstances, so cross-job comparisons are possible. Although the scale anchors are defined in terms of behavior, the behavioral specificity is low.

Threshold Trait Analysis (TTA). The objective of the TTA (Lopez, 1988) is to identify the personal characteristics that are important to perform a job acceptably. It is based on the trait-oriented approach and distinguishes 33 personal qualities divided into five groups: physical, mental, learned, motivational, and social. The physical, mental, and learned traits are called ability or "can do" factors. The motivational and social traits are labeled attitudinal or "willing to do" factors. The latter are particularly scarce in job analysis instruments and they are an extension of the abilities included in the ARS. Subject matter experts (SMEs), such as supervisors or incumbents of the job to be rated, estimate the relevance, the level, and the practicality of the 33 traits for acceptable job performance. To guarantee an adequate level of reliability a minimum of five SMEs is recommended. The method is appropriate for cross-job comparisons. The behavioral specificity of the method is high because the required level of each trait is specified in detail. For example, level 2 of the trait strength is described as follows: "the incumbent can: lift, push, pull, etc. objects of over 50 pounds readily" (Lopez, 1988, p. 883).

Task Inventory Analysis.   Task inventory approaches start with the identification of tasks in order to develop a questionnaire or checklist for a specific job. Tasks can be described as activities or sequences of related activities directed at specified job objectives (Levine, 1983). They are generated through interviewing SMEs or discussions in SME panels. Task inventories consist of lists of activities or task statements. In general a statement is at least a description of what the worker does in terms of an action verb, the purpose of that action, and the methods and equipment used. In short: What does the worker do, how does he or she do it, and why? Each task is rated on one or more scales: relative-time-spent (relative to the other tasks), importance, difficulty, and criticality. When using more than one scale per task it is possible to calculate a task importance value, for example by adding and/or multiplying the different scale values. Task inventories are behavioral specific and comparisons between jobs are not possible.

Job Element Method (JEM).   Primoff and Dittrich Eyde (1988, p. 807) described the purpose of the Job Element Method of job analysis as "to identify the behaviors and their evidences, as revealed in achievements, that are significant to job success." So, elements refer to behaviors and their evidences, or to the well-known Knowledge, Skills, Abilities, and Other characteristics (KSAOs) and their evidences. Elements that are relevant for a job are identified and evaluated by subject matter experts. The experts use four scales to rate the elements: "Barely acceptable worker," "Superior worker," "Trouble if not considered," "Practical." "Barely acceptable worker" indicates to what extent even barely acceptable workers have the ability (or skill, etc.). "Superior worker" indicates whether the element is very important to identify superior workers. "Trouble if not considered" refers to the amount of trouble that is likely to occur if the element is ignored when selecting applicants (e.g., safe driving in a chauffeur's job). Ratings for "Practical" refer to the extent that the organization can fill its openings if the element is required. Most elements are expressed in terms of job-specific KSAOs; because of the job specificity some of them can be considered as work-oriented (e.g., an element for the job of police officer is "ability to enforce laws"). The elements show a moderate or low level of behavioral specificity. The elements for each job are gathered in a rather unstructured way in sessions of SME panels, and therefore cross-job comparisons are very limited.

Personality-Related Position Requirements Form (PPRF).   Raymark et al. (1997) view the existing methods as lacking the possibility to identify some aspects of personality-related position requirements to formulate selection hypotheses. They stated that if personality traits are relevant to job performance, and if they are not identified and measured because job analysis instruments do not cover these variables, they will be overlooked for selection. The authors developed an instrument that is meant to generate hypotheses about relevant personality variables: the Personality-Related Position Requirements Form (PPRF). The PPRF is meant as an addition to other job analysis instruments that cover other job-related information. The twelve sub-dimensions are linked to the "Big Five" (Barrick & Mount, 1991), which are the basis of the instrument. General leadership, Interest in negotiation, and Achievement striving are the sub-dimensions of Surgency; Agreeableness covers: Friendly disposition, Sensitivity to interest of others, and Cooperative or collaborative work tendency; General trustworthiness, Adherence to a work ethic, and Thoroughness and attentiveness to details are parts of Conscientiousness; Emotional stability is covered by Emotional stability, Desire to generate ideas, and Tendency to think things through. Items are statements that refer to position requirements. Respondents are asked to indicate the extent to which the requirements are necessary for effective performance ("Effective performance in this position requires the person to . . ."; 0 = not required, 1 = helpful, 2 = essential). The instrument is low on behavior specificity and high on cross-job comparability.

Combination of methods.   None of the described or other instruments or methods can be said to be the best. Which method (or combination of methods) is appropriate in a specific context depends on the purpose of the analysis. However, only two studies report results of comparisons between job analysis methods with respect to specific purposes (Levine, Ash, & Bennett, 1980; Levine, Ash, Hall, & Sistrunk, 1983). Levine et al. (1983) compared the instruments presented above (except for the PPRF, which did not exist at the time of their study); the task inventory that was to be evaluated in their study was paired with the Comprehensive Occupational Data Analysis Program (CODAP). They asked experienced job analysts to rate the effectiveness (quality and comprehensiveness) of seven instruments in relation to eleven purposes on a five-point scale (a score of 1 indicates that a method is not at all comprehensive and is low in quality; 3 means that the method is moderately high in quality for the stated purpose and provides information that

TABLE 2.1   Purpose and suited job analysis method

Purpose	*Method*
Selection/placement (Levine et al.:** Personnel requirements/specifications)	TTA*, ARS*, PPRF, PAQ, FJA*
Development of AC exercises	PAQ, CIT, Task inventories, FJA
Job design and restructuring	TI/CODAP*, FJA*
Job evaluation	PAQ*, FJA*
Performance appraisal	CIT*, FJA*
Training	TI/CODAP*, CIT*
Validity generalization (Levine et al.:** Job classification)	TTA, PAQ*, TI/CODAP*, FJA*

* Mean > 3.5 in the study of Levine et al. (1983).
** Terminology of Levine et al.

covers about half of the job's features). Table 2.1 gives examples of possible combinations of job analysis methods and the purposes they might serve. The instruments marked with an asterisk had a mean higher than 3.5 in Levine et al.'s study.

Besides purpose, time and cost may guide the choice for the use of specific job analysis methods. The application of some methods is very time-consuming and thus expensive, for example: the CIT, task inventories, FJA, and JEM. Another characteristic of these methods is job specificity. This makes them less suited to identifying similarities between jobs or to discovering the more abstract and stable requirements of jobs that are relevant even after the job has changed. For the latter purposes the methods that focus on traits and abilities, such as the ARS, TTA, and PPRF, are more appropriate. However, as stated earlier, Harvey (1991) argues against these types of instruments because he considers worker traits and attributes to be too dependent on the personal characteristics of the employees who perform the job; furthermore, they are not observable, not verifiable, and not replicable. A combination of methods may be the solution to the problems attached to the specific instruments. In Levine et al.'s study, 86% of the 93 respondents preferred the use of a combination of job analysis methods. To cover the content of jobs in full, and moreover to cover work that goes beyond the borders of "traditional" jobs, a combination of different methods might be even more appropriate today.

FUTURE-ORIENTED JOB ANALYSIS AND COMPETENCY MODELING

In answer to the increased instability of jobs and the supposed inadequacy of job analysis to cover changes in jobs, in the past decennia several "new" techniques have been developed, techniques that pretend to grasp the content of existing but changing work and to predict work yet to be created: strategic job analysis, strategic job modeling, future-oriented job modeling, competency modeling. Whether these techniques are really new or whether they are a rearrangement or adaptation of existing techniques is not always clear. Schneider and Konz (1989) introduced the term strategic job modeling referring to "a process through which the skills required by jobs in the future can be identified" (p. 53). Their approach is based on a combination of traditional job analysis procedures ("Multimethod Job Analysis"). Information about jobs in the future and required KSAs is gathered by "simply" asking subject matter experts (e.g., job incumbents and supervisors) and job analysts about their expectations for the future. The method resembles the Combined Job Analysis Method (C-JAM) described by Levine (1983). Whereas in the C-JAM the task statements, their importance ratings, and the identification of KSAOs are related to existing jobs, in strategic job analysis they refer to the expected content of future jobs. A comparable but extended approach was applied by Landis, Fogli, and Goldberg (1998). They used a future-oriented job analysis (FOJA) procedure to gain an understanding of three newly formed entry-level positions. This procedure includes seven developmental steps that were based on a combination of traditional job analysis methods (task inventories, task–KSA linkage questionnaires) and new instruments. A unique characteristic of this procedure was the development and use of the Task Sort Questionnaire (TSQ). The TSQ consisted of a list of 459 task statements for the three jobs, which were gathered in the preceding steps. SMEs were asked to indicate in which of the three future positions each task was likely to be performed. The percentages of correct sorts (that is: tasks attributed to the job it was written for) were considered as indicators of accuracy and were input for discussions about misunderstandings and differences of opinions about the content of the jobs. Because Landis et al. collected only future-oriented information this procedure could be completed within six weeks. However, if practitioners followed the recommendations of Schneider and Konz to analyze the jobs as they currently exist as well, the procedure would be very time-consuming.

Schippmann (1999, p. x) uses the term strategic job modeling to describe a job analysis approach that focuses on "the strategic and future-oriented needs of today's organizations . . ." The term modeling underlines the creative, developmental character of the approach. The method is considered as a worker-oriented approach: competencies are one of the building blocks of strategic job modeling.

Competency modeling seems to be the most extreme "replacement" for job analysis. A problem with this technique is that definitions of the term competency are not univocal and sometimes even contradictory. McClelland (1973) introduced the term as a predictor of job performance because he doubted the predictive validity of cognitive ability tests. He proposed to replace intelligence testing by competency testing. Although he did not define the term competency, he made it clear that the term did not include intelligence. Today, we know that general mental ability is the most valid predictor of job performance (Schmidt & Hunter, 1998), and there is no empirical support yet for the validity of competency testing as a replacement for intelligence testing (e.g., Barrett & Depinet, 1991). This does not mean that the concept of competency is worthless. It is beyond doubt that there is more than cognitive intelligence. We all know the banal example of the shy genius who never leaves his study to tell the world about his brilliant ideas. The question is how to define and measure the characteristics that one needs in addition to intelligence. Is the answer the Big Five or do we need other concepts, such as competencies? The definition of a competency from Boyatzis (1982) is based on McClelland's data and refers to KSAs, motives, and traits related to job performance. Other authors refer to competencies as behaviors. For example, Tett et al. (2000, p. 215) describe a competency as: "an identifiable aspect of prospective work behaviour attributable to the individual that is expected to contribute positively and/or negatively to organizational effectiveness." They conclude: "In short, a competency is future-evaluated work behaviour" (p. 215). So, the definitions vary from abstract psychological constructs to direct observable behavior. Because of this lack of clarity and the rapid growth of competency-driven applications in practice, the Job Analysis and Competency Modeling Task Force (JACMTF; Schippmann et al., 2000) investigated the antecedents of competency modeling. The members of the JACMTF compared and contrasted competency modeling and job analysis. They conducted a literature search and interviewed 37 subject matter experts, such as human resources consultants, former presidents of the Society for Industrial and Organizational Psychology, leaders in the area of competency modeling, and industrial and organizational psychologists who represent a traditional job analysis perspective. The sample of experts represented advocates as well as opponents of either job analysis or competency modeling. The task force asked the experts to define a competency and to describe the differences between job analysis and competency modeling. Their search revealed, again, a variety of definitions of a competency. Schippmann et al. reasoned that the lack of consensus is obvious

TABLE 2.2   Differences between job analysis and competency modeling

Job analysis	Competency modeling
Focus on	Focus on
a. work and tasks	a. worker
b. technical skills	b. personal values, personality
c. differences between jobs	c. core competencies, common for several jobs
d. short-term job match	d. long-term organizational fit
Advantage: Psychometrically sound	Advantage: Link to business goals and strategies

Source: Schippmann et al. (2000).

considering the diverse areas in which the term was developed and used. The comparison of job analysis and competency modeling resulted in a superior overall evaluation of job analysis: job analysis is considered to be more psychometrically sound. Based on the interviews with the experts, the task force members rated both approaches on ten evaluative criteria, for example: method of investigation, procedures for developing descriptor content, detail of descriptor content. The differences are summarized in Table 2.2.

Except for the evaluation variable "link to business goals and strategies," job analysis demonstrates medium/high and high rigor with reference to the criteria. In contrast, competency profiling has a strong link to business goals and strategies but demonstrates low/medium to medium rigor with respect to the other criteria. The link to business goals and strategies is also reflected in the opinions of the experts about other characteristics of both approaches: competency modeling is more focused on core competencies that are common for several jobs (or even for the whole organization), and on aspects that are related to long-term organizational fit; the focus of job analysis is supposed to be on differences between jobs and on short-term job match. Furthermore, job analysis focuses more on technical skills whereas competency modeling tends to emphasize personal values and personality orientations. The findings of Schippmann et al. are no reason to replace job analysis with competency modeling. In the opinion of Sparrow and Bognano (1993), job analysis is necessary to identify competencies. Sanchez and Levine (2001) state that the difference between these two approaches is blurry. They also point out that the methodology in developing competency models is less rigorous than the traditional job analysis methodology. However, they state, like Schippmann et al., that traditional job analysis fails to reflect the strategy, goals, and future needs of the organization.

Job or work analysis in a changing world of work

Considering the changing world of work, in general the term work analysis may be preferred above the term job analysis. However, in several work settings a tight and detailed description of tasks and duties within jobs is inevitable. For example, in areas with high safety risks, such as an oil refinery, safety rules prescribe in detail the actions of the workers. Creativity and flexibility might result in disasters in this kind of industry. Similar examples can be found in the medical world; imagine the surgical nurse who is exploring the boundaries of her job during surgery. Less disastrous but yet embarrassing consequences are to be expected if tasks and responsibilities are not prescribed in detail in hierarchical settings and in settings where people work under time pressure. An example of the latter setting is the kitchen of a restaurant wherein the cook and the apprentice stay within the boundaries of their responsibilities as given by the job description and "the chef." Arnold (2001) and Weick (1996) note that those "strong" situations, that is, situations where there are clear guidelines and rules about how one should behave, also are quite common in cultures high in power distance and collectivism. However, many future work situations are more ambiguous and need adaptations in the focus of job analysis. Possible adaptations are discussed below.

Several authors stress the necessity of a shift away from a task-based analysis in the direction of identification of generalized work activities and worker characteristics (e.g., Dye & Silver, 1999; Sanchez, 1994) that are necessary to reach the goals of the organization (Hough & Oswald, 2000; Lawler, 1994; Schippmann, 1999). These activities and characteristics should be relevant to different jobs, situations, and even different departments.

Smith (1994) distinguishes three domains of individual characteristics that are in varying degrees relevant for performance in different work situations: universals, occupationals, and relationals. Universals are characteristics that are relevant to almost all work, such as cognitive ability, and vitality. Occupationals are characteristics that are relevant to particular jobs or occupations, such as specialized knowledge and certain aspects of personality. Relationals are characteristics relevant to the relationship between the individual and the work settings, for example the interpretation of the job ("some shared meaning about the tasks and skills involved," p. 23) and values ("ideas that are held in esteem . . . ," p. 23).

To identify universals and occupationals, analysis of work should focus on similarities and underlying communalities of different jobs (job families, occupations, etc.). As Fleishmann and Mumford (1988, 1991) stated, the successful performance of a large number of tasks performed in different jobs may require a limited amount of abilities. In their approach, tasks and task performance serve as a basis for the identification of required abilities. They claim that their use of established ability dimensions resulted in a taxonomic system that is reasonably stable in a changing environment. So, although specific tasks and behaviors may change, the derived abilities necessary to perform the work successfully might be the same. It may, however, not be sufficient to limit the analysis to established abilities. Sanchez (1994) argues that work analysis may result in the identification of new KSAOs that contribute to the process of business planning, such as openness to innovation.

To identify relationals and specific occupationals, a more detailed method of job analysis than the abilities requirements approach may be necessary. Regarding relationals, for example, two dimensions need to be explored: the direction and the content of the relationship. It needs, for example, to be assessed with whom (e.g., colleagues, superiors, subordinates, clients) and about what the individual communicates (Smith, 1994). It must be emphasized that relationals are important for teamwork. Employees have become highly interdependent in teamwork; therefore it requires cooperation and interaction between team members. These aspects were not included in traditional job analysis. Other consequences of changes in the nature of work in relation to teamwork and in relation to the level of person–environment fit (person–job, person–team, or person–organization) are discussed elsewhere in this volume (see Chapter 19 by Van Vianen and Chapter 22 by Allen & West, this volume). Sanchez (1994) states that the greater the emphasis on analyzing task interdependencies and workflows, the better the teamwork.

Task interdependencies and workflows are related to another trend in the description of work: a focus on descriptions of broad roles (Altink, Visser, & Castelijns, 1997; Snow & Snell, 1993) or work processes (Cascio, 1995). Role descriptions should reflect the strategies and goals of the organization and go beyond the tasks within traditional jobs. Cascio notices that there is a shift from clusters of tasks to a process-based organization of work. He wonders whether process-based structures require more attention to the environmental, contextual, and social dimensions of work.

Finally, in order to be able to adapt continuously to changing information about work and workers it is advisable to develop or optimize automated work-analytic systems and databases (e.g., Cunningham, 1996; Sanchez, 2000). Relations between different categories of information within a system, for example between work characteristics and worker characteristics, can be explored (Hanson, Borman, Kubisiak, & Sager, 1999). This could be a major step in the direction of closing the gap between the world of work and the world of persons, as Dunnette described in 1976.

CONCLUDING REMARKS AND SUGGESTIONS

This paper described the consequences of new developments in the structure of work for the choice of job descriptors and methods of analysis of work, and the use of the resulting data. Summarized, the suggestions made by different authors are:

- Realize a shift from detailed task-based approaches to the identification of:
  - strategic and future-oriented needs and goals of the organization, business unit, team (etc.), and the strategies to reach those goals and meet those needs;
  - values and personality variables that are relevant for the goals and needs of the organization, especially "universals" (e.g., intelligence), "new" worker characteristics (e.g., openness to innovation), and characteristics that are relevant for teamwork (e.g., interpersonal skills);
  - roles and processes in which people are engaged in order to reach the goals of the organization;
  - generalized worker activities;
  - similarities between jobs to make cross-job transitions and comparisons possible.
- Use different types of job descriptors (e.g., generalized work activities *and* knowledge and skills), including contextual and environmental dimensions, in order to cover jobs in their broadest meaning, with possibilities to capture continuous changes.
- Develop and use electronic systems of work analysis.

O*NET is a good example of most of the recommendations mentioned. It is a product from the application of diverse descriptors and methods. It is an automated job classification system that replaces the Dictionary of Occupational Titles (DOT). In the 1980s the task-based DOT was evaluated as no longer able to reflect changes in the nature and conditions of work (Dye & Silver, 1999). O*NET is based on a content model that consists of five categories of job descriptors: a) worker requirements (e.g., basic skills, cross-functional skills); b) worker characteristics (e.g., abilities, values); c) experience requirements (e.g., training); d) occupational requirements (e.g., generalized work activities, work context); e) occupation-specific requirements (e.g., tasks, duties). A sixth category, occupation characteristics (e.g., labor market information, occupational outlook), is not included in the system, but connections can be made to relevant databases (Mumford & Peterson, 1999).

The description of the existing job analysis methods shows that combinations of (parts of) these methods are able to cover the changes in work. There is no need to avoid the term job. A job can be described in as broad and abstract or in as detailed and specific a manner as one chooses, depending on the purpose of the analysis. For example, one may need detailed information for the design of a training program and general information for the development of predictors of potential for management progress. Also, it is possible to describe jobs in terms of variables that cut across jobs.

Job analysis is still the basis for personnel decisions and focuses on answers to questions such as: Selection for what? Compensation for what? Appraisal of what? And as Sanchez (2000, p. 207) stated: "the analysis of work continues to be an important management tool in a fast-evolving business world. Information about current work activities and work organization is the starting point to innovate and improve them."

Future research needs

Although extensions of existing job analysis methods might cover the recent and future developments in work, several questions that should be subject of additional research remain. Some examples are listed below:

♦ How to translate strategic and future-oriented needs and goals of the organization, or at lower levels of business units and teams, to the level of work of individuals?

♦ How to translate teamwork to the work of the individual team members? That is, what is the relation of tasks and requirements of individual jobs to the assignment of a team and what is the relation between jobs within teams?

♦ Which KSAOs are stable and transferable to different jobs and which need to be learned for specific assignments, and what is role of work experience?

♦ How to design jobs in such a way that they stimulate learning and change the orientation of behavior?

♦ Does work analysis on a higher level of abstraction than the level of traditional jobs, such as occupations and/or task clusters that exceed traditional jobs, differentiate between what different people actually do?

Most of these questions are based on the assumption that the content of work changes fast. However, systematic empirical studies on the speed and direction of changes in, for example, specific tasks are scarce or non-existent. Longitudinal research on a great variety of jobs should reveal what has changed and how fast. It may turn out that the (needed) tempo and content of changes vary from very slow and minor (e.g., truck driver) to very fast and far-reaching (e.g., jobs in or related to information technology); the consequences for the required KSAOs might vary as well. Results of such studies will show whether and for which work situations new job analysis procedures should be developed.

NOTE

I wish to thank my fellow editors for their valuable comments on an earlier version of this chapter.

REFERENCES

Altink, W. M. M., Visser, C. F., & Castelijns, M. (1997). Criterion development: The unknown power of criteria as communication tools. In N. Anderson & P. Herriot (Eds.), *International handbook of selection and assessment* (pp. 287–302). New York: Wiley.

Arnold, J. (2001). Careers and career management. In N. Anderson, D. S. Ones, H. K. Sinangil, & C. Viswesvaran (Eds.), *Handbook of industrial, work & organizational psychology: Vol. 2. Organizational psychology* (pp. 115–132). London: Sage.

Ash, R. A. (1988). Job analysis in the world of work. In S. Gael (Ed.), *The job analysis handbook for business, industry and government* (Vol. 1, pp. 3–13). New York: Wiley.

Ashton, M. C. (1998). Personality and job performance: The importance of narrow traits. *Journal of Organizational Behaviour, 19,* 289–303.

Barrett, G., & Depinet, R. (1991). Reconsideration of testing for competence rather than intelligence. *American Psychologist, 46,* 1012–1023.

Barrick, M. R., & Mount, M. K. (1991). The big five personality dimensions and job performance: A meta-analysis. *Personnel Psychology, 44,* 1–26.

Boyatzis, R. E. (1982). *The competent manager.* New York: Wiley.

Cascio, W. F. (1995). Whither industrial and organizational psychology in a changing world of work? *American Psychologist, 50,* 928–939.

Cascio, W. F. (1991). *Applied psychology in personnel management.* London: Prentice-Hall.

Cornelius, E. T., III, DeNisi, A. S., & Blencoe, A. G. (1984). Expert and naive raters using the PAQ: Does it matter? *Personnel Psychology, 37,* 453–464.

Cornelius, E. T., III, & Lyness, K. S. (1980). A comparison of holistic and decomposed judgments strategies in job analysis by job incumbents. *Journal of Applied Psychology, 65,* 155–163.

Cunningham, J. W. (1996). Generic job descriptors: A likely direction in occupational analysis. *Military Psychology, 8,* 247–262.

Dierdorff, E. C., & Wilson, M. A. (2003). A meta-analysis of job analysis reliability. *Journal of Applied Psychology, 88,* 635–646.

Dunnette, M. D. (1976). Aptitudes, abilities and skills. In M. D. Dunnette (Ed.), *Handbook of industrial and organizational psychology* (pp. 473–520). Chicago: Rand McNally.

Dye, D., & Silver, M. (1999). The origins of O*NET. In N. G. Peterson, M. D. Mumford, W. C Borman, P. R. Jeanneret, & E. A. Fleishman (Eds.), *An occupational information system for the 21st century: The development of O*NET* (pp. 9–19). Washington, DC: APA.

Fine, S. A. (1988). Functional job analysis. In S. Gael (Ed.), *The job analysis handbook for business, industry and government* (Vol. 2., pp. 1019–1035). New York: Wiley.

Fine, S. A., & Wiley, W. W. (1971). *An introduction to functional job analysis, methods for manpower analysis (monograph no. 4).* Kalamazoo, MI: W. E. Upjohn Institute.

Fiske, S. T., & Neuberg, S. L. (1990). A continuum of impression formation, from category-based to individuating processes: Influences of information and motivation on attention and interpretation. In M. P. Zanna (Ed.), *Advances in experimental social psychology* (Vol. 2., pp. 1–74). New York: Academic Press.

Flanagan, J. C. (1954). The critical incidents technique. *Psychological Bulletin, 51*, 327–358.

Fleishman, E. A., & Mumford, M. D. (1988). Ability Requirement Scales. In S. Gael (Ed.), *The job analysis handbook for business, industry and government* (Vol. 2, pp. 917–935*)*. New York: Wiley.

Fleishman, E. A., & Mumford, M. D. (1991). Evaluating classifications of job behaviour: A construct validation of the ability requirements scales. *Personnel Psychology, 44*, 523–575.

Gael, S. (Ed.). (1988). *The job analysis handbook for business, industry and government.* New York: Wiley.

Hanson, M. A., Borman, W. C., Kubisiak, U. C., & Sager, C. E. (1999). Cross-domain analyses. In N. G. Peterson, M. D. Mumford, W. C Borman, P. R. Jeanneret, & E. A. Fleishman (Eds.), *An occupational information system for the 21st century: The development of O*NET* (pp. 247–258). Washington, DC: APA.

Harvey, R. J. (1991). Job analysis. In M. D. Dunnette & L. M. Hough (Eds.), *Handbook of industrial and organizational psychology* (Vol. 2, pp. 71–162). Palo Alto: Consulting Psychologists Press.

Harvey, R. J., & Wilson, M. A. (2000). Yes Virginia, there *is* an objective reality in job analysis. *Journal of Organizational Behavior, 21*, 829–854.

Herriot, P., & Anderson, N. (1997). Selecting for change: How will personnel and selection psychology survive? In N. Anderson & P. Herriot (Eds.), *International handbook of selection and assessment* (pp. 1–34). New York: Wiley.

Hogan, J., & Roberts, B. W. (1996). Issues and non-issues in the fidelity–bandwidth tradeoff. *Journal of Organizational Behavior, 17*, 627–637.

Hough, L. M., & Oswald, F. L. (2000). Personnel selection; Looking toward the future – remembering the past. *Annual Review of Psychology, 51*, 631–664.

Huffcutt, A. I., Weekley, J. A., Wiesner, W. H., Groot, T. G., & Jones, C. (2001). Comparison of situational and behavior description interview questions for higher-level positions. *Personnel Psychology, 54*, 619–644.

Landis, R. S., Fogli, L., & Goldberg, E. (1998). Future-oriented job analysis: A description of the process and its organizational implications. *International Journal of Selection and Assessment, 6*, 192–197.

Landy, F. J., & Vasey, J. (1991). Job analysis: The composition of SME samples. *Personnel Psychology, 44*, 27–51.

Lawler, E. E. (1994). From job-based to competency-based organizations. *Journal of Organizational Behavior, 15*, 3–15.

Levine, E. L. (1983). *Everything you always wanted to know about job analysis.* Tampa, FL: Mariner Publishing.

Levine, E. L., Ash, R. A., & Bennett, N. (1980). Exploratory comparative study of four job analysis methods. *Journal of Applied Psychology, 65*, 524–535.

Levine, E. L., Ash, R. A., Hall, H., & Sistrunk, F. (1983). Evaluation of job analysis methods by experiences job analysts. *Academy of Management Journal, 26*, 339–348.

Lopez, F. M. (1988). Threshold traits analysis system. In S. Gael (Ed.), *The job analysis handbook for business, industry and government* (Vol. 2, pp. 880–901). New York: Wiley.

McClelland, D. C. (1973). Testing for competence rather than for intelligence. *American Psychologist, 28*, 1–14.

McCormick, E. J. (1976). Job and task analysis. In M. D. Dunnette (Ed.), *Handbook of industrial and organizational psychology* (pp. 651–697). Chicago: Rand McNally.

McCormick, E. J., DeNisi, A. S., & Shaw, J. B. (1979). Use of the Position Analysis Questionnaire for establishing the job component validity of tests. *Journal of Applied Psychology, 64*, 51–56.

McCormick, E. J., Jeanneret, P. R., & Mecham, R. C. (1972). A study of job characteristics and job dimensions as based on the Position Analysis Questionnaire (PAQ). *Journal of Applied Psychology, 56*, 347–368.

Morgeson, F. P., & Campion, M. A. (1997). Social and cognitive sources of potential inaccuracy in job analysis. *Journal of Applied Psychology, 82*, 627–655.

Morgeson, F. P., & Campion, M. A. (2000). Accuracy in job analysis: Toward an inference-based model. *Journal of Organizational Behavior, 21*, 819–827.

Mumford, M. D., & Peterson, N. G. (1999). The O*NET content model: Structural considerations in describing jobs. In N. G. Peterson, M. D. Mumford, W. C Borman, P. R. Jeanneret, & E. A. Fleishman (Eds.), *An occupational information system for the 21st century: The development of O*NET* (pp. 21–30). Washington, DC: APA.

Offermann, L. R., & Gowing, M. K. (1993). Personnel selection in the future: The impact of changing demographics and the nature of work. In N. Schmitt & W. C. Borman (Eds.), *Personnel selection in organizations* (pp. 385–417). San Francisco: Jossey-Bass.

Ones, D. S., & Viswesvaran, C. (1996). Bandwith–fidelity dilemma in personality measurement for personal selection. *Journal of Organizational Behavior, 17*, 609–626.

Paunonen, S. V., Rothstein, M. G., & Jackson, D. N. (1999). Narrow reasoning about the use of broad personality measures for personnel selection. *Journal of Organizational Behavior, 20*, 389–405.

Primoff, E. S., & Dittrich Eyde, L. (1988). Job element analysis. In S. Gael (Ed.), *The job analysis handbook for business, industry and government* (Vol. 2, pp. 807–824). New York: Wiley.

Peterson, N. G., Mumford, M. D., Borman, W. C., Jeanneret, P. R., & Fleishman, E. A. (1999). *An occupational information system for the 21st century: The development of O*NET*. Washington, DC: APA.

Raymark, P. H., Schmit, M. J., & Guion, R. M. (1997). Identifying potentially useful personality constructs for employee selection. *Personnel Psychology, 50*, 723–736.

Rosenthal, R., & Rosnov, R. L. (1991). *Essentials of behavioral research methods and data analysis*. London: McGraw-Hill.

Sanchez, J. I. (1994). From documentation to innovation: Reshaping job analysis to meet emerging business needs. *Human Resource management Review, 4*, 51–74.

Sanchez, J. I. (2000). Adapting work analysis to a fast-paced electronic business world. *International Journal of Selection and Assessment, 8*, 207–215.

Sanchez, J. I., & Levine, E. L. (1994). The impact of raters' cognition on judgment accuracy: An extension to the job analysis domain. *Journal of Business and Psychology, 9*, 47–57.

Sanchez, J. I., & Levine, E. L. (1999). Is job analysis dead, misunderstood or both? New forms of work analysis and design. In A. Kraut & A. Korman (Eds.), *Evolving practices in human resource management*. San Francisco: Jossey-Bass.

Sanchez, J. I., & Levine, E. L. (2000). Accuracy or consequential validity; which is the better standard for job analysis data? *Journal of Organizational Behavior, 21*, 809–818.

Sanchez, J. I., & Levine, E. L. (2001). The analysis of work in the 20th and 21st centuries. In N. Anderson, D. S. Ones, H. K. Sinangil, & C. Viswesvaran (Eds.), *Handbook of industrial, work & organizational psychology: Vol. 1. Organizational psychology* (pp. 71–89). London: Sage.

Sanchez, J. I., Zamora, A., & Viswesvaran, C. (1997). Moderators of agreement between incumbent and non-incumbent ratings of job characteristics. *Journal of Occupational and Organizational Psychology, 70*, 209–218.

Schippmann, J. S. (1999). *Strategic job modelling: Working at the core of integrated human resources*. London: Lawrence Erlbaum.

Schippmann, J. S., Ash, R. A., Battista, M., Carr, L., Eyde, L. D., Hesketh, B., et al. (2000). The practice of competency modeling. *Personnel Psychology, 53*, 703–739.

Schmidt, F. L. (1993). Personnel psychology at the cutting edge. In N. Schmitt & W. C. Borman (Eds.), *Personnel selection in organizations*. San Francisco: Jossey-Bass.

Schmitt, N., & Borman, W. C. (Eds.). (1993). *Personnel selection in organizations.* San Francisco: Jossey-Bass.

Schmidt, F. L., & Hunter, J. E. (1998). The validity and utility of selection methods in personnel psychology: Practical and theoretical implications of 85 years of research findings. *Psychological Bulletin, 124,* 262–274.

Schneider, B. S., & Konz, A. M. (1989). Strategic job analysis. *Human Resource Management, 28,* 51–63.

Schuler, H. (1989). Some advantages and problems of job analysis. In M. Smith & I. Robertson (Eds.), *Advances in selection and assessment* (pp. 31–42). London: Wiley.

Smith, M. (1994). A theory of the validity of predictors in selection. *Journal of Occupational and Organizational Psychology, 67,* 13–31.

Snow, C. C., & Snell, S. A. (1993). Staffing as strategy. In N. Schmitt & W. C. Borman (Eds.), *Personnel selection in organizations* (pp. 448–478). San Francisco: Jossey-Bass.

Sparrow, J. (1989). The utility of PAQ in relating job behaviors to traits. *Journal of Occupational Psychology, 62,* 151–162.

Sparrow, J., Patrick, J., Spurgeon, P., & Barwell, F. (1982). The use of job component analysis and related aptitudes in personnel selection. *Journal of Occupational Psychology, 55,* 157–164.

Sparrow, P. R., & Bognanno, M. (1993). Competency requirement forecasting: Issues for international selection and assessment. *International Journal of Selection and Assessment, 1,* 50–58.

Tett, R. P., Guterman, H. A., Bleier, A., & Murphy, P. J. (2000). Development and content validation of a "hyperdimensional" taxonomy of managerial competence. *Human Performance, 13,* 205–251.

Theologus, G. C., Romashko, T., & Fleishman, E. A. (1973). Development of a taxonomy of human performance: A feasibility study of ability dimensions for classifying human tasks. *JSAS Catalog of Selected Documents in Psychology, 3,* 25–26.

Thorndike, R. L. (1949). *Personnel selection: Test and measurement techniques.* New York: Wiley.

Uniform guidelines on employee selection procedures. (1978). *Federal Register, 43,* 38290–38315.

US Department of Labor. (1965). *Dictionary of Occupational Titles* (Vol. 2). Washington, DC: US Government Printing Office.

Voskuijl, O. F., & Van Sliedregt, T. (2002). Determinants of inter-rater reliability of job analysis: A meta-analysis. *European Journal of Psychological Assessment, 18,* 52–62.

Weick, K. E. (1996). Enactment and the boundaryless career: Organizing as we work. In M. B. Arthur & D. Rousseau (Eds.), *The boundaryless career: A new employment principle for a new organizational era* (pp. 40–55). Oxford, UK: Oxford University Press.

3

The *Im*practicality of Recruitment Research

ALAN M. SAKS

During the 1990s, many writers began to sound alarm bells about impending labor short-ages of skilled and professional workers (Jackson & Schuler, 1990; Offermann & Gowing, 1990). At the same time, it became increasingly clear that human capital and the man-agement of employees is a critical factor in an organization's success and competitiveness (Pfeffer, 1994). The increasing importance of human capital, combined with continuing concerns about labor shortages, has made applicant attraction and recruitment more important than ever.

The 21st century has arrived and sure enough, so has the labor shortages. Not sur-prisingly, many organizations are already having trouble finding qualified employees. It is predicted that there will be a 30 percent shortfall of workers between the ages of 25 and 44. In Canada, it is predicted that a critical shortage of skilled workers could reach one million by the year 2020. There are already shortages in scientific, technical, and high-tech industries, and in senior management, communications, and marketing positions. The problem is so serious that three-quarters of chief executive officers (CEOs) say they can't find enough competent employees, and Canada's top CEOs believe that retaining employ-ees has become their number one priority. Attracting new employees is their fourth prior-ity just behind financial performance and profitability (McLaren, 2002).

The problem is just as severe in the United States where 80 percent of employers say they are having trouble attracting and retaining employees with critical skills. Some organ-izations are even experiencing difficulty hiring employees with non-critical skills (McLaren, 2002). According to the US Bureau of Labor Statistics, there will be a shortage of 10 million workers between 1998 and 2008 (Cascio, 2003). Demographic trends such as the decline in the number of young workers combined with the retirement of baby boomers will make it increasingly difficult for organizations to fill job openings (Collins & Stevens, 2002).

The increasing importance of human capital for an organization's success and com-petitiveness, not to mention its very survival, coupled with the increasing difficulty of recruiting and retaining skilled employees, has suddenly made recruitment a top priority for many organizations. Furthermore, because recruitment influences the characteristics and quality of the applicant pool, it has implications for all other human resource practices (Turban & Cable, 2003). For example, the recruitment of a large pool of qualified applicants from which to choose has implications for the utility of an organization's selection system (Boudreau & Rynes, 1985; Murphy, 1986).

Thus, as noted by Taylor and Collins (2000), "recruitment has emerged as arguably the most critical human resource function for organizational survival and success" (p. 304). This is arguably a critical time for both recruitment research and practice (Taylor & Collins, 2000). In fact, many organizations have already increased their budget for recruitment (Turban, 2001).

Recruitment research has become more important than ever and there have been several excellent reviews and critiques of recruitment research in the last six years (Barber, 1998; Breaugh & Starke, 2000; Rynes & Cable, 2003; Taylor & Collins, 2000). In this chapter, I provide a brief summary of recruitment research, with particular emphasis on the practical implications. This will then set the stage for a discussion of how to close the gap between recruitment research and practice. Less attention will be given to the design and methodology of recruitment research and intervening-process variables. These topics have been thoroughly discussed in other reviews (see, for example, Breaugh & Starke, 2000, and Rynes & Cable, 2003).

What is Recruitment?

A number of definitions have been provided to describe recruitment. For example, in his book on recruitment, Breaugh (1992) provides the following definition: "Employee recruitment involves those organizational activities that (1) influence the number and/or the types of applicants who apply for a position and/or (2) affect whether a job offer is accepted" (p. 4). According to Barber (1998), "recruitment includes those practices and activities carried on by the organization with the primary purpose of identifying and attracting potential employees" (p. 5). Breaugh and Starke (2000) used Barber's (1998) definition and Taylor and Collins (2000) slightly modified it as follows: "Recruitment includes the set of activities undertaken by the organization for the primary purpose of identifying a desirable group of applicants, attracting them into its employee ranks, and retaining them at least for the short term" (p. 306).

For the most part, each definition refers to recruitment in terms of certain activities and practices that are carried out to achieve certain outcomes. Given the increasing emphasis on strategic human resource management, a definition of recruitment might include a focus on achieving an organization's strategic objectives. Thus, retaining employees might or might not be part of an organization's strategy. Therefore, for the purpose of this paper and more practically speaking, recruitment is defined as follows:

> Recruitment involves actions and activities taken by an organization in order to identify and attract individuals to the organization who have the capabilities to help the organization realize its strategic objectives. In particular, such activities should generate a pool of desirable candidates; enhance their interest in and attraction to the organization as an employer; and increase the probability that they will accept a job offer.

This definition has a number of important characteristics. First, it indicates that recruitment involves specific actions and activities that are undertaken to achieve particular outcomes. Second, it indicates that the purpose of those actions and activities is to generate an applicant pool of desirable candidates, enhance their interest in and attraction to a job and the organization, and increase the probability that applicants will accept a job offer. These three outcomes are based on Barber's (1998) description of the three phases of recruitment (generating applicants, maintaining applicant status, and job choice). Third, this definition clearly separates recruitment from the selection function by acknowledging that those persons who are attracted to the organization "might" have the capabilities desired. It is the purpose of selection to determine whether applicants have the required capabilities. Fourth, the definition does not specify any particular post-hire criteria or outcomes (e.g., retention) because recruitment is ultimately about activities designed to influence the number and type of applicants who apply for a job and accept job offers (Rynes & Barber, 1990). Furthermore, desired post-hire outcomes will depend on the strategy and objectives of the organization. Fifth, this definition links recruitment to strategy, thus making it clear that recruitment can and should play an important role in helping an organization achieve its strategic objectives. Thus, this definition is meant to signify the strategic importance of recruitment and the recruitment function (Taylor & Collins, 2000).

MODELS OF RECRUITMENT

Several models of the recruitment process have been proposed in recent years. Rynes (1991) presented a model for future recruitment research in her chapter in the second edition of the *Handbook of Industrial & Organizational Psychology* (Dunnette & Hough, 1991). Her model presents five recruitment activities including recruiters, sources, vacancy characteristics, selection standards, and administrative procedures (realistic job previews, timing, expenditures). The activities are linked to recruitment processes (self-selection, time-related processes, information-related processes, post-hire adjustment processes, and individual differences), which in turn lead to pre-hire (perceptions, intentions, and behaviors) and post-hire (attitudes, behaviors, effects on insiders) outcomes. In addition, the model also includes three context variables (external environment, organization characteristics, and institutional norms) that can influence recruitment activities and decisions, recruitment processes, and recruitment outcomes.

Rynes and Barber (1990) expressed concern that research on recruitment had been framed from the applicant's perspective rather than the organization's perspective and developed a model of the attraction process from the organization's perspective. Their model includes three strategies for applicant attraction (i.e., recruitment practices, modifying employment inducements, and targeting nontraditional applicants) that are predicted to lead to pre-employment and post-employment outcomes (i.e., quantity, quality, and spillover). The recruitment strategies include: organizational representatives, messages, sources, and timing. The model shows how the attraction strategies interact with other human resource practices, and includes contingency variables (i.e., labor market conditions, vacancy characteristics, organizational characteristics, phase of attraction process, and legal considerations) that can affect the choice and effectiveness of the attraction strategies.

In Breaugh and Starke's (2000) model of the organizational recruitment process, recruitment objectives (e.g., retention rate) lead to a recruitment strategy (e.g., whom to recruit?); recruitment strategy leads to recruitment activities (e.g., recruitment sources); recruitment activities lead to intervening-process variables (e.g., applicant attention), which in turn lead to recruitment results (e.g., greater retention rate). The strategy stage involves determining the type of individual that an organization wants to recruit (e.g., knowledge, skills, and abilities). This is consistent with the definition of recruitment presented earlier in that it takes into consideration an organization's goals and objectives. As noted by Breaugh and Starke (2000), this is a fundamental question because it will influence where and how an organization recruits as well as other strategy-related issues. For this reason, the establishment of objectives is the first stage of the recruitment process.

An organization's recruitment strategy determines the type of recruitment activities required to achieve the objectives. Recruitment activities include recruitment sources, recruiters, and the recruitment message (i.e., realism, completeness, and timeliness). These activities influence a number of intervening-process variables such as applicant interest (job and organizational attractiveness) that will lead to recruitment results.

In summary, extant models of the recruitment process describe the links between recruitment practices, processes, and outcomes. While these models help to identify different recruitment practices and outcomes, they do not clearly identify the stages of recruitment. Furthermore, they tend to focus on either the applicant's or organization's perspective. Therefore, models of the recruitment process should include the stages of recruitment as well as the applicant's and organization's perspective at each stage.

Figure 3.1 presents a Dual-Stage Model of the Recruitment Process. The model is based on Barber's (1998) description of the three phases of the recruitment process (generating applicants, maintaining applicant status, and influencing job choice decisions). The model presents three similar stages of the recruitment process: the application stage, the interaction stage, and the job offer stage. In addition, the model also highlights the perspective of both the applicant and the organization along with the relevant outcomes for both. For example, during the first stage, organizations must generate applicants for positions and applicants must decide whether they will apply for jobs. In the second stage in which organizations and applicants interact with each other, applicants and organizations must try to find out about each other, make themselves attractive, and assess their fit to each other. In the job offer stage, organizations want to increase the chances that applicants accept job offers, and applicants want to receive job offers and then decide whether they should accept or reject them. The arrows that connect the applicant and the organization at each stage demonstrate that they influence each other throughout the process.

RECRUITMENT RESEARCH AND PRACTICE

While there is much to be excited about in terms of the high-priority status of recruitment and the resurgence of recruitment research, there remains one very important question: What are the practical implications of recruitment research for organizations? In order to answer this question, a brief review of the main topic areas in recruitment research follows, along with the practical implications that stem from the main research findings.

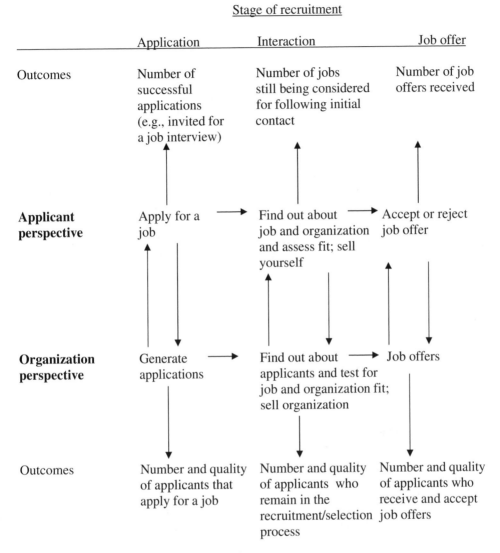

FIGURE 3.1   Dual-stage model of the recruitment process

Until recently, recruitment research has been dominated by three main topics which might be called the "3 R's" – realistic job previews, recruitment sources, and recruiter behaviors. Most research on recruitment has focused on these three topics. Furthermore, each topic has been studied in isolation from the others and has resulted in what some have called a piecemeal and fragmented approach to recruitment research (Barber, 1998; Breaugh & Starke, 2000; Rynes, 1991).

The "3 R's" of recruitment research

Realistic job previews.   Just over thirty years ago, Wanous (1973) published the first experiment on the effects of realistic job previews (RJPs). The basic premise behind RJP research is that if you tell job applicants the positive and negative features of a job rather than just the positive features (a traditional job preview), they will be less likely to quit. Although Wanous (1973) did not find a significant RJP effect on turnover, telephone operators who received an RJP film had lower job expectations and higher job satisfaction.

Over the past two decades, there have been dozens of studies on RJPs, four meta-analyses (McEvoy & Cascio, 1985; Meglino, Ravlin, & DeNisi, 2000; Phillips, 1998; Premack & Wanous, 1985), as well as numerous reviews (Breaugh, 1983). A great deal of RJP research has also focused on the psychology or mechanisms that underlie the effects of RJPs, such as lower expectations and self-selection as well as the methods of communicating RJPs (written versus video). The main finding from all three meta-analyses and review articles is that RJPs have a modest effect on turnover reduction. In addition, a recent meta-analysis found that RJPs have a positive effect on job performance and attrition from the recruitment process, and they lower job expectations (Phillips, 1998). Research on the mechanisms of RJP effects has provided some support for the met expectations and self-selection hypotheses. There is also some evidence that RJPs can lower job acceptance rates under certain conditions (Bretz & Judge, 1998; Meglino et al., 2000; Saks, Wiesner, & Summers, 1994, 1996). However, from a practical perspective, the practical implications of RJP research are straightforward:

> *Provide job applicants with an accurate and realistic picture of the job and organization that includes both the positive and negative attributes.*

Recruitment sources.   Research on recruitment sources focuses on the effects of different sources of recruitment on post-hire outcomes such as job satisfaction, job performance, and turnover. As well, most studies have included new hires rather than job applicants (Breaugh & Starke, 2000). For the past thirty years, the main finding is that employees recruited through informal sources (i.e., employee referrals and direct applications) have higher job satisfaction and lower turnover than employees recruited through formal sources (i.e., newspaper advertisements and employment agencies) (Breaugh & Starke, 2000). In addition, a number of studies have also investigated the psychological processes for the effects of recruitment sources, particularly the individual difference hypothesis and the realistic information hypothesis. Although there are a number of additional hypotheses that have been suggested in the literature, they have seldom been studied (Zottoli & Wanous, 2000). As well, only two studies have investigated the quality of applicants and found that informal sources result in more qualified applicants (Kirnan, Farley, & Geisinger, 1989; Williams, Labig, & Stone, 1993). Only one study has investigated pre-hire outcomes and found that the rate of job offer acceptance was higher among informal sources (Kirnan et al., 1989).

Finally, an interesting new development in this area is the use of company web pages and online recruiting as recruitment sources. This is an important extension of recruitment source research given that it is estimated that more than one million people apply for jobs over the Internet (Cascio, 2003). In one study, Williamson, Lepak, and King (2003) found that website orientation influenced organizational attractiveness. In particular, company websites with a recruiting-orientation were perceived as more favorable than screening-oriented websites, in part because the recruitment-oriented website contained more useful information. The ease of use of the website was also related to organizational attractiveness. In another innovative study, Dineen, Ash, and Noe (2002) found that Web-based recruitment that provided feedback to individuals regarding their potential person–organization fit was positively related to attraction.

Overall, the main conclusion from recruitment source research is that informal sources have more positive effects on a number of post-hire outcomes. Given that so few studies have investigated the characteristics of applicants recruited through different sources as well as pre-hire outcomes, and research on Web-based recruitment is still in its infancy, it is not possible to make any firm conclusions regarding these effects. Therefore, for now the main practical implication from recruitment source research is as follows:

Use informal sources of recruitment such as employee referrals, direct applications, as well as rehires to recruit employees rather than formal sources (i.e., newspaper advertisements and employment agencies).

Recruiter behaviors. The effect of recruiter behaviors on job applicants' reactions has been on the recruitment agenda for over thirty years. In one of the first studies, Alderfer and McCord (1970) found that job applicants were more likely to expect a job offer and to accept an offer when the recruiter was perceived to show interest in the applicant and provided information about the job.

Many other studies on recruiter effects have been conducted during the past three decades and even though research in this area has become more complex and methodologically sound (Breaugh & Starke, 2000), most studies have reached the same general conclusion: Job applicants perceive jobs and organizations more positively and are more likely to expect to receive and to accept a job offer when recruiters are personable and informative. The effects of recruiter characteristics have also been investigated; however, the results have been mixed and weak (Barber, 1998). Furthermore, recruiter effects are not only modest, but they become non-significant when compared to job attributes or vacancy characteristics (Rynes, 1991; Rynes & Barber, 1990), and they have been found to be strongest during early recruitment and to wane during the later stages (Taylor & Bergmann, 1987).

A number of explanations have been offered and tested to explain the effects of recruiters on applicant reactions and intentions. One popular view holds that recruiters act as signals for unknown characteristics of organizations. Some evidence has been found in support of signaling theory (Rynes, Bretz, & Gerhart, 1991). For example, Turban, Forret, and Hendrickson (1998) found that although recruiter behaviors did not have a direct effect on applicant attraction, they did have an indirect effect by influencing perceptions of job and organizational attributes.

That friendly, personable, and informative recruiters have a positive effect on applicant reactions leads to a fairly straightforward practical implication:

Recruiters should be knowledgeable about job openings and the organization and they should be personable and friendly when meeting and interacting with job candidates.

Summary

The almost exclusive focus on the "3 R's" of recruitment research has not only left many important questions unanswered, but it has produced few substantive practical implications for recruiters and organizations. Furthermore, even though a great deal of research has investigated the psychological mechanisms or theories for the effects of RJPs, recruitment sources, and recruiter behaviors, we still know very little about why they have the "modest" effects they do. To make matters worse, the practical implications that stem from research on the "3 R's" have been known for decades and are probably considered by most practitioners to be obvious if not trivial.

RECENT DEVELOPMENTS IN RECRUITMENT RESEARCH

In recent years, there have been some new and exciting developments in recruitment research. In fact, since Barber (1998) published her book which provided a comprehensive review of the recruitment literature and an agenda for research, there has been a dramatic resurgence of recruitment research that has not only resulted in the publication of more recruitment research than any other period, but also a greater diversity of topics than ever before. In this section, I will briefly review each of these areas and their implications for practice.

Employment inducements.   In their model of the attraction process, Rynes and Barber (1990) included employment inducements as a strategy for enhancing applicant attraction. Although the terms job attributes and vacancy characteristics are often used interchangeably, they used the term *employment inducements* "to convey the notion of deliberately modifying attributes for the explicit purpose of enhancing the attractiveness of a job to potential applicants" (p. 294). They argued that employers can improve attraction by raising starting salaries, improving benefits, offering flextime, child or eldercare, internal career paths, and by making improvements in working conditions.

Research on vacancy characteristics has generally found that both job and organizational attributes are related to applicant attraction and are considered among the most important factors in the recruitment-attraction process (Rynes, 1991; Turban et al., 1998). As indicated earlier, job attributes have generally been found to be stronger predictors of applicant attraction compared to recruiter behaviors, especially during the latter stages of recruitment when recruiter effects often become non-significant (Rynes & Barber, 1990; Powell, 1984; Taylor & Bergmann, 1987).

Among the various employment inducements, applicants appear to be most attracted to jobs with higher pay. Pay levels have been found to be positively related to the number of applications received and job acceptance rates (Williams & Dreher, 1992). As well, at least one study has also shown that applicants prefer individual-based rather than team-based pay and fixed pay rather than variable pay (Cable & Judge, 1994). According to Rynes and Barber (1990), "verifiable inducements with calculable pecuniary value are likely to be particularly effective motivators of job application and job acceptance decisions" (p. 295). Although some studies have found individual differences in applicants' preferences for vacancy characteristics (e.g., Cable & Judge, 1994; Trank, Rynes, & Bretz, 2002), the practical implication of research on employment inducements is for the most part, fairly clear:

Offer a variety of employment inducements to potential job applicants (e.g., flexible work arrangements, opportunities for training, benefits, etc.), especially high pay.

Recruitment activities. One of the most important research areas to emerge in recent years is research on the effects of recruitment activities. Research on recruitment activities that can increase the probability that applicants apply for positions, the attractiveness of the organization, and the likelihood that applicants will accept job offers can have real practical value for recruiters and organizations.

Turban (2001) examined the relationship between recruitment practices (campus activity, recruitment materials, recruitment process) and firm attractiveness in a sample of the *applicant population* (i.e., engineering students) of a large petrochemical company. He found that recruitment activities were positively related to perceptions of organizational attributes, and that organizational attributes fully mediated the effects of recruitment activities on attraction to the firm. Turban (2001) also found that firm familiarity was positively related to firm attractiveness and suggested that recruitment activities might be used to increase applicants' familiarity with a firm, thereby increasing firm attractiveness.

Collins and Stevens (2002) employed a brand equity approach to examine the relationship between four early recruitment activities (i.e., publicity, sponsorship, word-of-mouth endorsements, advertising) and application intentions and decisions. Their results indicated that early recruitment activities are indirectly related to application intentions and decisions through employer brand image (i.e., general attitudes toward the company and perceived job attributes). Further, employer brand image mediated the relationships between recruitment activities and application intentions and decisions. In addition, the recruitment activities interacted with each other such that employer brand image was strongest when publicity was used with the other recruitment activities, suggesting that "early recruitment-related practices may have their greatest effects when companies use them in conjunction with one another" (Collins & Stevens, 2002, p. 1130).

In an interesting study on the factors that influence job acceptance decisions, Turban, Campion, and Eyring (1995) found that evaluations of the site visit were positively related to job acceptance decisions. In addition, the likeableness of the site visit host was also positively related to job acceptance decisions. Thus, this study highlights the importance of the site visit for job acceptance decisions and is one of the few studies to test the relationship between recruitment activities and job acceptance decisions.

The timing of recruitment activities has also been shown to be an important factor throughout the recruitment process. The basic premise is that delays between recruitment stages might discourage applicants who then decide to drop out of the recruitment process. Several studies have found that delays during the recruitment process can have a number of negative effects on applicants. For example, Rynes et al. (1991) found that applicants were more likely to drop out of the recruitment-selection process when there were delays between phases.

In summary, research on recruitment activities holds great promise from a practical standpoint because it tests the effects of different recruitment practices on recruitment outcomes at different stages of the recruitment process. However, as noted by Turban (2001), recruitment research has not provided much evidence regarding those recruitment activities that have the greatest utility in attracting applicants. Nonetheless, research in this area does suggest a number of very practical implications:

Use a variety of recruitment activities (e.g., campus activity, recruitment materials, recruitment process, publicity, sponsorship activities, word-of-mouth endorsements, advertising) to increase applicant familiarity of and attractiveness to the organization, brand image, and application intentions and decisions.

The site visit should be carefully planned and conducted in a professional manner with particular attention paid to what is communicated to applicants; how applicants are treated; the people who meet with applicants; and the site visit host.

Avoid delays during the recruitment process and maintain contact with applicants throughout the process.

Recruitment advertising.   In recent years, a number of studies have investigated the effects of recruitment advertisements on applicant reactions and job choice intentions. It is generally believed that recruitment advertising can have a positive effect on job applicants' attitudes toward jobs and organizations, especially when they include specific information (Breaugh & Starke, 2000).

In one of the first studies, Belt and Paolillo (1982) found that applicants reacted more positively to a restaurant advertisement when it presented a favorable image of the organization. Gatewood, Gowan, and Lautenschlager (1993) found that an organization's recruitment image was strongly related to the amount of information provided in the company's advertisement. Yuce and Highhouse (1998) found that job advertisements that contained more job attributes increased the attractiveness of the vacancy being advertised.

Research on recruitment advertising has also examined the use of advertisements for attracting certain types of applicants. For example, Highhouse, Stierwalt et al. (1999) investigated the effects of job advertisement characteristics on minority job-seeker perceptions of an organization's attractiveness as a place to work. Two samples of African Americans (student members of a society for African American engineers and currently employed engineers) responded to hypothetical job advertisements for an engineering consultant. The advertisements differed in terms of staffing policy (identity-blind/equal employment opportunity vs. identify-conscious/affirmative action employer), work structure (individual based versus team based), and compensation system (individual performance based or group performance based). The results indicated that both samples were more attracted to an organization with an identity-conscious/affirmative action staffing policy than an identity-blind/equal-employment opportunity and to an individual-performance-based compensation system than a group-performance-based system. As well, the student sample was more attracted to the team-based work advertisement than to the individual-based work one.

Recruitment advertising research has also tested the effects of diversity information for attracting minority applicants. There is some evidence that racial similarity between applicants and the employees shown in recruitment advertisements enhances organizational attractiveness (Avery, 2003). In fact, Avery (2003) found that Black applicants were indeed more attracted to an organization that used a diversity advertisement but only when it depicted Blacks in higher-status supervisory positions as well as entry-level positions. Kim and Gelfand (2003) found that individuals with higher levels of ethnic identity responded more positively toward an organization and had greater job pursuit intentions when a recruitment brochure contained a diversity initiative. The results of these studies suggest that if organizations want to target minority group applicants, recruitment brochures should include diversity initiatives and minority group employees should be depicted in recruitment advertisements.

One of the problems with recruitment advertising research is that it confounds vacancy characteristics with advertising. To some extent, it is no different than research on vacancy characteristics except that an advertisement is used as the method for describing the characteristics of the job and organization. In effect, this research does not tell us anything about recruitment advertising. One would hope that future research in this area would investigate the effects of different kinds of advertisements (e.g., newspaper versus targeted magazines) or the effect of specific features of an advertisement (e.g., design, color, photos, etc.) while holding job and organizational attributes constant.

A recent study by Allen, Van Scotter, and Otondo (2004) is one of the first to begin to consider these kinds of issues. They investigated the effects of recruitment communication media on pre-hire recruitment outcomes. They found that different media (face-to-face, video, audio, text) result in differences in media features (amount of information, two-way communication, personal focus, social presence, symbolism). The media features were positively related to communication outcomes (credibility and satisfaction), which were positively related to attitudes toward the organization. Positive attitudes toward the organization were related to positive attitudes toward joining the organization which were related to intentions to pursue employment which were in turn related to behavior associated with joining. Overall, the results of this study indicate that recruitment communication media can influence applicants' attitudes, intentions, and behaviors.

Another problem with recruitment advertising research is the difficulty of separating the advertisement from organizational practices and policies. For example, whether or not an organization has an identity-blind versus identity-conscious staffing policy has more to do with an organization's values, goals, and human resource policies than recruitment advertising. The implication for recruitment advertising is simply to include this information in recruitment advertisements and materials. If a particular staffing policy will be more effective for attracting more or certain applicants, then the implication is to first change the staffing policy and then the recruitment message. The recruitment message is obviously dependent upon organizational policies and practices.

Thus, as of this time the basic finding from recruitment advertising research is similar to research on employment inducements: Recruitment advertisements that include more specific and positive information about a job and organization result in more positive applicant reactions. The practical implication of this is as follows:

Provide specific and positive information about job and organization attributes in recruitment advertisements and materials including information about diversity.

Organizational characteristics. A number of studies have examined the relationship between organizational characteristics and recruitment practices. For example, Rynes, Orlitzky, and Bretz (1997) investigated the factors that predict the recruitment of experienced workers versus recent college graduates. They found that the hiring of experienced workers was associated with organizational growth, short-term staffing strategies, an older workforce, and less dynamic business environments. Barber, Wesson, Roberson, and Taylor (1999) investigated the relationship between firm size and recruitment practices and found that the recruitment practices of large firms are more formal and bureaucratic compared to small firms. Given that so few studies have been conducted in this area and the descriptive nature of this research, it is not possible to state any practical implications for organizational recruitment.

Strategic human resources management. During the 1990s, research on strategic human resources management (SHRM) began to receive a great deal of research attention. For the most part, this stream of research examined the relationship between bundles of HR practices and organizational-level outcomes. In one of the earliest studies, Huselid (1995) found that high-performance human resource practices were associated with lower turnover, as well as higher productivity and corporate financial performance. However, the only measure of recruitment was the selection ratio (i.e., for the five positions that your firm hires most frequently, how many qualified applicants do you have per position on average?), which arguably is more of an outcome variable than a recruitment practice.

While several other studies have reported similar results, thereby attesting to the benefits of innovative and high-performance HRM practices and systems, relatively little has been learned about the role of recruitment in the SHRM literature. This is in part because the emphasis has been on the bundling of HR practices, complementarities, and HRM systems, thus making it difficult to determine the effects for any particular HR practice. In addition, most studies do not even include recruitment as a strategic HR practice and most include it as part of the selection or staffing dimension. For example, Ichniowski, Shaw, and Prennushi (1997) examined the effects of HRM practices on the productivity of steel finishing lines. Among the seven HRM practices was "extensive recruiting and selection," which was a measure of selection that measured how extensive the screening process is in the hiring of new workers.

Another problem is that recruitment measures often focus on the outcomes of recruitment such as the selection ratio rather than actual recruitment practices. For example, in a study by Harel and Tzafrir (1999), recruitment was measured as the number of candidates that an organization considered in the past year for each opening in several job categories. This measure was not, however, related to organizational or market performance.

In summary, while research on SHRM involves the organizational-level analysis, it has not provided much in the way of research or practical advancements in the area of recruitment. The measures of recruitment are often combined with indicators of selection and they tend not to measure actual recruitment practices or activities. Furthermore, organizational-level outcomes such as firm and market performance are quite distal from recruitment, and it is difficult if not impossible to determine the effect of recruitment on these kinds of outcomes. Therefore, at this time it is premature to conclude that recruitment practices influence organizational performance. Furthermore, because recruitment activities have not been measured in SHRM research, it is not possible to state any definitive practical implications.

Organizational image, reputation, and symbolic attributes.   One topic in recruitment research to emerge in recent years has been the effects of an organization's image, reputation, and symbolic attributes on applicant perceptions and intentions. Several studies have found that these subjective factors are related to applicant reactions and attraction to organizations (Cable & Graham, 2000).

As indicated earlier, Belt and Paolillo (1982) found that applicants were more attracted to a fast-food restaurant with a more favorable organization image. In a study on corporate and recruitment images, Gatewood et al. (1993) found that an organization's overall corporate image and recruitment image was positively related to a potential applicant's probability of pursuing contact with an organization. Furthermore, they also found that recruitment image was strongly related to the amount of information provided in the company's advertisement, suggesting that a greater amount of information enhances image, and image is positively related to intentions to pursue employment. Because the content of most of the advertisements was positive, this finding essentially suggests that providing more positive information will result in greater interest on the part of applicants.

Interestingly, the practical implication of this finding (i.e., provide applicants with lots of positive information about the organization) is somewhat at odds with the RJP literature and the realism hypothesis. In fact, Gatewood et al. (1993) make the following conclusion: "In many ways, these findings support the commonly held assumption of traditional recruitment advertising, which is that the presentation of favorable information will positively influence potential applicants" (p. 426).

As indicated earlier, Collins and Stevens (2002) studied the effects of early recruitment practices on engineering students' perceptions of employer brand image (applicants' general attitudes toward the company and perceived attributes) and their application intentions and decisions. Publicity, word-of-mouth endorsements, and recruitment advertising were significantly related to employer brand image, especially when they were used together. This was particularly the case when publicity was used with the other recruitment practices. In addition, employer brand image was found to mediate the relationships between the recruitment practices and application intentions and decisions.

In order to learn more about the most relevant dimensions for understanding the impressions that applicants hold about an organization's employment image, Highhouse, Zickar, Thorsteinson, Stierwalt, and Slaughter (1999) conducted a study on the dimensions of company employment image (CEI) in the fast-food industry. Using samples of teenagers and retirees, the results indicated that respectability, product image, hearsay, and atmosphere were the strongest predictors of CEI, suggesting that these factors are the most critical for applicant attraction in the fast-food industry. Further, most of the dimensions predicted CEI equally well for teenagers and retirees.

Several studies have also investigated the effects of firm reputation in the recruitment process. For example, Turban et al. (1998) found that firm reputation was positively related to applicant perceptions of job and organizational attributes and recruiter behaviors, but was negatively related to applicant attraction.

Cable and Graham (2000) conducted a series of studies demonstrating that job seekers' perceptions of an organization's reputation is a function of the type of industry in which an organization operates, opportunities for personal development, and organizational culture. Turban and Cable (2003) reported on two studies that looked at the effect of firm reputation on applicant pool size and quality. Using samples of senior undergraduates and MBA students, they found that firms with better reputations not only attract more applicants, but those applicants who applied for a position as well as those interviewed were of a higher quality in terms of grade point average, foreign language skills, and overall rating. Overall, these results provide support that firm reputation influences the number and quality of applicants who are attracted to an organization and actually apply for a job.

Lievens and Highhouse (2003) used the instrumental–symbolic framework from the marketing literature to examine the effects of instrumental job/organizational attributes (e.g., pay, benefits, location) and symbolic attributes on perceived attractiveness of an employer. While instrumental attributes are similar to those typically studied in research on vacancy characteristics and involve objective, concrete, and factual attributes, symbolic attributes involve more subjective and intangible attributes such as imagery and trait inferences that applicants assign to organizations (e.g., prestige, innovativeness).

Samples of students and bank employees were asked to rate banks in terms of their instrumental and symbolic attributes and to indicate the attractiveness of the bank as an employer. The results indicated that instrumental attributes significantly predicted the attractiveness of the bank as an employer and symbolic attributes explained a significant amount of incremental variance in the prediction of employer attractiveness. They also found that at least within a particular industry, applicants are better able to differentiate organizations on the basis of symbolic or trait inferences than more tangible job and organizational attributes.

Taken together, the studies reviewed in this section demonstrate that there are subjective attributes that attract applicants to organizations besides the more objective vacancy characteristics. Clearly, this is an important finding. However, from a practical perspective, it is not clear what it means. It would seem that if an organization wants to differentiate itself from its competitors, it should focus on these more subjective and intangible attributes. But how do you create a positive reputation and get applicants to perceive an organization as innovative, competent, or sincere? How do you change an organization's "symbolic meaning" in the minds of applicants? It would seem that these more subjective attributes develop over time and are partly a function of an organization's history and culture. Furthermore, attempts to change them extend far beyond recruitment and involve strategic decisions. As well, some factors that predict reputation perceptions cannot be easily changed or changed at all (e.g., industry, profitability, culture).

The more immediate implication seems to be to convey and reinforce the existing subjective attributes that differentiate the organization from its competitors. While certain images might seem especially likely to attract desired applicants (innovative, exciting, prestige), the RJP literature suggests that recruitment materials should only indicate what is realistic and accurate. It would seem that this is where one must differentiate the implications for marketing from recruitment. Clearly, to sell a product, whether it's a soft drink or clothing, you can create any image you want to capture the imagination and attention of the consumer (just look at how tobacco companies have advertised cigarettes over the decades). However, you can't create a flashy image to sell a job and organization just because it will attract applicants if the reality does not live up to the message. Therefore, the practical implication of this research is the following:

Communicate subjective attributes of the organization, especially those that differentiate it from its competitors, as well as positive but realistic information about the organization's image and reputation in recruitment materials.

Summary

Table 3.1 presents a summary of the practical implications of each area of recruitment research. While the past five years have seen a resurgence of recruitment research, the practical implications of recruitment research for recruiters and organizations is at best limited and at worst impractical.

Overall, the most meaningful practical implications stem from the growing research on recruitment activities and on organizational image, reputation, and symbolic attributes. The use of a number of recruitment activities can increase the number of applications, perceptions of job attributes and attractiveness, and job pursuit intentions and decisions. As well, organizations can benefit by including more symbolic information in their recruitment materials. This might not only improve applicant attraction and job acceptance decisions, but it might also enable an organization to better differentiate itself from its competitors. An important area for future research is to investigate the effect of recruitment practices on symbolic attributes as well as image and reputation. The study by Collins and Stevens (2002) is a good example of the kind of research that is needed.

Finally, it is worth noting that recruitment research has been primarily concerned with the application stage of the recruitment process, with much less attention on the interaction and job choice stages. In addition, with only one exception (Taylor & Bergmann, 1987), recruitment research has not studied applicants' movement across recruitment stages. As a result, it is not known how practices at one stage impact outcomes at subsequent stages or the combined effects of multiple practices across recruitment stages.

WHY HAS RECRUITMENT RESEARCH BEEN SO IMPRACTICAL?

As the above review demonstrates, recruitment research has not made much of a contribution to practice, a conclusion that has been noted by others (Barber, 1998; Rynes, 1991; Taylor & Collins, 2000). Given the very practical nature of recruitment (after all, every organization must continuously recruit and hire new employees), this is rather odd to say the least, especially when compared to other areas in industrial–organizational psychology such as training. In their recent review in the *Annual Review of Psychology*, Salas and Cannon-Bowers (2001) noted the many advances that have been made in the past decade in both the quantity and quality of training research. They concluded their review by stating that, "The stage for the application of training research is set" and "a new era of training has begun – one in which a truly reciprocal relationship between training research and practice will be realized" (p. 492). Clearly, the same cannot be said about recruitment research.

Why has recruitment research been so impractical? There are a number of factors that help us to understand this and to begin to consider how to close the recruitment research-to-practice gap.

TABLE 3.1   Practical implications of recruitment research

Recruitment research topic	Practical implication
Realistic job previews *Recruitment stage*: Interaction	Provide job applicants with an accurate and realistic picture of the job and organization that includes both the positive and negative attributes.
Recruitment sources *Recruitment stage*: Application	Use informal sources of recruitment such as employee referrals, direct applications, as well as rehires rather than formal sources (i.e., newspaper advertisements and employment agencies).
Recruiter behavior *Recruitment stage*: Interaction	Recruiters should be knowledgeable about job openings and the organization and they should be personable and friendly when meeting and interacting with job candidates.
Employment inducements *Recruitment stage*: Application and job offer	Offer a variety of employment inducements to potential job applicants (e.g., flexible work arrangements, opportunities for training, benefits, etc.), especially high pay.
Recruitment activities *Recruitment stage*: Application, interaction, and job offer	Use a variety of recruitment activities (e.g., campus activity, recruitment materials, recruitment process, publicity, sponsorship activities, word-of-mouth endorsements, advertising) to increase applicant familiarity with and attractiveness to the organization, brand image, and application intentions and decisions.
	The site visit should be carefully planned and conducted in a professional manner with particular attention paid to what is communicated to applicants; how applicants are treated; the people who meet with applicants; and the site visit host.
	Avoid delays during the recruitment process and maintain contact with applicants throughout the process.
Recruitment advertising *Recruitment Stage*: Application	Provide specific and positive information about job and organization attributes in recruitment advertisements and materials including information about diversity.
Organizational characteristics *Recruitment stage*: Application	None.
Strategic human resources management *Recruitment stage*: Application	None.
Organizational image, reputation, and symbolic attributes *Recruitment stage*: Application	Communicate subjective attributes of the organization, especially those that differentiate it from its competitors, as well as positive but realistic information about the organization's image and reputation in recruitment materials.

First, as indicated earlier, there has been an overwhelming concentration on the "3 R's" of recruitment research. As a result, only recently have researchers begun to explore new areas of recruitment. Most of what we know today about recruitment has its basis in research on the "3 R's."

There are a number of other reasons why recruitment research has not produced more practical information and guidelines for recruiters: 1) Recruitment research has traditionally been considered part of the selection function, 2) it has often focused on distal or post-hire outcomes rather than more relevant proximal pre-hire outcomes, 3) the level of analysis has been the individual rather than the organization, 4) finding applicants has, until recently, not been a major problem for organizations, and 5) recruitment and the human resource function has lacked a strategic focus. Since the latter two issues have already been discussed, in this section I will focus on the first three.

Recruitment versus selection

Several recent reviews have made note of the increasing interest in recruitment research by pointing out that in the first edition of the *Handbook of Industrial and Organizational Psychology* (Dunnette, 1976), the topic of recruitment was covered in less than one page, and by the time of the publication of the second edition, an entire chapter was devoted to it (Breaugh & Starke, 2000; Rynes & Cable, 2003).

While this certainly highlights the resurgence of interest in recruitment research, it also demonstrates how the topic of recruitment has traditionally been subsumed as a component of the larger topic of selection. Guion's (1976) article in the first edition of the Handbook was primarily about selection, of which recruitment was treated as one "small" part. One only has to look at the number of textbooks on selection compared to recruitment to get an idea of how recruitment has traditionally been treated within the field of industrial–organizational psychology. Most colleges and universities offer courses on staffing or selection but not on recruitment. They use textbooks on staffing that usually include one chapter or less on recruitment. There have been only two academic books written on recruitment in the past decade or so (Barber, 1998; Breaugh, 1992).

Furthermore, even recent research on strategic human resources management has given low priority to the role of recruitment. As indicated earlier, many studies do not even include measures of recruitment and when they do they are usually considered part of selection. Thus, recruitment has at best been considered as a sub-discipline of selection and, at worst, not even worthy of consideration.

Pre-hire versus post-hire outcomes

One of the most surprising problems with recruitment research is the emphasis on post-hire outcomes and perceptual pre-hire outcomes. Although some studies have measured pre-hire outcomes, too often the measures have been applicant reactions, perceptions of attractiveness, and job pursuit and acceptance intentions (Rynes, 1991; Rynes & Barber, 1990; Turban & Cable, 2003). In fact, most recruitment research has used measures of firm attractiveness and job acceptance intentions rather than actual job acceptance decisions (Turban et al., 1995).

In addition, both the RJP and recruitment source literature have been largely driven by a focus on retention or turnover reduction. From a research perspective, there is no doubt that collecting longitudinal data that tracks applicants throughout the organizational entry process is highly desirable. However, from a practical perspective it does not address the main goals of recruitment – *the identification and attraction of individuals to organizations*. Furthermore, post-hire outcomes such as job satisfaction and turnover are influenced by many other variables that occur on the job and are much stronger predictors of post-hire outcomes. As well, there are many other more effective things an organization can do to retain employees as part of a turnover reduction program. Furthermore, when it comes to recruitment, employers are not so concerned about post-hire outcomes. Rather, they are concerned about pre-hire outcomes such as the quality of applicants who apply for positions and the number who accept job offers (Breaugh & Starke, 2000; Williams et al., 1993). Thus, research that focuses almost exclusively on post-hire outcomes such as turnover will not contribute to the practice of recruitment.

Individual versus organizational level of analysis

A major limitation of recruitment research has been the almost exclusive reliance on the individual level of analysis (Rynes & Cable, 2003) or what Rynes and Barber (1990) described as the applicant's rather than the organization's perspective. This is odd to say the least, given that recruitment is an organizational-level phenomenon. That is, organizations not job applicants recruit. Job applicants search for work and their efforts and experiences are best studied in research on job search. However, the primary emphasis of recruitment research has been on job applicants' reactions, intentions, job choices, and post-hire attitudes and behaviors. As noted by Taylor and Collins (2000), there has been practically no recruitment research conducted at the macro or organizational level of analysis.

To understand the problem of the almost exclusive focus on the individual level of analysis, consider research on recruitment source effects. As indicated earlier, the major finding has been that employees recruited through employee referrals have greater job survival. However, because the data for many studies was collected from individuals rather than organizations, it is impossible to know how organizations actually differ in their use of recruitment sources and whether such differences have an effect on an organization's recruitment success. Furthermore, the collection of data from individuals rather than organizations also makes it very difficult to interpret the results of recruitment source research. For example, although employee referrals have been found to be the most effective recruitment source, the use of an employee referral might actually say more about the job seeker who provides the data than the organization that hired him or her. That is, employee referrals might be more effective because individuals who find employment through them might be more effective job seekers. If this is the case, the effectiveness of employee referrals might have more to do with job search or job applicants' characteristics and behavior than an organization's recruitment efforts. In fact, by focusing on the individual level of analysis, it is possible for a study to find that employee referrals are the most effective recruitment source, even though an organization might not even have an employee referral program. This is because many job seekers find employment through networking and word of mouth and this might have absolutely nothing to do with how an organization recruits.

Thus, by focusing on the individual level of analysis, it is difficult to know what organizations can do to improve the success of their recruitment efforts. The almost exclusive reliance on an individual level of analysis in recruitment research has produced very little in the way of practical implications for organizations.

WHAT DO ORGANIZATIONS NEED TO KNOW ABOUT RECRUITMENT?

Given the continued challenges that organizations will face in attracting and recruiting qualified applicants, how can future research inform recruitment practice? There are a number of avenues for future research that might lead to more practical implications than previous studies.

First, organizations can benefit from research on the effects of current and innovative recruitment programs. There is ample evidence that many organizations are using new and innovative recruitment practices. For example, Taylor and Collins (2000) described several strategies that some employers are using, including casting a wider net to target a broader range of applicants (e.g., attracting applicants across larger geographical areas), using technology to recruit applicants (e.g., Internet-based job search services), offering financial incentives (e.g., a signing bonus to new recruits, higher wage levels), and enhancing the desirability of the organization as a place to work (e.g., career opportunities, work–life balance programs). Cascio (2003) describes the creative recruitment tactics being used by Cisco Systems, Home Depot, GE Medical Systems, and MasterCard. In Canada, the Ontario Provincial Police (OPP) recently staged a five-day recruiting camp for one hundred women selected from close to 3,000 applicants interested in a career in policing. During the five-day recruiting camp, the women experienced typical OPP policing activities such as shooting a handgun, completing 6 a.m. fitness drills, and responding to mock crimes. Eighty-three of the women will go on to complete the first stage of testing and if they are successful they begin a lengthy application and selection process (Harding, 2003).

While these are just some examples of the many new strategies and tactics that organizations are now using for recruitment, there have been few examples of research on the effects of such creative recruitment practices. Thus, researchers can help organizations by conducting studies on the effectiveness of their new and innovative recruitment strategies. This appears to be one area where practice is far ahead of research and science.

Organizations would also benefit from research that develops and tests new recruitment practices and strategies. For example, training research has developed new strategies and interventions for improving the transfer of training (Machin, 2002). As a result, organizations can now look to the training literature to learn about how they can diagnose transfer problems and develop and implement interventions to improve transfer (Holton, 2003). In this regard, the past decade of training research can serve as a model for future recruitment research and practice. Along these lines, the next section provides a model and agenda for recruitment research-to-practice.

A RESEARCH MODEL AND AGENDA FOR RECRUITMENT RESEARCH-TO-PRACTICE

In this final section of the chapter, a model and agenda for future recruitment research is presented. In order to address some of the limitations of previous research and close the research-to-practice gap, future research should focus on the following issues.

Focus on innovative recruitment practices.   An important direction for future research is to stop the continued over-researching of the three traditional topics and begin to focus on new and innovative recruitment practices and processes that are likely to lead to practical implications. As indicated earlier, organizations are far ahead of the research in the use of innovative and creative recruitment strategies. Therefore, future research might identify new and untested strategies being used by organizations and conduct studies to test the effectiveness of them. Researchers might also develop new approaches for recruitment in the same way that training research has developed new approaches for needs analysis, evaluation, and transfer of training interventions (Salas & Cannon-Bowers, 2001).

Focus on objective pre-hire outcomes.   A second and related issue is the need to shift the focus of recruitment research toward pre-hire outcomes. Such an emphasis is not only consistent with the definition and meaning of recruitment, but it also addresses the primary concerns of organizations – how to attract and motivate the kind of job applicants desired by an organization (e.g., Knowledge, Skills and Abilities – KSAs, personality, experience, demographics, etc.) to apply for a job and accept a job offer. As noted by Rynes and Barber (1990), for organizations the most important objective of recruitment is to fill vacancies. Similarly, Turban and Cable (2003) recently stated that the primary objective of recruitment and the most important measure of recruitment success is the size and quality of the applicant pool. Therefore, future research should measure pre-hire outcomes such as the number of applicants that apply for a job opening; the quality of applicants that apply; the number of applicants that receive job offers; the number of applicants that accept job offers; the quality of applicants that accept job offers; and the number of vacancies that remain open.

In general, future research should measure the quantity and quality of applicants and job acceptors as well as more objective and behavioral outcomes of job applicants (e.g., job choice decisions) (Rynes & Barber, 1990).

Focus on organizational-level and multilevel analysis.   A third area is a greater emphasis on organizational-level analysis. As noted by Taylor and Collins (2000), there is a critical need for recruitment research to focus on the organizational level of analysis. While individual level of analysis remains important, especially for learning more about recruitment processes (e.g., applicant self-selection, person–organization fit; Breaugh & Starke, 2000; Rynes & Cable, 2003), an organizational level of analysis is necessary for recruitment research to inform recruitment practice. There is also a need for multilevel research that gathers data from both applicants and organizations.

Focus on the links between recruitment, individual, and organizational outcomes.   As indicated earlier, most recruitment research has focused on post-hire outcomes and has not examined the links between recruitment practices and various types and levels of outcome. Therefore, there is a need for research that connects recruitment practices to recruitment outcomes, individual outcomes, and organizational outcomes. Although there is some evidence that recruitment practices *might* influence organizational performance (Taylor & Collins, 2000), direct evidence is lacking. At best, one can conclude that recruitment as well as other HR practices is related to organizational performance. Research is needed that adequately demonstrates how recruitment practices and outcomes lead to both individual and organizational outcomes.

As a guide for future recruitment research, Figure 3.2 presents a Multilevel Model of the Recruitment Process. The model incorporates the three stages of recruitment from Figure 3.1 and shows how recruitment practices at each stage influence applicant outcomes (i.e., reactions, perceptions, and intentions), which in turn impact recruitment outcomes and might mediate the effect of recruitment practices on recruitment outcomes. The model also shows the links between recruitment outcomes and individual-level outcomes, and the link between individual-level outcomes and organizational-level outcomes. The model calls for future recruitment research to be both multilevel and longitudinal and to include both applicant and organizational data.

In summary, future research on recruitment needs to focus on the following questions:

♦ What is the effect of specific recruitment practices and activities on applicant outcomes (i.e., reactions, perceptions, and intentions) and recruitment outcomes such as applicant attraction (quantity and quality), applicant interest and motivation during the recruitment process, and applicant job acceptance rates (quantity and quality of applicants)?

♦ What recruitment practices and activities are most effective for attracting applicants, increasing their interest and motivation during recruitment, and enhancing the probability of job offer acceptance rates? Further, are there contextual factors (e.g., firm size, reputation, industry, labor market, etc.) that moderate the effectiveness of particular recruitment practices on certain outcomes?

♦ What is the effect of recruitment practices and outcomes on individual-level outcomes such as job attitudes, job performance, and turnover? Do applicant and/or recruitment outcomes mediate the effect of recruitment practices on individual-level outcomes?

♦ What is the effect of recruitment practices, applicant outcomes, recruitment outcomes, and individual-level outcomes on organizational-level outcomes (i.e., turnover rate, firm performance)? Do applicant, recruitment, and/or individual-level outcomes mediate the effect of recruitment practices on organizational-level outcomes? Do individual-level outcomes mediate the effect of recruitment outcomes on organizational-level outcomes?

Conclusion

Several recent reviews of the recruitment literature have made note of the numerous problems in the design and methodology of recruitment research (Barber, 1998; Breaugh & Starke, 2000). A similar conclusion can be made about the practical implications of

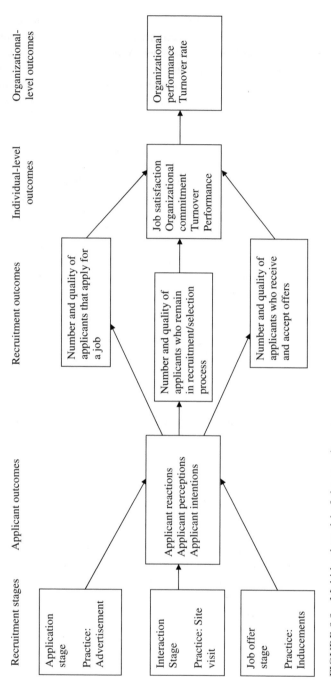

FIGURE 3.2 Multi-level model of the recruitment process

recruitment research. That is, even though there has been a great deal of research on recruitment over the last thirty years (Breaugh & Starke, 2000), it is fair to say that a) there are few practical implications for recruiters and organizations, b) the practical implications that can be gleaned from recruitment research have been known for more than a decade, and c) the main practical implications are at best obvious and at worst trivial.

Thus, there is good reason to be pessimistic about previous recruitment research (Breaugh & Starke, 2000) as well as its implications for practice. While other reviews have focused on the need to improve the design and methodology of recruitment research (e.g., Breaugh & Starke, 2000; Rynes & Cable, 2003), it is also important to shift the focus of recruitment research to issues and concerns that are relevant and practical for organizations. Along these lines, a multilevel model of recruitment was presented as a guide for future research. In particular, future research needs to investigate the effects of creative and innovative recruitment practices on applicant and recruitment outcomes as well as the links between these outcomes to post-entry individual-level and organizational-level outcomes. Until research along these lines is conducted, it will be difficult to defend the assertion that recruitment is one of the most important human resource systems and can provide an organization with a sustained competitive advantage (Taylor & Collins, 2000).

For the time being, organizations that wish to learn about creative, innovative, and effective recruitment practices are best advised to find out what other companies are doing and to consult the practitioner rather than the research literature. Thus, while the science of *training* is now ripe for practice, research on recruitment has a long way to go before we can begin to consider how to translate recruitment science into practice. The good news is that there has been a significant increase in the quantity and quality of recruitment research in the past five years, not to mention three review articles and Barber's (1998) book. If things continue at this pace, we will know a great deal more about the science and practice of recruitment by the end of this decade. If the last decade sets the stage for the application of training research, then the current decade might well be the decade that sets the stage for the application of recruitment research.

REFERENCES

Alderfer, C. P., & McCord, C. G. (1970). Personal and situational factors in the recruitment interview. *Journal of Applied Psychology, 54*, 377–385.

Allen, D. G., Van Scotter, J. R., & Otondo, R. F. (2004). Recruitment communication media: Impact on prehire outcomes. *Personnel Psychology, 57*, 143–171.

Avery, D. R. (2003). Reactions to diversity in recruitment advertising – are differences Black and White? *Journal of Applied Psychology, 88*, 672–679.

Barber, A. E. (1998). *Recruiting employees: Individual and organizational perspectives.* Thousand Oaks, CA: Sage.

Barber, A. E., Wesson, M. J., Roberson, Q. M., & Taylor, M. S. (1999). A tale of two job markets: Organizational size and its effect on hiring practices and job search behavior. *Personnel Psychology, 52*, 841–867.

Belt, J. A., & Paolillo, J. G. P. (1982). The influence of corporate image and specificity of candidate qualifications on response to recruitment advertisements. *Journal of Management, 8*, 105–112.

Boudreau, J. W., & Rynes, S. L. (1985). Role of recruitment in staffing utility analysis. *Journal of Applied Psychology, 70*, 354–366.

Breaugh, J. A. (1983). Realistic job previews: A critical appraisal and future research directions. *Academy of Management Review, 8*, 612–619.

Breaugh, J. A. (1992). *Recruitment: Science and practice.* Boston: PWS-Kent.

Breaugh, J. A., & Starke, M. (2000). Research on employee recruitment: So many studies, so many remaining questions. *Journal of Management, 26*, 405–434.

Bretz, R. D., Jr., & Judge, T. A. (1998). Realistic job previews: A test of the adverse self-selection hypothesis. *Journal of Applied Psychology, 83*, 330–337.

Cable, D. M., & Graham, M. E. (2000). The determinants of job seekers' reputation perceptions. *Journal of Organizational Behavior, 21*, 929–947.

Cable, D. M., & Judge, T. A. (1994). Pay preferences and job search decisions: A person–organization fit perspective. *Personnel Psychology, 47*, 317–348.

Cascio, W. F. (2003). Changes in workers, work, and organizations. In W. C. Borman, D. R. Ilgen, & R. J. Klimoski (Eds.), *Handbook of psychology: Industrial and organizational psychology* (Vol. 12, pp. 401–422). Hoboken, NJ: John Wiley & Sons.

Collins, C. J., & Stevens, C. K. (2002). The relationship between early recruitment-related activities and the application decisions of new labor-market entrants: A brand equity approach to recruitment. *Journal of Applied Psychology, 87*, 1121–1133.

Dineen, B. R., Ash, S. R., & Noe, R. A. (2002). A web of applicant attraction: Person–organization fit in the context of web-based recruitment. *Journal of Applied Psychology, 87*, 723–734.

Dunnette, M. D. (1976). Aptitudes, abilities and skills. In M.D. Dunnette (Ed.), *Handbook of industrial and organizational psychology* (pp. 473–520). Chicago: Rand McNally.

Dunnette, M. D., & Hough, L. M. (Eds.). (1991). *Handbook of industrial and organizational psychology* (2nd ed., Vol. 2). Palo Alto, CA: Consulting Psychologists Press.

Gatewood, R. D., Gowan, M. A., & Lautenschlager, G. J. (1993). Corporate image, recruitment image, and initial job choice decisions. *Academy of Management Journal, 36*, 414–427.

Guion, R. M. (1976). Recruiting, selection, and job placement. In M. D. Dunnette (Ed.), *Handbook of industrial and organizational psychology* (pp. 777–828). Chicago: Rand-McNally.

Harding, K. (2003, July 16). Police aim to hire officers. *The Globe and Mail*, C1.

Harel, G. H., & Tzafrir, S. S. (1999). The effect of human resource management practices on the perceptions of organizational and market performance of the firm. *Human Resource Management, 38*, 185–200.

Highhouse, S., Stierwalt, S. L., Slaughter, J. E., Bachiochi, P., Elder, A. E., & Fisher, G. (1999). Effects of advertised human resource management practices on attraction of African American applicants. *Personnel Psychology, 52*, 425–442.

Highhouse, S., Zickar, M. J., Thorsteinson, T. J., Stierwalt, S. L., & Slaughter, J. E. (1999). Assessing company employment image: An example in the fast food industry. *Personnel Psychology, 52*, 151–172.

Holton, E. F., III. (2003). What's *really* wrong: Diagnosis for learning transfer system change. In E. F. Holton III & T. T. Baldwin (Eds.), *Improving learning transfer in organizations* (pp. 59–79). San Francisco: Jossey-Bass.

Huselid, M. A. (1995). The impact of human resource management practices on turnover, productivity, and corporate financial performance. *Academy of Management Journal, 38*, 635–672.

Ichniowski, C., Shaw, K., & Prennushi, G. (1997). The effects of human resource management practices on productivity: A study of steel finishing lines. *The American Economic Review, 87*, 291–313.

Jackson, S. E., & Schuler, R. S. (1990). Human resource planning: Challenges for industrial/organizational psychologists. *American Psychologist, 45*, 223–239.

Kim, S. S., & Gelfand, M. J. (2003). The influence of ethnic identity on perceptions of organizational recruitment. *Journal of Vocational Behavior, 63*, 396–416.

Kirnan, J. P., Farley, J. A., & Geisinger, K. F. (1989). The relationship between recruiting source, applicant quality, and hire performance: An analysis by sex, ethnicity, and age. *Personnel Psychology, 42*, 293–308.

Lievens, F., & Highhouse, S. (2003). The relation of instrumental and symbolic attributes to a company's attractiveness as an employer. *Personnel Psychology, 56*, 75–102.

Machin, M. A. (2002). Planning, managing, and optimizing transfer of training. In K. Kraiger (Ed.), *Creating, implementing, and managing effective training and development* (pp. 263–301). San Francisco: Jossey-Bass.

McEvoy, G. M., & Cascio, W. F. (1985). Strategies for reducing employee turnover: A meta-analysis. *Journal of Applied Psychology, 70*, 342–353.

McLaren, C. (2002, February 8). Ways to win top talent. *The Globe and Mail*, C1.

Meglino, B. M., Ravlin, E. C., & DeNisi, A. S. (2000). A meta-analytic examination of realistic job preview effectiveness: A test of three counterintuitive propositions. *Human Resource Management Review, 10*, 407–434.

Murphy, K. A. (1986). When your top choice turns you down: Effect of rejected job offers on the utility of selection tests. *Psychological Bulletin, 99*, 128–133.

Offermann, L. R., & Gowing, M. K. (1990). Organizations of the future: Changes and Challenges. *American Psychologist, 45*, 95–108.

Pfeffer, J. (1994). Competitive advantage through people. *California Management Review, 36*, 9–28.

Phillips, J. M. (1998). Effects of realistic job previews on multiple organizational outcomes: A meta-analysis. *Academy of Management Journal, 41*, 673–690.

Powell, G. N. (1984). Effects of job attributes and recruiting practices on applicant decisions: A comparison. *Personnel Psychology, 37*, 721–732.

Premack, S. L., & Wanous, J. P. (1985). A meta-analysis of realistic job preview experiments. *Journal of Applied Psychology, 70*, 706–719.

Rynes, S. L. (1991). Recruitment, job choice, and post-hire consequences: A call for new research directions. In M. D. Dunnette & L. M. Hough (Eds.), *Handbook of industrial and organizational psychology* (2nd ed., Vol. 2, pp. 399–444). Palo Alto, CA: Consulting Psychologists Press.

Rynes, S. L., & Barber, A. E. (1990). Applicant attraction strategies: An organizational perspective. *Academy of Management Review, 15*, 286–310.

Rynes, S. L., Bretz, R. D., Jr., & Gerhart, B. (1991). The importance of recruitment in job choice: A different way of looking. *Personnel Psychology, 44*, 487–521.

Rynes, S. L., & Cable, D. M. (2003). Recruitment research in the twenty-first century. In W. C. Borman, D. R. Ilgen, & R. J. Klimoski (Eds.), *Handbook of psychology: Industrial and organizational psychology* (pp. 55–76). Hoboken, NJ: John Wiley & Sons.

Rynes, S. L., Orlitzky, M. O., & Bretz, R. D., Jr. (1997). Experienced hiring versus college recruitment: Practices and emerging trends. *Personnel Psychology, 50*, 309–339.

Saks, A. M., Wiesner, W. H., & Summers, R. J. (1994). Effects of job previews on self-selection and job choice. *Journal of Vocational Behavior, 44*, 297–316.

Saks, A. M., Wiesner, W. H., & Summers, R. J. (1996). Effects of job previews and compensation policy on applicant attraction and job choice. *Journal of Vocational Behavior, 49*, 68–85.

Salas, E., & Cannon-Bowers, J. A. (2001). The science of training: A decade of progress. *Annual Review of Psychology, 52*, 471–499.

Taylor, M. S., & Collins, C. J. (2000). Organizational recruitment: Enhancing the intersection of theory and practice. In C. L. Cooper & E. A. Locke (Eds.), *Industrial and organizational psychology: Linking theory and practice* (pp. 304–334). Oxford, UK: Blackwell.

Taylor, M. S., & Bergmann, T. J. (1987). Organizational recruitment activities and applicants' reactions at different stages of the recruitment process. *Personnel Psychology, 40*, 261–285.

Trank, C. Q., Rynes, S. L., & Bretz, R. D., Jr. (2002). Attracting applicants in the war for talent: Individual differences in work preferences by ability and achievement levels. *Journal of Business and Psychology, 16,* 331–345.

Turban, D. B. (2001). Organizational attractiveness as an employer on college campuses: An examination of the applicant population. *Journal of Vocational Behavior, 58,* 293–312.

Turban, D. B., & Cable, D. M. (2003). Firm reputation and applicant pool characteristics. *Journal of Organizational Behavior, 24,* 733–751.

Turban, D. B., Campion, J. E., & Eyring, A. R. (1995). Factors related to job acceptance decisions of college recruits. *Journal of Vocational Behavior, 47,* 193–213.

Turban, D. B., Forret, M. L., & Hendrickson, C. L. (1998). Applicant attraction to firms: Influences of organization reputation, job and organizational attributes, and recruiter behaviors. *Journal of Vocational Behavior, 52,* 24–44.

Wanous, J. P. (1973). Effects of a realistic job preview on job acceptance, job attitudes, and job survival. *Journal of Applied Psychology, 58,* 327–332.

Williams, M. L., & Dreher, G. F. (1992). Compensation system attributes and applicant pool characteristics. *Academy of Management Journal, 35,* 571–595.

Williams, C. R., Labig, C.E., Jr., & Stone, T. H. (1993). Recruitment sources and posthire outcomes for job applicants and new hires: A test of two hypotheses. *Journal of Applied Psychology, 78,* 163–172.

Williamson, I. O., Lepak, D. P., & King, J. (2003). The effect of company recruitment website orientation on individuals' perceptions of organizational attractiveness. *Journal of Vocational Behavior, 63,* 242–263.

Yuce, P., & Highhouse, S. (1998). Effects of attribute set size and pay ambiguity on reactions to "Help wanted" advertisements. *Journal of Organizational Behavior, 19,* 337–352.

Zottoli, M. A., & Wanous, J. P. (2000). Recruitment source research: Current status and future directions. *Human Resource Management Review, 10,* 353–382.

4

The Design of Selection Systems: Context, Principles, Issues

ROBERT A. ROE

This chapter addresses the design of systems for personnel selection which enable organizations to build up and maintain a competent and well-motivated workforce. While the use of selection systems is seen as a task for HRM specialists and managers, their design is typically depicted as a task for psychologists. They are expected to develop selection systems in such a way that valid predictions of performance and effective employee decisions are attained. There is an extensive psychological literature on selection, most of which describes systems design as a linear sequence of steps that include job analysis, choosing tests, administering tests, conducting a validation study, and composing a test battery (e.g., Guion, 1998; Schmitt & Chan, 1998; Smith & Robertson, 1989; Thorndike, 1949). Owing to its strong focus on predictive tools and statistical prediction techniques the perspective of these publications has been labeled as a "psychometric paradigm" (McCourt, 1999). Although this perspective has much to offer, it also has some limitations. First, it ignores much of the context of selection, in particular the fact that there are different stakeholders in organizations with diverging interests in selection. Secondly, it overlooks the fact that a variety of demands have to be met in designing selection systems, and that the search for a solution requires an iterative rather than a linear series of steps. Third, it disregards design facets other than prediction that may nonetheless have a strong impact on the effectiveness of the system. This chapter presents a view of selection systems design that aims at overcoming these limitations. It describes the context of the design process, including the roles of stakeholders, presents a methodology that tackles multiple demands in an iterative process, and demonstrates the importance of facets other than prediction.

THE CONTEXT OF SELECTION

For people in organizations selection usually matters. That is, they find it important who is selected for a particular job, who is involved in decision making, on what grounds candidates are accepted or rejected, etc. This is especially true for positions that are highly visible, in which great power is vested, or on which many others or the organization as a whole depends. Selection for such key positions is far from neutral. On the contrary, various parties struggle to influence job descriptions, requirements, procedures, and actual decisions. Psychologists charged with the design of selection systems for situations like this find themselves in a political arena in which "rationality" is readily perceived as the pursuit of specific interests and therefore difficult to achieve.

While power and politics do not fit well in the "psychometric paradigm," they are an obvious part of organizational life. Organizations are sites of power games between various types of stakeholders striving for dominance (Clegg, 1975; Mintzberg, 1983). Clearly, the area of selection is not exempted from such power games, nor does the design of selection systems take place in a political vacuum. Thus, when a manager proposes to design a new selection system (which usually means the redesign of an existing system), this is likely to be seen as a political move which can mobilize various actors in favor or against. Likewise, the decision to involve an expert (the psychologist) and to allocate resources to the project will be understood in political terms and be responded to accordingly. Such political responses may exert strong influences on the design and use of selection systems. All this suggests that the role of stakeholders has to be acknowledged and that their views have to be taken into account when designing selection systems.

In addition, selection systems must be designed in a manner compatible with the organization's structure and modus operandi. Thus, in a hierarchical and mechanical organization the design process will be rolled out top-down and be highly proceduralized, whereas in a flat and organic organization the design process may proceed more informally. Moreover, the system itself will have to fit within the organization's culture, be compatible with other HRM systems, be acceptable to line, staff, employees, customers, etc. A fit to available resources is also important; that is, the size and scope of the system will have to match available resources, in terms of staff, time and budgets. We will show that most of these issues can be addressed by involving stakeholders in the design process.

Selection Systems and Their Development

In the context of personnel selection we prefer to *define a selection system as a configuration of instruments, procedures, and people created with the purpose of selecting candidates for certain positions, in such a way that they can be expected to optimally fulfill pre-defined expectations.* Thus, the selection system enables the organization to interact with a pool of candidates and to identify those who most likely match standards of future performance. There are three essential *components* of the selection system, representing its hardware, software, and human resources, namely 1) instruments, such as tests and job samples, 2) procedures for administering these instruments and handling information, and 3) people using the instruments and applying procedures.

Although selection instruments receive much attention in the literature, and choosing reliable and valid tests is often described as the designer's key task, this is *not* the most critical factor for a successful design in our view. Strictly speaking, the instruments themselves do not predict. Prediction is achieved by processing information from the instruments according to a certain procedure. When used appropriately and combined well, good instruments will lead to high overall effectiveness, but when used or combined improperly effectiveness will be low. There are several more reasons why good predictors may *not*

TABLE 4.1 Components of the selection system

Selection system components

Instruments (hardware)
    Paper-and-pencil tests
    Computer tests
    Other apparatus tests
    Simulators
    Test and staff rooms
    Infrastructure (e.g., Web access)

Procedure (software)
    Processing rules for tests and other instruments (scoring, norms)
    Prediction model
    Decision model
    Report generator
    Rules for contact with candidates
    Rules for contacts with commissioners
    Internal script (and timetable)

People (humanware)
    Test administrators
    Selectors (incl. psychologists)
    Technical and secretarial staff

produce good results. For example, there may be too much redundancy in the test battery, weights may be chosen inadequately, cutoffs may be set too high or vary over time, the prediction may target the wrong type of criteria, the composition of the battery or the manner of administration may be at odds with candidates' expectations and lead to unwanted withdrawals, users may be doubtful about the adequacy of the selection procedure and therefore disregard its outcomes, and so on. One might say that a well-chosen procedure adds value to the instruments and that the art of design is to maximize this added value. The human component of the selection system should not be overlooked either. Good selection tools in the hands of people without proper qualifications or attitudes cannot be expected to produce good results. The presence of knowledgeable and competent staff certainly adds to the effectiveness of selection. Table 4.1 describes the three components of the selection system and lists a number of typical elements to be considered in the design process.

Developing a selection system is a process encompassing various stages and requiring considerable time and resources. We focus on the design of the system as the most critical part of this process, and will not dwell upon its actual construction and implementation.

DESIGN METHODOLOGY

Descriptions of a methodology for the design of personnel selection systems have been given elsewhere (Roe, 1989, 1998). Here, we limit ourselves to a brief description of the design process and a discussion of design tools.

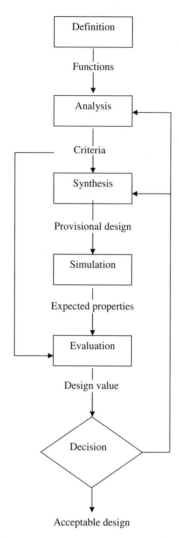

FIGURE 4.1   Basic design model (after Roozenburg & Eekels, 1991; Roe, 1998)

The design cycle

A useful notion originating from design methodology in the technical sciences (Eekels, 1983; Roozenburg & Eekels, 1991) is the "design cycle." The basic version of the design cycle model, depicted in Figure 4.1, comprises the following six steps.

1. *Definition.* The first step is defining the goals and functions of the selection system. Goals refer to the effects to be attained by using the system, while functions refer to the way in which these effects are brought about. Identifying goals and functions

requires a study of stakeholder views. A certain level of performance among selected candidates, a sufficient supply of candidates to fill vacancies, and a limited degree of attrition are examples of goals that stakeholders typically want to see fulfilled. Making valid predictions of performance and providing information that is useful for decisions about an individual's career are examples of functions.

2. *Analysis.* In the next step goals and functions are analyzed and spelled out in terms of requirements the system should meet and constraints it should observe. Requirements pertain to the system's functionality (what it is used for; e.g., predictive validity), constraints refer to limitations that should be taken into account (e.g., time or costs). Knowing requirements and constraints is important, as they guide the next step of the design process and provide criteria for later evaluation. Both notions will be clarified when we discuss the "Program of Requirements."

3. *Synthesis.* The third step represents the creative core of the design process. It consists of inductively generating possible solutions for the design problem as embodied in the requirement and constraints. Although the designer may be familiar with existing solutions and tools, there is usually a need to "invent" new solutions that optimally match the unique conditions of every case (applicant population, training and job content, organizational setting, etc.). The term "synthesis" is used to indicate that separate or known parts are combined to make a new whole. The result of this step is a provisional design of the selection system (or a part of it).

4. *Simulation.* The fourth step is of a deductive nature and consists of establishing the expected operational, predictive, and economic properties of the provisional design. Examples of such properties are duration, capacity, validity, levels of performance, decision errors, utility etc. Simulation can be done by means of reasoning, running experimental try-outs, performing validation studies, or using models.

5. *Evaluation.* After the expected properties of the selection system have been established they are evaluated, using the criteria in the "Program of Requirements." The result of this step is a judgment about the value of the proposed system for the stakeholders. This step should answer the question whether the system is or is not satisfactory.

6. *Decision making.* The final step is taking a decision about accepting the selection system for operational use or rejecting it. In case of rejection the process may continue with step 3, and make an effort to modify and improve the previous solution. When shortcomings in the "Program of Requirements" appear, one may return to step 2 and reformulate requirements and constraints first. The design cycle comes to an end when the proposed design has finally been accepted.

The model described here shows only the general logic of the design process. In practice, several parts of the system may be designed in parallel or sequentially, and the cycle may be run through several times. Also, the actual course of affairs may deviate in the sense that synthesis and simulation become closely intertwined or that other shortcuts are applied. The main advantage of the design cycle model is that it helps to understand that design has reductive and deductive moments and that a larger or smaller number of iterations are necessary to find an adequate solution. The model is also helpful in clarifying the importance of establishing design criteria beforehand and using them for evaluation afterwards.

TABLE 4.2   Design tools and inventories

	Design tools
Design process tools	Program of Requirements
Analytical tools	Selection flow analysis
	Job and task analysis
	Competence analysis
Synthetic tools	Prediction modeling tools
	Decision modeling tools (segmented and non-segmented)
	Compound prediction–decision models
Simulation tools	Flow models
	Selection effect models
	Validity simulation (incl. synthetic validation)
Prototyping tools	Visualization of tests
	Report formats

Design tools

Like in other areas in which design is used, such as architecture and product development, there are several tools that designers of personnel selection systems can rely on. In Table 4.2 we have listed a number of these tools. Here we will briefly clarify each of the table's entries. Some tools will be discussed in subsequent sections, when we address a number of specific issues related to analysis and synthesis. For information on predictors, criteria, and predictor–criterion relationships we refer to other chapters of this book.

1. Design process tools.   Apart from common project management tools, such as the project plan and the project structure, there is one tool that is particularly useful in structuring and controlling the design process, namely the "Program of Requirements" (or PoR). The PoR is basically a list of demands which the to-be-designed artifact – here the selection system – should meet. These demands derive from the goals and functions identified in a dialogue with stakeholders. It would be wrong to assume that the main goal for a selection system is to fill a limited number of positions with well-performing candidates and that the main function is making valid predictions, an assumption often made in the selection literature. Discussions with stakeholders may reveal many diverging goals and functions. For example, Wise (1994), in a chapter on military selection and classification, mentions: seat fill, training success, reduced attrition, job proficiency, job performance, qualified months of service, total career performance, performance utility, total MOS (military occupational specialty), unit performance/readiness, social benefit/problem avoidance, and accommodating recruit preferences (pp. 354–356). In design projects that we have conducted such aspects were normally part of the PoR. Some other aspects were: the fit of the system into employers' overall HRM policy, its integration with the training system, the avoidance of discrimination, the fair treatment of candidates, the handling of

TABLE 4.3   Example of items from a "Program of Requirements"

Requirements

R1. *Fulfillment of quota*

The selection system must yield a sufficient number of qualified candidates to fill the annual number of vacancies.

R5. *Success in training*

The system must maximize the success rate in initial training; the success rate should not be lower than 80%.

R12. *Multilingual examination*

The system must allow the examination of candidates in English as well as French.

Constraints

C2. *Treatment of candidates*

Candidates must be treated correctly and with due personal attention.

C7. *Operational reliability*

The system and its hardware must be minimally vulnerable to malfunction. It must be possible to restore the system within 24 hours in case of breakdown.

C13. *Cost-effectiveness*

The system must be cost-effective, taking account of direct costs, depreciation of equipment, overhead and personnel.

candidates' complaints, the supply of information to commissioners and candidates, legal aspects, flexibility of use, time demands, costs, etc. PoRs, as we have used them, typically contain several dozen items, classified into requirements and constraints, depending on whether they refer to goals and functions or to conditions to be taken into account. Each item is given a code and a label for easy identification and its content is described in a short statement. Some examples are given in Table 4.3.

It is helpful to assign weights to these items based on stakeholders' ratings. We have used the following three-point scale – "absolutely essential" (3), "desirable" (2) and "not really needed" (1) – and based weights on average ratings and degree of consensus. This helps to differentiate between more and less important aspects, and offers a possibility to identify and manage diversity of opinions among stakeholders.

PoRs sometimes contain a few items that are "specifications" rather than requirements or constraints. Specifications are in fact partial solutions to the design problem, as they designate particular properties the system must have. Examples of specifications are particular tests (e.g., NEO-PR), rating scales (e.g., C-scale), cutoff scores (e.g., 6 points), etc. The number of specifications in a PoR should be kept low, so as not to restrict the designer's degrees of freedom unnecessarily.

The PoR has a dual function. As is shown in Figure 4.1, it helps to give direction to the design process from the start onward (feedforward), and it serves to evaluate and modify results obtained during the design process (feedback).

2. Tools for analysis.   After the PoR has been set the designer will do some analyses in order to identify the desired properties of the selection system. Three types of analytical tools are useful at this stage: trajectory analysis, job and task analysis, and competence analysis. We use the term *trajectory analysis* to refer to the activity of identifying the positions candidates can occupy between the moment of application and some "final" point in their career, the transitions between these positions, the duration of these transitions, and the numbers involved. We recommend making a trajectory analysis for the current system of recruiting, selecting, training, allocating, and promoting personnel, as well as for the new system of which the selection system will be part. The analysis provides the designer with useful information regarding 1) quota and selection ratios and 2) the positions which are pivotal for the selection system. Many texts on personnel selection assume that there is only one pivotal position (or job) to be filled and that there is only one criterion or set of criteria to be predicted. Although this may sometimes be true, it is much more common that candidates are subsequently treated as entrants, trainees, occupants of position A (junior), job B (senior), and the like. An exemplary description of a trajectory is given below (see Figure 4.4). In such a case the selection system is not only expected to improve job performance but also to enhance successful transitions and reduce dropout.

Identifying positions is a crucial step that must precede job analysis and setting criteria. It is particularly important to identify diverging requirements and possible conflicts stemming from different positions. Quite often there is a discrepancy between the requirements for training and job success. For a student or trainee, characteristics such as verbal and numerical ability, achievement motivation, and submissiveness may be important, while for the fulfillment of the position entered after completing the training, communicative skills, technical competence, and independence are more important.

Methods for *job and task analysis* serve as tools for identifying training and job criteria to be predicted as well as candidate attributes that can play a role as predictors. *Competence analysis* can be seen as an extension to job and task analysis. It concentrates on candidate attributes that are to be considered when deciding on the composition of the selection battery. For methods for job and task analysis we refer to Fine and Cronshaw (1999), Landau and Rohmert (1989), as well as to Voskuijl (Chapter 2, this volume). Competence analysis, which we think is needed (Roe, 2002), is less extensively treated in the literature. We will give a brief coverage of this topic below.

3. Tools for synthesis.   A key issue in the design of a selection system is which predictors to use for predicting the appropriate criteria, and how to make decisions that produce the desired numbers of suitable candidates. The designer's task is to explore and compare alternative ways of composing selection batteries and establishing decision rules, taking account of the outcomes of analyses and available techniques.

Two types of tools are especially useful here. First, *prediction modeling tools* help to create "prediction models" (Roe, 1983) by means of which candidates' predictor scores can be transformed into estimates of future criterion scores. Some authors speak of performance modeling and performance models (Campbell, 1990, 1994; Greuter, 1988). Prediction modeling tools are in fact generic versions of prediction models in algebraic, graphic, or tabular (spreadsheet) form. As the prevailing format of the prediction model is algebraic, the main modeling tool is a multiple linear regression function (or density function). The actual prediction model is constructed by identifying the number of criteria and predictors, the type of measurement scale, compensatory or non-compensatory combination of predictors, the type of weights, etc. We refer to selection handbooks (e.g., Guion, 1998; Schmitt & Chan, 1998; Roe, 1983), which also provide examples of graphical tools, such as bivariate scatter plots, and tabular tools, such as expectancy charts.

Secondly, *decision modeling tools* help to create "decision models" that spell out how predicted values of criterion variables link to choice options. A good example is the generic multi-attribute-utility model, which can be turned into a model specifically geared to the selection problem at hand by specifying choice options, utility functions, etc. (Cabrera & Raju, 2001). In building explicit decision models the designer can also use tabulation tools to specify decisions for various (combinations of) predicted criterion scores or predictor scores. When it comes to determining cutoff scores, an important part of decision models, several methods can be used (see Roe, 1983).

Prediction and decision models can, but need not be, fully specified. Parts of the prediction process and/or parts of the decision making can be left to the judgment of people fulfilling the role of "selector." In other words, the selection system can be based on a combination of statistical and clinical selection methods. See, for example, the semi-clinical selection method by Roe (1998).

An important issue for designers is the *linkage between prediction model and decision models.* Older publications in selection have routinely opted for simple solutions based on the assumption that utility is a linear function of the predictor variable (Cronbach & Gleser, 1965). Thus, there are standard recipes for setting a cutoff score on a predictor composite or a cutoff profile when using multiple tests in parallel. With more complex selection systems comprising several sequential modules there are more options to consider, and the designer will need a *compound modeling tool* to build a combined prediction–decision model that produces valid predictions and adequately tailors the applicant stream simultaneously. We will give an example later in this chapter.

4. Simulation tools.   Every time the designer considers a particular set of predictors and a particular manner of predicting and decision making, he or she will have to establish the properties of the resulting selection system. We differentiate between three types of tools for simulating the systems' properties: flow models, selection effect models, and validity simulation models. *A flow model* is a spreadsheet tool that shows the effects of selection on the applicant stream. This is most useful when there are several stages of selection. Given an estimate of the number of candidates entering the system and selection ratio for each stage, the model shows the numbers of candidates surviving each stage. This information can subsequently be used for evaluating costs and capacity requirements. Of course, the tool can also serve to compare various selection scenarios involving different combinations of cutoffs, or variable numbers of applicants entering the system or withdrawing from the system voluntarily.

We use the term *selection effect model* to refer to a tabular or graphical tool for establishing the effect of selection on predictor and/or criterion variables. An example of a simple graphical format is given in Figure 4.2. Graphs like this have been used to illustrate the

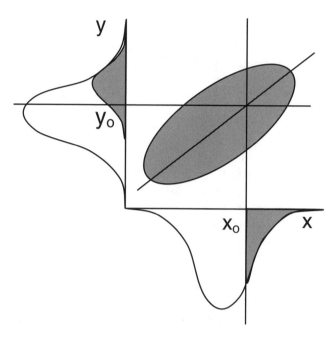

FIGURE 4.2   Example of simple selection effect model (graphical form)

phenomenon of "restriction of range" (Roe, 1983; Rydberg, 1962), but they are also helpful in visualizing the performance increments, that is, upward shifts in the (expected) criterion score distribution. Tabular effect models, also known as "expectancy tables," are more informative and make it easy to compare effects. Obviously, selection effect models rest on certain assumptions regarding the bivariate (or multivariate) distribution of predictor and criterion scores. Probably the best-known expectancy tables are those by Curtis and Alf (1969) and Taylor and Russell (1939), which show selection effects on the criterion variable for varying cutoffs/selection ratios and predictive validities.

All simulations involving expected levels of criterion scores require knowledge of predictive validity. Since empirical validation is only possible *after* completing the design and implementing a system, the designer will have to rely on estimates of predictive validity. Apart from simply assuming a certain level of validity for a particular composite or battery, he or she can derive estimates from published correlation data, for example by meta-analysis or validity generalization. However, the use of these methods is usually not sufficient since intercorrelations must also be known. Unless data on intercorrelations can be obtained from an applicant sample, one has to work on the basis of assumptions. Because of the assumptions involved we refer to methods producing validity estimates as "*validity simulation.*" They include multiple regression analysis based on hypothetical correlation matrices and synthetic validation.

It should be noted that methods for simulating validities and selection effects are not only useful for evaluating a particular variant of the selection system under consideration by the designer, but may also be used for a comparison of variants. As part of this, the designer may engage in sensitivity analysis to find out whether modifications of a design will make a difference in selection outcomes.

5. Prototyping tools. While much of the design is oriented to the conceptual framework and content of the selection system, the appearance and "feel" of the systems in the hands of candidates and users should be given due attention as well. Now that much of selection testing takes place by means of computers, it is feasible to use computer technology to develop an early prototype. Prototyping can help to visualize test formats, report formats, the administrator's console, etc., and in this way support the design of the system's interfaces.

COMPETENCE ANALYSIS

An important issue facing every designer of a selection system is how to make the inferential leap from job content to performance criteria and candidate attributes. The suggestion offered in selection textbooks (e.g., Guion, 1998) is to use a job analysis method that provides attribute ratings, to rely on sources that have made such ratings in the past (line O*Net), or to make direct ratings. None of these approaches is wholly satisfactory since they do not answer the question of which aspects of performance differentiate between successful and non-successful workers, and fail to give a clear rationale for the choice of candidate attributes. Although job analysis remains a necessary first step at the analytical stage of the design process, *competence analysis* may complement it and help to identify criteria and predictors. In this context competence is defined as "*an acquired ability to adequately perform a task, role or mission*" (Roe, 2002). The notion of competence is closely linked to the activities that individuals, groups, or larger entities in organizations are expected to undertake in order to fulfill the organizations' missions. Competences are formulated in the "technical" language of the organization (grinding, selling, leading, etc.), not in the vocabulary of the behavioral scientist (perceiving, interpreting, manipulating, etc.). They relate to the molar level of paid-for actions, not to psychological abstractions that cut through these actions. Competences are acquired in a process of learning-by-doing, either on the job or in a simulated environment, in interaction with the real work environment, including equipment, clients, colleagues, etc.

A distinctive feature of this learning process is its integrative character. That is, relevant knowledge, skills, and attitudes which were acquired earlier become integrated while building a behavior pattern optimally suited to perform the task at hand. For example, knowledge of medical terms, writing skills, and a prudent attitude become integral parts of a doctor's competence of writing prescriptions, along with other bits of knowledge, skill, and attitude. Our conception is markedly different from that Boyatzis (1982) or Spencer and Spencer (1993), who define competence as "an underlying characteristic of an individual that is causally related with criterion-referenced effective and/or superior performance in a job or situation" and thus use it as a container notion embracing all kinds of human attributes. We not only differentiate competence from knowledge, skills, and attitudes, but also from abilities, personality traits, and other characteristics (including values, interests, and biographical characteristics). With reference to theories from educational and

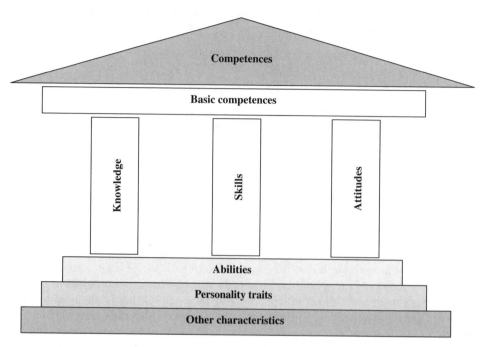

FIGURE 4.3   Model of competence architecture (Roe, 2002)

work psychology, we consider these latter characteristics, which are largely dispositions, as factors facilitating or constraining the learning processes by which knowledge, skills, and attitudes, as well as competences, are built (Roe, 2002). While acknowledging that dispositions influence everyday work performance directly, we assume that their influence is at least partly indirect, that is, through the attained mastery of competences (also knowledge, skills, and attitudes).

In this view competences are conceptually close to performance. They can be seen as immediate antecedents of performance that will express themselves in the way the person fulfills his or her duties, given a sufficient level of motivation and situational resources. Figure 4.3 illustrates our view on the architecture of competences, showing the seven types of concepts we have mentioned.[1]

Competence analysis based on this view follows a different route in the search for relevant attributes than traditional methods. It poses a series of questions, first about on-the-job learning experiences necessary for mastering critical duties (competences), next about knowledge, skills, and attitudes that are essential in this learning process, and finally about the abilities and personality dispositions that are likely to influence learning processes and/or to affect performance once the critical competences have been attained. The search for dispositional attributes thus focuses on aptitude–treatment interactions (Snow, 1989) in work-relevant learning, rather than on direct contributions to performance itself. The analysis gives a conceptual underpinning to the identification of KSAOs as recommended by other authors (e.g., Guion, 1998; Schmitt & Chan, 1998). In addition, it emphasizes the role that learned attributes – knowledge and skills, but also attitudes and (basic) competences – can play as predictors, as far as candidates have had relevant learning and work experiences.

Competence analysis may also be used to identify *criteria* for selection, since competences are useful proxies for performance. In the next section we will discuss the use of competences as criteria for selection. There we will focus on competences which have not yet been attained by all candidates but will have to be learned after selection and admission to on-the-job training.[2]

Of course, the logic of competence analysis as proposed here can only demonstrate its value when there is evidence on requisite knowledge, skills, and attitudes, and on aptitude–treatment interactions in work-related learning. To date this evidence is scarce and dispersed, and sometimes little else avails but reports from subject-matter experts involved in work-related education. But to the extent that such information is available, it can supplement or support inferences about candidate attributes derived by traditional methods.

ARCHITECTURAL DESIGN

The description of design in terms of job analysis, choosing tests, administering tests, conducting a validation study, etc., offers a fairly good description when creating simple selection systems. However, it does not do so when large numbers of applicants are involved and stakes in terms of scarce competence, attrition, turnover, malfunction, or safety are very high. In such situations, which exist in many large corporations, the government, the military, aviation, and other special sectors, the designer's task is much more complex. Here, an approach is needed that is both flexible and systematic, and that helps to establish an architecture that matches major requirements without going into detail. In this section we will list a number of steps that may help to arrive at a suitable architecture. Although these steps are described serially, it is important to stress their interdependence. The essence of architectural design is to consider the relationships between design options and to arrive at an optimal set of choices for the system as a whole. Steps 1 through 4 will address structural facets of the selection system (*how will the system be composed?*), whereas steps 5 through 7 deal with operational facets (*how will the system work?*). Step 8 addresses the integration of structural and operational facets in a global overall design (*what will the system look like?*). In our discussion we will refer to tools discussed above.

Step 1. Trajectories and positions

The first step is to decide whether selection will aim at one or more trajectories, and whether there are one or more pivotal positions to consider. A single position should not be taken as the default. First, for any significant position there is usually a preceding position that has to be successfully fulfilled (e.g., as trainee) and/or a subsequent position to which successful candidates are expected to move. Taking such positions into account as well may increase overall effectiveness. Second, it is worth while to see whether there is a secondary track that can absorb candidates who are not suitable to occupy a pivotal

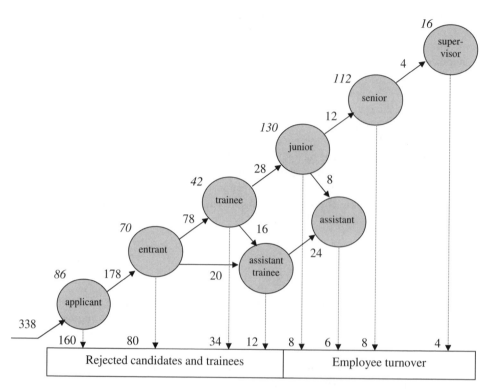

FIGURE 4.4   Positions and transitions in a trajectory. Numbers indicate average occupancy *(roman)* and transition *(italic)* within 6-month time interval (Example)

position in the primary trajectory but who are sufficiently qualified to fulfill other needs. This is especially useful for jobs that pose very high demands on candidates, such as fighter jet pilot or air traffic controller. The very low selection ratios at later selection stages imply high sunk costs spent on rejected but highly qualified candidates. Opening a second trajectory, containing related jobs, may therefore add considerably to the overall utility of selection within the HRM system as a whole. A scheme illustrating a career trajectory within a fictive company is given in Figure 4.4.

Step 2. Criteria

The second step is deciding on the number of criteria. Rather than making an a priori choice for single or multiple criteria we suggest looking at competences, and asking ourselves two questions. First, which competences are critical in the sense that insufficient mastery leads to unacceptable cost, damage, or risk? Second, which competences will be sufficiently mastered if no selection is applied? Obviously, competences that are not critical, and competences that are either present or can be learned by all candidates within a reasonable amount of time, should not be included in a selection system. The system should focus exclusively on critical competences that are unattainable without special precautions. The number of such competences should define the number of criteria for selection. Normally, there will be more than one criterion.[3]

Of course, the designer should at this stage keep an eye on the nature of the criteria, especially whether they are meant to be dynamic or not. Dynamic criteria gauge learning performance (acquisition of competence), static criteria performance at the end of learning (attained competence).[4] Other aspects of criteria and the means of measuring them can be addressed later in the design process.

Step 3. Predictors

In the third step the designer will look for potential predictors and decide on the types of predictors to be used, in terms of the underlying prediction principle (Wernimont & Campbell, 1968) and content. Relevant questions are: 1) Will the criteria require the use of sign instruments, sample instruments or both? 2) Which types of attributes are likely to contribute most to the prediction of the criteria? Competence analysis may help in answering these questions, giving suggestions about the contribution that abilities and personality traits (and other stable characteristics) can make, and about the degree to which success depends on acquiring competences on the job. The first points at sign prediction, the latter at sample prediction (cf., assessment exercises, job samples, or simulators). It is sufficient for the designer to know the types of predictive information the system will have to gather; a specification in terms of variables and instruments can follow at a later stage.

Step 4. Selection stages and batches

In the fourth step the designer will have to decide about segmenting the selection system in stages and batches. Stages refer to system parts that correspond to phases in the selection process, batches to groups of candidates being processed. As for *stages*, the most important questions to answer are: 1) Can all information on candidates be gathered "at once," for example within the time-span of one or two days? 2) Will it be cost-effective to examine all candidates with the total system, or will substantive savings be obtained by reducing the number of candidates flowing through parts of the system? Regardless of the precise content the selection procedure may get later on, it is important to think about the system's scope and to determine whether it is practically and economically feasible to conduct a full examination of all candidates. If the answer is yes, a relatively simple architecture with a single test battery may suffice. But if the answer is no, the designer will have to look into options for segmenting the system, that is, splitting it up into modules, and designing the corresponding parts of the overall prediction and decision model.

With regard to *batches* the following questions are relevant: 3) Will all candidates be available within one period of time, for example a month of the year? 4) Can the examination of candidates take place in one location (testing site, Internet)? Although the focus of these questions seems purely on logistics, they imply design choices that can have marked effects on the system's effectiveness. For instance, if the number of candidates is large and all of them apply within a short time period (e.g., the end of a school year), the designer might opt for a system that quickly reduces numbers to manageable size. A steady flow of candidates during the year, on the other hand, enables one to process them with a uniform procedure. The first may reduce effectiveness by high numbers of false negatives, the second may raise costs by not optimally using system resources (e.g., personnel, test equipment). In the second case it might be preferable to accumulate candidates and examine them in larger batches.

Step 5. Compensation

Apart from the structural features of the selection system, the designer should also look at operational aspects. The fifth step, then, is taking a decision about how to deal with compensation. Compensation can be looked at from two angles: prediction and decision making. In the context of prediction compensation is customary. Thus, a compensatory prediction model is adopted in which the same (predicted) criterion performance can result from different combinations of predictor scores. However, in exceptional cases, the designer can also opt for conjunctive or disjunctive prediction models in which the (predicted) level of the criterion is determined by the lowest or highest predictor score (see Guion, 1998, p. 53). As a rule, decisions follow predictions; thus, in the first case decisions are based on a single cutoff score for the weighted predictor sum, in the second case on multiple cutoffs.

Compensation in the case of multiple criteria is another issue. Here, the focus is typically on decisions, not on prediction (as the very use of multiple criteria points at the absence of a single overarching criterion). Often, compensation in decisions is not considered appropriate and separate cutoffs are preferred. For example, air traffic controllers are not supposed to perform with greater efficiency at the expense of lower safety. They must satisfy separate standards for these criteria.

Although practitioners are sometimes skeptical about compensation and favor multiple cutoffs, designers should be prudent and avoid using multiple cutoffs without justification. The reason is that multiple cutoffs can easily lead to high numbers of false negatives, that is, candidates who are unduly rejected, and thereby to a waste of human resources.

Step 6. Weights

The sixth step involves choosing the parameters for prediction. Although designers may sometimes opt for non-linear prediction models (e.g., Roe, 1983), a system with a linear prediction model will do well in most cases.[5] Regarding the parameters, two questions are to be answered: 1) Are there reasons to prefer unequal weighting over equal weighting? 2) If so, are empirical weights to be preferred over rational weights? Given the properties of the linear model and the statistical limitations of small and medium-sized samples, equal weights may be considered as the default. For a practical reason, namely the comparability of scores from different instruments, this rule is applied to standardized rather than raw scores. Designers do well to opt for unequal weights when validities of predictors are likely to show substantial differences (e.g., .10 or more). A rule of thumb is that weights that are roughly proportional to the expected validity give good results. Weights may, however, be rounded off to integers without much loss of overall predictive validity (Wherry, 1975). These wisdoms run counter to the recommendation in much of the older literature that weights be determined empirically by means of multiple regression analysis. Since there are usually no empirical data at the design stage – apart from estimated or simulated validities – the designer has little choice but to begin with rational (i.e., self-set) weights, and can decide to introduce empirical weights at a later stage after the appropriate empirical information has been collected. This is normally after the selection system has been put to use.

Step 7. Cutoffs

The seventh step is about decision parameters, that is, cutoffs. Here the question for the designer is whether the selection should be based on absolute (fixed) cutoff scores, relative (variable) cutoff scores, or semi-absolute cutoff scores, which can be seen as a compromise between the two. Absolute cutoffs give stable results and are seemingly "fair" to candidates, but the number of selected candidates may be too high or too low. In the absence of criterion evidence they may be set too high or too low. Relative cutoffs (based on selection ratios) give the right numbers of selected candidates, but may also be set too high or too low. When applied to separate batches, relative cutoffs may vary and be seen as unfair by candidates. In such cases one can "freeze" cutoffs as established in one batch and apply them to other batches. These semi-absolute cutoffs resemble the method of "predicted yield" (Guion, 1998). From a practical perspective the best approach is to set relative cutoffs for a limited period of time, and to replace them by semi-absolute or absolute cutoffs when possible.

Step 8. Integration

The preceding steps guide the designer through a number of interdependent choices and provide some support in taking decisions on structural and operational features of the selection system. The list does not spell out all issues to be considered. For instance, the predictors to be included, the precise structure of the prediction and the decision model, etc., are still to be decided upon. Yet, the designer will be able to develop an overall view of the system and make a composite description that integrates all aspects mentioned. Thus a design document can be made that describes positions, criteria, predictors, stages, as well as choices regarding quota, selection ratios, cutoffs, etc. The format for the description can be textual but also abstract or symbolic. For instance, components can be referred to as criteria A, B, C, . . . ; stages I, II, III . . . ; predictors 1, 2, 3, . . . , etc., without further specification. The document may also contain tables or flow charts that highlight particular parts of the design. A document outlining the system's architecture should stimulate critical discussions in the design team and promote sound decision making, before engaging in further design.

EXEMPLARY DESIGN ISSUES

In this section we discuss three issues which illustrate the kind of problems designers may encounter when designing a selection system in practice. They relate to sequential selection, batch-wise selection, and compensation. We will draw attention to some non-trivial implications that certain design options may have and the reasoning the designer may apply in searching a solution.

Sequential selection

Many advanced selection systems comprise a series of modules that offer successive hurdles to the candidates. After each module a number of candidates are rejected while the remaining candidates move on to the next module. Thus the group of candidates gradually shrinks until the final hurdle has been taken. Modules can be composed of different types of tests, an assessment center, a job simulation, but also a training course. For instance, the selection of future military pilots includes several tests modules, a set of assessment exercises, flying a basic simulator (grading), and even flying a real airplane. All these modules precede entry into the ground school, which is the first phase of a training trajectory leading to a pilot career.

Segmenting a selection process like this has a number of implications which the designer should consider carefully. A first issue is the nature of the prediction model. Will the test module have to predict success in the basic simulator and success in the first real flight? Figure 4.5 illustrates some options in *choosing a prediction model* for sequential selection. Theoretically there are several ways to build a prediction model. On the one hand (panel a), one can use predictive information from module I to predict performance in module II, and use performance in module II to predict performance in module III, etc. On the other hand (panel b), one can use information from every module to build a growing composite that predicts the performance in the pivotal position entered after passing the last module. Combinations of these two principles are also conceivable.

It is important to note that the second model is potentially more effective than the first because every new step brings a further increase in predictive validity. Predictive validity of the first model will be equal to the predictive validity of its last module. Although some-

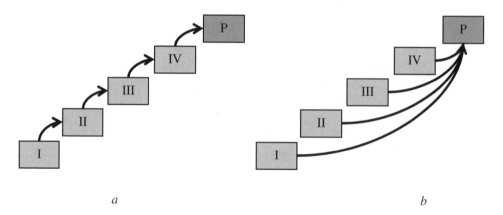

a   b

FIGURE 4.5   Alternative prediction models for sequential selection (*a* = criterion is next module performance, *b* = criterion is performance in pivotal position)

times favored by practitioners who expect colleagues earlier in the chain to "stop sending us the wrong people," this model leads to a waste of predictive power that limits overall selection effectiveness.

A second issue in sequential selection relates to *cutoff scores*. Practitioners often expect best results from high cutoffs, both in terms of the performance of those ultimately selected and lower capacity demands and costs in subsequent modules. When these expectations are not met the usual response is to raise cutoffs and to select more strictly. Theoretically this way of thinking is flawed, since it ignores the fact that later selection steps can only operate on candidates who have passed earlier steps, and that errors made in earlier steps – especially false negatives – cannot be corrected for. In fact there is a "selection paradox" in the sense that lower initial cutoffs give more room for selecting candidates with high criterion scores than higher initial cutoffs. This paradox manifests itself in two ways: 1) The criterion scores of the strictly selected candidates become even lower, and 2) the number of acceptable candidates declines. The latter can pose a pernicious problem for organizations that go to great lengths to recruit and select highly qualified personnel and continue to suffer from scarcity. When responding by raising selection standards further, especially in early stages, the result will be opposite to what they aim for and scarcity will only increase.

What can designers do about this problem? First, they can look into the sequence of predictive modules and try to optimize it. Second, they can devise a series of cutoffs tailored to the expected increase in predictive validity. Cutoffs for early modules will be low to moderate; only cutoffs for later modules will be high.

The third issue concerns the *sequence* of modules. Although this may not be perceived as important by practitioners, designers do well to take a close look at it, since it may have a great impact on the system's effectiveness. Several aspects have to be considered simultaneously. First, the flow of candidates through the modules, which can be modeled by multiplying the selection ratios. At each stage, the cumulative selection ratio is the product of the selection ratios of the preceding stages. The second aspect is the cost associated with administering each module. Fixed and variable costs should be included in a cost accounting calculation, on the basis of the expected flow of candidates as shown by a flow model. Cheap modules should be put at the beginning, when the number of candidates is still large, and expensive modules at the end. The third aspect is the logistic one. Modules with a large capacity (e.g., Internet testing) that can be operated at any moment in time will precede modules that assume group-wise testing. Modules requiring administration in small groups or individually will usually be put at the very end. The fourth aspect is predictive validity. Other things being equal, one would place modules with high validity early in the system. But given the payoff relationships between these four aspects, designers will have to play around with various options and look for an acceptable solution. There are some other aspects, such as the intrusion of privacy (see Roe, 1989), which should also be considered.

Batch-wise selection

Selection usually occurs in batches. That is, applicants for a given type of job present themselves at moments spaced in time, rather than at once. Therefore, the selection process has

TABLE 4.4   Simulated selection effects for batch-wise selection. Means and standard deviations for selected applicants on predictor (X) and criterion (Y) variables for different numbers of batches and two levels of validity; selection ratio = .50 (after Roe, 1983; p. 474)

Selection method				$r_{xy} = .30$		$r_{xy} = .60$	
		M_x	sd_x	M_y	sd_y	M_y	sd_y
Fixed cutoff population		.7978	.6029	.2400	.9427	.4787	.8780
Relative cutoffs	# of Batches						
1000/2000	1	.7899	.5846	.2483	.9484	.5017	.8698
5/10	200	.7309	.6573	.2284	.9465	.4746	.8555
4/8	250	.7162	.6758	.2197	.9594	.4508	.8704
3/6	333	.6948	.6940	.2239	.9674	.4320	.8591
2/4	500	.6601	.7305	.2061	.9755	.4236	.8836
1/2	1000	.5636	.8046	.2038	.9663	.3595	.8815

to be repeated, each time producing a number of selected candidates. Although batch-wise segmentation of selection is hard to avoid, because it reflects the inherent dynamics of the labor market, it represents an issue that designers should consider. The reason is that there are different ways to organize batches which affect the systems effectiveness differently.

The potential impact of batch-wise selection can be illustrated by considering a situation in which selection is based on a relative cutoff, that is, the best $p\%$ of the candidates is selected. How does this compare to a situation where all candidates applied at once and the same proportion of candidates would be selected? A simulation study by Roe (see Roe, 1983) provides the answer to this question. In this study random scores based on a bivariate normal distribution were generated. Selection was based on the total sample of 2,000 candidates and on sub-samples varying in size from 2 to 10.

Table 4.4 shows the results of the selection in terms of the means and standard deviations of the selected candidates for both X (predictor) and Y (criterion). As the results for Y depend on the validity a comparison is made between $r = .30$ and $r = .60$. The table shows that selecting from batches is less effective than selecting at once. If all selected candidates are taken together their mean score on the criterion is lower while the standard deviation is higher. For the predictor the effect is more dramatic, of course. The size of the batch also matters. In this study the focus was on very small batches, but larger batches generally give better results than smaller batches.

Designers can exercise some control over batch sizes. This requires an analysis of vacancies and the yield of recruitment over time, the costs and logistic aspects of testing candidates in smaller and larger batches, and the selection effects of smaller and larger batches. One way to increase the batch size is by accumulating candidates, that is, to ask them to stay available until a certain moment in time at which the pool will be large enough for efficient examination. Alternatively, one may conduct examinations immediately but keep the scores in reserve until a sufficient number of candidates have been processed to make a solid decision.

It might seem that relative cutoffs make batch-wise selection cumbersome. This is only partially true. Of course, selection effects would be stable if fixed cutoffs were used. But fixed cutoffs combined with smaller batch sizes may lead to situations in which no suitable candidates are selected while vacancies have still to be filled. This issue has been discussed earlier, but it appears more difficult to resolve in the case of batch-wise selection.

Compensation

Many people involved in the practice of selection appear to favor the use of multiple cutoffs. Thus, candidates for pilot training may first be selected on the basis of test scores, next on the basis of assessment center scores, then on the basis of simulator scores, and so on, without considering the relationships between the scores from the successive stages, and without applying compensatory rules. Whether it is useful to compensate for scores from earlier selection stages depends on the underlying prediction model. When the prediction model is of the type depicted in Figure 4.5a, that is, when every module is used to predict performance at the next stage, compensation is obviously not needed and separate successive cutoffs can be applied. However, when modules are incorporated in a single cumulative prediction model of the type shown in Figure 4.5b, compensation is preferable. We have already noted that the second model is preferable to the first since it can achieve higher predictive validity. When it comes to decision making, we can add that it is also preferable because it leads to fewer false negatives.

But how does compensation work with the second kind of prediction model? Let us take the example of three modules each producing a composite score X_i, thus: X_I, X_{II} and X_{III}. At stage I one would use the prediction model $Y' = W_{0I} + W_I.X_I$ and set a cutoff score for selecting the $q\%$ best candidates. At stage II one would use the prediction model $Y' = W_{0II} + W_I.X_I + W_{II}.X_{II}$ and set a cutoff score in a similar way. At stage III the prediction model would expand into $Y' = W_{0III} + W_I.X_I + W_{II}.X_{II} + W_{III}.X_{III}$, and a cutoff would have to be set. And so on.

This approach to compensation implies that a weak score in X_I can always be compensated, provided that the scores X_{II} and X_{III} are high enough. Such "full" compensation may not always be desirable, though. Candidates with too low scores on the tests may not be qualified enough ever to be considered successful in subsequent stages. Therefore, designers may want to set a minimum score for each module's composite, acting as a threshold. Such a (semi-)absolute cutoff can be used in conjunction with the compensatory cutoffs just discussed. This combined approach to sequential selection can be quite effective in maximizing the contributions of each module, while reducing false negatives. We give an example in Table 4.5. Here selection is based on relative cutoffs or selection ratios. In each step one first selects the $p_i\%$ candidates with the highest scores on the score for the specific module, and next the $q_i\%$ candidates with the highest scores on the accumulated composite. For example, in the third phase one will select 75% on the basis of X_{III} and 80% on the basis of $Y' = W_{0III} + W_I.X_I + W_{II}.X_{II} + W_{III}.X_{III}$. The total selection ratio of the third phase is .75 × .80 = .60. The last three columns of the table illustrate

TABLE 4.5   Example of dual cutoff scores in sequential selection, using selection ratio p for each module and selection ratio q for the composite derived from the accumulating prediction model. Selection flow in terms of cumulative selection ratio and numbers of in-flowing and out-flowing candidates at each phase

Phase	Module score	Prediction model	p	q	$p \times q$	Cumulative selection ratio	# of Candidates in	# of Candidates out
I	X_I	$W_I.X_I$	.90	–	–	.900	1,000	900
II	X_{II}	$W_I.X_I + W_{II}.X_{II}$	.85	.8	.68	.612	900	612
III	X_{III}	$W_I.X_I + W_{II}.X_{II} + W_{III}.X_{III}$	.75	.8	.60	.367	612	367
IV	X_{IV}	$W_I.X_I + W_{II}.X_{II} + W_{III}.X_{III} + W_{IV}.X_{IV}$	.70	.6	.42	.154	367	154
V	X_V	$W_I.X_I + W_{II}.X_{II} + W_{III}.X_{III} + W_{IV}.X_{IV} + W_V.X_V$	.60	.7	.42	.065	154	65
VI	X_{VI}	$W_I.X_I + W_{II}.X_{II} + W_{III}.X_{III} + W_{IV}.X_{IV} + W_V.X_V + W_{VI}.X_{VI}$	.50	.5	.25	.016	65	16

the drastic selective effect of sequential selection, even when seemingly mild cutoffs are used.

CONCLUSION

It is almost universally agreed that positions in organizations should be offered to people on the basis of demonstrated competence or expected performance. The larger the responsibilities vested in positions and the greater the risks of damage to people and their possessions, the more it is demanded that candidates are carefully selected. The message of this chapter is that effective selection requires serious preparation. Decades of research and development have resulted in a large body of knowledge and tools that can be applied for selecting personnel. But all this is little more than a stock of ingredients from which a proper choice has to be made and a system has to be created that can adequately separate candidates into those who will and will not perform well. The focus of this chapter has been on the process by which effective selection systems can be built. We have discussed the context of selection and the role of stakeholders, the nature and process of design, some design tools, and some typical design issues. Although this is very limited and does not give the reader a comprehensive picture of the development of selection systems, we hope that we have pointed out a way forward in an area that is sparsely covered in the selection literature.

In our view, the time and resources spent on design can be seen as an investment in effective selection. This is especially true when design is understood as anticipating the future in an open-minded and experimental way. We cannot put enough emphasis on the necessity of a thorough analysis to clarify the aim and context of selection. Such analysis, based on a dialogue with stakeholders, is a step toward a good result. But exploring options, subjecting them to desk-based simulations and making comparisons, is another essential part of the design process. This activity certainly involves the use of tools and data from the literature, but it also calls for inventiveness in finding solutions that uniquely match the technical requirements and practical conditions that the system has to meet.

What will normally not be included in the design process, or only at a very late stage, is a validation study. Here, our description of the design process deviates from what is commonly recommended in the selection literature. Although we assign great importance to a well-conducted validation study as a means to verify the predictive value of a selection system, we think that effective selection systems can be designed without doing a validation study and that the conditions under which systems have to be designed normally do not allow for a preceding validation study. In our view there is sufficient research evidence and a good-enough set of design tools to postpone validation research until after the implementation of the system. We dare to make a comparison with building a bridge or aircraft. Like these artifacts, selection systems can be built on the basis of existing knowledge and simulations during the development process. We would like to add that more effort should be spent on developing test-benches, in the sense of both statistical models and simulation tools, which would facilitate the designers' work and enhance the quality of its outcomes.

NOTES

1. In Roe (2002) we also distinguish basic (or partial) competences which are of a lower degree of complexity. Basic competences can be seen as building blocks for several higher-order competences.
2. The notion of competence sheds another light on so-called "dynamic criteria" (Steele Johnson, Osburn, & Pieper, 2000). Since it takes some time to fully master competences, the repeated measurement of competences (i.e., at the start, during, and at the end of on-the-job learning) will reveal candidates' differential progress. The competence framework can help to understand diverging requirements posed by different positions in a career trajectory, especially those between the position of student or trainee and those of employee. At an initial stage the emphasis is on acquiring knowledge and skills, and a greater role will be played by dispositions required for scholastic learning and fulfillment of the student role. At a later stage differences in knowledge and skills turn into predictors, along with dispositions needed for learning at the workplace and fulfilling the specific work role.
3. For practical reasons the designer may want to limit the number of criteria to four or five. A larger number of criteria will add disproportionately to the complexity of the system and reduce its overall transparency and effectiveness.
4. The notion of "dynamic criteria" as used here designates criterion constructs that relate to a desired change of performance over time, especially learning. It should be distinguished from changes in predictor–criterion relationships over time, which have also been referred to as "dynamic criteria" (Steele Johnson et al., 2000).
5. For some personality variables the scale may be transformed in such a way that the resulting score can be used as a linear predictor. For instance, when both high and low extroversion is undesirable a new variable may be created by taking the deviation from the scale midpoint.

References

Boyatzis, R. E. (1982). *The competent manager. A model for effective performance.* New York: John Wiley.

Cabrera, E. F., & Raju, N. S. (2001). Utility analysis: Current trends and future directions. *International Journal of Selection and Assessment, 9,* 92–102.

Campbell, J. P. (1990). Modeling the performance-prediction problem in industrial and organizational psychology. In M. D. Dunnette & L. M. Hough (Eds.), *Handbook of industrial & organizational psychology* (Vol. 1, pp. 687–732). Palo Alto, CA: Consulting Psychologists Press.

Campbell, J. P. (1994). Alternative models of job performance and their implications for selection and classification. In M. G. Rumsey, C. B. Walker, & J. H. Harris (Eds.), *Personnel selection and classification* (pp. 33–51). Hillsdale, NJ: Lawrence Erlbaum.

Clegg, S. (1975). *Power, rule, and domination: A critical and empirical understanding of power in sociological theory and organizational life.* London: Routledge & Paul.

Cronbach, L. J., & Gleser, G. C. (1965). *Psychological tests and personnel decisions* (2nd ed.). Urbana, IL: University of Illinois Press.

Curtis, E. W., & Alf, E. F. (1969). Validity, predictive efficiency, and practical significance of selection tests. *Journal of Applied Psychology, 53,* 327–337.

Eekels, J. (1983). *Design processes seen as decision chains: Their intuitive and discursive aspects.* Paper presented at the International Conference on Engineering Design, Copenhagen.

Fine, S. A., & Cronshaw, S. F. (1999). *Functional job analysis: A foundation for human resources management.* Mahwah, NJ: Erlbaum.

Greuter, M. A. M. (1988). *Personeelsselektie in perspektief* [Personnel selection in perspective]. Haarlem, The Netherlands: Thesis.

Guion, R. M. (1998). *Assessment, measurement, and prediction for personnel decisions.* Mahwah, NJ: Lawrence Erlbaum.

Landau, K., & Rohmert, W. (Eds.). (1989). *Recent developments in job analysis.* Philadelphia, PA: Taylor & Francis.

McCourt, W. (1999). Paradigms and their development: The psychometric paradigm of personnel selection as a case study of paradigm diversity and consensus. *Organization Studies, 20,* 1011–1033.

Mintzberg, H. (1983). *Power in and around organizations.* Englewood Cliffs, NJ: Prentice Hall.

Roe, R. A. (1983). *Grondslagen der personeelsselectie* [Foundations of personnel selection]. Assen, The Netherlands: Van Gorcum.

Roe, R. A. (1989). Designing selection procedures. In P. Herriot (Ed.), *Assessment and selection in organizations* (pp. 127–142). Chichester, UK: John Wiley & Sons.

Roe, R. A. (1998). Personnel selection: Principles, models and techniques. In P. J. D. Drenth, H. Thierry, & C. J. De Wolff (Eds.), *Handbook of work and organizational psychology* (Vol. 3, pp. 5–32). Hove, UK: Psychology Press.

Roe, R. A. (2002). Competenties – Een sleutel tot integratie in theorie en praktijk van de A&O-psychologie [Competencies – A key to the integration of theory and practice in Work and Organizational psychology]. *Gedrag & Organisatie, 15,* 203–224.

Roozenburg, N. F. M., & Eekels, J. (1991). *Produktontwerpen: Structuur en methode* [Product design: Structure and method]. Utrecht, The Netherlands: Lemma.

Rydberg, S. (1962). Methods of correcting correlations for indirect restriction of range with non-interval data. *Psychometrika, 27,* 49–58.

Schmitt, N., & Chan, D. (1998). *Personnel selection: A theoretical approach.* Thousand Oaks, CA: Sage.

Smith, M., & Robertson, I. T. (Eds.). (1989). *Advances in selection and assessment.* Chichester, UK: John Wiley & Sons.

Snow, R. E. (1989). Aptitude–treatment interaction as a framework for research on individual differences in learning. In R. J. Sternberg (Ed.), *Learning and individual differences: Advances in theory and research* (pp. 13–59). A series of books in psychology. New York: W. H. Freeman & Co.

Spencer, L. M., & Spencer, S. M. (1993). *Competence at work: Models for superior performance.* New York: Wiley.

Steele Johnson, D., Osburn, H. G., & Pieper, K. F. (2000). A review and extension of current models of dynamic criteria. *International Journal of Selection and Assessment, 8,* 110–136.

Taylor, H. C., & Russell, J. T. (1939). The relationship of validity coefficients to the practical effectiveness of tests in selection. Discussion and tables. *Journal of Applied Psychology, 23,* 565–578.

Thorndike, R. L. (1949). *Personnel selection.* New York: Wiley.

Wernimont, P. F., & Campbell, J. P. (1968). Signs, samples and criteria. *Journal of Applied Psychology, 52,* 372–376.

Wherry, R. J. (1975). Underprediction from overfitting: 45 years of shrinkage. *Personnel Psychology, 28,* 1–18.

Wise, L. L. (1994). Goals of the selection and classification decision. In M. G. Rumsey, C. B. Walker, & J. H. Harris (Eds.), *Personnel selection and classification* (pp. 351–361). Hillsdale, NJ: Lawrence Erlbaum.

5

Is the Obvious Obvious? Considerations About Ethical Issues in Personnel Selection

Olga F. Voskuijl, Arne Evers, and Sacha Geerlings

In most American textbooks on personnel selection or in a broader context on human resource management, ethical and legal issues are comprehensively covered (e.g., Cascio, 1998; Guion, 1998). Ethical issues are often related to legal standards, especially to privacy Acts and equal employment opportunity Acts; for example, in the USA, Title VII of the Civil Rights Act of 1964, which specifies several unlawful employment practices, and in the UK, the Sex Discrimination Act 1975 and the Race Relations Act 1976. Violation of the laws in the USA may have great financial consequences for the organizations and individuals involved. Although many European countries and the European Community have comparable laws or regulations (e.g., The Equal Treatment Directive 1976), the accompanying sanctions are less of a deterrent and suing practices are less common and less effective. This may explain the difference between the USA and Europe in the focus on legal and ethical matters in textbooks.

Ethical guidelines as well as legal directives cover what is considered right or wrong behavior in specific situations. Both are based on value systems of respectively a more or less loose group (like a professional association or a group of people with the same ideology) or a nation. The purpose of both laws and ethical codes is to direct behavior and to control for misbehavior. The differences between both "systems" seem a matter of degree. First, laws have more force and the consequences may be more extreme, while ethical codes may have more the character of advisory guidelines. Second, the scope of ethical guidelines seems smaller in terms of the number of people to whom it applies. What is considered as ethical behavior is in the eye of the beholder, depending on characteristics such as group membership, the social norms of the group, and shared interests. The likelihood of the occurrence of unethical behavior depends, for instance, on the opinion of other group members (e.g., severe disapproval of the other group members) and the consequences of unethical behavior (hurting an applicant or losing the organization that pays for the assessment of the applicant). On the other hand, the domain of ethics is much broader. Unlawful behavior is almost always unethical, but unethical behavior is often not against the law. Examples of unlawful and unethical behavior are the violation of the copyright of tests and direct discrimination. However, the boundaries between unethical and ethical behaviors are vague, as can be illustrated by the case of direct discrimination.

Although this seems a clear-cut example of unethical behavior, direct discrimination in personnel selection might be justified from an economic point of view (the hypothesis of rational discrimination, Riach & Rich, 2002). According to this point of view, direct discrimination could be classified as a (rare) example of unlawful but ethical behavior. In the context of selection more examples can be found of behavior or procedures which are lawful but which are perceived as unethical: Positive discrimination to attract members of minority groups is often perceived as unethical by members of majority groups, while members of minority groups as well as organizations striving for diversity may perceive it as fair. Another example is the use of unstructured interviews, whose predictive validity is known to be generally low; this is perfectly legal, but from a best practice point of view, selection psychologists should strive to maximize the validity of selection procedures, and thus abandon unstructured interviews. Because principles of morale and values are not fixed and because they often are conflicting and complex, associations of professional psychologists found it wise and necessary to develop sets of guidelines in order to protect clients and to support and guide psychologists. Ethical standards often seem obvious and luckily they often are, but it seems that in numerous situations there exist different opinions about the degree to which behaviors are ethical.

This chapter focuses on ethical standards in general and on specific ethical dilemmas of psychologists in the area of personnel selection. As our focus is psychological, legal issues are outside the scope of this chapter. Reese and Fremouw (1984) distinguish two forms of ethics: "normal" (descriptive) and "normative" (prescriptive). They state that the ethical standards for psychologists are a set of normative rules. These rules describe what psychologists should (not) do. Normal ethics of psychologists refer to what they in fact do, that is, to observable behavior. We give an overview of (the development of) normative ethics in Europe and the USA. In addition, we present the results of an e-mail survey of members of the European Federation of Psychologists' Association (EFPA) to identify the differences and similarities between ethical guidelines of the affiliate members. Specific dilemmas in the psychology of personnel selection and the "normal" ethics in professional practice are presented, based on a survey of a sample of Dutch psychologists involved with the selection of applicants. In this survey the respondents were asked to indicate the degree to which described behaviors in critical incidents were considered acceptable.

ETHICAL GUIDELINES FOR PSYCHOLOGISTS

Besides the term "ethical guidelines," several other terms are used to cover rules or recommendations concerning ethical professional behavior, such as "ethical standards," "ethical codes," or "codes of professional conduct." The terms may differ somewhat in the degree to which the contents are mandatory. Codes of conduct are more obligatory and guidelines are more exhortatory and refer more to the proper thing to do (Lindsay & Colley, 1995). However, we will treat them here as interchangeable. Ethical guidelines for psychologists are in general developed by an association of psychologists and the members of the association are expected to act according to those guidelines.

These guidelines serve several purposes, for example: "to set standards of behavior for psychologists with respect to clients, colleagues, and the public in general" (Francis,

1999, p. 7), or more specifically, as Lindsay (1996, p. 80) puts it: "1) Regulation of inappropriate behavior and 2) Promotion of optimal behavior." The second purpose means seeking the optimal, not that which is just acceptable (called "best practice"). One could argue that what is appropriate is self-evident to professionals but even when it is, there appears to be a difference between normative (what is appropriate) and normal (what is done) behavior, as the examples presented below will show.

Ethical standards are not always seen as beneficial for all psychologists. Golann noticed in 1969 that there might exist a gap between the requirements of practitioners and the earliest American Ethical Standards for Psychologists (APA, 1953). Clinical psychologists, in particular, felt that the standards interfered with their professional activities. In 1985 Schuler put forward some possible negative consequences of the existence of a professional ethical code: a) to bind professional psychologists and to restrain developments in research and practice, b) to feed public suspicion against psychology and psychologists, and c) to offer criteria for complaints by clients against psychologists. A more recent example, in the area of work and organizational psychology, shows that psychologists might feel that they harm their own business by acting according to the guidelines: Over a period of several months in 1997/1998 four members of the Dutch Association of Psychologists (NIP, Nederlands Instituut van Psychologen) resigned their membership because they thought that they could not compete with non-members who were not tied to ethical guidelines. This illustrates the limited scope of ethical guidelines in some countries (such as the Netherlands, Belgium, Denmark, and Slovenia), where the membership of the professional association is not obligatory. On the other hand, the examples illustrate that the benefits for psychologists are often underestimated by practitioners, benefits such as clarity about how to behave in complex situations, applying the code as a quality mark, and as a protection against misbehaving colleagues. Or, as Schuler (1985) suggests, to socialize students and young members, to clarify the relationships between the parties concerned to these parties and to other professions and institutions.

Apart from protection of clients, the first ethical guidelines in the Netherlands were developed in 1952 to protect psychologists from each other (Veldkamp & Van Drunen, 1988). It was not uncommon in those days for psychologists to "steal" each others' clients, students, and tests; competition between practitioners and academics was not always "fair and clean." Therefore one of the clauses in these early guidelines stated that blackening the good name of a colleague was not allowed. Fortunately, relations between professionals nowadays are more civilized and, in general, at least neutral.

The American Psychological Association developed the first ethical guidelines (APA, 1953), nowadays referred to as the Ethical Principles of Psychologists and Code of Conduct (APA, 2002). These guidelines were based on critical incidents generated by APA members, which resulted in six main principles (Competence, Integrity, Professional & scientific responsibility, Respect for people's rights and dignity, Concern for others' welfare, and Social responsibility) and eight standards, divided into 89 sub-standards.[1] The general principles are "aspirational goals to guide psychologists towards the highest ideals of psychology" (APA, 2002, p. 3). The standards are enforceable rules for conduct as psychologists and they apply to specific areas of psychology, such as Therapy and Forensic activities, and cover a variety of topics, such as Privacy and confidentiality, Human relations, and Assessment. Although the principles are not defined as enforceable rules, they should be considered by psychologists "in arriving at an ethical course of action" (p. 3).

The first overview of common domains in ethical codes in Europe is from Schuler (1985). He distinguished five categories to describe the similarities and differences between the (in those days) eleven European codes and the standards of the American Psychological Association: Basic values, Responsibility, Competence, Honesty, and Confidentiality. He emphasized that these categories should be considered as preliminary because in the majority of the countries the codes were under revision. In a more recent survey Lindsay (1992) found a high level of similarity of content across the codes of the European psychological associations and the APA, although they varied in specificity, length, and coverage of specific topics. Leach and Harbin (1997) compared 19 codes representing 24 countries to APA guidelines. Their survey covered countries worldwide. They calculated the percentage of US principles and standards covered in the ethical codes of the other countries. The APA principles were fully covered in four countries (Australia, Canada, Israel, and South Africa). The mean coverage of the principles across countries was 70.2%. The coverage of the more specific standards was much lower ($M = 34.4\%$). Privacy and Confidentiality (APA standard V) showed the highest percentage of overlap across countries (34.3%). Forensic activities (standard VII) showed the lowest percentage of similarity ($M = 7.8\%$). Overall the degree of overlap of standards across countries varied greatly. The aspects *Disclosures* and *Maintaining confidentiality* (standard: Privacy and confidentiality) appeared to be (almost) universal standards, at respectively 100% and 95% overlap.

In 1981, representatives of 12 European psychology associations founded the European Federation of Psychologists Associations (EFPA). Today there are 31 member associations. One of the aims of the EFPA was to develop a common European ethical code. This appeared to be too ambitious a goal. However, the member associations agreed on a Meta-Code, which was approved by the EFPA General Assembly in 1995. "It is aimed at associations and specifies what the code of each association must contain, rather than what individual members must do" (Lindsay, 1996, p. 82). The EFPA Meta-Code specifies four basic ethical principles: 1) Respect for a person's rights and dignity, 2) Competence (psychologists develop and maintain high standards in their work), 3) Responsibility (to their clients, to the community, and to the society in which they work and live), and 4) Integrity (in the science, teaching, and practice of psychology). The Meta-Code is more value oriented than rule based (Koene, 1997). The categories of Schuler coincide with, or are included in, those of the Meta-Code. For example, Confidentiality is specified under the basic principle Respect for a person's rights and dignity. These principles are divided into a total of 21 sub-dimensions. For example, the principle Respect for a person's rights and dignity covers the following sub-dimensions: General respect, Privacy and confidentiality, Informed consent and freedom of consent, Self-determination. The Meta-Code is less specific than the APA guidelines, because it is meant to guide associations instead of individuals.

Recently we compared the codes of individual EFPA member associations to the Meta-Code. The 31 member associations were asked by e-mail to respond to a small questionnaire about their association (e.g., number of members, year of foundation, the existence of an ethics committee). In addition, they were asked to send us an English version of their ethical guidelines. In cases of non-response (e.g., an insufficient e-mail address), a fax and/or letter was sent or some individual members were approached through and by personal contacts,[2] for example at a meeting of the Standing Committee on Tests and Testing of the EFPA. Eventually, 15 countries responded to the questionnaire and the codes of 19 countries were obtained. Three codes were obtained directly from the Internet. Another six were retrieved from the website of the Italian psychological association (marked with an asterisk in Table 5.5.). The national codes were analyzed by the third author. Each principle and sub-principle from the Meta-Code was compared with the principles and sub-principles from each national code to determine their consistency with the Meta-Code. An X in Table 5.1 indicates consistency of sub-principles. Absence of a particular sub-principle of the Meta-Code is indicated by a dash. Cases of doubt were resolved through discussion (first and third author). Comparisons were based on the thematic content of the statements and the exact wording did not have to be equivalent. Table 5.1 shows that the codes of all participating countries covered the four main principles of the Meta-Code. The mean percentage of coverage of the sub-principles was also high (85%). It must be noted that the scoring of the sub-principles was relatively lenient. For example, when a part of a sub-principle of the Meta-Code was described, or a principle was only described for a specific category of activities (e.g., research), it was considered to be consistent with the Meta-Code. Furthermore, the sub-principles 1.1, 2.1, and 3.1 appeared to be summary statements of the corresponding main principles; consequently they were evaluated as covered by all national codes. Since the code of Malta only describes the four main principles, only these three "summary sub-principles" could be identified.

The analysis of the national codes in relation to the Meta-Code revealed some ambiguities in the definitions of the sub-principles (either in the Meta-Code or in a national code), which resulted in relatively many dashes for some sub-principles. For example, some of the principles of the Meta-Code show some overlap (e.g., 4.1, 4.2, and 4.3). Therefore parts of the national codes could be assigned to more sub-principles. In these cases it was decided to choose one of the principles through discussion. Thus, when a sub-principle is indicated to be absent in a national code it does not mean that there is no attention at all paid to that sub-principle. There might be ambiguity or overlap in formulations.

Some of the countries followed the Meta-Code very closely, for example Belgium, the Nordic Countries, the Netherlands, and Slovenia. Other countries show a completely different structure, different accents, and different levels of specificity for particular topics. Germany, for example, focuses more on research and education and less on practicing psychologists. The code of the United Kingdom pays special and extensive attention to sexual harassment at work and working with animals; these topics are not explicitly covered in the Meta-Code. Despite these differences, there appears to be "a high level of similarity of content across the codes of the European psychological associations . . ." (Lindsay, 1996, p. 81) and the Meta-Code might have stimulated consistency between the European countries.

ETHICAL DILEMMAS

What are the ethical dilemmas psychologists feel they are confronted with? In a study by Pope and Vetter (1992), APA members were asked to describe situations (critical incidents) that they found ethically challenging or troubling. The categories with the highest percentages of troubling incidents were: 1) Confidentiality (18%), 2) Blurred, dual or

TABLE 5.1 A comparison of European ethical codes for psychologists with the EFPA Meta Code

Country								Sub-principles													%Main principles[1]	% Sub-principles[2]
	1.1	1.2	1.3	1.4	2.1	2.2	2.3	2.4	2.5	3.1	3.2	3.3	3.4	3.5	3.6	4.1	4.2	4.3	4.4	4.5		
Belgium	X	X	X	X	X	X	X	X	X	X	X	X	X	X	X	X	X	X	X	X	100	100
Croatia*°	X	X	X	–	X	X	X	X	X	X	X	X	X	X	X	X	X	X	X	X	100	95
Germany	X	X	X	X	X	X	X	X	–	X	X	X	–	X	–	–	X	–	X	X	100	75
Italy	X	X	X	X	X	X	X	X	X	X	–	X	X	X	–	–	–	–	X	–	100	75
Latvia*	X	X	X	X	X	X	X	X	X	X	X	X	–	X	X	X	X	X	X	X	100	90
Lithuania*	X	X	X	X	X	X	X	X	X	X	–	X	X	–	–	–	X	–	X	–	100	70
Malta*	X	–	–	–	X	X	–	–	–	X	–	–	–	–	–	–	–	–	X	–	100	15
The Netherlands	X	X	X	X	X	X	X	X	X	X	X	X	X	X	X	X	X	X	X	X	100	100
Nordic countries	X	X	X	X	X	X	X	X	X	X	X	X	X	X	X	X	X	X	X	X	100	100
Poland	X	X	X	X	X	X	X	X	X	X	–	X	–	X	X	X	X	–	X	X	100	85
Slovenia	X	X	X	X	X	X	X	X	X	X	X	X	X	X	X	X	X	–	X	X	100	95
Switzerland	X	X	X	–	X	X	–	X	X	X	–	X	–	–	–	–	X	–	X	–	100	55
United Kingdom	X	X	X	X	X	X	X	X	X	X	X	X	–	X	X	–	X	X	X	X	100	85
%	100	94	94	82	100	94	88	94	88	100	71	94	65	82	59	65	94	59	94	71	M = 100	M = 85

Note: * = Retrieved (June 2004) from the website of Ordine Nazionale Psicologi: http://www.psy.it/normativa_ue.
° Under revision.
X = in national code; – = not in national code.
[1] Main principles: Respect, Competence, Responsibility, Integrity.
[2] Sub-principles: 1.1 = General respect; 1.2 = Privacy/confidentiality; 1.3 = Informed consent/freedom of consent; 1.4 = Self-determination; 2.1 = Ethical awareness; 2.2 = Limits of competence; 2.3 = Limits of procedures; 2.4 = Continuing development; 2.5 = Incapability; 3.1 = General responsibility; 3.2 = Promotion of high standards; 3.3 = Avoidance of harm; 3.4 = Continuity of care; 3.5 = Extended responsibility; 3.6 = Resolving dilemmas; 4.1 = Recognition of professional limitations; 4.2 = Recognition of professional limitations; 4.3 = Honesty/accuracy; 4.3 = Straightforwardness and openness; 4.4 = Conflicts of interests/exploitation; 4.5 = Actions of colleagues.

conflictual relationships (17%), and 3) Payment sources, plans, settings, and methods (14%). Then there is a drop to 5% for a category labeled Forensic. Other categories, such as Supervision, Publishing, and Ethnicity only had 1–3% of the mentioned incidents. A comparable survey among the members of the British Psychological Society (Lindsay & Colley, 1995) resulted in a similar percentage of dilemmas in the category Confidentiality: 17%. In the other high-scoring APA categories the British sample scored much lower: Dual relationships: 3%, Payment matters: 3%, and Forensic: 2%. In this sample the troubling incidents were more evenly distributed over the other categories: Research: 10% (APA: 4%), Questionable intervention: 8% (APA: 3%), Colleagues' conduct: 7% (APA: 4%), School psychology: 7% (APA: 2%), Sexual issues: 6% (APA: 4%), Assessment: 6% (APA: 4%), Organizational: 5% (APA: 1%), with the remaining categories with less than 4%. Lindsay and Colley concluded that two kinds of dilemma could be distinguished. They refer to the first as a category of traditional dilemmas that focuses upon the interests of the client; this category includes confidentiality. The second category focuses upon psychologists as employees. This includes conflicts between what the psychologist considers as correct professional behavior and the employers' expectations.

Test Development and Test Use

It appears that specific matters referring to assessment and the development and use of psychological tests or other instruments (i.e., assessment center exercises) did not particularly bother the psychologists who participated in the surveys. Although the APA's Ethical Standards of Psychologists includes principles for test development and test use (London & Bray, 1980), Koene (1997) noted that specific guidelines on assessment or test use are absent in most European ethical guidelines. However, several associations have separate regulations or guidelines concerning the development of psychological tests and the use of tests and assessment center exercises, in addition to the ethical codes.

The *Technical recommendations for psychological tests and diagnostic techniques* (APA, AERA, NCME, 1954) and several revisions, known as the *Standards for educational and psychological testing* (the most recent version was published in 1999: AERA, APA, NCME, 1999), have had a major impact on standards for other countries. For example, similar publications were released by the respective psychological associations in Australia (Kendall, Jenkinson, De Lemos, & Clancy, 1997), Belgium (Belgische Federatie van Psychologen, Commissie Psychodiagnostiek, 1993), Canada (Canadian Psychological Association, 1987), and the Netherlands (Evers et al., 1988). Some of these publications are based on, or adapted from, the APA *Standards* and all include a detailed set of rules concerning test development and/or test use in a broad area of applications. Guidelines that are specifically relevant for the field of personnel selection can be found in the chapter on employment testing in the 1985 and 1999 editions of the APA *Standards*, and in the standards for the use of psychological tests in occupational settings that were developed in the UK (Bartram, 1995). For the use of assessment centers specific guidelines were published by the International Task Force on Assessment Center Guidelines (2000).

The *International Guidelines for Test Use* of the International Test Commission (Bartram, 2001; ITC, 2000) are partly based on some of the publications mentioned earlier. They relate to the competencies needed by test users. These competencies are specified in terms of assessable performance criteria and cover such issues as: professional and ethical standards in testing; rights of the test taker and other parties involved in the testing process; fairness; security and confidentiality; choice and evaluation of alternative tests; test administration, scoring, and interpretation; and report writing and feedback. The aim of the *ITC Guidelines* is described as: "The guidelines should be considered as benchmarks against which existing local standards can be compared for coverage and international consistency" (ITC, 2000, p. 4). So far, translations into 13 languages have been authorized by the ITC. Though the *ITC Guidelines* are meant to apply to all areas of psychology, they are highly relevant for the field of personnel selection.

Recent years have shown a rapid increase in the provision of stand-alone and Internet-delivered computer-based testing (see also Bartram, Chapter 18, this volume). As this raises a number of issues related to standards of administration, security of the tests and test results, control over the testing process, and psychometric qualities (such as equivalence with former paper-and-pencil versions), the *International Guidelines on Computer-Based and Internet Delivered Testing* (ITC, 2004) have been developed to complement the *International Guidelines for Test Use*. Although this document is a draft version and has not yet been endorsed by the Council of the ITC, its status seems well advanced and close to the final version. The CBT/Internet Guidelines have different guidelines for test developers, test publishers, and test users. The guidelines are formulated indiscriminately with respect to field of application, but are highly relevant for personnel selection as far as computer- or Internet-based testing is concerned.

The content of the special guidelines for test development and test use often overlaps with the content of the ethical guidelines and the content of privacy Acts, for example as far as it concerns the rights of the individual to know his or her test results. Bartram and Coyne (1998b) reported that about 55% of their sample of 29 countries (European and non-European) stated that there are statutory controls relating to the protection of the rights of individuals taking tests. These results are based on a survey of the Task Force on Tests and Testing of the EFPA (Bartram & Coyne, 1998a). The task force approached experts on test use (e.g., representatives of professional associations and publishers) in different countries to survey the importance of, and problems with, the seven factors indicating potential test misuse, identified by Eyde et al. (1993). Overall, 70 participants in 19 European and 17 non-European countries completed the survey. The questionnaire consisted of two sections: 1) Information on testing, tests, and test use, and 2) Indicators of lack of competence in test use. Data were analyzed for the four testing areas separately: Educational, Clinical, Forensic, and Work. Section 1 of the questionnaire covered six topics: 1) Proportion of test users who are psychologists, 2) The training of test users, 3) Availability of adaptations/translations of tests, 4) Access to information on test quality, 5) Statutory controls (e.g., legislation), 6) Non-statutory controls (e.g., certification by the psychological association). The authors clustered the countries according to the reactions to these topics. The data are too complex and the results too diverse to present the content of the clusters for each topic and each area. However, an important conclusion is "that the clusters do not represent geographical proximity of countries, nor do cultural or language features emerge" (Bartram & Coyne, 1998b, p. 259). The indicators of lack of competence (section 2) were presented as mean ratings and standard deviations over all countries. Participants were asked to evaluate 86 incidents (taken from the results of Eyde et al., 1993) in the context of test use, for example: "Not considering errors of measurement of a test score" (Bartram & Coyne, 1998a, Appendix 4, p. 10). They were asked to indicate for each incident how common (5-point scale, from rare to common) and how serious (5-point scale, from trivial to serious) the described (negative) behavior was; the incidents were combined into the seven factors identified by Eyde et al. Most common were problems referring to "Psychometric knowledge" (M = 3.25; SD = .95). "Accuracy of scoring" was considered the least common (M = 2.22; SD = .65). The mean values indicating perceived extent of misuse were around the midpoint (= 3) of the scale. The mean values indicating the seriousness of the presented problems were about 4, with the highest value for problems associated with proper test use (M = 4.19; SD = .62) and the lowest for accuracy of scoring (M = 3.92; SD = .87). Bartram and Coyne concluded that all of the factors related to potential test misuse were considered to be fairly serious by the sample of countries, and although there were differences between countries in the mean ranks, these differences were considered to be the consequences of sampling error.

ETHICAL CONSIDERATIONS IN PERSONNEL SELECTION AND ASSESSMENT

Although most psychologists will agree that ethical guidelines are valuable in some way, there are several reasons why some individuals might be tempted not to comply with all of them, for example commercial interests, ignorance, fame and fortune (research funds, merit increases in the case of research), inconvenience, or indolence. Francis (1999) stated that it is obvious that the ethical dilemmas in different areas of practice will not be the same, and the reasons not to comply with the guidelines will similarly vary with the specific area. Already in 1979 Mirvis and Seashore pleaded for ethical guidelines for organizational research because, especially in this field, the researcher could become entangled in a network of multiple roles and conflicting expectations derived from them. Jeanneret (1998) stresses the importance of an ethical code, especially for psychologists providing consultation to organizations based on individual assessment. He points to the dual client relationship of the assessing psychologist in which the assessee and the organization sponsoring the assessment are both clients of the assessor. This brings us to the number and diversity of stakeholders involved in personnel selection, which may lead to conflicts of interest: 1) the sponsoring organizations, which are in search of new employees, 2) the applicants, 3) the psychologists who conduct the assessment, 4) the employers of the psychologists, 5) the test developers' publishers.

All parties have their own interests at stake, but as Jeanneret noticed, it is especially the first category, the *sponsoring organization* (organizational clients, who are the paying clients), that might lead to ethical dilemmas that are absent in other branches of psychology. It is probably not as bad as the old English saying: "He who pays the piper calls the tune," but there are certainly commercial interests involved that may at least ask for special attention to ethical issues. The organizations are, especially in times of unemployment, the strongest party: they have one or more jobs to offer to individuals who are looking for a job, and they have work to offer to the psychologists who "may" assess the candidates. Psychologists are regularly confronted with the choice between loyalty to the sponsoring organization and loyalty to the assessee (the latter is in line with most of the ethical codes), as complaints against psychologists involved in selection illustrate (Carroll, Schneider, & Wesley, 1985). Furthermore, the organizational client might ask for information about a specific characteristic of applicants, for example emotional intelligence (see Woodruffe, Chapter 9, this volume), that the psychologist cannot or does not want to provide, because valid instruments to measure the characteristic are not (yet) available. In this case, the requirements of the organizational client conflict with the requirements of the professional society.

The second category of stakeholders, the *applicants* (the non-paying clients), differs from clients of psychologists in other branches. Applicants are the most vulnerable party, especially in times of unemployment. The services of the psychologist are forced upon them. Apparently they need or, at least, want the job for which they are assessed: they have to participate in the assessment procedure to be eligible for the position. Although there are several possibilities to prepare for a selection procedure, for instance test preparation books and tests on the Internet, these procedures are often perceived as stressful. Even when part of the procedure is perceived as unfair, unprofessional, or in any other way negative, the applicant might not complain in order not to lower his or her chances of getting the job.

The third category of stakeholders in the selection process, and the one that is at risk of getting caught between conflicting responsibilities, is the *assessing psychologists*. Nowadays, the selection of applicants through psychological assessment is an accepted procedure. However, in the Netherlands in the 1960s and early 1970s, organizational psychologists were accused of "playing the tune" of the sponsoring organization. The "anti-test movement" started ten years earlier in the USA (e.g., Packard, 1964). It was said that the interests of the applicants were considered as subordinate to those of the organizations. In 1971, critical comments in newspapers and criticism of the trade unions resulted in questions in the Lower House of Parliament in the Netherlands and the adoption of a motion in which psychological selection was described as unnecessary intrusion into personal privacy. In addition, the motion stated that the results and conclusions of psychological tests often were not clearly explained to applicants and that there were not enough guarantees that results were properly protected against unqualified or unauthorized people. In reaction to this motion the Minister of Social Affairs installed a task force to investigate whether it was necessary to take measures to protect the personal interests of applicants. The activities of the task force resulted in a report, called "An applicant is also a human being" (Commissie Selectieprocedure, 1977), which included a set of guidelines for employers and consultants who were looking for new employees and for applicants. These guidelines never got legal status like the American Uniform Guidelines on Employee Selection Procedures, as was intended initially. However, since the revision of 1976, the Dutch ethical code has covered the topics addressed in the report, such as the rights of the assessee to get information about procedures and tests, to confidentiality, to inspect the report, and to receive feedback about the assessment results. Unfortunately, severe dilemmas caused by the dual client relationship of assessing psychologists resulted in the resignation of membership of a professional psychological association. If members think that non-members attract the big paying clients at their expense, because they can deliver more and sooner, there is a real problem. Jeanneret (1998) argues that the assessing psychologist as well as the organizational client should have a strong appreciation of the same ethical considerations associated with the assessment of individuals.

The fourth party, the *employers of the assessing psychologists*, can be the same as the first, the sponsoring organization, otherwise it is often a consultancy agency specializing in assessment for selection and career development. When the psychologist is an employee of the sponsoring organization he or she is probably a member of a human resource department. In both cases the psychologist seeks to act according to the expectations and interests of the sponsoring organization. Even when the sponsoring organization is not the employer, the interests of the organization will be appreciated in order not to lose that organization as a client. In both cases commitment to his or her employer can result in ethical dilemmas. For example, the right of the assessee to inspect the report before the sponsoring manager gets the information is, for a lot of psychologists, a bother (Mulder, 1999). They feel that it is not service-oriented and are afraid that the assessee might prevent the sponsoring organization from getting the information, leaving the psychologist without a product to deliver. Another example of possible conflicts of interest between psychologists and their employers refers to sub-optimal use of tests: the employer urges the employed psychologist to use tests that are not the most valid available (or even tests with unacceptably low validity), because of commercial or personal interests. To solve the conflict the psychologist could ask his or her employer to purchase valid, but expensive, tests. Another option is to ignore the problem of validity, which often happens.

Test developers and test publishers, the fifth and last stakeholders in the métier of personnel selection, often use their own instruments. Numerous consultancy agencies in recruitment and personnel selection develop their own instruments and in some cases they also function as their own publishers. It might be tempting to apply those instruments in practice before empirical studies proved the instruments to be valid and reliable: development costs are high and the sooner one can yield the fruits of the investments the better.

London and Bray (1980) summarized the ethical dilemmas with which the different stakeholders are confronted by stating that balancing between obligations to the employer (including the sponsoring organization), the profession, and those evaluated for personnel decisions is difficult, but that maintaining ethical standards is paramount.

Most ethical guidelines cover some principles referring to the relations and possible conflicting roles with which work and organizational psychologists might be confronted. Some of them have or had additional or separate guidelines for this area of psychology in order to emphasize the importance of the specific problems, for example in the USA the *Standards for Providers of Industrial and Organizational Psychological Services* (APA, 1979). These standards for industrial and organizational psychologists covered topics such as anticipating and resolving conflicts of interest arising from dual user relationships (e.g., individuals and organizations) and establishing a system to protect confidentiality of records (London & Bray, 1980). In the Netherlands a similar set of principles was attached to the general ethical code, but this supplement disappeared with the last revision of the code in 1998, being under revision since then. An example of standards in the context of personnel selection is the document entitled *Principles for the Validation and Use of Personnel Selection Procedures* (Society for Industrial and Organization Psychology, 2003). These standards are primarily concerned with validity and psychometric "fairness." As already mentioned, regulations concerning discrimination and the adverse impact of personnel selection are often covered in laws or in guidelines deduced from those laws (e.g., in the USA the *Uniform Guidelines on Employee Selection Procedures* issued by the Equal Employment Opportunity Commission to govern compliance with Title VII in 1978). However, these laws and regulations apply not only to psychologists, but to all personnel experts in organizations subject to federal regulations regarding equal employment opportunity (London & Bray, 1980).

Probably because of the number of different non-psychologists that are involved in assessment centers, practitioners felt the need for standards or guidelines for users of assessment centers (Lievens & Thornton, Chapter 11, this volume). In 1975 the International Task Force on Assessment Center Guidelines presented the *Guidelines and Ethical Considerations for Assessment Center Operations* (International Task Force on Assessment Center Guidelines, 2000). After several revisions the last version of these guidelines was endorsed in 2000. The task force contained mainly practitioners from North America. Lievens and Thornton notice that a meeting of European practitioners to consider the applicability of the guidelines to Europe has not (yet) resulted in an adapted or totally different version. The purpose of the guidelines is to provide guidance to experts designing and conducting assessment centers, to give information to managers deciding whether or not to use assessment centers, and to provide guidance on the use of technology in assessments. It can be seen that the guidelines aim at a broad range of individuals, from I/O psychologists to managers in the sponsoring organization. The guidelines describe the essential elements of assessment centers in terms of requirements, for example the role of job analysis, classification of dimensions, design of techniques, and assessor training. The rights of the participants are specified in relation to the American Freedom of Information Act and the Privacy Act of 1974.

Table 5.2 displays the ethical codes, guidelines, and standards described in this chapter. We distinguish general guidelines and codes of conduct, standards for test use, and guidelines and standards for personnel psychologists.

TABLE 5.2 Ethical codes, guidelines and standards mentioned in this chapter

General ethical guidelines and codes of conduct		
1953–2002	APA – USA	Ethical principles of psychologists and code of conduct
1995	EFPA – Europe	Meta-Code
General standards for test use		
1954–1999	APA – USA	Standards for educational and psychological testing
	Several countries	Translations or adaptations
2000	ITC	International guidelines for test use
2004	ITC	International guidelines on computer-based and Internet-delivered testing (in development)
Guidelines and standards specific for personnel psychologists		
1975	APA – USA	Principles for the validation and use of personnel selection procedures
1978	EEOC – USA	Uniform guidelines on employee selection procedures
1979	APA – USA	Standards for providers of industrial and organizational psychological services
1995	BPS – UK	Standards for the use of psychological tests in occupational settings

Study into Ethics in Selection Psychology in the Netherlands

In the Netherlands a substantial percentage of the total amount of officially filed complaints against psychologists were against personnel selection psychologists. From 1993 to 2002 a mean number of 41 complaints a year were filed, of which 32% were in the area of work and organizational psychology. In the years 1993 to 1999 separate records were kept of the sub-disciplines within work and organizational psychology; these showed that 29% of the complaints in this area were related to personnel selection. Because this substantial number of complaints may be an indication of loose ethical norms, we recently undertook a survey of Dutch selection psychologists on attitudes on ethical matters in selection procedures. This study is described below.

Procedure. The survey form was developed by means of the critical incident technique. To collect the incidents semi-structured interviews were conducted with 17 individuals who were confronted with personnel selection as: a) an organizational client (e.g., a member of an HRM department), b) an apprentice in a consultancy agency (graduate student work and organizational psychology), c) psychology student and former assessee, or d) an employee of a consultancy agency. The interview was structured according to the respective phases in a selection procedure: a) resumé selection, b) interview, c) the use of assessment instruments (tests, assessment exercises), d) feedback, e) written reports, f) communication with candidates. The participants were asked to describe incidents in which the acting individual performed either extremely well, sub-optimally, or inadequately. The reported incidents referred to, for example, the use of unreliable tests, the use of unstructured interviews, or discrepancies between the immediate feedback to the applicant and the written report. The interviews resulted in a questionnaire with 75 statements or descriptions of actions that one can observe or perform in the context of selection. Some examples: "To make selection decisions based on first impressions"; "To use a test for another purpose than it is meant for." All actions are meant to present an example of (a mild form of) unethical behavior, although some items appeared to be somewhat ambiguous. Respondents were asked to indicate for each statement to what degree they considered the described behavior as acceptable (five-point scale: 1 = very unacceptable, 5 = very acceptable).

Sample. A total of about[3] 450 questionnaires were mailed to psychologist recruiters employed at consulting firms in recruitment and selection or at HRM departments in large organizations. Replies were received from 143 psychologists, so the response rate was about 32%. In earlier studies on ethical dilemmas response rates varied between 28% (Lindsay & Colley, 1995) and 51% (Pope & Vetter, 1992). The majority of the respondents (93%) were members of the Dutch association of psychologists. As mentioned before, in the Netherlands membership of the association is not obligatory to practice psychology. This high percentage of members might be the consequence of the fact that addresses of members were easy to trace through the registration of the association. We hoped that non-members would be reached indirectly (see note) and in HRM departments. Unfortun-

TABLE 5.3 Means, standard deviations and internal consistency of categories of ethical aspects

	N items	α	M	SD
Psychometric properties of tests	8	.80	2.36	.60
Quality of assessment procedure	10	.76	2.20	.54
(Un)informed consent	5	.77	1.19	.33
Report	5	.66	2.03	.58
Conscientiousness	4	.68	3.05	.82
Objectivity	4	.72	2.64	.83
Discrimination	5	.83	1.92	.77
Privacy candidate	3	.78	2.37	1.02

Note: $N = 143$.

ately, the response in the non-member category is low (13.6% of the sample); some of those potential respondents reported being too busy to participate in this survey. The ratio members/non-members of work and organizational psychologists in the Netherlands is unknown.

Other characteristics of the respondent group: 56 male (39.2%) and 87 female (60.8%); mean age: 40.3 years ($SD = 10.2$); mean number of years' experience as a selection psychologist: 9.6 ($SD = 7.6$); branch of psychology: work and organizational psychology and/or psychology of work and health 106 (74.6%); clinical psychology: 15 (10.5%); miscellaneous: 22 (15.4%).

Results. Based on the content of the statements and the homogeneity (Cronbach's alpha) of the responses of the sample, eight scales were developed: 1) Psychometric properties of the instruments (e.g., matters of validity and reliability), 2) Quality of the assessment procedure and evaluation (e.g., decision making based on first impression), 3) (Un)informed consent (e.g., informing the organizational client before informing the candidate), 4) Report (e.g., use of woolly language), 5) Conscientiousness (e.g., faxing the written report to the organization), 6) Objectivity (e.g., considering irrelevant characteristics of the applicant to influence the selection decision), 7) Discrimination (e.g., rejecting minority candidates regardless of their suitability), 8) Privacy (e.g., interview questions about children or partner). The results are presented in Table 5.3. All scales showed adequate to good internal consistencies. As all of the statements were meant to describe sub-optimal behaviors from an ethical point of view, the means below 3.00 indicate that the respondents disapproved of the described behaviors.

The only category that did not seem to worry the respondents too much was Conscientiousness. This category refers to activities that could be denoted as thoughtlessness, such as leaving confidential information on one's desk at the end of an office day (thus the office cleaner might read the information). Probably most of the respondents do not realize the possible consequences of those actions and therefore they do not disapprove of them. The mean opinion on the other categories varied from strong disapproval (Uninformed consent) to mild disapproval (Objectivity). From an ethical point of view it is good to see that most respondents disapprove strongly of informing the organizational client about an applicant's

TABLE 5.4   Differences between male and female respondents

Scale			Male		Female	
	F	p	M	SD	M	SD
Psychometric properties of tests	5.44	.02	2.50	.56	2.26	.61
Quality of assessment procedure	8.23	.01	2.36	.56	2.10	.50
(Un)informed consent	.78	.38	1.22	.35	1.17	.32
Report	3.08	.08	2.13	.60	1.96	.56
Conscientiousness	13.76	.00	3.35	.75	2.85	.81
Objectivity	.64	.43	2.71	.94	2.60	.76
Discrimination	.57	.45	1.98	.90	1.88	.69
Privacy candidate	6.62	.01	2.64	1.13	2.20	.91

Note: $N_{male} = 56$; $N_{female} = 87$.

assessment results without the explicit consent of the assessee (even when the incident is an exception, in case of time pressure). The respondents are less extreme, but still negative, concerning discrimination matters and issues referring to the content of written reports, such as using unclear language. The lowest agreement exists concerning the opinion on the privacy of candidates. Although the mean is below the neutral point of the scale, the standard deviation is relatively high. In particular, asking questions about having a partner tends to be evaluated as neutral ($M = 2.84$).

Further analyses by sex revealed significant differences between males and females. The multivariate effect of sex was significant ($F(8, 134) = 2.60$, $p = .01$) and differences were shown at the scales: Psychometric properties tests, Quality assessment procedure, Conscientiousness, and Privacy candidate (see Table 5.4). The mean scores of females were consistently lower than the mean scores of males, indicating that the female participants evaluated the described (unethical) behaviors as less acceptable than the male participants. The differences between men and women are in line with the results of Franke, Crown, and Spake (1997). They concluded that women are more likely than men to disapprove of specific hypothetical business practices.

Experience, expressed as the number of years practicing personnel selection, also showed a significant multivariate effect ($F(24, 383) = 1.62$, $p = .04$), which is caused by the differences on the scales Conscientiousness ($F = 4.31$, $p = .01$) and Objectivity ($F = 3.56$, $p = .02$). However, the differences between the experience categories ($\leq$4 yrs, 5–9 yrs, 10–14 yrs, $\geq$15 yrs) do not show a consistent pattern. For example, for Objectivity the category of 5–9 years of experience has the highest mean (2.93) and 10–14 years has the lowest mean (2.35).

Discussion.   Overall, the results of this survey are positive. Actions that are considered suboptimal ethical behavior are evaluated as unacceptable by the respondents, with the strongest disapproval by the female participants. However, limitations of this study should be noted. First, the sample consisted almost exclusively of members of the Dutch association of psychologists. As already said, in the Netherlands non-members are allowed to practice psychology. Just the fee might hold back a number of psychologists from becoming a member. It is possible, though, that members are more conscious about ethical matters because they are supposed to act according to the ethical code, developed by the association. The second limitation concerns the phrasing of the statements in the survey. All statements were meant to present an example of (a mild form of) unethical behavior. In an effort to make the description of the actions not too obviously unethical, some items may have appeared somewhat ambiguous. As Hofstee (1976) noted, in order to be not too obvious a certain degree of ambiguity is almost inevitable in formulating items to measure unethical behavior. Given the sensitive nature of the topic, respondents might have chosen a supposed ethical answer, especially in case of ambiguity. The results of this study are difficult to compare with the results of the survey of members of the American Psychological Association (Pope & Vetter, 1992) and of members of the British Psychological Society (Lindsay & Colley, 1995), because in those surveys the respondents were asked to describe situations that they found ethically challenging or troubling, while in our survey respondents were asked to give their opinion about specific incidents. Furthermore, the categories of ethical dilemmas in the different studies are not similar. Therefore, it is interesting to notice that the category of (un)ethical behaviors that is disapproved of most in our study, Uninformed consent, corresponds with the category with the highest percentage of troubling incidents in the other studies, namely Confidentiality.

CONCLUSIONS AND RECOMMENDATIONS

As Jeanneret (1998) concludes, "the entire scope of assessment services in an organizational context offered by a psychologist is a continuing matter of ethical practice" (p. 125). Where do all these reflections and study results lead us? Is ethical behavior obvious or do we need formal regulations to guide psychological behavior, and in particular the behavior of the selection psychologist? Incidents do occur and complaints are filed (Koene, 1997), showing that violations of ethical guidelines do occur, even by psychologists who are bound by professional ethical rules. One might wonder whether these violations are rooted in ignorance, in which case the ethical principles are not obvious, or whether psychologists ignore the guidelines on purpose, for example because they do not agree with their content or their consequences (e.g., competitive drawbacks). In the last case they may be obvious but inconvenient. Of course, ethical guidelines do not guarantee ethical behavior. As mentioned above, there are a lot of reasons not to comply with the guidelines. London and Bray (1980, p. 900) stressed the need for research on conditions leading to unethical conduct and "on ways to enforce ethical principles, particularly when these principles are promulgated in the profession but not supported by legislation."

Interesting in this context are the studies in the area of marketing. Akaah and Lund (1994) state that marketing has been identified as the branch of business most often charged with unethical practices. Therefore, much of the ethics research in business has focused on the ethical behavior of marketing professionals. Akaah and Lund studied the influence of personal and organizational values on marketing professionals' behavior. Their results indicated that personal and organizational values explain variance in the ethical behavior of marketing professionals. They found a small but significant relationship between organizational values and ethical behavior. However, the relationship between personal values and ethical behavior appeared to be insignificant. They concluded that personal as well as organizational values are potential antecedents of ethical behavior, but that more research is needed. These results may apply to psychologists as well. With respect to incorporating ethical values in the values of organizations, the results of a survey by the American Management Association (2002) are promising: 76% of the respondents indicated that ethics and integrity are core corporate values. So, one of the conditions to stimulate ethical behavior by psychologists might be the incorporation of ethical values in the core values of the organizations they work for, provided that these ethical values are not inconsistent with those expressed in the ethical guidelines of psychological associations.

We can conclude that ethical codes and/or guidelines are necessary. Several authors (Jeanneret, 1998; Lindsay, 1996; London & Bray, 1980) stress the importance of the relation between the requirements in ethical codes and the reality of professional practice. In terms of Reese and Fremouw (1984): the normative ethics should not diverge too much from the normal ethics; there must be a balance between how it should be and how it is, with explicitly formulated minimum standards. Lindsay (1996) proposes "good practice" guidelines to promote exemplary practice, which may result in normal normative behavior, or even beyond that – in optimal behavior.

Ethical guidelines and codes should follow developments in psychology and society; periodic revisions are necessary because opinions about what is ethical may change as a result of changed legal and professional requirements. An example of the influence of developments in society is the role of the unions in the development of changing opinions about freedom of information and individual privacy of employees (London & Bray, 1980). These principles were not incorporated in the earlier ethical guidelines; nowadays, they are part of a substantial percentage of ethical codes worldwide. Furthermore, the results of psychological studies might affect the perception of the ethicality of specific behavior or procedures. For example, according to many ethical guidelines applicants have the right to be informed about their assessment results. In these situations, giving detailed personal feedback would have been considered to be ethical behavior. However, the experimental studies of Schinkel, Van Dierendonck, and Anderson (2004) and Ployhart, Ryan, and Bennett (1999) showed that feedback about substandard performance could be harmful to the self-perception of rejected individuals. Since harming individuals is unethical, one could consider giving no detailed personal information to rejected applicants; thus, the ethical might become unethical. Therefore Schinkel et al. (p. 204) conclude that "the standard provision of performance measures after selection tests should be reconsidered." There should be continuous reflection upon such developments in relation to ethical guidelines in order to adapt the guidelines.

Another matter of concern is the way to enforce ethical principles. Little is known of disciplinary processes worldwide (Koene, 1997). Lindsay (1996) stresses the need to develop disciplinary procedures, or improve those already in being. The effect of disciplinary procedures in the context of professional associations is limited in countries, like the Netherlands, where membership is not obligatory. Non-members are not affected by disciplinary measures by the association. However, some ethical principles are covered by laws such as civil laws and privacy Acts (covering confidentiality). The Civil law in the Netherlands, for example, contains sections referring to the obligations of individuals delivering services. Clients of psychologists can go to court when they feel damaged by the actions of a psychologist in his or her role of deliverer of services. According to the law, the professional practitioner has the responsibility to act conscientiously and competently. Of course, it is better that ethical guidelines prevent clients feeling that they have to go to court.

The surveys comparing the ethical codes of different countries show that there are similarities in the main ethical principles across countries all over the world; at the level of sub-sections the diversity across countries is high. That is understandable and acceptable: as there is variability in selection practices due to nation and culture (Ryan, McFarland, Baron, & Page, 1999), variability in specific ethical accents was to be expected. However, there appears to be a striking understanding about the importance of *Confidentiality*; confidential treatment of individuals can be considered as a universal attainment, that is, information about individuals should be managed with the utmost care and safeguarded against inappropriate disclosure to third parties.

Answering the question in the title of this chapter: *Is the obvious obvious?*, the answer is "yes" and "more or less." The four to six main principles are in general acknowledged; when it comes to more specific behavior in specific situations the right thing to do is not always evident or convenient, and ethical guidelines and enforceable rules might help in diffuse and difficult situations.

NOTES

1. The new code from 2002 has five general principles, ten standards, and 102 sub-standards.
2. With our special thanks to Casper Koene, member of the Standing Committee on Ethics of the EFPA.
3. A number of questionnaires were delivered indirectly, through contacts in organizations who handed over an unknown number of questionnaires to colleagues. It appeared that not all questionnaires were distributed and some respondents received the form twice. Furthermore, some of the addressees were not selection psychologists (e.g., students, career counselors). The exact number of forms that eventually reached individual selection psychologists was unknown.

REFERENCES

Akaah, I. P., & Lund, D. (1994). The influence of personal and organizational values on marketing professionals' ethical behavior. *Journal of Business Ethics, 13*, 417–430.

American Educational Research Association, American Psychological Association, & National Council on Measurement in Education. (1985). *Standards for educational and psychological testing.* Washington, DC: Author.

American Educational Research Association, American Psychological Association, & National Council on Measurement in Education. (1999). *Standards for educational and psychological testing.* Washington, DC: Author.

American Management Association. (2002). *2002 Corporate values survey.* Retrieved June 24, 2004, from http://www.amanet.org/research/index.htm.

American Psychological Association. (1953). *Ethical standards of psychologists.* Washington, DC: Author.

American Psychological Association (Division of Industrial and Organizational Psychology). (1975). *Principles for the validation and use of personnel selection procedures.* Dayton, OH: APA.

American Psychological Association (Committee on Standards for Providers of Industrial and Organizational Psychological Services). (1979). *Standards for providers of industrial and organizational psychological services.* Washington, DC: APA.

American Psychological Association. (1992). *Ethical principles of psychologists and code of conduct.* Retrieved June 25, 2004, from www.apa.org/ethics/code1992.html.

American Psychological Association. (2002). *Ethical principles of psychologists and code of conduct.* Retrieved June 25, 2004, from www.apa.org/ethics/code2002.html.

American Psychological Association, American Educational Research Association, & National Council on Measurements Used in Education. (1954). Technical recommendations for psychological tests and diagnostic techniques. *Psychological Bulletin, 51* (Suppl. 2, part 2), 1–38.

Bartram, D. (1995). The development of standards for the use of psychological tests in occupational settings: The competence approach. *The Psychologist, May*, 219–223.

Bartram, D. (2001). The development of international guidelines on test use: The International Test Commission project. *International Journal of Testing, 1*, 33–53.

Bartram, D., & Coyne, I. (1998a). *The ITC/EFPPA survey of testing and test use in countries world-wide: Narrative report.* Unpublished manuscript, University of Hull, UK.

Bartram, D., & Coyne, I. (1998b). Variations in national patterns of testing and test use: The ITC/EFPPA international survey. *European Journal of Psychological Assessment, 14*, 249–260.

Belgische Federatie van Psychologen vzw, Commissie Psychodiagnostiek. (1993). *Richtlijnen voor het maken, publiceren en gebruiken van tests in psychologische en opvoedkundige context* [Standards for the construction, publication and use of tests in psychological and educational situations]. Alsemberg, Belgium: BFP-FBP.

Canadian Psychological Association. (1987). *Guidelines for educational and psychological testing.* Ottawa, ON: Author.

Carroll, M. A., Schneider, H. G., & Wesley, G. R. (1985). *Ethics in the practice of psychology.* Upper Saddle River, NJ: Prentice Hall.

Cascio, W. F. (1998). *Applied psychology in human resource management.* London: Prentice Hall.

Commissie Selectieprocedure. (1977). *Een sollicitant is ook een mens* [An applicant is also a human being]. The Hague, The Netherlands: Staatsuitgeverij.

EFPA. *Meta-Code of ethics.* Retrieved May 10, 2004, from http://www.cop.es/efppa/metacode.htm.

Equal Employment Opportunity Commission, Civil Service Commission, Department of Labor, & Department of Justice. (1978). Uniform guidelines on employee selection procedures. *Federal Register, 43* (166), 38290–38315.

Evers, A., Caminada, H., Koning, R., ter Laak, J., van der Maesen de Sombreff, P., & Starren, J. (1988). *Richtlijnen voor ontwikkeling en gebruik van psychologische tests en studietoetsen* [Standards for the development and use of psychological and educational tests]. Amsterdam: NIP.

Eyde, L. D., Robertson, G. J., Krug, S. E., Moreland, K. L., Robertson, A. G., Shewan, C. M., et al. (1993). *Responsible test use: Case studies for assessing human behavior.* Washington, DC: American Psychological Association.

Francis, R. D. (1999). *Ethics for psychologists: A handbook.* Leicester, UK: BPS Books.

Franke, G. R., Crown, D. F., & Spake, D. F. (1997). Gender differences in ethical perceptions of business practices: A social role theory perspective. *Journal of Applied Psychology, 82*, 920–934.

Golann, S. E. (1969). Emerging areas of ethical concern. *American Psychologist, 24*, 454–459.

Guion, R. M. (1998). *Assessment, measurement, and prediction for personnel selection.* London: Lawrence Erlbaum.

Hofstee, W. K. B. (1976). Verwerking van de vragenlijst selectie-ethiek [Data analysis of the questionnaire on ethics in personnel selection]. In P. J. Van Strien (Ed.), *Personeelselectie in discussie* [Personnel selection in discussion] (pp. 61–66). Meppel, The Netherlands: Boom.

International Task Force on Assessment Center Guidelines. (2000). Guidelines and ethical considerations for assessment center operations. *Public Personnel Management, 29,* 315–331.

International Test Commission. (2000). *International guidelines for test use.* Retrieved May 10, 2004, from http://www.intestcom.org.

International Test Commission. (2004). *International guidelines on computer-based and Internet delivered testing* (Draft Version 0.5, March 2004). Retrieved May 10, 2004, from http://www.intestcom.org.

Jeanneret, R. (1998). Ethical, legal, and professional issues for individual assessment. In R. Jeanneret & R. Silzer (Eds.), *Individual psychological assessment. Predicting behavior in organizational settings* (pp. 89–131). San Francisco: Jossey-Bass.

Kendall, I., Jenkinson, J., De Lemos, M., & Clancy, D. (1997). *Supplement to guidelines for the use of psychological tests.* Sydney: Australian Psychological Society.

Koene, C. J. (1997). Tests and professional ethics and values in European psychologists. *European Journal of Psychological Assessment, 13,* 219–228.

Leach, M. M., & Harbin, J. J. (1997). Psychological ethics codes: A comparison of twenty-four countries. *International Journal of Psychology, 32,* 181–192.

Lindsay, G. (1992). Educational psychologists and Europe. In S. Wolfendale, T. Bryans, M. Fox, & A. Sigston (Eds.), *The profession and practice of educational psychology.* London: Cassell.

Lindsay, G. (1996). Psychology as an ethical discipline and profession. *European Psychologist, 1,* 79–88.

Lindsay, G., & Colley, A. (1995). Ethical dilemmas of members of the society. *The Psychologist, 8,* 448–453.

London, M., & Bray, D. W. (1980). Ethical issues in testing and evaluation for personnel decisions. *American Psychologist, 35,* 890–901.

Mirvis, P. H., & Seashore, S. E. (1979). Being ethical in organizational research. *American Psychologist, 34,* 766–780.

Mulder, J. (1999). Inzagerecht in de A&O-praktijk: wat een gedoe! [The right of inspection of the psychological report in the practice of IO: what a bother!]. *De Psycholoog, 34,* 85–86.

Ordine Nazionale Psicologi. (2004). *Psychology in the European Union.* Retrieved June 24, 2004, from: http://www.psy.it/normativa_ue.

Packard, V. (1964). *The naked society.* New York: McKay.

Ployhart, R. E., Ryan, A. M., & Bennett, M. (1999). Explanations for selection decisions: Applicants' reactions to informational and sensitivity features of explanations. *Journal of Applied Psychology, 84,* 87–106.

Pope, K. S., & Vetter, V. A. (1992). Ethical dilemmas encountered by members of the American Psychological Association. *American Psychologist, 47,* 397–411.

Reese, H. W., & Fremouw, W. J. (1984). Normal and normative ethics in behavioral sciences. *American Psychologist, 39,* 863–876.

Riach, P. A., & Rich, J. (2002). Field experiments of discrimination in the market place. *The Economic Journal, 112,* 480–518.

Ryan, A. M., McFarland, L., Baron, H., & Page, R. (1999). An international look at selection practices: Nation and culture as explanations for variability in practice. *Personnel Psychology, 52,* 359–391.

Schinkel, S., Van Dierendonck, D., & Anderson, N. (2004). The impact of selection encounters on applicants: An experimental study into feedback effects after a negative selection decision. *International Journal of Selection and Assessment, 12,* 197–205.

Schuler, H. (1985). Synopsis of ethical codes for psychologists in Europe. *De Psycholoog, 20,* 88–92.

Society for Industrial and Organization Psychology. (2003). *Principles for the validation and use of personnel selection procedures* (4th ed.). Bowling Green, OH: Author.

Veldkamp, T., & Van Drunen, P. (1988). *50 jaar Nederlands Instituut van Psychologen* [50 years Dutch Association of Psychologists]. Assen, The Netherlands: Van Gorcum.

Part II

DEVELOPMENTS IN THE USE OF DIFFERENT KINDS OF PREDICTORS

6

The Selection/Recruitment Interview: Core Processes and Contexts

Robert L. Dipboye

Given the frequency with which interviews are used in selection (Keenan, 1995; Barclay, 1999), it is not surprising that work and organizational psychologists have devoted considerable attention to assessing their validity, reliability, and underlying dynamics. There have been several narrative reviews of this research literature in recent years (Jelf, 1999; Judge, Higgins, & Cable, 2000; Posthuma, Morgeson, & Campion, 2002). All are thorough, informative, and required reading for the serious scholar or practitioner of the interview. However, they are, for the most part, atheoretical and depict the interview as a series of disconnected and unrelated events. Typically, the social context is treated as a source of cues and the impact on the interview is framed from an information processing perspective. There are very few reviews that have examined the interrelationships among the cognitive and social processes and interview outcomes. Consequently, the major finding of interview research over the past century – that structured interviews achieve superior assessments than unstructured interviews – remains largely unexplained.

This chapter reviews the research on the separate assessment, social, and cognitive components of the interview process, building on previous theorizing about the interrelationships among these components (Dipboye, 1992, 1994; Dipboye & Gaugler, 1993). The model presented in Figure 6.1 expands on previous approaches by depicting the core process of the interview as a dynamical system that is embedded within several contexts. In part this means that processes and outcomes are reciprocally related at the level of the dyadic interaction of interviewer and interviewee. What this also means is that events at the level of the interview are intertwined with the organization, the environment of the organization, the human resource management function, and the interview task context. In the review that follows I will first consider each of the separate components of the core interview process and then the contexts in which this process is located.

THE CORE PROCESS OF THE INTERVIEW

As depicted in Figure 6.1, interviewer and interviewee come to the session with expectations, beliefs, needs, and intentions that influence the subsequent interaction and the

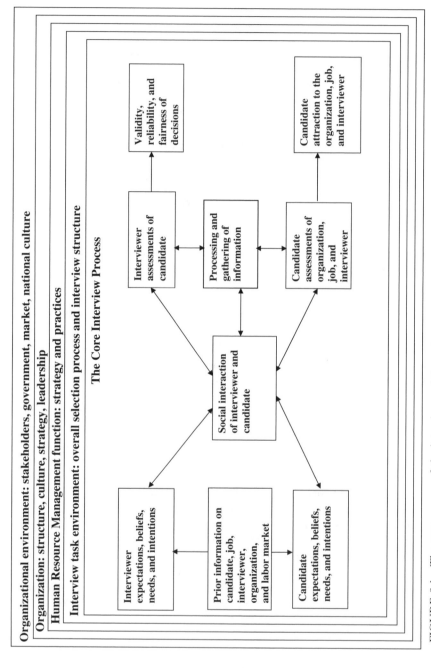

Organizational environment: stakeholders, government, market, national culture

Organization: structure, culture, strategy, leadership

Human Resource Management function: strategy and practices

Interview task environment: overall selection process and interview structure

The Core Interview Process

Interviewer expectations, beliefs, needs, and intentions

Prior information on candidate, job, interviewer, organization, and labor market

Candidate expectations, beliefs, needs, and intentions

Social interaction of interviewer and candidate

Interviewer assessments of candidate

Processing and gathering of information

Candidate assessments of organization, job, and interviewer

Validity, reliability, and fairness of decisions

Candidate attraction to the organization, job, and interviewer

FIGURE 6.1   The core process of the interview and its contexts

processing of information. Before, during, and after the interview, both interviewer and interviewee are engaged in information processing, judgment, and decision making. All this culminates after the session in final decisions on the part of the interviewer that can be evaluated in terms of their reliability, validity, accuracy, and fairness. Likewise, the applicant assesses the employment opportunity and forms an opinion of the interview experience, the interviewer, and the position.

Expectations, beliefs, needs, and intentions prior to the interview

Interviewers and applicants bring to the interview session expectations, beliefs, needs, and intentions that influence subsequent processes and are in turn influenced by interview events. On the interviewer side I would include expectations regarding the specific candidate based on prior knowledge as well as general expectations based on the interviewer's knowledge of the applicant pool, prior experience, and other sources of information. I also include the intentions of the interviewer such as whether the interviewer intends to emphasize selection or recruiting. The interviewer's personal needs may dictate their conduct of the session as in the case of an introverted interviewer who prefers minimal interaction and an extroverted, agreeable interviewer who relishes a two-way, wide-ranging conversation. Finally, interviewers have implicit theories of what the ideal and typical applicant are like, beliefs about their ability to assess the interviewee, the procedures needed to provide the most accurate assessment, and the appropriateness of various behaviors in the interview setting. On the side of the interviewee, there are expectations as to what will occur in the interview session and the likelihood of receiving a job offer, as well as the needs and intentions of the interviewee. Interviewees who have a desperate need for a job and who intend to accept a job if offered are likely to behave and process information differently than those who do not intend to accept the position if offered. The interviewees also have beliefs about what is appropriate and desirable behavior in the interview and their own fit to the position.

Perhaps the greatest attention has been given to the beliefs that individual interviewers bring to the session concerning the position and applicants (Rowe, 1984). In selecting applicants, interviewers rely on their implicit theories and prototypes of job requirements (Anderson & Shackleton, 1990; Hakel & Schuh, 1971). One might expect cognitive structures to be shaped by the experiences of the interviewer within the organization in which the interviewer is employed. However, Adkins, Russell, and Werbel (1994) found that interviewers held general conceptions of the ideal applicant that were uninfluenced by the organization. Experienced interviewers do appear to differ from inexperienced interviewers (e.g., Parton, Siltanen, Hosman, & Langenderfer, 2002) and in some instances are superior to inexperienced interviewers in their evaluation of applicants (Maurer, 2002). However, the findings are mixed and it is apparent that experience brings problems as well as benefits (Dipboye & Jackson, 1999).

Not many studies have explored the influence of the applicant's needs, beliefs, intentions, and expectations on the interview. Even fewer have explored how the congruence of interviewer and interviewee on these factors influence the effectiveness of the interview in recruiting and selection. An untested hypothesis is that when interviewer and interviewee conflict on these factors the interview is not as effective from the perspective of either participant as when these factors are complementary.

The social interaction of the interviewer and interviewee

Most of the attention in the research has been given to acts in interviews such as verbal, nonverbal, and paralinguistic behaviors exhibited by the interviewer and by the interviewee. Jablin, Miller, and Sias (1999) have described the typical interviewer as asking mostly closed-ended questions early in the interview and open-ended questions later in the interview. The interviewer does most of the talking in the session, with the conversation consisting of questions by the interviewer and answers by the interviewee. The interviewee typically asks few or no questions of the interviewer. Interviewees who receive favorable decisions tend to have a shorter latency of response to the interviewer, spend more time engaged in conversation other than answers to questions, have less hesitancy, fewer interruptions, more positive nonverbal behavior, and less negative nonverbal behavior than interviewees who do not receive offers or who receive unfavorable evaluations.

Acts often come as intentional attempts to shape the impressions of the other party to the interview (Ellis, West, Ryan, & DeShon, 2002; Kacmar & Carlson, 1999). Analyses of actual interviews have shown that assertive utterances are much more frequent than defensive acts of impression management and, among assertive tactics, applicants tended to use self-promotion more frequently than ingratiation (Ellis et al., 2002; Stevens & Kristof, 1995). McFarland, Ryan, and Kriska (2002) found that soft impression management tactics (e.g., ingratiation, rational persuasion) were used more frequently than hard tactics (e.g., pressure, coalition). Self-serving explanations for past behavior are another tactic. Applicants are more likely to attribute negative events to stable, internal, personal, and controllable sources than they are positive events (Silvester, 1997).

Acts are at the level of the individual. Interacts and double interacts are at the level of interviewer–interviewee dyad and consist of sequences or patterns of behaviors that vary on the symmetry of their interaction and the relational control expressed by each person. Tullar (1989) found more positive outcomes for dominance when there was complementary interaction (i.e., dominant utterance by interviewer followed by a submissive response by applicant, submissive utterance by interviewer followed by a dominant utterance by applicant). Engler-Parish and Millar (1989) further observed that the most satisfying interviews achieved a balance between the interviewer trying to acquire information and the interviewee trying to get the interviewer to deviate from questioning and provide information on the job and organization.

The third category of social process is the enactment of interview systems/structure in which the interviewer and interviewee not only act and interact but also make sense of their own and the other's behavior. Enactment involves both cognition and behavior as interviewer and interviewee make attributions for each other's acts and construct schemas, scripts, norms, and rules to interpret and represent the interaction. Ramsay, Gallois, and Callan (1997) identified one product of enactment in the form of nine implicit rules that interviewers use in judging the social behavior of the applicant (e.g., display self-confidence, take an active role in the interview, show evidence of preparation for the interview questions). Also emerging from the interaction is a relationship between the interviewer and interviewee that can be described in terms of its general quality and mutuality. Given the short duration of the employment interview and the formality of the setting, interviewer and interviewee are unlikely to develop a close relationship. Nevertheless, even within the short span of the typical session, interviewer and interviewee form an impression of the extent to which they have established rapport, trust, openness, authenticity, and other aspects of a high-quality relationship.

Information processing, judgment, and decision making

The interviewer is engaged in information processing, judgment, and decision making related to assessing the applicant's qualifications and fit. Likewise the interviewee is involved in processing information on the job and organization, judging the attractiveness of the job and organization based on this information, and deciding whether to accept an offer of a position. Both interviewers and interviewees are influenced by irrelevant cues that can lead them to deviations from the ideal, but the research and theory have dealt mostly with the impact on interviewer information processing.

A dual process approach such as that proposed by Fiske and Neuberg (1990) is useful in describing information processing, judgment, and decision making in the interview. According to this model, interviewers first *categorize* the applicant in a relatively unthinking way. They then engage in a process of *characterization* in which traits are inferred from the applicant's answers to questions and other behavior. As information is encountered that contradicts initial categorization, interviewers engage in a process of *correction* and change their impressions to incorporate new information on an applicant. Several factors often viewed as irrelevant to the job are seen as important cues influencing categorization, characterization, and correction.

Nonverbal, verbal, and paralinguistic cues. The findings are consistent in showing that "good" nonverbal and paralinguistic behaviors lead to more positive ratings by the interviewer of the applicant than negative nonverbal and paralinguistic behavior (Burnett & Motowidlo, 1998; DeGroot & Motowidlo, 1999; Howard & Ferris, 1996; Motowidlo & Burnett, 1995; Wright & Multon, 1995). Also, powerful speech style results in more positive attributions of competence and employability than a less powerful style (Parton et al., 2002). The interviewer's general impressions of the applicant are believed to mediate the effects of nonverbal, paralinguistic, and verbal acts on ratings of the applicant and hiring decisions (DeGroot & Motowidlo, 1999; Wade & Kinicki, 1997; Young & Kacmar, 1998).

Race, ethnicity, sex, age, disability. Ethical and legal restrictions make these dimensions inappropriate for the purposes of judging applicant qualifications except in rare circumstances. Although there are studies showing biases on the basis of these factors (e.g., Bragger, Kutcher, Morgan, & Firth, 2002; Frazer & Wiersma, 2001; Miceli, Harvey, & Buckley, 2001; Prewett-Livingston, Field, Veres, & Lewis, 1996), the findings are quite mixed. Sacco, Scheu, Ryan, and Schmitt (2003) have gone so far as to conclude from their field study "that organizations using carefully administered highly structured interviews may not need to be concerned about bias due to the mismatch between interviewer and applicant race or sex" (p. 852).

I suspect there is insufficient research to justify this conclusion. Given the strong pressures on interviewers to appear fair and nondiscriminatory, the transparent nature of much of this research, and the reluctance of organizations that do discriminate to allow such research, it is not surprising that the research literature shows so little convincing evidence of bias. Rather than concluding that all interviewers are fair in their judgments, a more fruitful approach to understanding discrimination in the interview may be to give greater attention to the work in social psychology on subtle and covert discrimination (Dipboye & Halverson, 2004). Prejudices appear to be deeply ingrained and, while usually suppressed, emerge to influence events in the interview where the discrimination can be rationalized and attributed to factors other than prejudice. For instance, Monin and Miller (2001) found that interviewers in simulated interviews were more likely to show bias against women and minorities when they were given the opportunity prior to the interview to make general egalitarian assertions. Specifically, enabling them to first disagree with a sexist or racist statement allowed them to appear nonprejudiced and provided license to subsequently discriminate.

Attractiveness.   Among the most consistent factors found to influence interviewer judgments is physical attractiveness. Interviewers are influenced more by general attractiveness and tend to assess applicants on their P–O fit. A recent meta-analysis has demonstrated that unattractive applicants are evaluated less favorably than attractive applicants in both the lab and the field and across employment interviews, promotion decisions, and performance evaluations (Hosada, Stone-Romero, & Coats, 2003).

Impressions of impression management.   The desirability of impression management depends on the appropriateness of the impression management tactics for the situation (Kacmar & Carlson, 1999) and whether fit to the position or organization is the focus of the evaluation (Kristof-Brown, Barrick, & Franke, 2002). Still, there are tactics that seem to be well received across a variety of situations. Interviewers are more positively impressed with applicants to the extent that they use self-promotion, nonverbal tactics (e.g., smiling and appropriate eye contact), expressions of fit to the organization such as interest in the position and the organization (Stevens & Kristof, 1995), and soft tactics as opposed to hard tactics (McFarland et al., 2002). Applicants are also better received if they take some degree of responsibility for their own past failures and shortcomings than if they try to explain them away (Silvester, 1997; Silvester, Anderson-Gough, Anderson, & Mohamed, 2002).

The linkages among the components of the core interview process

The core interview process presented in Figure 6.1 describes the various components as reciprocally related. Indicative of the dynamic nature of the interview are the interrelationships among the prior impressions, the social processes within the interview, and information processing.

Linkages of initial impressions with social and cognitive processes.   Several studies have shown that there is a substantial correlation between pre-interview ratings of applicants' qualifications and post-interview evaluations (Macan & Dipboye,1990) and the decision to interview applicants (Thoms, McMasters, Roberts, & Dombkowski, 1999). Cable and Gilovich (1998) found that recruiters evaluated job applicants they had prescreened into interviews more favorably than those who were not prescreened. This effect was independent of applicant qualifications and the accuracy of pre-interview assessments of applicant–job "fit."

In some circumstances, self-fulfilling prophecies can occur in which interviewer impressions bias applicant behavior in the direction of confirming these impressions (Biesanz, Neuberg, Judice, & Smith, 1999; Dougherty, Turban, & Callender, 1994; Judice & Neuberg, 1998; Reich, 2001; Ridge & Reber, 2002). Although most of the research has focused on interviewer expectations, there is also evidence that applicant expectations are self-fulfilling (Stevens, 1997). Confirmatory bias appears more likely when interviewers are unaware of the bias (Reich, 2001), are given a confirmatory orientation (Biesanz et al., 1999; Judice & Neuberg, 1998), and rely on their memory rather than taking notes (Biesanz et al., 1999).

The research has shown that interviewer impressions can bias the interviewing process and interviewee behavior but the effects are not as simple as some models imply. In some situations, prior impressions can trigger a disconfirmatory process and in other situations a diagnostic process (Dipboye, 1992). Moreover, confirmatory biases can occur for behaviors without affecting information processing or can impact information processing without affecting behavior (Biesanz et al., 1999; Reich, 2001).

Linkages among social and cognitive processes. Social and cognitive processes are unlikely to unfold in a serial fashion. Rather, they seem more likely to occur simultaneously and in parallel rather than serially. Thus, interviewer and interviewee interact, and the effects of one on the other are reciprocal. An important linkage between social and cognitive processes is the mental load placed on the interviewer and applicant as a consequence of social processes. To the extent that interviewer and interviewee are "cognitively busy" as the result of distraction or mental overload, they appear less likely to correct initial characterizations (Nordstrom, Hall, & Bartels, 1998). Another hypothesis that is untested concerns the impact of the interact/double interact sequences on the accuracy with which information is processed. It would be reasonable to expect interviews consisting of question–answer sequences with little chance for follow-ups by the interviewer to lead to personality judgments that are less complex and less accurate than the impressions that emerge from two-way, open communications (Powell & O'Neal, 1976). Consistent with these findings, structured interviews that are one-way interrogations lead to judgments of personality that are less accurate and valid than those reached in unstructured interviews (Blackman, 2002a; Blackman & Funder, 2002).

Perhaps more important than the sequencing of social process is the relationship that emerges from the interaction and that exists prior to the interaction. One might expect a high-quality relationship to lead to more accurate perceptions than a relationship characterized by mistrust or conflict. Partly this could be the consequence of more and better information exchange (e.g., interviewers ask good questions and applicants are honest and open in their answers). It could also reflect to some extent the likelihood that high-quality relationships characterized by trust and openness place fewer cognitive demands on the interviewer and interviewee. In possible support of this contention, Kolk, Born, and van der Flier (2003) found an improvement in construct-related validity when the intent of the interview was shared with interviewees rather than concealed. Much of this is speculation that remains to be explored in future research.

Outcomes of the core process

Among the outcomes of the core interview process are the judgments and the decisions of the interviewer and interviewee. There are several criteria of particular concern to psychologists and human resource management scholars in evaluating these outcomes: 1) the quality of interviewer judgments: validity, reliability, and accuracy, 2) success in recruiting desired applicants, 3) the quality of interviewee judgments of the job and the organization, and 4) the fairness of selection outcomes. These core criteria can conflict in the sense that achieving one may be at the cost of another.

In considering the measurement quality of interviewer judgments, a frequent assumption is that any information other than knowledge, skills, and abilities biases interviewer judgment and lowers the quality of the assessment. However, several studies have shown that so-called irrelevant factors can positively impact validity and reliability to the extent that they are in fact related to performance on the job. Sears and Rowe (2003) show how the similar-to-me effect can provide the basis for more valid interviewer judgments. Motowidlo and his colleagues have shown that nonverbal behaviors in simulated interviews with managers were predictive of performance on the job (Burnett & Motowidlo, 1998; DeGroot & Motowidlo, 1999; Motowidlo & Burnett, 1995). Langlois et al. (2000) concluded on the basis of a comprehensive meta-analysis that attractive adults were more successful in their careers, higher in self-esteem, more socially skilled, and slightly more intelligent than unattractive persons. Impression management tactics can reflect applicant characteristics that are related to performance in the job such as anxiety about communication (Ayres, Keereetaweep, Chen, & Edwards, 1998), extroversion and agreeableness (Kristof-Brown et al., 2002), and self-monitoring and locus of control (Delery & Kacmar, 1998). Also, favorable interviewer impressions of the applicant are positively related to traits that predict job performance, such as extroversion (Caldwell & Burger, 1998; Cook, Vance, & Spector, 2000; Osborn, Field, & Veres, 1998; van Dam, 2003), openness (Caldwell & Burger, 1998; van Dam, 2003), conscientiousness (Caldwell & Burger, 1998; van Dam, 2003), emotional intelligence (Fox & Spector, 2000), and emotional stability, locus of control, and low trait anxiety (van Dam, 2003).

Although the influence of so-called irrelevant factors does not necessarily lower the validity and accuracy of judgments, legal and ethical concerns often override concerns about psychometric quality of the judgment. If an interviewer is systematically discriminating against minorities, for instance, attempts to eliminate this bias are justified to avoid lawsuits and to ensure ethical practices.

CONTEXTS OF THE INTERVIEW

The interview itself has most often been treated as if it were a closed system uninfluenced by contextual factors. This assumption is not entirely inappropriate. It seems realistic, for the sake of exploring the causal links in this process and evaluating specific interventions, to approach the interview "as if" it were self-contained. This is especially appropriate if the sole concern is with how well the interview serves as an accurate, valid, reliable, and fair means of selection and enables the attraction of qualified applicants.

Nevertheless, the interview is in fact not closed and is embedded within several other contexts. A comprehensive understanding of the effects of the core processes on the outcomes of the interview requires a consideration of the contexts of the interview. These contexts include the interview tasks imposed on the core process, the overall human resource management function, the organization, and the environment of the organization.

Task context: The elements of imposed task structure

The immediate context of the social interaction and information processing of interviewer and applicant is the interview task. There are a variety of characteristics imposed on the interviewer and applicant that are important determinants of what occurs in the interview. I will discuss each of these elements and then consider how they potentially relate to the overall dimension of interview structure.

1. *Job relatedness*. Possibly the most important aspect of the interview task is the extent to which the interview is designed to focus on the knowledge, skills, abilities, and other characteristics required in the job. Interviews that are based on job analysis achieve higher levels of predictive validity than those that are less job-related (McDaniel, Schmidt, & Hunter, 1988; Wiesner & Cronshaw, 1988).

2. *Question focus*. There is evidence that experience-based questions in which interviewers ask about what the interviewee has done in the past are superior to future-based questions such as situational questions that ask applicants what they would do in hypothetical circumstances (Campion, Campion, & Hudson, 1994; Pulakos & Schmitt, 1995; Taylor & Small, 2002). One possible explanation is that experience-based questions evoke forms of impression management that might mislead or distract the interviewer. For example, compared to their responses to situational questions, applicants appear less likely to ingratiate in response to behavior-based questions and more likely to self-promote (Ellis et al., 2002).

3. *Behaviorally based rating scales*. With the behaviorally based rating scales used in structured interviews, applicants are evaluated on dimensions of performance identified on the basis of critical incidents analyses. The scales used in evaluating applicant answers are then anchored with behavioral incidents representative of each level of performance on a dimension. These behaviorally anchored scales (BARS) are generally considered preferable to graphic scales in structuring behavioral interviews (Vance, Kuhnert, & Farr, 1978).

4. *Restraints on questioning*. Another aspect of the interviewing task is the extent to which interviewers are constrained in the phrasing of questions and the use of follow-ups and probes (Huffcutt & Arthur, 1994). In highly structured interviews, interviewers ask exactly the same questions in the same order with no follow-ups or probes allowed. In support of this element of structure, interrater agreement is higher when interviewers are restricted in what they can ask and prohibited from asking follow-up questions (Schwab & Heneman, 1969).

5. *The use of alternative media*. The research so far is quite limited, but relatively lean media (e.g., telephone, online computer-based interviews) do appear to yield

assessments that differ from face-to-face interviews. Ratings of interviewees in telephone interviews, relative to face-to-face interviews, are more affected by attractiveness (Straus, Miles, & Levesque, 2001) and personal attributions (Silvester & Anderson, 2003) and are harsher (Silvester, Anderson, Haddleton, Cunningham-Snell, & Gibb, 2000). Interviewees in telephone interviews sometimes appear to compensate for the leaner medium by engaging in more impression management in the form of personal causal attributions (Silvester & Anderson, 2003). On the other hand, interviewees engage in less impression management with computer assessment than in face-to-face interview, an effect that seems to be declining as people become more acquainted with computers (Dwight & Feigelson, 2000). This declining effect of the medium suggests that interviewees are becoming less intimidated by computers and more willing to manage impressions.

The actual impact on the quality of assessments of alternative media is not clear. The lack of nonverbal cues in telephone interviews could reduce the accuracy of personality judgments relative to face-to-face interviews (Blackman, 2002b). Also, face-to-face interviews are perceived as superior to teleconferencing in conveying verbal and nonverbal cues, immediate feedback, and natural language and, as a consequence, interviewees in videoconference interviews are perceived to be at a disadvantage (Chapman & Webster, 2001).

6. *Using multiple interviewers.* Previous meta-analyses have concluded that the use of multiple interviewers yields levels of validity that are either the *same as* (Marchese & Muchinsky, 1993; Wiesner & Cronshaw, 1988) or *lower* than (Huffcutt & Woehr, 1999; McDaniel, Whetzel, Schmitt, & Maurer, 1994) the validities found with single interviewers. Unfortunately, previous research has failed to distinguish among the various forms of group interviews or the methods used in reaching a decision (e.g., simple averaging, consensus decision making, nominal group technique). This remains a relatively unexplored task dimension.

7. *Accountability.* Brtek and Motowidlo (2002) tested the effects on interviewer validity of holding interviewers accountable for either the procedure they follow to make interview judgments (procedure accountability) or the accuracy of their judgments (outcome accountability). Results showed that while procedure accountability increased the validity of interviewer judgments, outcome accountability lowered the validity of these judgments. Participant attentiveness fully mediated the effects of procedure accountability on interview validity.

8. *Note taking.* The most structured interviews not only have note taking but also impose a consistent framework for taking notes. Although a meta-analysis yielded inconclusive results (Huffcutt & Woehr, 1999), more recent research has demonstrated the benefits for note taking (Biesanz et al., 1999; Burnett, Fan, Motowidlo, & DeGroot, 1998; Middendorf & Macan, 2002).

9. *Statistical combination of ratings to form judgments.* Interviewers typically form an overall judgment in unstructured interviews, whereas in more structured behavioral interviews, they provide numerical ratings on each of several dimensions. The interviewee is "scored" by statistically combining the interviewer's ratings of the applicant across the separate dimensions (e.g., by averaging or adding the separate ratings). Previous research has consistently shown that using statistical combinations of data to

form judgments yields more accurate and valid results than using clinical combinations of data (Grove, Zald, Lebow, Snitz, & Nelson, 2000).

10. *Limited access to ancillary data.* The most structured behavioral interviews typically do not make biographical information, test scores, references, and other ancillary data available to the interviewer at the time that the applicant is evaluated and decisions rendered. In the typical unstructured procedure, interviewers are given access to other data such as test scores and biographical data and are free to use this information as they wish. Previous meta-analyses have shown higher validities when interviewers do not have access to test scores and do not have access to ancillary data (McDaniel et al., 1994).

11. *Consistent use of a decision model.* Once all applicants are judged on the knowledge, skills, abilities, and other characteristics required in the job, a decision has to be made as to which ones to hire, reject, or subject to further interviewing. Structured approaches apply an explicit rule in deciding among applicants that have been interviewed (Heneman, Judge, & Heneman, 2000).

12. *Training and instruction.* Another important aspect of the interview task context is the training provided to interviewers and applicants. On the interviewee side, coaching and preparation encourage the use of strategies that are positively associated with performance in the interview (Maurer, Solamon, Andrews, & Troxtel, 2001). Benefits of training also have been demonstrated on the interviewer side as well, in both structured and unstructured interviews (Huffcutt & Woehr, 1999; Stevens, 1998).

Impact of interview structure on the core outcomes of interviews

The various task components that are imposed on the interview process are thought to improve interview outcomes, and the usual assumption is that a single dimension of structure underlies these various task elements (Campion, Palmer, & Campion, 1997; Dipboye & Gaugler, 1993). An interesting and potentially important direction for future research is to determine if a uni-dimensional model of structure is sufficient to capture the various task elements. Although previous treatments of structure take a uni-dimensional approach, Dipboye, Wooten, and Halverson (2003) suggest three dimensions based on the life cycle of an interview along with factors specifically related to implementation (e.g., training). Another issue for future research is the impact of structure on other core outcomes, including recruiting effectiveness, fairness, and the quality of the interviewee's assessments. The research so far suggests that while structure enhances the quality of interviewer judgments, it is not always beneficial to other outcomes.

Quality of assessments: validity, reliability. A major conclusion emerging from several recent meta-analyses is that structured interviews are more valid and reliable than interviews that are unstructured (Conway, Jako, & Goodman, 1995; Huffcutt & Arthur, 1994; McDaniel et al., 1994; Wiesner & Cronshaw, 1988). As encouraging as these results are, the accuracy of the estimates of validity in meta-analyses has been questioned in recent reviews (Jelf, 1999; Judge et al., 2000).

Quality of assessments: construct validity.   Several recent meta-analyses have addressed the question of what traits are reflected in interviewer ratings. Conventional structured interviews differ from behavioral structured interviews in the constructs they tap, but a clear pattern of results has not yet emerged (Moscoso, 2000). I would suggest that the search for the specific traits that are measured by structured interviews is misguided and perhaps flawed because of the failure to distinguish between job-relatedness and procedural standardization in structured interviews. Questioning and evaluation procedures in an interview can be standardized to allow the assessment of traits that are irrelevant to the job as well as those that are relevant to a job. Thus, the standardization dimension of interview structure is independent of the constructs an interview is designed to assess. As an example, values are not usually measured in a structured interview. Yet, Parsons, Cable, and Wilkerson (1999) describe a structured interview that allowed an accurate assessment of values that were related to success in the organization.

Quality of assessments: accuracy of structured and unstructured interviews.   There is evidence that structure can improve accuracy. Maurer and Lee (2000) found that the accuracy of ratings of job candidates was greater in situational interview (SI) ratings of police sergeants and lieutenants. On the other hand, Blackman and Funder (2002) speculate, and Blackman (2002a) provides supporting evidence, that personality ratings are more accurately assessed with unstructured interviews than with structured interviews.

Recruiting outcomes.   The quality of assessments is obviously important, but attaining a good fit of the applicant to the position is likely to be achieved only if the best applicants are attracted to join the organization. Structured interview procedures that provide higher quality of assessments are not always optimal for recruiting because they are impersonal, inflexible, and allow the applicant little control over the situation (Latham & Finnegan, 1993; Schuler, 1993). For instance, applicants have been shown to prefer general interview questions to situational and behavioral questions (Conway & Peneno, 1999). There is even some evidence for a preference for interviews that are low on job relevance and standardization and high on voice and warmth (Kohn & Dipboye, 1998). Moscoso (2000) concluded, based on these and other findings, that negative applicant reactions are more likely associated with behavioral structured interviews than conventional structured interviews. Perhaps for the same reason, applicants tend to prefer face-to-face interviews over video-conference (Chapman, Uggerslev, & Webster, 2003; Straus et al., 2001) and telephone (Chapman et al., 2003) interviews. Videoconference interviews are more favorably received if they are structured, whereas face-to-face interviews are more favorably received if they are unstructured (Chapman & Rowe, 2002).

Fairness.   Fairness can be evaluated in terms of the adverse impact of the procedures on the selection of various groups as well as perceptions of the fairness of the procedures. Several meta-analyses of the interview research have concluded that structured interviews achieve high levels of validity without the adverse impact against minority groups found for cognitive ability tests (Huffcutt & Arthur, 1994; Huffcutt & Roth, 1998; McDaniel et al., 1994; Moscoso, 2000; Wiesner & Cronshaw, 1988). Roth, Van Iddekinge, Huffcutt,

Eidson, and Bobko (2002) and Bobko, Roth, and Potosky (1999) question this conclusion, and provide evidence that the adverse impact of interviewer judgments is larger than usually estimated. This is especially likely with many commonly used selection ratios and when the interview is used as an initial screening device or as part of a battery of other screening devices.

Regardless of the actual adverse impact of the procedures used in the selection process, procedures may or may not be perceived as fair by interviewees, interviewer, and other observers. Structured interviews should be more consistent, more job-related, and less vulnerable to improper questioning, but unstructured interviews are likely to have more two-way communication, a higher quality of interaction, and more opportunity to perform. Moreover, unstructured interview may be *perceived* as fairer because they allow the decision maker the flexibility to implement whichever rule seems to fit the situation (e.g., equality, equity, need). An area for future research to explore is the impact of the various facets of structure on perceptions of procedural and distributive justice.

Quality of the interviewee's decisions. An important objective in the interview from the perspective of the interviewee is whether sufficient information is gathered on the job and organization to allow an informed decision. There are at least two reasons that unstructured procedures may allow the applicant to make better choices among organizations and jobs at the same time as they lessen the quality of the interviewer's assessments. In an unstructured procedure the interviewer can provide realistic previews of the job. The applicant is able to ask questions about whether there is a match to his or her abilities, interests, goals, values, and needs. Additionally, the interviewer and applicant are better able to negotiate a mutually agreeable psychological contract. By contrast, a highly structured interview allows the applicant little opportunity to gather information or influence the conditions of employment. Whether unstructured procedures can actually lead to better applicant decisions remains untested.

Human resource management practices and strategies

Among the most important drivers of interview processes and design is likely to be the human resource management function. The power of the human resource management function relative to the individual units in the organization is one factor to consider. One might expect that a strong human resource function that is centralized and professionalized might be more likely to impose on subunits of the organization structured procedures. On the other hand, to the extent that the human resource function is decentralized and relatively weak one might expect a preference for unstructured interview procedures that allow departments discretion in their selection practices. In these cases, maintaining and increasing power become stronger than concerns over picking the person with the right knowledge, skills, abilities, and other characteristics.

The human resource strategies of the organization play a particularly important role in determining the design, implementation, and evaluation of the core interview. To achieve competitive advantage, one suggestion is to adopt bundles of human resource practices that fit the strategic aims of the organization (Baron & Kreps, 1999). The decision to adopt structured or unstructured interviews could depend as much on their consistency with the other tactics that are part of this bundle as on their accuracy and validity. Moreover, the adoption and successful implementation of a structured interview is probably facilitated to the extent that human resource strategy is consistent with and reinforces structured procedures. To the extent that human resource strategy is inconsistent with these procedures, structured interviews are less likely to be adopted and more likely to fail in implementation. The resource-based theory of the firm would suggest that competitive advantage comes from human resource practices that not only create value but are also rare and not easily imitated (Barney, 2002). This theory would suggest that instead of adopting standardized procedures that are easily transportable from one organization, an organization might choose novel, idiosyncratic, and even bizarre procedures to obtain competitive advantage. On the basis of an application of resource based theory by Wright, McMahan, and McWilliams (1994) one could speculate that unstructured procedures having less than optimal reliability and validity might be good enough to add value because they are rare, inimitable, and non-substitutable.

The most proximal influence on the core interview process in the human resource management function is overall staffing and recruiting process. Social process, information processing, and judgments are all intertwined in the interview with other selection tools and other phases of the selection process. In some types of interview situations, the interviewer's judgment is the lens through which many of the selection procedures influence decisions to reject or hire. In these situations, the interview is the "human" component at the heart of the overall selection process. Thus, it is often difficult to separate information collected in the interview from information originating from other sources such as the application, tests, and references. Despite the frequency with which other measures accompany interviews (Barclay, 1999), only a few researchers have given attention to the combined effects of interview judgments and other selection instruments (Chuang, 2001; Dalessio & Silverhart, 1994; Harland, Rauzi, & Biasotto, 1995). The importance of considering the overall selection process is also demonstrated in the research showing that the adverse impact of the interview is influenced by whether the interview is part of a process in which other selection procedures are used (Roth et al., 2002; Bobko et al., 1999).

Organizational context: Culture, structure, strategy, leadership, power

Among the most important factors at the level of the organization are formal and informal structure, organizational culture, leadership, and strategy. At the level of the culture and subcultures are the core values and assumptions of the organization as well as the myths, rituals, material artifacts, and ceremonies that communicate and sustain these values and assumptions. The early contacts of new members with the organization are crucial to socializing the new member and ensuring a good fit to the organization (Miller & Jablin, 1991). As the first significant encounter with the organization, the interview is often the initial attempt to "unfreeze" potential new hires, shaking them loose from previous attitudes, values, and norms, and bringing them in line with the culture. In a strong culture, the interview is potentially among the important means of communicating and reinforcing the culture.

Environmental context: National culture, stakeholders, institutions, and economy

Organizations operate within environmental contexts that consist of a national culture, stakeholders, other institutions, and an economic environment. The interview practices adopted by the organization can reflect the attempt of the organization to achieve legitimacy and perceived status in the eyes of these stakeholders. From the perspective of Institutional Theory (Meyer & Rowan, 1977), the practices of high-status institutions are imitated to maintain the firm's reputation and position in its environment. The interview procedures that are prevalent among these exemplary firms are those that are adopted. Economic forces are another environmental factor to consider. Among the most important and most neglected in the research is the labor market. When there are more positions than applicants, the emphasis is on recruitment, but when there are more applicants than positions, the emphasis shifts to selection. One could also expect interview procedures to conform to the values and norms of the national culture. There is speculation and evidence to support the contention that structured, behavioral interviews are more compatible in masculine, collectivist cultures than in feminine, individualistic cultures (Spence & Petrick, 2000), in universalistic than in particularistic cultures (Nyfield & Baron, 2000), and in cultures high on uncertainty avoidance than in cultures low on this dimension (Ryan, McFarland, Baron, & Page, 1999). In a case study of a clash of the national culture with the interview, Lee (1998) examined how structured selection procedures in South Korea conflicted with the traditional Confucian influence of *yon-go* which means a special social relationship or special connection based on family ties (*hyul-yon*), school-ties (*hakyon*) and birthplace (*ii-yon*).

The limited research conducted so far suggests that national culture may well affect adoption of structured interviews, but whether it moderates validity remains to be tested. Recent meta-analyses of general mental ability test validities indicate that test validities do not vary substantially across European cultures (Salgado et al., 2003). A similar examination of the generalization of interview validities across cultures has yet to be conducted.

Contextual influences on implementation of interview practices

Based on results such as these, one might expect that resistance to structured interviewing is the result of the attitudes, knowledge, and beliefs of the people who implement the procedures. The solution would seem to be to educate and persuade practitioners. However, the contexts of the interview that I have reviewed here suggest that interview procedures serve other functions that reside in the contexts of the interview. Thus, unstructured interviews that are less than ideal in their reliability, validity, and accuracy may be preferred over structured interviews because the unstructured procedures are superior in fulfilling these system functions.

CONCLUSIONS

The research reviewed here shows no shortage of research on the interview, but also reveals major gaps in the empirical literature. Most of the research has dealt with information processing of the interviewer and the impact of the interview task context on the quality of interviewer assessments. There is also a substantial amount of research providing descriptions of social processes in interview sessions. Where the research is quite limited is with regard to the relation of core interview processes with outcomes such as the quality of the interviewee's assessments or the success of recruiting efforts. Where the research is non-existent is with regard to contextual influences such as the impact of the human resource management, organization, or the environment contexts on interview processes and outcomes.

A thesis of this review is that future research would benefit from conceptualizing the selection/recruitment interview as more than the core processes and outcomes, which are so often the focuses of the research. The core of the interview is embedded within contexts that are in turn embedded within other contexts. What is observed to occur reflects a dynamic interplay among elements of the core process and the interview task context, the human resource function, the organization, and the environment of the organization. On the basis of this conceptualization, I would suggest that interviews should be evaluated not only on the basis of the quality of assessments, but also in terms of how well they function in reference to the contexts in which they are embedded. While radical, this is a possibility that deserves serious attention in the research on the selection/recruitment interview.

NOTE

This chapter was completed while the author was on the faculty at Rice University, Houston, TX.

REFERENCES

Adkins, C. L., Russell, C. J., & Werbel, J. D. (1994). Judgments of fit in the selection process: The role of work value congruence. *Personnel Psychology*, *47*, 605–623.

Anderson, N. H., & Shackleton, V. J. (1990). Decision making in the graduate selection interview: A field study. *Journal of Occupational Psychology*, *63*, 63–76.

Ayres, J., Keereetaweep, T., Chen, P., & Edwards, P. A. (1998). Communication apprehension and employment interviews. *Communication Education*, *47*, 1–17.

Barclay, J. M. (1999). Employee selection: A question of structure. *Personnel Review*, *28*, 134–151.

Barney, J. B. (2002). *Gaining and sustaining competitive advantage* (2nd ed). Upper Saddle River, NJ: Prentice Hall.

Baron, J. N., & Kreps, D. M. (1999). *Strategic human resources: Frameworks for general managers*. New York: John Wiley & Sons.

Biesanz, J. C., Neuberg, S. L., Judice, T. N., & Smith, D. M. (1999). When interviewers desire accurate impressions: The effect of notetaking on the influence of expectations. *Journal of Applied Social Psychology*, *29*, 2529–2549.

Blackman, M. C. (2002a). Personality judgment and the utility of the unstructured employment interview. *Basic and Applied Social Psychology*, *24*, 241–250.

Blackman, M. C. (2002b). The employment interview via the telephone: Are we sacrificing accurate personality judgments for cost efficiency? *Journal of Research in Personality*, *36*, 208–223.

Blackman, M. C., & Funder, D. C. (2002). Effective interview practices for accurately assessing counterproductive traits. *International Journal of Selection and Assessment, 10*, 109–116.

Bobko, P., Roth, P. L., & Potosky, D. (1999). Derivation and implications of a meta-analytic matrix incorporating cognitive ability, alternative predictors, and job performance. *Personnel Psychology, 52*, 561–589.

Bragger, J. D., Kutcher, E., Morgan, J., & Firth, P. (2002). The effects of the structured interview on reducing biases against pregnant job applicants. *Sex Roles, 46*, 215–226.

Brtek, M. D., & Motowidlo, S. J. (2002). Effects of procedure and outcome accountability on interview validity. *Journal of Applied Psychology, 87*, 185–191.

Burnett, J. R., Fan, C., Motowidlo, S. J., & DeGroot, T. (1998). Interview notes and validity. *Personnel Psychology, 51*, 375– 396.

Burnett, J. R., & Motowidlo, S. J (1998). Relations between different sources of information in the structured selection interview. *Personnel Psychology, 51*, 963–983.

Cable, D. M., & Gilovich, T. (1998). Looked over or overlooked? Prescreening decisions and postinterview evaluations. *Journal of Applied Psychology, 83*, 501–508.

Caldwell, D. F., & Burger, J. M. (1998). Personality characteristics of job applicants and success in screening interviews. *Personnel Psychology, 51*, 119–136.

Campion, M. A., Campion, J. E., & Hudson, J. P., Jr. (1994). Structured interviewing: A note on incremental validity and alternative question types. *Journal of Applied Psychology, 79*, 998–1002.

Campion, M. A., Palmer, D. K., & Campion, J. E. (1997). A review of structure in the selection interview. *Personnel Psychology, 50*, 655–702.

Chapman, D. S., & Rowe, P. M. (2002). The influence of videoconference technology and interview structure on the recruiting function of the employment interview: A field experiment. *International Journal of Selection and Assessment, 10*, 185–197.

Chapman, D. S., Uggerslev, K. L., & Webster, J. (2003). Applicant reactions to face-to-face and technology-mediated interviews: A field investigation. *Journal of Applied Psychology, 88*, 944–953.

Chapman, D. S., & Webster, J. (2001). Rater correction processes in applicant selection using videoconference technology: The role of attributions. *Journal of Applied Social Psychology, 31*, 2518–2537.

Chuang, A. (2001). The perceived importance of person–job fit and person–organization fit between and within interview stages. *Dissertation Abstracts International: Section B: The Sciences and Engineering, 62* (3-B), 1626.

Conway, J. M., Jako, R. A., & Goodman, D. F. (1995). A meta-analysis of interrater and internal consistency reliability of selection interviews. *Journal of Applied Psychology, 80*, 565–579.

Conway, J. M., & Peneno, G. M. (1999). Comparing structured interview question types: Construct validity and applicant reactions. *Journal of Business and Psychology, 13*, 485–506.

Cook, K. W., Vance, C. A., & Spector, P. E. (2000). The relation of candidate personality with selection-interview outcomes. *Journal of Applied Social Psychology, 30*, 867–885.

Dalessio, A. T., & Silverhart, T. A. (1994). Combining biodata test and interview information: Predicting decisions and performance criteria. *Personnel Psychology, 47*, 303–315.

DeGroot, T., & Motowidlo, S. J. (1999). Why visual and vocal interview cues can affect interviewers' judgments and predict job performance. *Journal of Applied Psychology, 84*, 986–993.

Delery, J. E., & Kacmar, K. M. (1998). The influence of applicant and interviewer characteristics on the use of impression management. *Journal of Applied Social Psychology, 28*, 1649–1669.

Dipboye, R. L. (1992). *Selection interview: Process perspective.* Cincinnati, OH: South-Western Publishing Co.

Dipboye, R. L. (1994). Structured and unstructured selection interviews: Beyond the job-fit model. In G. Ferris (Ed.), *Research in Personnel and Human Resources Management* (Vol. 12, pp. 79–123). Greenwich, CT: JAI Press.

Dipboye, R. L., & Gaugler, B. B. (1993). Cognitive and behavioral processes in the selection interview. In N. Schmitt & W. Borman (Eds.), *Personnel selection in organizations* (pp. 135–170). San Francisco: Jossey-Bass.

Dipboye, R. L., & Halverson, S. K. (2004). Subtle (and not so subtle) discrimination in organizations. In R. W. Griffin & A. M. O'Leary-Kelly (Eds.), *The dark side of organizational behavior* (pp. 131–158). San Francisco: Jossey-Bass.

Dipboye, R. L., & Jackson, S. (1999). The influence of interviewer experience and expertise on selection decisions. In R. W. Eder & M. M. Harris (Eds.), *The employment interview handbook: Theory, research and practice* (2nd ed., pp. 229–292). Beverly Hills, CA: Sage.

Dipboye, R. L., Wooten, K. C., & Halverson, S. K. (2003). Behavioral and situational interviews. In J. C. Thomas (Ed.), *Comprehensive handbook of psychological assessment* (Vol. 4, pp. 297–318). New York: John Wiley.

Dougherty, T. W., Turban, D. B., & Callender, J. C. (1994). Confirming first impressions in the employment interview: A field study of interviewer behavior. *Journal of Applied Psychology, 79,* 659–665.

Dwight, S. A., & Feigelson, M. E. (2000). A quantitative review of the effect of computerized testing on the measurement of social desirability. *Educational and Psychological Measurement, 60,* 340–360.

Ellis, A. P. J., West, B. J., Ryan, A. M., & DeShon, R. P. (2002). The use of impression management tactics in structured interviews: A function of question type? *Journal of Applied Psychology, 87,* 1200–1208.

Engler-Parish, P. G., & Millar, F. E. (1989). An exploratory relational control analysis of the employment screening interview. *Western Journal of Speech Communication, 53,* 30–51.

Fiske, S. T., & Neuberg, S. L. (1990). A continuum of impression formation from category-based to individuating processes: Influences of information and motivation on attention and interpretation. In M. P. Zanna (Ed.), *Advances in experimental social psychology* (Vol. 23, pp. 1–74). New York: Academic Press.

Fox, S., & Spector, P. E. (2000). Relations of emotional intelligence, practical intelligence, general intelligence, and trait affectivity with interview outcomes: It's not all just 'G'. *Journal of Organizational Behavior, 21,* 203–220.

Frazer, R. A., & Wiersma, U. J. (2001). Prejudice versus discrimination in the employment interview: We may hire equally, but our memories harbour prejudice. *Human Relations, 54,* 173–191.

Grove, W. M., Zald, D. H., Lebow, B. S., Snitz, B. E., & Nelson, C. (2000). Clinical versus mechanical prediction: A meta-analysis. *Psychological Assessment, 12,* 19–30.

Hakel, M. D., & Schuh, A. J. (1971). Job applicant attributes judged important across seven diverse occupations. *Personnel Psychology, 24,* 45–52.

Harland, L. K., Rauzi, T., & Biasotto, M. M. (1995). Perceived fairness of personality tests and the impact of explanations for their use. *Employee Responsibilities and Rights Journal, 8,* 183–192.

Heneman, H. G., Judge, T. A., & Heneman, R. L. (2000). *Staffing organizations.* Boston: Irwin McGraw Hill.

Hosada, M., Stone-Romero, E. F., & Coats, G. (2003). The effects of physical attractiveness on job-related outcomes: A meta-analysis of experimental studies. *Personnel Psychology, 56,* 431–462.

Howard, J. L., & Ferris, G. R. (1996). The employment interview context: Social and situational influences on interviewer decisions. *Journal of Applied Social Psychology, 26,* 112–136.

Huffcutt, A. I., & Arthur, W., Jr. (1994). Hunter and Hunter (1984) revisited: Interview validity for entry-level jobs. *Journal of Applied Psychology, 79,* 184–190.

Huffcutt, A. I., & Roth, P. L. (1998). Racial group differences in employment interview evaluations. *Journal of Applied Psychology, 83,* 179–189.

Huffcutt, A. I., & Woehr, D. J. (1999). Further analysis of employment interview validity: A quantitative evaluation of interviewer-related structuring methods. *Journal of Organizational Behavior, 20,* 549–560.

Jablin, F. M., Miller, V. D., & Sias, P. M. (2002). Communication and interaction processes. In R. W. Eder & M. M. Harris (Eds.), *The employment interview handbook: Theory, research and practice* (2nd ed., pp. 297–320). Beverly Hills, CA: Sage.

Jelf, G. S. (1999). A narrative review of post-1989 employment interview research. *Journal of Business and Psychology, 14,* 25–58.

Judge, T. A., Higgins, C. A., & Cable, D. M. (2000). The employment interview: A review of recent research and recommendations for future research. *Human Resource Management Review, 10,* 383–406.

Judice, T. N., & Neuberg, S. L. (1998). When interviewers desire to confirm negative expectations: Self-fulfilling prophecies and inflated applicant self-perceptions. *Basic and Applied Social Psychology, 20,* 175–190.

Kacmar, K. M., & Carlson, D. S. (1999). Effectiveness of impression management tactics across human resource situations. *Journal of Applied Social Psychology, 29,* 1293–1315.

Keenan, T. (1995). Graduate recruitment in Britain: A survey of selection methods used by organizations. *Journal of Organizational Behavior, 16,* 303–317.

Kohn, L., & Dipboye, R. L. (1998). The effects of interview structure on recruiting outcomes. *Journal of Applied Social Psychology, 28,* 821–843.

Kolk, N. J., Born, M. P., & van der Flier, H. (2003). The transparent assessment centre: The effects of revealing dimensions to candidates. *Applied Psychology: An International Review, 52,* 648–668.

Kristof-Brown, A. L., Barrick, M. R., & Franke, M. (2002). Applicant impression management: Dispositional influences and consequences for recruiter perceptions of fit and similarity. *Journal of Management, 28,* 27–46.

Langlois, J. H., Kalakanis, L., Rubenstein, A. J., Larson, A., Hallam, M., & Smoot, M. (2000). Maxims or myths of beauty? A meta-analytic and theoretical review. *Psychological Bulletin, 126,* 390–423.

Latham, G. P., & Finnegan, B. J. (1993). Perceived practicality of unstructured, patterned, and situational interviews. In H. Schuler, J. L. Farr, & M. Smith (Eds.), *Personnel selection and assessment: Individual and organizational perspectives* (pp. 41–55). Hillsdale, NJ: Lawrence Erlbaum.

Lee, H. (1998). Transformation of employment practices in Korean businesses. *International Studies of Management and Organization, 28,* 26–39.

Macan, T. H., & Dipboye, R. L. (1990). The relationship of interviewers' preinterview impressions to selection and recruitment outcomes. *Personnel Psychology, 43,* 745–768.

Marchese, M. C., & Muchinsky, P. M. (1993). The validity of the employment interview: A meta-analysis. *International Journal of Selection and Assessment, 1,* 18–26.

Maurer, S. D. (2002). A practitioner-based analysis of interviewer job expertise and scale format as contextual factors in situational interviews. *Personnel Psychology, 55,* 307–327.

Maurer, S. D., & Lee, T. W. (2000). Accuracy of the situational interview in rating multiple job candidates. *Journal of Business and Psychology, 15,* 73–96.

Maurer, T. J., Solamon, J. M., Andrews, K. D., & Troxtel, D. D. (2001). Interviewee coaching, preparation strategies, and response strategies in relation to performance in situational employment interviews: An extension of Maurer, Solamon, and Troxtel (1998). *Journal of Applied Psychology, 86,* 709–717.

McDaniel, M. A., Schmidt, F. L., & Hunter, J. E. (1988). A meta-analysis of the validity of methods for rating training experience in personnel selection. *Personnel Psychology, 41,* 283–314.

McDaniel, M. A., Whetzel, D. L., Schmidt, F. L., & Maurer, S. D. (1994). The validity of employment interviews: A comprehensive review and meta-analysis. *Journal of Applied Psychology, 79,* 599–616.

McFarland, L. A., Ryan, A. M., & Kriska, S. D. (2002). Field study investigation of applicant use of influence tactics in a selection interview. *Journal of Psychology, 136,* 383–398.

Meyer, J. W., & Rowan, B. (1977). Institutionalized organizations: Formal structure as myth and ceremony. *American Journal of Sociology, 83*, 340–363.

Miceli, N. S., Harvey, M., & Buckley, M. R. (2001). Potential discrimination in structured employment interviews. *Employee Responsibilities and Rights Journal, 13, 15–38.*

Middendorf, C. H., & Macan, T. H. (2002). Note-taking in the employment interview: Effects on recall and judgments. *Journal of Applied Psychology, 87*, 293–303.

Miller, V. D., & Jablin, F. M. (1991). Information seeking during organizational entry: Influence, tactics, and a model of the process. *Academy of Management Review, 16*, 92–120.

Monin, B., & Miller, D. T. (2001). Moral credentials and the expression of prejudice. *Journal of Personality and Social Psychology, 81*, 33–43.

Moscoso, S. (2000). A review of validity evidence, adverse impact and applicant reactions. *International Journal of Selection and Assessment, 8*, 237–247.

Motowidlo, S. J., & Burnett, J. R. (1995). Aural and visual sources of validity in structured employment interviews. *Organizational Behavior and Human Decision Processes, 61*, 239–249.

Nordstrom, C. R., Hall, R. J., & Bartels, L. K. (1998). First impressions versus good impressions: The effect of self-regulation on interview evaluations. *Journal of Psychology, 132*, 477–491.

Nyfield, G., & Baron, H. (2000). Cultural context in adapting selection practices across borders. In J. F. Kehoe (Ed.), *Managing selection in changing organizations: Human resource strategies* (pp. 242–270). San Francisco: Jossey-Bass.

Osborn, S. M., Field, H. S., & Veres, J. G. (1998). Introversion-extraversion, self-monitoring and applicant performance in a situational panel interview: A field study. *Journal of Business and Psychology, 13*, 143–156.

Parsons, C. K., Cable, D., & Wilkerson, J. M. (1999). Assessment of applicant work values through interviews: The impact of focus and functional relevance. *Journal of Occupational and Organizational Psychology, 72*, 561–566.

Parton, S. R., Siltanen, S. A., Hosman, L. A., & Langenderfer, J. (2002). Employment interviews outcomes and speech style effects. *Journal of Language and Social Psychology, 21*, 144–161.

Posthuma, R. A., Morgeson, F. P., & Campion, M. A. (2002). Beyond employment interview validity: A comprehensive narrative review of recent research and trends over time. *Personnel Psychology, 55*, 1–81.

Powell, R. S., & O'Neal, E. C. (1976). Communication feedback and duration as determinants of accuracy, confidence, and differentiation in interpersonal perception. *Journal of Personality and Social Psychology, 34*, 746–756.

Prewett-Livingston, A. J., Field, H. S., Veres, J. G., III, & Lewis, P. M. (1996). Effects of race on interview ratings in a situational panel interview. *Journal of Applied Psychology, 81*, 178–186.

Pulakos, E. D., & Schmitt, N. (1995). Experience-based and situational interview questions: Studies of validity. *Personnel Psychology, 48*, 289–308.

Ramsay, S., Gallois, C., & Callan, V. J. (1997). Social rules and attributions in the personnel selection interview. *Journal of Occupational and Organizational Psychology, 70*, 189–203.

Reich, D. A. (2001). Behavioral confirmation of generalized future-event expectancies: The moderating roles of perceivers' awareness of bias and targets' Expectancies. *Dissertation Abstracts International: Section B: The Sciences and Engineering, 61* (8-B), 4479.

Ridge, R. D., & Reber, J. S. (2002). "I think she's attracted to me": The effect of men's beliefs on women's behavior in a job interview scenario. *Basic and Applied Social Psychology, 24*, 1–14.

Roth, P. L., Van Iddekinge, C. H., Huffcutt, A. I., Eidson, C. E., Jr., & Bobko, P. (2002). Corrections for range restriction in structured interview ethnic group differences: The values may be larger than researchers thought. *Journal of Applied Psychology, 87*, 369–376.

Rowe, P. M. (1984). Decision processes in personnel selection. *Canadian Journal of Behavioral Science, 16*, 326–337.

Ryan, A. M., McFarland, L., Baron, H., & Page, R. (1999). An international look at selection practices: Nation and culture as explanations for variability in practice. *Personnel Psychology, 52,* 359–391.

Sacco, J. M., Scheu, C. R., Ryan, A. M., & Schmitt, N. (2003). An investigation of race and sex similarity effects in interviews: A multilevel approach to relational demography. *Journal of Applied Psychology, 88,* 852–865.

Salgado, J. F., Anderson, N., Moscoso, S., Bertua, C., De Fruyt, F., & Rolland, J. P. (2003). A meta-analytic study of general mental ability validity for different occupations in the European community. *Journal of Applied Psychology, 88,* 1068–1081.

Schuler, H. (1993). Social validity of selection situations: A concept and some empirical results. In H. Schuler, J. L. Farr, & M. Smith (Eds.), *Personnel selection and assessment: Individual and organizational perspectives* (pp. 11–26). Hillsdale, NJ: Lawrence Erlbaum.

Schwab, D. P., & Heneman, H. G. (1969). Relationship between interview structure and interviewer reliability in an employment situation. *Journal of Applied Psychology, 53,* 214–217.

Sears, G. J., & Rowe, P. M. (2003). A personality-based similar-to-me effect in the employment interview: Conscientiousness, affect-versus competence-mediated interpretations, and the role of job relevance. *Canadian Journal of Behavioural Science, 35,* 13–24.

Silvester, J. (1997). Spoken attributions and candidate success in graduate recruitment interviews. *Journal of Occupational and Organizational Psychology, 70,* 61–73.

Silvester, J., & Anderson, N. (2003). Technology and discourse: A comparison of face-to-face and telephone employment interviews. *International Journal of Selection and Assessment, 11,* 206–214.

Silvester, J., Anderson, N., Haddleton, E., Cunningham-Snell, N., & Gibb, A. (2000). A cross-modal comparison of telephone and face-to-face selection/interviews in graduate recruitment. *International Journal of Selection and Assessment, 8,* 16–21.

Silvester, J., Anderson-Gough, F. M., Anderson, N. R., & Mohamed, A. R. (2002). Locus of control, attributions and impression management in the selection interview. *Journal of Occupational and Organizational Psychology, 75,* 59–76.

Spence, L. J., & Petrick, J. A. (2000). Multinational interview decisions: Integrity capacity and competing values. *Human Resource Management Journal, 10,* 49–67.

Stevens, C. K. (1997). Effects of preinterview beliefs on applicants' reactions to campus interviews. *Academy of Management Journal, 40,* 947–966.

Stevens, C. K. (1998). Antecedents of interview interactions, interviewers' ratings, and applicants' reactions. *Personnel Psychology, 51,* 55–85.

Stevens, C. K., & Kristof, A. L. (1995). Making the right impression: A field study of applicant impression management during job interviews. *Journal of Applied Psychology, 80,* 587–606.

Straus, S. G., Miles, J. A., & Levesque, L. L. (2001). The effects of videoconference, telephone, and face-to-face media on interviewer and applicant judgments in employment interviews. *Journal of Management, 27,* 363–381.

Taylor, P. J., & Small, B. (2002). Asking applicants what they would do versus what they did do: A meta-analytic comparison of situational and past behaviour employment interview questions. *Journal of Occupational and Organizational Psychology, 75,* 277–294.

Thoms, P., McMasters, R., Roberts, M. R., & Dombkowski, D. A. (1999). Resume characteristics as predictors of an invitation to interview. *Journal of Business and Psychology, 13,* 339–356.

Tullar, W. L. (1989). Relational control in the employment interview. *Journal of Applied Psychology, 74,* 971–977.

van Dam, K. (2003). Trait perception in the employment interview: A five-factor model perspective. *International Journal of Selection and Assessment, 11,* 43–55.

Vance, R. J., Kuhnert, K. W., & Farr, J. L. (1978). Interview judgments: Using external criteria to compose behavioral and graphic ratings. *Organizational Behavior and Human Performance, 22,* 279–294.

Wade, K. J., & Kinicki, A. J. (1997). Subjective applicant qualifications and interpersonal attraction as mediators within a process model of interview selection decisions. *Journal of Vocational Behavior, 50*, 23–40.

Wiesner, W. H., & Cronshaw, S. F. (1988). A meta-analytic investigation of the impact of interview format and degree of structure on the validity of the employment interview. *Journal of Occupational Psychology, 61*, 275–290.

Wright, G. E., & Multon, K. D. (1995). Employer's perceptions of nonverbal communication in job interviews for persons with physical disabilities. *Journal of Vocational Behavior, 47*, 214–227.

Wright, P. M., McMahan, G. C., & McWilliams, A. (1994). Human resources and sustained competitive advantage: A resource-based perspective. *International Journal of Human Resource Management, 5*, 301–327.

Young, A. M., & Kacmar, K. M. (1998). ABCs of the interview: The role of affective, behavioral, and cognitive responses by applicants in the employment interview. *International Journal of Selection and Assessment, 6*, 211–221.

7

Cognitive Ability in Personnel Selection Decisions

Deniz S. Ones, Chockalingam Viswesvaran,
and Stephan Dilchert

Cognitive ability (CA) or intelligence testing has been hailed "as the most practical contribution made to humanity by all of psychology (e.g., Cronbach, 1960)" (Roberts, Markham, Matthews, & Zeidner, in press). Spearman's paper from 100 years ago, "'General Intelligence', Objectively Determined and Measured," was the initial turning point in directing attention to the construct of CA. Fascinating, detailed historical reviews of CA testing may be found in Carroll (1993) and Roberts et al. (in press).

CA is unique as a construct in that a century of scientific research has shown that it predicts an extensive range of important behaviors and life outcomes such as academic achievement, health-related behaviors, moral delinquency, socioeconomic status, racial prejudice, divorce, accident proneness, occupational status and even death, among others (see Brand, 1987; Gottfredson, 1997b; Jensen, 1998; Lubinski, 2000; Ree & Carretta, 2002; Schmidt, 2002, for reviews of variables that are related to cognitive ability). CA is perhaps the most important individual differences determinant of work performance (Viswesvaran & Ones, 2002). As such, the broad societal value of CA is undeniable. Yet, ability testing has had a checkered history in psychological sciences. Nevertheless, the mountain of data accumulated in applied psychology supports the pragmatic usefulness of cognitive ability tests. Attesting to the durability and usefulness of the construct, CA tests have been utilized as predictors in selection settings for approximately the past 100 years.

Our main objective in this chapter is to provide an overview of the vast literature on CA tests in selection contexts. We first discuss the unique status of CA in selection, and clarify its psychometric and psychological meaning. We then review information on the prevalence of CA test use in personnel selection from around the world. We also discuss acceptability of ability testing and applicant reactions. Next, we review the evidence supporting the use of CA tests for selection by summarizing results from meta-analyses examining their criterion-related validity in occupational settings, across national boundaries. The overwhelming evidence suggests that CA tests are predictive of job performance across jobs and cultures. Given this conclusion, we explore the causal mechanisms through which CA comes to influence job performance. Next, we briefly note research on race, ethnic group, gender, and age differences on CA tests and their implications for adverse impact. We conclude our chapter with a discussion of current and new directions for research on CA, including the assessment of CA using various selection methods such as interviews, assessment centers, situational judgment tests (SJTs), and newly proposed intelligences (such as practical intelligence, emotional intelligence, etc.).

Several terms such as CA, general mental ability, and *g*-factor have been used to refer to the same construct (Viswesvaran & Ones, 2002). We use the term cognitive ability to refer to the construct domain covered by tests of CA. We reserve the terms *g* and general mental ability (GMA) to refer to the general factor that spans across CA tests.

PREVALENCE OF USE AND ACCEPTANCE

Attitudes toward cognitive ability testing

Despite widespread recognition of CA's importance, varying attitudes toward the use of CA measures in personnel selection exist. A number of studies have investigated applicants' reactions toward various personnel selection methods, including paper-and-pencil-based tests of GMA and specific abilities, in different countries (for a review see Anderson, Born, & Cunningham-Snell, 2001). CA measures tend to receive moderate favorability ratings from applicants as well as the general population. Fairness ratings of selection methods might be strongly influenced by perceived job-relatedness of the measures. In general, selection measures with apparent job-relatedness (e.g., work sample tests) as well as measures that have high perceived job-relatedness (e.g., assessment centers, interviews) are judged more favorably (i.e., as fair and valid) by job candidates than are paper-and-pencil tests of CA (Marcus, 2003; Smither, Reilly, Millsap, Pearlman, & Stoffey, 1993; Steiner & Gilliland, 1996). Lounsbury, Borrow, and Jensen (1989), in a phone survey among 546 participants, found that positive attitudes toward employment testing increase when people are told how a test relates to job performance. Also, a moderating factor in the acceptability of CA tests seems to be item specificity of instruments, with tests that contain more concrete items being perceived as more job related than abstract tests (Rynes & Connerley, 1993; Smither et al., 1993).

Applicants also express a preference for specific ability tests. Schmidt (2002) notes that a focus on specific abilities might lead testees to believe that they can find their own niche ability (i.e., some ability to score high on). This, of course, is a fallacy, as specific abilities are positively correlated, giving rise to a general ability factor.

Prevalence of cognitive ability tests in personnel selection

Although there is evidence that ratings of acceptability of CA measures show at least some stability across countries (Anderson et al., 2001), the extent of their use varies considerably. Salgado, Viswesvaran, and Ones (2001) summarized recent surveys of organizations in the USA, Canada, Australia, and across Europe. Proportions of companies using CA measures for means of personnel selection ranged from below 10% to as much as above 70% of organizations surveyed. Salgado and Anderson (2002) reviewed the available studies and surveys across the European community and, using data from Ryan, McFarland, Baron, and Page (1999), established a rank order among European countries and the USA with regard to frequency of cognitive test use. Surprisingly, their results indicate that test use is less prevalent in the United States than in many European countries (the USA ranking only 15th among 18 countries for which data were available). They attribute this to be a possible effect of the ongoing debate over group differences in CA and resulting adverse impact that is much more dominant in the USA than in Europe. However, results of such surveys should be viewed with some caution. As Salgado and Anderson (2002) point out, the range of frequency differences in test use varies considerably by level of applicant group (e.g., graduate and managerial level versus general selection). Also, as the summary by Anderson et al. (2001) shows, there is a notable difference in use of general CA tests versus tests of specific aptitudes. Where the information was available, studies included in their review showed that specific aptitude tests see wider use than do tests of GMA. This trend might be attributable to the higher perceived job-relatedness of specific versus general measures of CA. Generalizing the existing evidence from the available surveys and reviews, it appears that CA measures see wide use across countries, yet the frequency of their use in comparison to other selection instruments is disproportionately low, considering their comparatively high predictive validities.

Definitions

Cognitive ability can be described as a fundamental reasoning capability (Cattell, 1943). It incorporates the components of ability to learn and adapt (Jensen, 1980; Schmidt, 2002; Sternberg & Detterman, 1986; Terman, 1916). Its core appears to be complex information processing capability (see Stankov, in press). Flynn (1987) interprets this capability as "real-world problem solving ability" (p. 188).

A group of 52 experts on CA have converged on the following definition of the construct:

> Intelligence is a very general mental capability that, among other things, involves the ability to reason, plan, solve problems, think abstractly, comprehend complex ideas, learn quickly and learn from experience. It is not merely book learning, a narrow academic skill, or test-taking smarts. Rather, it reflects a broader and deeper capability for comprehending our surroundings – "catching on," "making sense" of things, or "figuring out" what to do. (Gottfredson, 1997a, p. 13)

Psychometric meaning

CA test scores are highly correlated with each other. For example, while verbal and quantitative ability tests correlate in the .70s–.80s among themselves, correlations between them are "only .10 to .20 smaller than are the within-trait correlations" (Drasgow, 2003, p. 110). Intercorrelations among a multitude of CA measures exhibit what is referred to as a positive manifold. A positive manifold arises as a consequence of a general factor of CA (Spearman, 1904). Despite widely varying content across cognitive tests (e.g., remembering words, doing arithmetic, estimating lengths), the same common, general factor heavily influences performance on all of them. Most of the variance in ability batteries is due to a general factor called g or general mental ability (see Jensen, 1998; Ree & Carretta, 2002).

This result has been found for both paper-and-pencil tests and computerized cognitive tests (Kranzler & Jensen, 1991; Kyllonen, 1993). GMA can be regarded as a general information processing capacity and is typically extracted as the first unrotated factor from a battery of specific ability tests. Although a single general factor is responsible for explaining much of the association among CA tests, it is not sufficient. Incidentally, general factors emerging from a broad variety of CA measures are highly correlated (Johnson, Bouchard, Krueger, McGue, & Gottesman, 2004). Group factors such as quantitative and verbal ability and specific factors are needed to more accurately model scores on CA tests.

Organization of abilities

Scores on CA tests co-vary due to a general factor. Yet, the structure of the CA domain is hierarchical (Carroll, 1993; Spearman, 1904). Different measures of CA show different levels of saturation with, or loadings on, a general factor. This general factor lies at the apex of the CA hierarchy (Stratum III, Carroll, 1993), representing the communality among measures of cognitive abilities. At the next level are group factors such as fluid intelligence, crystallized intelligence, memory, visual perception, auditory perception, retrieval, cognitive speed, and processing speed (Stratum II, Carroll, 1993). At the next lower level, first-order common factors may be found (Stratum I, Carroll, 1993). For example, verbal ability, reading comprehension, and lexical knowledge are located among the Stratum I factors related to crystallized intelligence. On the other hand, deduction, induction, and quantitative reasoning are examples of Stratum I factors related to fluid intelligence (i.e., "basic processes of reasoning and other mental activities that depend only minimally on learning and acculturation"; Carroll, 1993, p. 624). First-order factors include specific components unique to a test or limited set of tests and they cannot be measured without simultaneously measuring g (Spearman, 1937). It is worth noting that numerous first-order factors can be identified. That is, responses to CA test items can be interpreted as assessing successively more specific abilities. However, as Kelley (1939) aptly recognized, "evidence of existence of a factor" should not be "cited as evidence that it is important" (p. 141). Fractionated or splintered factors may or may not be important in prediction and explanation. "Only those group factors shown to have significant practical value in daily life are worth incorporating in the picture" (Vernon, 1950, p. 25).

Nature of the construct and psychological meaning

Often, scholarly critics of CA tests refer to "psychometric g" as though the construct is ephemeral and can only be defined and described as a psychometric entity. However, there is a psychological meaning that can be attached to the GMA construct.

Gottfredson (2004) defines GMA as a "highly general ability to learn, reason and solve problems" (p. 175). It is a general-purpose ability that spans across cognitive abilities such as problem solving, conceptual thinking, learning, and reasoning. Fluid intelligence "reflects basic abilities in reasoning and related higher mental processes," while crystallized intelligence "reflects the extent of an individual's base of knowledge" (Drasgow, 2003, p. 114). Individuals are born with capacities to reason and learn; however, these capacities are invested in "all kinds of complex learning situations" leading to the acquisition of different crystallized abilities (Cattell, 1971, p. 118).

At the heart of GMA is the ability to process information. In information processing models of CA, performance on cognitive tasks, including producing responses to test items, is a function of four processes: declarative knowledge, procedural knowledge, cognitive processing speed, and working memory capacity (Kyllonen & Christal, 1989, 1990). Given the widespread applicability of GMA, more research should be directed at understanding its theoretical underpinnings (Campbell, 1996; Lubinski, 2000). In the personnel selection arena, criterion-related validities offer some evidence on the psychological import of the construct.

CRITERION-RELATED VALIDITY

Criterion-related validity is relied on to demonstrate the usefulness of CA tests in applied settings. It is one line of evidence in showing the job relatedness of the CA construct. Over the past century, thousands of studies have been carried out aiming to document the criterion-related validity of CA tests for predicting behaviors, performances, and outcomes in both educational and organizational settings. Up until the mid-1970s, it was believed that validities of CA tests varied widely even for the same test and the same job across settings. The doctrine of situational specificity (cf., Hunter & Schmidt, 1976; Schmidt & Hunter, 1998, for details) was invoked to assert the uniqueness of each situation and conclude that findings from one situation could not be transported or generalized to other situations.

Hunter and Schmidt (1976) pointed out that observed criterion-related validities will deviate from their population value due to the distorting effects of statistical artifacts such as sampling error, criterion unreliability, and range restriction (see Hunter & Schmidt, 1990, for a description of statistical artifacts). Psychometric meta-analysis was invented to estimate the population values of validities and to determine how much of the observed variability in validities across studies is due to sampling error variance and variability attributable to differences in other artifacts. The first applications of the technique revealed that the criterion-related validity of CA tests has been systematically and severely underestimated in individual studies and that criterion-related validities can be transported across situations and settings (i.e., validity generalizes) (Schmidt & Hunter, 1977). Numerous additional meta-analyses have examined the validities of CA tests and results have repeatedly disconfirmed the situational specificity hypothesis. To provide an accurate overview of this momentous literature, we summarize results from dozens of CA meta-analyses reported to date. We also include results from large-scale investigations.

Predicting learning

CA tests are demonstrably useful in predicting learning in both educational settings and job training. The results consistently indicate that CA measures are valid for predicting learning in education (Kuncel, Hezlett, & Ones, 2001, 2004). Relationships between CA test scores and learning have also been documented in meta-analyses of ability test validities for job training performance.

CA is the main individual differences trait that predicts the successful acquisition of job knowledge. Training constitutes a major activity that is unquestionably linked to learning. Table 7.1 summarizes the results from meta-analyses that have examined the criterion-related validity of CA tests for training performance. Across the 17 meta-analyses summarized in Table 7.1, training performance was most commonly assessed through supervisory ratings of training success or through training course grades. Both these assessments during training tap into the amount of job knowledge acquired during training. Meta-analytic validity estimates have been reported for GMA as well as for specific ability measures. The results summarized are across different jobs, industries and countries.

Criterion-related validities of quantitative and verbal abilities as well as GMA are high, ranging from the high .30s to .70s. A comparison of the criterion-related validity of GMA vis-à-vis specific abilities indicates that GMA has at least as much if not larger predictive value than its dimensions, both for single job families and across jobs and settings. For GMA tests, the validities for training performance converge around the .50–.60 range. An important trend to note in the data is that the validity of CA tests for learning cognitively demanding tasks is higher than learning for relatively simple tasks. Criterion-related validities tend to increase for higher levels of complexity (Hunter, 1983b; Salgado et al., 2003).

Predicting job performance

Jobs have knowledge and information processing demands that necessitate the use of cognitive abilities in performing work behaviors (Reeve & Hakel, 2002). Job performance is perhaps the most important criterion in all of industrial, work and organizational psychology (see Viswesvaran & Ones, Chapter 16, this volume). Most of our efforts in selection, training, and other organizational interventions aim to influence this important variable. It is perhaps for this reason that the largest numbers of primary studies examining the criterion-related validities of CA tests have been conducted for the criterion of job performance. Hence, several meta-analyses have been carried out on the criterion-related validity of CA tests for predicting job performance. These are summarized in Table 7.2. Across the analyses, supervisory ratings have been most relied on in measuring job performance, although objective measures of task performance (e.g., counts of output) have also been utilized.

Validities for predicting job performance are somewhat lower than those for predicting training success. This is to be expected, as training success is a more proximal outcome of learning and is therefore better predicted by CA, which has often been referred to as "the ability to learn" (Schmidt, 2002, p. 188). On the other hand, general CA has been linked to job performance through the key construct of job knowledge. As such, it is a more distal determinant of performance than of learning. Nevertheless, GMA and more specific abilities display substantial correlations with job performance. For large-scale investigations, across heterogeneous jobs, the estimates of operational validity converge around .50.

Table 7.2 is organized such that a comparison of the operational validities that have been reported for GMA versus specific abilities is possible. Large-scale meta-analyses reveal

TABLE 7.1 Meta-analytic findings summarizing the validity of CA tests for learning in job training

Study	Predictor	Job/setting	N	k	ρ	SD_ρ	80% CI	
Hunter (1983b)	GMA	Heterogeneous jobs	6,496	90	.55	.16	.37	– .74
Salgado et al. (2003a) which	GMA	Heterogeneous jobs, Europe	16,065	97	.54	.19	.30	– .78
Salgado & Anderson (2002)	GMA	Heterogeneous jobs, Spain	2,405	25	.47	.17	.25	– .69
Salgado & Anderson (2002)	GMA	Heterogeneous jobs, UK	20,305	61	.56	.08	.46	– .66
Salgado & Anderson (2002)	GMA	Heterogeneous jobs, Spain + UK	22,710	86	.53	.09	.41	– .65
Hunter (1985)	GMA	Heterogeneous jobs; military	472,539	828	.62[a]			.65
Hunter (1983b)	GMA	High CJ	235	4	.65	.00	.65	– .65
Hartigan & Wigdor (1989)	GMA	High CJ	64		.60[b,c]			
Salgado et al. (2003b)	GMA	High CJ; Europe	2,619	13	.74	.00	.74	– .74
Hunter (1983b)	GMA	Moderately high CJ	1,863	24	.50	.20	.29	– .71
Hunter (1983b)	GMA	Medium CJ	3,823	54	.57	.16	.36	– .78
Hartigan & Wigdor (1989)	GMA	Medium CJ	347		.33[b,c]			
Salgado et al. (2003b)	GMA	Medium CJ; Europe	4,304	35	.53	.22	.25	– .81
Hunter (1983b)	GMA	Moderately low CJ	575	8	.54	.04	.49	– .59
Hartigan & Wigdor (1989)	GMA	Moderately low CJ	3,169		.40[b,c]			
Hartigan & Wigdor (1989)	GMA	Low CJ	106		.00[b,c]			
Salgado et al. (2003b)	GMA	Low CJ; Europe	4,731	21	.36	.15	.17	– .55
Salgado et al. (2003b)	GMA	Apprentices, Europe	1,229	9	.49	.08	.39	– .59
Salgado et al. (2003b)	GMA	Chemical workers, Europe	1,514	4	.72	.00	.72	– .72
Pearlman et al. (1980)	GMA	Clerical jobs	32,157	65	.71	.12	.56	– .86
Hunter (1985)	GMA	Clerical jobs; military	42,832	104	.58[a]			.48
Salgado et al. (2003b)	GMA	Drivers, Europe	2,252	9	.40	.06	.32	– .48
Salgado et al. (2003b)	GMA	Electrical Assistants, Europe	353	4	.63	.12	.48	– .78
Hunter (1985)	GMA	Electronic jobs; military	92,758	160	.67[a]			.78
Salgado et al. (2003b)	GMA	Engineers, Europe	1,051	8	.74	.00	.74	– .74
Hunter (1985)	GMA	General technical jobs; military	180,806	287	.62[a]			.74
Salgado et al. (2003b)	GMA	Information jobs, Europe	579	4	.69	.00	.69	– .69

TABLE 7.1 *Continued*

Study	Predictor	Job/setting	N	k	ρ	SD_p	80% CI	
Hunter (1985)	GMA	Mechanical jobs; military	156,143	277	.62[a]			
Salgado et al. (2003b)	GMA	Mechanics, Europe	549	4	.40	.08	.30	– .50
Callender & Osburn (1981)	GMA	Petroleum industry	1,694	14	.54	.00	.54	– .54
Salgado et al. (2003b)	GMA	Policemen, Europe	392	3	.25	.26	-.08	– .58
Salgado et al. (2003b)	GMA	Skilled workers, Europe	2,276	12	.27	.12	.12	– .42
Salgado et al. (2003b)	GMA	Typists, Europe	1,651	12	.57	.26	.24	– .90
Hirsh et al. (1986)	Verbal + RA	Policemen and detectives	1,151	7	.71	.00	.71	– .71
Barrett et al. (1999)	Cognitive + mechanical comprehension	Firefighters	1,027	9	.77	.12	.62	– .92
Sager et al. (1997)	Computerized cognitive ability battery	17 jobs; military		17	.73[a]			
Schmidt et al. (1981)	Arithmetic reasoning	35 jobs, time 1; military	10,488	35	.56[a]	.12[a]	.41	– .71
Schmidt et al. (1981)	Arithmetic reasoning	35 jobs, time 2; military	10,534	35	.57[a]	.14[a]	.39	– .75
Callender & Osburn (1981)	Arithmetic reasoning	Petroleum industry	1,378	13	.52	.15	.33	– .71
Salgado et al. (2003a)	QA	Heterogeneous jobs, Europe	10,860	58	.48	.18	.25	– .71
Pearlman et al. (1980)	QA	Clerical jobs	50,751	107	.70	.12	.55	– .85
Hirsh et al. (1986)	QA	Police and detectives	1,206	9	.63	.20	.37	– .89
Pearlman et al. (1980)	RA	Clerical jobs	4,928	25	.39	.18	.16	– .62
Kuncel et al. (2004)	RA	Internships in graduate school	300	4	.22	.00	.22	– .22
Hirsh et al. (1986)	RA	Police and detectives	4,374	24	.61	.11	.47	– .75
Salgado et al. (2003a)	VA	Heterogeneous jobs, Europe	11,123	58	.44	.19	.20	– .68
Pearlman et al. (1980)	VA	Clerical jobs	44,478	102	.64	.13	.47	– .81
Hirsh et al. (1986)	VA	Police and detectives	3,943	26	.64	.21	.37	– .91
Schmidt et al. (1981)	Vocabulary	35 jobs, time 1; military	10,488	35	.51[a]	.11[a]	.37	– .65
Schmidt et al. (1981)	Vocabulary	35 jobs, time 2; military	10,534	35	.52[a]	.13[a]	.35	– .69
Verive & McDaniel (1996)	Short-term memory test	Heterogeneous jobs	16,521	35	.49	.09	.37	– .61
Salgado et al. (2003a)	Memory	Heterogeneous jobs, Europe	3,323	15	.34	.20	.08	– .60

Study	Predictor	Criterion	N	k	ρ	SD_ρ	80% CI	
Hirsh et al. (1986)	Memory	Police and detectives	801	6	.41	.00	.41	.41
Schmidt et al. (1981)	Automotive information	35 jobs, time 1; military	10,488	35	.41[a]	.15[a]	.22	.60
Schmidt et al. (1981)	Automotive information	35 jobs, time 2; military	10,534	35	.38[a]	.18[a]	.15	.61
Callender & Osburn (1981)	Chemical comprehension	Petroleum industry	1,378	13	.47	.00	.47	.47
Schmidt et al. (1981)	Clerical speed	35 jobs, time 1; military	10,488	35	.39[a]	.10[a]	.26	.52
Schmidt et al. (1981)	Clerical speed	35 jobs, time 2; military	10,534	35	.42[a]	.12[a]	.27	.57
Schmidt et al. (1981)	Electronics information	35 jobs, time 1; military	10,488	35	.45[a]	.10[a]	.32	.58
Schmidt et al. (1981)	Electronics information	35 jobs, time 2; military	10,534	35	.44[a]	.13[a]	.27	.61
Schmidt et al. (1981)	Mechanical aptitude	35 jobs, time 1; military	10,488	35	.51[a]	.10[a]	.38	.64
Schmidt et al. (1981)	Mechanical aptitude	35 jobs, time 2; military	10,534	35	.50[a]	.11[a]	.36	.64
Barrett et al. (1999)	Mechanical comprehension	Firefighters	869	5	.62	.17	.40	.84
Callender & Osburn (1981)	Mechanical comprehension	Petroleum industry	1,419	11	.52	.07	.43	.61
Schmidt et al. (1981)	Radio information	35 jobs, time 1; military	10,488	35	.32[a]	.11[a]	.18	.46
Schmidt et al. (1981)	Radio information	35 jobs, time 2; military	10,534	35	.32[a]	.13[a]	.15	.49
Schmidt et al. (1981)	Radiocode aptitude	35 jobs, time 1; military	10,488	35	.34[a]	.04[a]	.29	.39
Schmidt et al. (1981)	Radiocode aptitude	35 jobs, time 2; military	10,534	35	.35[a]	.04[a]	.30	.40
Schmidt et al. (1981)	Shop mechanics	35 jobs, time 1; military	10,488	35	.48[a]	.14[a]	.30	.66
Schmidt et al. (1981)	Shop mechanics	35 jobs, time 2; military	10,534	35	.48[a]	.13[a]	.31	.65
Schmidt et al. (1980)	Programmer aptitude test	Computer programmers	1,635	9	.91	.17	.69	1.00
Barrett et al. (1999)	Cognitive ability – unspecified	Firefighters	2,007	14	.77	.03	.73	.81
Levine et al. (1996)	Cognitive ability – unspecified	Craft jobs; utility industry	5,872	52	.67	.00	.67	.67
Vineberg & Joyner (1982)	Aptitude – unspecified	Military		51	.27			

Note: N = total sample size; k = number of studies; ρ = estimate of operational validity; SD_ρ = standard deviation of ρ; 80% CI = 80% credibility interval. CJ = complexity jobs; QA = quantitative ability; RA = reasoning ability; VA = verbal ability.
[a] Not corrected for unreliability in the criterion. [b] Not corrected for range restriction. [c] Corrected for criterion unreliability using conservative criterion reliability estimates.

TABLE 7.2   Meta-analytic findings summarizing the validity of cognitive abilities for predicting job performance

Study	Predictor	Criterion	Job/setting	N	k	ρ	SD_p	80% CI	
Hunter (1983b) a and b	GMA	JP	Heterogeneous jobs		515	.47	.12	.31	– .63
Hunter (1983b)	GMA	JP	Heterogeneous jobs	32,124	425	.45	.08	.34	– .56
Salgado & Anderson (2002)	GMA	JP	Heterogeneous jobs, Spain	1,239	9	.61	.00	.61	– .61
Salgado & Anderson (2002)	GMA	JP	Heterogeneous jobs, UK	7,283	45	.41	.23	.12	– .70
Salgado & Anderson (2002)	GMA	JP	Heterogeneous jobs, Spain + UK	8,522	54	.42	.23	.13	– .71
Hunter (1983b)	GMA	JP	High CJ	1,114	17	.56	.03	.52	– .60
Hartigan & Wigdor (1989)	GMA	JP	High CJ	3,900		.17[a,b]			
Hunter (1983b)	GMA	JP	Moderately high CJ	2,455	36	.58	.15	.38	– .78
Hartigan & Wigdor (1989)	GMA	JP	Moderately high CJ	200		.21[a,b]			
Hunter (1983b)	GMA	JP	Medium CJ	12,933	151	.51	.15	.31	– .69
Hartigan & Wigdor (1989)	GMA	JP	Medium CJ	630		.28[a,b]			
Hunter (1983b)	GMA	JP	Moderately low CJ	14,403	201	.40	.03	.36	– .44
Hartigan & Wigdor (1989)	GMA	JP	Moderately low CJ	19,206		.23[a,b]			
Hartigan & Wigdor (1989)	GMA	JP	Low CJ	10,862		.20[a,b]			
Hunter (1983b)	GMA	JP	Low CJ	1,219	20	.23	.06	.15	– .31
Pearlman et al. (1980)	GMA	JP	Clerical jobs	17,539	194	.52	.24	.21	– .83
Schmidt et al. (1979b)	GMA	JP	Clerical jobs	5,433	58	.49	.21	.22	– .76
Schmidt et al. (1979b)	GMA	JP	Clerical jobs	3,986	65	.61	.36	.15	– 1.00
Schmidt et al. (1979b)	GMA	JP	First-line Supervisors	5,143	75	.64	.23	.35	– .93
Callender & Osburn (1981)	GMA	JP	Petroleum industry jobs	3,219	37	.32	.13	.15	– .49
Schmidt et al. (1981a)	GMA	JP	Petroleum maintenance workers	821	13	.30	.18	.07	– .53

Study		Criterion	Sample	N	k					
Schmidt et al. (1981a)	GMA	JP	Petroleum operators	1,486	16	.26	.19	.02	—	.50
Salgado et al. (2003a)	GMA	SR	Heterogeneous jobs; Europe	9,554	93	.62	.19	.38	—	.86
Salgado et al. (2003b)	GMA	SR	High CJ; Europe	1,604	14	.64	.24	.33	—	.95
Salgado et al. (2003b)	GMA	SR	Medium CJ; Europe	4,744	43	.53	.26	.20	—	.86
Salgado et al. (2003b)	GMA	SR	Low complexity job; Europe	864	12	.51	.10	.38	—	.64
Nathan & Alexander (1988)[c]	GMA	SR	Clerical jobs	11,987	142	.44[a,d]	.20[a,d]	.18	—	.70
Salgado et al. (2003b)	GMA	SR	Drivers; Europe	394	5	.45	.19	.21	—	.69
Salgado et al. (2003b)	GMA	SR	Electrical assistants; Europe	280	3	.54	.17	.32	—	.76
Salgado et al. (2003b)	GMA	SR	Engineers; Europe	837	9	.63	.00	.63	—	.63
Salgado et al. (2003b)	GMA	SR	Information clerks; Europe	890	5	.61	.00	.61	—	.61
Salgado et al. (2003b)	GMA	SR	Managers; Europe	783	6	.67	.41	.15	—	1.00
Salgado et al. (2003b)	GMA	SR	Police; Europe	619	5	.24	.15	.05	—	.43
Vinchur et al. (1998)	GMA	SR	Salespeople	1,770	25	.31	.12	.20	—	.46
Vinchur et al. (1998)	GMA	SR	Salespeople	1,231	22	.40		.27	—	.53
Salgado et al. (2003b)	GMA	SR	Salespeople; Europe	394	5	.66	.00	.66	—	.66
Salgado et al. (2003b)	GMA	SR	Skilled workers; Europe	994	7	.55	.00	.55	—	.55
Salgado et al. (2003b)	GMA	SR	Typists; Europe	1,870	23	.45	.26	.12	—	.78
Schmitt et al. (1984)	GMA	Performance ratings	Heterogeneous jobs	3,597	25	.22[e]	.10[e]	.09	—	.35
Martinussen (1996)	GMA	Global performance	Pilots; mostly military	15,403	26	.16[e]	.10[e]	.03	—	.29
Schmidt & Hunter (1977)	GMA	Proficiency	Clerical jobs		72	.67				
McHenry et al. (1990)	GMA	Soldiering proficiency	Heterogeneous jobs; military	4,039	9	.65[f]				
McHenry et al. (1990)	GMA	Effort and leadership	Heterogeneous jobs; military	4,039	9	.31[f]				
McHenry et al. (1990)	GMA	Fitness + bearing	Heterogeneous jobs; military	4,039	9	.20[f]				
McHenry et al. (1990)	GMA	Personal discipline	Heterogeneous jobs; military	4,039	9	.16[f]				
Nathan & Alexander (1988)[c]	GMA	Ranking	Clerical jobs	689	12	.66[a,d]	.33[a,d]	.24	—	1.00

TABLE 7.2 Continued

Study	Predictor	Criterion	Job/setting	N	k	ρ	SD_ρ	80% CI	
Funke et al. (1987)	GMA	Research achievement	Research and science	949	11	.16[a]	.07[a]	.07 —	.25
McHenry et al. (1990)	GMA	Technical proficiency	Heterogeneous jobs; military	4,039	9	.63[f]			
Schmitt et al. (1984)	GMA	Status change	Heterogeneous jobs	21,190	9	.28[e]	.09[e]	.16 —	.40
Nathan & Alexander (1988)[c]	GMA	Production quality	Clerical jobs	438	6	–.01[a,d]	.02[a,d]	–.04 —	.02
Nathan & Alexander (1988)[c]	GMA	Production quantity	Clerical jobs	1,116	22	.35[a,d]	.13[a,d]	.18 —	.52
Nathan & Alexander (1988)[c]	GMA	Work sample	Clerical jobs	747	9	.60[a,d]	.34[a,d]	.16 —	1.00
Schmitt et al. (1984)	GMA	Work sample	Heterogeneous jobs	1,793	3	.43[e]	.07[e]	.34 —	.52
Barrett et al. (1999)	Cognitive + mechanical	SR	Firefighters	3,637	23	.56	.12	.41 —	.71
Hunter & Hunter (1984)	Ability composite	SR	Entry-level jobs	32,124	425	.53	.15	.34 —	.72
Schmidt et al. (1980)	Programmer aptitude test	Proficiency	Computer programmers	1299	42	.73	.27	.38 —	1.00
Callender & Osburn (1981)	Arithmetic reasoning	JP	Petroleum industry jobs	1,850	25	.20	.20	–.06 —	.46
Schmidt et al. (1981a)	Arithmetic reasoning	JP	Petroleum maintenance workers	628	11	.15	.16	–.05 —	.35
Schmidt et al. (1981a)	Arithmetic reasoning	JP	Petroleum operators	1,067	12	.26	.20	.00 —	.52
Schmidt et al. (1980)	Arithmetic reasoning	Proficiency	Computer programmers	535	33	.57	.34	.13 —	1.00
Schmidt et al. (1979b)	QA	JP	Clerical jobs	12,368	130	.51	.10	.38 —	.64
Schmidt et al. (1979b)	QA	JP	Clerical jobs	10,631	140	.52	.15	.33 —	.71
Pearlman et al. (1980)	QA	JP	Clerical jobs	39,584	453	.47	.14	.29 —	.65
Hirsh et al. (1986)	QA	JP	Police and detectives	1,188	8	.26	.18	.03 —	.49
Salgado et al. (2003a)	QA	SR	Heterogeneous jobs; Europe	5,241	48	.52	.00	.52 —	.52
Vinchur et al. (1998)	QA	SR	Salespeople	783	6	.12	.09	.06 —	.24
Nathan & Alexander (1988)[c]	QA	SR	Clerical jobs	24,913	284	.40[a,d]	.11[a,d]	.26 —	.54

Nathan & Alexander (1988)[c]	QA	Ranking	Clerical jobs	1,392	32	.64[a,d]	.14[a,d]	.46	—	.82
Nathan & Alexander (1988)[c]	QA	Production quality	Clerical jobs	647	12	.17[a,d]	.30[a,d]	-.21	—	.55
Nathan & Alexander (1988)[c]	QA	Production quantity	Clerical jobs	630	15	.44[a,d]	.02[a,d]	.41	—	.47
Nathan & Alexander (1988)[c]	QA	Work sample	Clerical jobs	1,114	15	.55[a,d]	.02[a,d]	.52	—	.58
Pearlman et al. (1980)	RA	JP	Clerical jobs	11,586	116	.39	.15	.20	—	.58
Kuncel et al. (2004)	RA	JP	Graduate School	598	7	.41	.12	.26	—	.56
Hirsh et al. (1986)	RA	JP	Police and detectives	3,175	29	.17	.07	.08	—	.26
Kuncel et al. (2004)	RA	Potential ratings	Graduate School	494	11	.37	.00	.37	—	.37
Kuncel et al. (2004)	RA	Counseling potential	Graduate School	192	6	.49	.00	.49	—	.49
Kuncel et al. (2004)	RA	Counseling work sample	Graduate School	92	2	.51	.00	.51	—	.51
Kuncel et al. (2004)	RA	Administrative perf.	Graduate School	225	10	.27	.15	.08	—	.46
Kuncel et al. (2004)	RA	Ratings of creativity	Graduate School	1,104	6	.36	.00	.36	—	.36
Schmidt et al. (1979b)	VA	JP	Clerical jobs	16,176	175	.43	.24	.12	—	.74
Schmidt et al. (1979b)	VA	JP	Clerical jobs	8,670	110	.39	.24	.08	—	.70
Pearlman et al. (1980)	VA	JP	Clerical jobs	39,187	450	.39	.23	.10	—	.68
Hirsh et al. (1986)	VA	JP	Police and detectives	2,207	18	.18	.14	.00	—	.36
Salgado et al. (2003a)	VA	SR	Heterogeneous jobs; Europe	4,781	44	.35	.24	.04	—	.66
Nathan & Alexander (1988)[c]	VA	SR	Clerical jobs	24,620	277	.32[a,d]	.20[a,d]	.06	—	.58
Distefano & Paulk (1990)	VA	Supervisory rating	Psychiatric aides	273	5	.50				
Vinchur et al. (1998)	VA	SR	Salespeople	597	4	.14	.18	.08	—	.37
Nathan & Alexander (1988)[c]	VA	Ranking	Clerical jobs	639	19	.52[a,d]	.27[a,d]	.17	—	.87
Nathan & Alexander (1988)[c]	VA	Production quality	Clerical jobs	1,134	16	.15[a,d]	.11[a,d]	.01	—	.29

TABLE 7.2 Continued

Study	Predictor	Criterion	Job/setting	N	k	ρ	SD_ρ	80% CI	
Nathan & Alexander (1988)[c]	VA	Production quantity	Clerical jobs	931	19	.28[a,d]	.02[a,d]	.25 —	.31
Nathan & Alexander (1988)[c]	VA	Work sample	Clerical jobs	1,387	19	.50[a,d]	.21[a,d]	.23 —	.77
Verive & McDaniel (1996)	Short-term memory test	JP	Heterogeneous jobs	17,741	106	.41	.09	.29 —	.53
Verive & McDaniel (1996)	Short-term memory test	JP	High CJ	983	20	.29	.00	.29 —	.29
Verive & McDaniel (1996)	Short-term memory test	JP	Medium CJ	6,785	31	.51	.27	.16 —	.86
Verive & McDaniel (1996)	Short-term memory test	JP	Low CJ	10,000	55	.34	.14	.16 —	.52
Pearlman et al. (1980)	Memory	JP	Clerical jobs	7,764	117	.38	.17	.16 —	.60
Hirsh et al. (1986)	Memory	JP	Police and detectives	3,028	25	.10	.13	-.07 —	.27
Salgado et al. (2003a)	Memory	SR	Heterogeneous jobs; Europe	946	14	.56	.19	.32 —	.80
Nathan & Alexander (1988)[c]	Memory	SR	Clerical jobs	5,637	73	.32[a,d]	.16[a,d]	.12 —	.52
Nathan & Alexander (1988)[c]	Memory	Ranking	Clerical jobs	198	8	.35[a,d]	.03[a,d]	.31 —	.39
Nathan & Alexander (1988)[c]	Memory	Production quality	Clerical jobs	462	7	.32[a,d]	.34[a,d]	-.12 —	.76
Nathan & Alexander (1988)[c]	Memory	Production quantity	Clerical jobs	274	6	.38[a,d]	.02[a,d]	.35 —	.41
Nathan & Alexander (1988)[c]	Memory	Work sample	Clerical jobs	171	5	.53[a,d]	.24[a,d]	.22 —	.84
Schmidt et al. (1980)	Figure analogies	Proficiency	Computer programmers	535	33	.46	.32	.05 —	.87
Schmidt et al. (1980)	Number series	Proficiency	Computer programmers	535	33	.43	.38	-.06 —	.92
Callender & Osburn (1981)	Chemical comprehension	JP	Petroleum industry jobs	2,016	28	.28	.00	.28 —	.28
Schmidt et al. (1981a)	Chemical comprehension	JP	Petroleum maintenance workers	605	10	.25	.00	.25 —	.25

Reference	Predictor	Criterion	Sample	N	k	ρ	SD_ρ	80% CI
Schmidt et al. (1981a)	Chemical comprehension	JP	Petroleum operators	1,138	13	.30	.05	.24 – .36
Schmidt et al. (1979b)	Mechanical comprehension	JP	First-line supervisors	2,710	36	.48	.27	.13 – .83
Callender & Osburn (1981)	Mechanical comprehension	JP	Petroleum industry jobs	3,230	38	.31	.17	.09 – .53
Schmidt et al. (1981a)	Mechanical comprehension	JP	Petroleum maintenance workers	706	12	.33	.17	.11 – .55
Schmidt et al. (1981a)	Mechanical comprehension	JP	Petroleum operators	1,800	18	.33	.12	.18 – .48
Barrett et al. (1999)	Mechanical comprehension	SR	Firefighters	3,087	26	.54	.29	.17 – .91
Schmidt et al. (1984)	Specific abilities	Performance ratings	Heterogeneous jobs	838	14	.16[c]	.11[c]	.02 – .30
Martinussen (1996)	Specific abilities	Global performance	Pilots; mostly military	17,900	35	.24[c]	.13[c]	.07 – .41
Schmidt et al. (1984)	Specific abilities	Work sample	Heterogeneous jobs	1,793	3	.28[c]	.05[c]	.22 – .34
Levine et al. (1996)	Cognitive tests – unspecified	JP	Craft jobs; utility industry	12,504	149	.43	.14	.25 – .61
Barrett et al. (1999)	Cognitive tests – unspecified	SR	Firefighters	2,791	24	.42	.35	-.03 – .87
Churchill et al. (1985)	Aptitude – unspecified	JP	Salespeople	820		.19[a]	.09[a]	.07 – .31
Vineberg & Joyner (1982)	Aptitude – unspecified	SR	Military	101		.21[a]		

Note: N = total sample size; k = number of studies; ρ = estimate of operational validity; SD_ρ = standard deviation of ρ; 80% CI = 80% credibility interval. CJ = complexity jobs; QA = quantitative ability; RA = reasoning ability; VA = verbal ability; JP = job performance; SR = supervisory ratings.
[a] Not corrected for range restriction. [b] Corrected for criterion unreliability using conservative criterion reliability estimates. [c] Same data as Pearlman et al. (1980). [d] Corrected for unreliability in the predictor. [e] Not corrected for range restriction or unreliability in the criterion. [f] Not corrected for unreliability in the criterion.

consistent results for GMA and more specific abilities. The validities for GMA are as large, if not larger than those validities found for specific abilities. In addition, higher operational validities are found for higher-complexity jobs.

Implications for productivity

The predictive validity of CA tests has direct implications for organizational productivity. The higher the criterion-related validity of any selection measure in predicting job performance, the higher the level of performance that can be expected from those selected on the basis of the measure. The utility of any measure or selection system will also depend on the variability in job performance among the applicant pool, as well as the proportion of applicants hired (see Schmidt & Hunter, 1998). Job performance variability among job applicants as measured in dollar value of output is most often substantial (Schmidt & Hunter, 1983; Schmidt, Hunter, McKenzie, & Muldrow, 1979a).

The economic benefits for organizations can be enormous when maximizing the predictive validity of selection procedures through the choice of the right predictors. This gain in productivity can be quantified in percent of output or dollar value by means of utility analysis (see Hunter & Hunter, 1984; Schmidt & Hunter, 1998). In predicting job performance, when moving from one selection measure to one of higher predictive value, the gain in utility will be directly proportional to the size of the difference between the validities of these two measures. In this light, the substantial criterion-related validity of CA tests in predicting job performance has colossal economic implications. To consider just one example, Hunter and Hunter (1984), based on data from the US Bureau of Labor Statistics from 1980, estimated the utility of hiring on the basis of CA tests to be $15.61 billion for one year in US federal government jobs alone.

POTENTIAL MODERATORS OF COGNITIVE ABILITY VALIDITIES

Criterion-related validities of CA tests generalize across situations and settings (Schmidt, Ones, & Hunter, 1992). Nevertheless, there have been several hypothesized moderators of cognitive test validities.

Influence of validation strategy

An important question is whether or not concurrent validities estimate predictive validities. For cognitive abilities, it could be hypothesized that validities obtained using employee samples might differ from using job applicant samples due to 1) missing data, 2) range restriction, 3) motivational and demographic differences, and 4) job experience. The comparability of concurrent and predictive validities was empirically examined in a study by Barrett, Phillips, and Alexander (1981). The results suggested that in the CA domain, concurrent validities are similar to predictive validities. The same question was also addressed in Project A using concurrent and longitudinal data from the US Army (Oppler, McCloy, Peterson, Russell, & Campbell, 2001), reaching the same conclusion. Hence, concurrent vs. predictive validation designs do not appear to moderate the criterion-related validities of CA tests.

Influence of criterion and its measurement

CA measures display substantial validities for both learning and job performance criteria. However, stronger relations are found with learning criteria than with more distal performance criteria. Whether or not job performance measurement method moderates validities of CA tests is a question that has been meta-analytically examined by Nathan and Alexander (1988). Their study showed that supervisory ratings, rankings, work samples, production quantity, and production quality were all positively predicted by CA tests. Highest validities were found for work samples and supervisory rankings of performance (rs in the .60s). Lower validities were reported for supervisory ratings (.40s). Lowest and non-generalizable validities were found for production quality measures, calling into question the reliability of this particular criterion.

Recent theories recognize that the job performance construct is multidimensional (Campbell, 1990), but also hierarchically organized (Campbell, Gasser, & Oswald, 1996), with general, overall job performance at the apex of the hierarchy (Viswesvaran, Schmidt, & Ones, in press). Are there dimensions of performance for which CA tests are not likely to be valid? Though this is a legitimate question, both theoretical arguments and empirical data suggest that CA is a valid predictor of all performance dimensions. Empirically, the largest investigation of this issue was carried out using data collected for Project A (McHenry, Hough, Toquam, & Ashworth, 1990; Oppler et al., 2001). GMA tests were found to predict technical proficiency, soldiering proficiency, as well as effort and leadership, personal discipline, and fitness and military bearing with positive, substantial validities. There is, therefore, empirical evidence of validity generalization for GMA tests across dimensions of job performance. Even for the criterion of contextual performance, the meta-analytic correlation is .24 (Alonso, 2001). Theoretically, Viswesvaran et al. (in press) have hypothesized that one reason for the presence of a general job performance factor is the contribution of GMA to all performance dimensions. The fact that GMA is a major determinant for all job performance dimensions is the chief reason for hypothesizing a valid, non-artifactual, general factor in job performance measures (see also Viswesvaran & Ones, Chapter 16, this volume). Even in very specific performance domains there is evidence for positive and quite substantial correlations with CA measures. For example, a recent meta-analysis reported the true score correlation between CA and objectively measured leadership effectiveness as .33 (Judge, Colbert, & Ilies, in press).

Prediction using GMA versus specific abilities

Specific abilities cannot be measured without measuring GMA in applied settings and GMA cannot be measured without measuring specific abilities (Carroll, 1993). Measures of GMA and specific abilities are generalizably valid. Several large-scale primary studies have been conducted to directly investigate whether or not specific cognitive abilities show incremental validity over GMA.

Hunter (1986) found that the specific ability composites derived for specific occupations from the Armed Services Vocational Aptitude Battery (ASVAB) scores did not provide any improved validity over the general composite. In Project A, McHenry et al. (1990) found the incremental validity of specific ability measures over GMA to be in the .02 range. Ree and Earles (1991) showed that specific abilities do not account for any additional variance beyond a general factor extracted from the ASVAB for predicting training performance. Ree, Earles, and Teachout (1994) reached the same conclusion in predicting job performance ratings. The average incremental validity of the orthogonal specific abilities over GMA was .02. In other research replicating these findings, Olea and Ree (1994) reported incremental validities of specific abilities to be in the .02 to .08 range. Hunter's (1983a) structural equations models indicate that the only causal paths between specific abilities and performance are through GMA ($N = 20,256$).

From a criterion-related validity point of view, there does not appear to be an advantage associated with using specific ability measures rather than GMA. However, it might be worth noting again that it is impossible to measure specific abilities without assessing GMA and vice versa. From a practical point of view, there may be an advantage to using tests of GMA. Selection in the 21st century is rarely for specific positions and rarely do employees stay in the same position for which they are hired. Further, the nature of jobs changes over time. Therefore, the relative importance of specific abilities varies over time, necessitating a workforce high on GMA, not only on specific abilities.

Differential validity by gender

Based on the results of meta-analyses and large-scale studies reporting criterion-related validities for men and women separately, there appears to be little support for the differential validity of CA measures for men and women (Carretta & Doub, 1998; Hartigan & Wigdor, 1989).

One interesting moderator of the differential validity of CA tests by gender might be the gender composition of the job. Rothstein and McDaniel (1992) found some existence of differential validity for males and females depending on the gender roles dominating the occupations investigated. For job performance, for male-dominated jobs, GMA appears to be more predictive for men than for women (validities of .34 and .25, respectively). GMA appears to be more predictive for women than for men for female-dominated jobs (validities of .22 and .38, respectively). CA test validity differences by gender vanish when investigating sex-neutral occupations.

Differential validity by race and ethnicity

Are there differences in validities of CA tests for different racial and ethnic groups? Test critics who allege unfair discrimination in personnel selection posit potential differences in test validity across racial groups (Outtz, 2002). Meta-analyses and large-scale studies refute the hypothesis of single group validity (Hartigan & Wigdor, 1989; Hunter, Schmidt, & Hunter, 1979). Furthermore, there appears to be little support for the differential validity of CA measures for different racial groups in predicting learning and performance criteria. There is no evidence that CA tests cause disadvantages for minority groups due to predictive bias (Evers, te Nijenhuis, & van der Flier, Chapter 14, this volume; Hunter & Schmidt, 2000; Rotundo & Sackett, 1999; Schmidt et al., 1992).

Generalizability beyond the North American context

Cultural differences have often been cited as a potential obstacle to the validity generalization of CA tests across countries. Most of the evidence supporting the criterion-related validities of CA tests has been reported in the USA and Canada. The past decade has seen an increase in the numbers of primary studies and meta-analyses that report cognitive test validities in other countries around the world (e.g., Bartram & Baxter, 1996, in the UK; Salgado & Anderson, 2002, in Spain and the UK; Schuler, Moser, Diemand, & Funke, 1995, in Germany). In a series of meta-analyses examining the validity of CA tests in Europe, Salgado, Anderson, and colleagues (Salgado & Anderson, 2002, 2003; Salgado et al., 2003) have reported validities for training success and job performance across European Union countries. The findings suggest that CA tests retain high validity across cultural contexts, offering evidence of international validity generalization.

Job complexity moderators of cognitive ability test validities

As can be seen in Tables 7.1 and 7.2, an important moderator of cognitive test validities is job complexity. Criterion-related validity increases with task or job complexity levels. This is true for both training and job performance. Highest validities are found for highest-complexity jobs where tasks are more cognitively loaded. There are two reasons for the moderating influence of complexity on CA test validities. First, more complex jobs require the worker to acquire knowledge of greater complexity (e.g., learning a computer programming language versus memorizing food menu items). Second, more complex jobs require more difficult information processing (e.g., composing a piece of chamber music versus keeping time when boiling eggs).

Many hypothesized moderators of CA test validities have failed to be supported when empirically examined. These include race, gender, and culture. To date, the strongest moderator of validities empirically identified and documented is job complexity.

How g is Important: Causal Models in Predicting Job Performance

In explaining the predictive validity of GMA, the main process that has been invoked involves learning (cf., Schmidt, Hunter, & Outerbridge, 1986). Intelligence is the ability to learn and thus has implications for the acquisition of job knowledge, both declarative and procedural (i.e., what to do and how to do it) (see Hunter, 1986, for a discussion of CA and learning).

GMA predicts job performance across jobs and settings primarily because it predicts learning and acquisition of knowledge, which is a necessary determinant of task completion. Unless an employee can learn what to do and how to do it, even for the simplest tasks, work cannot be completed. Hunter (1983b) presented a causal model where GMA was predictive of job knowledge, which partially mediated the relationship between ability and job performance. In a large sample of US Army personnel, Schmidt et al. (1986) confirmed this mediating role for job knowledge. Borman, Hanson, Oppler, Pulakos, and White (1993) found similar mechanisms to be explanatory of supervisory performance. Further, using a more recent, large sample of US Army enlistees, McCloy, Campbell, and Cudeck (1994) demonstrated that GMA was indirectly related to job performance through its influence on declarative knowledge and procedural knowledge.

The substantial validities of CA tests for predicting job performance can be attributed to the fact that those who are higher on GMA acquire more declarative and procedural knowledge, and do so more quickly than those lower on GMA. This is probably related to their ability to process complex information quickly, more efficiently and with greater accuracy.

GROUP DIFFERENCES

The inquiry into the question of whether certain groups differ in their standing on a certain trait is a major part of exploring the nomological net of any construct. However, the study of group differences in CA has provoked particularly strong, polarized reactions unlike for any other individual differences construct. The distributions for all population subgroups investigated overlap substantially, and at any level of the ability distribution one can find individuals from any given group. However, the fact that there are subpopulation mean differences on CA stirs considerable controversy among some researchers and the public alike. To a great extent, this is due to the important role that CA plays in determining many educational, economic, and social criteria. Group mean differences on a trait can result in adverse impact against subgroups when an outcome (e.g., promotions, job offers) is distributed on the basis of measured standings on this trait.

Age differences

Although common wisdom suggests that individual levels of GMA begin to decline after peaking in early adulthood, there is now evidence that CA levels are at least somewhat stable for the most of individuals' working lives (cf., Hough, Oswald, & Ployhart, 2001). Differential patterns of age-related decline in CA test scores can be found for specific cognitive abilities. It has been suggested that the observed decline in cognitive functioning with old age is mainly due to a decline in aspects of fluid intelligence, while levels of crystallized intelligence remain considerably stable over the lifespan (Horn & Donaldson, 1976). Adverse impact effects against older working adults are most likely to be found on tests highly saturated with the general factor of mental ability.

A major factor influencing the magnitude of age differences findings is study design. Longitudinal studies, tracking the same individuals and comparing their levels of cognitive abilities over time, yield smaller estimates of age-related decline than do those with cross-sectional designs, comparing individuals from different birth cohorts at the same point in time. While these are important for detecting cohort effects such as rising levels of cognitive abilities through improved education or absence of negative environmental influences (e.g., malnutrition), they are less suited for evaluating the stability of trait-levels over time. There is now considerable evidence for rising IQ levels over time (Flynn, 1984, 1987, 1998), confounding estimates of temporal stability of CA in cross-sectional studies.

Gender differences

Gender differences in CA seem to be small and disappearing over time (Feingold, 1988). Hyde and Linn (1988), in a meta-analysis of gender differences in verbal ability, found that women tend to score higher than men on most aspects of verbal ability, most notably speech production. However, effect sizes were small to negligible. The authors concluded, "the magnitude of the gender difference in verbal ability is currently so small that it can effectively be considered to be zero" (p. 64). This pattern of near-zero differences seems to hold for quantitative abilities, as well. In a meta-analysis including more than 3 million men and women, Hyde, Fennema, and Lamon (1990) report a d-value of .15 on quantitative ability, with males on average scoring only slightly higher than females. The largest group mean differences on quantitative abilities were reported for problem solving, $d = .32$, with males scoring higher.

Racial and ethnic group differences

Although CA tests have not been found to be predictively biased against racial and ethnic subgroups, moderate to large mean-score differences on most tests have been reported, depending on the groups under investigation. Estimates of group mean differences in GMA have ranged between .7 standard deviation units for the Hispanic–White comparison to around 1 standard deviation unit for the Black–White comparison. In general, Hispanics and Blacks on average score lower than Whites on tests of both GMA as well as tests of specific abilities, while Asians tend to score slightly higher (see Ones, Viswesvaran, & Dilchert, in press, for a comprehensive summary of the meta-analytic evidence; see also Evers et al., Chapter 14, this volume).

Implications for adverse impact

Group differences on scale scores of any selection instrument are the main source of adverse impact, the disproportional hiring of a minority group when compared to the majority group. The ascertainment of adverse impact creates the need "to produce compelling evidence of the job relatedness" of the instruments in question (Sackett & Wilk, 1994). The job relatedness of CA tests has been well established (Hunter & Schmidt, 1996; Schmidt et al., 1986). Yet, given the group mean differences for various demographic subgroups described above, depending on the selectiveness of an organization, the economic mandate of selecting personnel based on CA might create adverse impact, particularly against ethnic minorities (see Evers et al., Chapter 14, this volume). Today's organizations will have to balance the need for maximally productive employees with that for diversity in the demographic composition of their workforces.

Current and New Directions

The above-described dilemmas, particularly those relating to group differences, have led to a search for alternative predictors in occupational and educational settings.

Other predictors and their relationship with cognitive ability

There are predictors other than tests of CA that show substantial validity in predicting job performance (e.g., integrity tests, structured interviews, assessment centers, see Schmidt & Hunter, 1998; Schmidt et al., 1992). However, in evaluating the utility of a given selection instrument over the predictive value of an existing measure, both its validity and amount of overlap between the two measures have to be considered. The higher the overlap between the measure and CA (as expressed by the correlation between scores on both measures), the lower the incremental validity. Therefore, we will briefly discuss some of the commonly used assessment methods in personnel selection as well as what is known about their overlap with CA. We focus our attention on selection tools and methods (i.e., assessment centers [AC], interviews, and SJTs) rather than constructs, as the distinctiveness of popular construct-based predictors is already well established (for an example, see Ackerman & Heggestad, 1997, on the relationships between ability and personality domains).

Assessment centers. There have been four published meta-analyses exploring the nomological net as well as criterion-related validities of the AC method (Arthur, Day, McNelly, & Edens, 2003; Collins et al., 2003; Gaugler, Rosenthal, Thornton, & Bentson, 1987; Scholz & Schuler, 1993). Gaugler et al. (1987) reported a corrected mean validity of .36 for the prediction of job performance criteria, while the validity for the prediction of ratings of potential was notably higher, .53. Arthur et al. (2003) also reported the estimated true validity of overall AC ratings to be .36.

A comprehensive meta-analysis investigating the nomological net of AC dimensions found the observed correlation between overall AC ratings and GMA to be .43 ($N = 17,373$) (Scholz & Schuler, 1993). In a second meta-analysis, Collins et al. (2003) reported the estimated operational validity of CA in predicting overall AC rating to be .65, corrected for unreliability in the criterion but not in the CA measures. This indicates substantial overlap between the constructs assessed by overall AC ratings and GMA. It seems reasonable to conclude that the incremental validity of overall AC ratings over measures of GMA is relatively small, most likely in the range of .02 reported by Schmidt and Hunter (1998).

Interviews. Meta-analytic evidence indicates the overall validity of employment interviews in predicting job performance is .37 ($k = 160$, $N = 25,244$) (McDaniel, Whetzel, Schmidt, & Maurer, 1994). However, there are a number of moderators influencing validities. Interviews with situational content show higher mean validities than do those with job-related or psychological content (ρ = .50, .39, and .29, respectively). Also, structured interviews are substantially more valid than unstructured ones; ρs = .44 and .33, respectively. The relationships between interview ratings and CA measures also have been meta-analytically investigated. Huffcutt, Roth, and McDaniel (1996), in a meta-analysis specifically targeting the question to what extent employment interview ratings reflect CA, report a corrected mean true score correlation of .40 (k = 49; N = 12,037). The relationship between interview ratings and CA seems to be somewhat stronger when the interview is less structured; also, employment interviews for low complexity jobs seem to overlap more substantially with CA. Based on correlations reported in Huffcutt et al. (1996) and the validity estimates reported by McDaniel et al. (1994), Schmidt and Hunter (1998) estimated the incremental validity of employment interviews over tests of CA to be .12 and .04 for structured and unstructured interviews, respectively.

Situational judgment tests. SJTs are paper-and-pencil measures that aim to assess judgment in work situations. Typically items are comprised of scenarios that are followed by response alternatives that the test takers must choose from. McDaniel, Morgeson, Finnegan, Campion, and Braverman (2001) meta-analytically examined the criterion-related validity of SJTs. The operational validity across 102 samples was .34 (N = 10,640) and the lower 90% credibility value was positive. As such, it appears that SJTs are moderately, but generalizably valid. The limited pool of primary studies contributing to the meta-analyses, and hence second-order sampling error, precluded any firm moderator conclusions. Although it is theoretically possible to build SJTs to assess different constructs, typical SJTs display substantial correlations with measures of CA. McDaniel et al.'s (2001) meta-analysis reported a true score correlation (i.e., mean correlation corrected for unreliability in both SJTs and CA measures) of .46 (k = 79; N = 16,994). In a follow-up study, McDaniel (2003) reported that SJTs that use knowledge instructions (e.g., what is the most effective/best response?) are more highly correlated with CA measures than SJTs that use behavioral tendency instructions (e.g., what would you do?). The respective true score correlations were .55 and .23. There is overlap between constructs assessed by SJTs and GMA, even when behavioral tendency instructions are used.

Newly proposed intelligences

The urge to explore the nomological net of the CA domain has led researchers not only to investigate the factorial structure of the intelligence construct, but also to propose a number of new intelligences in order to explain proportions of variance in behavior yet unaccounted for. These newly proposed constructs differ not only in scope but also in the methodological soundness with which they were developed and the amount of data offered to support claims of their utility. Legitimate scientific curiosity is only one reason for exploring the construct space. Societal discontent with standardized testing of cognitive abilities is another. It has been suggested that the most successful proponents of competing constructs are those that tap into "the popular preference for an egalitarian plurality of intelligences . . . and a distaste for being assessed, labeled, and sorted by inscrutable mental tests" (Gottfredson, 2003, p. 392). It is therefore a matter of the highest import to carefully evaluate newly proposed constructs not only with regard to their face validity, but also with regard to their predictive value, divergent and convergent validity with GMA and specific abilities, as well as the psychometric soundness of their measures.

Practical intelligence.   One newly proposed intelligence for which utility in predicting both occupational as well as everyday life outcomes has been claimed is practical intelligence. Its core component is tacit knowledge (Sternberg & Wagner, 1993), "the procedural knowledge one learns in everyday life that usually is not taught and often is not yet even verbalized" (Sternberg et al., 2000, p. 111). It is usually conceptualized as internalized rules of thumb about what behavior to exert depending on the environmental context and is claimed to be a powerful predictor of an individual's success in specific settings (Sternberg, 1999). Practical intelligence has been claimed to be distinct from GMA, and tacit knowledge has been claimed to be more than just job knowledge.

Sternberg and colleagues state that "tacit knowledge generally increases with experience but is not simply a proxy for experience; that tacit knowledge tests measure a distinct construct from that measured by traditional abstract intelligence tests; that scores on tacit knowledge tests represent a general factor, which appears to correlate across domains; and finally, that tacit knowledge tests are predictive of performance in a number of domains and compare favorably with those obtained for IQ" (Sternberg et al., 2000, p. 161). Despite more than two decades of research, the data offered in support of the practical intelligence construct remains sparse and spans only a handful of occupational domains. Moreover, primary studies are afflicted with small, heavily restricted samples. A meta-analytic estimate of the operational validity of practical intelligence in predicting task performance is .39 (Dilchert & Ones, 2004).

The utility of any construct is mainly a function of the incremental validity its measures will add over existing and currently employed measures of other constructs. Incremental validity will be a function of both the new construct's predictive validity and a lack of construct overlap with currently employed constructs (divergent validity). Dilchert and Ones (2004) have reported a meta-analytic estimate for the true score correlation between practical intelligence and GMA as .58, indicating that there is substantial overlap between the two constructs. This suggests that the incremental validity over *g*-loaded tests of CA for predicting job performance that can be expected from tacit knowledge inventories will range around .03, casting doubt on whether the enthusiasm around practical intelligence is justified.

Emotional intelligence.   There are currently two views on the nature of emotional intelligence. One describes emotional intelligence as encompassing personality characteristics (Bar-On & Parker, 2000; Goleman, 1995; see also Woodruffe, Chapter 9, this volume). Emotional intelligence as proposed by this school of thought is mostly unrelated to general intelligence (e.g., Derksen, Kramer, & Katzko, 2002). Positing the appropriateness of an ability model, another view postulates that emotional intelligence is (1) a form of intelligence, (2) reliably measured, and (3) rather distinct from personality (e.g., Caruso, Mayer, & Salovey, 2002; Mayer, Salovey, Caruso, & Sitarenios, 2003). Typically, the former conceptualization of emotional intelligence has relied on self-report measures, while the latter has been assessed using task-based procedures (Petrides & Furnham, 2000; Roberts,

Zeidner, & Matthews, 2001). Interestingly, task-based and self-report measures show a small correlation (Van Rooy & Viswesvaran, in press). It has been shown that the ability-based approach to defining emotional intelligence yields a construct that shows discriminant validity from personality (Caruso et al., 2002) and moderate convergent validity with CA (Roberts et al., 2001). In a meta-analysis investigating the nomological net of the emotional intelligence construct, Van Rooy and Viswesvaran (in press) reported a true score correlation of .33 between ability-based measures of emotional intelligence and GMA. Based on the meta-analytically obtained estimate of the validity of emotional intelligence for predicting job performance (operational validity = .24, based on $N = 2,652$; Van Rooy & Viswesvaran, in press), it is unlikely that substantial incremental validity can be expected by emotional intelligence measures above measures of GMA in employment settings. On the other hand, tests of GMA demonstrate substantial incremental validity over emotional intelligence measures.

CONCLUSIONS

The voluminous data and research studies published in the area of CA testing present some broad conclusions as well as areas for future exploration. First, although future research could explore the nuances of different definitions of CA, there is a broad consensus as to what constitutes CA and what GMA is. Any assertion of the contrary, with implications that there is substantive disagreement in defining the construct, is erroneous. Scientists and practitioners have a fairly good understanding of the construct, despite some potential areas of disagreement.

Second, the amount of empirical data available to support the assertion that CA is correlated with several important life outcomes is overwhelming (Brand, 1987; Gottfredson, 2002). Assertions that CA is nothing but academic ability, without any relevance to real-world tasks, are not supported by empirical data. CA tests are predictive of training and job performance. The predictive validity of CA is not moderated by situational influences, setting, validation strategy, criterion measurement, or cultural context. The predictive validities of CA tests increase with increasing job complexity. Utility losses to employers and national economies will be large if CA tests are not utilized in personnel selection.

Several new types of intelligence are being introduced. While worth while to explore potential supplements to CA, exaggerated claims, as we find them for constructs like practical intelligence and emotional intelligence, are not helpful. Employers are unlikely to forgo the use of CA testing, especially in a highly competitive global market. GMA is the most powerful individual differences trait in predicting job performance across situations, organizations, and jobs. Hopefully, this chapter has adequately stressed the importance of CA and provided a glimpse of its vast supporting literature.

NOTE

Order of authorship is arbitrary; all three authors contributed equally to this chapter.

REFERENCES

Ackerman, P. L., & Heggestad, E. D. (1997). Intelligence, personality, and interests: Evidence for overlapping traits. *Psychological Bulletin, 121*, 219–245.

Anderson, N., Born, M., & Cunningham-Snell, N. (2001). Recruitment and selection: Applicant perspectives and outcomes. In N. Anderson, D. S. Ones, H. K. Sinangil, & C. Viswesvaran (Eds.), *Handbook of industrial, work, and organizational psychology* (Vol. 1, pp. 200–218). London: Sage.

Alonso, A. (2001). *The relationship between cognitive ability, big five, task and contextual performance: A meta-analysis*. Unpublished Master's Thesis, Florida International University, Miami, FL.

Arthur, W., Jr., Day, E. A., McNelly, T. L., & Edens, P. S. (2003). A meta-analysis of the criterion-related validity of assessment center dimensions. *Personnel Psychology, 56*, 125–154.

Bar-On, R., & Parker, J. D. A. (Eds.). (2000). *Handbook of emotional intelligence*. San Francisco: Jossey-Bass.

Barrett, G. V., Phillips, J. S., & Alexander, R. A. (1981). Concurrent and predictive validity designs: A critical reanalysis. *Journal of Applied Psychology, 66*, 1–6.

Barrett, G. V., Polomsky, M. D., & McDaniel, M. A. (1999). Selection tests for firefighters: A comprehensive review and meta-analysis. *Journal of Business and Psychology, 13*, 507–514.

Bartram, D., & Baxter, P. (1996). Validation of the Cathay Pacific Airways pilot selection program. *International Journal of Aviation Psychology, 6*, 149–169.

Borman, W. C., Hanson, M. A., Oppler, S. H., Pulakos, E. D., & White, L. A. (1993). Role of early supervisory experience in supervisor performance. *Journal of Applied Psychology, 78*, 443–449.

Brand, C. (1987). The importance of general intelligence. In S. Modgil & C. Modgil (Eds.), *Arthur Jensen: Consensus and controversy* (pp. 251–265). New York: Falmer.

Callender, J. C., & Osburn, H. G. (1981). Testing the constancy of validity with computer-generated sampling distributions of the multiplicative model variance estimate: Results for petroleum industry validation research. *Journal of Applied Psychology, 66*, 274–281.

Campbell, J. P. (1990). Modeling the performance prediction problem in industrial and organizational psychology. In M. D. Dunnette & L. M. Hough (Eds.), *Handbook of industrial and organizational psychology* (2nd ed., Vol. 1, pp. 687–732). Palo Alto, CA: Consulting Psychologists Press.

Campbell, J. P. (1996). Group differences and personnel decisions: Validity, fairness, and affirmative action. *Journal of Vocational Behavior, 49*, 122–158.

Campbell, J. P., Gasser, M. B., & Oswald, F. L. (1996). The substantive nature of job performance variability. In K. R. Murphy (Ed.), *Individual differences in behavior in organizations* (pp. 258–299). San Francisco: Jossey-Bass.

Carretta, T. R., & Doub, T. W. (1998). Group differences in the role of *g* and prior job knowledge in the acquisition of subsequent job knowledge. *Personality and Individual Differences, 24*, 585–593.

Carroll, J. B. (1993). *Human cognitive abilities: A survey of factor-analytic studies*. New York: Cambridge University Press.

Caruso, D. R., Mayer, J. D., & Salovey, P. (2002). Relation of an ability measure of emotional intelligence to personality. *Journal of Personality Assessment, 79*, 306–320.

Cattell, R. B. (1943). The measurement of adult intelligence. *Psychological Bulletin, 40*, 153–193.

Cattell, R. B. (1971). *Abilities: Their structure, growth, and action*. Oxford, UK: Houghton Mifflin.

Churchill, G. A., Ford, N. M., Hartley, S. W., & Walker, O. C. (1985). The determinants of salesperson performance: A meta-analysis. *Journal of Marketing Research, 22*, 103–118.

Collins, J. M., Schmidt, F. L., Sanchez-Ku, M., Thomas, L., McDaniel, M. A., & Le, H. (2003). Can basic individual differences shed light on the construct meaning of assessment center evaluations? *International Journal of Selection and Assessment, 11*, 17–29.

Cronbach, L. J. (1960). *Essentials of psychological testing* (2nd ed.). Oxford, UK: Harper.

Derksen, J., Kramer, I., & Katzko, M. (2002). Does a self-report measure for emotional intelligence assess something different than general intelligence? *Personality and Individual Differences, 32*, 37–48.

Dilchert, S., & Ones, D. S. (2004, April). *Meta-analysis of practical intelligence: Contender to the throne of g?* Poster session presented at the annual conference of the Society for Industrial and Organizational Psychology, Chicago, IL.

Distefano, M. K., & Paulk, K. D. (1990). Further evaluation of verbal ability selection test and work performance validity with psychiatric aides. *Psychological Reports, 67*, 845–846.

Drasgow, F. (2003). Intelligence and the workplace. In W. C. Borman, D. R. Ilgen, & R. J. Klimoski (Eds.), *Handbook of psychology: Industrial and organizational psychology* (Vol. 12, pp. 107–130). New York: John Wiley & Sons.

Feingold, A. (1988). Cognitive gender differences are disappearing. *American Psychologist, 43*, 95–103.

Flynn, J. R. (1984). The mean IQ of Americans: Massive gains 1932 to 1978. *Psychological Bulletin, 95*, 29–51.

Flynn, J. R. (1987). Massive IQ gains in 14 nations: What IQ tests really measure. *Psychological Bulletin, 101*, 171–191.

Flynn, J. R. (1998). IQ gains over time: Toward finding the causes. In U. Neisser (Ed.), *The rising curve: Long-term gains in IQ and related measures* (pp. 25–66). Washington, DC: American Psychological Association.

Funke, U., Krauss, J., Schuler, H., & Stapf, K.-H. (1987). Zur Prognostizierbarkeit wissenschaftlich-technischer Leistungen mittels Personvariablen: Eine Metaanalyse der Validitaet diagnostischer Verfahren im Bereich Forschung und Entwicklung [Predictability of scientific-technical achievement through personal variables: A meta-analysis of the validity of diagnostic procedures in research and development]. *Gruppendynamik, 18*, 407–428.

Gaugler, B. B., Rosenthal, D. B., Thornton, G. C., III, & Bentson, C. (1987). Meta-analysis of assessment center validity. *Journal of Applied Psychology, 72*, 493–511.

Goleman, D. (1995). *Emotional intelligence*. New York: Bantam Books.

Gottfredson, L. S. (1997a). Mainstream science on intelligence: An editorial with 52 signatories, history and bibliography. *Intelligence, 24*, 13–23.

Gottfredson, L. S. (1997b). Why g matters: The complexity of everyday life. *Intelligence, 24*, 79–132.

Gottfredson, L. S. (2002). Where and why g matters: Not a mystery. *Human Performance, 15*, 25–46.

Gottfredson, L. S. (2003). Dissecting practical intelligence theory: Its claims and evidence. *Intelligence, 31*, 343–397.

Gottfredson, L. S. (2004). Intelligence: Is it the epidemiologists' elusive "fundamental cause" of social class inequalities in health? *Journal of Personality & Social Psychology, 86*, 174–199.

Hartigan, J. A., & Wigdor, A. K. (Eds.). (1989). *Fairness in employment testing: Validity generalization, minority issues, and the General Aptitude Test Battery.* Washington, DC: National Academy Press.

Hirsh, H. R., Northrop, L. C., & Schmidt, F. L. (1986). Validity generalization results for law enforcement occupations. *Personnel Psychology, 39*, 399–420.

Horn, J. L., & Donaldson, G. (1976). On the myth of intellectual decline in adulthood. *American Psychologist, 31*, 701–719.

Hough, L. M., Oswald, F. L., & Ployhart, R. E. (2001). Determinants, detection and amelioration of adverse impact in personnel selection procedures: Issues, evidence and lessons learned. *International Journal of Selection and Assessment, 9*, 152–194.

Huffcutt, A. I., Roth, P. L., & McDaniel, M. A. (1996). A meta-analytic investigation of cognitive ability in employment interview evaluations: Moderating characteristics and implications for incremental validity. *Journal of Applied Psychology, 81*, 459–473.

Hunter, J. E. (1983a). *The prediction of job performance in the military using ability composites: The dominance of general cognitive ability over specific aptitudes.* Report for Research Applications in partial fulfillment of Department of Defense Contract F41689-83-C-0025.

Hunter, J. E. (1983b). *Test validation for 12,000 jobs: An application of job classification and validity generalization of the General Aptitude Test Battery* (USES Test Research Report No. 45). Washington, DC: United States Department of Labor.

Hunter, J. E. (1985). *Differential validity across jobs in the military*. Report for Research Applications, Inc., in partial fulfillment of DOD Contract No. F41689-83-C-0025.

Hunter, J. E. (1986). Cognitive ability, cognitive aptitude, job knowledge, and job performance. *Journal of Vocational Behavior, 29*, 340–362.

Hunter, J. E., & Hunter, R. F. (1984). Validity and utility of alternative predictors of job performance. *Psychological Bulletin, 96*, 72–98.

Hunter, J. E., & Schmidt, F. L. (1976). Critical analysis of the statistical and ethical implications of various definitions of test bias. *Psychological Bulletin, 83*, 1053–1071.

Hunter, J. E., & Schmidt, F. L. (1990). *Methods of meta-analysis: Correcting error and bias in research findings*. Thousand Oaks, CA: Sage.

Hunter, J. E., & Schmidt, F. L. (1996). Intelligence and job performance: Economic and social implications. *Psychology, Public Policy, and Law, 2*, 447–472.

Hunter, J. E., & Schmidt, F. L. (2000). Racial and gender bias in ability and achievement tests: Resolving the apparent paradox. *Psychology, Public Policy, and Law, 6*, 151–158.

Hunter, J. E., Schmidt, F. L., & Hunter, R. (1979). Differential validity of employment tests by race: A comprehensive review and analysis. *Psychological Bulletin, 86*, 721–735.

Hyde, J. S., Fennema, E., & Lamon, S. J. (1990). Gender differences in mathematics performance: A meta-analysis. *Psychological Bulletin, 107*, 139–155.

Hyde, J. S., & Linn, M. C. (1988). Gender differences in verbal ability: A meta-analysis. *Psychological Bulletin, 104*, 53–69.

Jensen, A. R. (1980). *Bias in mental testing*. New York: Free Press.

Jensen, A. R. (1998). *The g factor: The science of mental ability*. Westport, CT: Praeger Publishers/Greenwood Publishing Group.

Johnson, W., Bouchard, T. J., Jr., Krueger, R. F., McGue, M., & Gottesman, I. I. (2004). Just one *g*: Consistent results from three test batteries. *Intelligence, 32*, 95–107.

Judge, T. A., Colbert, A. E., & Ilies, R. (in press). Intelligence and leadership: A quantitative review and test of theoretical propositions. *Journal of Applied Psychology*.

Kelley, T. L. (1939). Mental factors of no importance. *Journal of Educational Psychology, 30*, 139–142.

Kranzler, J. H., & Jensen, A. R. (1991). The nature of psychometric *g*: Unitary process or a number of independent processes? *Intelligence, 15*, 397–422.

Kuncel, N. R., Hezlett, S. A., & Ones, D. S. (2001). A comprehensive meta-analysis of the predictive validity of the graduate record examinations: Implications for graduate student selection and performance. *Psychological Bulletin, 127*, 162–181.

Kuncel, N. R., Hezlett, S. A., & Ones, D. S. (2004). Academic performance, career potential, creativity, and job performance: Can one construct predict them all? *Journal of Personality and Social Psychology, 86*, 148–161.

Kyllonen, P. C. (1993). Aptitude testing inspired by information processing: A test of the four-sources model. *Journal of General Psychology, 120*, 375–405.

Kyllonen, P. C., & Christal, R. E. (1989). Cognitive modeling of learning abilities: A status report of LAMP. In R. F. Dillon & J. W. Pellegrino (Eds.), *Testing: Theoretical and applied perspectives* (pp. 146–173). New York: Praeger.

Kyllonen, P. C., & Christal, R. E. (1990). Reasoning ability is (little more than) working-memory capacity? *Intelligence, 14*, 389–433.

Levine, E. L., Spector, P. E., Menon, S., Narayanan, L., & Cannon-Bowers, J. A. (1996). Validity generalization for cognitive, psychomotor, and perceptual tests for craft jobs in the utility industry. *Human Performance, 9*, 1–22.

Lounsbury, J., Borrow, W., & Jensen, J. (1989). Attitudes toward employment testing: Scale development, correlates, and "known-group" validation. *Professional Psychology: Research and Practice, 20*, 340–349.

Lubinski, D. (2000). Scientific and social significance of assessing individual differences: "Sinking shafts at a few critical points." *Annual Review of Psychology, 51*, 405–444.

Marcus, B. (2003). Attitudes towards personnel selection methods: A partial replication and extension in a German sample. *Applied Psychology: An International Review, 52*, 515–532.

Martinussen, M. (1996). Psychological measures as predictors of pilot performance: A meta-analysis. *International Journal of Aviation Psychology, 6*, 1–20.

Mayer, J. D., Salovey, P., Caruso, D. R., & Sitarenios, G. (2003). Measuring emotional intelligence with the MSCEIT V2.0. *Emotion, 3*, 97–105.

McCloy, R. A., Campbell, J. P., & Cudeck, R. (1994). A confirmatory test of a model of performance determinants. *Journal of Applied Psychology, 79*, 493–505.

McDaniel, M. A. (2003). *Practical intelligence: The emperor's new clothes.* Paper presented at the International Symposium on emotional and practical intelligence, Berlin.

McDaniel, M. A., Morgeson, F. P., Finnegan, E. B., Campion, M. A., & Braverman, E. P. (2001). Use of situational judgment tests to predict job performance: A clarification of the literature. *Journal of Applied Psychology, 86*, 730–740.

McDaniel, M. A., Whetzel, D. L., Schmidt, F. L., & Maurer, S. D. (1994). The validity of employment interviews: A comprehensive review and meta-analysis. *Journal of Applied Psychology, 79*, 599–616.

McHenry, J. J., Hough, L. M., Toquam, J. L., & Ashworth, S. (1990). Project A validity results: The relationship between predictor and criterion domains. *Personnel Psychology, 43*, 335–354.

Nathan, B. R., & Alexander, R. A. (1988). A comparison of criteria for test validation: A meta-analytic investigation. *Personnel Psychology, 41*, 517–535.

Olea, M. M., & Ree, M. J. (1994). Predicting pilot and navigator criteria: Not much more than *g. Journal of Applied Psychology, 79*, 845–851.

Ones, D. S., Viswesvaran, C., & Dilchert, S. (in press). Cognitive ability in selection decisions. In O. Wilhelm & R. W. Engle (Eds.), *Understanding and measuring intelligence.* London: Sage.

Oppler, S. H., McCloy, R. A., Peterson, N. G., Russell, T. L., & Campbell, J. P. (2001). The prediction of multiple components of entry-level performance. In J. P. Campbell & D. J. Knapp (Eds.), *Exploring the limits in personnel selection and classification* (pp. 349–388). Mahwah, NJ: Erlbaum.

Outtz, J. L. (2002). The role of cognitive ability tests in employment selection. *Human Performance, 15*, 161–172.

Pearlman, K., Schmidt, F. L., & Hunter, J. E. (1980). Validity generalization results for tests used to predict job proficiency and training success in clerical occupations. *Journal of Applied Psychology, 65*, 373–406.

Petrides, K. V., & Furnham, A. (2000). On the dimensional structure of emotional intelligence. *Personality and Individual Differences, 29*, 313–320.

Ree, M. J., & Carretta, T. R. (2002). g2K. *Human Performance, 15*, 3–24.

Ree, M. J., & Earles, J. A. (1991). Predicting training success: Not much more than *g. Personnel Psychology, 44*, 321–332.

Ree, M. J., Earles, J. A., & Teachout, M. S. (1994). Predicting job performance: Not much more than *g. Journal of Applied Psychology, 79*, 518–524.

Reeve, C. L., & Hakel, M. D. (2002). Asking the right questions about *g. Human Performance, 15*, 47–74.

Roberts, R. D., Markham, P. M., Matthews, G., & Zeidner, M. (in press). Assessing intelligence: Past, present, and future. In O. Wilhelm & R. W. Engle (Eds.), *Understanding and measuring intelligence.* London: Sage.

Roberts, R. D., Zeidner, M., & Matthews, G. (2001). Does emotional intelligence meet traditional standards for an intelligence? Some new data and conclusions. *Emotion, 1*, 196–231.

Rothstein, H. R., & McDaniel, M. A. (1992). Differential validity by sex in employment settings. *Journal of Business and Psychology, 7*, 45–62.

Rotundo, M., & Sackett, P. R. (1999). Effect of rater race on conclusions regarding differential prediction in cognitive ability tests. *Journal of Applied Psychology, 84*, 815–822.

Ryan, A. M., McFarland, L., Baron, H., & Page, R. (1999). An international look at selection practices: Nation and culture as explanations for variability in practice. *Personnel Psychology, 52*, 359–391.

Rynes, S. L., & Connerley, M. L. (1993). Applicant reactions to alternative selection procedures. *Journal of Business and Psychology, 7*, 261–277.

Sackett, P. R., & Wilk, S. L. (1994). Within-group norming and other forms of score adjustment in preemployment testing. *American Psychologist, 49*, 929–954.

Sager, C. E., Peterson, N. G., Oppler, S. H., Rosse, R. L., & Walker, C. B. (1997). An examination of five indexes of test battery performance: Analysis of the ECAT battery. *Military Psychology, 9*, 97–120.

Salgado, J. F., & Anderson, N. (2002). Cognitive and GMA testing in the European Community: Issues and evidence. *Human Performance, 15*, 75–96.

Salgado, J. F., & Anderson, N. (2003). Validity generalization of GMA tests across countries in the European Community. *European Journal of Work and Organizational Psychology, 12*, 1–17.

Salgado, J. F., Anderson, N., Moscoso, S., Bertua, C., & de Fruyt, F. (2003a). International validity generalization of GMA and cognitive abilities: A European community meta-analysis. *Personnel Psychology, 56*, 573–605.

Salgado, J. F., Anderson, N., Moscoso, S., Bertua, C., de Fruyt, F., & Rolland, J. P. (2003b). A meta-analytic study of general mental ability validity for different occupations in the European Community. *Journal of Applied Psychology, 88*, 1068–1081.

Salgado, J. F., Viswesvaran, C., & Ones, D. S. (2001). Predictors used for personnel selection: An overview of constructs, methods, and techniques. In N. Anderson, D. S. Ones, H. K. Sinangil, & C. Viswesvaran (Eds.), *Handbook of industrial, work, and organizational psychology* (Vol. 1, pp. 165–199). London: Sage.

Schmidt, F. L. (2002). The role of general cognitive ability and job performance: Why there cannot be a debate. *Human Performance, 15*, 187–210.

Schmidt, F. L., Gast-Rosenberg, I., & Hunter, J. E. (1980). Validity generalization results for computer programmers. *Journal of Applied Psychology, 65*, 643–661.

Schmidt, F. L., & Hunter, J. E. (1977). Development of a general solution to the problem of validity generalization. *Journal of Applied Psychology, 62*, 529–540.

Schmidt, F. L., & Hunter, J. E. (1983). Individual differences in productivity: An empirical test of estimates derived from studies of selection procedure utility. *Journal of Applied Psychology, 68*, 407–414.

Schmidt, F. L., & Hunter, J. E. (1998). The validity and utility of selection methods in personnel psychology: Practical and theoretical implications of 85 years of research findings. *Psychological Bulletin, 124*, 262–274.

Schmidt, F. L., Hunter, J. E., & Caplan, J. R. (1981a). Validity generalization results for two job groups in the petroleum industry. *Journal of Applied Psychology, 66*, 261–273.

Schmidt, F. L., Hunter, J. E., McKenzie, R. C., & Muldrow, T. W. (1979a). Impact of valid selection procedures on work-force productivity. *Journal of Applied Psychology, 64*, 609–626.

Schmidt, F. L., Hunter, J. E., & Outerbridge, A. N. (1986). Impact of job experience and ability on job knowledge, work sample performance, and supervisory ratings of job performance. *Journal of Applied Psychology, 71*, 432–439.

Schmidt, F. L., Hunter, J. E., & Pearlman, K. (1981b). Task differences as moderators of aptitude test validity in selection: A red herring. *Journal of Applied Psychology, 66,* 166–185.

Schmidt, F. L., Hunter, J. E., Pearlman, K., & Shane, G. S. (1979b). Further tests of the Schmidt–Hunter Bayesian validity generalization procedure. *Personnel Psychology, 32,* 257–281.

Schmidt, F. L., Ones, D. S., & Hunter, J. E. (1992). Personnel selection. *Annual Review of Psychology, 43,* 627–670.

Schmitt, N., Gooding, R. Z., Noe, R. A., & Kirsch, M. (1984). Meta-analyses of validity studies published between 1964 and 1982 and the investigation of study characteristics. *Personnel Psychology, 37,* 407–422.

Scholz, G., & Schuler, H. (1993). Das nomologische Netzwerk des Assessment Centers: eine Meta-analyse [The nomological network of the assessment center: A meta-analysis]. *Zeitschrift für Arbeits- und Organisationspsychologie, 37,* 73–85.

Schuler, H., Moser, K., Diemand, A., & Funke, U. (1995). Validitaet eines Einstellungsinterviews zur Prognose des Ausbildungserfolgs [Validity of an employment interview for the prediction of training success]. *Zeitschrift für Paedagogische Psychologie, 9,* 45–54.

Smither, J. W., Reilly, R. R., Millsap, R. E., Pearlman, K., & Stoffey, R. W. (1993). Applicant reactions to selection procedures. *Personnel Psychology, 46,* 49–76.

Spearman, C. (1904). "General intelligence," objectively determined and measured. *American Journal of Psychology, 15,* 201–293.

Spearman, C. (1937). *Psychology down the ages* (Vol. 2). Oxford, UK: Macmillan.

Stankov, L. (in press). "*g*" factor: Issues of design and interpretation. In O. Wilhelm & R. W. Engle (Eds.), *Understanding and measuring intelligence.* London: Sage.

Steiner, D. D., & Gilliland, S. W. (1996). Fairness reactions to personnel selection techniques in France and the United States. *Journal of Applied Psychology, 81,* 134–141.

Sternberg, R. J. (1999). What do we know about tacit knowledge? Making the tacit become explicit. In R. J. Sternberg & J. A. Horvath (Eds.), *Tacit knowledge in professional practice: Researcher and practitioner perspectives* (pp. 231–236). Mahwah, NJ: Erlbaum.

Sternberg, R. J., & Detterman, D. K. (1986). *What is intelligence? Contemporary viewpoints on its nature and definition.* Norwood, NJ: Ablex.

Sternberg, R. J., Forsythe, G. B., Hedlund, J., Horvath, J. A., Wagner, R. K., Williams, W. M., et al. (2000). *Practical intelligence in everyday life.* New York: Cambridge University Press.

Sternberg, R. J., & Wagner, R. K. (1993). The *g*-ocentric view of intelligence and job performance is wrong. *Current Directions in Psychological Science, 2,* 1–5.

Terman, L. M. (1916). *The measurement of intelligence: An explanation of and a complete guide for the use of the Stanford revision and extension of the Binet–Simon Intelligence Scale.* Boston: Houghton Mifflin.

Van Rooy, D. L., & Viswesvaran, C. (in press). Emotional intelligence: A meta-analytic investigation of predictive validity and nomological net. *Journal of Vocational Behavior.*

Verive, J. M., & McDaniel, M. A. (1996). Short-term memory tests in personnel selection: Low adverse impact and high validity. *Intelligence, 23,* 15–32.

Vernon, P. E. (1950). *The structure of human abilities.* New York: Methuen.

Vinchur, A. J., Schippmann, J. S., Switzer, F. S., III, & Roth, P. L. (1998). A meta-analytic review of predictors of job performance for salespeople. *Journal of Applied Psychology, 83,* 586–597.

Vineberg, R., & Joyner, J. N. (1982). *Prediction of job performance: Review of military studies.* Alexandria, VA: Human Resources Research Organization.

Viswesvaran, C., & Ones, D. S. (2002). Agreements and disagreements on the role of general mental ability (GMA) in industrial, work, and organizational psychology. *Human Performance, 15,* 212–231.

Viswesvaran, C., Schmidt, F. L., & Ones, D. S. (in press). Is there a general factor in ratings of job performance? A meta-analytic framework for disentangling substantive and error influences. *Journal of Applied Psychology.*

8

Personality in Personnel Selection

Jesús F. Salgado and Filip de Fruyt

The purpose of this chapter is to review the current research on personality in personnel selection. Many things have changed over the past fifteen years and many conclusions, which for years were taken for granted, are now rejected. In this chapter we review the current theoretical models of personality used in IWO psychology and the empirical evidence relating personality and personnel selection. More specifically, we will review the relationships between personality and job performance, personality and training, personality and occupational choice, personality and job satisfaction, personality and leadership, and finally personality and occupational health.

Personality in Industrial, Work and Organizational Psychology: A summary of the first 65 years

Personality measures have been used in industrial, work and organizational (IWO) psychology since 1920, when they were initially used in industry for personnel selection purposes. Over the decades, hundreds of validity studies were conducted and, until 1990, the main conclusion of the narrative and quantitative literature reviews was that personality measures were poor predictors of organizational criteria, including job performance, training proficiency, job satisfaction, and many other criteria (Ghiselli, 1973; Ghiselli & Barthol, 1953; Guion & Gottier, 1965; Schmitt, Gooding, Noe, & Kirsh, 1984). However, despite these negative conclusions, different surveys conducted in Europe and the United States showed that, paradoxically, personality measures were frequently used in IWO psychology (Levy-Leboyer, 1994; Ryan & Sackett, 1987; Spriegel & Dale,1953). In summary, when taking into account the researchers' conclusions and what was put into practice by the practitioners, we find that researchers and practitioners have followed different paths. The most recent research, however, shows that practitioners do have a good theoretical basis for using personality measures in organizations. More specifically, the research on the Five Factor Model of personality and new developments in related areas led to a changing opinion on the validity and utility of personality at work (see Anderson, Chapter 1, this volume).

Models of personality: The Five Factor Model (FFM) and other alternative models

The Five Factor Model of personality served as one of the flagships for the examination of trait–occupational criteria relationships over the past fifteen years (De Fruyt & Salgado, 2003a, 2003b). At first, the model and its dimensions were used as a taxonomy for the classification of different personality scales that were applied in occupational criteria validity research. Scales were grouped as markers of the FFM dimensions and their validity to predict occupational criteria was subsequently meta-analytically examined. In a second phase, the validity of direct operationalizations of the FFM, including the NEO-FFI, NEO-PI, and NEO-PI-R (Costa & McCrae, 1992), Goldberg's Big Five markers (Goldberg, 1992), the Hogan Personality Inventory (HPI; Hogan & Hogan, 1995), the Personal Characteristics Inventory (PCI; Barrick & Mount, 1993), and the IP/5F (Salgado, Moscoso, & Lado, 2003a) were meta-analytically investigated. In addition, moderators such as job families (sales, customer service, managers, and skilled and semi-skilled workers) and different job performance criteria, including task performance, job dedication, and interpersonal facilitation, were taken into account (Hurtz & Donovan, 2000). A further refinement was to align FFM traits to a personality-oriented account of different criterion measures. Hogan and Holland (2003) meta-analytically examined job–performance relationships from a socio-analytic perspective and organized criterion measures into the socio-analytic dimensions of "getting along" and "getting ahead" (Hogan, 1983), further classifying occupational criteria according to the Big Five personality content categories.

It is clear that the FFM provided a new and massive impetus to personality research for different applications in IWO psychology, and that the potential of the model to guide research has not come to an end. First, it would be of interest to look at studies examining trait–occupational performance criteria relationships at lower levels of the trait hierarchy, further examining the validity of broad versus narrow traits and the bandwidth–fidelity dilemma (Hogan & Roberts, 1996). An additional promising area is the examination of interactions among FFM dimensions. Witt, Burke, Barrick, and Mount (2002) studied the interactive effects of conscientiousness and agreeableness for predicting job performance. So far, the majority of personality–criterion association studies only considered the effect of single traits. A future challenge will be to study traits in interaction with each other (De Fruyt, 2002). Finally, another potential area of study from an FFM perspective is to examine the impact of the traits of individuals comprising a team-on-team performance. With regard to this, exemplary research has been done by Barry and Stewart (1997) describing different models on how individual differences operate in teams.

Personality and clinical psychologists have studied the areas of normal and dysfunctional personality characteristics rather independently, initially considering adaptive and maladaptive traits as qualitatively different systems. The FFM conceptualized the normal variation of traits, whereas the dysfunctional and pathological domain was represented by a categorical system, distinguishing ten more or less discrete symptom configurations, described as Axis-II of the *Diagnostic and Statistical Manual of Mental Disorders* (DSM-IV; American Psychiatric Association, 1994). More recently, there is growing evidence that allows us to consider adult personality disorders as extreme variants of FFM dimensions, with differences between abnormality and normality being gradual and quantitative rather than qualitative. Maladaptive trait models might be of interest to IWO psychologists for studying work outcomes such as negative emotions at work (Rolland & De Fruyt, 2003), a range of counterproductive behaviors, including theft, voluntary absenteeism, industrial vandalism, and drug abuse, and adherence to professional ethics and standards.

Few alternative operationalizations of personality received broad attention in IWO psychology in comparison to the FFM, with the exception of a number of commercially available alternatives that were frequently redesigned to assess the five-factor traits. The Occupational Personality Questionnaire (OPQ; SHL, 1999) and the Personality and Preference Inventory (PAPI; PA Consulting Group, 1998), for example, underwent considerable changes, making them more FFM-linked or look-alikes than their original conceptualizations. Additional alternatives have strong temperamental links, such as Watson, Clark, and Tellegen's PANAS model (1988), including two dimensions referring to positive and negative emotions, or they adopt a type approach for representing individual differences, such as the Myers–Briggs Type Indicator (Myers & Briggs, 1962).

PERSONALITY AND PERSONNEL SELECTION: THE STATE-OF-THE-ART

In the past fifteen years many primary studies and dozens of meta-analyses have examined the validity of personality measures as predictors in personnel selection. The FFM proved to be a successful taxonomy for classifying the various measures included in the validity studies, and we now have greater knowledge regarding the validity of the Big Five. Furthermore, the validity of other personality measures (e.g., integrity tests, managerial scales) was also examined. In this section, we will review the validity of three types of personality measures: (a) the personality measures based on the FFM, (b) composites of personality measures, and (c) personality measures not based on the FFM.

Personality measures based on the Five Factor Model in personnel selection

The Five Factor Model and job performance. The seminal work on the validity of the Big Five for predicting job performance was carried out by Barrick and Mount in 1991. This study was the origin of several meta-analytic studies conducted by these authors and many others (Barrick & Mount, 1991; Barrick, Mount, & Judge, 2001; Hough, 1992; Hurtz & Donovan, 2000; Mount & Barrick, 1995; Salgado, 1997, 1998, 2002, 2003; Tett, Rothstein, & Jackson, 1991) during the next twelve years. In the initial study, Barrick and Mount hypothesized that conscientiousness and emotional stability would be valid predictors of job performance for all occupational groups. They sustained that conscientiousness would be related to job performance because this personality dimension assesses personal characteristics such as persistence, reliability, responsibility, or work effort and all of these are relevant attributes in the execution of job tasks in all occupations. Barrick and Mount also sustained that emotional stability would be a predictor of job performance because employees displaying characteristics such as being worrisome, neurotic, anxious, or emotionally unstable would be less performing than employees displaying the opposite characteristics. Barrick and Mount expected to find that the validity of these two dimensions would generalize across occupational groups and all criterion categories. Furthermore, they hypothesized that extroversion and agreeableness would be predictors of job performance in occupations with frequent interpersonal interactions (e.g., sales and managerial occupations) and that openness to experience would be a valid predictor of training proficiency.

The results partially supported these hypotheses. The main finding was that conscientiousness proved to be a valid predictor for all occupational groups and for all criteria and that it generalized validity across studies. However, the magnitude of the validity coefficient was relatively small ($\rho = .22$). Barrick and Mount also found that extroversion and agreeableness predicted job performance in managerial occupations and that openness to experience was a valid predictor for training proficiency. Other predictions were not supported by the results. For example, emotional stability did not show a relevant validity coefficient and did not generalize validity across occupations and criteria. Therefore, Barrick and Mount's conclusions were slightly optimistic based on the results found for conscientiousness, while the Five Factor Model of personality proved to be a very useful tool for researching personality at work.

In those years, two additional studies had an important impact on this area. Tett, Rothstein, and Jackson (1991) carried out a small-scale meta-analysis using only confirmatory studies. Their findings showed that the five personality dimensions were valid predictors of job performance. Hough and her colleagues (Hough, 1992; Hough, Eaton, Dunnette, Kamp, & McCloy, 1990) conducted another meta-analysis containing two important variations. In the first place, they did not correct validity for reliability and range restriction, and second, they used six criterion types: education, training, job commitment, job efficiency, delinquency, and substance abuse. In the case of job efficiency, Hough et al. found that conscientiousness and emotional stability were valid predictors. Indeed, due to the fact that Hough et al. made no corrections for artifactual errors, the magnitude of the validity coefficients was smaller than Barrick and Mount's coefficients.

In sum, these three studies showed that the conclusions of the previous narrative and meta-analytic researches were not correct and that they were probably due to two types of error: a) artifactual errors pointed out by the validity generalization hypothesis (Hunter & Schmidt, 1990), and b) the lack of a theoretical framework for classifying the various personality measures included in the primary validity studies.

In the next few years, several meta-analyses reinforced and extended the conclusions of these pioneer studies. For example, Salgado (1997, 1998) examined the validity of the Big Five in the European Community. Most existing meta-analyses have been conducted using American primary studies, thus their international generalizability could not be taken for granted. The results of Salgado's study essentially replicated the former findings by Barrick and Mount, with an important addition: emotional stability proved to be a valid predictor for all occupational groups and it generalized validity across samples and criteria. This finding confirmed that Barrick and Mount's hypothesis for emotional stability was correct. Salgado's results also showed a slight increment in the magnitude of the validity coefficient (e.g., conscientiousness displayed a validity coefficient equal to .25). Hurtz and Donovan (2000) examined the validity of the Big Five when they were assessed using personality measures explicitly developed for this purpose. Their results replicated previous findings, confirming that conscientiousness and emotional stability generalized validity across occupations and criteria.

Barrick et al. (2001) re-analyzed all the previous meta-analyses and conducted a second-order meta-analysis with all the primary meta-analyses carried out during the 1990s. The main conclusion by Barrick et al. was that two personality dimensions, conscientiousness and emotional stability, were valid predictors of job performance for all occupational groups and that the other three personality dimensions were valid predictors for some jobs and some criteria. Therefore, the accumulated empirical evidence left no room for doubts concerning the relevancy of the Big Five personality dimensions (and personality measures in general) as tools for personnel selection. Recently, in the largest primary-order meta-analysis conducted until now, in which the most recent advances in meta-analytic methods were used (Hunter, Schmidt, & Le, 2002; Le & Schmidt, 2003), Salgado (2004a) found that the magnitude of the Big Five validity was substantially underestimated in previous quantitative studies. Exclusively using studies in which explicitly developed Big Five measures were used, Salgado found validities of .33, .21, .19, .10, and .09 for conscientiousness, emotional stability, agreeableness, extroversion, and openness to experience, respectively.

Three recent studies have added new information regarding the use of the Big Five in this area. Salgado (2002) showed that conscientiousness and agreeableness were predictors of counterproductive behaviors (i.e., deviant behaviors at work) and that the five dimensions predicted turnover. Salgado (2003), using meta-analysis, compared the validity of the personality measures based on the Five Factor Model with those that were not based on the FFM. He found that in both cases conscientiousness and emotional stability proved to be valid predictors of job performance but that the validity magnitude of the measures based on the FFM were remarkably larger. Hogan and Holland (2003) examined the validity of the Big Five for predicting two types of organizational criteria, getting along and getting ahead, as they are conceptualized in the socioanalytic theory of personality (R. Hogan, 1983). Getting along was defined as *"behavior that gains the approval of others, enhances cooperation, and serves to build and maintain relationships"* (Hogan & Holland, 2003, p. 103). This criterion has a great parallelism with the concept of contextual performance as defined by Borman and his colleagues (Borman & Motowidlo, 1993; Borman, Penner, Allen, & Motowidlo, 2001). Getting ahead was defined as *"behavior that produces results and advances an individual within the group and the group within its competition"* (Hogan & Holland, 2003, p. 103). This kind of criterion has a parallelism with the promotion criterion used in other meta-analyses (e.g., Hough, 1992; Mount & Barrick, 1995). For the getting along criterion, adjustment (emotional stability) showed a validity of .34, likeability (agreeableness) showed a validity of .23, and prudence (conscientiousness) showed a validity of .31. For the getting ahead criterion, adjustment produced a validity of .22, ambition (one of the sub-dimensions of extroversion) produced a validity of .26, and prudence produced a validity of .20. Further differentiation among the criterion domain showed once again that emotional stability and conscientiousness were valid predictors of job performance.

In a more recent study, Salgado (2004b) examined the moderating effects of job complexity on the validity of the Big Five, applying the most recent developments in meta-analytic methodology (e.g., the correction for indirect range restriction). The findings showed that job complexity is a relevant validity moderator of personality measures and that the magnitude of validity coefficients was much larger than previously believed. For example, in the case of occupations with a medium level of complexity (around 68% of all occupations), three personality dimensions showed validity generalization: conscientiousness, emotional stability, and agreeableness. The magnitude of the validity coefficients was .36, .24, and .25, respectively. These coefficients were remarkably larger than the coefficients found in any previous meta-analytic study conducted with large samples.

A related and at the same time very promising line of research for the future has been carried out by Judge and his colleagues (Judge & Bono, 2001; Judge, Locke, & Durham, 1997), who proposed that a higher-order factor could include four traits: emotional stability, self-esteem, self-efficacy, and locus of control. Judge et al. (1997) termed this factor "core self-evaluation" and Barrick et al. (2001) described this factor as a wider conceptualization of neuroticism (reversed emotional stability).

The research on the relationship between individual differences in personality and training has also increased in the past ten years, examining both the role of personality in process and outcome variables of training (Hough & Ones, 2001). The examination of these relations was done with both the Big Five personality dimensions and composite personality variables. In recent years, many primary studies and various meta-analyses have examined the role of Big Five personality variables for training in organizations. In fact, training proficiency was used as a criterion in some of the meta-analyses reviewed in the prior section. For example, in the USA, Barrick and Mount (1991) reported that extroversion (ρ = .26), openness to experience (ρ = .25), and conscientiousness (ρ = .23) were predictors of training proficiency. In the European Community, Salgado (1997) found that emotional stability (ρ = .27), openness to experience (ρ = .26), agreeableness (ρ = .31), and conscientiousness (ρ = .39) were predictors of training proficiency. More recently, Barrick et al. (2001), integrating all the prior meta-analyses, found that openness to experience (ρ = .33), extroversion (ρ = .28), conscientiousness (ρ = .27), and agreeableness (ρ = .14) were predictors of training proficiency.

Therefore, the conclusions of the cumulated research in the past fourteen years is that Big Five personality dimensions are important variables for predicting and explaining job performance and training proficiency and that they can be used confidently in personnel selection by practitioners. In Table 8.1, we report a summary of the main results of the various meta-analyses. In each case, we report the meta-analyses conducted with the largest sample size.

Incremental validity of the Big Five for predicting job performance and training. Typically, personality measures are not used alone in personnel selection processes but in conjunction with other instruments, often GMA tests, but also assessment center exercises. Therefore, it is relevant to estimate whether the Big Five showed added validity beyond GMA. The incremental validity of conscientiousness and emotional stability over and beyond GMA for predicting job performance and training proficiency was examined by Salgado (1998) using data from the European Community. The results of this meta-analysis showed that the two personality dimensions added validity over GMA. Conscientiousness showed incremental validity over GMA by 11% and over emotional stability by 10%. However, this initial analysis has three limitations: a) the incremental validity of only two of the five personality dimensions was reported, b) it was limited to the European studies, and c) the data base was small and the meta-analytic techniques are now improved. Currently, we have more accurate estimates of the Big Five validity, as well as better estimates of the relationships between the Big Five and GMA tests. Therefore, it is possible to conduct a new

TABLE 8.1 Summary of the meta-analytic results on the relationship between the Big Five personality dimensions and organizational criteria and variables

Dimension	K	N	ρ
Job performance[a]			
Conscientiousness	133	33,668	.33
Emotional stability	108	19,880	.21
Extroversion	111	21,916	.10
Openness to experience	82	13,895	.09
Agreeableness	110	21,911	.19
Training[b]			
Conscientiousness	20	3,909	.31
Emotional stability	25	3,753	.09
Extroversion	21	3,484	.28
Openness to experience	18	3,177	.33
Agreeableness	24	4,100	.14
Leadership emergence[c]			
Conscientiousness	17	na	.33
Emotional stability	30	na	.24
Extroversion	37	na	.33
Openness to experience	20	na	.24
Agreeableness	23	na	.05
Leadership effectiveness[c]			
Conscientiousness	18	na	.16
Emotional stability	18	na	.22
Extroversion	23	na	.24
Openness to experience	17	na	.24
Agreeableness	19	na	.16
Job satisfaction[d]			
Conscientiousness	79	21,719	.26
Emotional stability	92	24,527	.29
Extroversion	75	20,184	.25
Openness to experience	50	15,196	.02
Agreeableness	38	11,856	.17
Deviant behavior (reversed)[e]			
Conscientiousness	13	6,276	.26
Emotional stability	15	3,107	.06
Extroversion	12	2,383	−.01
Openness to experience	8	1,421	−.14
Agreeableness	9	1,299	.20
Turnover (reversed)[e]			
Conscientiousness	5	748	.31
Emotional stability	4	554	.35
Extroversion	4	554	.20
Openness to experience	4	554	.14
Agreeableness	4	554	.22

Note: K = number of studies; N = total sample size; na = not available; [a] Salgado (2004a); [b] Barrick, Mount, & Judge (2001); [c] Judge, Bono, Ilies, & Gerhardt (2002); [d] Judge, Heller, & Mount (2002); [e] Salgado (2002).

and more complete analysis of the incremental validity of the Big Five. The cumulative evidence of the validity of the Big Five as predictors of job performance is currently very strong and, when considered with the cumulative evidence that General Mental Ability is the best single predictor of job performance, allows for the examination of the incremental validity of the Big Five beyond GMA. With regard to this, two meta-analyses of GMA validity are especially relevant. Hunter and Hunter (1984) demonstrated that the validity of GMA for medium-complexity jobs (68% of the total jobs in the US economy and a similar percentage in Europe) was .53. Recently, Salgado et al. (2003) have demonstrated that the validity of GMA in the European Community for medium-complexity jobs is exactly .53. Therefore, we can confidently consider that .53 is the best estimate of GMA validity for the majority of jobs in Europe and America. Based on this estimate, we have analyzed the contribution of each personality dimension for predicting job performance beyond GMA. In order to conduct this analysis, we have used the estimates of the Big Five validity reported for the medium level of complexity (Salgado, 2004b). The results of the incremental validity analysis are reported in Table 8.2. As can be seen, for the job performance criterion, three personality dimensions showed incremental validity: conscientiousness, agreeableness, and emotional stability. The first two dimensions resulted in strong additions of explained variance beyond GMA, i.e., 30.30% and 20.12% for conscientiousness and agreeableness, respectively. Emotional stability also added validity over GMA but the percentage was smaller, 9.07%. Therefore, the result for emotional stability is very similar to the one found by Salgado (1998), but the current estimate for conscientiousness is remarkably larger than the value found by him.

With regard to the training proficiency criterion, three personality dimensions showed an important increment in the explained variance over GMA: conscientiousness, openness to experience, and extroversion. Agreeableness also showed added validity, but the size of the increment was modest. Table 8.2 shows that conscientiousness, openness, and extroversion displayed incremental validity by 24.20%, 22.24%, and 18.04% respectively, and that agreeableness added validity by 7.47% over GMA.

The results of these last two analyses suggest that in most cases the practitioner should opt to combine GMA measures with measures of conscientiousness, emotional stability, and agreeableness for predicting job performance and to combine GMA tests with measures of conscientiousness, extroversion, and openness to predict training proficiency.

The FFM and the prediction of job satisfaction and leadership.   Recently the role of personality variables in job satisfaction has been acknowledged and many studies have been conducted in this area, clearly contrasting with the emphasis on the topic in past decades. Judge and his colleagues must be credited as the main researchers in this area. For example, Judge, Heller, and Mount (2002) have meta-analytically examined the relationships between the Big Five and job satisfaction. They found that four personality dimensions were correlated with job satisfaction: emotional stability, extroversion, agreeableness, and conscientiousness. The correlations were .29, .25, .17, and .16 for emotional stability, extroversion, agreeableness, and conscientiousness, respectively. The multiple correlation was strong ($R = .41$) suggesting that individuals' personality characteristics have a causal impact on job satisfaction.

The relationship between personality traits and leadership was hypothesized for many years, but the empirical findings only weakly supported this conjecture (Stogdill, 1974). For

TABLE 8.2 Incremental validity of the Big Five over GMA explained variance for predicting job performance and training proficiency

Variable	Validity	Correlation with GMA	R mult.	R^2	ΔR	% Suppl.	β GMA	β Suppl.
Job performance								
GMA	.53							
GMA + conscientiousness	.36	.02	.63	.40	.10	30.30	.53	.36
GMA + emotional stability	.24	.14	.56	.31	.03	9.07	.58	.19
GMA + agreeableness	.25	-.03	.59	.35	.06	20.12	.52	.26
GMA + extroversion	.08	.06	.53	.28	.00	.00	.56	-.05
GMA + openness	.09	.09	.53	.28	.00	.00	.57	-.05
Training proficiency								
GMA	.53							
GMA + conscientiousness	.31	.02	.61	.37	.08	24.20	.53	.31
GMA + emotional stability	.09	.14	.53	.28	.00	.00	.60	-.02
GMA + agreeableness	.14	-.03	.55	.30	.02	7.47	.52	.15
GMA + extroversion	.28	.06	.59	.34	.06	18.04	.55	.26
GMA + openness	.33	.09	.60	.36	.07	22.24	.55	.31

example, qualitative reviews suggested that traits such as dependability, sociability, initiative, achievement orientation, and emotional stability were typical personality characteristics of effective leaders, and they were found in some empirical studies but not in others (Stogdill, 1974).

The largest meta-analytic study on personality and leadership was carried out by Judge, Bono, Ilies, and Gerhardt (2002). They examined the relation between the Big Five personality dimensions, including a number of sub-dimensions and leadership. With regard to the Big Five, Judge et al. found that emotional stability ($\rho = .24$), extroversion ($\rho = .31$), openness to experience ($\rho = .24$), and conscientiousness ($\rho = .28$) were correlated with leadership, while agreeableness showed a very small correlation ($\rho = .08$). Furthermore, emotional stability, extroversion, openness, and conscientiousness generalized the correlation across the studies and samples, but agreeableness did not. The multiple correlation between the Big Five and leadership was robust ($R = .48$), suggesting that the Big Five taxonomy is very useful for explaining the dispositional basis of leadership.

With regard to the personality sub-dimensions, Judge et al. found that two of the conscientiousness sub-dimensions (achievement orientation and dependability) correlated with leadership, that two of the extroversion sub-dimensions (sociability and dominance) correlated with leadership, and that one of the emotional stability sub-dimensions (self-esteem) correlated with overall leadership.

Judge et al. also examined the relationships between the Big Five and two leadership criteria: leadership emergence and leadership effectiveness. According to Hogan, Curphy, and Hogan (1994), leadership emergence refers to the characteristics linked to someone who is perceived as a leader, while leadership effectiveness refers to the leader's performance. With regard to leadership emergence, once again, emotional stability, extroversion, openness, and conscientiousness were correlated with this criterion. The magnitude of the correlation was .24, .33, .24, and .33 for emotional stability, extroversion, openness, and conscientiousness, respectively. The multiple correlation was also robust ($R = .53$). In the case of leadership effectiveness, all the Big Five were correlated with this criterion but the magnitude of the correlations was smaller. The correlations were .22, .24, .24, .21, and .16 for emotional stability, extroversion, openness, agreeableness, and conscientiousness, respectively. The multiple correlation was also strong ($R = .39$). This last analysis showed that the important difference between leadership emergence and leadership effectiveness is agreeableness, which, although not relevant for the emergence, is important for maintaining leadership.

Personality composites in personnel selection

A second line of research, carried out in recent years, was the examination of construct and criterion validity of personality composites used in personnel selection. Ones and her colleagues are responsible for the majority of the meta-analytic contributions in this area (Ones, 1993; Ones & Viswesvaran, 1998a, 2001a, 2001b; Ones, Viswesvaran, & Schmidt, 1993). Ones and Viswesvaran (2001a) classified the composites in two large groups: Criterion-focused Occupational Personality Scales (COPS) and Job-focused Occupational Personality Scales (JOPS). The COPS are occupational personality scales created for the purpose of predicting specific organizational criteria, such as honesty, stress tolerance, counterproductive behaviors, accidents, violent behaviors, customer service orientation, security orientation, and others. The JOPS are occupational personality scales explicitly developed for the purpose of predicting performance in specific occupational groups, such as managerial occupations, sales occupations, clerical occupations, and others.

Personality composites and job performance and training. Integrity tests are probably the most researched of the COPS in personnel selection, with various meta-analyses having been recently conducted on this subject. Based on the content of the items, integrity tests are usually classified in two groups, i.e., overt integrity tests and personality-based tests (Sackett, Burris, & Callaham, 1989). Because this chapter is restricted to personality measures, we will present only findings concerning personality-based integrity tests. The most comprehensive meta-analysis so far was carried out by Ones et al. (1993). These researchers found that the validity of personality-based integrity tests was .37 for predicting overall job performance rated by the supervisor and .35 for predicting all performance criteria (job performance ratings plus production records). Ones and Viswesvaran (1998a) investigated the relationship between integrity and training proficiency and found that the correlation was .38. In this meta-analysis, training was measured mainly with objective tests (75% of the studies) at the end of the training period.

Ones and Viswesvaran (2001a) also examined the validity of other COPS for predicting job performance. For example, they found validities of .19, .42, and .39 for drug and alcohol scales, stress tolerance scales, and customer service scales, respectively. Ones and Viswesvaran (2001b) also reported a validity coefficient of .41 for the violence scales. Therefore, we can conclude that all COPS have substantial validity for predicting job performance. In fact the COPS validity is generally larger than the conscientiousness validity, which is the personality dimension with the largest validity. A possible explanation resides in the nomological net of the COPS. Ones (1993) has demonstrated that both types of integrity tests consisted of a combination of conscientiousness, emotional stability, and agreeableness. Ones and Viswesvaran (2001a) showed that customer service scales also correlated considerably with agreeableness ($\rho = .70$), emotional stability ($\rho = .58$), and conscientiousness ($\rho = .43$). Ones and Viswesvaran (2001a) also found that the drug and alcohol scales and the stress tolerance scales showed a similar pattern of relationships with the Big Five. For example, the drug and alcohol scales correlated .39, .28, and .48 with emotional stability, agreeableness, and conscientiousness, respectively, and the stress tolerance scales correlated .65, .48, and .38 with these same dimensions. Consequently, we can speculate with some foundation that COPS showed greater validity than any other single personality dimension because they are a linear combination of three or four personality dimensions, mainly emotional stability, conscientiousness, and agreeableness, and, in some cases, extroversion. A summary of the main results of the meta-analyses commented above appears in Table 8.3.

Personality composites and counterproductive behaviors. Ones and her colleagues have also extensively researched the validity of COPS for predicting counterproductive behaviors, both as an overall criterion of counter-productivity and as specific disruptive behaviors such as theft or absenteeism. In this review, we will concentrate on the validity of the personality-based COPS. A summary of the results commented in this section is shown in Table 8.3.

TABLE 8.3 Summary of the meta-analytic results on the relationship between COPS and JOPS and organizational criteria and variables

Dimension	K	N	ρ
Job performance			
Integrity (personality-based tests)[a]	102	27,081	.37
Drug and alcohol scales[b]	7	1,436	.19
Stress tolerance scales[b]	13	1,010	.42
Customer service scales[b]	33	6,944	.39
Violence scales[c]	14	4,003	.41
Training			
Integrity (personality-based tests)[d]		2,364	.38
Counterproductive behaviors			
Integrity (personality-based tests)[a]	138	158,065	.32
Stress tolerance scales[b]	5	594	.42
Customer service scales[b]	5	740	.42
Violence scales[c]	4	533	.46
Absenteeism			
Integrity (personality-based tests)[e]	16	5,435	.36

Note: K = number of studies; N = total sample size; [a] Ones, Viswesvaran, & Schmidt (1993); [b] Ones & Viswesvaran (2001a); [c] Ones & Viswesvaran (2001b); [d] Ones & Viswesvaran (1998a); [e] Ones, Viswesvaran, & Schmidt (2003).

In the comprehensive meta-analysis mentioned in the previous section, Ones et al. (1993) found that personality-based integrity tests predicted counterproductive behaviors very efficiently, given that the validity was .32 when the criterion included both narrow and broad disruptive behaviors such as actual theft, admitted theft, illegal activities, absenteeism, tardiness, dismissals for actual theft, and violence. Recently, Ones, Viswesvaran, and Schmidt (2003) have examined the validity of personality-based integrity tests for predicting voluntary absenteeism. They have shown that personality-based integrity tests are good predictors of this kind of absenteeism. The validity coefficient was .36. This coefficient contrasts with the very small validities found by Salgado (2002) for the Big Five for predicting absenteeism and clearly suggests that the personality-integrity test is a good option for predicting absenteeism in personnel selection contexts.

In addition to the validity of integrity tests, Ones and Viswevaran (2001a, 2001b) have also analyzed the validity of other types of COPS. For example, they reported a validity of .29 for drug and alcohol scales, .42 for stress tolerance and costumer service scales, and .46 for violence scales. All these coefficients are substantial and suggest that COPS are robust predictors of counterproductive behaviors at work. These findings allow us to recommend personality measures to practitioners for personnel selection purposes when the objective is to prevent or reduce dysfunctional behaviors at work.

Incremental validity of personality composites for predicting job performance and counterproductive behaviors. The results of the various meta-analyses described in the previous sections allow us to examine whether COPS show incremental validity over GMA for predicting job

TABLE 8.4   Incremental validity of the COPS over GMA explained variance for predicting job performance and training proficiency

Variable	Validity	Correlation with GMA	R mult.	R^2	ΔR	% Suppl.	β GMA	β Suppl.
Job performance								
GMA	.53							
GMA + integrity	.37	.02	.64	.41	.11	31.51	.53	.37
GMA + drug & alcohol	.19	−.18	.60	.36	.07	23.06	.48	.24
GMA + stress tolerance	.42	.15	.63	.40	.10	29.69	.55	.40
GMA + customer service	.39	−.10	.69	.48	.16	41.37	.32	.40
Training proficiency								
GMA	.53							
GMA + integrity	.37	.02	.65	.42	.12	32.70	.53	.38

performance. Once again, the findings by Ones and her colleagues are basic for computing the incremental validity of COPS. Together with the reported operational validity, it is necessary to know the correlation of COPS with GMA. Ones and Viswesvaran (2001a) reported the correlation coefficients of −.18, .15 and −.10 between GMA and drug and alcohol scales, stress tolerance scales, and customer service scales, respectively. Ones et al. (1993) pointed out that the correlation between integrity tests and GMA is practically zero. Therefore, using the data reported in Table 8.3, together with these correlations and the correlation of .53 between GMA and job performance, the optimal combination between the GMA measures and the COPS measures can be estimated. The results of the multiple regression analyses are reported in Table 8.4.

As can be seen, all COPS produced important gains in the prediction of job performance when they were combined with GMA tests. The multiple correlation ranges from .60 to .69 and the percentage of explained variance added by the COPS was 31.51%, 23.06%, 29.69%, and 41.37% for personality-based integrity tests, drug and alcohol scales, stress tolerance scales, and customer service scales, respectively. With regard to the prediction of training proficiency, personality-based integrity tests proved to be an important source of explained variance as the increment of the variance over GMA was 32.70%. Based on the results of the cumulated evidence, we suggest that COPS can assuredly be used for predicting job performance, especially when the criteria of interest are counterproductive behaviors.

Non-based FFM personality measures

As already mentioned, there are alternative models next to the Five Factor Model, and the validity of these models for use in personnel selection was also examined in the period reviewed in this chapter. A first examination was conducted by Hough (1992; Hough et al., 1990), who evaluated the validity of the locus of control and masculinity–femininity measures. After that review, new concepts were developed and examined in work contexts.

In this section we will review the validity of three groups of personality measures: a) maladaptive personality styles, b) emotional intelligence measures, and c) other personality measures (locus of control, self-esteem, self-efficacy, positive affectivity and negative affectivity).

It is also relevant to mention in this section the results of the meta-analysis in which Salgado (2003) compared the validity of the Big Five measures explicitly developed to assess the Big Five and other measures developed with other models (e.g., 16PF, Occupational Personality Questionnaire) when they tried to assess the Big Five. With regard to these measures, they can be organized using the Five Factor Model taxonomy, and they either assess the Big Five partially (e.g., some facets) or entirely (the complete dimension). The meta-analysis showed that the validity for predicting job performance was .18, .05, .08, .08, and .13 for conscientiousness, emotional stability, extroversion, openness, and agreeableness, respectively. These results mean that the validity of measures that are explicitly developed to assess the Big Five is substantially larger than the validity for alternative models. Therefore, we suggest that practitioners use measures explicitly developed to assess the Big Five when they wish to measure the five personality dimensions. The summary of the findings on these measures appears in Table 8.5.

Maladaptive personality styles and job performance. As we stated previously, the FFM sustains that its dimensions comprehensively describe the normal variation of traits in adults. However, we have also displayed that there are alternative models based on clinical and psychopathological conceptualizations of personality. For example, DSM-III-R and DSM-IV suggest that there are a number of maladaptive personality styles and further offer an alternative classification system for personality. Nevertheless, at present, only a small number of studies have examined the criterion-related validity of these taxonomies of maladaptive personality styles for predicting job performance. Research has also shown that the number of individuals presenting dysfunctional personality styles at work is very small, but it is also true that the negative consequences of the maladaptive personality styles may be greater in terms of the negative effects on productivity than the consequences of normal personality dimensions. Furthermore, the number of individuals presenting maladaptive tendencies at work could be larger than the number of individuals presenting personality disorders. Additionally, Hogan and Hogan (2001) have recently shown that maladaptive personality styles were correlated with leadership behaviors. More specifically, they found that narcissistic styles were positively associated with leadership. Salgado, Moscoso, and Lado (2003b) speculated on possible relations between the maladaptive personality styles and job performance. They hypothesized that the maladaptive personality styles mainly related to neuroticism and that conscientiousness would be a predictor of job performance. More specifically they hypothesized that 1) avoidant, depressive, passive-aggressive, self-defeated, schyzotypal, borderline, antisocial, and dependent traits and symptoms would show a negative relation with task performance, contextual performance, and overall job performance, and that 2) the compulsive personality style would correlate positively with task, contextual, and overall performance. Salgado et al.'s results supported the hypothesis regarding the styles related to emotional stability, as they found that all the styles that consisted of emotional stability were found to be predictors of the three criteria of job performance. The magnitude of the correlations ranged from −.24 to −.35 for task

TABLE 8.5 Summary of the meta-analytic results on the relationship between the various personality variables (and models) and organizational criteria and variables

Dimension	K	N	ρ
Job performance			
Conscientiousness-NFFM[a]	36	5,874	.18
Emotional stability-NFFM[a]	25	4,541	.05
Extroversion-NFFM[a]	26	4,338	.08
Openness to experience-NFFM[a]	29	4,364	.08
Agreeableness-NFFM[a]	31	4,573	.13
Generalized self-efficacy[b]	11	1,506	.43
Locus of control[c]	35	4,310	.22
Self-esteem[c]	40	5,145	.26
Training			
Generalized self-efficacy[b]	4	422	.29
Employment performance (b)			
Emotional intelligence[d]	19	2,652	.24
Job satisfaction			
Positive affectivity[e]	15	3,326	.49
Negative affectivity[e]	27	6,233	−.33
Generalized self-efficacy[c]	8	1,411	.29
Locus of control[c]	80	18,491	.32
Self-esteem[c]	56	20,819	.26
Salary			
Generalized self-efficacy[b]	5	468	.28
Absenteeism			
Generalized self-efficacy[b]	4	718	.21

Note: K = number of studies; N = total sample size; [a] Salgado (2003); [b] Salgado & Moscoso (2000); [c] Judge & Bono (2001); [d] Van Rooy & Viswesvaran (in press); [e] Connolly & Viswesvaran (2004).

performance, from −.27 to −.43 for contextual performance, and from −.27 to −.45 for overall job performance. An interesting result was found for the antisocial (risky) style. They found that this style was negatively correlated with task, contextual, and job performance. This may be explained by the fact that the risky style is negatively correlated with agreeableness and conscientiousness. Previous research has shown that conscientiousness plus agreeableness plus emotional stability produces a composite of integrity. Therefore, the antisocial style could be reflecting the opposite pole of integrity and, consequently, be negatively predicting job performance. Up until now little research has been conducted in this area, and we suggest that more studies be carried out in order to reach more conclusive results.

Emotional intelligence and job performance. In the past few years, emotional intelligence (EI) has been a topic that has received much attention in organizations and in the popular literature. The meta-analysis conducted by Van Rooy and Viswesvaran (in press) has shown that EI correlated .22 with General Mental Ability (GMA), .23 with agreeableness, .31 with conscientiousness, .33 with emotional stability, .34 with extroversion, and .23 with openness to experience. These results suggest that EI is a composite of GMA and the Big Five. Schulte, Ree, and Carretta (in press) have examined this hypothesis, finding that the multiple correlation was .81. With regard to the criterion-oriented validity of EI measures in organizational settings, the meta-analysis by Van Rooy and Viswesvaran showed that EI has a validity of .24 for predicting performance in employment and .14 for predicting organizational records. Taken together, these results are very important for the debate on the nature of EI and its utility in applied contexts and, more specifically, in personnel selection.

We have examined the incremental validity of EI for predicting job performance in various combinations of predictors: GMA–EI, conscientiousness–EI, emotional stability–EI and agreeableness–EI. The results of this examination have many implications for the practice of personnel selection using EI measures. In connection with GMA, the results suggest that EI measures do not add relevant variance when they are combined with GMA measures because the increment in the multiple correlation is only .01 ($R^2 = .30$). This result clarifies the debate on the relations between GMA and EI and the utility of EI measures when GMA is used in a personnel selection process. These results show that, for purposes of predicting job performance, the combination of a measure of GMA with a measure of EI is a waste of time and money. Exactly the same result was found for conscientiousness. The increment in the multiple correlation by adding EI was .01 ($R^2 = .14$). Only the combination of EI measures with measures of emotional stability or agreeableness has practical utility. In these cases, EI showed relevant increments of validity over emotional stability (.04; $R^2 = .08$) and agreeableness (.07; $R^2 = .10$). However, a personnel selection process based on the combination of EI measures with measures of emotional stability or agreeableness is not an optimal combination of predictors. Furthermore, measures of emotional stability and agreeableness are typically included in all Big Five questionnaires and, therefore, it is not necessary to include a specific EI scale along with an FFM and a GMA measure. In conclusion, this suggests that EI measures are only useful for predicting job performance when they are used alone; in any other case their contribution is practically zero.

Other personality measures and organizational criteria: locus of control, self-esteem, self-efficacy, positive affectivity and negative affectivity.   In the years reviewed in this chapter, research has been published on other personality constructs besides the measures reviewed in the previous sections that can be useful for personnel selection. These personality variables, which were related to job performance and job satisfaction, included locus of control, self-esteem, and self-efficacy. Judge et al. (1997) concluded that these three constructs were sub-dimensions of a bigger construct called core self-evaluation or a more extensively conceptualized notion of neuroticism. However, two meta-analyses have analyzed the correlations of these variables with organizational criteria. Salgado and Moscoso (2000) found that generalized self-efficacy correlated .43 ($K = 11, N = 1506$) with job performance, .28 ($K = 5, N = 468$) with salary, .29 ($K = 8, N = 1411$) with job satisfaction, .29 ($K = 4, N = 422$) with training, and .21 ($K = 4, N = 718$) with absenteeism (reversed). For their part, Judge and Bono (2001) found that self-efficacy correlated .23 ($K = 10, N = 1122$) with job performance and .45

($K = 12$, $N = 12903$) with job satisfaction. With regard to locus of control, Judge and Bono found a correlation of .22 ($K = 35$, $N = 4310$) with job performance and a correlation of .32 ($K = 80$, $N = 18491$) with job satisfaction. Finally, Judge and Bono found that self-esteem correlated .26 ($K = 40$, $N = 5145$) with job performance and .26 ($K = 56$, $N = 20819$) with job satisfaction. A summary of these findings is presented in Table 8.5.

As Rolland and De Fruyt (2003) observed, interest in emotions in the workplace has rapidly increased in the past decade and the role of affectivity at work has become a theme of major interest. Affective styles are the general tendency to experience a given mood over time and across situations (Rolland & De Fruyt, 2003). The affective styles are structured in two dimensions: positive affectivity and negative affectivity. These two dimensions are relatively independent from each other. Positive affectivity is defined as a dimension related to positive emotional states such as joy, enthusiasm, excitement, and pride, and some authors have seen positive affectivity as the same domain captured by extroversion. Negative affectivity is defined as a dimension related to negative emotional states such as sadness, anger, guilt, and disgust, and, therefore, it has been considered as the same domain captured by neuroticism. Recently, Connolly and Viswesvaran (2004), using meta-analysis, examined the relationship between job satisfaction and positive affectivity and negative affectivity. They found that the two variables predict job satisfaction and that 10–25% of the variance in job satisfaction could be due to individual differences in affectivity. More specifically, Connolly and Viswesvaran found that positive affectivity correlated .49 with job satisfaction and negative affectivity correlated −.33 with job satisfaction. These results show the relevance of the affective styles for explaining emotions at work.

PERSONALITY AND OCCUPATIONAL CHOICE

There has been a long research tradition linking personality traits and vocational interests (Darley & Hagenah, 1955; Holland, 1973, 1999; Hogan & Blake, 1999). Years ago, one of the major contributors to research on the structure of interests, John Holland (1973), suggested that interest inventories are personality inventories. Expressing a preference for a particular occupation, or demonstrating interest in particular activities, was assumed by Holland to reveal something of the individual's personality. Since the inception of Holland's RIASEC interest model distinguishing six vocational interest types, i.e., the Realistic, Investigative, Artistic, Social, Enterprising, and Conventional types, several studies have examined the associations with personality, in particular with the dimensions of the Five Factor Model. Both RIASEC and the FFM are well-researched and robust models that provide a comprehensive account of the structure of interests and personality traits, respectively.

Several individual studies on RIASEC–FFM associations have been reported over the past years, showing a number of consistent, but also conflicting findings, warranting the use of meta-analytic techniques to describe the overall association picture (see De Fruyt & Mervielde, 1997). Larson, Rottinghaus, and Borgen (2002) and Barrick, Mount, and Gupta (2003) recently and independently conducted meta-analyses examining FFM–RIASEC relationships, also investigating moderating influences of sex, type of RIASEC measure (Self-Directed Search versus Strong Interest Inventory or Vocational Preference Inventory), type of personality inventory (FFM-based or lower-level personality tests), and participant status (students or working adults). The results were convergent across analyses showing four replicable interest–trait associations, and the absence of a relationship between the Realistic interest type and the FFM, and the Neuroticism dimension and the RIASEC types. Consistent positive correlations were described between: (a) Extroversion and the Enterprising type, (b) Openness to Experience and the Investigative and especially the Artistic type, (c) Agreeableness and the Social type, and finally (d) Conscientiousness and the Conventional type. The effect of moderators was rather minimal, suggesting robust and overall patterns. The major conclusion from the individual studies and the meta-analyses is that interests and personality traits are related in a consistent way, but cannot be considered as isomorphic constructs (Barrick et al., 2003).

Indeed, there is empirical evidence that both interests and traits predict different vocational criteria. Examining the validity of both RIASEC and the FFM to predict employment status and nature of employment in a sample of graduating college seniors entering the job market, De Fruyt and Mervielde (1999) demonstrated that Holland's RIASEC interest dimensions were more effective at predicting the kind of work individuals were doing, whereas the FFM had greater validity to predict employment status of applicants. This study and the previously reviewed meta-analytic work on trait–performance relationships suggest that the FFM is probably better at predicting performance in a job, whereas RIASEC is probably more effective to describe nature of employment. Taking this perspective, personality traits are probably more employer oriented, whereas interests can be considered to be more employee driven: ultimately, employers are seeking well-performing collaborators, whereas employees want jobs they are interested in to facilitate their job satisfaction (De Fruyt & Mervielde, 1999). These results are very much in line with Hogan and Blake's (1999) interpretation of the agenda for interest and personality measurement. They suggest that interest measurement is about predicting individual differences in satisfaction with various vocational choices, whereas personality assessment is about the individual's performance in an occupation, expressed in his/her ability or potential to get along and get ahead.

The previous paragraphs described the considerable progress that has been made linking the trait–occupational choices domains. Two new challenges have been recently proposed by Barrick and colleagues. First, Barrick et al. (2003) re-conceptualized the congruence construct. Originally, Holland (1973, 1999) invented the congruence concept to describe the fit between an individual's interests and the RIASEC pattern characterizing the environment. Barrick et al. (2003) suggest additionally considering congruence between traits and interests within the individual. They argue that congruence, conceptualized this way, may have important consequences for understanding work outcomes. A second challenge is to conduct a higher-order analysis of traits and interests together (Mount, Barrick, Scullen, & Rounds, 2004).

Conclusions

As Hough (2001) has stated, the past decade has been the decade of personality in Industrial, Work and Organizational Psychology and personnel selection. The cumulated evidence in the past fourteen years has demonstrated that personality variables have a strong impact on job performance and other relevant criteria for organizations (e.g., absenteeism, counterproductive behaviors, promotions, turnover) and, consequently, are now accepted as useful tools for personnel selection and included in many models of job performance (see Hunter, Schmidt, Rauschenberger, & Jayne, 2001). In great part, the advances in the domain of personality at work were due to the use of a construct-oriented approach in which the Five Factor Model of personality has become the preferred model of IWO psychology researchers (Hough & Ones, 2001). The seminal work by Barrick and Mount (1991), Hough (1992), and Tett et al. (1991) was crucial for demonstrating that personality dimensions are relevant predictors of job performance and, on the basis of these pioneer investigations, many studies were conducted in the following years. Furthermore, many surveys conducted around the world since the 1950s have shown that practitioners typically included personality measures in the personnel selection processes. Therefore, as Anderson and Cunningham-Snell (2000) concluded, the current evidence suggests that personality tests measure variables that are not assessed by other selection methods, and hence provide unique and non-overlapping variance for explaining the criterion space.

Based on the empirical evidence reviewed in this chapter, the following conclusions can be formulated:

1.   The taxonomy of the personality traits derived from the FFM has proved to be a very useful framework for organizing the various single measures and is now accepted as the paradigm of the area. The use of this taxonomy allowed personnel selection researchers to adequately respond to the concerns of Ghiselli (1973) and Guion and Gottier (1965) regarding the lack of a widely accepted personality model.

With regard to conscientiousness, the meta-analytic research has shown that it is the best personality predictor of job performance, training proficiency, and counterproductive behaviors. This personality dimension has shown validity generalization across samples, occupations, and countries. The validity of conscientiousness is moderated by the occupational groups and by job complexity, but for most occupations a coefficient of .36 is the best estimate of its true validity for predicting job performance. The meta-analytic research has also shown that emotional stability was the second most relevant personality predictor of job performance, although the magnitude of its true validity was only modest. The best estimate is .24. The validity of emotional stability is also moderated by the occupational group and job complexity. Emotional stability is also a good predictor of turnover. With relation to agreeableness, the meta-analytic evidence showed that it is a useful predictor of job performance for occupations with a medium level of job complexity. For this range of complexity, the validity of agreeableness is .25. Agreeableness was also found to be a predictor of counterproductive behaviors, such as deviant behaviors and turnover. For the prediction of training proficiency, extroversion and openness to experience proved to be good predictors of this criterion. The validity of extroversion was. 28 and was .33 for openness to experience. These two variables were also predictors of turnover. Curiously, these values were found when the Big Five were assessed with measures explicitly derived from the FFM. When the Big Five were assessed with measures developed with alternative models, the validity was substantially lower.

2.   Conscientiousness, emotional stability and agreeableness showed incremental validity over GMA for predicting job performance, adding validity by 10–30% over the validity explained by GMA. The multiple correlation of GMA plus a supplement consisting of conscientiousness, emotional stability, or agreeableness ranged from .56 to .63. Three personality dimensions also showed incremental validity over GMA for predicting training proficiency. Conscientiousness, extroversion, and openness to experience added validity over GMA and the multiple correlation ranged from .55 to .61.

3.   The Big Five were found to be predictors of other relevant organizational criteria, such as leadership and job satisfaction. Personality dimensions related to both leadership emergence and leadership effectiveness. Conscientiousness, emotional stability, extroversion, and openness predicted leadership emergence and all the Big Five predicted leadership effectiveness. The meta-analytic evidence showed that four personality dimensions, conscientiousness, emotional stability, extroversion, and agreeableness, determine job satisfaction.

4.   The COPS are very good predictors of job performance and counterproductive behaviors. The most researched COPS were integrity tests. The research has revealed that the personality-based integrity tests showed a validity of .37 for predicting job performance, .38 for training success, and .32 for overall counterproductive behaviors. Other COPS which showed strong validity for predicting job performance and counterproductive behaviors were stress tolerance scales, violence scales, and customer service scales. The validity of these scales was .42, .39, and .31 for predicting job performance and .42, .42, and .46 for predicting counterproductive behaviors. The nomological net of these measures suggests hypotheses for explaining why they predict job performance and counterproductivity. Ones and her colleagues (1993; Ones & Viswesvaran, 2001a, 2001b) have found that the COPS mainly consisted of conscientiousness, emotional stability, and agreeableness. Consequently, the conjoint effect of these three basic personality dimensions explains the large validity of the COPS.

5.   Other personality measures which have shown very promising results for predicting job performance are the core self-evaluations, as they are called by Judge and his colleagues (e.g., Judge & Bono, 2001). Self-esteem and self-efficacy showed very relevant validity sizes and appear to extend to the neuroticism (emotional stability) domain. Therefore, new measures of emotional stability should include scales assessing these facets. Also, positive and negative affectivity appear to be of interest for predicting mood and emotions at work.

The maladaptive personality styles are beginning to be researched in employment settings. The first primary studies suggest that these measures can be useful for predicting overall job performance, task performance, contextual performance, and leadership. However, many more studies are needed before solid conclusions can be reached.

Another measure examined in this review was EI, given that many authors have suggested that EI measures assess personality characteristics. The meta-analytic evidence showed that the validity of EI measures is modest, similar to the validity of emotional stability and agreeableness and much lower than the validity of GMA measures. The meta-analytic evidence also showed that the EI measures mainly consisted of GMA and the Big

Five. When we examined the incremental validity of EI measures over GMA and the Big Five, we found that this variable did not add validity when combined with GMA or conscientiousness and that they only added some validity when combined with emotional stability or agreeableness.

IMPLICATIONS FOR PRACTICE

We have included some suggestions for practitioners throughout this chapter. A summary of those suggestions and recommendations is given below.

1. If you wish to predict job performance, training proficiency, counterproductive behaviors, leadership, and emotions at work, the Big Five are important variables you should consider. Owing to the fact that conscientiousness, emotional stability, and agreeableness were found to be predictors of job performance for the majority of occupations, and that they added validity over GMA, an optimal combination of measures for personnel selection purposes should include one GMA test and a Big Five questionnaire.
2. If you decide to assess the Big Five in the workplace, you should take into account the model on which the measure is based. The findings of the meta-analytic research have shown that the model used to develop the personality measures grossly affects the validity. Therefore, our suggestion is that, if the practitioner wishes to assess the Big Five, the best option is to use a questionnaire explicitly developed for assessing the five factors, given that the alternative measures (e.g., 16PF, OPQ, MMPI, CPI) producing estimates of the Big Five showed smaller operational validities.
3. If you wish to use emotional intelligence measures, you should know that its validity is only modest at best and that it is not a single or primary dimension of ability or personality (see also Woodruffe, Chapter 9, this volume). With regard to emotional intelligence, the current research has shown that EI measures have a modest validity, much lower than the validity of GMA (.53 vs. .24) and also lower than the validity of conscientiousness (.36 vs. 24). In combination with other measures, EI has little or no practical utility. Therefore, our suggestion for practitioners is to use EI measures only when no other measures are available.
4. If you wish to use measures of maladaptive personality styles, you should take into account that the current research is still very limited. They appear to be good for predicting job performance and leadership but these findings were only found for a small number of occupations.
5. If you wish to use personality measures, you should use questionnaires with norms specifically developed for job applicants (Ones & Viswesvaran, 1998b) in order to avoid the effects of the intentional distortion on the test scores. Intentional distortion does not affect the validity of the personality measures and, therefore, can be confidently used for personnel selection purposes.

NOTE

Jesús F. Salgado's work for this chapter was partially supported by grant BSO2001-3070 from Ministerio de Ciencia y Tecnologia (Spain).

References

American Psychiatric Association. (1994). *Diagnostic and statistical manual of mental disorders* (4th ed.). Washington, DC: Author.

Anderson N., & Cunningham-Snell, N. (2000). Personnel selection. In N. Chmiel (Ed.), *Introduction to work and organizational psychology. A European perspective* (pp. 69–99). Oxford, UK: Blackwell.

Barrick, M. R., & Mount, M. K. (1991). The Big Five personality dimensions and job performance: A meta-analysis. *Personnel Psychology, 44,* 1–26.

Barrick, M. R., & Mount, M. K. (1993). Autonomy as a moderator of the relationships between the Big Five personality dimensions and job performance. *Journal of Applied Psychology, 78,* 111–118.

Barrick, M. R., Mount, M. K., & Gupta, R. (2003). Meta-analysis of the relationship between the Five-Factor Model of personality and Holland's occupational types. *Personnel Psychology, 56,* 45–74.

Barrick, M. R., Mount, M. K., & Judge, T. A. (2001). Personality and performance at the beginning of the new millennium: What do we know and where do we go next? *International Journal of Selection and Assessment, 9,* 9–30.

Barry, B., & Stewart, G. L. (1997). Composition, process, and performance in self-managed groups: The role of personality. *Journal of Applied Psychology, 82,* 62–78.

Borman, W. C., & Motowidlo, S. J. (1993). Expanding the criterion domain to include elements of contextual performance. In N. Schmitt & W. C. Borman (Eds.), *Personnel selection in organizations.* San Francisco: Jossey-Bass.

Borman, W. C., Penner, L. A., Allen, T. D., & Motowidlo, S. (2001). Personality predictors of citizenship performance. *International Journal of Selection and Assessment, 9,* 52–69.

Connolly, J. J., & Viswesvaran, C. (2004). The role of affectivity in job satisfaction: A meta-analysis. *Personality and Individual Differences, 29,* 265–281.

Costa, P. T., Jr., & McCrae, R. R. (1992). *Professional Manual: Revised NEO Personality Inventory (NEO-PI-R) and NEO Five-Factor-Inventory (NEO-FFI).* Odessa, FL: Psychological Assessment Resources.

Darley, J. B., & Hagenah, T. (1955). *Vocational interest measurement: Theory and practice.* Minneapolis, MN: University of Minnesota Press.

De Fruyt, F. (2002). A person-centered approach to P-E fit questions using a multiple trait model. *Journal of Vocational Behavior, 60,* 73–90.

De Fruyt, F., & Mervielde, I. (1997). The Five-Factor model of personality and Holland's RIASEC interest types. *Personality and Individual Differences, 1,* 87–103.

De Fruyt, F., & Mervielde, I. (1999). RIASEC types and Big Five traits as predictors of employment status and nature of employment. *Personnel Psychology, 52,* 701–727.

De Fruyt, F., & Salgado, J. (2003a). Personality and IWO Applications: Introducing personality at work. *European Journal of Personality, 17,* S1–S3.

De Fruyt, F., & Salgado, J. (2003b). Applied personality psychology: Lessons learned from the IWO field. *European Journal of Personality, 17,* 123–131.

Ghiselli, E. E. (1973). The validity of aptitude tests in personnel selection. *Personnel Psychology, 26,* 461–477.

Ghiselli, E. E., & Barthol, R. P. (1953). The validity of personality inventories in the selection of employees. *Journal of Applied Psychology, 38,* 18–20.

Goldberg, L. R. (1992). The development of markers of the Big Five factor structure. *Psychological Assessment, 4,* 26–42.

Guion, R. M., & Gottier, R. F. (1965). Validity of personality measures in personnel selection. *Personnel Psychology, 18,* 135–164.

Hogan, J., & Holland, B. (2003). Using theory to evaluate personality and job-performance relations: A socioanalytic perspective. *Journal of Applied Psychology, 88,* 100–112.

Hogan, J., & Roberts, B. W. (1996). Issues and non-issues in the fidelity–bandwidth trade-off. *Journal of Organizational Behavior, 17*, 627–637.

Hogan, R. (1983). A socioanalytic theory of personality. In M. M. Page (Ed.), *Nebraska symposium on motivation 1982. Personality: Current theory and research* (pp. 55–89). Lincoln: University of Nebraska Press.

Hogan, R., & Blake, R. (1999). John Holland's vocational typology and personality theory. *Journal of Vocational Behavior, 55*, 41–56.

Hogan, R., Curphy, G. J., & Hogan, J. (1994). What we know about leadership: Effectiveness and personality. *American Psychologist, 49*, 493–504.

Hogan, R., & Hogan, J. (1995). *Hogan Personality Inventory manual.* Tulsa, OK: Hogan Assessment Systems.

Hogan, R., & Hogan, J. (2001). Assessing leadership: A view from the dark side. *International Journal of Selection and Assessment, 9*, 40–51.

Holland, J. L. (1973). *Making vocational choices: A theory of careers.* Englewood Cliffs, NJ: Prentice-Hall.

Holland, J. L. (1999). Why interest inventories are also personality inventories. In M. Savickas & A. Spokane (Eds.), *Vocational interests: Their meaning, measurement, and use in counseling* (pp. 87–101). Palo Alto, CA: Davies-Black.

Hough, L. M. (1992). The "Big Five" personality variable-construct confusion: Description versus prediction. *Human Performance, 5*, 139–155.

Hough, L. M. (2001). I/owes its advances to personality. In B. E. Roberts & R. Hogan (Eds.), *Personality psychology in the workplace* (pp. 19–44). Washington, DC: American Psychological Association.

Hough, L. M., Eaton, N. K., Dunnette, M. D., Kamp, J. D., & McCloy, R. A. (1990). Criterion-related validities of personality constructs and the effects of response distortion on those validities. *Journal of Applied Psychology, 75*, 581–595.

Hough, L. M., & Ones, D. S. (2001). The structure, measurement, validity, and use of personality variables in Industrial, Work, and Organizational Psychology. In N. Anderson, D. S. Ones, H. K. Sinangil, & C. Viswesvaran (Eds.), *Handbook of industrial, work, and organizational psychology* (Vol. 1, pp. 233–267). London: Sage.

Hunter, J. E., & Hunter, R. F. (1984). Validity and utility of alternative predictors of job performance. *Psychological Bulletin, 96*, 72–98.

Hunter, J. E., & Schmidt, F. L. (1990). *Methods of meta-analysis.* Newbury Park, CA: Sage.

Hunter, J. E., Schmidt, F. L., & Le, H. (2002). *Implications of direct and indirect range restriction for meta-analysis methods and findings.* Unpublished manuscript, Department of Management and Organizations, University of Iowa.

Hunter, J. E., Schmidt, F. L., Rauschenberger, J. M., & Jayne, M. E. A. (2001). Intelligence, motivation, and job performance. In C. L. Cooper & E. A. Locke (Eds.), *Industrial and organizational psychology* (pp. 278–303). Oxford, UK: Blackwell.

Hurtz, G. M., & Donovan, J. J. (2000). Personality and job performance: The big five revisited. *Journal of Applied Psychology, 85*, 869–879.

Judge, T., & Bono, J. E. (2001). Relations of core self-evaluations traits – self-esteem, generalized self-efficacy, locus of control, and emotional stability – with job satisfaction and job performance: A meta-analysis. *Journal of Applied Psychology, 86*, 80–92.

Judge, T. A., Bono, J. E., Ilies, R., & Gerhardt, M. W. (2002). Personality and leadership: A qualitative and quantitative review. *Journal of Applied Psychology, 87*, 765–780.

Judge, T. A., Heller, D., & Mount, M. K. (2002). Five-factor model of personality and job satisfaction: A meta-analysis. *Journal of Applied Psychology, 87*, 530–541.

Judge, T. A., Locke, E. A., & Durham, C. C. (1997). The dispositional causes of job satisfaction: A core evaluations approach. *Research in Organizational Behavior, 19*, 151–188.

Larson, L. M., Rottinghaus, P. J., & Borgen, F. (2002). Meta-analyses of Big Six interests and Big Five personality factors. *Journal of Vocational Behavior, 61,* 217–239.

Le, H., & Schmidt, F. L. (2003). *Development and test of a new meta-analysis method for indirect range restriction.* Paper presented at the 16th Annual Conference of the Society for Industrial and Organizational Psychology, Orlando, FL.

Levy-Leboyer, C. (1994). Selection and assessment in Europe. In H. C. Triandis, M. D. Dunnette, & L. M. Hough (Eds.), *Handbook of industrial and organizational psychology* (Vol. 4, pp. 173–190). Palo Alto, CA: Consulting Psychologists Press.

Mount, M. K., & Barrick, M. R. (1995). The Big Five personality dimensions: Implications for research and practice in human resources management. In K. M. Rowland & G. Ferris (Eds.), *Research in personnel and human resources management* (Vol. 13, pp. 153–200). Greenwich, CT: JAI Press.

Mount, M. K., Barrick, M. R., Scullen, S. M., & Rounds, J. (2004, April). *Higher order dimensions of the Big Five personality traits and the Big Six vocational interest types.* Poster presented at the 19th Annual Conference of the Society for Industrial and Organizational Psychology, Chicago.

Myers, I., & Briggs, K. C. (1962). *Myers–Briggs Type Indicator.* Oxford, UK: Oxford Psychologists Press.

Ones, D. S. (1993). *Construct validity of integrity tests.* Unpublished doctoral dissertation: University of Iowa.

Ones, D. S., & Viswesvaran, C. (1998a). Integrity testing in organizations. In R. W. Griffin, A. O'Leary-Kelly, & J. Collins (Eds.), *Dysfunctional behavior in organizations: Vol. 2. Nonviolent behaviors in organizations* (pp. 243–276). Greenwich, CT: JAI Press.

Ones, D. S., & Viswesvaran, C. (1998b). The effects of social desirability and faking on personality and integrity assessment for personnel selection. *Human Performance, 11,* 245–269.

Ones, D. S., & Viswesvaran, C. (2001a). Personality at work: Criterion-focused occupational personality scales (COPS) used in personnel selection. In B. Roberts & R. T. Hogan (Eds.), *Applied personality psychology* (pp. 63–92). Washington, DC: American Psychological Association.

Ones, D. S., & Viswesvaran, C. (2001b). Integrity tests and other criterion-focused occupational personality scales (COPS) used in personnel selection. *International Journal of Selection and Assessment, 9,* 31–39.

Ones, D. S., Viswesvaran, C., & Schmidt, F. L. (1993). Comprehensive meta-analysis of integrity test validities: Findings and implications for personnel selection and theories of job performance. *Journal of Applied Psychology (Monograph), 78,* 679–703.

Ones, D. S., Viswesvaran, C., & Schmidt, F. L. (2003). Personality and absenteeism: A meta-analysis of integrity tests. *European Journal of Personality, 17,* 19–38.

PA Consulting Group. (1998). *Personality and Preference Inventory (PAPI). Technical manual.* Brussels: PA Consulting Group Cubiks.

Rolland, J. P., & De Fruyt, F. (2003). The validity of FFM personality dimensions and maladaptive traits to predict negative affects at work: A 6 months prospective study in a military sample. *European Journal of Personality, 17,* 101–121.

Ryan, A. M., & Sackett, P. R. (1987). A survey of individual assessment practices by I/O psychologists. *Personnel Psychology, 40,* 455–488.

Sackett, P. R., Burris, L. R., & Callaham, C. (1989). Integrity testing for personnel selection: An update. *Personnel Psychology, 42,* 491–529.

Salgado, J. F. (1997). The five factor model of personality and job performance in the European Community. *Journal of Applied Psychology, 82,* 30–43.

Salgado, J. F. (1998). The Big Five personality dimensions and job performance in army and civil occupations: A European perspective. *Human Performance, 11,* 271–288.

Salgado, J.F. (2002). The Big Five personality dimensions and counterproductive behaviors. *International Journal of Selection and Assessment, 10,* 117–125.

Salgado, J. F. (2003). Predicting job performance using FFM and non-FFM personality measures. *Journal of Occupational and Organizational Psychology*, *76*, 323–346.

Salgado, J. F. (2004a). *La hipótesis de especificidad situacional, la hipótesis de la generalización de la validez y la predicción del desempeño ocupacional: influencia de la personalidad.* [Situational specificity hypothesis, validity generalization hypothesis and the prediction of job performance: The influence of personality]. Unpublished manuscript, Department of Social Psychology, University of Santiago de Compostela, Spain.

Salgado, J. F. (2004b). *Moderator effects of job complexity on the Big Five validity.* Poster presented at the Conference of the Society for Industrial and Organizational Psychology, Chicago, Illinois.

Salgado, J. F., Anderson, N., Moscoso, S., Bertua, C., De Fruyt, F., & Rolland, J. P. (2003). A meta-analytic study of GMA validity for different occupations in the European Community. *Journal of Applied Psychology*, *88*, 1068–1081.

Salgado, J. F., & Moscoso, S. (2000). Autoeficacia y criterios organizacionales de desempeño [Self-efficacy and organizational performance criteria]. *Apuntes de Psicología*, *18*, 179–191.

Salgado, J. F., Moscoso, S., & Lado, M. (2003a). Evidence of cross-cultural invariants of the Big Five personality dimensions in Cork settings. *European Journal of Personality*, *17*, 67–76.

Salgado, J. F., Moscoso, S., & Lado, M. (2003b, May). Maladaptive personality styles and job performance. In D. Bartram & J. F. Salgado (Chairs), *Personality at work across the European Community.* Symposium conducted at the 11th European Congress of Work and Organizational Psychology, Lisbon, Portugal.

Schmitt, N., Gooding, R. Z., Noe, R. A., & Kirsch, M. (1984). Metaanlyses of validity studies published between 1964 and 1982 and the investigation of study characteristics. *Personnel Psychology*, *37*, 407–422.

Schulte, M. J., Ree, M. J., & Carretta, T. R. (in press). Emotional intelligence: Not much more than *g* and personality. *Personality and Individual Differences.*

SHL (1999). *OPQ32 manual and user's guide.* Surrey, UK: SHL.

Spriegel, W. R., & Dale, A. G. (1953). Trends in personnel selection and induction. *Personnel*, *30*, 169–175.

Stogdill, R. M. (1974). *Handbook of leadership.* New York: Free Press.

Tett, R. P., Rothstein, M. G., & Jackson, D. J. (1991). Personality measures as predictors of job performance: A meta-analytic review. *Personnel Psychology*, *44*, 703–742.

Van Rooy, D. L., & Viswesvaran, C. (in press). Emotional intelligence: A meta-analytic investigation of predictive validity and nomological net. *Journal of Vocational Behavior.*

Watson, D., Clark, L. A., & Tellegen, A. (1998). Development and validation of brief measures of positive and negative affect – The PANAS scales. *Journal of Personality and Social Psychology*, *54*, 1063–1070.

Witt, L. A., Burke, L. A., Barrick, M. R., & Mount, M. K. (2002). The interactive effects of conscientiousness and agreeableness on job performance. *Journal of Applied Psychology*, *87*, 164–169.

9

Emotional Factors as Selection Criteria

Charles Woodruffe

Focusing on people's emotions might not seem an obvious part of a selection process. We tend to rely on candidates' behavior, either manifested at an assessment center, observed and discussed at an interview, or self-reported in a personality inventory. Looking at the emotions behind behavior or the psychological characteristics that generate the emotions might seem intrusive and inappropriate. You might also say that the emotional arena is adequately addressed by personality models and inventories. However, a moment's reflection confirms that variables other than emotion (such as learning and cognition) also contribute to the regularities in behavior that give rise to personality dimensions. In looking specifically at emotion in this chapter, we are undoubtedly focusing on a part of personality but, at the same time, we are trying to focus more deeply on the emotional causes of behavior than do many models of personality. They tend to go no further than imputing traits from summaries of behavior (Mischel, 1968).

The immediate cause of behavior to be considered is people's feelings. Feelings that are typically contrasted with thoughts. Feelings that are as much a part of us as rational thought processes. As Rafaeli (2002) observes, "the bottom line is that people *are* emotions" (p. xii). Although, as Kiefer and Briner (2003) observe, "the workplace is supposed to be where rationality rules – emotions are meant to be contained in our lives outside work" (p. 48), it is inconceivable that emotions can simply be suspended for eight hours on entry to the workplace.

Emotion affects work behavior very directly in our obvious expression of it – for example, negative and positive sentiments. Affective Events Theory (Weiss & Cropanzano, 1996) aims to specify which emotion is provoked by an event. Emotion also affects work behavior through the range of behavior less obviously the result of emotion, such as resistance to change. Oreg (2003) developed a Resistance to Change scale, made up of four factors. One factor is the emotional reactions to imposed change. The factor refers to the tension and stress that change can induce in people. It results from a combination of a lack of psychological resilience as well as reluctance to lose control. Paterson and Härtel (2002) describe how these and other emotions come into play in downsizing and Kiefer (2002) examines the emotional response to being involved in a merger.

In short, emotion is an inescapable and necessary contributor to all behavior, including behavior at work. Emotion is a fundamental and functional aspect of people. The fact that emotion is ubiquitous might cause us to argue that manifestations of emotions are unremarkable, just part of office life and certainly not the subject of selection. There are five reasons to take the opposite tack which I will outline first in this chapter. Then, I turn to models of emotion that might be useful in selection. One is positive and negative affectivity; the other is attachment theory. The control of emotion is the subject of the next section. It is an aspect of the emotional domain made popular under the label of emotional intelligence and I aim to make clear the complexity of control as well as to stress that it is not necessarily a desirable quality, particularly when it involves habitual suppression. Finally, I debate the fairness of selecting – or, more particularly, – rejecting people for their emotional status.

SELECTING FOR EMOTION

First of all, then, the reasons to make emotional factors criteria for selection. There seem to me to be five distinct arguments.

1. Identifying extremes

First, emotions can become remarkable because of the intensity and circumstances of their expression. Some people get angrier than others; some resist change more than others. In short, some express emotions (directly or indirectly) that seem inappropriate either in their type or in their intensity. Making a speech to a large conference for the first time engenders appropriate trepidation. A malfunctioning computer evokes an inappropriate outburst of anger. Ultimately, the appropriateness of emotional experiences is the domain of psychotherapy. Therapy gives people insights into how they have come to feel – or not feel – the way they do. According to this model, we start life with a few basic emotions and they gradually evolve in the light of experience. The experiences we have might cause our emotions to evolve in a way that results in them being appropriate for our adult life. In which case, we need no therapy. Alternatively, our emotions might evolve in a way that was right at the time for the particular circumstances we were in, but wrong for our dealing with the world in general. They are wrong in that they thwart our ability to have productive interpersonal relationships and to be happy – wrong often by involving the display of perfectly legitimate emotions but to an inappropriate target. Perhaps, in childhood, we have been the victim of aggression. We become hypersensitive to cues of aggression in others. At work, when receiving feedback, we defend before we are attacked, but, in defending, we are ourselves attacking. Perversely, we evoke a defense in others that serves to justify our belief that they are attacking. It is this sort of self-fulfilling prophecy that psychotherapy seeks to ablate.

We could advance an argument for deselecting people who express emotions that are inappropriate and detrimental to performance. Someone who is always getting angry is unlikely to build good relationships with colleagues or clients. If emotions and emotionality affect behavior at work in ways that make a difference to performance and if people differ in the emotions they feel, the intensity with which they experience them, and their ability to manage them, then there is a clear argument for choosing between people on the basis of emotions.

2. Identifying the source of behavior

At the time of selection, knowing the reasons for behavior might well be helpful to predicting future behavior. For example, someone may appear quite welcoming of change at the time of selection but turn out to be quite anxious and stressed by change when they are employed. It would be helpful at the time of selection to know about the person's base level of anxiety. Another person might appear slightly brusque in a group exercise. It would be useful to know if this was due to a feeling of nervousness, a general anger, or having had a bad night's sleep in a noisy hotel. We might, then, give more weight to the brusqueness if it is caused by anger because it is more likely to be repeated than the brusqueness from a lack of sleep.

3. Authentic expression

Brotheridge and Lee (2003) note that particular emotions are expected for successful performance at work. For example, someone in a customer-facing role is expected to be reasonably cheerful. If these are not the emotions the person actually feels, then the person has two remedies. The first is faking the emotion (surface acting) and the second is to get into a state of mind whereby the appropriate feelings are felt (deep acting). Either solution requires emotional labor and Brotheridge and Lee have set about developing an Emotional Labour Scale to help explore the management of emotions at work. The scale has six factors, namely: surface acting, deep acting, intensity, variety, duration, and frequency of emotional display. Administering the scale with other measures to a sample of people in various occupations showed that surface acting was related to both emotional exhaustion and depersonalization. Surface acting was also shown to differ from the straightforward suppression of emotions but was associated with Snyder's (1974) self-monitoring scale. The conclusion from this would seem to be that it is helpful to specify the emotions that are needed in a job and to select people disposed to display them. Otherwise, jobholders will run the risk of stress from surface acting. They are also quite likely, one might think, to appear inauthentic (airline crew smiles and the "have a happy day" syndrome).

4. Developmental prognosis

If you understand the person's psychology, you can estimate the likelihood of him or her growing and developing. The prognosis for a person who is a poor presenter because of an omission to learn basic presentation skills is very different to the prognosis for the person with a chronic lack of self-esteem. More generally, if someone is failing to manifest the behavior of a competency it is helpful to know if this is due to a deep-seated emotional issue or a skill-deficiency.

5. Parsimony

It is economical to know about the general source of behavior rather than each specific behavior. Rather than measuring, say, all the emotional intelligence (EI) competencies

(Goleman, 1998), it would seem obviously more efficient to measure a small number of qualities that lie behind them. The measurement of the source qualities will enable generalizations to be made about the person. The problem is that the EI capacities do not seem to fulfill this requirement. They either deal with the management of emotion (e.g., self-regulation) rather than emotion itself or they appear to be re-statements of the behavior itself.

To pursue the goal of parsimony, we need to find a clear distinction between behavior on the one hand and the supposed source-emotions on the other. This might seem easy. The emotion is a feeling and behavior is the result of the feeling. For example, it might seem obvious that angry behavior is caused by feeling angry and that feeling angry also intrudes on an array of other behaviors as well. Therefore, we should measure whether the person feels angry. However, we then have to decide where feelings end and behavior begins. Can we know a person has an emotion other than through the observation or report of behavior? Furthermore, how does the fact that the person feels or does not feel angry right now at the time of measurement relate to their feelings and behavior in future? We can see that measuring the feelings themselves is not the way forward. What we need to measure is the propensity to have the feelings. This might sound pedantic but it is a most important point. We cannot proceed in selection by measuring a feeling in the here and now (i.e., when selecting someone). We can only proceed by measuring the propensity to have the feeling which in turn will be expressed by behavior.

However, we immediately have to narrow the focus. Do we look at all of personality or home in on particular aspects? Many models of personality are either simply models of the major dimensions along which behavior varies (e.g., 16PF and "Big Five" measures) or models of those dimensions of behavior of particular interest to the modeler of personality (e.g., OPQ). They do not seem to be good models of the emotional domain. Of course, they include the emotional by including dimensions such as neuroticism. At the same time, they include dimensions such as conscientiousness and agreeableness that are affected to some degree or other by emotion but also by learning. Certainly, we could not seriously argue that, as a whole, the Big Five offered a comprehensive model of the emotional causes of behavior.

MAPPING THE EMOTIONAL DOMAIN

To make progress, we need to find a useful taxonomy of emotions that can be applied to the world of work. Otherwise we are left in the morass of the lexicon of emotions. Different writers provide different answers. As noted already, Frank and Stennett (2001) identified six emotions as "basic." These are: anger, disgust, fear, happiness, sadness, and surprise. These six had earlier been shown by Ekman and his co-researchers (1987) to be universally recognized. Lowe and Bennett (2003) adopted a four-emotion distinction: anger, guilt, anxiety, sadness. Anderson, Keltner, and John (2003) assessed three positive emotions: happiness, amusement, and pride, as well as seven negative emotions: anger, contempt, discomfort, disgust, fear, guilt, and sadness. Trierweiler, Eid, and Lischetske (2002) focused upon six emotions: love, joy, fear, anger, shame, and sadness. Clearly, there is overlap between these lists but, equally, there is not consensus on a list of "basic" emotions.

The difficulty of reducing the emotional domain is emphasized by Trierweiler et al. (2002). They compared three models of emotional expressivity, one based on a general factor, a second dividing positive and negative expressivity, and the third which was the emotion-specific model. They found "very strong support for the multidimensionality of emotional expressivity" (p. 1033). In particular, they found that negative emotions are differentiated such that "the expression of anger and shame, especially, is quite different from the expression of the other negative emotions" (p. 1033). Although the expressivity of emotions is not the same as the emotions themselves, Trierweiler et al.'s work would seem to caution against oversimplification. Yet, in dealing with emotions relevant to work and especially at the time of selection, one has to choose either to focus on emotions of particular relevance to the particular role or to reduce the cornucopia of emotions in some way. The reduction alternative offers the benefit of homing in on fundamental differences between people. I will consider two of what seem to me to be the most fruitful schemas for the emotional domain: the first is positive and negative affectivity and the second is attachment theory.

Positive and negative affectivity

Although Trierweiler et al. are, no doubt, correct in pointing out that the specific positive emotions are not interchangeable with each other and nor are negative emotions, it also seems true that positive and negative affect are basic dimensions of emotional functioning. Positive affect is associated with perceiving as challenges those situations that the person with negative affect would see as threats. Mendes, Reis, Seery, and Blascowich (2003) describe threat as the sense that we are in a situation that is beyond our capacity, whereas challenge is a situation that will stretch us but with which we can cope. They say that people recover physiologically more slowly from threat and that it is threat that is associated with pathophysiological cardiovascular responses, while the responses to challenge are likely to be beneficial.

If some people habitually see situations as a threat whereas others see them as a challenge, then there is a distinction upon which one might choose to select people. The justification for doing so is that the arousal of the autonomic system by negative emotions is also associated with a narrowing of cognitive attention so people can focus upon specific action tendencies such as attack or escape. On the other hand, positive emotional experience is associated with a broadening of attention, thinking, and behavioral repertoires possibly due to an increase in circulating brain dopamine. In other words, one might expect the person disposed to negative emotions to be less good at creative problem solving than the more positive person. More generally, they might be less ready to embrace the norm of change that applies in many organizations.

Positive affect would seem to be related to a positive view of the self. In turn, this view might necessarily be based on a degree of self-enhancement. Again, in turn, self-enhancement was shown by Taylor, Lerner, Sherman, Sage, and McDowell (2003) to "regulate the experience of stress" (p. 203). In short, self-enhancers benefited from their rosy interpretation of themselves; they were not stressed by hiding from "the truth" about themselves. So, in selection, perhaps we should not take against the person who self-enhances. Within reason, their embellishments might act against stress and thus act to the employer's benefit.

Additional positive and negative consequences of affect are identified by Ambady and Gray (2002). They describe how mood colors people's judgments, with sad and depressed people exhibiting "a negative bias when interpreting the behavior of those around them" (p. 948). In addition, "happy people tend to process information in a more heuristic and less systematic manner, relying more on cognitive short cuts" whereas "sad people tend to use systematic and detailed information-processing styles" (p. 948). Although, on the face of it, this might enable sad people to be more accurate in their judgments, in fact many judgments of others do not need – and can be downgraded by – deliberation. Ambady and Gray confirmed that "sadness produces a significant impairment in the ability to draw valid inferences about others on the basis of brief observations" (p. 956). This will be as true at work as elsewhere, though I am not, of course, suggesting that all judgments should be without deliberation.

Fredrickson, Tugade, Waugh, and Larkin (2003) point out that the effects of positive emotional experience extend to helping people be in a position that will let them feel good in the future. They link this idea to their "broaden-and-build" theory of positive emotions by which positive emotions help to build "a range of personal resources including physical resources (e.g., physical skills, health, longevity), social resources (e.g., friendships, social support networks), intellectual resources (e.g., expert knowledge, intellectual complexity), and psychological resources (e.g., resilience, optimism, creativity" (p. 367). Fredrickson et al. continue by noting the circular relationship between resilience and positive emotions. Resilient people are characterized by more positive emotionality which in turn can be used to achieve their effective coping. They suggest that resilient people are buffered from depression by, and thrive through, positive emotions. In the face of adversity, they find the positive and "bounce back stronger than before" (p. 373). All of these correlates of resilience – and of positive affect – would seem to be useful in the context of work.

Resilience is associated with low neuroticism, extroversion, and openness, a set of traits that yields a predisposition to positive affectivity. Trierweiler et al. (2002) confirmed that "people who express their positive emotions are extroverted and agreeable and have a relatively high intellect. People who show their negative emotions are more neurotic" (pp. 1037–1038).

Harker and Keltner (2001) traced how the lives unfolded of women who had expressed different degrees of positive emotion in their college yearbook photos. They found that the women who had expressed more positive emotion were stronger in terms of affiliation and competence. Over time, these more positive women also "became more organized, mentally focused and achievement-oriented and less susceptible to repeated and prolonged experiences of negative affect" (p. 120). The authors suggest that people expressing more positive emotion might well be more enjoyable to be with and so are sought out by others, setting up a virtuous circle.

Where might the differences in positive and negative affect come from? Emotion must have a purpose. At its most fundamental, emotions presumably had and continue to have survival value. The presumption is that objects that give us pleasurable emotions, say happiness, are good for our survival and those that make us feel pain, say being afraid, are deleterious. The further presumption is that we operate according to the hedonic principle of being motivated to approach pleasure and avoid pain. As Higgins (1998) says, this has been "the basic motivational principle throughout the history of psychology" (p. 1).

Higgins explores the hedonic principle, making the distinction between self-regulation systems that have desired and undesired end states. He also distinguishes between two self-guides, those that represent ideals to aspire to and those that represent attributes the person ought to possess. Ideals are maximal goals whereas "oughts" are minimal. Aspiring to the ideals yields the presence or absence of positive outcomes whereas trying to adhere to the oughts yields the presence or absence of negative outcomes. The absence of positive outcomes is accompanied by dejection-related emotions such as disappointment, dissatisfaction, or sadness whereas the presence of negative outcomes is associated with agitation-related emotions such as feeling uneasy, threatened, or afraid. Aspiring to the ideal involves self-regulation concerned with nurturance and with a focus on promotion, whereas abiding by the oughts involves security and a prevention-focused regulation. People might emphasize one focus or the other, resulting in characteristic differences. In particular, "with a promotion focus, the state should be eagerness to attain advancement and gains. With a prevention focus, the state should be vigilance to assure safety and nonlosses" (p. 27).

The distinction between a promotion and prevention focus would appear to be one that will have an impact on work, maybe giving rise to the distinction between achievement motivation and fear of failure that are discussed later. As such, the focus might profitably be assessed at selection.

But, like unpacking the Russian doll, why do some people have a promotion focus and others a prevention focus? What is the source of emotions and emotional expression? We need to find a model of people that explains the emotions that are displayed and the propensity to display them. There are two aspects to the explanation, nature and nurture. Dealing first with nurture, it is quite clear that our upbringing – either independently or in interaction with our physiology – contributes powerfully to the emotional behavior we produce as adults. One model of the results of upbringing that seems particularly useful at the time of selection is provided by attachment theory.

Attachment theory

There is a huge literature on people's sense of security, based around the attachment theory of Bowlby (1973). Following Bowlby, the categorization of people has been developed by Bartholomew and Horowitz (1991) into a four-fold choice which can be summarized by saying that people appear to be one of the following:

- *Secure.* These people feel secure in themselves and are comfortable making commitments.
- *Anxious ambivalent.* These people have a high need for reassurance.
- *Fearful avoidant.* People who keep away from relationships because they do not want the pain that might be involved.
- *Dismissive avoidant.* These people see no need for intense relationships with others.

Attachment styles are based on history. The less secure person starts off less secure for a reason. The seed is sown in their mind that their attachment figure is not reliable.

Unfortunately, once their view of the world as a less "safe" place has been set up, it perpetuates itself. People build up "working models" of the world and use these as a guide to their interactions in a way that begets behavior from others that only serves to confirm the working model. Anxious-ambivalent people behave in an anxious-ambivalent manner and this evokes responses from others that reinforce the view of the world as a risky place. They also interpret behavior from the world in a way that is congruent with their view. The secure person does not even perceive the threat in another's actions which is discerned by the insecure.

These differences have been applied particularly to children's relationships with their parents and other attachment figures and extended to adult romantic relationships. There have also been speculative extensions of attachment theory into employment relationships (Feeney & Noller, 1996). It seems reasonable to suppose that attachment styles will generalize and carry forward into the workplace. The secure person might behave in a less edgy way towards others at work and perceive less sinister motives in their actions. Anxious-ambivalent and avoidant people might behave in an insecure way that others tire of. Such people are likely to get passed over for positions requiring high levels of interpersonal skills.

A further inferential link to the workplace can be extracted from a study by Vorauer, Cameron, Holmes, and Pearce (2003). They linked attachment theory to people's tendency to exaggerate in their own minds the explicitness with which they made their romantic feelings clear to another person. They suggest that the less securely attached are likely to have a greater fear of rejection and will exhibit greater signal amplification. In turn, the failure of the other person to respond to the unnoticed overture only serves to heighten the insecure person's sense of rejection. As the authors note, the same phenomenon might apply to ongoing relationships and it is quite conceivable that it extends to communication of feelings at work. The insecure person, for example, might feel they have quite clearly signaled their pleasure or displeasure but to the receiver the message is equivocal and/or faint.

The application of attachment theory to work is not all speculation. Empirical studies are now being reported. Of particular interest is research by Johnston (2000) that looked at delegation and organizational structure in relation to the attachment style of owner-managers. Johnston found that secure managers "tended to be the most likely to report the highest levels of delegation. Avoidant managers reported the lowest levels of delegation. Preoccupied managers generally fell in the middle" (p. 11). She also reports very strong associations between secure attachment and having a decentralized structure, avoidant attachment and a centralized structure, and preoccupied attachment and a disorganized structure.

Although attachment theory started out referring to the relationship between individuals, Smith, Murphy, and Coats (1999) extended it to the relationship between a person and group. They suggest that people build models in their minds based on their history with groups. Smith et al. hypothesize that attachment to groups has two underlying dimensions, namely attachment anxiety and avoidance. People low on both could be characterized as secure in group attachment whereas people high on anxiety will be worried about acceptance and therefore conforming. In contrast, people high on avoidance will remain aloof. They found that anxiety was related to negative affect, affective extremity, and perceptions of fewer and less satisfying social supports within the group. Avoidance was related to lower positive affect, perceptions of fewer and less satisfying social supports, and plans to leave the group. They speculate that avoidance may relate to promotion focus for motivation while anxiety may relate to a prevention focus (Higgins, 1998).

Woodruffe (1999) extended the focus of attachment to organizations. He suggested that people will build an attachment history with organizations analogous to that with individuals and groups. Depending upon their personal and vicarious history, people might regard organizations as basically reliable and they will feel secure about them. Alternatively, they might regard them as unreliable and display anxiety about the organization's commitment. Finally, they might have developed sufficient suspicion to be avoidant of commitment to an organization, preferring for example to work as a contractor.

The foci for attachment are likely to be related and build on each other. For example, the person who is not secure might well have less favorable outcomes at work because of their way of relating to others. In turn, this could give rise to a less secure attachment to organizations. However, to some extent, they might develop an independence. For example, Smith et al. (1999) found that group attachment was related to interpersonal attachment but not to such a degree that the two could be said to be identical. Similarly, it is possible to conceive of a person who is secure at work and yet insecure in their personal life or vice versa. A person who is perfectly content with others but who has been made redundant might develop a cynicism about organizations.

So, we might choose to look at any or all of the domains of security in seeking to understand a person's behavior and potential. An example of using the interpersonal attachment styles in organizational research is provided by Lyons (1999). She measured attachment style as well as people's preference for a transactional versus relational psychological contract. In a correlational study, she found that secure people tended to prefer a relational contract. She also found that those with a relational orientation expressed less intent to leave and also avowed to have more trust in their employer. Of course, all these variables might mutually influence each other. However, in theory at least, attachment style is born from infancy and comes before psychological contracting with employers.

A consequence of attachment is exploratory behavior. Securely attached children will engage in more care-free exploration. On the other hand, avoidant attachment is suggested to result in exploration motivated more by the desire to get away from the attachment figure than to find out about the world. In contrast, anxious/ambivalent attachment might result in more diffident exploration. Elliot and Reis (2003) built on these ideas, within the conceptual framework that exploration is a manifestation of the motive to be competent which, in adulthood, is expressed in terms of achievement motivation. They look at four achievement goals. The first is mastery-achievement goals, defined by "striving to attain task-based standards of competence" (p. 319). The second is mastery-avoidance goals, defined as "striving to avoid task-based standards of incompetence" (p. 319). Third, there are performance-approach goals, defined as "striving to attain norm-based standards of competence" (p. 319), and finally there are performance-avoidance goals, defined as "striving to avoid norm-based standards of incompetence" (p. 319). Of these, they suggest that the first is the optimal form of achievement motivation, with the avoidance-oriented form as non-optimal. The achievement goals are associated with high need for achievement whereas the avoidant goals are associated with fear of failure. In their study, Elliot and Reis found that securely attached people tended to adopt more approach-oriented goals than the insecure. In particular, they had more mastery-approach goals than avoidant people and fewer performance-avoidant goals than anxious-ambivalent people. So the secure are higher than the insecure in need for achievement and the insecure are higher than the secure in fear of failure. The authors speculate that maybe being securely attached helps a person withstand "a difficult day at the workplace" (p. 328) and it "may also facilitate appetitive engagement in the work itself" (p. 328).

As a basis for selection, a psychologist might assess people's attachment style or at least employ the constructs of attachment in considering someone's suitability. Clearly, the precise focus of attachment needs to be appropriately work-related and not intrude into people's domestic lives. Nonetheless, it would seem quite appropriate to uncover a candidate's sense of security both with other people at work and with groups and organizations.

Physiology and Emotions

Differences in attachment styles seem to have pervasive consequences for our behavior. So too do inherited differences and it is quite possible that our inheritance predisposes us to an attachment style. Inheritance could encourage us to behave in a way that evokes a response that sets up the attachment style. Indeed, just such a chain of events seems to have been demonstrated by van den Boom (1989). She assessed infant irritability at 15 days of age and found that irritable babies after one year were more likely to be classified as insecurely attached whereas non-irritable babies were more likely to be classified as securely attached. Furthermore, in a follow-up study van den Boom (1994) trained the parents of some irritable babies on how to soothe and play with them. A year later these babies were more likely to be classified as securely attached than the irritable babies whose mothers had received no such training.

A detailed account of the physiology of emotion is beyond the scope of this chapter but there appear to be three main issues. The first is the physiological correlates of emotion such as the heart rate increasing with fear. Clearly, if the physiological correlate is unique to a specific emotion, the information could be used in selection. Measuring the physiological reaction would indicate the emotion. The hurdles, of course, are acceptability to candidates and the availability of technicians to monitor physiological responses. The second issue is the physiology that gives rise to emotional predisposition. Again though, it is hard to imagine measuring a person's physiology at selection and rejecting them upon the results. It is hard because it is unlikely to be seen as legitimate and acceptable. Interestingly, of course, on the face of it, we would be deciding on the basis of far more reliable data than a personality inventory. However, the perceived immutability of one's physiology would make it very tough to be told that one has been rejected on the basis of it and I suspect the toughness of the telling will stop employers from the attempt.

The third issue is the extent to which the physiological predisposers to emotion are inherited. Knowing the heritability of physiology is of interest at the time of selection because the more that is due to inheritance the less it would seem open to change. If selection is based upon some behaviors that are known to be contributed to considerably by inherited physiology then the employer is advised not to overlook "development needs" on these behaviors as they are less likely to change.

There seems little doubt that people do indeed differ in inherited temperament and that much of temperament is firmly in the domain of the emotional. The case is argued particularly forcefully by a group of researchers led by McCrae and Costa (2000). They describe personality as biologically based and "more or less immune to environmental influences" (p. 175). They go on to say that "personality traits have a substantial genetic component" (p. 176) and assert that all the Big Five factors are heritable. In a similar vein, Rothbart, Ahadi, and Evans (2000) describe research that yielded the dimensions of "fear, anger or frustration, positive affect and approach, activity level, and attentional persistence or duration of orienting" (p. 124) as distinguishable in infants. Furthermore, they found "strongly reliable relationships" (p. 127) between some of these dimensions measured in infancy and the same or similar dimensions measured at age seven. These relationships can be taken as evidence of heritability.

The work-related results of inheritance were demonstrated by Ilies and Judge (2003) in research entitled "On the heritability of job satisfaction." The notion of a genetic config-uration operating directly upon job satisfaction might seem a little fanciful. Nonetheless, the paper presents good evidence that somehow or other our propensity to feel job satis-faction, which Ilies and Judge see as an emotional state, is influenced by our inheritance. They look at the link between inheritance and job satisfaction as mediated by the traits of positive and negative affectivity and by the 'Big Five' personality traits. As we have seen, the two are not entirely independent as positive affectivity is an indicator of extroversion and negative affectivity is an indicator of neuroticism. Ilies and Judge summarize very clearly how our genotype determines the range within which our phenotypic behavior is constrained to develop. They estimate that roughly 30% of the variation in job satisfac-tion can be accounted for by genetics and that around a quarter of this genetic effect is mediated by the Big Five traits, with approximately 45% mediated by positive and nega-tive affectivity.

From this, we might conclude that inheritance has a major influence upon our emo-tions, acting via our physiology. For selection, this has the implication, at the very least, that we should choose people carefully as the possession of emotional predispositions unsuitable for the role will be hard if not impossible to change.

CONTROL OF EMOTIONS

So far, we have concentrated on differences between people in the emotions they are dis-posed to feel. However, the sole reason for investigating this when selecting people is that emotions will affect behavior which will affect performance. Clearly, this chain can be broken to the extent that emotion can be controlled. There are three aspects to this: exert-ing control; recognizing the emotion that you are about to or need to control; recognizing others' emotions so that you can tailor yourself accordingly.

Exerting control

A superficial understanding of emotional intelligence might lead us to think that all control is intelligent and desirable. This is not so, and if control is the basis for selection, we need

INDIVIDUAL DIFFERENCES IN EMOTION REGULATION

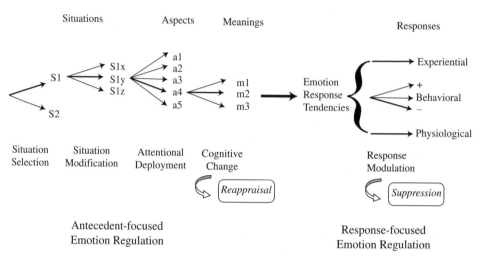

FIGURE 9.1   A process model of emotion regulation. (Source: from Gross, 2001). Copyright ©
American Psychological Society

to ensure it is the right sort of control. Eisenberg, Fabes, Guthrie, and Reiser (2000) draw
a distinction between emotion regulation, emotion-related behavior regulation, and niche
picking. The first is regulation of the emotion that is felt whereas the second is the regulation of behavior following the emotion. Niche picking is regulating exposure to situations that will provoke emotions. This distinction is built upon by Gross and John (2003)
who note that emotions might be controlled at a variety of points from their provocation
to expression. They distinguish between antecedent-focused and response-focused strategies for regulating emotions. Antecedent strategies, such as cognitive reappraisal, work
before the emotional response has been provoked by acting on the way in which the
situation is appraised. On the other hand, response-focused strategies, such as expressive
suppression, are aimed at the emotional response itself. Their model is reproduced in
Figure 9.1.

Reappraisal seems to be the healthier path to emotional control. Gross and John found
that suppression was related to people seeing themselves as inauthentic and to a general
"shutting down" of emotions. Suppressors reported themselves and were seen by peers to
be more likely to experience negative emotion and peers were able to detect this method
of regulation. Suppression was associated with less likelihood of sharing both negative and
positive emotions with others and substantially more avoidance of attachment. Suppressors were not generally disliked but they were recipients of less social support, particularly
emotional support, from peers. Suppression of emotion was also examined by Mendes
et al. (2003). They confirmed that it tended to produce the cardiovascular reaction of threat
rather than challenge.

On the other hand, Gross and John found that reappraisal was related to a lack of neuroticism and to a greater experience of positive emotions as reported by the respondents
and their peers. Reappraisal was related positively to sharing emotions and "reappraisers

had closer relationships (as rated by peers) and were also better liked by their peers" (p. 358). Reappraisal was associated with fewer symptoms of depression, whereas suppression was related negatively with well-being.

The management and control of emotion has, of course, over the last decade been popularized by writers on "emotional intelligence." Unfortunately, as the American Psychological Association has commented (Benson, 2003), this is "a popular idea that some researchers are struggling to keep grounded in science" (p. 52). For example, it might be too simple to regard "emotional intelligence" as a general quality. Trierweiler et al.'s work cautions against seeing the ability to control emotional expression as a general trait. Rather, they say, "regulation abilities do not generalize across emotions" (p. 1037), citing as an example the person who is well able to control anger but who might not be so able to control shame or anxiety. In addition, the work considered above suggests that the habitual suppression of emotion has negative side effects. We are probably better selecting people who feel appropriate emotions than those who suppress inappropriate ones.

Recognizing one's emotions

Nonetheless, managing the expression of emotion will clearly be called for on occasion. Part and parcel of being able to regulate the expression of emotion is the clarity with which emotions are experienced. Gohm (2003) reports a thorough study in which she examined three aspects of the experience: emotional clarity, attention to emotions, and emotional intensity. With regard to clarity, Gohm suggests the person who lacks clarity "may be likely to find his or her reactions in emotional situations to be unpredictable and often problematic" (p. 595). She also suggests that people at the extremes of attention to emotions will be less likely than mid-scorers to regulate their moods whereas people who experience emotions with the greatest intensity "might seek to dampen their moods" (p. 595). These three aspects of emotional experience are seen as independent. Different patterns of the three yield four types, which Gohm labels: hot, overwhelmed, cerebral, and cool. Hot individuals are high on all three dimensions and cool are low on all three. Overwhelmed are high on attention and intensity but low on clarity whereas the cerebral are the opposite: high on clarity and low on attention and intensity. Gohm asked people to read a positive or negative news story, report how it made them feel, and write about a recent happy or sad event (happy or sad in congruence with the nature of the news item). They then carried out a third unrelated task and also estimated the likelihood of a negative event happening to them (a judgment task). Finally, they reported how they felt at the end of the experiment and how they felt when writing about the event. She found that the overwhelmed made judgments that were different to the other three "types." Unlike others, the overwhelmed estimated lower (rather than higher) risk in the negative than in the positive mood condition. Their contrarian judgments appeared to be due to the fact that their moods reversed in the course of a session, in contrast to the others whose moods either dissipated (cerebral and cool) or continued (hot). The judgments were in keeping with the reversed moods.

Gohm draws attention to the fact that her sample (introductory psychology students) included 30% who could be labeled overwhelmed – people who experience emotions but do not have clarity about them – and she suggests these people be taught emotional intelligence. Overwhelmed people seem to be at a "normal" point on a continuum that ends with alexithymia. Gohm says that high scorers on alexithymia "report difficulty in describing and identifying their feelings, and they attempt to avoid emotional experience by replacing feelings with abstract thoughts" (p. 594).

The ability to perceive others' emotions

The ability – preferably to anticipate or at least to read – others' emotional reactions is, prima facie, conducive to good interpersonal relations. It appears to be more an interpersonal skill than a direct emotional factor in the perceiver. It is part of the sensitivity to interpersonal situations that enables high-performing leaders to vary their leadership styles appropriately to the situation.

There is a body of evidence suggesting that the ability resides in the amygdala (Killcross, 2000). People with damage to the amygdala have difficultly in recognizing the facial expression of fear, anger, and disgust (but not happiness, sadness, and surprise). However, these findings do not mean that in undamaged people there is a continuum of amygdala functioning which sets in train a continuum of emotional "intelligence." Instead, it seems to me more likely that, for people without physiological damage, the recognition of emotions in others is learned rather than varying with the "hardware" of the amygdala. I believe the same is true of the anticipation of others' emotions. Some families seem to put a great stress on emotion and emotion-recognition and others do not, and it seems more parsimonious to attribute differences in the "skill" to such learning differences than to amygdala differences.

COMPARISON WITH EMOTIONAL INTELLIGENCE

The control of emotion is central to emotional intelligence which in turn is associated most strongly with Goleman (1998). In their most recent book, Goleman, Boyatzis, and McKee (2002) present six styles of leadership, namely:

Pacesetting
Commanding
Affiliative
Coaching
Democratic
Visionary.

The leadership styles are related by Goleman and his co-writers to the competencies – or more specifically, the emotional intelligence competencies – the person has to draw upon. There are 20 of these, grouped into four clusters labeled:

Self-awareness
Self-management
Social awareness
Relationship management.

It is my belief (Woodruffe, 2000, 2001) that Goleman has set out extremely well the influence of the emotional on behavior and particularly on success at work. However, although, in a sense, Goleman's account is beyond criticism, that is also its weakness. The styles of leadership are but amalgams of competencies; the competencies are "often little more than a dating-agency list of desirable qualities" (Matthews, Zeidner, & Roberts, 2002, p. 531); and it is obvious that the competencies and styles are influenced by the emotional. However, we are really no closer from reading Goleman to specifying clear links between particular emotional capacities and particular competencies; and we certainly are misleading ourselves if we think there is a continuum of amygdala functioning related to a continuum of emotional capacities.

Most people would agree that virtually all behavior is influenced by emotion. The EI contribution seems limited by not generating clear measures of the presumably independent emotional variables that give rise to competent behavior. Matthews et al. (2002) conclude with respect to the use of EI in occupational settings that "the ratio of hyperbole to hard evidence is rather high, with overreliance on anecdote and unpublished surveys" (p. 542). They continue by observing that "currently, EI mostly serves a cheerleading function, helping to whip up support for potentially (though not always actually) useful interventions focused on a heterogeneous collection of emotional, cognitive and behavioral skills" (p. 544).

"Tests" of emotional intelligence

Given the above general conclusion on the status of emotional intelligence, is there any sense in buying commercial "tests" to measure it for selection? On the face of it, the answer would seem to be "no." Emotional intelligence amounts to something of a rainbow of competencies which may or may not be relevant to any particular role or organization. There seems no more point in buying a generic measure of these EI competencies than a measure of any other generic competency set. Certainly, any practitioner considering investing in a commercial "test" of EI would be well advised first to buy Matthews et al.'s (2002) *Emotional Intelligence: Science and myth*, which contains a very thorough review of the issue. In brief, Matthews et al. review the three main measures of EI. They are:

- *Performance-based tests by Mayer, Salovey and colleagues.* The Mayer–Salovey–Caruso Emotional Intelligence Test (MSCEIT) consists of sub-tests, each of which asks the candidate to carry out tasks (such as recognizing the emotion in a face) to which there are right and wrong answers. The final score is based on how the candidate performed. There are different versions of the MSCEIT, as well as an earlier test by the same authors. For the HR practitioner, the most important point must be whether the qualities measured actually predict performance at work. As with any other test, this one should only be used after its predictive validity has been confirmed.
- *Emotional Quotient Inventory (EQ-i) by Bar-On.* This self-report of 15 subscales of EI is seen by Matthews et al. to overlap so heavily with personality measures (particularly the Big Five) for them to conclude that this "should be a cause of concern for those organizations prepared to employ it in personnel selection" (p. 213). Certainly, there seems little reason to use it as well as a Big Five inventory.

♦ *Emotional Competence Inventory (ECI)*. This inventory, marketed by the Hay consultancy, aims to provide a measure of Goleman's model of EI competencies. Matthews et al. speculate that commercialization has been a high priority and conclude that "it is difficult not to be cynical of this measure" (p. 218).

Using any of these measures for selection – either of external or internal applicants – seems contentious. Most fundamentally, the HR practitioner must check empirically that the qualities purportedly measured actually matter to job performance and that they cannot be measured just as well or better by a carefully developed measure of personality such as those aimed at the "Big Five."

Conclusion on controlling emotions

We might conclude from this section that the ability to control emotion needs to be approached carefully at selection. The discussion supports the argument that we should look behind behavior to try to gain insights into the causes of behavior. If someone is calm because they are suppressing anger their calmness seems very different to the person who is "naturally" calm. For example, at the time of writing the British Prime Minister's former press secretary (Alastair Campbell) has gained some notoriety for going to a parliamentary committee holding a nail in his hand. His purpose was to create pain to subdue his anger if he began to feel enraged. Presumably it is preferable to select people who do not have an habitual need for the nail. Instead we should select people who by appraisal or reappraisal of the situation feel the appropriate emotion for the role. Of course, everyone might find themselves in Alastair Campbell's shoes occasionally and need to use the nail. When they do, the ability to perceive one's emotions is a prerequisite to controlling them and the ability to perceive others' emotions serves as a guide to what is appropriate.

But Is It Fair?

Before concluding, I would like to raise some issues on the justification of blighting someone's chances because of their emotional functioning. In particular, I am acutely reluctant to extend the notion of a quotient to emotion. The implication is that the more you have the better, and so the person with the highest EI should always be chosen. More generally, while clearly positively disposed to examining emotional factors at selection, I would also make the following observations in the cause of balance:

1. There is a recurrent finding that the 'g' of intellectual ability is the dominant correlate of occupational and job performance (Schmidt & Hunter, 2004). If anything, this association might increase as we become increasingly embedded in an information age (Lubinski, 2004). We should not assume that success is all about or even mostly about emotion. It is mostly about intellectual ability, albeit with some "impossible" people having their potential quite nullified by their emotional nature.
2. Although some people are "a nightmare," most people's emotional imperfections can be worked around. The perfectly balanced individual loses individuality and proba-

bly a lot of their drive and creativity. Taking the EI route carries the danger of populating offices with Stepford Wives.

3. As a society, we run the risk of creating an underclass of the unemployable purely because these people do not have the personalities that are – at least in part – a matter of fashion.

4. Maybe we should give greater consideration to designing jobs around people as well as people around jobs. Indeed, this is just what some organizations already do. For example, technically brilliant staff who demonstrate interpersonal development needs are left to work quite happily without a team.

Overall Conclusions

In selecting for emotion, it will be clear that I advocate following a different path to that set out in the popular EI literature. The measurement of competencies is a perfectly valid approach and the one that will probably continue to be adopted for most selection decisions. In taking this approach we check the person's behavior rather than the reasons behind the behavior. However, for some vacancies there would seem to be added value in finding out about relevant aspects of a person's emotional functioning. In doing so, we can screen out the person who is likely to behave inappropriately when not on "best behavior." We can also seek to identify whether the source of a particular behavior is ephemeral or deep-seated and we can choose people who will produce the appropriate emotions for the role in an authentic way. Knowing about the source of behavior also enables us to estimate the ease with which it can be developed and yields a more parsimonious insight into the person than studying behavior itself.

Two particular approaches to emotion that I think offer mileage are on the one hand positive and negative affectivity and on the other attachment and the person's sense of security. Both of these seem to address profound differences between people that have pervasive consequences for their behavior. They can be measured and if relevant to the role there is a good case for considering employing a psychologist to give the employer insight into them. It seems perfectly fit and proper to assess these when they are relevant for a particular job or career track. In particular, it seems reasonable to think in terms of there being a range for these emotional factors beyond which the person becomes a risk in the role. For example, some people are so defensively aggressive or bullying that they are decidedly unpleasant to work with.

Finally, there is merit in determining the candidate's ability to control emotion, with the emphasis less upon suppression than reappraisal so that the appropriate emotion is felt rather than faked.

Notes

1. The first four points of regulation are antecedent-focused and the fifth is response-focused. The number of options at each point in the illustration is arbitrary and the heavy lines trace the series of options that might be selected.

2. Reproduced with permission from Gross, J. J. (2001), Emotion regulation in adulthood: Timing is everything, *Current Directions in Psychological Sciences*, *10*, p. 215, copyright by Blackwell Publishing.

References

Ambady, N., & Gray, H. M. (2002). On being sad and mistaken: Mood effects on the accuracy of thin-slice judgements. *Journal of Personality and Social Psychology*, *83*, 947–961.

Anderson, C., Keltner, D., & John, O. P. (2003). Emotional convergence between people over time. *Journal of Personality and Social Psychology*, *84*, 1054–1068.

Bartholomew, K., & Horowitz, L. M. (1991). Attachment styles among young adults: A test of a four-category model. *Journal of Personality and Social Psychology*, *61*, 226–244.

Benson, E. (2003). Breaking new ground. *Monitor in Psychology*, *34*, 52–54.

Bowlby, J. (1973). *Attachment and loss: Vol. 2. Separation: Anxiety and anger.* New York: Basic Books.

Brotheridge, C. M., & Lee, R. T. (2003). Development and validation of the Emotional Labour Scale. *Journal of Occupational and Organizational Psychology*, *76*, 365–379.

Eisenberg, N., Fabes, R. A., Guthrie, I. K., & Reiser, M. (2000). Dispositional emotionality and regulation: Their role in predicting quality of social functioning. *Journal of Personality and Social Psychology*, *78*, 136–157.

Ekman, P., Friesen, W. J., O'Sullivan, M., Chan, A., Diacoyanni-Tariatzis, I., Heider, K., et al. (1987). Universals and cultural differences in the judgments of facial expressions of emotion. *Journal of Personality and Social Psychology*, *53*, 712–717.

Elliot, A. J., & Reis, H. T. (2003). Attachment and exploration in adulthood. *Journal of Personality and Social Psychology*, *85*, 317–331.

Feeney, J. A., & Noller, P. (1996). *Adult attachment.* Thousand Oaks, CA: Sage.

Frank, M. G., & Stennett, J. (2001). The forced-choice paradigm and the perception of facial expressions of emotion. *Journal of Personality and Social Psychology*, *80*, 75–85.

Fredrickson, B. L., Tugade, M. M., Waugh, C. E., & Larkin, G. R. (2003). What good are positive emotions in crises? A prospective study on resilience and emotions following the terrorist attacks on the United States on September 11th 2001. *Journal of Personality and Social Psychology*, *84*, 365–376.

Gohm, C. L. (2003). Mood regulation and emotional intelligence: Individual differences. *Journal of Personality and Social Psychology*, *84*, 594–607.

Goleman, D. (1998). *Working with emotional intelligence.* London: Bloomsbury.

Goleman, D., Boyatzis, R., & McKee, A. (2002). *Primal leadership: Realizing the power of emotional intelligence.* Boston: Harvard Business School Press.

Gross, J. J. (2001). Emotion regulation in adulthood: timing is everything. *Current Directions in Psychological Science*, *10*, 214–219.

Gross, J. J., & John, O. P. (2003). Individual differences in two emotion regulation processes: Implications for affect, relationships, and well-being. *Journal of Personality and Social Psychology*, *85*, 348–362.

Harker, L.-A., & Keltner, D. (2001). Expressions of positive emotion in women's college yearbook pictures and their relationship to personality and life outcomes across adulthood. *Journal of Personality and Social Psychology*, *80*, 112–124.

Higgins, E. T. (1998). Promotion and prevention: Regulatory focus as a motivational principle. In M. P. Zanna (Ed.), *Advances in experimental social psychology* (Vol. 30, pp. 1–46). New York: Academic Press.

Ilies, R., & Judge, T. A. (2003). On the heritability of job satisfaction: The mediating role of personality. *Journal of Applied Psychology, 88*, 750–759.

Johnston, M. A. (2000). Delegation and organizational structure in small businesses: Influences of manager's attachment patterns. *Group and Organization Management, 25*, 4–21.

Kiefer, T. (2002). Analysing emotions for a better understanding of organizational change: Fear, joy, and anger during a merger. In N. M. Ashkanasy, W. J. Zerbe, & C. E. J. Härtel (Eds.), *Managing emotions in the workplace* (pp. 45–69). New York: M E Sharpe.

Kiefer, T., & Briner, R. (2003). Handle with care. *People Management, 23*, 48–50.

Killcross, S. (2000). The amygdala, emotion and learning. *The Psychologist, 13*, 502–507.

Lowe, R., & Bennett, P. (2003). Exploring coping reactions to work-stress: Application of an appraisal theory. *Journal of Occupational and Organizational Psychology, 76*, 393–400.

Lubinski, D. (2004). Introduction to the special section on cognitive abilities: 100 years after Spearman's (1904) "'General Intelligence,' objectively determined and measured." *Journal of Personality and Social Psychology, 86*, 96–111.

Lyons, W. (1999). *Attachment styles and the psychological contract.* Unpublished MSc dissertation, University of Surrey, UK.

McCrae, R. R., Costa, P. T., Jr., Ostendorf, F., Angleitner, A., Hřebíčková, M., Avia, M.D., et al. (2000). Nature over nurture: Temperament, personality, and life span development. *Journal of Personality and Social Psychology, 78*, 173–186.

Matthews, G., Zeidner, M., & Roberts, R. D. (2002). *Emotional intelligence: Science and myth.* Cambridge, MA: MIT Press.

Mendes, W. B., Reis, H. T., Seery, M. D., & Blascovich, J. (2003). Cardiovascular correlates of emotional expression and suppression: Do content and gender context matter? *Journal of Personality and Social Psychology, 84*, 771–792.

Mischel, W. (1968). *Personality and assessment.* New York: Wiley.

Oreg, S. (2003). Resistance to change: Developing an individual difference measure. *Journal of Applied Psychology, 88*, 680–693.

Paterson, J. M., & Härtel, C. E. J. (2002). An integrated affective and cognitive model to explain employees' responses to downsizing. In N. M. Ashkanasy, W. J. Zerbe, & C. E. J. Härtel (Eds.), *Managing emotions in the workplace* (pp. 25–44). New York: M E Sharpe.

Rafaeli, A. (2002). Foreword to N. M. Ashkanasy, W. J. Zerbe, & C. E. J. Härtel (Eds.), *Managing emotions in the workplace* (pp. xi–xiii). New York: M E Sharpe.

Rothbart, M. K., Ahadi, S. A., & Evans, D. E. (2000). Temperament and personality: Origins and outcomes. *Journal of Personality and Social Psychology, 78*, 122–135.

Schmidt, F. L., & Hunter, J. (2004). General mental ability in the world of work: Occupational attainment and job performance. *Journal of Personality and Social Psychology, 86*, 162–173.

Smith, E. R., Murphy, J., & Coats, S. (1999). Attachment to groups: Theory and measurement. *Journal of Personality and Social Psychology, 77*, 94–110.

Snyder, M. (1974). Self-monitoring of expressive behavior. *Journal of Personality and Social Psychology, 30*, 526–537.

Taylor, S. E., Lerner, J. S., Sherman, D. K., Sage, R. M., & McDowell, N. K. (2003). Are self-enhancing cognition's associated with healthy or unhealthy biological profiles? *Journal of Personality and Social Psychology, 85*, 605–615.

Trierweiler, L. I., Eid, M., & Lischetzke, T. (2002). The structure of emotional expressivity: Each emotion counts. *Journal of Personality and Social Psychology, 82*, 1023–1040.

Van den Boom, D. C. (1989). Neonatal irritability and the development of attachment. In G. A. Kohnstamn, J. E. Bates, & M. K. Rothbart (Eds.), *Temperament in childhood* (pp. 299–318). Chichester, UK: John Wiley.

Van den Boom, D. C. (1994). The influence of temperament and mothering on attachment and exploration: An experimental manipulation of sensitive responsiveness among lower-class mothers with irritable infants. *Child Development, 65,* 1457–1477.

Vorauer, J. D., Cameron, J. J., Holmes, J. G., & Pearce, D. G. (2003). Invisible overtures: Fears of rejection and the signal amplification bias. *Journal of Personality and Social Psychology, 84,* 793–812.

Weiss, H. M., & Cropanzano, R. (1996). Affective events theory: A theoretical discussion of the structure, causes and consequences of affective experiences at work. *Research in Organizational Behavior, 18,* 1–74.

Woodruffe, C. W. E. (1999). *Winning the talent war: A strategic approach top attracting developing and retaining the best people.* Chichester, UK: Wiley.

Woodruffe, C. (2000). Emotional intelligence: Time for a time-out. *Selection and Development Review, 16,* 3–9.

Woodruffe, C. (2001). Promotional intelligence. *People Management, 11,* 26–29.

10

Situational Judgment Tests

David Chan and Neal Schmitt

The inclusion of situational judgment tests (SJTs) in a battery of predictor measures has become increasingly common in personnel selection research and practice (e.g., Chan & Schmitt, 2002; Phillips, 1992; Pulakos & Schmitt, 1996; Weekley & Jones, 1999). Unlike cognitive ability and personality measures which have an extensive literature and large database, the empirical evidence on SJTs is much less well established and the theoretical or conceptual underpinnings of SJTs are much less well understood. This chapter summarizes what we now know and do not know about SJTs and identifies specific directions for future research. We begin with a summary of the research on the criterion-related validity of SJTs. This is followed by a discussion of several important issues involving the construct validity of SJTs that have not been adequately addressed in extant research. The chapter ends with an agenda for future research that, if effectively implemented, should contribute to our understanding and effective use of SJTs in personnel selection.

CRITERION-RELATED VALIDITY OF SITUATIONAL JUDGMENT TESTS

Assessments of the quality of judgments or decisions made by applicants for jobs have been attempted during much of the time that industrial/organizational psychologists have sought to improve organizations' selection procedures. McDaniel, Morgeson, Finnegan, Campion, and Braverman (2001) identified three early tests of situational judgment that accounted for 48 of the 102 validity estimates that were the basis of their meta-analysis on the validity of SJTs. These tests, which provided the early seeds of situational judgment as a predictor construct in personnel selection, included the Supervisory Judgment Test (Richardson, Bellows, & Henry Co., 1949), the How Supervise (File, 1945), and the Supervisory Practices Test (Bruce & Learner, 1958). As their titles imply, all three involved supervisory judgments including the requirement that a respondent indicate the desirability of various actions or a choice among alternative actions in response to some situation.

Most modern versions of situational judgment tests derive from the work of Motowidlo, Dunnette, and Carter (1990) whose work was motivated by Sternberg and Wagner's concept of tacit knowledge (Wagner, 1987). According to Wagner, tacit knowledge was needed to accomplish everyday tasks that were usually not openly stated or a part of any formal instruction. Motowidlo et al. (1990) improved on the Wagner and Sternberg (1991) measure by using job analyses to identify the types of judgments made on a specific job and to improve their content and face validity. Motowidlo, Hanson, and Crafts (1997) outlined the steps involved in a typical development of SJTs. The development process usually involves the identification of a set of work-related constructs that are targeted in an SJT. Job incumbents are asked to generate critical incidents or situations that require ability or expertise related to these constructs. Other job incumbents provide a set of actions that could be taken to resolve or improve the situations and yet another group provides judgments about the best and worst of these solutions and ratings of their relative effectiveness. These judgments are used to develop a final item and scoring key that is applied to the items. Respondents are asked to indicate their most likely and least likely actions in one scenario. Other response formats are required in some SJT renditions. For example, the SJTs described in Chan and Schmitt (2002) and Clevenger, Pereira, Wiechmann, Schmitt, and Schmidt Harvey (2001, Sample 2) required respondents to rate each possible solution to an item on a five-point effectiveness scale, whereas the SJT described in McDaniel and Nguyen (2001) required respondents to indicate the best and worst alternative solution.

Validities of situational judgment tests were meta-analyzed by McDaniel et al. (2001). They found that the average observed validity of 102 validity coefficients was .26; the average validity corrected for criterion unreliability was .34. However, there remained substantial unexplained variability (55%) in coefficients around this population value, suggesting the presence of moderators. Moderator analyses indicated that measures developed as the result of job analyses yielded larger validity coefficients than those not based on a job analysis (.38 versus .29), but the results of other moderator analyses were inconclusive usually because of a small number of studies or small total sample size in one or more of the groups of studies formed by the moderator variable.

Studies conducted since the "reintroduction" of situational tests by Motwidlo et al. (1990) have produced validities very similar to the averages reported by McDaniel et al. (2001). Correlations between the SJT and ratings of interpersonal, problem-solving, communication, and overall effectiveness were .35, .28, .37, and .30 respectively for a group of externally hired managers in the Motowidlo et al. study. Similar correlations for a small ($N = 25$) group of internally promoted managers ranged from .28 to .45. Motowidlo and Tippins (1993) reported lower, but statistically significant predictive validity ($r = .25$) for a group of 36 managers and .20 in a concurrent study of marketing incumbents. The managers in both these studies were employed by telecommunications companies.

Several other large-scale studies involving employees in a wide variety of jobs have produced similar outcomes. Pulakos and Schmitt (1996) reported SJT validities of .20 and .14 (.38 and .25 corrected for range restriction and criterion unreliability) for the prediction of performance in core investigative and effort and professionalism dimensions among a group of federal investigative agents. Borman, Hanson, Oppler, Pulakos, and White (1993) reported an observed correlation of .22 (corrected for unreliability in the criterion, .28) between a situational judgment measure and supervisory ratings of the performance of 570 soldiers. In two separate studies, Weekley and Jones (1999) reported observed validities of .23 and .16 among nearly 4,000 service employees in retail and hotel industry jobs and observed validities of .22, .24, and .33 in a sample of retail employees and nursing home workers. Results across studies suggest observed validities in the low .20s with corrected validities of approximately .30. In only one of these studies were any corrections for range restriction employed, so the corrected coefficients may have been underestimates.

The concern expressed by McDaniel et al. (2001) as well as critics of earlier versions of SJT that they are simply cognitive ability tests (e.g., Thorndike & Stein, 1937) was assessed by Weekley and Jones (1999) who found that SJTs produced increments of .03 and .01 in a battery that included both cognitive ability and experience. Similar assessments of incremental validity by Weekley and Jones (1997) produced changes in squared multiple correlations of .025, .057, and .096. Clevenger et al. (2001) reported re-analyses of two previous studies as well as data on a new sample that indicated the situational judgment inventory added in a statistically significant fashion to batteries that included cognitive ability, experience, and simulations or job knowledge measures. The incremental R^2s ranged from .016 to .028. Chan and Schmitt (2002) provided additional evidence of incremental validity in that they showed that an SJT increased R^2 by .03 to .08 above cognitive ability and experience as well as measures of the Big Five personality constructs. The latter study was also unique in that the investigators examined the prediction of three conceptually and empirically distinct (although correlated) performance dimensions (core technical proficiency, interpersonal contextual performance, and job dedication) as well as overall performance. Observed correlations with these four criteria of the performance of Singaporean civil servants ranged from .27 to .38.

In two recent studies, researchers have examined the use of SJT in the prediction of college student performance. Lievens and Coetsier (2002) reported the use of two video-based SJTs in the selection of 941 Flemish medical and dental students. One of the two SJTs based on a patient–doctor interaction was significantly related to first year medical school grades (r corrected for restriction or range = .12), but the other SJT based on a medical expert discussion was not significantly related to medical school grades. Oswald, Schmitt, Kim, Gillespie, and Ramsay (in press) reported validities of .16 and −.27 between an SJT and first year college grades and self-reported absences respectively for a group of over 600 college freshmen. Empirically derived scales comprised of the most valid SJT items yielded validities of .23 and −.33 in cross validation samples. The Lievens and Coetsier study was a predictive study while the Oswald et al. study was concurrent and involved study participants who were already college students when predictor data were collected.

In summary, the criterion-related validity of SJTs in predicting performance seems well established both through the meta-analysis conducted by McDaniel et al. (2001) and the summary of primary studies conducted since Motowidlo et al. (1990) revived interest in the method. While SJTs do appear to be related to cognitive ability and, in some studies, personality measures as well, incremental validity of SJTs over and above personality and cognitive ability has been reported in multiple studies (e.g., Chan & Schmitt, 2002; Clevenger et al., 2001). The substantial variability in correlations may be because different constructs are being measured depending on the types of situations included on the SJT (Chan & Schmitt, 2002). When the situations require cognitive-based constructs such as planning, organizational ability, and analytical problem solving, then SJT scores correlate more highly with cognitive ability test scores than is the case when the situations require constructs associated with interpersonal or leadership skills, for example, which are more personality based.

Construct Validity of Situational Judgment Tests

SJTs appear to have high content validity and face validity (see Chan & Schmitt, 1997) and there is increasing evidence that SJTs can produce substantial zero-order and incremental criterion-related validities (Chan & Schmitt, 2002; Clevenger et al., 2001; McDaniel et al., 2001). However, it is important also to establish evidence of construct validity for SJTs for at least two reasons. First, establishing construct validity would help avoid a vacuous and circular translation of the concept of situational judgment into whatever is measured by situational judgment measures (i.e., SJTs). Second, explicating the constructs underlying SJTs would help locate SJTs or SJT constructs in models of job performance, including the specification of their interrelationships with other predictors such as cognitive ability and personality traits, thereby enriching our understanding and prediction of job performance.

Accordingly, we will first discuss the possibility of using SJTs as measures of contextual job knowledge. We will then address the fundamental issue of the construct-method distinction with respect to SJTs and relate the distinction to the concept of practical intelligence. We end by outlining a construct-oriented agenda that we propose for future research on SJTs.

SJTs as measures of contextual job knowledge

SJTs, as mentioned above, typically consist of questions in paper-and-pencil mode that present a hypothetical critical incident and several alternative courses of action in response to the situation. They have been assessed in several modes, including video-based items (e.g., Lievens & Coetsier, 2002), interview questions (e.g., Morgeson, Bauer, Truxillo, & Campion, 2003), as well as paper-and-pencil formats. As mentioned above, they can also require different instructional and response sets (McDaniel et al., 2001; Pereira & Harvey, 1999; Ployhart & Ehrhart, 2003).

Specific items in an SJT may also refer to a wide range of situations and include different types of content to which the test taker must attend or disregard when making a decision. Efforts to factor analyze situational judgment items typically produce little support for a priori factors that researchers have tried to incorporate into their items (e.g., Oswald et al., in press). The first factor in these analyses usually accounts for two to three times the variance of the second factor, but unless the scale is comprised of a large number of items, coefficient alpha reliabilities are typically low. One explanation for these results is that responses to a single SJT item with its varied options may be the result of a variety of individual difference constructs including both ability and motivational/personality constructs. This is consistent with empirical findings that indicate that SJTs are correlated with a variety of different variables including cognitive ability discussed above. Chan and Schmitt (2002) reported SJT correlations of .23, .24, and .29 with conscientiousness, extraversion, and agreeableness and −.20 with neuroticism. In the Lievens and Coetsier (2002) study none of the reported correlations between measures of the Big Five and the SJT exceeded .15. Clevenger et al. (2001) reported correlations of .00, .16, and .21 between SJTs and conscientiousness in three different samples. Correlations between an

SJT and measures of extraversion, agreeableness, conscientiousness, emotional stability, and openness of .17, .38, .28, .17, and .21 respectively were reported by Oswald et al. (in press). McDaniel et al. (2001) reported a meta-analytic estimate of .31 for the correlation between SJTs and cognitive ability, but their 90% credibility interval ranged from .09 to .69.

Adapting ideas first presented by Motowidlo (1999a), Kim, Schmitt, Oswald, Gillespie, and Ramsay (2003) tested a model of college student performance in which an SJT was treated as a measure of contextual knowledge. This model is built on similar models of job performance (e.g., Borman, White, Pulakos, & Oppler, 1991) in which job knowledge has been identified as a mediator of the relationship between cognitive ability and job performance. In the model tested by Kim et al., SJT performance, which is construed as indicating contextual knowledge, is hypothesized as a mediator of the relationship between personality and contextual job performance. There has been a popular claim that personality traits, rather than ability, relate more to contextual performance (e.g., Borman & Motowidlo, 1997). The mediation hypothesis in Kim et al.'s model is consistent with this claim. In addition, the hypothesis specified the criterion-relevant knowledge (i.e., contextual knowledge as measured by a SJT) posited as the more proximal predictor that intercedes between personality and contextual job performance. Some support for these hypothesized relationships was found in that agreeableness was related to SJT scores and the SJT, in turn, was related to peer ratings of contextual performance. However, the influence of extraversion and conscientiousness on contextual performance was not mediated by the SJT. Given previous support for the mediating role of job knowledge on ability–task performance relationships and the original conceptualization of SJT as measures of tacit knowledge, these models bear additional evaluation even though the results from Kim et al. (2003) are only moderately encouraging.

Kim et al. (2003) emphasized that their model was not an attempt at construct validation of SJTs in general and acknowledged that contextual knowledge is one of several constructs that can be potentially measured by SJTs. Indeed, we can always design an SJT to measure task knowledge in terms of technical core proficiency, such as describing a traffic accident and asking how a police officer should respond. However, as elaborated later in this chapter, we believe that contextual knowledge is one of the dominant constructs assessed by typical SJTs. Kim et al. (2003) represents a first step in an attempt to adopt a more theory-driven and construct-oriented approach to studying the validity of SJTs. However, more will need to be done beyond simply locating the SJT in a path model linking personality and ability predictors and job performance criteria. For example, in the study of SJTs as possible measures of contextual knowledge, features of contextual (tacit) knowledge such as experiential acquisition, procedural nature, and practical use (Sternberg et al., 2000) should be explicated and matched with the characteristics of the specific test content in the SJT.

Given the nature of SJTs and the extant research findings, we believe that it is unlikely that there will be strong evidence that SJTs measure any single unidimensional construct. SJTs, like interviews or many paper-and-pencil tests, may be better construed as a method of measurement that can be adapted to measure a variety of job-related constructs in different situations. However, as discussed in the next section, there may be some types of situational judgment constructs that are almost inherently assessed in typical SJTs.

SJT as construct versus method

The issue of SJT as construct versus method includes at least two different levels. The first and more specific level concerns distinguishing between the format of testing used by a given SJT (i.e., the specific test method) and the situation/item content of the SJT (i.e., the intended test construct(s)). This level of distinction between construct and method is important because it allows the researcher to isolate unintended constructs measured by a given SJT and thereby avoid several problems associated with construct contamination. The second and more general level concerns whether the SJT is a method of measurement that can be used to assess different constructs or an indicator of an identifiable and meaningful new construct (i.e., situational judgment).

In addressing the specific-level distinction between construct and method, Chan and Schmitt (1997) compared a video-based SJT with a written paper-and-pencil version (i.e., two different methods of testing) of the same test. Black–White subgroup differences on the video-based version of this SJT were substantially less than differences on the written version ($d = -.21$ versus $d = -.95$ favoring the White group). The authors also measured the perceptions of the face validity of these instruments and the reading comprehension levels of their participants. They found that part of the Black–White differences in performance across the two different methods of test presentation were attributable to Black–White differences in reading comprehension and reactions to the tests.

If the intent is to measure constructs other than reading comprehension, for example, the correlations with reading comprehension would be evidence that the test is contaminated. Even if reading comprehension were an important part of job performance, it would be best to measure it directly with another test and keep the SJT, which is usually intended to measure other constructs, as free of the influence of reading comprehension as possible. This would allow for better interpretation of predictor–performance relationships and the proper application of any weighting schemes used in combining various elements of a test battery. More fundamentally, the study highlighted the importance of making a clear distinction between test construct and test method and showed one way in which sources of variance due to construct versus method can be isolated.

Empirical studies in which the impact of construct and method are separately estimable are very difficult to devise especially in field situations, primarily because test methods differ in the ease with which they can be adapted to assess similar test content. However, the separation of the SJT into its construct versus method components is critical and an area in which much more work needs to be done to inform researchers as to the nature of the constructs they are measuring with an SJT, the validity of the construct measurement, and the nature of the observed relationships between SJT and job performance or other job-relevant criteria. Such work would need to directly address the more general-level distinction between construct and method to which we now turn our attention.

We propose that SJTs, like the interview, be construed as a method of testing that has constraints on the range of constructs measured, although the dominant constructs are different from those in the interview. Like the interview, SJTs have dominant constructs that are readily or almost inherently assessed. We propose that the primary dominant constructs are *adaptability constructs* that are likely a function of both individual difference traits and the result of acquisition through previous experiences and *contextual knowledge constructs* that may be gained through experience in various real-world contexts. Collectively, these SJT-dominant constructs can be represented by the global construct called *practical intelligence* (Chan & Schmitt, 2002; Motowidlo et al., 1990; Pulakos, Arad, Donovan, & Plamondon, 2000; Sternberg et al., 2000) which we elaborate below.

Unlike the interview, SJT-dominant constructs are not associated with the structural format of the SJT (i.e., candidates presented with a problem situation followed by the requirement to generate, endorse, or rate a series of response options). Instead, the dominant constructs are associated with the core characteristics of the test content of typical SJTs. A specification of these core characteristics and relating them to SJT performance as well as job performance is necessary to avoid the circular assertion that practical intelligence or situational judgment effectiveness is the global construct that is dominant in typical SJTs.

Based on our reading of the SJTs reported in the available literature and used in practice, as well as our personal experiences with the development of a joint total of over 1,000 SJT situations, we propose three distinct but interrelated core characteristics of SJT content: practical situational demands, multidimensionality of situational response, and criterion–correspondent sampling of situations and response options in test content development (Chan & Schmitt, 2002).

A core characteristic of a typical SJT is that the content describes realistic demands found in practical or everyday situations. In contrast to academic problems which tend to be well defined, complete in information provided, have one correct answer, and often solvable by only one correct method, practical problems are ill-defined, incomplete in information provided, do not have one clearly correct answer, and often have multiple "solutions" each with varying degrees of effectiveness as well as different liabilities and assets (Chan, 2000a; Hedlund & Sternberg, 2000). Practical or real-world situational demands on the job often go beyond technical task knowledge to include requirements of contextual knowledge and adaptability requirements (Chan, 2000a, 2000b; Chan & Schmitt, 2002; Kim et al., 2003; Pulakos et al., 2000; Sternberg et al., 2000). Successful SJT performance is defined as overall effectiveness in responses to a variety of these practical situational demands (as indexed by the composite test score) which reflects high levels of contextual knowledge of what to do and how to do it such that one adapts and functions in the practical situations and contexts.

Several researchers have argued that SJT performance is a manifestation of these knowledge and ability dimensions which collectively constitute what Sternberg and his colleagues have called *practical intelligence* (Chan & Schmitt, 2002; Motowidlo et al., 1990; Sternberg et al., 2000). Practical intelligence refers to the ability or expertise to effectively respond and successfully adapt to a variety of practical problems or situational demands. Practical intelligence refers to the contextual knowledge acquired from everyday experience and the ability to apply this knowledge effectively in practical situations to achieve personally valued goals (Sternberg et al., 2000). Practical intelligence, and contextual knowledge in particular, is typically procedural in nature. with an implicit learning/processing quality. The procedural nature refers to the characteristic structure of the knowledge representation. Specifically, the knowledge is represented in sets of multiple behavior-guiding condition–action procedural (production) rules in the form of "IF ⟨antecedent condition⟩, THEN ⟨consequent action⟩." The implicit quality refers to the expertise development process. Specifically, the sets or systems of procedural knowledge rules are acquired or learned tacitly through previous everyday experiences outside conscious awareness or focal attention and in the absence of deliberate intention to learn. Hence, given a practical situation or class of situations (such as those described in a SJT), individuals high on practical intelligence would activate their relevant contextual knowledge and apply one or more sets of multiple condition–action procedural rules to guide their behavioral response, often without explicit awareness of the sequences of rules or the ability to readily articulate the reasoning justifying the judged effectiveness of the response. Both implicit learning/processing and procedural knowledge have strong theoretical bases and the empirical evidence is well documented in studies on expertise and skill acquisition as well as other areas of cognitive psychology. Although less direct evidence is available for implicit learning and procedural knowledge at workplace situations such as the types of scenarios described on SJTs, the strong theoretical bases and robust empirical evidence from cognitive psychology provide a rich source of information for researchers to compose similar but higher-level constructs applicable at workplace (SJT) situations (i.e., contextual job knowledge and practical intelligence). It is noteworthy that the application of cognitive psychology constructs which are at the intrapersonal cognitive level to responses at workplace situations which are often at the interpersonal behavioral level involves moving across levels of analysis. To avoid various cross-levels fallacies and misleading inferences, the cross-levels application needs to be guided by adequate composition models (Chan, 1998b) and attend to multilevel conceptual and statistical issues (see Chan, in press; Klein & Kozlowski, 2000).

Another core characteristic of SJT content is the multidimensionality of the situational response, often even at the level of a single response option to a situation. This is consistent with the multidimensionality of the practical intelligence (or adaptability) construct. Because most practical situations are complex, good judgment in these situations is likely to be a function of multiple, more narrowly defined traits and abilities. This may explain the typical findings from SJT studies showing relatively low internal consistency estimates of reliability (despite large number of items) and low test variance accounted for by the single general factor in factor analyses. Factor analytic solutions that allow cross-loadings (i.e., an item is allowed to load on more than one factor) are probably more adequate factorial representations of the SJT content. Factor analytic solutions need to explicitly model the multidimensionality of the adaptive response (i.e., SJT item) and not just the multidimensionality of the entire test. Unfortunately, unambiguous interpretation of the substantive nature of factors is difficult in the presence of items with cross-loadings.

We believe that the multidimensionality of SJT situations and situation responses may be traced back to the multidimensionality of the criterion construct that the SJT is designed to predict. This brings us to the third core characteristic of SJT content: the criterion–correspondent sampling of situations and situational responses in test content development. When developing SJT content (i.e., situations and situation responses), most test developers adopt a domain-sampling approach, often with the help of subject matter experts. This approach consists of an analysis of the criterion domain (typically a job analysis, i.e., analyzing the job performance criterion) to establish an appropriate pool of criterion behaviors (i.e., job situations and responses to the situations) from which suitable situations and responses are then selected for inclusion as SJT content. The scoring of the responses is also directly based on the assessment of the level of effectiveness of the criterion behaviors (i.e., responses to the situation) in terms of their extent of adaptive functioning in the criterion situations. This close correspondence, as well as the multidimensionality of SJT content which allows the SJT to capture more of the criterion conceptual space which is itself multidimensional, could account for the substantial criterion-related validities of SJTs, in terms of both its zero-order validity and incremental validity over ability and personality tests.

Although internally coherent and consistent with the empirical findings, our statements above on the construct validity of SJTs are nevertheless speculative and tentative rather than based on empirical evidence. In addition, the core characteristics of the SJT, as we describe them, are not constructs in the same sense as the characteristics attributed to the interview (e.g., oral communication skill, interpersonal skills, motivation). In the remainder of this chapter we explore the implications of greater concentration on the constructs in SJT research and outline a proposed research agenda. Our proposed agenda includes four substantive issues and broaches three strategic approaches to designing SJT research.

AGENDA FOR FUTURE RESEARCH: FOUR SUBSTANTIVE ISSUES

The four substantive issues which are all construct validity concerns revolve around the variables or conditions that may influence the magnitude of criterion-related validities of SJTs. They include 1) relating the multidimensional nature of SJT constructs to KSAOs (knowledge, skills, attributes, and other personal characteristics) and job performance, 2) distinguishing "routine performance" and "adaptive performance," 3) distinguishing "maximum performance" and "typical performance," and 4) examining socially desirable responding on SJTs.

Relating the multidimensional nature of SJT constructs to KSAOs and job performance

An unresolved issue concerns the relationship linking SJT constructs, traditional predictor constructs (i.e., KSAOs: Knowledge, Skills, Abilities, and Other characteristics), and job performance or other criterion outcomes. We propose the general framework depicted in Figure 10.1 to address this issue.

Owing to the nature of their development, SJTs are probably better construed as "sample" tests rather than "sign" tests. However, as responses to sample tests, SJT responses are not the actual job or criterion outcome behaviors. We propose that SJT responses, as predictors of job performance criteria, are best construed as measures of job-related situational judgment competencies that are proximal causes of job performance and other job-relevant criteria. As we have argued above, SJT responses are multidimensional in nature. Hence, we propose that future research identifies or specifies situational judgment competencies (e.g., system thinking, interpersonal sensitivity, conflict resolution, and moral courage) which are multidimensional rather than unidimensional (factorially pure) in nature, with each competency modeled as a complex person attribute reflecting a specific combination of multiple unidimensional KSAOs. That is, each situational judgment

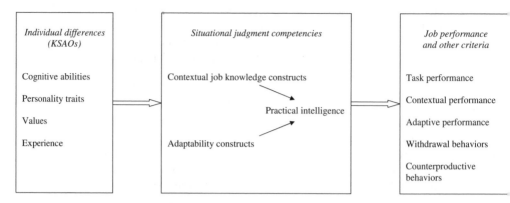

FIGURE 10.1   Framework for relating the multidimensional nature of SJT constructs to KSAOs and job performance

competency is in turn caused or predicted by a set of different unidimensional KSAOs with varying causal or predictive weights. The same KSAO could also cause or predict different competencies with varying weights. In order to adequately identify relevant KSAOs and derive their associated weights, each situational judgment competency should have a clear conceptual definition. For example, a situational judgment competency labeled conflict resolution may be defined as "resolving opposing viewpoints or disagreements between self and others or between others by achieving 'win–win' situations that take into consideration the needs, goals, and concerns of each party involved" and a situational judgment competency labeled moral courage may be defined as "courageously and tactfully standing up and speaking for what you believe to be right when you disagree with supervisors or others, or when you discover that things are wrong or not going the way it should." The conceptual definition would drive the search for relevant KSAO antecedents (i.e., causes or predictors). For example, the definition of conflict resolution may lead the researcher to identify KSAOs such as cognitive ability, openness to experience, proactive personality, and agreeableness as the relevant set of antecedents.

In our proposed framework as depicted in Figure 10.1, situational judgment competencies are multidimensional constructs each of which is a partial mediator of the predictive or causal effect of unidimensional KSAOs on job performance or other job-relevant criteria. The extant findings on the substantial zero-order validities and incremental validities of SJTs in predicting job performance over the prediction provided by cognitive ability and personality traits are consistent with the proximal status of situational judgment competencies (relative to the distal status of KSAOs) in this proposed framework. To obtain more direct evidence for our proposal of situational judgment competencies as multidimensional mediators in the relationship between KSAOs and job performance, we would need to specify and test hypothesized and alternative structural equation models linking KSAOs, SJT competencies, and job performance or other criterion outcomes. The structural equation models may be based on primary data from a single study or cumulation of results from past studies using meta-analyses. We believe that theory-driven models derived from the general framework depicted in Figure 10.1 could produce promising research on SJTs that would facilitate the interpretation of the zero-order and incremental validities of SJTs in predicting different criterion outcomes.

Distinguishing "routine performance" and "adaptive performance"

In the past decade, there has been increasing research interest relating to the need for individuals to continuously adapt to new or changing work circumstances and what that might imply for job performance and the types of abilities or competencies required to work effectively in a context requiring constant adaptation to a changing job situation. The notion of adaptability emerged as a hot topic and the distinction between routine and adaptive performance, first distinguished in the cognitive psychological research on expertise and skill acquisition (Hatano & Inagaki, 1986; Holyoak, 1991), became a popular performance distinction in organizational research (e.g., Chan, 2000a; Pulakos et al., 2000).

There is considerable conceptual overlap between the notion of practical intelligence (which we and many other researchers assume to underlie SJT performance) and the notion of adaptability. Although the central features of practical intelligence such as experiential acquisition and procedural nature of knowledge representation are not critical to the notion of adaptability, both adaptability and practical intelligence share the important elements of behavioral flexibility and striving to achieve optimal fit between behavior and situational demand. Hence, future research should consider how SJT responses relate to adaptability and adaptive performance dimensions.

In addition to directly generating adaptive performance dimensions from job analyses data and SJT responses (Pulakos et al., 2000), we suggest that researchers manipulate SJT content to study the linkages between SJT responses and adaptability/adaptive performance. Specifically, researchers could write situations with routine demands as well as situations with adaptive demands for an SJT and relate the test performance for the two types of situations to various individual difference predictors (e.g., ability, personality, thinking styles) and criterion outcomes (e.g., task job performance, contextual job performance, coping with change). SJT content could also be written to measure a priori defined adaptive work competencies. This would provide better construct validity than post hoc factor analyses of situations available in existing SJTs and written without the benefit of conceptual definitions of adaptive work competencies. Similarly, SJT content could be written to measure routine work competencies.

Using the framework we proposed earlier (Figure 10.1), these routine and adaptive SJT competencies could be located in path models as proximal antecedents of routine and adaptive job performance criteria, respectively. Each routine or adaptive competency would have multiple appropriately weighted linkages with more distal antecedents that are traditional KSAO predictors such as cognitive ability and personality traits. Such models would help us understand the adaptability constructs underlying SJT responses. For example, some adaptive competencies (e.g., empathy) but not others (e.g., system thinking) might be more influenced or better predicted by personality than cognitive ability. That is, specifying the appropriate paths linking KSAOs and competencies and deriving the associated parameter estimates would provide some construct validity evidence for SJT adaptive competencies. Many of the adaptive SJT competencies are likely to overlap with dimensions of contextual knowledge or practical intelligence. Thus, the models would also clarify the relationships linking SJT responses, practical intelligence, contextual knowledge, and adaptability dimensions.

Another direction for future research is to apply the critical features of adaptive expertise to the study of practical intelligence as measured by SJTs. As noted earlier, the use of procedural rules is an integral part of practical intelligence. However, while procedural rules could explain how the individual quickly or automatically applies well-practiced strategies or solutions to familiar and well-learned problem situations, by themselves they fail to provide an adequate account for situations in which the practically intelligent individual integrates multiple sources of information and solves novel and ill-defined problems. Moreover, procedural rules which are highly internalized may in fact inhibit adaptation through the mechanism of routinization. In such cases, the individual quickly or automatically applies well-practiced strategies or solutions to familiar and well-learned problem situations. However, in novel situations requiring new strategies or responses, similar but causally irrelevant (in terms of problem solution) features would match the condition in the individual's production, causing this *routine* (as opposed to adaptive) expert to automatically execute the action. The action executed would be inappropriate to meet the new demands in the novel situation. This would be an instance of a negative association between experience and adaptive performance. Alternatively, there could be a curvilinear (inverted-U shaped) relationship between the extent of rule proceduralization (or previous experience with similar situations) and adaptive performance such that adaptive performance increases with initial rule proceduralization but decreases with more extensive proceduralization (Chan, 2000b).

The cognitive research on adaptive expertise offers an explanatory account for situations in which the practically intelligent individual integrates multiple sources of information and solves novel and ill-defined problems. Specifically, adaptive experts are able to create new methods or strategies, and make new predictions based on their knowledge structures (Hatano & Inagaki, 1986). The critical component in the development of adaptive expertise is the development of an understanding of the deep structure/features of problems in the task domain. Structural features of a problem are functionally related to outcomes or goal attainment, whereas surface features are not (Gick & Holyoak, 1987). Novices tend to focus on surface features but not structure features.

Experts' understanding of structural features is developed through mindful processing and abstraction of underlying principles in task performance during training (Hatano & Inagaki, 1986). Understanding the deep structures allows the adaptive expert to recognize or identify situations in which existing procedures/behaviors apply or do not apply. When existing procedures/behaviors do not apply, the adaptive expert selects other appropriate ones from his or her repertoire of behaviors or creates new ones based on the repertoire. The assumption is that the adaptive expert would have developed some meta-cognitive or executive-level capabilities to monitor and regulate the various cognitive activities involved in matching situations to behavioral responses. Adaptive experts are assumed to have developed detailed and organized knowledge about the task domain and the meta-cognitive capabilities to regulate their cognitive activities (for more details, see Chan, 2000a, 2000b). Applying these features to practical intelligence, future research could hypothesize and test for the existence of meta-cognitive structures and self-regulatory processes that underlie individuals high on practical intelligence as indicated by high levels of SJT performance.

More specifically, research could examine how high SJT performers select appropriate behaviors from their repertoire of behaviors or create new ones based on the repertoire in order to achieve optimal fit between behavior and situation demand. As elaborated later in the chapter, such research would probably require the use of nontraditional techniques of data collection that would adequately assess meta-cognitive structures and self-regulatory processes.

The proposed directions for future research that we just described are much easier said than done. Given the many ambiguities and untested hypotheses and assumptions regarding adaptability (Schmitt & Chan, 1998), fruitful exploration of SJTs as measures of adaptability depends on the delineation of the critical features of adaptability such as meta-cognitive structures, self-regulatory processes, and the effective modification of behaviors to achieve optimal fit between new behaviors and novel situational demands, as well as how the various types of previous work experiences (cf. Quinones, Ford, & Teachout, 1995) may enhance or inhibit adaptive performance (Chan, 2000a, 2000b).

Distinguishing "maximum performance" and "typical performance"

One problem with using work sample tests is that they are likely to be measures of maximum performance rather than typical performance. While maximum performance is largely ability-based and refers to what the individual can do, typical performance is motivation-based and refers to what the individual will do in everyday job performance situations. Sackett, Zedeck, and Fogli (1988) argued that the motivational components associated with everyday performance probably play a minimal role in work sample test performance.

SJTs are conceptualized as "low fidelity" simulations or work samples (Motowidlo et al., 1990) in that they assess subsets of actual or close-to-actual job tasks. However, the issue of typical versus maximum performance is less clear for SJTs as compared to work sample tests. Given the promising SJT validities in predicting job performance, it appears that at least some substantial part of typical performance on the job must be captured by SJT responses. Yet, to the extent that SJTs measure contextual knowledge and practical intelligence which are both ability and capacity constructs, it seems that SJTs must also capture maximum performance. Perhaps the SJT is measuring both maximum and typical performance which may account for its substantial validities in predicting job performance. That is, SJTs measure what individuals can do and will do in practical situations.

Future researchers should try to decompose the SJT into its capacity and motivational bases and relate them respectively to the maximum and typical performance components of job performance. Maximum performance is likely to dominate in some work situations such as emergencies and those with high stakes (e.g., period of probation during which the newcomer is being evaluated for confirmation in the job position). In such situations, a SJT that largely measures what the individual is able to do given the work-related requirements should predict job performance better than one that largely measures what the individual will typically do in everyday work-related situations. The opposite should be true in everyday situations where typical performance dominates, such as motivating others, managing conflicts, and relating to colleagues.

It is by no means an easy task to tease out the maximum and typical performance components of SJTs. We believe that the relative proportions of the two performance components in a given SJT is a function of not only the substantive test content but also the social desirability response sets present and the response format. Socially desirable responding will be discussed in the next section and response format will be discussed later in this chapter.

Examining socially desirable responding on SJTs

Like other self-report measures, the use of SJTs is confronted with the criticism of validity threat due to faking or socially desirable responding (SDR). Insofar as SDR is not the intended test construct, the presence of SDR constitutes construct contamination in the SJT and the failure to model or take into account SDR would lead to model (measurement and structural) misspecification involving SJTs or distorted estimates of true SJT validities.

There is a growing consensus that fakeability is both conceptually and empirically distinct from actual faking. Primary and meta-analytic studies of non-cognitive tests have shown large differences in test scores between directed faking and honest/control conditions, with directed faking condition producing a higher test mean (Hough & Ones, 2001). On the other hand, studies have shown that test means obtained in naturalistic applicant settings are typically lower than in directed faking conditions, a difference which researchers interpreted as indicating less faking among actual applicants, although applicant means are typically higher than job incumbent means (e.g., Hough, 1998).

However, we think it is premature to directly apply the findings of the above studies to SJTs. The above between-groups comparisons of test means are based mostly on personality measures and several features of SJTs make direct extrapolation of findings problematic. For example, on one hand, we expect testing involving SJTs to be similar to testing involving personality tests and other types of selection tests in terms of the stakes in testing. However, unlike personality traits, SJT constructs are probably less stable and more malleable. Specifically, if SJT performance partly reflects contextual job performance and it appears reasonable to assume that at least some part of such knowledge is acquired on the job and changes with job experience, then we would expect incumbent SJT means to be higher than applicant SJT means if SDR is absent in both groups. That is, experience on the target job (which incumbents have but applicants have not) could influence the true score on the SJT constructs. In addition, if SJTs are indeed job-relevant and correlated with other selection tests used on incumbents (when they were applicants), then the SJT scores for incumbents should be range restricted with a higher mean as compared to SJT scores for applicants.

In short, differences between applicants and incumbents in stakes in testing (and therefore motivation to fake) on one hand and job experience and true SJT scores on the other are pulling the between-group test mean difference in opposing directions. Insofar as both the effects of SJT scores on the achievement of desired outcomes and job experience are operating, direct group comparison of test means between applicants and incumbents would not allow us to isolate the sources of variance and obtain accurate estimates of SDR on SJTs. More generally, our point is that to address SDR on SJTs (and more generally the study of SDR on personality or other tests), we need to do much more careful work in comparing applicants and incumbents because they may differ in multiple ways which often affect the test mean difference in opposite directions. Looking at mean difference in SJT scores between applicant and incumbent samples per se does not tell us much, if anything, about applicant faking on SJTs. To address SDR on SJTs (or other self-report measures), we need to go beyond direct comparisons of test means between groups. We propose the following directions for future research, some of which have already been undertaken by a few researchers.

We propose that studies of SDR on SJT or any other test using the self-report method examine the measurement model underlying the test responses of each group (i.e., applicants versus incumbents). Specifically, the factor structure of the measurement model should clearly distinguish between substantive factors and method factors representing SDR. Factor structures as well as the various corresponding parameter estimates could be compared between applicant and incumbent groups. There are two primary purposes for these between-group comparisons of measurement models. First, measurement invariance of test responses between groups, which is a statistical prerequisite for direct between-group comparison of test means, could be assessed (see Chan, 1998a). Second, theory-driven specification and comparison of measurement models between groups could test specific hypotheses concerning the nature and extent of between-group differences in SDR.

These techniques are highly flexible, and potentially misleading, so they are also easily misused, leading to incorrect inferences about SDR. Thus, we suggest that researchers begin with a "theory" of SDR and specify what factor structure should emerge when the sample (group) is faking versus when it is not. For example, a faking factor structure may include an impression management factor which loads on all or some of the test items in addition to the substantive dimensional structure (i.e., intended constructs) of the test. Alternatively, the faking factor structure may simply specify a one-factor impression management model loading with all test items representing faking with no substantive construct validity. However, while potentially useful, we think that these faking factor structure models are ambiguous as it is unclear what the "faking" factor in fact represents. The one-factor model is particularly problematic since it cannot be distinguished from a model that represents the single general factor as a global substantive construct underlying the intended test constructs. This is especially so in the case of SJTs if we believe that a global substantive construct such as practical intelligence accounts for SJT item responses.

SDR studies should include an independent measure of faking such as Paulhus' (1988) impression management scale. By specifying a faking factor that is independently (of test responses) measured, the impact of faking on test responses could be assessed more unambiguously and separated from the substantive test constructs, including the global substantive test construct underlying all test responses if there is one. In addition, we propose that SDR studies include the modeling of relationships linking both faking and substantive test constructs to relevant criterion constructs (and their measures) which are external to the test constructs. Comparing nested models with and without the specification of faking effects would provide a measure of the impact (i.e., sensitivity) of faking. In doing so, more convincing evidence of faking effects could be obtained and the practical impact of faking on the measurement of substantive constructs and the relationships between substantive constructs could be assessed.

Theory-driven models in SDR studies could be tested using the latent variable approach employed by Williams and Anderson (1994), Schmitt, Pulakos, Nason, and Whitney (1996), and Chan (2001) to model method effects including response sets. Another direction for future research is to focus on the susceptibility of SJT items to faking. We expect directed faking studies to show generally lower fakeability for SJTs than for personality tests, because SJTs typically appear less transparent. In this respect, an interesting question that arises is the substantive construct-relevant differences between individuals who are more able and those who are less able (but equally willing) to successfully fake good on the same SJT. In order to be successful in faking good, the individual must first have the ability to identify the desirable or effective response to select or endorse. Therefore, individuals with low ability to fake on an SJT that is not highly transparent may also tend to be those with low true score values on certain intended SJT constructs or some other job-relevant substantive constructs, especially those associated with knowledge requirements. Of course, the distinction between maximum performance (in this case it refers to knowing the correct answer rather than trying one's best on the test) and typical performance components of SJT scores remains a problem.

SJT items (even within the test) may vary in their SDR as well as susceptibility to SDR depending on item content. Items associated with situations that require the candidate to project him- or herself into a hypothetical situation which he or she has never experienced may be more susceptible to SDR compared to items associated with situations with which the candidate has had previous experience. This differential susceptibility to SDR need not always represent deliberate faking as it may also be due to non-deliberate self-deception (cf. Paulhus, 1986, 1988). Unlike familiar SJT situations similar to actual situations experienced by the candidate, unfamiliar SJT situations do not have the benefit of the candidate's memories of actual past situational responses and might thus be more susceptible to non-deliberate SDR such as self-deception. SJT situations and items (i.e., response alternatives) that are loaded with stereotypic descriptions are also more likely to induce SDR – both deliberate and non-deliberate. For example, items such as "Ignore the supervisor . . ." and "Calmly explain your problem to the supervisor . . ." are stereotypic descriptions of ineffective and effective responses, respectively, thereby increasing the likelihood of endorsement for the latter item over the former even if the candidate has little or no knowledge of the substantive difference in the responses represented by the two items.

In short, the effect of SDR on tests in general and SJTs in particular is not as straightforward as it might have been presented by many test-faking studies. Issues of SDR on SJTs, especially fakeability of items and actual faking, intentional distortion and non-deliberate self-deception, test-taking sets and examinee motive structures, and relationships linking SDR and response instruction ("should do" versus "would do") and the distinction between maximum and typical performance components are clearly important topics for SJT research. Understanding these issues has direct implications for interpretation and use of test scores as well as practical issues such as the effects of test-taking coaching on SJT performance.

AGENDA FOR FUTURE RESEARCH: THREE STRATEGIC APPROACHES

Perhaps the most significant research challenge regarding SJTs involves the attempt to understand and explain what it is that these tests are measuring. In addition to the substantive issues for future research described above, we propose several strategies for designing future research that would contribute to such understanding and explanation, some of which have already been pursued by different researchers. We organize these strategies in terms of three broad approaches. They are 1) using situation content to understand SJTs, 2) examining response instructions in SJTs, and 3) examining response processes in SJT performance.

Using situation content to understand SJTs

In the Motowidlo et al. (1990) study, the researchers sought to write items that reflected the interpersonal and problem-solving aspects of the jobs of the managerial positions for which they hoped to select personnel. They communicated and analyzed only a composite SJT score which had an alpha coefficient of .56. The alpha coefficient of .56 is consistent with the findings of multiple other studies (e.g., Weekley & Jones, 1997; Pulakos & Schmitt, 1996) unless the number of SJT items was very large. As mentioned above, one explanation for these findings is that responses on any individual SJT item can be determined by a variety of individual difference constructs.

Perhaps because of the evidence that the intended dimensionality of SJT measures does not match empirical results, few researchers have even reported evidence of the intercorrelations of SJTs that might have been designed to measure different content or construct dimensions. One attempt to do this was described by Gillespie, Oswald, Schmitt, Manheim, and Kim (2002). They attempted to write SJT items that reflected 12 dimensions thought to reflect 12 aspects of college student performance. Only items for which there was agreement among independent raters that the items reflected a given dimension were retained. Despite these efforts to produce homogenous sets of items based on their content, the alphas for the subscales produced in this manner ranged from .22 to .56. Correlations between subscales corrected for unreliability approached 1.00 in many instances. Not surprisingly, confirmatory factor analyses did not support the a priori hypothesized structure. Exploratory factor analyses did not reveal any interpretable multi-factor structure and alpha for the 57-item composite was .86. Since the subscales in this effort were all relatively short, low alphas might be expected, but there is no reason to expect the nearly complete absence of evidence for the expected multidimensionality of the items or some reasonable post hoc interpretation of the factor structure. Subsequent work in the academic prediction context conducted by this same group of researchers has provided some evidence of the meaningfulness of a distinction between academic and social judgment, though correlations corrected for unreliability in both dimensions exceeded .70.

Given the wide range in correlations between SJTs and a variety of measures including measures of cognitive ability described above, it seems reasonable to expect that the content of items would have some impact on the observed dimensionality. Since one of the reasons to use SJTs is to provide an instrument that adds incrementally in some way to the prediction and understanding of job performance, cognitive ability or the highly verbal demands of some SJTs might be considered unwanted contaminants insofar as those SJTs were developed to measure constructs other than cognitive ability or verbal ability. This would also be true in situations in which there are concerns about hiring underrepresented groups whose performance on cognitive or verbal ability is generally lower than Caucasian groups. This reasoning motivated the studies by Chan and Schmitt (1997) and Pulakos and Schmitt (1996).

The manipulation of situation content could be performed in even more sophisticated and innovative ways than simply writing different situation content as has usually been the practice. For example, we could develop SJT content that is dynamic by having evolving situations where new situations are "injected" after candidates have selected or endorsed their response option to the initial situation. Presenting evolving situations via the "inject" method is particularly suited for assessing certain adaptive competencies such as decision making in crisis situations. This is because effective response to the situational injects often requires the candidate to have high situation awareness, ability to separate important issues from unimportant details, and willingness to quickly make judgments and decisions based on incomplete information. Certain assessment centers have used a similar method for measuring adaptability by having assessors rate candidates' responses to new scenarios "injected" midway through an exercise (e.g., Chan, 1996). An interesting challenge for future research is to manipulate or use SJT content in various innovative ways to measure manifestations of situation awareness, meta-cognitive structures, self-regulatory processes, or transfer of learning to novel situations. However, such manipulations may result in an instrument that is very different from the typical SJT (in content or method of testing) described in this chapter.

Examining response instructions in SJTs

Motowidlo (1999b) raised the possibility that response instructions in SJTs may affect responses. McDaniel and Nguyen (2001) explicitly suggested that response instructions in SJTs will affect the constructs measured and the test's susceptibility to faking. If these authors are correct, then examining response instructions in SJTs is another broad strategy that would potentially yield productive research on SJTs.

The type of response instructions that have been used in SJTs varies considerably. One common instruction asks respondents to rate the effectiveness of each response option or select the most effective response option (e.g., Chan & Schmitt, 1997, 2002; Weekley & Jones, 1997, 1999) and another that asks respondents to indicate what he or she would most/least likely do (Motowidlo et al., 1990; Pulakos & Schmitt, 1996). These two specific instructions are prototypical of "should do" and "would do" types of instructions, respectively. In their meta-analytic study of response instructions as a moderator of SJT validities, McDaniel, Hartman, and Grubb III (2003) found that SJT instructions could be classified into these two categories which they labeled as knowledge ("should do") instruction types and behavioral tendency ("would do") instruction types.

McDaniel and Nguyen (2001) argued that SJTs with knowledge instructions are more resistant to faking than SJTs with behavioral tendency instructions. They reasoned that for knowledge instruction SJTs, the correct answers would be the same for honest and faking respondents. On the other hand, behavioral tendency instruction SJTs are more susceptible to faking because applicants may be motivated to select response options that are socially desirable even if the options do not correspond to what they would typically do at work. We are aware of only one primary study (Ployhart & Ehrhart, 2003) and one meta-analytic study (McDaniel et al., (2003) that have explicitly examined the effects of SJT response instructions. Using undergraduate samples with GPA as criterion, Ployhart and Ehrhart reported results showing higher validities for SJTs using behavioral tendency instructions than those using knowledge instructions. In contrast, McDaniel et al.'s (2003) meta-analysis showed lower validities for SJTs using behavioral tendency instructions than those using knowledge instructions.

On the surface, one may conclude that Ployhart and Ehrhart's results contradict, whereas McDaniel et al.'s results support, McDaniel and Nguyen's (2001) argument that SJTs using behavioral tendency instructions are more susceptible to faking (and therefore less valid) than those using knowledge instructions. We argue that such a conclusion is unwarranted. There are many differences in measures, samples, and contexts between Ployhart and Ehrhart's study and McDaniel et al.'s meta-analysis such that it is not very meaningful and probably misleading to make any direct comparison of validities. For example, Ployhart and Ehrhart's study used only undergraduates whereas McDaniel et al.'s meta-analysis was based exclusively on studies of actual job applicants and employees. As noted earlier in this chapter, differences in samples and contexts have associated with them substantial and probably even substantive differences in faking or socially desirable responding tendencies due to differences in stakes in testing and respondent motive structures. The two studies also differ in the nature of the criterion variable used in computing SJT validities. Ployhart and Ehrhart used undergraduates' GPA whereas McDaniel et al. used mostly supervisory ratings of job performance.

These two studies represent useful first steps in adopting the examination of SJT response instructions as a research strategy for understanding construct and criterion-related validities of SJTs. Future studies would need to begin with a priori hypotheses on the linkages connecting differences in response instructions (while keeping constant the substantive content of the situation and response option) and differences in faking (more generally, socially desirable responding) as well as differences in the nature of the constructs measured. These hypotheses would determine the type of focal variables and measures to include in a study and also the samples and settings to examine. For example, if knowledge and behavioral tendency instructions indeed reflect ability versus personality constructs, respectively, the magnitude and direction of the difference in their criterion-related validities may depend on whether the job performance criterion is dominated by core technical proficiency or contextual performance dimensions. It would be ideal if we could factorially cross SJT response instructions with type of content in the SJT situation/response option and relate it to individual difference constructs (e.g., ability and personality) and type of performance criterion. With appropriate theory and design, such results would provide a clearer picture of the effects of SJT response instructions on SJT validities and, more importantly, the constructs measured by SJTs. In short, we need to conceptually match predictor and criterion spaces before comparing validities across SJTs with different response instructions.

Finally, we believe that if the examination of response instructions is to yield productive research, future studies may need to examine the cognitive processes invoked by different SJT response instructions and relate them to the constructs measured, response sets, and individual differences so that linkages with specific criterion outcomes could be established. Examining cognitive processes invoked by response instructions is an example of the research strategy we support in the next section, namely, examining response processes in SJT performance.

Examining response processes in SJT performance

Like all other areas of personnel selection research involving self-report measures, SJT research has followed the traditional trait-based approach in data collection by focusing exclusively on the item response outcome (i.e., endorsement of response options on the test) without any explicit attempt to measure process underlying the item response. However, SJT performance clearly involves cognitive processes such as encoding the information conveyed in the SJT situation, constructing a mental representation of the situation, generating or retrieving from memory alternative mental models corresponding to the states of affairs represented by or resulting from the various response options, evaluating the various response options, and finally translating the evaluation into an endorsement of the response options. Endorsement of response options, which has been the sole focus of SJT research, is simply the final observed outcome of multiple substantive cognitive processes that transpired in the respondent's judgment and performance episodes leading to the SJT item response.

Addressing basic questions about these underlying cognitive processes and eventually understanding them could provide the key to explicating the constructs measured by SJTs. When respondents read a situation and the associated response options presented on a paper-and-pencil SJT, is the mental representational format primarily visual (imagery), propositional, or does the format vary across individuals or subgroups (e.g., ethnic/cultural groups)? Given what is known in cognitive science, the mental representational format should have implications for mental manipulation and hence the final evaluation outcome (i.e., endorsement of response option). If we could empirically demonstrate systematic differences in mental representational format associated with different testing methods (i.e., paper-and-pencil SJT versus video-based SJT) and different ethnic groups (i.e., Blacks versus Whites), we would have provided strong support of Chan and Schmitt's (1997) argument and results regarding the effects of test method on ethnic group differences in SJT performance as described earlier in the chapter.

Another basic question concerns the relationship between mental representations and the procedural and implicit nature of the practical intelligence or contextual knowledge that presumably underlie effective situational judgment. Assessments of proceduralization and implicit processing would provide the empirical data that is needed to build a stronger case for what we have argued earlier concerning the nature of SJT constructs. Also related are questions on the meta-cognitive structures and self-regulatory processes that may be involved in the SJT response process. Do subject matter experts and high SJT performers have similar meta-cognitive structures and self-regulatory processes that are qualitatively different from low SJT performers and novices? Do SJT coaching effects, if they exist, operate through modifications of these cognitive structures and processes? Are there differences in these cognitive structures and processes associated with the maximum versus typical performance components of SJT response? Are there differences associated with specific SJT competencies such as system thinking and adaptability constructs? In addition to mental representations, there are also cognitive process issues such as the assumptions, beliefs, values, and worldviews that may be activated and applied in the SJT response process.

We propose the examination of response processes in SJT performance using cognitive assessments that are nontraditional methods of data collection in personnel selection research such as probed verbal protocols (e.g., Kraiger, Ford, & Salas, 1993), knowledge structure elicitation techniques such as proximity-based methods (e.g., Schvaneveldt, Durso, & Dearholt, 1989), and subliminal priming techniques such as implicit association tests (e.g., Greenwald, Draine, & Abrams, 1996). Knowledge structure elicitation techniques, given appropriate data input, are well suited to assess meta-cognitive structures. Verbal protocols, when adequately implemented, may provide valid assessments of certain assumptions, beliefs, values, and worldviews that are activated in the response process but they will not be valid in the assessment of certain implicit processes.

Clearly, one major challenge facing our proposed strategy of examining response processes in SJT performance is that many SJT researchers may not be familiar with the use of such nontraditional methods of data collection and their potential pitfalls. For example, the valid use of verbal protocols is premised on the assumption that the focal process of interest is accessible to consciousness and that the respondent is able and willing to accurately report his or her thoughts while processing a SJT situation/response option without SDR and other reactivity effects. Effective application of knowledge structure elicitation techniques is premised on various conditions such as representative sampling of the input elements for proximity ratings and availability of relevant referent knowledge structures for comparisons. Notwithstanding these practical (although not insurmountable) challenges, we think the strategy of examining response processes in SJT performance provides SJT researchers a good opportunity to incorporate theory and methods of data collection in cognitive psychology to complement extant theory and data collection methods in personnel selection research so as to achieve a better understanding of the complexity of cognitive processing involved in situational judgment.

Concluding Remarks

In this chapter, we have adopted a more comprehensive view of SJTs than is usual in SJT research by moving beyond criterion-related validity to address in detail fundamental issues of construct validity. We have argued that it is insufficient for SJT research to focus on criterion-related validities per se and advocated that researchers adopt a theory-driven and construct-oriented approach to examine specific substantive issues. The detailed analyses led us to consider multiple variables such as the reading level of the SJT, the dimensionality of SJT scores, the various types of performance components in SJTs, the content of SJT situations, the format of the response instructions, the cognitive processes that transpire when examinees choose a response, the test-taking setting as well as the possible examination outcomes, motive structures and experiences of the respondents.

From the practical viewpoint of prediction, the multiple variables listed above are critical because they help identify the boundary conditions for the criterion-related validity of

SJTs. In addition, research that clarifies the effects of these variables would increase our understanding of the nature of SJT responses which in turn would help elucidate the processes underlying acquisition of SJT constructs and how to identify or develop these constructs in individuals. Given the current interest and increasing use of SJTs in personnel selection practice, more SJT research directed at construct validity issues is urgently needed to produce findings that would inform the use of SJTs. In this chapter, we have elaborated on several substantive issues and proposed several strategies that we hope will move future research in this direction.

REFERENCES

Borman, W. C., & Motowidlo, S. J. (1997). Task performance and contextual performance: The meaning for personnel selection research. *Human Performance, 10*, 99–109.

Borman, W. C., Hanson, M. A., Oppler, S. H., Pulakos, E. D., & White, L. A. (1993). Role of early supervisory experience in supervisor performance. *Journal of Applied Psychology, 78*, 443–449.

Borman, W. C., White, L. A., Pulakos, E. D., & Oppler, S. H. (1991). Models of supervisory job performance ratings. *Journal of Applied Psychology, 76*, 863–872.

Bruce, M. M., & Learner, D. B. (1958). A supervisory practices test. *Personnel Psychology, 11*, 207–216.

Chan, D. (1996). Criterion and construct validation of an assessment center. *Journal of Occupational and Organizational Psychology, 69*, 167–181.

Chan, D. (1998a). The conceptualization of change over time: An integrative approach incorporating longitudinal means and covariance structures analysis (LMACS) and multiple indicator latent growth modeling (MLGM). *Organizational Research Methods, 1*, 421–483.

Chan, D. (1998b). Functional relations among constructs in the same content domain at different levels of analysis: A typology of composition models. *Journal of Applied Psychology, 83*, 234–246.

Chan, D. (2000a). Understanding adaptation to changes in the work environment: Integrating individual difference and learning perspectives. *Research in Personnel and Human Resources Management, 18*, 1–42.

Chan, D. (2000b). Conceptual and empirical gaps in research on individual adaptation at work. *International Review of Industrial and Organizational Psychology, 15*, 143–164.

Chan, D. (2001). Modeling method effects of positive affectivity, negative affectivity, and impression management in self reports of work attitudes. *Human Performance, 14*, 77–96.

Chan, D. (in press). Multilevel research. In F. T. L. Leong & J. T. Austin (Eds.), *The psychology research handbook* (2nd ed.). Thousand Oaks, CA: Sage.

Chan, D., & Schmitt, N. (1997). Video-based versus paper-and-pencil method of assessment in situational judgment tests. *Journal of Applied Psychology, 82*, 143–159.

Chan, D., & Schmitt, N. (2002). Situational judgment and job performance. *Human Performance, 15*, 233–254.

Clevenger, J., Pereira, G. M., Wiechmann, D., Schmitt, N., & Schmidt Harvey, V. (2001). Incremental validity of situational judgment tests. *Journal of Applied Psychology, 86*, 410–417.

File, Q. W. (1945). The measurement of supervisory quality in industry. *Journal of Applied Psychology, 29*, 381–387.

Gick, M. L., & Holyoak, K. J. (1987). The cognitive basis of knowledge transfer. In S. M. Cormier & J. D. Hagman (Eds.), *Transfer of training: Contemporary research and applications* (pp. 9–46). New York: Academic Press.

Gillespie, M. A., Oswald, F. L., Schmitt, N., Manheim, L., & Kim, B. H. (2002). *Construct validation of a situational judgment test of college student success.* Paper presented at the 17th annual convention of the Society for Industrial and Organizational Psychology, Toronto, Canada.

Greenwald, A. G., Draine, S. C., & Abrams, R. L. (1996). Three cognitive markers of unconscious semantic activation. *Science, 273,* 1699–1702.

Hatano, G., & Inagaki, K. (1986). Two course of expertise. In H. Stevenson, H. Azuma, & K. Hakuta (Eds.), *Child development and education in Japan* (pp. 262–272). San Francisco: Freeman.

Hedlund, J., & Sternberg, R. J. (2000). Practical intelligence: Implications for human resources research. *Research in Personnel and Human Resources Management, 19,* 1–52.

Holyoak, K. J. (1991). Symbolic connectionism: Toward third-generation theories of expertise. In K. A. Ericsson & J. Smith (Eds.), *Toward a general theory of expertise* (pp. 301–336). Cambridge: Cambridge University Press.

Hough, L. M. (1998). Effects of intentional distortion in personality measurement and evaluation of suggested palliatives. *Human Performance, 11,* 209–244.

Hough, L. M., & Ones, D. S. (2001). The structure, measurement, validity, and use of personality variables in industrial, work, and organizational psychology. In N. Anderson, D. S. Ones, H. K. Sinangil, & C. Viswesvaran (Eds.), *Handbook of industrial, work, and organizational psychology* (Vol.1, pp. 233–277). Thousand Oaks, CA: Sage.

Kim, B. H., Schmitt, N., Oswald, F. L., Gillespie, M. A., & Ramsay, L. J. (2003). *Job knowledge tests on the path to successful performance.* Paper presented at the 18th Annual Conference of the Society for Industrial and Organizational Psychology, Orlando, FL.

Klein, K. J., & Kozlowski, S. W. J. (2000). *Multilevel theory, research, and methods in organizations: Foundations, extensions, and new directions.* San Francisco: Jossey-Bass.

Kraiger, K., Ford, J. K., & Salas, E. (1993). Application of cognitive, skill-based, and affective theories of learning outcomes to new methods of training evaluation. *Journal of Applied Psychology, 78,* 311–328.

Lievens, F., & Coetsier, P. (2002). Situational tests in student selection: An examination of predictive validity, adverse impact, and construct validity. *International Journal of Selection and Assessment, 10,* 245–257.

McDaniel, M. A., Hartman, N. S., & Grubb, W. L., III. (2003). *Situational judgment tests, knowledge, behavioral tendency, and validity: A meta-analysis.* Paper presented at the 18th Annual Conference of the Society for Industrial and Organizational Psychology, Orlando, FL.

McDaniel, M. A., Morgeson, F. P., Finnegan, E. B., Campion, M. A., & Braverman, E. P. (2001). Use of situational judgment tests to predict job performance: A clarification of the literature. *Journal of Applied Psychology, 80,* 730–740.

McDaniel, M. A., & Nguyen, N. T. (2001). Situational judgment tests: A review of practice and constructs assessed. *International Journal of Selection and Assessment, 9,* 103–113.

Morgeson, F. P., Bauer, T. N., Truxillo, D. M., & Campion, M. A. (2003). *Assessing situational judgment with a structured interview: Construct validity and adverse impact.* Paper presented at the 18th Annual Conference of the Society for Industrial and Organizational Psychology, Orlando, FL.

Motowidlo, S. J. (1999a). *Comments regarding symposium titled "Construct validity of the situational judgment inventory".* Presented at the 14th Annual Conference of the Society for Industrial and Organizational Psychology, Atlanta, GA.

Motowidlo, S. J. (1999b). Asking about past behavior versus hypothetical behavior. In R. W. Eder & M. M. Harris (Eds.), *Employment interview handbook* (pp. 179–190). Thousand Oaks, CA: Sage.

Motowidlo, S. J., Dunnette, M. D., & Carter, G. W. (1990). An alternative selection procedure: The low-fidelity simulation. *Journal of Applied Psychology, 75,* 640–647.

Motowidlo, S. J., Hanson, M. A., & Crafts, J. L. (1997). Low-fidelity simulations. In D. L. Whetzel & G. R. Wheaton (Eds.), *Applied measurement methods in industrial psychology* (pp. 241–260). Palo Alto, CA: Davies-Black Publishing.

Motowidlo, S. J., & Tippins, N. (1993). Further studies of the low-fidelity simulation in the form of a situational inventory. *Journal of Occupational and Organizational Psychology, 66,* 337–344.

Oswald, F. L., Schmitt, N., Kim, B. H., Gillespie, M. A., & Ramsay, L. J. (in press). Developing a biodata measure and situational judgment inventory as predictors of college student performance. *Journal of Applied Psychology*.

Paulhus, D. L. (1986). Self-deception and impression management in test responses. In A. Angleitner & J. S. Wiggens (Eds.), *Personality measurement via questionnaires: Current issues in theory and measurement* (pp. 143–165). Berlin: Springer-Verlag.

Paulhus, D. L. (1988). *Assessing self-deception and impression management in self-reports: The Balanced Inventory of Desirable Responding*. Unpublished manual, University of British Columbia, Vancouver, Canada.

Pereira, G. M., & Harvey, V. S. (1999). *Situational judgment tests: Do they measure ability, personality, or both?* Paper presented at the 14th Annual Convention of the Society for Industrial and Organizational Psychology, Atlanta, GA.

Phillips, J. F. (1992). Predicting sales skills. *Journal of Business and Psychology*, 7, 151–160.

Ployhart, R. E., & Ehrhart, M. G. (2003). Be careful what you ask for: Effects of response instructions on the construct validity and reliability of situational judgment tests. *International Journal of Selection and Assessment*, 11, 1–16.

Pulakos, E. D., Arad, S., Donovan, M. A., & Plamondon, K. E. (2000). Adaptability in the workplace: Development of a taxonomy of adaptive performance. *Journal of Applied Psychology*, 85, 612–624.

Pulakos, E. D., & Schmitt, N. (1996). An evaluation of two strategies for reducing adverse impact and their effects on criterion-related validity. *Human Performance*, 9, 241–258.

Quinones, M. A., Ford, J. K., & Teachout, M. S. (1995). The relationship between work experience and job performance: A conceptual and meta-analytic review. *Personnel Psychology*, 48, 887–910.

Richardson, Bellows, & Henry Co., Inc. (1949). *Test of Supervisory Judgment: Form S*. Washington, DC: Richardson, Bellows, and Henry.

Sackett, P. R., Zedeck, S., & Fogli, L. (1988). Relations between measures of typical and maximum job performance. *Journal of Applied Psychology*, 73, 482–486.

Schmitt, N., & Chan, D. (1998). *Personnel selection: A theoretical approach*. Thousand Oaks, CA: Sage.

Schmitt, N., Pulakos, E. D., Nason, E., & Whitney, D. J. (1996). Likeability and similarity as potential sources of predictor-related criterion bias in validation research. *Organizational Behavior and Human Decision Processes*, 68, 272–286.

Schvaneveldt, R. W., Durso, F. T., & Dearholt, D. W. (1989). Network structures in proximity data. In G. G. Bower (Ed.), *The psychology of learning and motivation* (Vol. 24, pp. 249–284). New York: Academic Press.

Sternberg, R. J., Forsythe, G. B., Hedlund, J., Horvath, J. A., Wagner, R. K., Williams, W. M., et al. (2000). *Practical intelligence in everyday life*. Cambridge, UK: Cambridge University Press.

Thorndike, R. L., & Stein, S. (1937). An evaluation of the attempts to measure social intelligence. *Psychological Bulletin*, 34, 275–285.

Wagner, R. K. (1987). Tacit knowledge in everyday intelligent behavior. *Journal of Personality and Social Psychology*, 32, 1236–1247.

Wagner, R. K., & Sternberg, R. J. (1991). *Tacit Knowledge Inventory for Managers*. Unpublished research instrument available from authors.

Weekley, J. A., & Jones, C. (1997). Video-based situational testing. *Personnel Psychology*, 50, 25–49.

Weekley, J. A., & Jones, C. (1999). Further studies of situational tests. *Personnel Psychology*, 52, 679–700.

Williams, L. J., & Anderson, S. E. (1994). An alternative approach to method effects by using latent-variable models: Applications in organizational behavior research. *Journal of Applied Psychology*, 79, 323–331.

11

Assessment Centers: Recent Developments in Practice and Research

FILIP LIEVENS AND GEORGE C. THORNTON III

In an assessment center, candidates who participate in various simulation exercises are evaluated by a multiple trained assessors on job-related dimensions. Examples of commonly used simulation exercises are role-plays, presentations, in-baskets, or group discussions. For nearly fifty years, assessment centers have remained a popular approach for managerial selection and development (Spychalski, Quinones, Gaugler, & Pohley, 1997), and they have been shown to have substantial validity (Thornton & Rupp, 2004). Assessment centers are also very much an international affair as they are used around the globe (Byham, 2001; Kudisch et al., 2001; Sarges, 2001). Over the past years, several innovative trends have emerged in assessment center practice. At the same time, various scholars (e.g., Arthur, Woehr, & Maldegen, 2000; Arthur, Day, McNelly, & Edens, 2003; Haaland & Christiansen, 2002; Kolk, Born, & Van der Flier, 2002; Lance et al., 2000; Lievens & Conway, 2001; Lievens & Klimoski, 2001) have given a new impetus to assessment center research. The aim of this chapter is to inform both practitioners and researchers of these recent intriguing developments. In particular, we focus on developments in assessment center practice and research that occurred in the past five years (1998–2003).

RECENT DEVELOPMENTS IN ASSESSMENT CENTER PRACTICE

In this section, we give an overview of recent developments in assessment center practice. To identify these recent developments we examined assessment center operations described in research studies, surveys of practitioners around the world, presentations at the International Congress on Assessment Center Methods, and innovations we learned about from colleagues around the world in recent years.

The following developments in assessment center practice are described: assessment centers for non-managerial jobs, assessment centers in cross-cultural settings, new methods of analyzing job requirements, assessment of new dimensions, types of exercises, use of technology and virtual assessment centers, integrating assessment centers with organizational strategy, using assessment centers for developmental purposes, and assessment centers as criterion measures. If relevant, we begin our discussion of each trend by out-lining the changes in business practices and organizations that have triggered the trend.

Assessing non-managerial jobs

Historically, assessment centers have been applied most frequently to managerial jobs ranging from supervisor to executive. More recently, they have been used to assess a wider range of non-managerial jobs. For many years, Diamond Star Motors has used an assessment center process to select manufacturing employees (Henry, 1988). This practice has spread to other manufacturing organizations such as Cessna (Hiatt, 2000) and BASF (Howard & McNelly, 2000). The State of Connecticut has used assessment center methods to certify the competence of teachers (Jacobson, 2000). Other organizations have used assessment centers to select entry-level police officers (Dayan, Kasten, & Fox, 2002) and airline pilots (Damitz, Manzey, Kleinmann, & Severin, 2003) and to assess and certify consultants (Howard & Metzger, 2002; Rupp & Thornton, 2003) and lawyers (Sackett, 1998).

These examples demonstrate the applicability of assessment center principles to a wide range of jobs. As noted below, the good news is that recent research has found evidence for the validity of some of these assessment centers in non-managerial populations.

Applying assessment centers in multinational and cross-cultural settings

The emergence of global businesses has increased the need to design assessment centers that have cross-cultural and cross-national applicability. Assessment centers have been implemented in an ever-increasing variety of countries around the world. Soon after their inception in England and the USA in the 1950s, assessment centers spread to selected organizations in Canada and Japan. Next came extension to Germany, Switzerland, Israel, South Africa, and Indonesia in the 1970s. But it was not until the past several years that assessment centers cropped up in virtually every industrialized country in the world.

The internationalization of assessment centers is also revealed by examination of the lists of persons attending the International Congress on Assessment Center Methods over the past 31 years. There has been a steady increase in the number and percentage of atten-dees coming from countries outside North America. In 1974 at the second Congress, only 5 of 76 attendees were from countries other than the USA and Canada. The percentage of attendees from outside North America grew steadily: 1974 to 1983 – approximately 5%; 1984 to 1993 – approximately 15%; 1994 to 2003 – approximately 25%. In 2003, 27 of the 104 attendees were from such diverse countries as Kuwait, Indonesia, Korea, and the Philippines.

Many challenging issues about the design and implementation of assessment centers arise when they are used in cross-cultural situations. Two approaches to these issues can be considered: etic and emic (Chawla & Cronshaw, 2002). The etic approach assumes that a) there are universal individual attributes that are relevant to organizational effectiveness, b) preexisting assessment techniques can be adapted in different countries, c) standardiza-tion and validity extension require that a fixed set of dimensions and procedures must be used, and d) the adoption of uniform selection procedures across cultures contributes to a homogeneous organizational culture. The emic approach assumes that a) generic assessment methods will be invalid (i.e., they under-specify unique aspects of criterion performance), b) each culture must be studied to identify its unique features, c) the acceptance of various assessment techniques varies across cultures, and d) assessor training must include an appreciation of contextual information. An unresolved issue in this discussion is the relative gains and losses that come from modifying assessment center elements. For example, modification of the exercises may accommodate unique local demands, but render comparisons of assessments across locations problematic.

The spread of assessment centers around the world, the cross-cultural applications of assessment centers, the globalization of businesses, the need for global executives (McCall, 2002), and the establishment of consultancies offering assessment center services in many other countries have raised questions about the application of assessment practices in diverse countries. Are assessment centers useful in selecting persons from a home country to serve in another country? Along these lines, Briscoe (1997) suggested that careful attention should be paid to the design of other exercises, the use of different dimensions, the use of assessors from both the home and host country, the evaluation of behaviors, and the provision of feedback. Briscoe (1997) and Howard (1997) also provided case studies that illustrated some of the challenges in using assessment centers to select international personnel. Kozloff (2003) discussed some of the complex issues of selecting leaders, along with their spouses and families, to live and work in diverse settings around the world. In the only empirical, predictive validity study on this topic of which we are aware, Lievens, Harris, Van Keer, and Bisqueret (2003) found that ratings from selected assessment exercises contributed to predictive accuracy over cognitive ability and personality tests in predicting success in a training program for European managers in Japan.

Another challenging question is whether the *Guidelines and Ethical Considerations for Assessment Center Operations* (International Task Force on Assessment Center Guidelines, 2000) apply universally around the world. Over the years there has been a trend to consider international issues. The task forces who wrote the 1975 and 1979 editions of the *Guidelines* contained only North American practitioners. The 1989 and 2000 task forces each included one Dutch representative, and there was increased input sought from practitioners from outside North America. In 2001, a group of practitioners in Europe met to consider whether the *Guidelines* needed revision for application in those countries (Seegers & Huck, 2001). In 2000, a task force was set up in Indonesia to write a code of conduct for assessment center operations for that country (Pendit & Thornton, 2001).

We predict that assessment centers will be used more frequently in international settings. This will occur in three different ways. Home-country organizations will use assessment centers to assess persons going to host countries. Home-country organizations will use their assessment methods to assess host-country persons in those other countries. Organizations in countries not currently using assessment centers will adopt the method. Each of these applications of the assessment center method presents unique challenges. Assessment center proponents and adopters will have to make choices about what elements and specific practices of the method can be kept the same from their points of origin to the new location, and what adaptations need to be made to accommodate the unique aspects of the new location.

Job analysis methods

Recently, the breakdown of rigid divisions of labor among jobs has led to the search for broader competencies to serve as the dimensions for assessment. Therefore, traditional methods of analyzing tasks involved in job accomplishment and the knowledge, skills, and other attributes needed for performance on specific current jobs have been supplemented by future-oriented methods such as strategic job analysis (Schneider & Konz, 1989) and by competency modeling to analyze more general competencies that organizations expect employees to possess in order to achieve broader organizational objectives (Schippmann et al., 2000; see also Voskuijl, Chapter 2, this volume). These broader objectives may be translated into the roles that employees are expected to play (Mahoney-Philips, 2002; Sackett & Tuzinski, 2000).

In our opinion, the current techniques of competency modeling have several advantages of aligning performance in specific jobs to broader organizational objectives, defining requirements of broader sets of jobs rather than isolated positions, and gaining acceptance from higher-level managers and executives. Conversely, competencies are often defined so broadly as to defy reliable and valid assessment. Thus, there is often a clear need to develop techniques to translate competencies into performance dimensions that can be assessed with reasonable accuracy.

Different dimensions

Traditionally, assessment centers have been designed to measure relatively specific sets of behaviors known as "dimensions" (Thornton & Byham, 1982). Recently, assessment center architects began to assess broader competencies (e.g., customer service orientation, teamwork) each of which is often a complex combination of traditional dimensions. In our opinion, broad organizational competencies do not provide specific, objective attributes appropriate for assessment in assessment centers. For example, "customer service" and "continuous quality improvement" are worthy organizational goals, but they need operationalization into behavioral dimensions. The former can be specified as behaviors classified into active listening, information seeking, and oral communication, and the latter as behaviors such as problem analysis, creativity, and decision analysis.

Other trends include increased emphasis on the assessment of interpersonal dimensions such as teamwork, cooperation, and informal leadership. These sorts of broader dimensions are especially relevant to success in international settings. Kozloff (2003) describes the need to consider broader sets of personality factors (e.g., tolerance for ambiguity and emotional balance) and family relations when selecting global leaders. Some organizations are also devising ways to assess sets of values, using systematic techniques such as Systematic Multiple Level of Observation of Groups (SYMLOG) (Wilson & Pilgram, 2000). Other programs have assessed roles that employees are expected to play (Mahoney-Phillips, 2002). On a grander scale, the US Office of Personnel Management has developed a national framework of dimensions defining all jobs in the US economy (Gowing, 1999). This taxonomy of jobs listed in the Standard Occupational Classification system provides a common language for the attributes needed for all jobs. Taking a quite different approach, some assessment center architects argue that no dimensions at all should be assessed (Thoreson, 2002), but rather that the performance of behavior in the exercise as a whole should be assessed.

In our estimation, virtually any performance attribute is amenable to assessment if two conditions are met: 1) the dimension is clearly defined in terms of behaviors on the job and behaviors observable in simulation exercises, and 2) the exercises are constructed carefully so as to elicit the relevant behaviors. The second condition implies that exercises can and should be constructed in different ways to assess different attributes. Techniques for constructing various types of exercises for various purposes and for eliciting behaviors relevant to different dimensions are described in *Developing Organizational Simulations* (Thornton & Mueller-Hanson, 2004).

Assessment exercises

One might think that new types of exercises would have been invented to assess new dimensions for new jobs in new settings, but this does not seem to be the case. Most of the old standby types of exercises seem to persist, including in-baskets, case studies, and inter-action simulations. There seems to be a trend toward lesser use of the group discussion technique. There may be three explanations. First, in police and fire departments where the assessments are used as one method in promotional examinations, there is a strong pressure for strict standardization that does not exist in the highly variable group dynamics that typically unfold in a leaderless group discussion. Second, there are practical, logistical problems of gathering all candidates at one specific location at one specific time. Designers often wish to have a process that does not require that a group of participants are at the same location at the same time. Third, the complex interactions among five or six persons in a group discussion are often difficult to observe and thus defy the systematic observation and evaluation by novice assessors.

The elimination of group discussion exercises is understandable when the assessment center is being used for selection or promotion, and legal challenges to standardization are highly likely. However, in light of organizations' interest in assessing the fit of individuals to teams and organizations, the group exercise is one of the more content valid assessment exercises.

Use of technology and virtual assessment centers

The availability of computers and electronic media has provided the opportunity to increase the use of technology in assessment centers. Initially, computers were used to compile and analyze ratings from a team of assessors. Recently, more sophisticated applications have emerged, primarily in the methods to present stimuli. Exercise stimuli have been presented via video monitors and on computer-based simulations (Bobrow & Schulz, 2002). At Sprint, a virtual office has been simulated on the company's intranet for the administration of exercises (Hale, Jaffee, & Chapman, 1999). Reynolds (2003) described the movement toward web-based delivery of exercises for the assessment of executives and leaders. Other applications of technology involve capturing behavior on audio and video recordings, sometimes from remote locations. These recordings can then be analyzed in a traditional manner by trained observers, or by using sophisticated software programs.

Other assessment programs have used the web to capture electronic records of various achievements, including text, audio, and video media (Richards, 2002). Automated analysis of written responses can evaluate the content and quality of writing samples (Ford, 2001). In addition, software can analyze voice tone (Bobrow & Schulz, 2002). Special software has been developed to automate the process of writing reports (Lovler & Goldsmith, 2002). Furthermore, the web can be used to facilitate all stages of an assessment process, including administration, exercise delivery, scoring, data tracking, report writing, and feedback (Smith & Reynolds, 2002). Reynolds (2003) traced the progression of technology applications toward a web services model of assessment using the manager's online desk to complete work in a simulated "day in the life" set of assessment activities.

A number of these technological developments increase the fidelity of exercise in terms of the stimuli presented to the participant (e.g., managers nowadays typically receive information via electronic media and respond online). Thus, in our estimation, high technology in an exercise may increase the realism of the exercise. Other aspects of high-tech assessment exercises may in fact decrease the fidelity of the assessment, especially response fidelity. For example, some computerized in-baskets call for the participant to respond by choosing among a number of pre-established alternatives. In real life, managers do not typically have the alternatives presented. In fact, they must generate alternatives and then overtly write a response. In some exercises a video depicts a subordinate's comments and the participant selects among a set of pre-established responses. This sort of assessment method does not have fidelity with dynamic interpersonal interactions. Computerized in-baskets and video-based assessment techniques may have predictive validity, but they are qualitatively different from the overt behaviors required in the typical interpersonal and decision-making simulations that have been the hallmark of the assessment center method.

Integrating assessment centers with HR management and organizational strategy

There has been increasing recognition in recent years that assessment centers must be integrated carefully with other human resource management practices and with the overall organizational strategy. Although this is not a new idea (Thornton, 1992), pressures to make all HRM practices more efficient have placed more emphasis on making assessment center practices more compatible with broader organizational strategies. Thus, we see a recent trend to more systematically build the assessment center into a larger system of recruitment, selection, promotion, development, and succession planning for management talent (Byham, 2002; Byham, Smith, & Pease, 2001; Roth & Smith, 2000). This trend is also manifest in organizations operating global HR practices (Eckhardt, 2001).

The integration of assessment centers into broader organizational strategic planning and the use of assessment centers to foster organizational change are also apparent in recent applications. For example, assessment centers have been used to help achieve redeployment of existing staff (Adler, 1995), downsizing (Gebelein, Warrenfeltz, & Guinn, 1995), executive team development (Fleisch & Cohen, 1995), restructuring from functional to product focus (Fleisch, 1995), and climate change (Dailey, Cohen, & Lockwood, 1999) in such diverse organizations as manufacturing, telecommunications, trucking, customer service, high-tech, and security. The integration of assessment centers into organizational change efforts requires involvement of high-level executives in the program (Dowell & Elder, 2002).

Assessment centers for developmental purposes

The most pronounced trend in assessment center activities in recent years is the shift in their predominant purpose from selection/promotion to development. This increased interest in using assessment centers to develop the talent of managers remaining in their current positions results, among other things, from the flattening and downsizing of organizations and the fewer promotional opportunities available. The original purpose of assessment centers (i.e., identification of managerial talent and decision making for promotion, Bray & Grant, 1966; Thornton & Byham, 1982) is still predominant in public safety organizations. Conversely, in most business organizations in recent years, the most frequent application is for developmental purposes (Kudisch et al., 2001; Spychalski et al., 1997). A more skeptical view of this application was presented by Tillema (1998) who found only minimal use of development centers in a survey of Dutch organizations because of lack of familiarity with, and difficulties in implementation of, this application.

There are several variants of developmental assessment centers. In some, the emphasis is on the diagnosis of training needs of individuals. The design of these centers, including the dimensions and exercises, is very similar to promotional centers. Another variant is a true *development* center in which the objective is to foster skill development (Ballantyne & Povah, 1995). To turn the program into a learning experience, steps are taken to provide immediate feedback, practice, reinforcement of learning, transfer of training, and follow-up developmental support in the organization. A third variant of developmental assessment centers is programs designed to promote development of organizational units. The use of simulation technology for development purposes typically involves the assessment of intact work groups participating in complex organization games (Thornton & Cleveland, 1990). The use of one assessment center program for dual purposes of selection and development is problematic (Arnold, 2002) and requires careful attention to factors beyond psychometric precision (e.g., motivated participants, clear feedback, supportive context) (Kudisch, Lundquist, & Smith, 2002).

Developmental assessment centers have become quite popular, but have met with numerous challenges. One of the primary challenges is the necessity to demonstrate adequate psychometric evidence of construct validity. As discussed in a later section of this chapter, there is mixed evidence regarding the ability of assessors' ratings to demonstrate evidence of construct validity. The second challenge of development assessment centers is to provide evidence that the program has some impact on participants. Impact may take the form of a) intentions to take action to develop, b) engagement in some form of developmental experience, c) change of understanding of the performance dimensions, d) improvement in skills, e) change of behavior on the job, or f) improvement in organizational effectiveness. Jones and Whitmore (1995) found that career advancement of assessed and non-assessed managers did not differ, except when the assessed managers engaged in developmental activities. Unfortunately, most managers do not follow up assessment center diagnoses with developmental activities (Byham, 2003). Only recently has research evidence begun to emerge that demonstrates the conditions under which developmental assessment centers are effective (Maurer et al., 2003). Positive effects do not automatically ensue and are likely to occur only if there are a number of other support systems in place in the organization to help the assessee after the assessment center experience (Bernthal, Cook, & Smith, 2001).

Assessment centers as criterion measures

Similar to work samples, assessment centers are increasingly used as criterion measures in studying various aspects of managerial and student performance. For example, Thomas, Dickson, and Bliese (2001) used an assessment center of leader effectiveness in a study of the role of values, motives, and personality among cadets. Barlay and York (2002) and Riggio, Mayes, and Schleicher (2003) used assessment centers to measure undergraduate student achievement. Recently, Atkins and Wood (2002) validated a 360-degree feedback program on the basis of assessment center ratings of the candidates.

The underlying rationale of the use of assessment centers as criterion measures is that they correspond closely to the job and therefore can be considered as miniaturized settings for observing job performance. Although this rationale makes sense, it is important to note that the criterion data obtained with assessment centers are also inherently different from more traditional job performance data (i.e., ratings). Assessment center performance reflects maximal performance, whereas job performance ratings represent typical performance.

Disturbing trends

Two disturbing trends have been noted in the implementation of assessment centers in recent years. First, in response to the economic downturn in recent years (2000–2003), organizations have sought ways to streamline the process. Unfortunately, in many cases, modifications of essential steps in the development and implementation of programs have led to short cuts that may affect accuracy and effectiveness. Caldwell, Thornton, and Gruys (2003) summarize ten errors that diminish assessment center validity (e.g., inadequate job analysis, ill-defined dimensions, inadequate assessor training).

A second disturbing trend is that the term "assessment center" has been used to refer to many methods that do not conform to the essential elements of the assessment center method. Examples that in our opinion do not qualify as assessment centers are methods that include only paper-and-pencil tests, methods that involve only one assessor, and methods that do not involve the observation of overt behavior. Thus, even though they are valid, the following methods do not constitute an assessment center: computerized in-baskets that call for the participant to pick among a set of predefined alternative behaviors; situational interviews that ask the respondent to state what he or she would do when faced with hypothetical situations; written "low fidelity" simulations or situational judgment tests that call for choosing among alternative actions; clinical or individual psychological assessments that are carried out by one assessor.

While there is no legal restriction, patent registration, or copyright proprietary claim for the words "assessment center," there are strong reasons for wishing to restrict the use of the term. First, for over fifty years the term has been used in the personnel assessment profession to refer to a common set of practices. Second, extensive research has been conducted on the method, and while there are certainly different instantiations of many elements of the method, there are enough commonalities to the claim that a coherent body of research exists. Summaries of that research have led to several meta-analyses of validity findings and comparisons with alternative assessment techniques. Such comparative studies are not meaningful if the alternative techniques cannot be clearly defined and classified. Third, for over twenty-five years, the International Congress on Assessment Center Methods has attracted hundreds of participants who have a common interest in the design, implementation, and evaluation of this commonly understood method. *Guidelines and Ethical Considerations for Assessment Center Operations* (International Task Force on Assessment Center Guidelines, 2000) clearly defines what is and what is not an assessment center. It provides a standard for students, practitioners, and researchers to follow.

RECENT DEVELOPMENTS IN ASSESSMENT CENTER RESEARCH

Whereas the first part of this chapter focused on recent developments in assessment center practice, this part delves into recent assessment center research. Inspection of assessment center research published between 1998 and 2003 showed that the vast majority of studies could be grouped under the following four broad themes: criterion-related validity research, incremental validity research, construct validity research, and process-related research. While these are recurring themes in the assessment center literature, recent research has often given a new twist to them.

Assessment centers and criterion-related validity

Over the past five years, further support for the criterion-related validity of assessment centers has been gathered. One set of studies extends validity evidence of the overall assessment rating, and another set of studies extends validity evidence of dimension ratings. Specifically, recent studies have provided evidence that the criterion-related validity of assessment centers holds across jobs, time, and contexts. With respect to jobs, two studies were most noteworthy. Damitz et al. (2003) broadened existing selection procedures for selecting airline pilots by including various assessment center exercises to assess both interpersonal and performance-related dimensions. The overall assessment rating was a valid predictor of peer criterion ratings. Similarly, Dayan et al. (2002) argued that assessment centers can be a vital tool to capture the interpersonally oriented dimensions of police work. Their assertion was supported among Israeli police force candidates using both supervisory and peer ratings as criteria. Other studies have also confirmed the relevance of assessment centers for student selection (Bartels, Bommer, & Rubin, 2000; Riggio et al., 2003).

With respect to the validity of assessment centers in the long run, Jansen and Stoop (2001) validated an assessment center over a seven-year period with average salary growth as the criterion. The corrected validity of the overall assessment rating was .39. An interesting contribution of Jansen and Stoop was that they also examined how the validity of assessment center dimensions changed over time. They found that the firmness dimension was predictive over the whole period, whereas the interpersonal dimension became valid only after some years. The latter finding is consistent with research showing that non-cognitive predictors become more important when the criterion data are gathered later on (Goldstein, Zedeck, & Goldstein, 2002).

In recent years, there has also been some evidence that assessment centers can be used in contexts other than domestic selection. Stahl (2000) developed an assessment center for selecting German expatriates. Although the criterion-related validity was not examined, Stahl found that candidates scoring high on different criteria of intercultural competence were also appraised by their peers as being more adaptable to a foreign environment. Lievens et al. (2003) developed and validated an assessment center for selecting European managers for a cross-cultural training program in Japan. Besides assessment center exercises, the procedure included cognitive ability and personality tests and a behavior description interview. The dimensions of adaptability, teamwork, and communication as measured by a group discussion exercise emerged as valid predictors, beyond cognitive ability and personality tests. Dimensions measured in a presentation did not emerge as significant predictors, showing that exercise design is an important issue in assessment centers for international applications (see above).

Finally, Arthur et al. (2003) conducted a meta-analysis of the criterion-related validity of assessment center dimensions. They distinguished six meta-dimensions: 1) consideration/awareness of others, 2) communication, 3) drive, 4) influencing others, 5) organizing and planning, and 6) problem solving. True criterion-related validities varied from .25 to .39. Moreover, a regression-based composite consisting of four out of the six dimensions accounted for the criterion-related validity of assessment center ratings and explained somewhat more variance in performance than the prior meta-analysis of Gaugler, Rosenthal, Thornton, and Bentson (1987). The assessment center dimensions yielded a multiple correlation of .45 ($R^2 = .20$). Thus, a focus on assessment center constructs (dimensions) instead of on the overall assessment rating seems to increase the predictiveness of assessment centers.

In summary, in the past five years, recent studies have found evidence that assessment center validities hold across a wide range of jobs, over longer time periods, and in international contexts. In addition, a recent meta-analysis has further supported the criterion-related validity of assessment centers. An important new finding was that assessment centers have higher predictive validity when they are not seen as a monolithic entity (cf., the overall assessment rating) but as a measure to provide information on various constructs (cf., assessment center dimensions). Despite this positive news, an intriguing finding is that the validity of assessment centers is not higher than the validity of less expensive predictors such as highly structured interviews or situational judgment tests. Two methodological issues might explain this. First, prior assessment center meta-analyses used values of .77 (Gaugler et al., 1987, p .496) and .76 (Arthur et al., 2003, p. 153), respectively, to correct for criterion unreliability. Hence, these values are much higher than the .52 inter-rater reliability value of job performance ratings that has typically been used in recent meta-analyses of selection procedures (e.g., structured interviews) (Viswesvaran, Ones, & Schmidt, 1996). Since prior meta-analyses used such conservative estimates for correcting criterion unreliability, their corrected values underestimate the "true" validity of assessment centers. For example, if we correct the validity coefficient of Gaugler et al. (1987)

with the usual .52 value instead of the more conservative values, the corrected validity of assessment centers rises to .45 instead of to .37. In a similar vein, the corrected validity coefficient of .45 of Arthur et al. (2003) would be higher when corrected with the usual .52 value. Another key methodological issue when interpreting assessment center validities relates to range restriction in the KSAOs measured. Typically, assessment centers are used in final selection stages so that assessment center candidates have been screened in prior selection stages on the basis of both cognitive ability and personality. Consequently, the variance in terms of both cognitively oriented and interpersonally oriented competencies among assessment center candidates is more limited, leading to a possible decrease in predictive validity (Hardison & Sackett, 2004). Future research should put all of this to the test.

Assessment centers and incremental validity

Despite the widespread agreement that assessment centers have strong predictive validity, there is more debate as to whether assessment centers have incremental validity over and above traditional selection procedures such as cognitive ability and personality tests. A meta-analysis of Collins et al. (2003) found that the multiple correlation of personality and cognitive ability tests with overall assessment center ratings was .84. In addition, Schmidt and Hunter (1998) reported that assessment centers had a small incremental validity (2%) when combined with cognitive ability tests. A recent study (Dayan et al., 2002), however, found the opposite results as assessment centers had significant unique validities beyond cognitive ability tests. In addition, O'Connell, Hattrup, Doverspike, and Cober (2002) found that role-play simulations added incremental validity over biodata in predicting retail sales performance.

How can these conflicting findings be reconciled? First, it should be noted that the assessment centers included in the two aforementioned large-scale reviews (Collins et al., 2003; Schmidt & Hunter, 1998) often incorporated cognitive ability and personality tests. Thus, the overall assessment ratings were partially based on information from cognitive ability and personality tests. Given this contamination, it is less surprising that assessment centers did not explain much additional variance over cognitive ability and personality tests. Second, both large-scale studies focused on the overall assessment rating. Although the overall assessment rating is of great practical importance (hiring decisions are contingent upon it), it is a summary rating of evaluations on a variety of dimensions in a diverse set of exercises (Howard, 1997). The fact that the overall assessment rating is such an amalgam of various ratings may reduce its conceptual value. Arthur et al. (2003) cogently argued that assessment centers are best conceptualized as a method for measuring a variety of constructs. Therefore, it makes little sense to state that assessment centers *per se* measure cognitive ability. Instead, depending on the job-related constructs measured, assessment centers might (or might not) have strong correlations with cognitive ability. For instance, if assessment center exercises (in-baskets, case-analyses) primarily measure cognitively oriented dimensions, strong correlations with cognitive ability tests are to be expected. If this is not the case, correlations with cognitive ability tests will be lower. In support of this, Goldstein, Yusko, Braverman, Smith, and Chung (1998) reported that the relationship between assessment centers and cognitive ability tests varied as a function of the cognitive "loading" of assessment center exercises. When exercises (e.g., in-basket exercise) tapped cognitively oriented dimensions (e.g., problem analysis), there were stronger relationships between the exercise and the cognitive ability test (see also Goldstein, Yusko, & Nicolopoulos, 2001).

In a similar vein, the relationship between an overall assessment rating and personality tests will differ according to the job-related constructs measured in assessment center exercises. Various recent studies (Craik et al., 2002; Lievens, De Fruyt, & Van Dam, 2001; Spector, Schneider, Vance, & Hezlett, 2000) support this reasoning. For instance, Spector et al. (2000) discovered that "interpersonal" exercises correlated with personality constructs such as emotional stability, extroversion, and openness, and that "problem-solving" exercises correlated with cognitive ability and conscientiousness. In another study, Craik et al. (2002) reported that in-basket performance was related to conscientiousness, openness, and strategic dimensions such as decision making. Conversely, group discussion performance was best described by interpersonal dimensions and personality constructs such as agreeableness, extroversion, and openness. Finally, Lievens et al. (2001) linked the personality and assessment center domains by scrutinizing the notes of assessors for personality-descriptive adjectives and by classifying them according to the Big Five. Again, results revealed that the distribution of the Big Five categories varied across exercises. For example, the in-basket elicited most frequently conscientiousness descriptors, whereas the group discussion was characterized by many extroversion descriptors.

In recent years, assessment centers have been challenged not only by personality and cognitive ability tests, but also by other assessment methods. In particular, situational judgment tests, situational interviews, and behavior description interviews have gained in popularity because they are easy to administer, good predictors of job performance, and not very expensive. Therefore, an important question is whether assessment centers have incremental validity over them. So far, research seems to support the continued use of assessment centers. In fact, Lievens et al. (2003) showed that dimensions measured by an assessment center had incremental validity over dimensions assessed in a behavior description interview for predicting cross-cultural training performance. Further, Harel, Arditi, and Janz (2003) reported that the validity of a behavior description interview was .53, whereas the assessment center's validity was .62.

In summary, recent studies have scrutinized the incremental validity of assessment centers over traditional selection procedures (personality and cognitive ability tests) and emerging ones (behavioral description interviews). Unfortunately, only a few studies have been conducted so far. A drawback of most incremental validity studies is that they confound methods (e.g., assessment centers, interviews, tests) with constructs (e.g., conscientiousness, sociability). For example, the validity of two constructs (cognitive ability and personality) was typically compared to the validity of a method (assessment center). As already noted, these comparisons are not meaningful unless one either holds the constructs constant and varies the method, or holds the method constant and varies the content (Arthur et al., 2003). For instance, future studies should examine whether sociability as measured by an assessment center exercise has incremental validity over sociability as measured by a personality inventory or situational interview.

Assessment centers and constructs measured

Generally, two analytical methods have been used for examining assessment center construct validity. First, final dimension ratings have been placed in a nomological network to investigate their relationships with similar constructs measured by other methods such as tests, interviews, etc. As described above, assessment center ratings have been found to correlate with the same or similar dimensions assessed by other methods. As a second analytical strategy, dimensional ratings made per exercise (i.e., within-exercise dimension ratings) have been cast as a multitrait-multimethod matrix in which dimensions serve as traits and exercises as methods. The general conclusion from the latter strategy has been that ratings on the same dimensions across exercises correlate lowly (i.e., low convergent validity), whereas ratings on different dimensions in a single exercise correlate highly (i.e., low discriminant validity, or method bias). This has led to the debate whether assessment centers actually measure the dimensions that they purport to measure. This is not to say that assessment centers do not have construct validity. Rather than questioning *if* there are constructs measured, the issue is *what* constructs are measured (Lievens & Klimoski, 2001; Sackett & Tuzinski, 2001).

Over the past five years, research on this theme has expanded (see Hoeft & Schuler, 2001; Lievens, 1998; Lievens & Conway, 2001; Sackett & Tuzinski, 2001; Woehr & Arthur, 2003, for reviews). Researchers have tried to unravel why the aforementioned construct validity results are found. Although the debate is still ongoing, current thinking seems to be that at least three factors are responsible.

First, poorly designed assessment centers seem to show less construct validity evidence. To examine the effects of assessment center design, Lievens and Conway (2001) reanalyzed a large number of studies. They reported significantly more evidence of construct validity when fewer dimensions were used and when assessors were psychologists. Use of behavioral checklists, a lower dimension–exercise ratio, and similar exercises also increased dimension variance. Recently, Woehr and Arthur (2003) confirmed the influence of many of these design considerations. These two large-scale studies demonstrate that assessment center design is important and matters. Therefore, we are generally enthusiastic regarding this body of research. Yet, a caveat is in order. It is important to consider which design recommendations are artificial and which are not. For instance, asking assessors to integrate behavior observations and ratings for each dimension across all exercises prior to evaluating the subsequent dimensions (see Arthur et al., 2000) might be stretching design changes too far. When assessors are first required to look at consistency of candidates across exercises, one might artificially inflate the correlations of the dimensions across exercises.

As a second factor affecting construct validity evidence, there should be high interrater reliability among assessors. If interrater reliability is at best moderate, variance due to assessors will be necessarily confounded with variance due to exercises because assessors typically rotate through the various exercises (they do not rate candidates in all exercises). Owing to this confounding, part of the large exercise variance observed in construct validity studies of operational centers might be assessor variance (Howard, 1997). To examine this, two recent studies (Kolk et al., 2002; Robie, Adams, Osburn, Morris, & Etchegaray,

2000) compared construct validity evidence when assessors rated all dimensions in a single exercise (as is often the case in practice) to construct validity evidence when an assessor rated only a single dimension across exercises. Construct validity evidence increased with the latter method. Although having one assessor per dimension may not be practically feasible, these studies do indicate that the large exercise variance typically found may at least partly be due to rating variability across assessors.

Recent studies have further revealed that the aforementioned factors (i.e., careful design and assessor reliability) might be necessary but insufficient conditions for establishing construct validity. Specifically, two studies (Lance et al., 2000; Lievens, 2002) identified the nature of candidate performances as a third key factor. Lance et al. examined whether exercise variance represented bias or true cross-situational performance differences. They correlated latent exercise factors with external correlates such as cognitive ability measures and concluded that exercise factors captured true variance instead of bias. Apparently, assessors provide relatively accurate assessments of candidates. These candidates, however, do not show performance consistency across exercises. Lievens (2002) reached similar conclusions, showing that convergent and discriminant validity evidence could be established only for candidates whose performances varied across dimensions and were relatively consistent across exercises. This suggests that assessors are capable of detecting performance differences on dimensions, when these differences truly exist.

Now that we know that candidate performances affect construct validity evidence, the next question becomes what makes candidates perform differently across exercises. To answer this question, recent studies have built on interactionist models in social psychology. In particular, Tett and Guterman (2000) used the principle of trait activation (Tett & Burnett, 2003) to emphasize how the behavioral expression of a trait requires arousal by trait-relevant situational cues (i.e., exercise demands). On the basis of this interactionist approach, Tett and Guterman (2000) and Haaland and Christiansen (2002) showed that cross-exercise consistency in assessor ratings is found only when exercises share trait-expressive opportunities.

In sum, in recent years substantial advancements have been made to unravel the puzzle of assessment center construct validity. We have better insight into the factors contributing to the typically low construct validity of operational assessment centers when an internal validation strategy is used. These findings seem to result from a combination of poor assessment center design, moderate interrater reliability, and inconsistent and undifferentiated performance levels of candidates. To shed further light on this issue, future research might especially benefit from using interactionist models in social psychology (e.g., trait activation). We also believe that trait activation theory might not only serve to understand what is happening in assessment centers, but also be useful as a prescriptive framework to modify assessment center design (e.g., design of exercise–dimension matrix, role-player instructions).

Assessment centers and process-related research

In the past five years, researchers have also shown a renewed interest in the assessment center process. A first group of studies has examined potentially biasing factors in this process. In particular, researchers have explored whether assessors' judgments are prone to effects related to repeated assessee participation (Kelbetz & Schuler, 2002), exercise order (Bycio & Zoogah, 2002), assessee impression management (Kuptsch, Kleinmann, & Köller, 1998; McFarland, Ryan, & Kriska, 2003), and assessor–assessee acquaintance (Moser, Schuler, & Funke, 1999). Many of these potentially biasing factors exerted relatively minor effects. For example, Bycio and Zoogah (2002) found that the order wherein candidates participated in exercises explained only about 1% of the rating variance. Kelbetz and Schuler (2003) reported that prior assessment center experience explained no more than 3% of the variance of the overall assessment rating. Generally, repeated participation in an assessment center provided candidates with a gain equivalent to an effect size of .40. McFarland et al. (2003) found less use of candidate impression management tactics in an assessment center exercise (a role-play) than in a situational interview. Apparently, candidates are already so busy acting out their designated role-play character that they have little cognitive resources left to engage in impression management. Whereas the aforementioned studies found only minor effects, Moser et al. (1999) found a large effect of assessor–assessee acquaintance. When acquaintance between the candidate and the assessor was less than or equal to two years, the criterion-related validity was .09. This value increased dramatically to .50 when assessor–assessee acquaintance was greater than two years. Although there might be drawbacks in terms of fairness, we believe that assessor–assessee acquaintance is not always bad. It might be beneficial in assessment centers for developmental purposes. To facilitate follow-up developmental actions, the best "assessor" might well be the participant's boss. In fact, this process is followed by a branch of Suisse Credit Bank in Italy (D. Hippendorf, personal communication, October 7, 1999).

Another group of process-related studies has confirmed the importance of assessor type (psychologist versus manager). Specifically, Lievens (2001a, 2001b) found that managers had more difficulty in discriminating among dimensions than psychology student assessors. However, managerial assessors also rated candidates with higher accuracy. Other studies found that psychologists outperformed non-psychologists only when the criterion-related validity of the interpersonal ratings made was examined ($r = .24$ versus $r = .09$) (Damitz et al., 2003) and that experienced assessors yielded significantly higher accuracy than inexperienced assessors (Kolk, Born, Van der Flier, & Olman, 2002). As a whole, these studies have shown that both types of assessors have their strengths and weaknesses. Therefore, it seems recommendable to continue the common practice of including a mix of experienced line managers and psychologists in the assessor team.

Third, recent studies have examined how assessors' observation and evaluation task can be facilitated. An obvious intervention consists of providing assessors with better training. There seems to be some evidence that especially schema-driven training might be beneficial in terms of increasing interrater reliability, dimension differentiation, differential accuracy, and even criterion-related validity (Goodstone & Lopez, 2001; Lievens, 2001a; Schleicher, Day, Mayes, & Riggio, 2002). Schema-driven training (frame-of-reference training) teaches raters to use a specific performance theory as a mental scheme to "scan" the behavioral stream for relevant incidents and to place these incidents – as they are observed – in performance categories. Such a training seems to be a useful complement to the traditional data-driven training that teaches assessors to strictly distinguish various rating phases (observation, classification, and evaluation) and to proceed to another phase only when the previous one is finished.

Other researchers have explored whether modifications to the existing observation and evaluation procedures might yield beneficial effects. Hennessy, Mabey, and Warr (1998) compared three observation procedures: note taking, behavioral checklists, and behavioral coding. The methods yielded similar outcomes in terms of accuracy, halo, and attitude toward the method, with a preference for behavioral coding. Kolk et al. (2002) found no positive effects of asking assessors to postpone note taking until immediately after the exercise on accuracy, interrater reliability, or halo.

In summary, in the past five years, research on the assessment center process has revealed valuable findings. Specifically, the importance of the type of assessor has been corroborated. Furthermore, frame-of-reference training has emerged as one of the best assessor training strategies. Results on different observation formats have not yielded beneficial effects. Although the studies reviewed have advanced our understanding of the assessment center process, they also constitute only the proverbial tip of the iceberg. Few studies have actually profited from current thinking in person perception, social information processing, interpersonal judgments, and decision making. More specifically, examples of interesting research avenues might involve the roles of social judgment accuracy, assessor expectancies, cognitive structures, motivated cognition, and accountability in assessor judgments (Lievens & Klimoski, 2001).

EPILOGUE

The assessment center method continues to be used in a variety of organizational settings and to generate numerous research studies. In recent years, assessment centers have been used for a variety of purposes with an increasingly diverse set of jobs in countries around the world. Developments in assessment center practice in the past few years include new dimensions being assessed, with innovations in assessment methods employing computer and web-based technology. Although these are often innovative applications, it is unfortunate that systematic research into their validity and utility in comparison with established practices is typically lacking.

Developments in research include innovative studies regarding the criterion-related validity of assessment centers and the unique contribution of assessment centers over alternative assessment procedures. Recent studies have also increased our understanding of the construct validity issue. Specifically, research identified that poor assessment center design, assessor unreliability, and lack of performance variability all contribute to poor measurement of constructs in assessment centers. Finally, process-related studies on assessment centers have emphasized the criticality of type of assessor and type of assessor training.

Additional research is needed to demonstrate the conditions under which developmental assessment centers have impact. Evidence is sorely lacking to demonstrate that participants take some follow-up action in response to developmental feedback, show changes in behavior on the job, in order to contribute to increasing levels of individual and organizational effectiveness. Initial research has demonstrated some of the individual characteristics and organizational support mechanisms that contribute to the positive impact of developmental assessment centers, but more studies in these areas are needed.

References

Adler, S. (1995, May). *Using assessment for strategic organization change.* Paper presented at the 23rd International Congress on the Assessment Center Method, Kansas City, MO.

Arnold, J. (2002). Tensions between assessment, grading and development in development centres: A case study. *International Journal of Human Resource Management, 13*, 975–991.

Arthur, W. A., Jr., Woehr, D. J., & Maldegen, R. (2000). Convergent and discriminant validity of assessment center dimensions: A conceptual and empirical re-examination of the assessment center construct-related validity paradox. *Journal of Management, 26*, 813–835.

Arthur, W., Jr., Day, E. A., McNelly, T. L., & Edens, P. S. (2003). A meta-analysis of the criterion-related validity of assessment center dimensions. *Personnel Psychology, 56*, 125–154.

Atkins, P. W. B., & Wood, R. E. (2002). Self- versus others' ratings as predictors of assessment center ratings: Validation evidence for 360-degree feedback programs. *Personnel Psychology, 55*, 871–904.

Ballantyne, I., & Povah, N. (1995). *Assessment and development centres.* Aldershot: Gower.

Barlay, L. A., & York, K. M. (2002, October). *Assessment centers for program evaluation: Assessing student academic achievement.* Paper presented at the 30th International Congress on Assessment Center Methods, Pittsburgh, PA.

Bartels, L. K., Bommer, W. H., & Rubin, R. S. (2000). Student performance: Assessment centers versus traditional classroom evaluation techniques. *Journal of Education for Business, 75*, 198–201.

Bernthal, P., Cook, K., & Smith, A. (2001). Needs and outcomes in an executive development program. *Journal of Applied Behavioral Science, 37*, 488–512.

Bobrow, W., & Schulz, M. (2002, October). *Applying technical advances in assessment centers.* Paper presented at the 30th International Congress on Assessment Center Methods, Pittsburgh, PA.

Bray, D. W., & Grant, D. L. (1966). The assessment center in the measurement of potential for business management. *Psychological Monographs, 80* (17, Whole No. 625), 1–27.

Briscoe, D. R. (1997). Assessment centers: Cross-cultural and cross-national issues. *Journal of Social Behavior and Personality, 12*, 261–270.

Bycio, P., & Zoogah, B. (2002). Exercise order and assessment centre performance. *Journal of Occupational and Organizational Psychology, 75*, 109–114.

Byham, T. (2003). *AC follow up.* Paper presented at the meeting of the Society for Industrial and Organizational Psychology, Orlando, FL.

Byham, W. C. (2001, October). *What's happening in assessment centers around the world.* Paper presented at the 29th International Congress on Assessment Center Methods, Frankfurt, Germany.

Byham, W. C. (2002, October). *Growing leaders: We must do better.* Paper presented at the 30th International Congress on Assessment Center Methods, Pittsburgh, PA.

Byham, W. C., Smith, A., & Paese, M. J. (2001). *Grow your own leaders.* Pittsburgh, PA: DDI Press.

Caldwell, C., Thornton, G. C., III, & Gruys, M. L. (2003). Ten classic assessment center errors: Challenges to selection validity. *Public Personnel Management, 32*, 73–88.

Chawla, A., & Cronshaw, S. (2002, October). *Top-down vs bottom-up leadership assessment: Practical implications for validation in assessment centers.* Paper presented at the 30th International Congress on Assessment Center Methods, Pittsburgh, PA.

Collins, J. M., Schmidt, F. L., Sanchez-Ku, M., Thomas, M. A., McDaniel, M. A., & Le, H. (2003). Can basic individual differences shed light on the construct meaning of assessment center evaluations? *International Journal of Selection and Assessment, 11*, 17–29.

Craik, K. H., Ware, A. P., Kamp, J., O'Reilly, C., III, Staw, B., & Zedeck, S. (2002). Explorations of construct validity in a combined managerial and personality assessment programme. *Journal of Occupational and Organizational Psychology, 75*, 171–193.

Dailey, L., Cohen, B. M., & Lockwood, W. (1999, June). *Using assessment centers as a change strategy in a global company*. Paper presented at the 27th International Congress on Assessment Center Methods, Orlando, FL.

Damitz, M., Manzey, D., Kleinmann, M., & Severin, K. (2003). Assessment center for pilot selection: Construct and criterion validity and the impact of assessor type. *Applied Psychology, An International Review*, *52*, 193–212.

Dayan, K., Kasten, R., & Fox, S. (2002). Entry-level police candidate assessment center: An efficient tool or a hammer to kill a fly? *Personnel Psychology*, *55*, 827–849.

Dowell, B. E., & Elder, E. D. (2002, October). *Accelerating the development of tomorrow's leaders*. Paper presented at the 30th International Congress on Assessment Center Methods, Pittsburgh, PA.

Eckhardt, T. (2001, October). *Implementing integrated human resource development globally*. Paper presented at the 29th International Congress on Assessment Center Methods, Frankfurt, Germany.

Fleisch, J. M. (1995, May). *The human side of reengineering*. Paper presented at the 23rd International Congress on the Assessment Center Method, Kansas City, MO.

Fleisch, J. M., & Cohen, B. M. (1995, May). *Organizational change: You want it? You got it!* Paper presented at the 23rd International Congress on the Assessment Center Method, Kansas City, MO.

Ford, J. (2001, October). *Automating the collection and scoring of written (non-multiple choice) assessment center data*. Paper presented at the 29th International Congress on Assessment Center Methods, Frankfurt, Germany.

Gaugler, B. B., Rosenthal, D. B., Thornton, G. C., III, & Bentson, C. (1987). Meta-analysis of assessment center validity. *Journal of Applied Psychology*, *40*, 243–259.

Gebelein, S., Warrenfeltz, W., & Guinn, S. (1995, May). *Change in organizations – assessment tools as solutions*. Paper presented at the 23rd International Congress on the Assessment Center Method, Kansas City, MO.

Goldstein, H. W., Yusko, K. P., Braverman, E. P., Smith, D. B., & Chung, B. (1998). The role of cognitive ability in the subgroup differences and incremental validity of assessment center exercises. *Personnel Psychology*, *51*, 357–374.

Goldstein, H. W., Yusko, K. P., & Nicolopoulos, V. (2001). Exploring Black–White subgroup differences of managerial competencies. *Personnel Psychology*, *54*, 783–807.

Goldstein, H. W., Zedeck, S., & Goldstein, I. L. (2002). *g*: Is this your final answer. *Human Performance*, *15*, 123–142.

Goodstone, M. S., & Lopez, F. E. (2001). The frame of reference approach as a solution to an assessment center dilemma. *Consulting Psychology Journal: Practice and Research*, *53*, 96–107.

Gowing, M. (1999, June). *Defining assessment center dimensions: A national framework for global use*. Paper presented at the 27th International Congress on Assessment Center Methods, Orlando, FL.

Haaland, S., & Christiansen, N. D. (2002). Implications of trait-activation theory for evaluating the construct validity of assessment center ratings. *Personnel Psychology*, *55*, 137–163.

Hale, B., Jaffee, C., & Chapman, J. (1999, June). *How technology has changed assessment centers*. Paper presented at the 27th International Congress on Assessment Center Methods, Orlando, FL.

Hardison, C. M., & Sackett, P. R. (2004, April). *Assessment center criterion related validity: A meta-analytic update*. Paper presented at the 18th Annual Conference of the Society for Industrial and Organizational Psychology, Chicago.

Harel, G. H., Arditi, V. A., & Janz, T. (2003). Comparing the validity and utility of behavior description interview versus assessment center ratings. *Journal of Managerial Psychology*, *18*, 94–104.

Hennessy, J., Mabey, B., & Warr, P. (1998). Assessment centre observation procedures: An experimental comparison of traditional, checklist and coding methods, *International Journal of Selection and Assessment*, *6*, 222–231.

Henry, S. E. (1988). *Nontraditional applications of assessment centers: Assessment in staffing plant start ups*. Paper presented at the meeting of the American Psychological Association, Atlanta, GA.

Hiatt, J. (2000, May). *Selection for positions in a manufacturing startup*. Paper presented at the 28th International Congress on Assessment Center Methods, San Francisco.

Hoeft, S., & Schuler, H. (2001). The conceptual basis of assessment centre ratings. *International Journal of Selection and Assessment, 9*, 114–123.

Howard, A. (1997). A reassessment of assessment centers: Challenges for the 21st century. *Journal of Social Behavior and Personality, 12*, 13–52.

Howard, A., & Metzger, J. (2002, October). *Assessment of complex, consultative sales performance*. Paper presented at the 30th International Congress on Assessment Center Methods, Pittsburgh, PA.

Howard, L., & McNelly, T. (2000). *Assessment center for team member level and supervisory development*. Paper presented at the 28th International Congress on Assessment Center Methods, San Francisco.

International Task Force on Assessment Center Guidelines. (2000). Guidelines and ethical considerations for assessment center operations. *Public Personnel Management, 29*, 315–331.

Jacobson, L. (2000, May). *Portfolio assessment: Off the drawing board into the fire*. Paper presented at the 28th International Congress on Assessment Center Methods, San Francisco.

Jansen, P. G. W., & Stoop, B. A. M. (2001). The dynamics of assessment center validity, Results of a 7-year study. *Journal of Applied Psychology, 86*, 741–753.

Jones, R. G., & Whitmore, M. D. (1995). Evaluating developmental assessment centers as interventions. *Personnel Psychology, 48*, 377–388.

Kelbetz, G., & Schuler, H. (2002). Verbessert Vorerfahrung die Leistung im Assessment Center? [Does practice improve assessment center performance?]. *Zeitschrift für Personalpsychologie, 1*, 4–18.

Kolk, N. J., Born, M. P., & Van der Flier, H. (2002). Impact of common rater variance on construct validity of assessment center dimension judgments. *Human Performance, 15*, 325–338.

Kolk, N. J., Born, M. Ph., Van Der Flier, H., & Olman, J. M. (2002). Assessment center procedures: Cognitive load during the observation phase. *International Journal of Selection and Assessment, 10*, 271–278.

Kozloff, B. (2003, October). *Expatriate selection*. Paper presented at the 31st International Congress on Assessment Center Methods, Atlanta, GA.

Kudisch, J. D., Avis, J. M., Fallon, J. D., Thibodeauz, H. F., Roberts, R. E., Rollier, T. J., et al. (2001). *A survey of assessment center practices in organizations worldwide: Maximizing innovation or business as usual?* Paper presented at the 16th Annual Conference of the Society for Industrial and Organizational Psychology, San Diego, CA.

Kudisch, J. D., Lundquist, C., & Smith, A. F. R. (2002, October). *Reactions to "dual purpose" assessment center feedback*. Paper presented at the 30th International Congress on Assessment Center Methods, Pittsburgh, PA.

Kuptsch, C., Kleinmann, M., & Köller, O. (1998). The chameleon effect in assessment centers: The influence of cross-situational behavioral consistency on the convergent validity of assessment centers. *Journal of Social Behavior and Personality, 13*, 102–116.

Lance, C. E., Newbolt, W. H., Gatewood, R. D., Foster, M. R., French, N., & Smith, D. E. (2000). Assessment center exercise factors represent cross-situational specificity, not method bias. *Human Performance, 13*, 323–353.

Lievens, F. (1998). Factors which improve the construct validity of assessment centers: A review. *International Journal of Selection and Assessment, 6*, 141–152.

Lievens, F. (2001a). Assessor training strategies and their effects on accuracy, inter-rater reliability, and discriminant validity. *Journal of Applied Psychology, 86*, 255–264.

Lievens, F. (2001b). Assessors and use of assessment center dimensions: A fresh look at a troubling issue. *Journal of Organizational Behavior, 65*, 1–19.

Lievens, F. (2002). Trying to understand the different pieces of the construct validity puzzle of assessment centers: An examination of assessor and assessee effects. *Journal of Applied Psychology, 87,* 675–686.

Lievens, F., & Conway, J. M. (2001). Dimension and exercise variance in assessment center scores: A large-scale evaluation of multitrait-multimethod studies. *Journal of Applied Psychology, 86,* 1202–1222.

Lievens, F., De Fruyt, F., & Van Dam K. (2001). Assessors' use of personality traits in descriptions of assessment centre candidates: A five-factor model perspective. *Journal of Occupational and Organizational Psychology, 74,* 623–636.

Lievens, F., Harris, M. M., Van Keer, E., & Bisqueret, C. (2003). Predicting cross-cultural training performance: The validity of personality, cognitive ability, and dimensions measured by an assessment center and a behavior description interview. *Journal of Applied Psychology, 88,* 476–489.

Lievens, F., & Klimoski, R. J. (2001). Understanding the assessment centre process: Where are we now? *International Review of Industrial and Organizational Psychology, 16,* 246–286.

Lovler, R., & Goldsmith, R. F. (2002, October). *Cutting edge developments in assessment center technology.* Paper presented at the 30th International Congress on Assessment Center Methods, Pittsburgh, PA.

Mahoney-Phillips, J. (2002, October). *Role profiling and assessment as an organizational management tool.* Paper presented at the 30th International Congress on Assessment Center Methods, Pittsburgh, PA.

Maurer, T. J., Eidson, C. E., Jr., Atchley, K., Kudisch, J. D., Poteet, M., Byham, T., et al. (2003). *Where do we go from here? Accepting and applying assessment center feedback.* Paper presented at the 31st International Congress on Assessment Center Methods, Atlanta, GA.

McCall, M. W., Jr. (2002, October). *Good news and bad news about developing global executives.* Paper presented at the 30th International Congress on Assessment Center Methods, Pittsburgh, PA.

McFarland, L. A., Ryan, A. M., & Kriska, S. D. (2003). Impression management use and effectiveness across assessment methods. *Journal of Management, 29,* 641–661.

Moser, K., Schuler, H., & Funke, U. (1999). The moderating effect of raters' opportunities to observe ratees' job performance on the validity of an assessment centre. *International Journal of Selection and Assessment, 7,* 133–141.

O'Connell, M. S., Hattrup, K., Doverspike, D., & Cober, A. (2002). The validity of "mini" simulations for Mexican retail salespeople. *Journal of Business and Psychology, 16,* 593–599.

Pendit, V., & Thornton, G. C., III. (2001, October). *Development of a code of conduct for personnel assessment in Indonesia.* Paper presented at the 29th International Congress on Assessment Center Methods, Frankfurt, Germany.

Reynolds, D. (2003, October). *Assessing executives and leaders through a technology-based assessment center.* Paper presented at the 31st International Congress on Assessment Center Methods, Atlanta, GA.

Richards, W. (2002, October). *A digital portfolio to support learning and development.* Paper presented at the 30th International Congress on Assessment Center Methods, Pittsburgh, PA.

Riggio, R. E., Mayes, B. T., & Schleicher, D. J. (2003). Using assessment center methods for measuring undergraduate business outcomes. *Journal of Management Inquiry, 12,* 68–78.

Robie, C., Adams, K. A., Osburn, H. G., Morris, M. A., & Etchegaray, J. M. (2000). Effects of the rating process on the construct validity of assessment center dimension evaluations. *Human Performance, 13,* 355–370.

Roth, E., & Smith, A. (2000, May). *The United States Postal Service: Reinventing executive succession planning.* Paper presented at the 28th International Congress on Assessment Center Methods, San Francisco.

Rupp, D. E., & Thornton, G. C., III. (2003). *Development of simulations for certification of competence of IT consultants.* Paper presented at the 18th Annual Conference of the Society for Industrial and Organizational Psychology, Orlando, FL.

Sackett, P. R. (1998). Performance assessment in education and professional certification: Lessons for personnel selection? In M. D. Hakel (Ed.), *Beyond multiple choice tests* (pp. 113–129). Mahwah, NJ: Lawrence Erlbaum.

Sackett, P. R., & Tuzinski, K. (2001). The role of dimensions and exercises in assessment center judgments. In M. London (Ed.), *How people evaluate others in organizations* (pp. 111–129). Mahwah, NJ: Lawrence Erlbaum.

Sarges, W. (2001, October). *The state of assessment centers in German speaking countries.* Paper presented at the 29th International Congress on Assessment Center Methods. Frankfurt, Germany.

Schippmann, J. S., Ash, R. A., Battista, M., Carr, L., Eyde, L. D., Hesketh, B., et al. (2000). The practice of competency modeling. *Personnel Psychology, 53,* 703–740.

Schleicher, D. J., Day, D. V., Mayes, B. T., & Riggio, R. E. (2002). A new frame for frame-of-reference training: Enhancing the construct validity of assessment centers. *Journal of Applied Psychology, 87,* 735–746.

Schmidt, F. L., & Hunter, J. E. (1998). The validity and utility of selection methods in personnel psychology: Practical and theoretical implications of 85 years of research findings. *Psychological Bulletin, 124,* 262–274.

Schneider, B., & Konz, A. M. (1989). Strategic job analysis. *Human Resource Management, 28,* 51–63.

Seegers, J., & Huck, J. (2001, October). *European review of new assessment center guidelines.* Paper presented at the 29th International Congress on Assessment Center Methods, Frankfurt, Germany.

Smith, A., & Reynolds, D. (2002, October). *Automating the assessment experience: The latest chapter.* Paper presented at the 30th International Congress on Assessment Center Methods, Pittsburgh, PA.

Spector, P. E., Schneider, J. R., Vance, C. A., & Hezlett, S. A. (2000). The relation of cognitive ability and personality traits to assessment center performance. *Journal of Social Psychology, 30,* 1474–1491.

Spychalski, A. C., Quinones, M. A., Gaugler, B. B., & Pohley, K. (1997). A survey of assessment center practices in organizations in the United States. *Personnel Psychology, 50,* 71–90.

Stahl, G. K. (2000). Using assessment centers as tools for international management development: An exploratory study. In T. Kuehlmann, M. Mendenhall, & G. Stahl (Eds.), *Developing global leaders: Policies, processes, and innovations* (pp. 197–210). Westport, CT: Quorum Books.

Tett, R. P., & Burnett, D. D. (2003). A personality trait-based interactionist model of job performance. *Journal of Applied Psychology, 88,* 500–517.

Tett, R. P., & Guterman, H. A. (2000). Situation trait relevance, trait expression, and cross-situational consistency: Testing a principle of trait activation. *Journal of Research in Personality, 34,* 397–423.

Thomas, J. L., Dickson, M. W., & Bliese, P. D. (2001). Values predicting leader performance in the US Army Reserve Officer Training Corps assessment center: Evidence for a personality-mediated model. *Leadership Quarterly, 12,* 181–196.

Thoreson, J. (2002, October). *Do we need dimensions? Dimensions limited unlimited.* Paper presented at the 30th International Congress on Assessment Center Methods, Pittsburgh, PA.

Thornton, G. C., III. (1992). *Assessment centers and human resource management.* Reading, MA: Addison-Wesley.

Thornton, G. C., III, & Byham, W. C. (1982). *Assessment centers and managerial performance.* New York: Academic Press.

Thornton, G. C., III, & Cleveland, J. N. (1990). Developing managerial talent through simulation. *American Psychologist, 45,* 190–199.

Thornton, G. C., III, & Mueller-Hanson, R. A. (2004). *Developing organizational simulations: A guide for practitioners and students.* Mahwah, NJ: Erlbaum.

Thornton, G. C., III, & Rupp, D. E. (2004). Simulations and assessment centers. In M. Hersen (Series Ed.) & J. C. Thomas (Vol. Ed.), *Comprehensive handbook of psychological assessment: Vol. 4. Industrial and organizational assessment* (pp. 319–344). Hoboken, NJ: Wiley.

Tillema, H. H. (1998). Assessment of potential, from assessment centers to development centers. *International Journal of Selection and Assessment, 6*, 185–191.

Viswesvaran, C., Ones, D. S., & Schmidt, F. L. (1996). Comparative analysis of the reliability of job performance ratings. *Journal of Applied Psychology, 81*, 557–574.

Wilson, L., & Pilgram, M. (2000, May). *Diagnose . . . then prescribe*. Paper presented at the 28th International Congress on Assessment Center Methods, San Francisco.

Woehr, D. J., & Arthur, W., Jr. (2003). The construct-related validity of assessment center ratings: A review and meta-analysis of the role of methodological factors. *Journal of Management, 29*, 231–258.

Part III

DECISIONS AND THEIR CONTEXT

12

Decision Making in Selection

MARISE PH. BORN AND DORA SCHOLARIOS

INTRODUCTION

While selection measures themselves may show good predictive validity and thus provide for excellent predictions of future job performance of candidates, problems can occur during the *decision-making phase* of the selection process. Difficulties first of all arise when individuals make final hiring decisions in a less than optimal way; for instance, under conditions of time pressure and an overload of information. Additional problems may emerge when conditions under which the hiring decisions take place are difficult; for instance, when relatively few or poorly qualified candidates apply for a large number of vacancies.

It is just this part of the selection process that forms the heart of the present chapter. The chapter's focus is on difficulties and challenges encountered in the selection decision-making process. In the classical distinction between the prediction phase and decision-making phase, it is the latter, particularly decision making by the organization, that is of interest here. The next chapter (Imus & Ryan, this volume) will deal with decision making by the applicant, stressing further the importance of decision-making issues in the selection process. Boudreau, Sturman, and Judge (1994) have already pointed out that the way in which recruiters, managers, and candidates make actual decisions during the selection process should become the focal point of selection research.

In its broadest sense, decision making in personnel selection may imply an array of issues, varying from whether to select or recruit, whether a thorough job analysis is needed, what selection measures to use, to deciding how much money and time can be made available for the selection procedure. Decision making in personnel selection in turn forms part of the larger system of decision events in the staffing cycle (Carlson & Connerley, 2003).

Less broadly, industrial and organizational psychologists traditionally have focused on decision making during the process one would actually undertake to determine what constructs should be measured when selecting personnel, how to measure them, how to develop these measures, and how to determine their quality (Whetzel & Wheaton, 1997). In essence, these decisions revolve around the issue of how to arrive at the most predictive measures. These issues will not be discussed in the present chapter.

In an even narrower sense, decision making in personnel selection is about deciding to which candidates the organization wishes to offer a job and which candidates will be rejected, based upon an evaluation of all relevant candidate information. As a selector, the individual's subjective decision making may be affected by a host of motivational and cognitive factors. These micro-level issues are important, as we need to understand how to minimize the subjectivity of the individual decision maker. Yet, at the same time selectors are representatives of the organization. The decision environment of the organization therefore forms an external constraint on the individual selector's decision-making process. Simultaneously this environment also is a venue for social construction processes impacting on selectors. These meso-level influences, and moreover even societal influences at large (e.g., characteristics of a particular industry, selection practices in different countries), exert an influence on the way decisions are made in selection. This chapter will discuss issues at each of these separate levels and will subsequently demonstrate that decision process dynamics need multilevel theorizing. To this end, a multilevel model of selection decision making will be introduced.

Prior to this, however, two vital matters will be discussed. First, we consider alternative decision strategies against the organization's wider business needs. Will decisions entail relatively straightforward person-to-job matching, involving only one position with several applicants, or more complex choices not only about whom to select but also in which job to place applicants? Second, the chapter discusses the stages of decision making that take place during selection. Three such stages can be discerned. The first, involving the ratings of assessors, is at stake as soon as the measures used in selection are of a subjective nature. A subjective measure involves one or more assessors who rate candidates on a series of competencies. Whereas tests of cognitive ability, background data, and self-report personality questionnaires do not require an assessor, employment interviews and assessment centers do. It is essential, therefore, to understand whether any bias occurs during these rating processes. The second decision-making stage involves the strategy choice of how to combine applicant information that has been collected. Will this be done by means of the subjective judgment of the selector, or will the combination be done statistically? The third stage is the hiring decision itself, including, for instance, what values the organization places on alternative decision outcomes. These three phases will be dealt with after a brief discussion of decision making in the initial phase of screening.

In the third section of the chapter, a multilevel model of selection decision making will be introduced, where the decision-maker level, the organizational level, and the societal level will be examined. The chapter concludes by drawing together these levels, considering the implications of the model for the decision choices discussed earlier, and suggesting avenues for future research.

TYPES OF DECISIONS

Decision strategies

Most organizations only consider recruiting and selecting when a vacancy arises for a specific post. In line with this reality, the vast majority of academic literature and advice to employers concerned with hiring decisions focuses on techniques for identifying the "best" person for the job in question. Witness, for example, the vast amounts of research within personnel psychology and HRM dedicated to designing valid and reliable selection methods (for a recent review of selection method research see Salgado, Viswesvaran, & Ones, 2001; for a more practitioner-oriented treatment see Cooper, Robertson, & Tinline, 2003). In most cases, expert advice and managerial wisdom promote a meritocratic and strategic approach to such decisions, where hiring is based on candidate ability and organizational needs as opposed to random selection or selection guided by criteria with little bearing on job performance (e.g., class, race, gender, group, or family membership).

Embedded within this advice, there is a range of choices for organizations faced with decisions regarding person–job fit. Iles (1999) describes some of these choices in terms of two dimensions: supply flow (the degree to which the organization is open to the external labor market) and assignment flow (whether decisions about internal movement – internal selection or promotion – are based on individual or group criteria). The choice whether to seek external selection is often linked to the organization's wider strategic intentions (Iles, 1999; Jayne & Rauschenberger, 2000; Snow & Snell, 1993). There are several strategic typologies or scenarios which have been developed to inform selection strategy; but the general relationship can be illustrated simply using Porter's (1980) typology of cost reduction, innovation, and quality enhancement strategies (see also Iles, 1999; Jackson, Schuler, & Rivero, 1989). "Cost reducers" will attempt to compete on price and so will hire according to narrow specialized job requirements usually at junior levels at minimal cost. This is likely to exclude expensive external recruitment and selection efforts. "Innovators" will tend to favor external selection in order to maximize workforce creativity and long-term sustainability of the company, searching for qualities such as propensity for risk-taking and tolerance for ambiguity (Williams & Dobson, 1997). Finally, quality enhancement strategies suggest internal selection and promotion in order to encourage employee loyalty, low risk-taking and a concern for quality.

Similar distinctions can be drawn between Miles and Snow's (1984) strategic types of defenders, prospectors, analyzers, and reactors. Sonnenfeld and Peiperl (1988) related each of these types to both supply flow and assignment flow. "Defenders," like cost reducers, will recruit externally only at junior levels and tend to promote staff on the basis of loyalty and contribution to the organization. "Prospectors" will follow an innovation strategy and search for relevant expertise at all levels. They will be more likely to recruit externally, with little emphasis on promotion and reward internally and a focus on individual job performance. "Analyzers" adopt a middle ground between "defenders" and "prospectors." In order to find competitive advantage in a niche market, for example through process improvements, they will search for people who take moderate risks but remain loyal to the organization. "Reactors," unlike the other strategic types, lack control over their environment and selection decisions will tend to be less strategic and focus internally on issues of retirement or redundancy in reaction to external demands.

Selection and classification

The approach to decision making also varies depending on the number of jobs to be filled. The classic selection problem involves identifying the "best" person for a single job and is based on top-down selection from a surplus of applicants on a continuum of ability and suitability for that job. In some situations, the goal is to make decisions about multiple job vacancies simultaneously. Obvious cases of this are large employers who are more likely to make strategic choices about staffing, hence show less concern for person–job fit and short-term decision making about specific vacancies (Jackson et al., 1989; Storey, 1995). This may apply, for example, to public sector organizations (Lowry, 1996), most notably the military, fire service, or police force (e.g., Cochrane, Tett, & Vandecreek, 2003) and corporations with annual intakes of graduates for management training programs (Hodgkinson & Payne, 1998).

When a group of applicants is considered for more than one job simultaneously, or if an individual who is rejected for one job can also be considered for a different job, the problem becomes one of differential classification or placement (Cronbach & Gleser, 1965). Classification from a single group of applicants involves an attempt to predict intrapersonal as well as interpersonal differences in suitability for more than one job (Cascio, 1998) and was distinguished from the single-job selection problem as far back as Brogden (1955) and Horst (1954). Thus, while selection is the control of entrance into the organization (the decision can only be "hire" or "do not hire"), classification implies that even if the decision on one job is to "not hire," individuals can still be considered for other jobs. (Placement applies the same principle to levels within jobs.)

The importance of classification decisions is most visible in the military context, where the hiring problem involves a continual flow of untrained youths who must be channeled into different types of specialized training programs or jobs. The US Army's 12-year Project A and Career Force research programs, which collected test, training, and job performance data from enlisted personnel with the goal of evaluating alternative procedures for efficient selection and classification to a range of Army jobs, illustrate the importance attached to this goal (Campbell & Knapp, 2001). The scale of this single coordinated research effort is unmatched; it began with a sample of 50,000 new recruits and considered the problem of matching them to 250 Army jobs (Military Occupational Specialties). There has been no other attempt to consider a number of jobs simultaneously on such a scale, partly because, for most management, selection for a specific job is the most common and immediate short-term problem (Shields, Hanser, & Campbell, 2001). Yet, as argued by the director of this research program (Campbell, 2001), a great deal of generalization regarding predictive validity or the construction of test and performance measures is possible from these findings to other complex organizations in both the public and private sectors. The breadth and detail of the data available have also stimulated new avenues of research, such as the elaboration and testing of Brogden's classification theories in different job contexts and the development of techniques (such as the construction of predictor composites and job families) to aid the prediction of suitability for multiple jobs (e.g., Scholarios, Johnson, & Zeidner, 1994; Zeidner, Johnson, & Scholarios, 2001).

Beyond the military, assessment of differential abilities is also significant when learning and development are more important than matching people's existing profiles to specific job requirements. In educational contexts, for instance, it is clear that the aim is to capture a broad picture of potential to inform effective vocational decision making, albeit that here there is not only one organization for which the decision is being made. In a work context, similarly, selection for specific, stable job requirements may be less important than identifying motivational and dispositional characteristics (e.g., versatility, interests) which allow the job to be shaped by individuals themselves (Ilgen, 1994; Murphy, 1994). This is consistent with Cronbach and Gleser's (1965) discussion of adaptive treatments suggesting the adaptation of job systems to individual talent and a differential classification approach to decision making. It has even been argued that the increasingly fluid, uncertain, and complex nature of jobs makes the adaptation of jobs to people, rather than the traditional selection approach of fitting people to specific jobs, the more relevant concern for the future. These suggestions apply to contexts as far removed from each other as the military (Rumsey, Walker, & Harris, 1994) and the service sector (Schmitt & Borman, 1993; Ilgen, 1994) and have also given rise to greater emphasis on achieving person–organization rather than person–job fit (Schneider, Kristof-Brown, Goldstein, & Smith, 1997).

STAGES OF DECISION MAKING

The employment process can be seen as a system of sequential, independent decisions on what to do with one or more individuals. The major two decisions are the decision of whether to initially screen an individual in or out, and the subsequent decision to select or reject an individual. We will focus only briefly on the screening phase and then more extensively on the selection phase.

Decision making during screening

Several studies have examined recruiter decision making (e.g., Brown & Campion, 1994; Hutchinson & Brefka, 1997; Rynes, Orlitzky, & Bretz, 1997; Thoms, McMasters, Roberts, & Dombkowski, 1999); but the results nevertheless remain somewhat problematic to interpret. Two recurring problems with studies in this area are: 1) the use of retrospective reports even though it has been shown that reports by decision makers of their own decisions are unrelated to what they actually decided (e.g., Stevenson, Busemeyer, & Naylor, 1990), and 2) the lack of external validity of research designs used, e.g., not using actual decision makers, or not using actual dichotomous screening decisions but a rank order of suitability. One of the primary factors in initial screening decisions is thought to be college grade point average (GPA). Recently, however, McKinney, Carlson, Mecham III, D'Angelo, and Connerley (2003) studied initial screening decisions by recruiters for 548 jobs. They demonstrated that probably more than half of the decisions did not rely on GPA or even selected against high GPA levels. This research suggests that many factors will influence recruiters' decision making. Examples of such factors are the capacity of a firm to attract high-quality applicants and to retain them once they are on the job (McKinney et al., 2003). Such factors are in need of better examination.

Decision making during selection

When candidates are hired, promoted, or placed in new jobs to achieve maximal productivity levels, the accuracy of the prediction of their job performance is at stake. These predictions are based on either their test performance during selection, or, for promotion or placement in new jobs, on the evaluations of their job performance. Formally, a prediction is different from a decision, as a prediction involves estimating a criterion (the candidate's future job performance), and a decision involves choosing among several courses of action (e.g., accepting or rejecting the candidate). Yet, the validity of a prediction is of great importance for the decision outcomes. Murphy and Davidshofer (2001, p. 170) therefore prefer to label the relationship between the prediction and the future job performance, or the criterion-related validity, as "validity for decisions." More specifically, the question arises regarding what ways assessors combine candidate information into a rating on a specific subjective selection measure (e.g., the interview and the assessment center; the *first stage* of decision making) and how, subsequently, candidate scores on a set of selection measures are combined in a prediction of future job performance (the *second stage* of decision making). Do alternative ways of combining information differ in their accuracy? After having addressed this issue, we will turn to the *third and last stage* of decision making, namely the actions that can be taken, their quality, and factors that influence this quality.

The first stage of decision making in selection.   At this stage, decision making concerns the way that assessors process information to rate applicants in the employment interview and the assessment center. Much and very varied research has been done in this area. This research ranges from examining contrast effects with other applicants, the influence of cognitive scripts or schemata (e.g., stereotypes) on assessors' ratings, decision makers' perception of their accountability, or cognitive load of the decision maker, to factors affecting group decision making during selection (e.g., Dose, 2003; Kolk, Born, & Van der Flier, 2002; Van Dam, 2003). Notwithstanding the influences of such variables on ratings by assessors, both the (structured) employment interview and the assessment center have relatively good predictive validity (see the overview by Robertson & Smith, 2001). For a discussion of the employment interview and the assessment center we refer to Chapter 6 (Dipboye) and Chapter 11 (Lievens & Thornton) of this volume.

The second stage of decision making in selection.   The prediction issue revolves around whether to use statistical techniques (e.g., multiple regression analysis) in which the information is used directly to make predictions, or whether the information is given to a decision maker (a clinician) who evaluates this information and combines it by judgment into an overall impression for decision making. In a statistical (or mechanical) combination of data, for example, test scores, interview ratings, and biographical data scores may be combined using a formula to predict job success. In a judgmental (or clinical) combination, the decision maker may look at the test scores, interview ratings, and biographical data, subsequently making an overall judgment about the candidate's likely success. The latter method of prediction doubtless is much more commonly used in practice than the former. In a famous publication, Meehl (1954) reviewed 20 studies that had compared the accuracy of these two general classes of data combination. The overall conclusion was that a statistical combination produced at least as accurate and often more accurate judgments than those of trained professionals. Meehl's review inspired many psychologists to conduct studies on this topic, which largely reached the same conclusion as Meehl had.

Recently, Grove, Zald, Lebow, Snitz, and Nelson (2000) conducted the first meta-analysis comparing clinical and mechanical prediction. They were able to include 136 primary studies, varying from the prediction of business start-up success to psychiatric diagnosis. The authors confirmed the conclusion of the overall superiority of mechanical prediction, regardless of the criterion to be predicted. Nonetheless, in half of the studies the clinical method appeared to be approximately as good as mechanical prediction. Interestingly, when a clinician had access to an interview, his or her prediction was outperformed to a substantially greater extent by mechanical prediction. The general reasons for the weaker clinical prediction, on the whole, are to be found in the susceptibility of humans to many errors. Such errors include ignoring base rates, failure to understand regression to the mean, the use of the availability heuristic (judging the commonality of behavioral occurrences from the ease of imagining such examples), and illusory correlations (overestimating the co-occurrence of rare behaviors or characteristics) (for an overview of such errors see Kunda, 1999). It is noteworthy that experienced psychologists often show little improvement relative to the judgment of psychology graduate students (e.g., Garb, 1989). In this light, Highhouse (2002) offers a good overview of clinical prediction practices in personnel decision making. In a later section on the decision maker, we will extend the theme of human judgment further, and we will demonstrate that in the phase where the selector decides whom to accept and whom to reject, several factors lead to less clear-cut decisions than we may think.

As a final point regarding the first stage of decision making, we refer to Dipboye (Chapter 6, this volume) and to Guion (1998) for different ways of mechanically combining predictor information in selection decision making. These include multiple regression (a conjunctive model), multiple cut-offs (a disjunctive model where applicants are rejected if any one of their scores is below a minimum cut-off), and the multiple hurdle strategy (sequential passing of each predictor).

The third stage of decision making in selection. This is the action itself with regard to a specific individual, the simplest version being whether to accept or reject that individual. The actual level of job performance of the individual in its simplest form will either be successful performance or unsuccessful performance. A combination of the two possible decisions and the two actual performance levels leads to the familiar fourfold table of possible decision outcomes, namely false negatives, true positives, true negatives, and false positives. Depending on the value ascribed by an organization to each possible outcome, the *quality* of the decisions may be defined as the percentage of true positives among the applicants accepted (the success ratio), or the percentage of true outcomes among all possible outcomes.

The accuracy of the prediction is a crucial factor for the quality of the decision. Yet, it is not the only factor of importance. The selection ratio, or the percentage of the population of candidates that is accepted, and the base rate, or the number of potential successes in the population of applicants, are further influences that may have a limiting effect on the quality of the decisions. When, for instance, the base rate is very high (or very low), such as when there are many qualified (or many unqualified) applicants for a vacancy, there may not be very much room for improvement by implementing a highly predictive selection device over merely flipping a coin. Moreover, when the selection ratio is very high because the organization cannot be very selective, there similarly will not be much room for improvement by using a highly predictive test. The result will be virtually the same, as there hardly is any choice but to accept almost everyone.

The Taylor–Russell (1939) utility model expresses the quality of decisions in terms of the success ratio, an index adequate for dichotomous criterion behavior. The quality of decisions, or the utility, can also be described in terms of the average standard score on a criterion measure for the selected group. To this end, the actual job performance does not have to be dichotomized into successful performance versus failure but can be seen more naturally as a continuous variable. This is the approach that the Naylor–Shine utility model (1965) takes. The more familiar Brogden–Cronbach–Gleser (BCG) utility model (Brogden, 1949; Cronbach & Gleser, 1965) extends the Naylor–Shine utility model further, by expressing utility in the most concrete, that is financial, terms. Here, the quality or utility is expressed as the dollar payoff of an employee to the organization and depends not only on validity of the prediction and the selection ratio, but also on the cost of testing and the standard deviation in financial value (dollars, euros) of the job performance of the (pre-screened) applicant group (SDy). The larger this standard deviation, the larger the potential gain associated with a valid selection procedure. It is the determination of the latter that has always been the most difficult aspect of the BCG model (see Cascio, 1998, for a succinct overview of utility models).

These well-known utility models have been in existence now for quite some time. After the rising interest in utility analysis in the 1980s and the early 1990s, as demonstrated by the work of, for instance, Schmidt, Hunter, McKenzie, and Muldrow (1979) (see Boudreau's (1991) overview), the overall decrease in attention to utility analysis since the 1990s is quite worrisome within industrial and organizational psychology (Boudreau & Ramstad, 2003). Nevertheless, some efforts to refine and modify utility analysis can be identified.

First, the issue of estimating the standard deviation of job performance in monetary terms remains an ongoing discussion. Schmidt et al. (1979) had proposed a global estimation procedure for SDy by having experts estimate the financial utility of employees at specific percentiles of a normal distribution of job performance. Yet, recently Myors, Carstairs, and Todorov (2002) demonstrated that participants individually but also as a group grossly err when they have to estimate these percentiles, implying that Schmidt et al.'s utility estimates probably are inaccurate. The estimation of SDy clearly has not been adequately resolved as yet.

Second, the line of research on utility estimation and maximization in the area of classification (Scholarios et al., 1994; Zeidner et al., 2001) has been given relatively little emphasis to date in the personnel selection area (e.g., Guion, 1998). This is primarily because the conceptual, mathematical, and practical problems in this domain generally are rather complex.

Third, a series of articles by De Corte concerns improvements in utility estimation and maximization under several specific circumstances (e.g., De Corte, 1994, 1999, 2000; De Corte & Lievens, 2003). One example is a refinement in the estimation of the success ratio, the index used in the Taylor–Russell approach. As was demonstrated by De Corte (1999) among others, the Taylor–Russell utility formula often leads to faulty estimations. For single-stage selection scenarios with fixed quota, threshold, and mixed quota/threshold decisions, De Corte (2002) offers solutions to these shortcomings.

Fourth, and most important for the impact of utility analysis, Boudreau and Ramstad (2003) propose a new focus away from refinements of utility models and measurement and toward a decision-process lens of looking at utility analysis. Central to this viewpoint is the connections that decision makers need to make between utility analysis, job performance, and organizational outcomes. For more detailed descriptions of current trends and future directions in utility analysis we refer to Cabrera and Raju (2001) and Boudreau and Ramstad (2003).

In closing this section, an important issue remains, for what if in practice the selection decision circumstances do not meet the requirements for building such intricate models? For instance, the organization may not be able to obtain the necessary applicant sample sizes, or the need for personnel selection decisions may only occur sporadically. This is a realistic scenario for a small company seeking an employee. The best thing to do in such cases is to systematize the decision making: by explicating important job-related knowledge, skills, and abilities (KSAs), attaching a weight to each of these, and systematically judging each candidate on these KSAs in an interview or by having them tested at a consultancy, the decision maker ensures the procedure is, at least, methodical. Then, by multiplying the rating given to each candidate on each K, S, or A with the weight given to each K, S, or A, and obtaining the sum of these products, each candidate will receive a total score which subsequently can be compared with the total scores of the other candidates to arrive at a selection decision.

A MULTILEVEL MODEL OF SELECTION DECISION MAKING

Presenting decision strategies and stages as we have done so far in this chapter suggests a largely rational approach to decision making where effective staffing decisions depend on the efficient processing of information about job-related human capacities. Surveys of organizational practice, however, consistently suggest that employers either ignore or are unaware of the supposed benefits from rigorously developed, methodically implemented, and validated assessment tools (e.g., Terpstra & Rozell, 1997). In the selection literature this is often treated as a problem of increasing practitioners' and especially small employers' awareness of valid techniques, such as testing, and of the potentially biasing components of methods such as the interview. As described in the previous section, we might also suggest relatively easy ways of systematizing the collection and organization of candidate information.

An alternative approach is to aim for greater understanding of the complexities of the selection decision problem. A bounded rationality view of human judgment suggests the need to look at the framing effects of context on the decision maker. Arguably, HRM's devolution of selection responsibilities to line management (IRS Management Review, 1998; Storey, 1992), who are likely to have limited training in selection techniques, heightens the importance of further analysis at this level of the decision process. Organizational context also may exert a constraining or facilitating influence on the conduct of decision making by selectors or on the strategic options available to the organization; and at a further aggregated level of analysis, factors which impact populations of organizations may directly impact decision makers or shape accepted organizational standards. For example, Spender (1989) used the term "industry recipes" to connote the rules, equivalent to tacit knowledge developed through experience within an industry, used to guide action and provide timesaving techniques for managers dealing with an uncertain and changing environment.

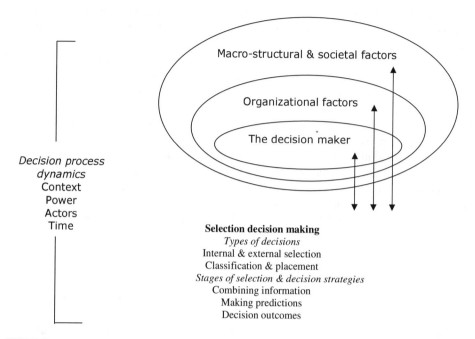

*Decision process
dynamics*
Context
Power
Actors
Time

Selection decision making
Types of decisions
Internal & external selection
Classification & placement
Stages of selection & decision strategies
Combining information
Making predictions
Decision outcomes

FIGURE 12.1   A multilevel selection decision-making model

Thus, we can conceptualize the process of selection decision making as a series of overlapping layers: the individual decision maker or selector, the organizational context, and the wider environment (see Ployhart & Schneider, 2002 and Chapter 23 of this volume, and Ramsay & Scholarios, 1999, for related approaches to selection). This model is depicted in Figure 12.1. Interactions between these layers will directly shape selection decisions. In addition, beyond these cross-level interactions, the model presented in Figure 12.1 also reflects the dynamics of an essentially social process which embodies the preferences and choices of several parties involved in the process – not only the selector acting on behalf of the organization. Interpretative traditions view organizational activity as a socially constructed phenomenon (Daft & Weick, 1984) and with respect to selection, it is also possible to think in terms of social relational processes, which reveal the power-laden, contested, negotiated, and transient nature of each aspect of the decision process (see, for example, Dachler & Hosking, 1995). Each element of this model is developed further below.

The decision maker

As pointed to earlier, in mainstream textbooks on personnel selection there generally is an implicit assumption that the decision-making process of the selector(s) is a *rational* and *orderly* one. At the least, no explicit mention commonly is made of possible factors influencing this process. The process is regarded as one where the decision maker picks the best candidate from a series of human resources presented on a conveyor belt. The only constraints to be taken into account in rational top-down selection procedures are civil rights regulations and equal opportunities laws as laid down by society at large, and the possibility that the best candidate may reject the job offer. Otherwise the decision maker tries to maximize the (financial) utility of the decision for the organization, and will rationally set about this task. Several decision theories and empirical studies on selection decisions nevertheless demonstrate that this may be an *overly simplistic* picture of the decision maker.

Models of decision making. Models of human decision making range from completely rational to irrational, where the decision maker is influenced by biases and judgmental heuristics. These models are general in their scope and therefore not only have relevance for the interpretation of decision makers representing the organization, but also for the interpretation of decision making by applicants (Anderson, Born, & Cunningham-Snell, 2001; Imus & Ryan, Chapter 13 of this volume).

The *classic economic rationality model* comes from economics and assumes a perfectly rational decision maker who is completely aware of all possible alternative choices, is able to work with probability calculations, and can deal with unlimited complex computations to determine the best alternatives and to reach the maximum outcome. The more detached and analytical the decision maker, the more effective the decision making. Most economists will not claim that this model is a realistic description of decision-making behavior under all circumstances, and amendments to this model have been made over time (see Luthans, 2005, for an overview). *Simon's bounded rationality model* (Simon, 1957), in contrast, states that decision makers will satisfice and do not have the ability to maximize; that is, they will choose an action that is "good enough." They are happy with simple rules of thumb and will not determine all possible alternatives before making their choice. In this model, Simon recognizes the cognitive, social, and organizational barriers to maximization.

Judgmental heuristics outlook. Cognitive psychological research into judgmental heuristics and biases has led to more insight into which biases may influence human decision making. Kahneman and Tversky demonstrated three major and well-known biases that are at work when humans are making decisions and that will hinder a fully rational decision-making process (e.g., Kahneman & Tversky, 1982; Tversky & Kahneman, 1974): the availability heuristic (the assessment of probability of an event depends on how readily it is remembered); the representativeness heuristic (the assessment of probability of an event depends on its resemblance to similar events that have occurred); and the anchoring and adjustment heuristic, where a judgment is made by starting from an initial value (this may be some accidental information, some historical precedent, etc.) and the decision subsequently is the result of adjustments to that initial value.

Social influences outlook. One of the most important findings to emerge from studies focusing on social influences during decision making is the phenomenon of escalation of commitment (Staw & Ross, 1989; Hantula & DeNicolis Bragger, 1999). This phenomenon refers to decision makers sticking with faulty decisions. Social forces such as the need to save face, but also defensively ignoring information, are some of the reasons thought to be behind the occurrence of commitment escalation.

Several exemplary empirical studies on selection decisions demonstrate how such cognitive and affective influences impact upon the decisions made. A study by Shafir (1993) showed that decision-making behavior may vary according to whether the type of decision involves *choosing* the very best candidates or *rejecting* the worst candidates. In the first type of decision, decision makers focus on information that makes one candidate superior to the other. Shafir's study illustrated that decision makers in this case favor complex individuals having striking strengths and weaknesses over more plain and unremarkable ones. This is because more reasons (i.e., strengths) are perceived for choosing the complex individuals. When having to reject the worst candidates, the complex individuals will be rejected as well, because more reasons are perceived (i.e., weaknesses) to reject these individuals. Therefore, a selector who puts together a shortlist of the very best candidates may end up with a very different list than a selector who constructs a shortlist by rejecting the worst candidates.

Other studies have focused on the impact of accuracy goals on decision makers. When decision makers will have to give a full account of their selection decisions to the organization, and explain the reasons for their choices, they will think longer and harder about their choices until they are satisfied that they have arrived at the best possible conclusion (Tetlock & Kim, 1987). But this more elaborate thinking does not always guarantee a better decision. Tetlock and Boettger (1989), for instance, showed that individuals who had to justify their judgments were more likely than others to show the so-called dilution effect. This effect is the tendency to make less extreme judgments about another person (e.g., is this candidate dishonest?) when given information about this person which is unrelated to dishonesty (e.g., candidate now works for Unilever). More generally, no amount of thought will improve decisions when people use faulty heuristics instead of good reasoning strategies.

Moving from cognitions to emotions, an experimental study by Baron (1987) shows interesting results, suggesting that mood variations between selectors may affect the careers of the people involved. Baron had participants develop an impression of an applicant during a face-to-face interview. First, Baron induced them to feel mildly elated, neutral, or dejected. The applicant supposedly applied for a middle-management job and each subject had to ask the applicant a list of pre-arranged questions in a structured interview. The applicant in fact was a confederate giving the same deliberately ambivalent answers. The elated interviewers subsequently rated the applicant as having greater potential for the job and would hire him, whereas the depressed interviewers rated the applicant worse and would not hire him. Such studies show that mood biases may have an impact in a realistic selection decision setting.

Sessa (2001) describes the process of executive promotion and selection, where the decision makers responsible for selection at the top are different people than the decision makers responsible for selection in the lower levels of the organization. At the top, the decision makers will often be the CEO, the chair of the board of directors, or other higher-level executives. Sessa reports that these selectors typically do not use psychometrically valid selection technique information but that their own values, beliefs, affects, and expectations instead will be influential in the choice of an executive. Ruderman and Ohlott

(1990; in Sessa, 2001) note that use of salient but irrelevant candidate characteristics and exclusion of summary data but inclusion of concrete, vivid information are among the factors that have the greatest potential to affect the choice of an executive. Executive selection situations form a clear demonstration of the possible influences of cognitions, motivations, and affect in selection decisions.

In sum, these and other studies reveal that individuals making decisions are affected by (automatic) cognitive and affective processes that result in less straightforward decisions than we may envision.

Organizations and selection decisions

A second layer of influence on the selection decision process is represented by the organizational context. A range of organizational characteristics can determine the nature of a selection process and its utility for the organization. The most commonly cited organizational contingencies include, for example, the size of the organization and resource availability (Terpstra & Rozell, 1993); departmental/functional structure (Olian & Rynes, 1984); employment patterns and turnover (Judge & Ferris, 1992); organizational values and culture (Sparrow, 1997); the organization's stage in the business cycle of growth, maturity, and decline (Williams & Dobson, 1997); and, as mentioned earlier in the chapter, the strategic direction of the organization (Jackson et al., 1989).

Each of these is likely to impact the specification of the formal procedures adopted, including choices about the number and type of jobs to be filled, internal versus external recruitment, the methods used to select, and to manage, candidate information. Thus, in general, research has shown that larger organizations are more likely to have institutionalized HRM departments and policies, to adopt systematic and formalized procedures based on psychometrically sound assessment techniques, and to display a more strategic approach to selection. This acceptance of scientific techniques means, usually, more selective hiring standards (Cohen & Pfeffer, 1986) and greater concern for rational hiring decisions based on choosing the best person for a job in an unbiased and impersonal way. Larger organizations and those with regular recruitment drives (e.g., those in the public sector or military) also are more likely to consider classification to multiple jobs rather than selection for a single job.

A strategic approach to selection decisions assumes a rational approach to identifying needs and making decisions. As mentioned in the discussion of types of decisions, strategy will inform whether to replace existing staff or to develop new areas of work, and whether internal or external recruitment is appropriate. Snow and Snell's (1993) depiction of selection as part of an organization's wider manpower delivery system argued that requirements should be defined for three types of jobs – existing, envisaged, and even those yet to be prescribed. Williams and Dobson (1997) also present a model of strategic personnel selection which aligns selection (along with other HRM functions) with current strategy, future strategy, or a change strategy, and the importance of identifying either operational, visionary, or transformational performance criteria to meet these needs. Sparrow (1997) similarly differentiates between core, transitional, emergent, and maturing behavioral competencies and links these to wider organizational developments. While core competencies (e.g., the generic qualities required of managers) are at the heart of effective performance regardless of changing business strategy, in an organization affected, for example, by downsizing, delayering, or increasing competition, it may be more important to identify those with the capacity to cope with uncertainty (a transitional competency), to adapt to a new business process (an emerging competency) or to reorient away from obsolescent skills, perhaps as a result of changing technology or product markets (maturing competencies).

In short, this view of selection decision making assumes a rational design process which matches choices to changing organizational needs, as well as other structural and resource constraints affecting the given organization (e.g., size, sector, employment contracts). As such, it draws from the contingency tradition of strategic HRM (Delery & Doty, 1996). Indeed, many of the most recent trends in selection practice, such as the use of competency-based assessment, reflect such a rational design of selection practice aligned with strategy, particularly the increasing emphasis on building more innovative, adaptable, and interdependent workforces (e.g., Pearlman & Barney, 2000). Performance criteria like contextual (discretionary) performance, team effectiveness, or the ability to perform in diverse jobs have become more important than task performance for many organizations forced to survive in a more competitive environment, and attention has shifted to the measurement of attitudes, personality, and values that match these changing organizational goals (for some accounts of this trend see Motowidlo & Van Scotter, 1994; Schneider et al., 1997).

Matching decision making to organizational contingencies, however, may not be as rational a process as such "best fit" models would suggest. As indicated in Figure 12.1, not only do organizational-level characteristics directly shape the formal selection process but also the decision maker is embedded within this organizational context, suggesting a dynamic interaction between these two spheres. The cognitive and affective processes described in the previous section, therefore, occur within, and are adaptive to, a dynamic organizational context (Payne, Bettman, & Johnson, 1993). This adds greater complexity to the way that organizational constraints are filtered and implemented by decision makers. For instance, individual decision makers' perceptions of their own accountability within the organizational context (Tetlock, 1985) may lead to the rejection of scientific information provided by assessment tools in favor of other less strategic or "rational" organizational decision criteria, such as maintaining their own status in the organization.

This complexity illustrates again the bounded rationality model of decision making within organizational constraints. Going further, though, it is also possible to reject a rational, albeit constrained, explanation of selection decisions. Alternative theoretical perspectives include more emergent and unpredictable accounts of strategy (for example, the resource-based theory of the firm (Grant, 1991)) and recognition that decision makers are actors within a socially constructed, rather than deterministic, context (Iles & Salaman, 1995). From the latter perspective, organizational context both shapes and is shaped by that individual's perspective, status, and influence. An implication of this alternative view is that decision makers may not act in maximizing ways for the organization, and the framework within which rational decisions need to be considered may be far wider than that encompassed by the narrow confines of the organization, strategic choice, and the selection moment itself. This non-rational interpretation of selection decisions is explored further in a later section of the chapter when we try to integrate the multiple levels in our model.

The wider context of selection decisions

The final layer in our multilevel model of selection decisions is the organization's external environment. Thompson (1967) defined the relevant "task environment" for an organization as composed of customers, suppliers, competitors, and regulatory agencies, although we can expand this to include any influence from outwith the organization.

Some environmental variables affect specific organizations or industries while others have a more global influence. The local labor market, business market, and trading relations (Rousseau & Tinsley, 1997) will shape an organization's overall staffing strategy, the applicant pool they can attract, the degree to which they can afford to be selective, and ultimately their choice of methods. At the industry level, patterns in market demand and requirements for sector-specific skills and qualifications, sources of potential candidates (Murphy, 1996), and traditions in practice (Born & Jansen, 1997) are important to consider. The selection methods and performance criteria of exemplary or large firms can be seen as models to be borrowed or copied by other firms with fewer resources (Johns, 1993). In practice, this has meant the wider use of psychological tests and competency-based assessment (Sparrow & Hiltrop, 1994).

Even more broadly, employment legislation (Pearn, 1993), national culture (Ryan, McFarland, Baron, & Page, 1999), and government employment policies have all been shown to account for variability in selection practice, although there is some suggestion that the spread of multinationals and globalization should reduce differences brought about by cultural preferences or access to resources (Ryan et al., 1999). It is possible to trace the emergence of patterns across organizations or industries, for example in governmental institutions where a culture of public and personal accountability tends to encourage greater standardization and monitoring of selection procedures than in private sector organizations (Pearn, 1993). Similar "recipes" (Spender, 1989) are just as likely to exist in other clusterings, for example within markets, regions, or cultures, each with their own rationality regarding the form that selection processes should take. One such emerging pattern was highlighted in our earlier discussion of environmental instability which encourages organizations to emphasize candidate fit with organizational culture and a greater focus on person qualities such as adaptability or market awareness. This conforms to Johns' (1993) proposal that the adoption of new personnel practices is less based on issues of technical merit than on the need to respond to global competition or external threat or to benchmark one's competitors.

Each of these examples conveys the impact of the external environment on decisions made within organizations. The arrows in Figure 12.1, however, indicate a mutual influence between each of our contextual layers and selection. Taking just one example of this bidirectional influence, organizational hiring decisions are both shaped by socio-political factors and themselves have broader societal consequences, most notably with respect to issues of equal opportunity and equal treatment. First, we can see that several general external forces have shaped the way in which organizations make selection decisions.

Employers' freedom to consider how best to satisfy their own organization's goals has evolved into a legislative right in most economies driven by the capitalist ideology of nine-teenth-century industrialism which gave rise to the principles of meritocracy and ration-alism. Most advanced industrialized economies acknowledge employers' rights to consider individual merit for their own purposes and may even discourage the equal distribution of jobs across the potential labor force or any overt favoritism for a particular group (Guest, 1990). Thus, the attempt to achieve meritocracy permeates research on selection decision making (take, for example, the attempts to limit the subjective biases of individual deci-sion makers and to ensure nondiscriminatory procedures). Recent organizational research which claims to show that "good" selection decisions are part of a human resource system which impacts many critical organizational outcomes, such as employee productivity, reten-tion, and adaptability (e.g., Pfeffer, 1994), also supports the position that employers have a right to maximize utility through systematic selection systems.

Further environmental impact is evident in the moderating effect of regulatory inter-vention. This has, in places, curbed the laissez-faire approach to employers in the USA through equal employment opportunity legislation which emerged from the Civil Rights Acts of 1964 and 1991. Public sector employers, such as the civil service, police force, or the military, tend to be more accountable to such regulation than those in the private sector (Pearn, 1993). Policies regarding employment contracts also still tend to be determined by national legislative frameworks (Roe & van den Berg, 2003; Torrington, 1994) or, as in the case of the European Union, supranational frameworks. Some governments remain more interventionist than others in their countries' labor market policy and employment rela-tions legislation (see, for example, Bamber's (Bamber, Park, Lee, Ross, & Broadbent, 2000) contrast between Asia Pacific's advanced industrial economies (Australia, New Zealand, and Japan), newly industrialized economies (South Korea and Taiwan), and recent indus-trializers (Indonesia and China).

Turning to the wider effects of organizations' actions on society, opinions are divided on whether an emphasis on always selecting the best is in society's overall interest. A dom-inant position over the last thirty years of selection research is that general cognitive ability, or g, is the most valid predictor of potential across a wide range of jobs and that addi-tional predictors add little in terms of incremental predictive validity (Ree, Earles, & Teachout, 1994). Thus, on the one hand, it has been argued that utility both for organi-zations and the economy as a whole is maximized through the use of the most valid pre-dictors as part of a top-down hiring process based on candidate scores for these predictors (e.g., Schmidt & Hunter, 1998).

The opposing view stresses the adverse impact of general cognitive ability tests which result in different hiring rates for different subgroups in society; for example, minority groups in the USA have tended to score lower on average on tests of ability than major-ity group members (Schmitt, Clause, & Pulakos, 1996). Chapter 14 in this volume (Evers, te Nijenhuis, & van der Flier) deals further with this issue. The question of relevance here is whether organizations can produce workforces that are both optimal performers and representative of diverse groups in society. There is some optimism at least that it is indeed possible both to maximize efficiency of prediction through the use of multiple or alterna-tive predictors and to minimize adverse impact (e.g., Sackett & Ellingson, 1997).

The issues discussed above highlight the different goals of assessment, of which rank-ordering candidates on the basis of the most valid predictors of potential performance in order to maximize selection efficiency is only one. Other goals include ensuring equity and equal opportunity and, as argued here, top-down hiring may not always be the most desirable from a societal perspective. This returns to our early distinction between selection, classification, and placement as distinct strategies for achieving different outcomes, but also places these decision choices within a wider societal context. Ilgen (1994) summarizes this position as follows:

> As employment is viewed more from a societal than from an organizational perspective, classification and placement along with other human resource practices, such as training, replace selection by definition . . . There is no repository for low g individuals. Therefore, shifting models away from selection to placement and classification is not only a desirable goal, it is the only goal. (p. 18 and p. 29)

Integrating the levels

Our multilevel model of selection decision making outlines three layers of influence on the decision strategies adopted by organizations and selectors. The micro level of the selector highlights the potential for affective and cognitive distortions, particularly as decision tasks become more complex or uncertain. The organizational context of selection decision making comprises various sources of information and pressures, which not only dictate the direction that an organization may take in terms of hiring strategy but also directly frames the task of the selector to either facilitate or constrain decision making. And recognition of the environment and its role in shaping organizational selection practice illustrates more macro-structural forces on decision making, and in turn how selection practice at the level of organizations has implications for society.

Selection decision making also can be conceptualized as a socially constructed process set within a context of different interests and competing pressures. Figure 12.1 illustrates this additional aspect under the label of "decision process dynamics" which is shown as having an influence at all levels of the model. Two non-positivistic theoretical approaches can be used to further analyze selection decision making in this way. First, borrowing from interpretive sociological and social psychological traditions (e.g., Berger & Luckmann, 1967; Daft & Weick, 1984), organizational activity is viewed as a process of meaning-creation characterized by inferences about events and causality. At the center of this meaning-creation process is the individual decision maker, even though in most selection literature the selector is indistinguishable from the organization they represent. The decision maker, as we have seen, is susceptible to a range of influences which may lead to less than optimal decision making. Going further than this constrained notion of individual decision making, though, some writers call for more explicit recognition of the essentially social character of selection (e.g., Dachler, 1989; Herriot, 1989). Social process models acknowledge the contextual, dynamic, and interactional nature of selection events and regard the recruitment and selection period as a continuous process of information gathering and sense-making involving all parties in the interaction. While a psychometric and utility perspective of selection decisions assumes the organization as the sole decision maker and information gathering to be unidirectional, social process models instead depict a two-way interaction with power resting also with the applicant (see Imus & Ryan, Chapter 13, this volume, for a further discussion of this topic).

The second approach, which leads us away from positivist and rationalist traditions in understanding selection (i.e., the psychometric or strategic management views), theorizes the relational quality of the interaction between key actors, such as decision makers, applicants, the organization, and sources of power within the organization (Dachler & Hosking, 1995). Dachler (1989) suggested that only by understanding how decision makers attach meaning to organizational realities (for instance, what performance criteria are valued, their own organizational position and status, or their role in decision making) against the backdrop of competing interests can the selection process be adequately modeled. Even more critical positions consider organizational selection processes as "technologies of power" which operate at all levels of analysis and use selection procedures to regulate and shape according to the (often unspoken) interests of those with power (Hollway, 1991). Jewson and Mason (1987) describe how line managers involved in selection decision making may be driven by maintaining existing patterns of allegiance and dependency and follow their own informal decision agenda rather than that formally dictated within the organization. We can see how this would directly conflict with the implementation of a strategy of external recruitment, for example, designed to facilitate strategic change. Also, the selectors' own training and experience, or network of contacts within and external to the organization, may increase their power to shape the selection process over and above organizational or environmental contingencies (Sparrow, 1994).

In Conclusion

In this chapter we have discussed selection decision making from the perspective of the organization. First, we presented a typology of broad decision strategies, including implications for the choice of external or internal candidate selection, and a comparison of classic selection with classification. We then distinguished between several decision-making stages, where one of the critical issues to emerge was the use of judgmental versus statistical methods of combining information for selection. A recent meta-analysis by Grove et al. (2000) of 136 studies generally confirms the superiority of statistical data combination.

The chapter presented a multilevel model which proposes one way to systematize the many factors that can influence selection decisions. The micro level shows that selectors are affected by cognitive and affective processes which result in less straightforward decisions. At the meso level, several organizational variables either constrain selectors' decision making or provide strategic direction for an organization's selection practice. Finally, the wider macro context of selection concerns external forces which impact organizational selection and the societal consequences of selection decisions.

We have identified some of the relationships between types and stages of decision making which will be impacted by the micro, meso, and macro levels of the selection context, and also the possibilities of different theoretical interpretations for the process dynamics which lead us to conclude that selection decision making is a more complex process than simply defining environmental, organizational, and decision-maker conditions and decision options.

While we have illustrated the different effects of each level on the decision choices, and sometimes interactions between levels themselves, we have not postulated that any one of these levels will have a greater impact than the others. Although this is, of course, an issue of great importance, it remains a challenge for those concerned with understanding selection decision processes to determine whether this is answerable at all.

References

Anderson, N., Born, M. Ph., & Cunningham-Snell, N. (2001). Recruitment and selection: Applicant perspectives and outcomes. In N. Anderson, D. S. Ones, H. K. Senangil, & C. Viswesvaran (Eds.), *Handbook of industrial, work and organizational psychology: Vol. 1. Personnel psychology* (pp. 200–218). London: Sage.

Bamber, G. J., Park, F., Lee, C., Ross, P. K., & Broadbent, K. (Eds.). (2000). *Employment relations in the Asia Pacific: Changing approaches.* Sydney: Allen & Unwin/London: Thomson Learning.

Baron, R. A. (1987). Interviewer's mood and reaction to job applicants: The influence of affective states on applied social judgments. *Journal of Applied Social Psychology, 17,* 911–926.

Berger, P. L., & Luckmann, T. (1967). *The social construction of reality.* Harmondsworth, UK: Allan Lane.

Born, M. P., & Jansen P. G. W. (1997). Selection and assessment during organizational turnaround. In N. Anderson & P. Herriot (Eds.), *International handbook of selection and assessment* (pp. 247–265). Chichester, UK: Wiley.

Boudreau, J. W. (1991). Utility analysis for decision in human resource management. In M. D. Dunnette & L. M. Hough (Eds.), *Handbook of industrial and organizational psychology* (2nd ed., Vol. 2, pp. 621–745). Palo Alto, CA: Consulting Psychologists Press.

Boudreau, J. W., & Ramstad, P. M. (2003). Strategic I/O psychology and the role of utility analysis models. In W. C. Borman, D. R. Ilgen, & R. J. Klimoski (Eds.), *Handbook of psychology: Vol. 12, Industrial and organizational psychology* (pp. 193–221). New York: Wiley.

Boudreau, J. W., Sturman, M. C., & Judge, T. A. (1994). Utility analysis: What are the black boxes and do they affect decisions? In N. Anderson & P. Herriot (Eds.), *Assessment and selection in organizations: Methods and practice for recruitment and appraisal* (pp. 77–96). New York: Wiley.

Brogden, H. E. (1949). When testing pays off. *Personnel Psychology, 2,* 171–183.

Brogden, H. E. (1955). Least squares estimates and optimal classification. *Psychometrika, 20,* 249–252.

Brown, B. K., & Campion, M. A. (1994). Biodata phenomenology: Recruiters' perceptions and use of biographical information in resume screening. *Journal of Applied Psychology, 79,* 897–908.

Cabrera, E. F., & Raju, N. S. (2001). Utility analysis: Current trends and future directions. *International Journal of Selection and Assessment, 9,* 1–11.

Campbell, J. P. (2001). Matching people and jobs: An introduction to twelve years of R & D. In J. P. Campbell & D. J. Knapp (Eds.), *Exploring the limits in personnel selection and classification* (pp. 3–20). Mahwah, NJ: Lawrence Erlbaum.

Campbell, J. P., & Knapp, D. J. (Eds.). (2001). *Exploring the limits in personnel selection and classification.* Mahwah, NJ: Lawrence Erlbaum.

Carlson, K. D., & Connerley, M. L. (2003). The staffing cycles framework: Viewing staffing as a system of decision events. *Journal of Management, 29,* 51–78.

Cascio, W. F. (1998). *Applied psychology in human resource management* (5th ed.). Upper Saddle River, NJ: Prentice Hall.

Cochrane, R. E., Tett, R. P., & Vandecreek, L. (2003). Psychological testing and the selection of police officers: A national survey. *Criminal Justice and Behavior, 30*, 511–537.

Cohen, Y., & Pfeffer, J. (1986). Organizational hiring standards. *Administrative Science Quarterly, 31*, 1–24.

Cooper, D., Robertson, I. T., & Tinline, G. (2003). *Recruitment and selection. A framework for success.* London: Thomson Learning.

Cronbach, L. J., & Gleser, G. C. (1965). *Psychological tests and personnel decisions* (2nd ed.). Urbana, IL: University of Illinois Press.

Dachler, H. P. (1989). Selection and the organizational context. In P. Herriot (Ed.), *Assessment and selection in organizations: Methods and practice for recruitment and appraisal* (pp. 45–70). London: John Wiley.

Dachler, H. P., & Hosking, D. (1995). The primacy of relations in socially constructing organizational realities. In D. M. Hosking, H. P. Dachler, & K. J. Gergen (Eds.), *Management and organization: Relational alternatives to individualism* (pp. 1–28). London: John Wiley.

Daft, R. L., & Weick, K. E. (1984). Toward a model of organizations as interpretation systems. *Academy of Management Review, 9*, 284–295.

De Corte, W. (1994). Utility analysis for the one-cohort selection-retention decision with a probationary period. *Journal of Applied Psychology, 79*, 402–411.

De Corte, W. (1999). A note on the success ratio and the utility of fixed hiring rate personnel selection decisions. *Journal of Applied Psychology, 84*, 952–958.

De Corte, W. (2000). Estimating the classification efficiency of a test battery. *Educational and Psychological Measurement, 60*, 73–85.

De Corte, W. (2002). Sampling variability of the success ratio in predictor-based selection. *British Journal of Mathematical and Statistical Psychology, 55*, 93–107.

De Corte, W., & Lievens, F. A. (2003). A practical procedure to estimate the quality and the adverse impact of single stage selection decisions. *International Journal of Selection and Assessment, 11*, 89–97.

Delery, J. E., & Doty, D. H. (1996). Modes of theorizing in strategic human resource management: Tests of universalistic, contingency, and configurational performance predictions. *Academy of Management Journal, 39*, 802–835.

Dose, J. J. (2003). Information exchange in personnel selection decisions. *Applied Psychology: An International Review, 52*, 237–252.

Garb, H. N. (1989). Clinical judgment, clinical training, and professional experience. *Psychological Bulletin, 105*, 387–396.

Grant, R. M. (1991). The resource-based theory of competitive advantage: Implications for strategy formulation. *California Management Review, 33*, 112–135.

Grove, W. M., Zald, D. H., Lebow, B. S., Snitz, B. E., & Nelson, C. (2000). Clinical versus mechanical prediction: A meta-analysis. *Psychological Assessment, 12*, 19–30.

Guest, D. (1990). Human resource management and the American dream. *Journal of Management Studies, 27*, 377–397.

Guion, R. M. (1998). *Assessment, measurement, and prediction for personnel decisions.* Mahwah, NJ: Lawrence Erlbaum.

Hantula, D. A., & DeNicolis Bragger, J. L. (1999). The effects of equivocality on escalation of commitment: An empirical investigation of decision dilemma theory. *Journal of Applied Social Psychology, 29*, 424–444.

Herriot, P. (1989). Selection as a social process. In M. Smith & I. T. Robertson (Eds.), *Advances in selection and assessment* (pp. 171–178). Chichester, UK: Wiley.

Highhouse, S. (2002). Assessing the candidate as a whole: A historical and critical analysis of individual psychological assessment for personnel decision making. *Personnel Psychology, 55*, 363–396.

Hodgkinson, G. P., & Payne, R. L. (1998). Graduate selection in three European countries. *Journal of Occupational and Organizational Psychology, 71*, 359–365.

Hollway, W. (1991). *Work psychology and organisational behaviour.* London: Sage.

Horst, P. (1954). A technique for the development of a differential predictor battery. *Psychometrika, 68,* Whole No. 380.

Hutchinson, K. I., & Brefka, D. S. (1997). Personnel administrators' preferences for resume content: Ten years after. *Business Communication Quarterly, 60,* 67–75.

Iles, P. (1999). *Managing staff assessment and selection.* Buckingham, UK: Open University Press.

Iles, P., & Salaman, G. (1995). Recruitment, selection and assessment. In J. Storey (Ed.), *Human resource management. A critical text* (pp. 203–234). London: Routledge.

Ilgen, D. R. (1994). Jobs and roles: Accepting and coping with the changing structure of organizations. In M. G. Rumsey, C. B. Walker, & J. H. Harris (Eds.), *Personnel selection and classification: New directions* (pp. 13–22). Hillsdale, NJ: Erlbaum.

IRS Management Review. (July 1998). *The evolving HR function.* Issue 10.

Jackson, S. E., Schuler, R. S., & Rivero, J. C. (1989). Organizational characteristics as predictors of personnel practices. *Personnel Psychology, 42,* 727–786.

Jayne, M. E. A., & Rauschenberger, J. M. (2000). Demonstrating the value of selection in organizations. In J. F. Kehoe (Ed.), *Managing selection in changing organizations* (pp. 123–157). San Francisco: Jossey-Bass.

Jewson, N., & Mason, D. (1986). Modes of discrimination in the recruitment process: Formalisation, fairness and efficiency. *Sociology, 20,* 43–63.

Johns, G. (1993). Constraints on the adoption of psychology-based personnel practices: Lessons from organizational innovation. *Personnel Psychology, 46,* 569–592.

Judge, T. A., & Ferris, G. R. (1992). The elusive criterion of fit in human staffing decisions. *Human Resource Planning, 15,* 47–68.

Kahneman, D., & Tversky, A. (1982). Variants of uncertainty. In D. Kahneman, P. Slovic, & A. Tversky (Eds.), *Judgments under uncertainty: Heuristics and biases* (pp. 414–421). New York: Cambridge University Press.

Kolk, N. J., Born, M. Ph., & Van der Flier, H. (2002). Assessment center rating procedures: Cognitive load during the observation phase. *International Journal of Selection and Assessment, 10,* 271–278.

Kunda, Z. (1999). *Social cognition: Making sense of people.* Cambridge, MA: The MIT Press.

Lowry, P. E. (1996). A survey of the assessment center process in the public sector. *Public Personnel Management, 25,* 307–321.

Luthans, F. (2005). *Organizational behavior* (10th ed.). New York: McGraw-Hill/Irwin.

McKinney, A. P., Carlson, K. D., Mecham, R. L., III, D'Angelo, N. C., & Connerley, M. L. (2003). Recruiters' use of GPA in initial screening decisions: Higher GPAs don't always make the cut. *Personnel Psychology, 56,* 823–845.

Meehl, P. E. (1954). *Clinical vs. statistical prediction: A theoretical analysis and a review of the evidence.* Minneapolis, MN: University of Minnesota Press.

Miles, R. E., & Snow, C. C. (1984). Designing strategic human resources systems. *Organizational Dynamics, 16,* 36–52.

Motowidlo, S. J., & Van Scotter, J. R. (1994). Evidence that task performance should be distinguished from contextual performance. *Journal of Applied Psychology, 79,* 475–480.

Murphy, K. R. (1994). Toward a broader conception of jobs and job performance: Impact of changes in the military environment on the structure, assessment and prediction of job performance. In M. G. Rumsey, C. B. Walker, & J. H. Harris (Eds.), *Personnel selection and classification: New directions* (pp. 85–102). Hillsdale, NJ: Erlbaum.

Murphy, K. R. (1996). Individual differences and behavior in organizations: Much more than g. In K. R. Murphy (Eds.), *Individual differences and behavior in organizations* (pp. 3–30). San Francisco: Jossey-Bass.

Murphy, K. R., & Davidshofer, C. O. (2001). *Psychological testing: Principles and applications* (5th ed.). Upper Saddle River, NJ: Prentice Hall.

Myors, B., Carstairs, J. R., & Todorov, N. (2002). Accuracy of percentile judgments used in the utility analysis of personnel selection procedures. *Australian Journal of Psychology*, *54*, 1–7.

Naylor, J. C., & Shine, L. C. (1965). A table for determining the increase in mean criterion score obtained by using a selection device. *Journal of Industrial Psychology*, *3*, 33–42.

Olian, J. D., & Rynes, S. L. (1984). Organizational staffing: Integrating practice and strategy. *Industrial Relations*, *23*, 170–118.

Payne, J. W., Bettman, J. R., & Johnson, E. J. (1993). *The adaptive decision maker*. Cambridge, UK: Cambridge University Press.

Pearlman, K., & Barney, M. F. (2000). Selection for a changing workplace. In J. Kehoe (Ed.), *Managing selection in changing organizations* (pp. 3–72). San Francisco: Jossey-Bass.

Pearn, M. (1993). Fairness in selection and assessment: A European perspective. In H. Schuler, J. L. Farr, & M. Smith (Eds.), *Personnel selection and assessment: Individual and organisational perspectives* (pp. 205–220). Hillsdale, NJ: Erlbaum.

Pfeffer, J. (1994). *Competitive advantage through people*. Harvard, MA: Harvard Business School.

Ployhart, R. E., & Schneider, B. (2002). A multilevel perspective on personnel selection: Implications for selection system design, assessment, and construct validation. In F. J. Yammarino, & F. Dansereau (Eds.), *Research in multi-level issues. The many faces of multi-level issues* (Vol. 1, pp. 95–140). Oxford, UK: Elsevier Science.

Porter, M. E. (1980). *Competitive strategy*. New York: Free Press.

Ramsay, H., & Scholarios, D. (1999). Selective decisions: Challenging orthodox analyses of the hiring process. *International Journal of Management Reviews*, *1*, 63–89.

Ree, M. J., Earles, J. A., & Teachout, M. S. (1994). Predicting job performance: Not much more than g. *Journal of Applied Psychology*, *79*, 518–524.

Robertson, I. T., & Smith, M. (2001). Personnel selection. *Journal of Occupational and Organizational Psychology*, *74*, 441–472.

Roe, R. A., & van den Berg, P. T. (2003). Selection in Europe: Contexts, developments and research agenda. *European Journal of Work and Organizational Psychology*, *12*, 257–287.

Rousseau, D. M., & Tinsley, C. (1997). Human resources are local. In N. Anderson & P. Herriot (Eds.), *International handbook of selection and assessment* (pp. 39–61). Chichester, UK: Wiley.

Ruderman, M. N., & Ohlott, P. J. (1990). *Traps and pitfalls in the judgment of executive potential* (Rep. No. 141). Greensboro, NC: Center for Creative Leadership.

Rumsey, M. G., Walker, C. B., & Harris, J. H. (Eds.). (1994). *Personnel selection and classification*. Hillsdale, NJ: Lawrence Erlbaum.

Ryan, A. M., McFarland, L., Baron, H., & Page, R. (1999). An international look at selection practices: Nation and culture as explanations for variability in practice. *Personnel Psychology*, *52*, 359–391.

Rynes, S., Orlitzky, M. O., & Bretz, R. D., Jr. (1997). Experienced hiring versus college recruiting: Practices and emerging trends. *Personnel Psychology*, *50*, 707–721.

Sackett, P. R., & Ellingson, J. E. (1997). The effects of forming multi-predictor composites on group differences and adverse impact. *Personnel Psychology*, *50*, 707–721.

Salgado, J. F., Viswesvaran, C., & Ones, D. S. (2001). Predictors used for personnel selection: An overview of constructs, methods and techniques. In N. Anderson, D. S. Ones, H. K. Sinangil, & C. Viswesvaran (Eds.), *Handbook of industrial, work and organizational psychology: Vol. 1. Personnel psychology* (pp. 165–199). London: Sage.

Schmidt, F. L., & Hunter, J. E. (1998). The validity and utility of selection methods in personnel psychology: Practical and theoretical implications of 85 years of research findings. *Psychological Bulletin*, *124*, 262–274.

Schmidt, F. L., Hunter, J. E., McKenzie, R. C., & Muldrow, T. W. (1979). Impact of valid selection procedures on work-force productivity. *Journal of Applied Psychology*, *64*, 609–626.

Schmitt, N., & Borman, W. (Eds.). (1993). *Personnel selection in organizations*. San Francisco: Jossey-Bass.

Schmitt, N., Clause, C. S., & Pulakos, E. D. (1996). Subgroup differences associated with different measures of some common job relevant constructs. In C. L. Cooper & I. T. Robertson (Eds.), *International review of industrial and organizational psychology* (pp. 115–140). New York: Wiley.

Schneider, B., Kristof-Brown, A. L., Goldstein, H. W., & Smith, D. B. (1997). What is this thing called fit? In N. Anderson & P. Herriot, (Eds.), *International handbook of selection and assessment* (pp. 393–412). Chichester, UK: Wiley.

Scholarios, D., Johnson, C. D., & Zeidner, J. (1994). Selecting predictors for maximizing the classification efficiency of a battery. *Journal of Applied Psychology, 79*, 412–424.

Sessa, V. I. (2001). Executive promotion and selection. In M. London (Ed.), *How people evaluate others in organizations* (pp. 91–110). Mahwah, NJ: Lawrence Erlbaum.

Shafir, E. (1993). Choosing versus rejecting: Why some options are both better and worse than others. *Memory and Cognition, 21*, 546–556.

Shields, J., Hanser, L. M., & Campbell, J. P. (2001). A paradigm shift. In J. P. Campbell & D. J. Knapp (Eds.), *Exploring the limits in personnel selection and classification* (pp. 21–30). Mahwah, NJ: Lawrence Erlbaum.

Simon, H. A. (1957). *Administrative Behavior* (2nd ed.). New York: Macmillan.

Snow, C. C., & Snell, S. A. (1993). Staffing as strategy. In N. Schmitt & W. C. Borman (Eds.), *Personnel selection in organizations* (pp. 448–478). San Francisco: Jossey-Bass.

Sonnenfeld, J. A., & Peiperl, M. A. (1988). Staffing policy as a strategic response: A typology of career systems. *Academy of Management Review, 13*, 588–600.

Sparrow, P., & Hilltrop, J. (1994). *European human resource management in transition*. Hemel Hempstead, UK: Prentice Hall.

Sparrow, P. R. (1994). The psychology of strategic management: Emerging themes of diversity and cognition. In C. L. Cooper & I. T. Robertson (Eds.), *International review of industrial and orgnanizational psychology* (pp. 147–181). Chichester, UK: John Wiley.

Sparrow, P. R. (1997). organizational competencies. Creating a strategic behavioural framework for selection and assessment. In N. Anderson & P. Herriot (Eds.), *International handbook of selection and assessment* (pp. 343–368). Chichester, UK: John Wiley.

Spender, J. C. (1989). *Industry recipes: The nature and sources of managerial judgement*. Oxford, UK: Basil Blackwell.

Staw, B. M., & Ross, J. (1989). Understanding behavior in escalation situations. *Science, 200*, 216–220.

Stevenson, M. K., Busemeyer, J. R., & Naylor, J. C. (1990). Judgment and decision-making theory. In M. D. Dunnette & L. M. Hough (Eds.), *Handbook of industrial and organizational psychology* (2nd ed., Vol. 1, pp. 283–374). Palo Alto, CA: Consulting Psychologists.

Storey, J. (1992). *Developments in the management of human resources*. Oxford, UK: Blackwell.

Storey, J. (1995). Human resource management: Still marching on, or marching out? In J. Storey (Ed.), *Human resource management. A critical text* (pp. 3–32). London: Routledge.

Taylor, H. C., & Russell, J. T. (1939). The relationship of validity coefficients to the practical effectiveness of tests in selection. *Journal of Applied Psychology, 23*, 565–578.

Terpstra, D. E. & Rozell, E. J. (1993). The relationship of staffing practices to organizational level measures of performance. *Personnel Psychology, 46*, 27–48.

Terpstra, D. E., & Rozell, E. J. (1997). Why some potentially effective staffing practices are seldom used. *Public Personnel Management, 26*, 483–495.

Tetlock, P. E. (1985). Accountability: The neglected social context of judgment and choice. In L. L. Cummings & B. M. Staw (Eds.), *Research in organizational behavior, 7* (pp. 297–332). Greenwich, CT: JAI Press.

Tetlock, P. E., & Boettger, R. (1989). Accountability: A social magnifier of the dilution effect. *Journal of Personality and Social Psychology, 57*, 388–398.

Tetlock, P. E., & Kim, J. I. (1987). Accountability and judgment processes in a personality prediction task. *Journal of Personality and Social Psychology, 52*, 700–709.

Thompson, J. D. (1967). *Organizations in action: Social science bases of administrative theory.* New York: McGraw-Hill.

Thoms, P., McMasters, R., Roberts, M. R., & Dombkowski, D. A. (1999). Resume characteristics as predictors of an invitation to interview. *Journal of Business and Psychology, 13*, 339–356.

Torrington, D. (1994). *International human resource management: Think globally, act locally.* Hemel Hempstead, UK: Prentice Hall International.

Tversky, A., & Kahneman, D. (1974). Judgment under uncertainty: Heuristics and biases. *Science, 185*, 1124–1131.

Van Dam, K. (2003). Trait perception in the employment interview: A five factor model perspective. *International Journal of Selection and Assessment, 11*, 43–55.

Whetzel, D. L., & Wheaton, G. R. (1997). *Applied measurement methods in industrial psychology.* Palo Alto, CA: Davies-Black.

Williams, A. P. O., & Dobson, P. (1997). Personnel selection and corporate strategy. In N. Anderson & P. Herriot (Eds.), *International handbook of selection and assessment* (pp. 219–245). Chichester, UK: John Wiley.

Zeidner, J., Johnson, C., & Scholarios, D. (2001). Matching people to jobs: New classification techniques for improving decision making. *Kybernetes, 30*, 984–1005.

13

Relevance and Rigor in Research on the Applicant's Perspective: In Pursuit of Pragmatic Science

ANNA L. IMUS AND ANN MARIE RYAN

In the past several years, there have been a number of reviews of the burgeoning applicant reactions literature (Chambers, 2002; Chan & Schmitt, 2004; Hausknecht, Day, & Thomas, in press; Ryan & Ployhart, 2000; Rynes, 1991, 1993; Schmitt & Chan, 1999; Steiner & Gilliland, 2001; Truxillo, Steiner, & Gilliland, 2004). This area of research focuses on the perceptions applicants hold of employee selection procedures, and the antecedents and consequences of those perceptions. Given the status of research on the applicant's perspective and the existence of several comprehensive qualitative and quantitative reviews, our aim in this chapter is not to provide yet another retrospection on what has occurred. Rather, we take these wide-ranging reviews as the starting point for identifying the key conclusions and research needs in the field. We caution that the objective of this chapter is not to serve as an all-inclusive detailing of applicant perspective studies, but to function as a launch pad for continued research in the domain. From this vantage point, our aim is to provide a more macro-level critique of the research endeavor: Based on the conclusions of these reviews, what can be said about the quality and usefulness of research on the applicant perspective?

We begin to address this question with a general summary of the research reviews – what has been found and what is lacking. Following from this, we highlight key issues from the reviews regarding research rigor and relevance, and indicate what we perceive as needed directions for future research.

SUMMARY OF SUMMARIES

The premise of research on applicant perceptions of the hiring process has been that applicants form judgments of the selection processes and procedures and these perceptions affect how the applicant views the organization, intentions to join the organization, performance in the process, and subsequent behaviors (Ryan & Ployhart, 2000). By gaining insight into when and why applicants form more or less positive impressions of the hiring process, we gain the ability to potentially influence these perceptions and related applicant attitudes and behaviors.

As noted, there have been at least a dozen reviews and chapters that have targeted the literature on applicant perspectives. Seminal book chapters and articles (Gilliland, 1993; Rynes, 1993; Schuler, 1993; Smither, Reilly, Millsap, Pearlman, & Stoffey, 1993) that appeared in the early 1990s all drew attention to how the selection process itself was something job candidates evaluate. One of the most influential pieces has been Gilliland's application of organizational justice to the selection context (1993). Gilliland asserted that factors such as the extent to which a test appears to be job-related or the type of test that is used in the selection procedure can lead an applicant to judgments regarding procedural justice or the fairness of the process. Perceptions of distributive justice arise based on the fairness of decisions made by the organization such as who was hired, as well as the outcome of tests used during the hiring process. Gilliland proposed that perceptions of fairness can lead to the decision to accept or refute a job offer, satisfaction on the job, and self-perceptions. Numerous studies in the applicant reactions area have been derived from Gilliland's treatment of organizational justice theory in the selection context (e.g., Bauer et al., 2001; Gilliland, 1994; Ployhart & Ryan, 1998; Truxillo, Bauer, Campion, & Paronto, 2002). Thus, the predominant framework in the area has been a justice one.

A second early direction in the applicant perspective literature related to how test-taking attitudes influenced performance. Early key pieces measuring perceptions included Arvey, Strickland, Drauden, and Martin's (1990) conceptualization of test-taker attitudes which has been frequently examined in studies of test-taker anxiety and motivation. A number of subsequent studies examined how test-taking attitudes affected performance (e.g., Chan, 1997; Chan, Schmitt, DeShon, Clause, & Delbridge, 1997). Thus, a second stream of applicant perceptions research lies outside of the focus on fairness as the focal interest and instead has concerned itself with how applicant perceptions influence performance in the selection process.

Since the seminal theory and measurement pieces in the early 1990s, there have been many studies of specific antecedents and consequences of applicant reactions. The current literature affirms that applicants do in fact come to the hiring process with certain expectations and beliefs about what should occur (e.g., Ployhart & Ryan, 1998) and that the content of selection procedures can interact with these perceptions to influence the way applicants react (see Ryan & Ployhart's 2000 review for a detailed description of findings). While few behavioral outcomes have been studied, perceptions of the hiring process have been linked to organizational attractiveness (e.g., Bauer, Maertz, Dolen, & Campion, 1998; Saks, Leck, & Saunders, 1995) and behavioral intentions (e.g., Ployhart & Ryan, 1998; Truxillo et al., 2002). Furthermore, individual differences such as motivation and anxiety influence performance on selection tests (e.g., Arvey et al., 1990; Chan et al., 1997). We provide a summation of the overarching findings from the literature in Table 13.1.

However, the many reviews of the applicant perspective literature all suggest that we cannot be very conclusive about the relative influence of various applicant perceptions. The short and global nature of the list in Table 13.1 follows from the tone of the reviews – despite the growing proliferation of studies, evidence regarding key antecedents and consequences of applicant perceptions is often equivocal. Each review has also produced some summary of the knowledge gaps and research limitations. Table 13.2 provides a summary of the major suggestions for improvement in the research in five areas. First, the quality,

TABLE 13.1   Key findings from applicant perspective research

Applicants bring expectations and beliefs to the selection context, i.e., perceptions are not just
   formed based on what occurs but on prior experiences and knowledge.
The content of selection procedures influences applicant reactions.
Perceptions of process fairness relate to organizational attractiveness and satisfaction with the
   hiring process and intentions; equivocal results exist with hard outcomes (i.e., behaviors).
Applicant perceptions of the selection process relate to their performance in the process, with the
   evidence supporting a self-serving bias in reactions.
Effects of specific person characteristics (demographics, personality) on applicant perceptions
   appear to be weak or non-existent.
Applicant motivation and anxiety can affect performance.

TABLE 13.2   Research needs indicated in reviews of applicant perspective research

Improve measure quality, specificity and focus	Improve the quality of measures of applicant perceptions.
	Provide for analysis of applicant perceptions within the context of job and organizational characteristics.
	Cover the entire recruitment and selection process, not just one step/component.
	Conduct studies that provide a better understanding of which justice rules are most critical and how and when they affect applicant perceptions and behavior.
Consider time of measurement	Use pre-measures to evaluate applicant perceptions and intentions prior to experiencing the selection process.
	Conduct longitudinal studies that evaluate changes in perceptions over time.
Study behaviors	Focus on a broader set of outcomes such as organizational success, post-hire attitudes, psychological well-being; in particular examine actual applicant behavior.
Use alternative designs	Conduct more experimental and intervention/quasi-experimental research.
Improve theory	Conduct studies involving a more expansive coverage of justice theory elements.
	Consider alternative theoretical perspectives to understanding applicant perceptions, such as attribution theory or psychological contract theory.

specificity, and focus of measurement need to be improved. Second, researchers should
consider the timing of the measurement. Third, research has looked at behavioral intentions, but actual behaviors are understudied. Fourth, alternative research designs should
be adopted. Fifth, new theories should be developed and tested. Each of these will be discussed in detail in subsequent sections of the chapter.

Although Table 13.2 indicates room for improvement, our guess is that most readers of
the applicant perspective literature would see this research as both rigorous and relevant.

Work is being published in top-tier journals, thus meeting standards for quality, and attending to applicant perceptions is easily argued as a relevant topic for organizations. In this chapter, we would like to provide a more critical examination of how well applicant perceptions research fares on these dimensions. After discussing a framework for this analysis, we highlight specific ways in which this domain of research could be enhanced in terms of rigor and relevance.

In the initial chapter in this volume, Anderson discusses a model of research relevance and rigor that may be applied to evaluating this research. Within the applicant perspective research field, we define relevance to equate to meaningfulness in terms of a) conceptual contributions to the knowledge base, b) practical usefulness for applicants, selection system designers, administrators, and hiring managers and c) leading to improvements to hiring processes from the applicant's perspective. Rigor can be evaluated against the traditional conceptions of research quality such as whether designs permit causal inferences, whether alternative explanations for results are adequately ruled out, the quality of construct specification and adequacy of measurement, and the appropriateness of research samples and settings. We review the current state of applicant perspective research in terms of these two dimensions, addressing the broader questions of whether the body of research represents pragmatic science, and how to better avoid building a literature that is either popularist or pedantic.

Rigor in Applicant Perspective Research

Given the competitive nature of the publishing process in top-tier IWO journals, one could say that researchers are forced to conduct research in a rigorous manner. Despite the fact that the publishing process does weed out less rigorous research, our review of the reviews has identified concerns regarding the rigor of applicant perceptions research. In this section, we provide a brief synopsis of the methodological challenges faced by applicant perspective researchers that have been noted in these reviews and how they may be effectively addressed.

Measure quality, specificity, and focus.   As indicated in Table 13.2, several of the reviews called for improvement in the quality of measures of applicant perceptions. As is true early on in many research areas, initial studies on applicant perceptions employed a wide variety of measures. To some extent, strides are being made in this area. Published studies of scale development include Bauer et al.'s (2001) measure of selection fairness perceptions, Colquitt's (2001) measures of organizational justice, Sanchez, Truxillo, and Bauer's (2000) measure of applicant motivation, and Derous, Born, and DeWitte's (2004) measure of selection treatment beliefs. As these more systematically developed measures gain wider usage, greater confidence may be placed in the findings of studies employing them.

However, there are still a number of ways to improve the construct validity of the research in this domain. Chan and Schmitt (2004) recently called for a construct-oriented approach to applicant reactions research, suggesting greater clarity regarding the specificity of measures in both level of evaluation and domain evaluated (e.g., whether applicable to a single justice rule or a global evaluation of fairness; whether addressing a specific test or a test type category) as a means to developing better predictive hypotheses. For example, looking across studies, one can see process fairness perceptions operationalized in terms of specific procedural elements (e.g., The treatment I received by selection system administrators was fair), overall processes (e.g., Overall, this was a fair process), the content of the selection system (e.g., The methods used to hire me were fair), a specific category of tests (e.g., Personality testing is fair) or a specific test (i.e., This test was fair). These different questions may yield different conclusions for the same context. Further, Ryan and Ployhart (2000) noted that all procedures of the same type (e.g., personality measures) are not interchangeable and applicants react differently to them. As Chan and Schmitt (2004) note, not only does this lack of consistency hinder the ability to accumulate research findings, but a lack of specificity likely limits appropriate matches between predictors and criteria that lead to finding relationships.

We would add one other angle to Chan and Schmitt's (2004) discussion of measure specificity. For many practitioners, there may be perceptions unique to a given selection context. For example, a multiple hurdle context might involve assessing perceptions of the placement of hurdles. A selection process that combines pass/fail with rank-ordering on predictors might necessitate questions regarding perceptions of scoring. Furthermore, a technological context such as using a video-testing procedure calls for questions regarding applicants' perceptions of how items are reviewed. That is, the key drivers of applicant reactions in a given selection context may not be the universally studied or more global perceptions. In their review, Ryan and Ployhart (2000) noted that context in terms of type of job, organizational factors, information provided to applicants, and the other procedures in the process all influenced applicant perceptions of a given procedure, suggesting that greater specificity is needed for research to be appropriately generalizable. Also, as we will note in our discussion of relevance, the practical value of information on process fairness, for example, lies in its being specific enough to be actionable (i.e., what is it about the process that applicants found unfair).

While research fields benefit immeasurably when well-developed, validated measures of constructs become common (e.g., organizational commitment, job satisfaction literatures), one must recognize that because the phenomenon of interest here is *reactions* to a selection process, measures may need to vary so as to consider the nature of the process more specifically. Note that this does not serve as a justification for using psychometrically unsound measures, but is a recognition that tackling research questions in one setting may require different measures of perceptions than in another setting. Less of an argument can be made for the need for unique measures of global evaluations (e.g., overall fairness), of preexisting beliefs or expectations, and of outcomes (e.g., attractiveness of the organization); therefore, the more recent development of sound measures of these concepts should aid research.

Understanding perceptions of applicant reactions necessitates the use of self-report measures. With the use of such measures, researchers must be cautious of how results are interpreted due to variance that may be a result of error associated with the measurement method rather than relationships represented by the measures (Podsakoff, MacKenzie, Lee, & Podsakoff, 2003). Podsakoff et al. caution that common method variance can come from single source data collection, the actual measurement items, the context of the items within a measure, and/or the context in which the measures are administered. Greater attention to these issues in applicant perspective research is warranted, given the need to rely on self-reports for many of the constructs of interest. Also, Podsakoff et al. recommend including measures of affectivity and/or social desirability so that constructs that may lead to similar patterns in responses across measures can be controlled for. It seems likely that both of these constructs may affect applicant responding to perception measures (i.e., applicants seeking a job will be motivated by socially desirable responding; individuals who receive negative feedback may report perceptions influenced by trait affectivity) and research evaluating their role is needed.

One other point regarding the focus of measurement deserves exposition. Truxillo et al. (2004) suggested that we direct our research focus to studying when treatment is unfair, rather than relative comparisons of when processes are "less" fair than others. That is, justice research has supported that injustice has more of an influence on outcomes than justice, and there may be thresholds when individuals will act on unfairness. For example, failing to follow up with an applicant's interview after one week may be perceived as less fair than a day or two, but it would not necessarily lead an individual to feel the selection process was "unfair." The implication for measurement and analysis is that we may need to refocus our measures from assessing relative fairness to differentiating "unjust" from "fair enough."

Time of measurement.   A number of reviews note the need for pretest measures and longitudinal studies (e.g., Rynes, 1993) as many of the existing studies on applicant perceptions do not consider that perceptions are dynamic and may change as the applicant interacts with the organization. Here again, we are seeing advances as more studies incorporate pre-measures and more longitudinal studies are appearing (Lam & Reeve, 2004; Truxillo et al., 2002; Van Vianen, Taris, Scholten, & Schinkel, 2004). Because applicants come to selection settings with beliefs regarding processes, tools, and expectations regarding what will occur (Bell, Ryan, & Wiechmann, 2004; Derous et al., 2004), our knowledge of applicant perceptions will remain limited if we cannot place those perceptions in the context of what occurs before the process itself. Hausknecht et al. (in press) demonstrated that correlations between perceptions measured at the same point in time (e.g., justice perceptions and organizational attractiveness) were much higher than when measured at separate points in time, suggesting the importance of understanding method variance as a potential source of inflated relationships. Further, evidence regarding how feedback affects perceptions (Schinkel, Van Dierendonck, & Anderson, 2004) suggests that some connections to intentions and behavior cannot be meaningfully studied prior to applicants learning the outcome of the process (exceptions would be application and withdrawal intentions and behavior). Thus, studies that inappropriately treat applicant perceptions as static and/or studies that fail to consider preexisting views lead to puerile science.

One last point regarding examinations of applicant views over time is a recognition of what change indicates. Chan and Schmitt (2004) argued that change can be in the magnitude of a perception (e.g., I become less motivated to obtain the job), but may also be a beta or gamma change, such as developing more or less differentiated reactions over time (e.g., at first not distinguishing consistency of processes from interpersonal treatment, but after several selection hurdles, making the distinction). A more sophisticated view of applicant perceptions that considers change in meaning and interrelationships of perceptions instead of just in level is called for.

Post-decision behaviors/attitudes. A number of review articles have noted that few studies measure actual applicant behavior (e.g., Chambers, 2002; Ryan & Ployhart, 2000). In their meta-analysis, Hausknecht et al. (in press) did not locate sufficient studies on any applicant behavior other than performance to conduct a meta-analysis, nor did they find sufficient research available on post-hire attitudes such as organizational commitment. Truxillo et al. (2004) noted that findings that do exist relating fairness perceptions and "hard" or behavioral outcomes have been ambiguous. While the lack of research on behavioral outcomes calls into question the rigor of the research, the equivocal findings that do exist call into question the relevance.

We feel that the applicant perception literature runs the risk of being categorized as much ado about little variance. In an earlier review (Ryan & Ployhart, 2000), one of us suggested that perhaps we have not sufficiently established that applicant perceptions matter. Recent summaries (e.g., Hausknecht et al., in press) suggest that they *do* relate to other attitudes and intentions; meta-analyses on test-taker perceptions such as anxiety clearly show connections to performance (e.g., Hembree, 1988; Seipp, 1991). However, much work needs to be done connecting applicant perceptions of selection processes to both pre- and post-hire behavioral criteria that are of interest to organizational decision makers (e.g., job acceptance decisions).

Lest this sound overly pessimistic, how applicant perceptions of the hiring process can affect post-hire behavior and attitudes has been addressed in some specific areas. For example, Heilman and her colleagues (e.g., Heilman & Alcott, 2001; Heilman, Kaplow, Amato, & Stathatos, 1993; Heilman, McCullough, & Gilbert, 1996) have focused their attention on how individuals who perceive they have benefited from unfair hiring procedures react post-hire. Collectively, they have found that beneficiaries are more susceptible to feeling the stigma of incompetence, demonstrate performance-limiting task decisions, and have negative self-regard toward their task ability levels. Other examples of post-decision behavioral studies are Juhasz and Mishken's (2004) examination of appeals of rejection decisions and Gilliland's (1994) study of job performance.

Truxillo et al. (2004) argue that a narrowly defined set of outcomes in terms of post-process behaviors and attitudes should be the focus of our study, rather than global evaluations of the organization. That is, the choice of post-decision outcomes to study should be based on a thoughtful matching of predictors and criteria (Chan & Schmitt, 2004) rather than an attempt to "prove" the value of applicant perceptions by attempting to link them with criteria traditionally studied in other areas of organizational research (e.g., job performance). We would urge applicant perspective researchers to focus more heavily on pre-hire behaviors and outcomes (e.g., decisions to apply; decisions to accept offers; selection system performance).

The value of alternative designs. Many of the studies on applicant reactions are non-experimental in nature. While a number of the reviews note the clear importance of examining reactions in actual selection contexts (e.g., Hausknecht et al., in press), the limitations of correlational research also need to be acknowledged (Chan & Schmitt, 2004; Ryan & Ployhart, 2000). Without experimental manipulation of features of selection processes, the inference of causality between procedures and applicant perceptions may be unjustified. For example, organizational attraction is often studied as an outcome of applicant perceptions but could just as easily be an antecedent of perceptions (Ryan & Ployhart, 2000). Further, because justice rules tend to covary in reality, it is difficult to tease apart whether a change in one aspect (e.g., two-way communication) might have an effect separate from a change in some other aspect (e.g., opportunity to perform). Truxillo et al. (2004) echo this concern regarding an over-reliance on correlational designs and call for the greater use of intervention designs.

However, a movement away from correlation research to more rigorous designs should not be accompanied by a loss of context or the research will become pedantic. Hausknecht et al. (in press) found considerable differences between magnitudes of relationships found in authentic versus simulated selection settings, although there was no consistent pattern as to which setting produced stronger effects. Thus, care must be taken in interpreting the generalizability of simulated setting research.

Relevance and Applicant Perspective Research

Every article and review piece of applicant perceptions provides a statement, and in many cases a litany, of reasons why the topic is relevant to organizations and individuals. Anderson (2004) noted that it is curious that for decades selection researchers hardly focused at all on the applicant's perspective, given how relevant it appears. While writers can speculate as to why research evolved in the manner it did, the relevance of examining the applicant's perspective seems unassailable. We take no issue with the relevance of the topic; what we wish to do here is to use the reviews and our own analysis to argue that the specific research studies in this domain may be more pedantic than acknowledged.

To evaluate relevance, Anderson (in this volume) noted that one must consider who the stakeholders to the research are and what their definitions of relevance are. Research from the applicant's perspective is often quick to point out two sets of stakeholders – the organization and individual applicant. The organization as a stakeholder might need to be further subdefined, as has been done by Gilliland and Cherry (2000), in terms of line managers and coworkers, who may have different needs, desires, and goals with regard to selection systems. Additional stakeholders that may have different perspectives would include selection system designers and selection system administrators. One other obvious stakeholder of applicant perspective research is the broader community of scholars that seeks to understand individual perceptions and behavior within the context of work.

When we ask the question of research relevance, then, we should consider its relevance to these six stakeholder groups: applicants, line managers, coworkers/other organization members, selection system designers, selection system administrators, and research scholars. Viewed from a multiple stakeholder perspective, we address the relevance of the research products emerging in the applicant perspective area.

Prescriptions regarding selection process design.   For selection system designers, selection system administrators, and line managers, a key relevance question is: How does this research inform decisions regarding selection system development? As noted above, most articles in the applicant perspective area discuss what organizations should do, such as "treat applicants well" or "provide information on the process in advance." While this advice is certainly appropriate, we would conclude that it is not "new news" to many, nor is it specific enough to be actionable.

For example, rather than suggesting that organizations "make selection processes consistent," researchers need to take an in-depth look at the meaning of consistency. What attributes of a process do applicants consider when making consistency judgments (e.g., time spent with individuals, information given to individuals)? What kinds of social and context cues can be managed by organizations to ensure perceptions of consistency (e.g., statements regarding interview time being strictly adhered to across candidates)? How should information regarding legitimate exceptions (e.g., disability accommodations) be conveyed? Further, there is research to suggest that inconsistency that is beneficial to an applicant does not necessarily engender negative perceptions (Ployhart & Ryan, 1998) – when is inconsistency okay?

Another example of where research relevance might be enhanced by more prescriptive studies involves informational justice and explanations in the selection context. There have been a number of studies that have examined explanations in the selection context (e.g., Horvath, Ryan, & Stierwalt, 2000; Lievens, DeCorte, & Brysse, 2003; Ployhart, Ryan, & Bennett, 1999). Truxillo et al. (2004) noted that despite these attempts, we need much more research on what information to provide and how to present it. Meta-analytic research in the organization justice area (Shaw, Wild, & Colquitt, 2003) has confirmed that explanation adequacy is more important than explanation provision, and that providing an inadequate explanation can be more damaging than providing no explanation. Thus, offering advice to selection system administrators and line managers to "provide explanations" is probably not sufficiently helpful and may even be harmful if the explanations for selection system decisions are not adequate. Shaw et al. (2003) suggest that researchers tap into dimensions of adequacy, such as legitimacy, reasonableness, and sincerity, to better address what aspects of explanations should be attended to. Note that the justice literature generally examines explanations for decisions made, not explanations for processes used, yet both can be important in the selection context. Research on determinants of adequacy for each is warranted.

For organizations that have engendered negative perceptions due to less controllable influences (e.g., a low selection ratio that leads to some elements of less personal treatment), the applicant perspective literature offers surprisingly little in the way of concrete suggestions. There is a need for examination of specific interventions to improve perceptions (Truxillo et al., 2004). For example, Bell et al. (2004) suggested application of an expectancy challenge program approach, as pursued in alcoholism prevention research, as a format for an organizational intervention to change applicants' expectations. To enhance the relevance of research on the applicant perspective, experimental and quasi-experimental evaluations of interventions designed to enhance perceptions are needed.

Evidence regarding self-serving biases in applicant perceptions (e.g., Chan, Schmitt, Sacco, & DeShon, 1998) indicates that applicant perceptions of the fairness of procedures and affect toward them is driven largely by their performance on them. Additionally, Van Vianen et al. (2004) have suggested that belief in test utility is a preventive self-serving bias, influencing perceptions across contexts. One could argue that applicant perspective research is of limited value for selection system designers and administrators if the key antecedent of perceptions is one that cannot be influenced by the organization. We argue that by underplaying the role of self-serving biases, applicant perspective researchers do a disservice; designs that fully consider this phenomenon are necessary to appropriately interpret what else influences perceptions.

Lest we provide too negative a portrayal of relevance, one example of directly applicable research involves how technology influences applicant reactions to a selection process (see Anderson, 2003, for a review). Studies by Bauer, Truxillo, Paronto, Campion, and Weekley (2004) and Chapman, Uggerslev, and Webster (in press) involve comparisons of content delivered via different modes and can be of value to those in organizations determining if new modalities that offer economic efficiencies also do not engender negative perceptions among applicants.

Prescriptions regarding selection system content. While the reviews discuss categories of measures as perceived more or less favorably, they offer little advice regarding specific selection system content. Despite the evidence that face validity is a key determinant of applicant reactions to selection systems (Smither et al., 1993; Steiner & Gilliland, 1996), research provides little in the way of *specific* advice for organizations on how to improve or manage face validity perceptions. Statements such as "make the process face valid" (e.g., Truxillo et al., 2004) are insufficiently actionable for a selection system designer faced with certain constructs to assess. While the way to follow this advice may be obvious for some procedures, it may be less clear for others. For example, will face validity be enhanced if one takes standardized math problems typical of cognitive ability measures and simply adds instructions regarding why these types of skills are needed on the job? Must item content also be changed to reflect job-related activities (e.g., putting items in dollars sold rather than simple computations)? How does an applicant's understanding of the job affect perceptions of face validity?

Back in 1947, Mosier recommended that the term "face validity" be abandoned because of its indiscriminate use, calling for fuller specification of intended concepts. Our current recommendation is to work to develop a better understanding of those drivers of face validity; models proposed by Schuler (1993), Nevo (1995), and Brutus (1996) may be helpful in designing more relevant research. For example, Brutus (1996) proposed that perceptions of tool job relatedness are influenced by physical fidelity and transparency of the correct response. Investigating more specific suggestions on how to increase these characteristics without sacrificing other important selection system characteristics (e.g., predictive validity, fakeability) would be relevant research on content.

Relevance across cultural contexts. Cultural differences in reactions to selection practices have been proposed and examined (e.g., Steiner & Gilliland, 1996). As we noted earlier, a dominant paradigm in the applicant perspective research domain has been justice theory. Researchers have empirically supported (e.g., Li, 2004) that the operationalization of justice is culturally defined. That is, while relationships between fairness perceptions and outcomes hold across cultural contexts, the nature and content of a fair process are likely to be culturally determined. Thus, the relevance of applicant perspective research across cultural contexts should remain a highly sensitive issue. Further, concrete suggestions for the selection system designer in the multinational organization will enhance the relevance of the research. For example, Steiner and Gilliland (1996) discussed differences in how one would "sell" a new selection tool in France versus the USA.

Relevance to the broader scholarly community.   Several of the review articles (Chambers, 2002; Chan & Schmitt, 2004; Ryan & Ployhart, 2000; Rynes, 1993) noted the need for a theoretical expansion of the process by which we view applicant reaction research. In response, theoretical frameworks for understanding employee perceptions and reactions have multiplied in the past few years. For example, Ployhart and Harold (2004) recently developed a framework which proposes that reactions to the selection process are guided by an attributional process; Herriot (2004) asserts that applicant reactions should be viewed through a social identity framework. Such efforts to think critically about why applicants react to selection processes in certain ways will advance our understanding and can contribute in meaningful ways to selection system design and organizational actions.

However, we wish to throw out a challenge to applicant perspective researchers: How can research on applicant perceptions inform psychological theory more broadly? For example, are findings on applicant perceptions of social justice merely replications of justice findings in other settings? Is the research simply an application of existing theory or does it provide for theoretical extension and refinement? For research to be truly relevant to the broader research community, it must serve the role of contributing to knowledge for more than a limited group of scholars. When the research conducted by applicant perspective researchers informs the development of broader theory, the relevance of this area will be enhanced.

Tangible advice for the individual applicant.   Anderson (2004) stresses the importance of focusing on the psychological well-being of applicants as they journey through the selection process. Ironically, an individual applicant might not find much he/she could use in the body of literature on applicant perceptions to help him/herself do well in the process. While the undercurrent of the research is to value and respect the applicant, the focus of most studies is on what the organization should do. Research that considers how and when applicant actions may lead to more favorable outcomes for the applicant (e.g., when is it appropriate to point out an inconsistency and ask for a reevaluation), or to valuable information for the applicant (e.g., how to request feedback from an organization that has rejected you), would be of relevance to the individual.

Murphy and Tam (2004) suggest that applicants often focus on irrelevant pieces of information during the selection process. For example, they assert that applicants often view experiences from the perspective of how each encounter is suspected to be representative of future events should they get hired. Murphy and Tam suggest that applicants who have been exposed to more selection settings may be more capable of determining which pieces of information they gather during the process are most relevant as signals of the fairness of the organization's treatment of employees. Furthermore, exposing oneself to many job application processes may be an essential way to understand the most important factors involved with the hiring practice.

Researchers have also found that psychological states such as anxiety and test-taking self-efficacy can have detrimental effects on performance during the hiring process (Ryan,

Ployhart, Greguras, & Schmit, 1998). Studies of interventions (e.g., test preparation programs) may assist in understanding how applicants can better manage the process. For example, meta-analyses of test anxiety reduction programs provide strong evidence of their effectiveness (Ergene, 2003).

Concluding Remarks

Literature on applicant reactions is relatively nascent. Not until the late 1980s and early 1990s did researchers fully embrace the importance of understanding how applicants view the selection process and the ramifications of such perceptions. The research has evolved to a point where multiple reviews have critiqued the state of knowledge. In this chapter, we attempted to delineate themes from those reviews that indicate the rigor and relevance of this research area. While we have indicated that rigor and relevance can be improved, we feel that research on the applicant perspective has great potential to be viewed as Pragmatic Science. A concerted effort to address the methodological issues presented here coupled with decisions to address more prescriptive topics should lead to the research domain being considered one of the most influential in IWO.

References

Anderson, N. (2003). Applicant and recruiter reactions to new technology in selection: A critical review and agenda for future research. *International Journal of Selection and Assessment, 11*, 121–136.
Anderson, N. (2004). The dark side of the moon: Applicant perspectives, negative psychological effects (NPEs), and candidate decision making in selection. *International Journal of Selection and Assessment, 12*, 1–8.
Arvey, R. D., Strickland, W., Drauden, G., & Martin, C. (1990). Motivational components of test-taking. *Personnel Psychology, 43*, 695–716.
Bauer, T. N., Maertz, C. P., Jr., Dolen, M. R., & Campion, M. A. (1998). Longitudinal assessment of applicant reactions to employment testing and test outcome feedback. *Journal of Applied Psychology, 83*, 892–903.
Bauer, T. N., Truxillo, D. M., Paronto, M. E., Campion, M. A., & Weekley, J. A. (2004). Applicant reactions to different selection technology: Face-to-face, interactive voice response, and computer-assisted telephone screening interviews. *International Journal of Selection and Assessment, 12*, 135–147.
Bauer, T. N., Truxillo, D. M., Sanchez, R. J., Craig, J., Ferrara, P., & Campion, M. A. (2001). Applicant reactions to selection: Development of the Selection Procedural Justice Scale (SPJS). *Personnel Psychology, 54*, 387–419.
Bell, B. S., Ryan, A. M., & Wiechmann, D. (2004). Justice expectations and applicant perceptions. *International Journal of Selection and Assessment, 12*, 24–38.
Brutus, S. (1996). The perception of selection tests: An expanded model of perceived job relatedness (Doctoral dissertation, Bowling Green University, 1996). *Dissertation Abstracts International, 57*, 741.
Chambers, B. A. (2002). Applicant reactions and their consequences: Review, advice, and recommendations for future research. *International Journal of Management Reviews, 4*, 317–333.
Chan, D. (1997). Racial subgroup differences in predictive validity perceptions on personality and cognitive ability tests. *Journal of Applied Psychology, 82*, 311–320.

Chan, D., & Schmitt, N. (2004). An agenda for future research on applicant reactions to selection procedures: A construct-oriented approach. *International Journal of Selection and Assessment, 12*, 9–23.

Chan, D., Schmitt, N., DeShon, R. P., Clause, C. S., & Delbridge, K. (1997). Reactions to cognitive ability tests: The relationships between race, test performance, face validity perceptions, and test-taking motivation. *Journal of Applied Psychology, 82*, 300–310.

Chan, D., Schmitt, N., Sacco, J. M., & DeShon, R. P. (1998). Understanding pretest and posttest reactions to cognitive ability and personality tests. *Journal of Applied Psychology, 98*, 471–485.

Chapman, D. S., Uggerslev, K. L., & Webster, J. (in press). Applicant reactions to face-to-face and technology-mediated interviews: A field investigation. *Journal of Applied Psychology.*

Colquitt, J. A. (2001). On the dimensionality of organizational justice: A construct validation of a measure. *Journal of Applied Psychology, 86*, 386–400.

Derous, E., Born, M. P., & DeWitte, K. (2004). How applicants want and expect to be treated: Applicants' selection treatment beliefs and the development of the social process questionnaire on selection. *International Journal of Selection and Assessment, 12*, 99–119.

Ergene, T. (2003). Effective interventions on test anxiety reduction: A meta-analysis. *School Psychology International, 24*, 313–328.

Gilliland, S. W. (1993). The perceived fairness of selection systems: An organizational justice perspective. *Academy of Management Review, 18*, 694–734.

Gilliland, S. W. (1994). Effects of procedural and distributive justice on reactions to a selection system. *Journal of Applied Psychology, 79*, 691–701.

Gilliland, S. W., & Cherry, B. (2000). Managing "customers" of selection processes. In J. F. Kehoe (Ed.), *Managing selection in changing organizations* (pp. 158–196). San Francisco: Jossey-Bass.

Hausknecht, J. P., Day, D. V., & Thomas, S. C. (in press). Applicant reactions to selection procedures: An updated model and meta-analysis. *Personnel Psychology.*

Heilman, M. E., & Alcott, V. B. (2001). What I think you think of me: Women's reactions to being viewed as beneficiaries of preferential selection. *Journal of Applied Psychology, 86*, 574–582.

Heilman, M. E., Kaplow, S. R., Amato, M. A., & Stathatos, P. (1993). When similarity is a liability: Effects of sex-based preferential selection on reactions to like-sex and different-sex others. *Journal of Applied Psychology, 78*, 917–927.

Heilman, M. E., McCullough, W. F., & Gilbert, D. (1996). The other side of affirmative action: Reactions of nonbeneficiaries to sex-based preferential selection. *Journal of Applied Psychology, 81*, 346–357.

Hembree, R. (1988). Correlates, causes, effects, and treatment of test anxiety. *Review of Educational Research, 58*, 47–77.

Herriot, P. (2004). Social identities and applicant reactions. *International Journal of Selection and Assessment, 12*, 75–83.

Horvath, M., Ryan, A. M., & Stierwalt, S. L. (2000). The influence of explanations for selection test use, outcome favorability, and self-efficacy on test-taker perceptions. *Organizational Behavior and Human Decision Processes, 83*, 310–330.

Juhasz, K., & Mishken, M. A. (2004). *Personality differences in accepting selection procedure decisions.* Poster presented at the meeting of the Society for Industrial and Organizational Psychology, Chicago, IL.

Lam, H., & Reeve, C. L. (2004). *A closer look at the relation between test perceptions, test-taking motivation, and ability-test performance: Do non-ability factors really matter?* Paper presented at the meeting of the Society for Industrial and Organizational Psychology, Chicago, IL.

Li, A. (2004). *Are reactions to justice cross-culturally invariant? A meta-analytic review.* Paper presented at the meeting of the Society for Industrial and Organizational Psychology, Chicago, IL.

Lievens, F., De Corte, W., & Brysse, K. (2003). Applicant perceptions of selection procedures: The role of selection information, belief in tests, and comparative anxiety. *International Journal of Selection and Assessment, 11*, 65–75.

Mosier, C. I. (1947). A critical examination of the concept of face validity. *Educational and Psychological Measurement, 7*, 191–206.

Murphy, K. R., & Tam, A. P. (2004). The decisions job applicants must make: Insights from a Bayesian perspective. *International Journal of Selection and Assessment, 12*, 66–74.

Nevo, B. (1995). Examinee feedback questionnaire: Reliability and validity measures. *Educational and Psychological Measurement, 55*, 499–504.

Ployhart, R. E., & Harold, C. M. (2004). The applicant attribution-reaction theory (AART): An integrative theory of applicant attributional processing. *International Journal of Selection and Assessment, 12*, 84–98.

Ployhart, R. E., & Ryan, A. M. (1998). Applicants' reactions to the fairness of selection procedures: The effects of positive rule violations and time of measurement. *Journal of Applied Psychology 83*, 3–16.

Ployhart, R. E., Ryan, A. M., & Bennett, M. (1999). Explanations for selection decisions: Applicants' reactions to informational and sensitivity features of explanations. *Journal of Applied Psychology, 84*, 87–106.

Podsakoff, P. M., MacKenzie, S. B., Lee, J. Y., & Podsakoff, N. P. (2003). Common method biases in behavioral research: A critical review of the literature and recommended remedies. *Journal of Applied Psychology, 88*, 879–903.

Ryan, A. M., & Ployhart, R. E. (2000). Applicants' perceptions of selection procedures and decisions: A critical review and agenda for the future. *Journal of Management, 26*, 565–606.

Ryan, A. M., Ployhart, R. E., Greguras, G. J., & Schmit, M. J. (1998). Test preparation programs in selection contests: Self-selection and program effectiveness. *Personnel Psychology, 51*, 599–622.

Rynes, S. L. (1991). Recruitment, job choice, and post-hire consequences: A call for new research directions. In M. D. Dunnette & L. M. Hough (Eds.), *Handbook of Industrial and Organizational Psychology* (2nd ed., Vol. 2, pp. 399–444). Palo Alto, CA: Consulting Psychologists Press.

Rynes, S. L. (1993). Who's selecting whom? Effects of selection practices on applicant attitudes and behavior. In N. Schmitt & W. C. Borman (Eds.), *Personnel selection in organizations* (pp. 240–274). San Francisco: Jossey-Bass.

Saks, S. M., Leck, J. D., & Saunders, D. M. (1995). Effects of application blanks and employment equity on applicant reactions and job pursuit intentions. *Journal of Organizational Behavior, 16*, 415–430.

Sanchez, R. J., Truxillo, D. M., & Bauer, T. N. (2000). Development and examination of an expectancy-based measure of test-taking motivation. *Journal of Applied Psychology, 85*, 739–750.

Schinkel, S., Van Dierendonck, D., & Anderson, N. (2004). The impact of selection encounters on applicants: An experimental study into feedback effects after a negative selection decision. *International Journal of Selection and Assessment, 12*, 197–205.

Schmitt, N., & Chan, D. (1999). The status of research on applicant reactions to selection tests and its implications for managers. *International Journal of Management Reviews, 1*, 45–62.

Schuler, H. (1993). Social validity of selection situations: A concept and some empirical results. In H. Schuler, J. L. Farr, & M. Smith (Eds.), *Personnel selection and assessment: Individual and organizational perspectives* (pp. 11–26). Hillsdale, NJ: Erlbaum.

Seipp, B. (1991). Anxiety and academic performance: A meta-analysis of findings. *Anxiety Research, 4*, 27–41.

Shaw, J. C., Wild, E., & Colquitt, J. A. (2003). To justify or excuse? A meta-analytic review of the effects of explanations. *Journal of Applied Psychology, 88*, 444–458.

Smither, J. W., Reilly, R. R., Millsap, R. E., Pearlman, K., & Stoffey, R. W. (1993). Applicant reactions to selection procedures. *Personnel Psychology, 46*, 49–76.

Steiner, D. D., & Gilliland, S. W. (1996). Fairness reactions to personnel selection techniques in France and the United States. *Journal of Applied Psychology, 81*, 134–141.

Steiner, D. D., & Gilliland, S. W. (2001). Procedural justice in personnel selection: International and cross-cultural perspectives. *International Journal of Selection and Assessment, 9*, 1–14.

Truxillo, D. M., Bauer, T. N., Campion, M. A., & Paronto, M. E. (2002). Multiple dimensions of procedural justice: Longitudinal effects on selection system fairness and test-taking self-efficacy. *International Journal of Selection and Assessment, 9*, 336–349.

Truxillo, D. M., Steiner, D. D., & Gilliland, S. W. (2004). The importance of organizational justice in personnel selection: Defining when selection fairness really matters. *International Journal of Selection and Assessment, 12*, 39–53.

Van Vianen, A. E., Taris, R., Scholten, E., & Schinkel, S. (2004). Perceived fairness in personnel selection: Determinants and outcomes in different stages of the assessment procedure. *International Journal of Selection and Assessment, 12*, 149–159.

14

Ethnic Bias and Fairness in Personnel Selection: Evidence and Consequences

ARNE EVERS, JAN TE NIJENHUIS, AND HENK VAN DER FLIER

Almost since the beginning of standardized psychological testing, differences between racial or ethnic groups have intrigued researchers (Galton, 1892). However, until the mid-1960s hardly any research had been carried out regarding the actual methods used in personnel selection in terms of bias and fairness for ethnic subgroups. Even Guion's classical handbook of personnel selection contains only two pages on "racial discrimination" (Guion, 1965, pp. 491–493), not referring to any research whatsoever. Although at the time cognitive tests in particular were criticized and accused of putting ethnic minorities at a disadvantage (Black, 1962; Gross, 1962), it seems that only the passage of the Civil Rights Act (1964) triggered research in this area in the USA. From then on, a rapid growth of research on bias and fairness in personnel selection can be seen, going hand in hand with a steady development and sophistication of research methods. Classical publications such as Cleary's study (1968) of differences in prediction of African American and White students and Bartlett and O'Leary's study (1969) describing differential prediction models mark the onset of this period.

The American studies on differential prediction generally focus on differences in test and criterion performance between native-born English-speaking minorities and Whites, and to a lesser extent between Hispanics and Whites. These groups have been part of multiracial American society as it existed for a long time. In Europe, however, problems with the selection of various ethnic groups are from a much more recent period, as these groups are formed by immigrants who only started to come to Europe in the 1950s. Probably this accounts for the fact that the first studies regarding ethnic bias in personnel selection in Europe were published 10–15 years later than in the USA (e.g., in the Netherlands, van der Flier & Drenth, 1980). It was in this period that difficulties were encountered with the selection of the growing numbers of first and second generation immigrants, a problem that had almost been non-existent 20 years before.

The basic objective of a selection procedure is to predict future performance of job candidates. Therefore, tests[1] have been developed that are supposed to have predictive validity. The higher the validity the better, because it will mean higher utility and fewer false selection decisions (Hunter, Schmidt, & Judiesch, 1990). A test can only reach a sufficient level of validity if the test scores show sufficient variability; in other words, the test should discriminate between individuals. Although the term *discrimination* usually has a negative connotation, its statistical meaning is neutral. In point of fact, the discriminating power of a test is the justification for the use of it.

The point is whether the discriminations are biased or unbiased. A test is *biased* "when mean criterion (e.g. job performance) predictions for groups differentiated on some other basis than criterion performance are systematically too high or too low relative to mean criterion performance of the groups" (Society for Industrial Organization Psychology, 1987, p. 18). It follows that if a difference between groups in mean test scores is associated with a corresponding difference in mean job performance, there is no evidence of bias. In this chapter we will adopt this definition of test bias which is based on the regression model of fair selection (Cleary, 1968).

Mean differences in psychological test scores between ethnic groups often result in selection rates that are to the disadvantage of ethnic minorities. This may give rise to questions such as: Are psychological tests biased against ethnic minorities? If tests prove to be unbiased, what can be done to reduce adverse impact? Does the amount of adverse impact differ for various types of tests? These, and other related questions are discussed in the review below which will cover almost forty years of research in this field. First, we will review the results of bias research in the USA and Europe with respect to four types of psychological instruments that are frequently used as sources of information in personnel selection. In the second section a possible solution to reduce adverse impact is discussed. The final section addresses the issue of criterion bias.

RESULTS OF BIAS RESEARCH

This section gives a review of bias research dealing with cognitive ability or general mental ability tests (CATs or GMA tests), work samples, personality inventories, and the selection interview. In this review we will rely heavily on the results of meta-analyses. Reported validity coefficients will have been corrected for range restriction and criterion unreliability, unless stated otherwise. Specifically for cognitive ability tests, three hypotheses on bias will be discussed.

Cognitive ability tests

Cognitive ability is well documented as the best predictor of job performance and training success, with predictive validity coefficients of .55 and .63 in the USA (Schmidt & Hunter, 2004), and .62 and .54 in Europe respectively (Salgado, Anderson, Moscoso, Bertua, & De Fruyt, 2003). As to cognitive ability tests, GMA is supposed to be responsible for the prediction of job and training performance, better than any specific cognitive ability (for a more comprehensive treatment of the validities of cognitive ability tests, see Ones, Viswesvaran, & Dilchert, Chapter 7, this volume).

These high validities for GMA tests seem to hold for various ethnic groups and countries. Moreover, no substantial predictive bias was found for this type of test. Hunter, Schmidt, and Hunter (1979) showed that for employment tests differential validity occurred no more frequently than chance for Blacks and Whites. Also, Jensen (1980) and Hunter (1983) provide extensive reviews of research on differential validity and differential prediction for

Blacks and found no evidence for prediction bias. Although several more recent studies do show some differential prediction (Harville, 1996; Houston & Novick, 1987; Linn, 1982; Young, 1994), adding the data-points of these studies to the meta-analysis by Hunter et al. (1979) would only slightly change the effect sizes and would not alter the conclusions to be drawn from this meta-analysis (see Schmidt, 1992). Therefore, there is consensus that in general differential prediction for Blacks is absent in tests (e.g., American Educational Research Association, American Psychological Association, & National Council of Measurement in Education, 1999; Hartigan & Wigdor, 1989; Neisser et al., 1996). There are cases, however, where the regression line of the Black group is slightly below that of the White group.

Accordingly, Schmidt, Pearlman, and Hunter (1980) showed that differential validity and differential prediction (slopes and intercepts) occur no more frequently than chance between Hispanics and Whites. Similar conclusions can be drawn from other studies on Hispanics (e.g., Durán, 1983; Eitelberg, Laurence, Waters, & Perelman, 1984; Pearson, 1993; Pennock-Román, 1992; Reynolds & Kaiser, 1990; Wigdor & Garner, 1982). In this subgroup too, small effects of over-prediction may occur, predicting somewhat higher grades for Hispanic students than they actually get.

In an overview of Dutch research te Nijenhuis and van der Flier (1999) conclude that if any differential prediction for intelligence tests in work settings is found, the effects tend to be only small and are mostly in favor of the immigrant groups. These findings were confirmed in a study by van den Berg (2001).

In a meta-analysis Salgado and Anderson (2003) compared the validities of GMA tests in six European countries. The validity coefficients ranged from .56–.68 for job performance criteria, for training success from .38–.65 (the .38 value, for France, was an underestimation, because it could not be corrected for range restriction; the other coefficients were in the range .58–.65). Because the differences in validity coefficients in these countries with clearly different cultural backgrounds were so small, the authors concluded that the validity of GMA measures can be generalized internationally. In all, the results of the European research seem to support the conclusion that "tests predict job performance of minority and majority persons in the same way" (Schmidt, 1988, p. 275). In this context it could be reformulated into: GMA tests predict job performance and training criteria of persons of different racial, ethnic, and cultural backgrounds in the same way.

Up to this point, tests for cognitive abilities seem to be the ideal selection tool: high validity and no bias. However, cognitive ability tests show large ethnic group differences, thereby inducing considerable adverse impact in the hiring rates for most minority groups. An overview of ethnic differences in cognitive abilities in the area of personnel selection in the USA, the UK and the Netherlands is presented in Table 14.1. The ethnic differences in Europe appear to be at least as big as in the USA. The finding that differences on specific ability factors are smaller than differences on g is in accordance with the general expectation that the higher the g-loading of a test the bigger the ethnic group differences will be (Jensen, 1998).

Three hypotheses on bias in cognitive ability tests

In the literature it is suggested that stereotype threat, language bias, and speed–accuracy trade-offs may differentially influence the performance of majority and minority groups

TABLE 14.1   Ethnic differences (d values) in cognitive abilities for industrial samples in three countries

Sample	g[1]	Verbal	Quantitative/Mathematical
USA			
Blacks/Whites	.99[2]	.76	.76
Hispanics/Whites	.58[2]	.40	.28
South East Asians/Whites	−.20[3]	–	–
United Kingdom			
Blacks/Whites	1.69[4]	1.30	1.36
Asians/Whites	1.02[4]	.92	.76
The Netherlands			
Turks & Moroccans/Dutch	1.39[5]	–	–
Surinamese & Antilleans/Dutch	1.08[5]	–	–

[1] A negative sign means the first-named group scoring higher; [2] Roth, Bevier, Bobko, Switzer III, & Tyler (2001); [3] Herrnstein & Murray (1994); [4] Scott & Anderson (2003); [5] te Nijenhuis, de Jong, Evers, & van der Flier (2004).

on cognitive ability tests, thereby causing bias in the measurement of GMA. This section gives a review of the research concerning each of these three constructs.

Stereotype threat.   Steele (Steele, 1997; Steele & Aronson, 1995) proposed a hypothesis, referred to as stereotype threat, thereby suggesting that performance on ability tests by individual members of a racial group may be undermined by stereotypes associated with that racial group. According to Steele, fear or anxiety about negative stereotypes interferes with performance on standardized tests of the stigmatized domain. Some 100 laboratory studies have now been carried out in this field, revealing the robustness of the stereotype threat issue in laboratory settings. Obviously, in a laboratory setting a statistically significant effect ($ES = -.40\,d$, Jones & Stangor, 2004) on test scores can be the result of factors other than the examinee's true level of skill and achievement.

These results give rise to the question whether findings of a laboratory setting can be generalized to the field. Strong experimental manipulations have been used in several published studies, such as the explicit information that the test is diagnostic of a particular construct and that performance of stereotyped groups is less good. Obviously, such statements would never be part of employment testing. Moreover, in these experiments in general only the most difficult items from the most difficult tests with strict time limits are used. These strong manipulations may limit the generalizability to selection settings where standard IQ tests or scholastic ability tests with a wide range of g-loadings are being used, and suggest that the effects from laboratory studies may become smaller or disappear completely in the field. Four laboratory studies simulating settings of personnel selection or assessment tested generalizability and failed to find an effect (Mayer & Hanges, 2003; McFarland, Lev-Arey, & Ziegert, 2003; Nguyen, O'Neal, & Ryan, 2003; Ployhart, Ziegers, & McFarland, 2003). It may be that the motivational context of these studies accounted for the anomalous findings (Sackett, 2003). The only two field studies, using the Advanced

Placement Calculus (Stricker, 1998) and the Computerized Placement Tests (Stricker & Ward, 1998), failed to find any significant statistical and practical effect on the test performance of Blacks.

There is more strong evidence from field studies that seriously questions the phenomenon of stereotype threat. If stereotype threat explained the lower average test scores of groups, then these test scores would necessarily reveal predictive bias in the prediction of educational and occupational performance (Sackett, Schmitt, Ellingson, & Kabin, 2001; Schmidt, 2002). Stereotype threat is hypothesized to artificially lower minority scores, resulting in an underestimate of g. It is obvious that any artificial reduction of the scores of a group should result in under-prediction of performance. As shown above, the empirical literature is clear in showing no substantial predictive bias against minority groups; any effects that are found tend to be very small and to over-predict, instead of under-predicting performance. Sackett, Hardison, and Cullen (in press) state that according to stereotype theory, a) stereotype threat affects those test takers highly identified with the domain in question, and b) domain identification correlates positively with performance in the domain in question. So, test takers with low true scores in the domain should not produce observed scores that differ systematically from their true scores. If this were the case, then one would expect that the regression lines using observed scores to predict a criterion would show an intercept difference between higher scorers affected by the threat and lower scorers not affected by the threat. Contrary to what this model predicts, Sackett et al. found a linear relationship between Scholastic Aptitude Test scores and grades throughout the score range.

Although research clearly demonstrated that an effect can indeed be produced in the laboratory, the mechanisms of this effect as yet remain unclear. Several potential mediators have been examined, including anxiety, effort, performance expectancies, external attributions, and withdrawal from the performance domain, but to date no consistent support for any of these mediators has been found (Steele, Spencer, & Aronson, 2002). In fact, the phenomenon of stereotype threat may be explained in terms of a more general construct (Jensen, 1998, pp. 513–515): Test anxiety tends to lower performance levels in proportion to the degree of complexity and the amount of mental effort they require of the subject. The maximum test performance occurs at decreasing levels of anxiety or drive as the complexity or difficulty level of the test increases. Practically all studies fit into the pattern of the stereotyped group differing from the non-stereotyped group on a variable known to influence the outcome measured. One would expect stereotyped groups to score better than non-stereotyped groups on easy tasks, which has been confirmed in a recent study (O'Brien & Crandall, 2003).

Language bias. When comparing test scores of bilinguals and of people who do not have a desirable level of proficiency in the target language (i.e., most immigrants) with test scores of native speakers, two questions are relevant. The first concerns how well the test scores reflect cognitive skills and the second concerns predictive value with regard to future performance. However, as to the required level of proficiency in the second language at which a test with content or instruction in that language can be used, evidence is scarce.

With regard to the first question, a distinction is usually made between verbal and non-verbal tests. Subtests with a substantial verbal component may measure target-language proficiency to an extent that is undesirable, and underestimate the level of g of the non-native speakers. The lower the language proficiency, the larger the underestimate. This is supported by the findings of several studies. In several Dutch studies on the effect of length of residence in the Netherlands on the scores on various intelligence tests, the influence of language proficiency for immigrants was demonstrated. Tests without a verbal component show small to negligible correlations with length of residence, whereas high correlations are found with language tests, and moderate correlations with tests that have a verbal component (te Nijenhuis & van der Flier, 1999; van den Berg, 2001). For tests without a verbal component comparable effects were found by Ramos (1981), who designed a study to determine whether Spanish test instructions would facilitate the performance of Hispanic employment applicants on a predominantly nonverbal, clerical test battery. The 29% of the Hispanic applicants who indicated a preference for receiving the employment test battery with Spanish instructions were allocated to two groups. The group with Spanish instructions scored better than the group with English instructions, but with all effects being small, between $.12\,d$ and $.27\,d$, with a mean of $.19\,d$. Ramos states that the generalizability of these results is probably limited to individuals born and educated in Spanish-speaking countries, being people who are Spanish-language oriented and with a limited proficiency in English. Using a mixture of culture-loaded and culture-reduced tests, te Nijenhuis and van der Flier (2003) found that the highly verbal subtest Vocabulary of the General Aptitude Test Battery is so strongly biased against immigrants that it suppresses the score on Vocabulary with $.92\,d$, leading to an underestimate of g based on GATB IQ with 1.8 IQ points, due to this single biased subtest alone. The other seven, predominantly nonverbal subtests show on average a small bias effect that is negligible: they each underestimate g based on GATB IQ with .2 IQ point. In sum, for many non-native speakers, nonverbal tests do not or only very slightly underestimate g, whereas verbal tests generally underestimate g.

Different speed–accuracy trade-offs. Two types of speed factors play a role in timed tests; one is the speed of mental operations and is strongly linked to g, and the other is a general attitude or preference for speed in performing any task, which might be called personal tempo, and is not linked to g (Jensen, 1980). A slower personal tempo is claimed to be a factor in the lower scores of minority groups. However, no support is found for the notion that the condition of speeded versus power tests of mental ability actually is of influence on the observed mean differences in test scores between majority and minority groups, as we will see below.

First, there is no consistent variation in the size of the Black–White difference in terms of untimed versus timed tests (Jensen, 1980). Second, one can measure a speed factor almost in its pure form by divesting the timed task of any cognitive difficulty as much as possible, as happens for example in the Making X's test. Subjects are asked to make X's in rows of boxes within a time-limit of three minutes. Research does not show meaningful Black–White differences on this test (Jensen, 1974). Third, extended testing time results in higher scores for all groups, but generally does not favor minority groups more than the majority group; and differential effects found tend to be very small (e.g., Dubin, Osburn, & Winick, 1969; Evans & Reilly, 1973; Knapp, 1960; Llabre & Froman, 1987; Wild, Durso, & Rubin, 1982). Fourth, in an exploratory study by Wilson (1990) on the relationship between speededness and predictive validity for Hispanics and students of other linguistic minority groups, he hypothesized that speed is a valid component for the majority group, but a source of error for Hispanic and bilingual examinees. He assumed that the first part of a verbal test was less speeded than the second part, and correlated the two scores with self-reported grades within groups. Wilson found that the less speeded section was .03 to .04 more valid for Hispanics, and that the speeded section was .01 to .02 more valid for the majority group. However, the small effects found in this exploratory study can hardly be interpreted as convincing evidence for Wilson's hypothesis. Fifth, research using differential item functioning (DIF) techniques shows that differential response rates between minority group members and majority group members matched for sum scores to items appearing at the end of a timed test instead of at the beginning (Dorans, Schmitt, & Bleistein, 1992; Schmitt & Dorans, 1990). This might be interpreted as differential speededness: minorities choose to work more accurately and therefore focus more strongly on the items at the beginning, leaving less time for the items at the end of the test. The results of other studies contradict explanations of differential speededness; for instance, presenting items one at a time with standard time length did not differentially improve performance for Hispanic students (Llabre & Froman, 1988). Fundamental criticism of this kind of item bias research is that the effects per item are generally extremely small (usually .05 of an item less correct), resulting in scores a few hundredths of an SD lower for a subtest sum score. Sixth, attempts have been made to construct measures of preference for speed or accuracy based on test scores alone. Phillips and Rabbitt's (1995) measure of impulsivity was computed as the difference between z scores for speed and for accuracy. Speed of performance on time-limited tests can be assessed by simply counting the number of questions attempted within the time limit. Percentage accuracy can be calculated by dividing the number of questions answered correctly by the number attempted and multiplying by 100. Van den Berg (2001) applied this measure of preference for speed or accuracy to immigrant samples' test scores, suggesting a stress on speed for immigrants, whereas all other studies suggest a stress on accuracy for minority groups. This line of research looks rather unpromising; measures of preference for speed or accuracy should probably be based on experimental, rather than correlational designs.

Work samples

A general definition of a work sample test is "a standard sample of a job content domain taken under standard conditions" (Guion, 1998, p. 509). Examples of typical work sample assignments are simulations, role-play exercises, in-baskets, and portfolio assessments. However, work sample tests can vary in the degree of abstraction from the actual work behavior (Motowidlo, Dunnette, & Carter, 1990), and in practice many types of tests are categorized as work or job sample tests, ranging from hands-on performance tests of job-related tasks to situational judgment tests and written tests of job-related knowledge (Schmitt, Clause, & Pulakos, 1996). In the terminology of Motowidlo et al., hands-on performance tests usually will be classified as high-fidelity simulations (low abstraction) and situational judgment and job knowledge tests as low-fidelity simulations (high abstraction). Most often, work samples have been used as predictor measures for the purpose of personnel selection, but also as criterion measures to validate training outcomes, performance ratings, and predictor measures used in selection such as interviews and cognitive ability tests (Callinan & Robertson, 2000).

In their review of meta-analytical studies, Schmidt and Hunter (1998) report a mean predictive validity coefficient of .54 for work sample tests, which is the highest coefficient for all individual selection procedures included in their review. Although predictive validities may vary within this rather heterogeneous category of tests, higher-fidelity simulations need not necessarily show higher predictive validities. For instance, Robertson and Kandola (1982) report validities of .28, .34, .39, and .40 for tests classified as respectively Situational decision making, Group discussion, Psychomotor, and Job-related information, showing the lowest as well as the highest validity coefficient for low-fidelity simulations (Robertson and Kandola do not mention whether these coefficients were corrected for restriction of range and criterion unreliability). To the best knowledge of the authors, no meta-analysis reports explicitly on the differential validity or the differential prediction of work sample tests. However, some of the older meta-analyses of differential validity studies (Hunter et al., 1979; Schmidt et al., 1980) deal with "employment tests." Under this generic term some unequivocal examples of work sample tests, besides cognitive ability tests, are classified. Therefore, the conclusion from these meta-analyses that no predictive bias was found can probably be extended to work sample tests. Moreover, Robertson and Kandola (1982) review three studies in which no predictive bias for work sample tests for different ethnic groups was found. No comparable data on immigrant groups in Europe are available.

Work sample tests tend to produce smaller mean score differences between ethnic groups than do cognitive ability tests. In a meta-analysis Schmitt et al. (1996) report a d value of .38 for Black–White comparisons (Blacks scoring lower) and of .00 for Hispanic–White comparisons. However, the large range in effect sizes suggests the presence of some moderators. Hough, Oswald, and Ployhart (2001) suggest mode of stimulus presentation to be one of these moderators, showing that situational judgment tests presented in video-form produce less adverse impact than when presented in paper-and-pencil form.

So far, work sample tests seem to have an advantage over cognitive ability tests in showing less adverse impact, whereas predictive validity is at least as high. The question then is why are cognitive ability tests not replaced by work sample tests in most of the selection procedures? First of all, some characteristics of work sample tests limit their use, such as:

♦ Work sample tests, contrary to cognitive ability tests, are not suitable for the assessment of applicants without job experience, whereas most hiring is done at the entry level (Schmidt, 2002).

♦ Work sample tests are expensive, because they need to be individually developed for each job, and usually require specific arrangements and individual administration.

♦ The validity of work sample tests does seem to attenuate more in the course of time than other selection measures (Callinan & Robertson, 2000), whereas Schmidt and Hunter (2004) conclude that the predictive validity of GMA is at least stable over time and does not decrease.

A more theoretical argument is put forward by Schmidt (2002), who states that performance on work sample tests is a consequence of GMA. Causal modeling studies (Schmidt & Hunter, 2004) suggest that GMA is responsible for the acquisition of job knowledge, which in turn is the major cause of performance on work sample tests. The essential point is that GMA is fundamental for acquiring the knowledge and mastering the skills required in most jobs. Therefore, GMA tests should constitute the core of most selection procedures, and should not be replaced by work sample tests despite the higher adverse impact for ethnic minority groups. However, a combination of GMA tests with work sample tests in order to reduce adverse impact may be a strategy worth considering. We will address this issue in another section of this chapter.

Personality inventories

Whereas the criterion-related validity of personality measures is much lower than that of cognitive ability tests and work samples, meta-analytic studies based on the Five Factor Model (FFM) and related classification systems have convincingly demonstrated their usefulness as predictors of job performance and training success. Summarizing the results of fifteen prior meta-analytic studies based on data sets from both the United States and European countries, Barrick, Mount, and Judge (2001) conclude that conscientiousness is a valid predictor across all performance measures in all occupations studied and that emotional stability is a generalizable (but much weaker) predictor when overall work performance is the criterion. The other three Big Five traits (extroversion, agreeableness, and openness to experience) were found to predict success in specific occupations or to relate to specific criteria (see also Barrick & Mount, 1991; Hough, 1992; Salgado, 1997; for a more comprehensive discussion on the validities of personality inventories, see Salgado & De Fruyt, Chapter 8, this volume).

Very little research has addressed the differential predictive validity of personality questionnaires for ethnic minority groups. For example, Saad and Sackett (2002) reported no prior instances of examining differential prediction by race or gender in the personality domain. In the Netherlands, te Nijenhuis and van der Flier (2000) investigated the predictive validity of the General Aptitude Test Battery (GATB) and the Amsterdamse Biografische Vragenlijst (ABV)[2] for the training results of 78 immigrant and 78 Dutch trainee truck drivers. The ABV consists of four scales: neuroticism, neurosomatism, extroversion, and social conformity or lie. In this study on differential prediction only the scales for neuroticism and extroversion were taken into account. Training results were clustered to form three composite criteria: examination marks, professional attitude, and practice skills. As to the ABV, differential prediction was found for two of the six predictor–criterion combinations: The neuroticism scale was negatively related to practice skills in the Dutch group, but positively related to practice skills in the immigrant group. Only the relation in the Dutch group was significant. The extroversion scale was positively related to practice skills in the Dutch group but negatively in the group of immigrants. Only the negative relation in the group of immigrants was significant. Thus, the relationships in the Dutch group were more or less in line with expectations, while the relationships in the minority group clearly were not. The authors argue that since the dimensional comparability of the ABV scales for majority and immigrant group members in the Netherlands had been illustrated in earlier research (see later in this section), this result might point to a difference in the assessment of immigrants during the training, meaning that precise (worried) and less extroverted immigrants are considered to be more serious trainees/employees.

In a recent article, Sackett, Laczo, and Lippe (2003) argue that, when using multiple predictors in a selection system, differential prediction analysis should not be conducted on each predictor individually, but on the set of predictors in combination. Analyzing predictors individually may lead to the so-called omitted variables problem. An omitted variable can influence conclusions about differential prediction when it is correlated with the criterion and with subgroup membership. This problem is especially relevant for personality measures in situations where these measures are used as supplements to measures of cognitive ability in order to reduce subgroup differences. Sackett et al. (2003) illustrated the omitted variables problem with a differential prediction study for American Blacks and Whites using predictor and criterion data for 13 separate jobs from the US Army's Project A. The omitted variable in this study was the general factor of the Armed Services Vocational Aptitude Battery (ASVAB). Three personality constructs from the Assessment of Background and Life Experiences (Peterson et al., 1990) were used: adjustment, dependability, and surgency. Criterion measures were core technical proficiency, general soldiering proficiency, effort and leadership, and personal discipline. Analyzing the personality predictors individually for 79 predictor–criterion combinations indicated predictive bias by intercept in 45 cases and by slope in 7 cases. Inclusion of the ASVAB general factor as an additional predictor reduced occurrence of bias by intercept to 14 cases and by slope to 4 cases. The remaining differential prediction was predominant in the form of overpredicting the performance of Blacks (i.e., higher intercepts for Whites). However, a reanalysis of the data used in the study by te Nijenhuis and van der Flier (2000), including the general factor of the GATB as an additional predictor, did not alter the above conclusion for the two cases of slope bias.

In the Netherlands, studies into the dimensional comparability of scores on personality questionnaires for immigrant and native Dutch job applicants were carried out by van Leest (1997) and te Nijenhuis, van der Flier, and van Leeuwen (1997, 2003). For some of the scales the reliabilities were clearly lower for immigrants, but in general the differences were not large. All studies revealed that the scales have a strong dimensional comparability and that the influence of cultural background on the measurement of dimensions is limited. As to the incidence of differential item functioning (DIF), te Nijenhuis and van der Flier (1999, p. 170) conclude that "Although there are some items that clearly measure something different in the immigrant groups, leaving out the biased items results in relatively small score improvements for the immigrants. The overall picture is that most items measure what they are supposed to measure."

With regard to the possibility of adverse impact, a meta-analysis of ethnic group differences on personality inventories used in personnel selection in the USA has been reported by Hough et al. (2001). This study included the data from an earlier quantitative overview by Hough (1998) and from more recent studies by Goldberg, Sweeney, Merenda, and Hughes (1998) and Ones and Viswesvaran (1998). While the meta-analysis was based on the FFM, the factors extroversion and conscientiousness were considered to be too heterogeneous (see also Hough, 1997). Extroversion was therefore divided into affiliation and surgency (potency) and conscientiousness into achievement and dependability. In addition, results were presented for social desirability scales and for integrity and managerial potential, two variables that combine FFM factors. Score differences were calculated for Blacks and Whites, Hispanic and Whites, American Indians and Whites, and Asian Americans and Whites. On openness to experience the largest difference was between Blacks and Whites, Blacks scoring about .21 *d* lower than Whites. On the subfactors of extroversion and conscientiousness some larger differences were found. Blacks scored .31 *d* lower than Whites on affiliation and Asian Americans scored .29 *d* lower than Whites on dependability. The largest mean score differences between different ethnic groups were found for the social desirability scales. Hispanics and Asian Americans scored respectively .56 and .40 *d* higher than Whites. For Blacks and American Indians the differences with Whites were minimal. Differences on the integrity scales were also minimal; however, on the managerial potential scales Blacks scored .30 *d* lower than Whites.

In a study among university students in the UK, Ones and Anderson (2002) reported ethnic group differences on three popular work-related personality inventories: the Hogan Personality Inventory (HPI), the Occupational Personality Questionnaire (OPQ), and the Business Personality Indicator (BPI). Ethnic group comparisons were carried out for Black–White, Chinese–White, and Asian/Indian–White subgroups. For Black–White comparisons the largest effect sizes were found for the managerial potential, emotionally controlled, decisive, and stamina scales (*d* = .36, .46, −.36, and −.40, respectively), the first two in favor of Blacks and the last two in favor of Whites. The largest effect sizes for Chinese–White differences in mean scores were found for the prudence (conscientiousness), managerial potential, traditional, achieving, and methodical scales (*d* = .64, .52, .59, .69, and .55, respectively, in favor of the Chinese). The Chinese scored lower on the competitive and the stamina scales (*d* = −.41 and −.38, respectively). The largest Asian–White differences were found for the school success (openness to experience), innovative, methodical, and risk-taking scales (*d* = .43, .37, .45, and .67, respectively, all favoring the Asian/Indians). The overall conclusion of the study was that ethnic group differences on personality inventories are not large enough to cause concern about adverse impact. It was also concluded that there is little consistency in the constructs that showed different means across the groups compared. However, as indicated by the authors, caution is warranted with respect to the interpretation of the findings since the ethnic subgroup comparisons were based on small sample sizes for the minority groups (*N*'s between 30 and 56).

For the situation in the Netherlands, the studies by van Leest (1997) and te Nijenhuis et al. (1997, 2003) provide information about score differences between immigrant and native Dutch job applicants. Van Leest, using the RPDV, the standard personality questionnaire of the Dutch Civil Service personnel selection consultancy, compared the scores of first generation Turkish immigrants who applied for jobs in the Dutch Public Service with the scores of native Dutch applicants. The largest effect sizes were found for assertiveness (*d* = −1.15), distrust (*d* = 1.05), routine in methods (*d* = 1.16), work attitude (*d* = −.84), and internal control (*d* = .98).

In a second study, applying the NPVJ, a newly developed personality test, van Leest (1997) compared the mean scores of Turks, Moroccans, Antillians, and Surinams who applied for jobs in the police force with the mean scores of native Dutch applicants. The applicants of the minority group scored much higher on inadequacy (d values ranging from 1.06 to 1.43), perseverance (d values ranging from .62 to .98), and recalcitrance (d values ranging from 1.00 to 1.29). With regard to dominance the differences were rather small (d values ranging from −.34 to .05). The overall conclusion of these two studies was that the average score profiles of immigrants was considered to be less favorable for job applicants.

Te Nijenhuis et al. (1997, 2003) compared the scores of first generation immigrants from Turkey, North Africa, Netherlands Antilles, and Surinam versus native Dutch on two personality questionnaires, the Amsterdam Biographical Questionnaire (ABV) and the ICIP (Institute for Clinical and Industrial Psychology) Rigidity Test (IRT; Tellegen, 1968), using a large sample of applicants from the Dutch Railways and from regional public transport companies. The immigrants showed higher mean scores on the scales corresponding with the neuroticism dimension (neuroticism, $d = .62$; neurosomatic complaints, $d = .63$; and emotional perseveration, $d = .28$), the rigidity dimension (dogmatism, $d = .84$, and order, $d = .52$), and social desirability (social conformity or lie, $d = .56$, and test attitude, $d = .48$) and lower mean scores on scales corresponding with the extroversion dimension (extroversion, $d = −.19$; achievement orientation, $d = −.22$; social adaptation, $d = −.37$; and variation need, $d = −.11$). The differences were larger for Turks and North Africans than for Antillians and Surinams. The largest effect sizes for Turks and North Africans were found for neuroticism ($d = .79$ and .93, respectively), neurosomatic complaints ($d = 1.05$ and 1.19, respectively), social conformity or lie ($d = .78$ and .69, respectively), and dogmatism ($d = 1.03$ and 1.15, respectively). The average score profiles of the immigrant groups, and especially those of Turks and North Africans, are considered less favorable for job applicants and imply a lower mean level of suitability for most positions.

In summary, it can be concluded that the empirical results do not give strong indications of differential prediction or non-comparability of personality inventories in different ethnic groups. Besides, the results of studies in the USA and in the UK suggest that the adverse impact of personality inventories with respect to ethnic minority groups is not very strong or even negligible. This means that these inventories may have some potential for reducing adverse impact in selection procedures, especially in situations where personality-related job performance aspects such as contextual performance, service orientation, and teamwork are included in the overall performance measures. However, research among first generation immigrant job applicants in the Netherlands shows much higher differences in mean scale scores than in the USA and the UK, leading to less favorable mean score profiles, especially for immigrants from Turkey and North Africa. These differences may have to do with language problems, the level of education, the socioeconomic position, or the specific cultural background of these groups. Whatever the case, there is little reason for optimism about the possibilities of reducing adverse impact for these groups by including personality inventories in the selection program.

The selection interview

Interviews are the most popular selection device (Huffcutt & Roth, 1998). There are several types (see also Dipboye, Chapter 6, this volume), mostly categorized according to degree of structure, types of questions used, or kind of information collected (Huffcutt, Roth, &

McDaniel, 1996). Examples of different question types are situational questions, behavior description questions, job simulation questions, and questions about worker requirements. Although the meta-analysis of Hunter and Hunter (1984) showed a mean validity coefficient of the interview for the prediction of job performance of only .14, more recent meta-analytic research resulted in much higher coefficients. Methodological problems in the older meta-analyses seem to account for the differences (Huffcutt & Arthur, 1994). Wiesner and Cronshaw (1988) report a mean validity coefficient of .47 for the prediction of job performance, based on a worldwide search for validity studies. Huffcutt and Arthur (1994) and McDaniel, Whetzel, Schmidt, and Maurer (1994) both mention a mean value of .37, primarily based on North-American studies. In general, more highly structured interviews result in higher validity coefficients. Mean predictive validity for the least structured interviews is .20, whereas the best structured interviews have a mean validity coefficient of about .60 (Huffcutt & Arthur, 1994; Wiesner & Cronshaw, 1988). However, there is a point at which additional structure stops increasing validity. Furthermore, McDaniel et al. showed that interview content was related to validity: Situational interviews have the highest validity (.50) and psychological interviews the lowest (.29).

Surprisingly, ethnicity is not used as a moderator in these meta-analyses, which prohibits conclusions about differential validity. Two studies report on mean score differences between ethnic groups in employment interviews. Schmitt et al. (1996) summarized six Black–White and three Hispanic–White comparisons of interviews that measured mostly motivational factors. The d values were .15 and .19, respectively (minority groups scoring lower). In their meta-analysis Huffcutt and Roth (1998) mention somewhat higher d values of .25 and .26 for the same ethnic group comparisons. Therefore, the employment interview shows considerably less adverse impact compared to cognitive ability tests. Particular interesting is the fact that highly structured interviews produced smaller differences between ethnic groups than did unstructured interviews. This can be explained by the higher correlation between interview ratings and GMA scores in unstructured interviews versus structured interviews (Huffcutt et al., 1996; Salgado & Moscoso, 2002). Thus, when the focus in an interview is less on cognitive ability, adverse impact will be lower. Consequently, the structured interview is a useful selection tool with high validity and relatively low adverse impact.

The Use of Alternative Predictors

The preceding review of research has shown ethnic group differences for some popular selection instruments. In addition, it was shown that the size of these differences varied according to the type of instrument used. Subgroup differences are largest for cognitive ability tests and smallest for personality inventories. Larger differences in mean scores will translate into larger adverse impact; yet, even small differences may lead to considerable adverse impact when selection ratios happen to be very selective (Sackett & Ellingson, 1997). However, it has also become clear in the preceding review that these tests generally do not exhibit predictive bias. This justifies the use of these tests irrespective of the ethnicity of the applicant, since it appeared that higher scores on a valid unbiased test will equally predict higher job performance for applicants of all ethnic groups. The question now is: What is fair when it comes to equal opportunities? What can be done to enhance ethnic diversity within organizations? The answers to these kinds of questions are not at all simple, because in a multi-ethnic society the values of maximum job performance and diversity may come into conflict.

Some strategies to reduce adverse impact, as discussed in the review of Sackett et al. (2001), are clear examples of this conflict of values. For instance, setting quotas, within-group norming, or the technique of banding will more or less reduce adverse impact, but simultaneously mean job performance will be reduced. The effects of other strategies are small, such as the removal of items on the basis of the outcomes of item-bias research, or await further research, such as the use of alternative modes of item presentation. The most promising strategies to reduce adverse impact seem to be those that intervene in the content or composition of the predictor. One method is to modify cognitive ability tests specifically to reduce group differences, for instance by eliminating certain cognitive components such as subtests with high verbal loadings. However, this procedure will either result in a decrease in predictive validity (e.g., te Nijenhuis, Evers, & Mur, 2000), or is likely to cause differential prediction where it was previously absent in the unmodified GMA test (Kehoe, 2002). A more radical procedure is to abandon cognitive ability tests completely and replace them by other predictors which are known to show smaller ethnic differences. A serious drawback of this strategy is that most alternative tests will have lower, less stable, or less generalizable validities. Besides, as argued above, GMA is fundamental for learning to perform in a job and therefore should be part of any selection procedure.

A more promising strategy to reduce adverse impact seems to be the combination of various predictors. Because of their special status, cognitive ability tests should constitute the core element combined with other personnel measures that may be referred to as supplements (Schmidt & Hunter, 1998). The idea behind this strategy is straightforward: Combining a low-adverse impact predictor with a high-adverse impact predictor should lower adverse impact over using the high-adverse impact predictor alone. Moreover, it can be expected that combining a cognitive ability test with a non-cognitive predictor, which in itself is related to the criterion, will result in an increase in validity, particularly when the correlation between the predictors is low. Indeed, several studies have shown that adding one or more predictors to cognitive ability tests will result in substantial incremental validity in the prediction of job performance or training success (Cortina, Goldstein, Payne, Davison, & Gilliland, 2000; De Corte, 1999; Ones, Viswesvaran, & Schmidt, 1993; Pulakos & Schmitt, 1996; Schmidt & Hunter, 1998; Schmitt, Rogers, Chan, Sheppard, & Jennings, 1997). The highest gains in validity came from the inclusion of integrity tests, work sample tests, conscientiousness tests, structured interviews, and/or job knowledge tests. For instance, Cortina et al. (2000) show that a combination of measures for cognitive ability and conscientiousness and a highly structured interview can result in a multiple validity coefficient of .75.

Sackett et al. (2001) distinguish three different approaches for the examination of the effects of combining predictors on the size of ethnic differences. One is to estimate the effect of a supplemental strategy on the basis of the psychometric theory of composites (De Corte, 1999; Sackett & Ellingson, 1997). A second approach is the empirical tryout of different composite alternatives (Pulakos & Schmitt, 1996; Ryan, Ployhart, & Friedel, 1998). The third approach relies on meta-analytic findings of predictive validities, predictor intercorrelations, and subgroup differences for the estimation of the effects of predictor combinations (Bobko, Roth, & Potosky, 1999; Ones et al., 1993; Schmitt et al., 1997). The results of all three approaches were similar: Composite measures invariably reduced subgroup differences, but the size of the reduction was smaller than what one would intuitively expect. Thus, Sackett and Ellingson show that a composite of two uncorrelated measures, where $d_1 = 1.0$ and $d_2 = .0$, will reduce the difference to .71, where .50 might be expected. Likewise, in an empirical study Pulakos and Schmitt show that the Black–White difference of $d = 1.03$ for a verbal ability test is only reduced to .63 when three alternative predictors are supplemented (biodata, a situational judgment test, and a structured interview), where one might have expected a more substantial reduction when adding three predictors. Within the meta-analytic approach, Bobko et al. computed a d value of .76 for subgroup differences for a composite of four predictors (cognitive ability, conscientiousness, biodata, and interview) when $d = 1.00$ for the cognitive ability test alone. Comparably, Ones et al. come to a d value of .78 for a composite of a cognitive ability test and an integrity test. When the balance in the criterion shifts from task performance to contextual performance, these figures can become more positive (that is, result in smaller group differences), because in that case alternative predictors should be weighted more heavily (De Corte, 1999).

Researchers seem a bit pessimistic in the interpretation of the effects of adding alternative predictors to cognitive ability tests. One reason may be that effects are slightly disappointing; another may be that the resulting subgroup differences will still result in considerable adverse impact for the most common selection ratios, thereby not meeting the four-fifths rule. However, the above-mentioned research shows that this strategy in general will result in a reduction in ethnic group differences of 20 to 40%, which will translate into an even greater drop in percentage in adverse impact ratios (e.g., Ones et al., 1993; Sackett & Ellingson, 1997). To attain this improvement predictive validity need not be sacrificed; on the contrary, the predictive power of these combined predictor sets will be higher compared to cognitive ability alone. Personnel psychologists should cherish this strategy and resign themselves to the existence of subgroup differences, the consequences of which cannot be eliminated completely by the use of alternative predictors. The reduction of subgroup differences in cognitive abilities is beyond their influence.

BIAS IN THE CRITERION

All studies and models of prediction bias assume that criterion measures are unbiased. However, if the criterion contains some kind of bias that runs parallel to the bias in the predictor, that is to say that it equally disfavors one of the groups, the predictor may be wrongly considered unbiased.

A common research design to investigate the possibility of criterion bias is to compare the degree of association between ethnic group and subjective performance measures on the one hand versus the degree of association between ethnic group and objective performance measures on the other, the idea being that criteria which can be objectively determined (e.g., figures on absenteeism, scores on job knowledge tests, sales figures) are less susceptible to bias as no judgments are involved. When the differences between ethnic groups on the objective criteria appear to be smaller than on the subjective criteria (e.g., ratings by supervisors on overall performance or on specific criterion aspects), this may be an indication of bias in the subjectively determined criteria. Information on bias of subjective criteria is of special interest, because ratings are the prevailing method of performance appraisal (Landy, Shankster, & Kohler, 1994), and are therefore used as criterion measures in most validity studies. In a meta-analysis, Ford, Kraiger, and Schechtman (1986) compared objective and subjective performance measures for Whites and Blacks on several types of criterion measures (work performance, absenteeism, and cognitive criteria). Whites scored higher than Blacks on all measures (higher scores meaning better performance); the overall correlation between group membership and criterion score was .20. The overall effect sizes for the objective and subjective measures were virtually identical, although Ford et al. found that the ethnicity–performance relationship for the subjective measures of work performance and absenteeism were larger than the objective measures in the same category. Roth, Huffcutt, and Bobko (2003) re-analyzed the Ford et al. data, meanwhile including many new studies. Roth et al. also found Whites scoring higher than Blacks on all types of criterion measures (quality measures, quantity measures, job knowledge, and absenteeism), but contrary to the findings of Ford et al. the ethnic differences within each criterion type were larger for the objective measures than for the subjective measures. Assuming that objective criteria are relatively unbiased measures, these results may lead to the conclusion that subjective criteria showed no rater bias to the disadvantage of the minority group. In fact, on the basis of their results Roth et al. supposed that there may be some pressure on raters to minimize ethnic group differences.

Another research design to study the possibility of criterion bias is to investigate the influence of the ethnicity of the rater–ratee interaction on the performance rating. Meta-analyses by Kraiger and Ford (1990), Sackett and DuBois (1991), and Waldman and Avolio (1991) fit within this strategy. The conclusion of this line of research is that raters do not appreciably favor ratees of their own race when generating performance ratings, although an exception may be made for minority group supervisors appraising minority group employees. Moreover, when the effects of cognitive abilities, education, and experience on the criterion scores were partialed out (as was done in the Waldman & Avolio study), the mean criterion scores of Whites and Blacks were almost equal. This finding supports indirectly the unbiasedness of the ratings, as cognitive abilities, education, and experience are strong predictors of job performance. Therefore, one would expect that neutralizing ethnic differences in these variables would indeed eliminate the difference in the criterion.

All in all, the results of the above studies indicate that "the criterion is not the problem" (Schmidt, 2002, p. 206). First, the effects on objective criteria are equal to or even larger than those on supervisory ratings. Second, these ratings seem to be relatively free of ethnic rater bias. Third, when the effects of cognitive ability and education are controlled for, the criterion differences between ethnic groups almost disappear. The conclusion that subjective criterion measures – being the prevailing measure used in research on prediction bias – in general are unbiased supports the evidence presented in the first section of this chapter that prediction bias is absent.

Finally, the size of the criterion differences between ethnic groups needs to be discussed. The effect sizes of the reported criterion differences between Whites and Blacks in the USA usually are in the range of .2–.6 d (e.g., Ford et al., 1986; DuBois, Sackett, Zedeck,

& Fogli, 1993; Roth et al., 2003; Waldman & Avolio, 1991); the White–Hispanic differences seem to be somewhat smaller, especially when subjective measures are involved (Roth
et al., 2003). In an English study (Dewberry, 2001), the results showed that ethnic minority trainees were more likely to fail the compulsory training for lawyers and got lower performance scores than White trainees, the effect sizes being .50 d and .54 d, respectively. Te
Nijenhuis, de Jong, Evers, and van der Flier (2004) reviewed eight Dutch studies in which
work performance and job-related training results of Dutch and immigrant employees are
compared. The differences are generally within the range of .25 to .50 d, and even higher
for language-related performance aspects. The findings of the European studies are consistent with the results of the US studies in showing lower performance by ethnic minorities. Even the effect sizes seem to generalize, with modal values of d in the .40–.50 range,
although the effect size may vary a bit for the specific ethnic groups involved.

Apart from the specific ethnic group effect, it seems that the most important factor that
influences the size of the differences is the type of the criterion measure. The largest differences are to be found for criteria such as training performance, job knowledge, technical proficiency, and work samples (Dewberry, 2001; Ford et al., 1986; Kraiger & Ford,
1990; Roth et al., 2003; Sackett & DuBois, 1991; te Nijenhuis et al., 2004). The smallest
differences are for criteria such as discipline (Sackett & Dubois, 1991) and absenteeism
(Ford et al., 1986; Roth et al., 2003; te Nijenhuis et al., 2004). These differential effects
may be explained by presumed differences in cognitive complexity or g-loading of the criterion types (Gottfredson, 2002). As mentioned in the previous section, the predictive validity of GMA tests for job performance in general is about .50 and the difference in GMA
between African Americans and Whites in the USA and between various immigrant and
majority groups in Europe (see Table 14.1) is about 1 d. Schmidt (2002) notes that, in view
of these values, a difference of .5 d in criterion performance can be expected. The empirical modal value of .4 to .5 corresponds very well to this expected value, the d values of
criterion types with supposed relatively high g-loadings (training performance and job
knowledge) being above and the d values of criterion types with supposed relatively low
g-loadings (discipline and absenteeism) being below this value. As cognitive complexity of
the criterion increases, so will the differences between the majority and the minority group.

CONCLUSION

This chapter gives a review of research on ethnic bias in personnel selection in North
America and Europe. Fortunately, a considerable amount of research shows no predictive
bias for four of the most popular types of selection measures, i.e., cognitive ability tests,
work sample tests, personality inventories, and selection interviews (though an exception
may be the use of personality inventories for immigrant groups). At the same time, research
on criterion bias has provided evidence that the most popular type of criterion measure,
i.e., performance ratings, is not biased either. This evidence supports the finding that there
is no predictive bias, as it rules out the possibility of parallel bias in predictor and criterion measures.

A serious matter of concern appears to be the large differences in mean scores for
various ethnic groups, especially on cognitive ability tests. They cause considerable adverse

impact in the hiring rates for ethnic minority groups. Three hypotheses to explain these differences are discussed, namely 1) stereotype threat, 2) language bias, and 3) speed–accuracy trade-offs. No conclusive evidence has been found for any of these hypotheses. Nevertheless, especially for immigrant groups, language bias may produce small effects on cognitive test scores.

Consequently, the possibility of reducing adverse impact by supplementing cognitive ability tests with other predictor measures is discussed. This strategy may lead to both a considerable reduction in adverse impact and an increase in predictive validity. However, the presented research findings also have shown that equal representation of all ethnic groups in all jobs is unrealistic, as long as these groups differ in job-related skills and abilities. A more valid strategy would be to try to reduce the differences in skills and abilities themselves by providing special training and education, bearing in mind that these differences have appeared to be rather stubborn (Gottfredson, 1988). For the moment, the best a personnel psychologist can do is to optimize the predictor measures used, realizing that "fairness" – in terms of equal representation – cannot be achieved at present.

NOTES

1. In this text the words "test" and "predictor" are used interchangeably. Both words are used as a general term for all kinds of selection instruments (e.g., cognitive tests, work samples, interviews, personality inventories, assessment centers, biodata).
2. The ABV is a frequently used Dutch personality questionnaire, mainly based on the Maudsley Personality Inventory (MPI; Eysenck, 1959).

REFERENCES

American Educational Research Association, American Psychological Association, & National Council of Measurement in Education. (1999). *Standards for educational and psychological testing.* Washington, DC: American Psychological Association.

Barrick, M. R., & Mount, M. K. (1991). The Big Five personality dimensions and job performance: A meta analysis. *Personnel Psychology, 44,* 1–26.

Barrick, M. R., Mount, M. K., & Judge, T. A. (2001). Personality and performance at the beginning of the new millennium: What do we know and where do we go next. *International Journal of Selection and Assessment, 9,* 9–29.

Bartlett, C. J., & O'Leary, B. S. (1969). A differential prediction model to moderate the effects of heterogeneous groups in personnel selection and classification. *Personnel Psychology, 22,* 1–17.

Black, H. (1962). *They shall not pass.* New York: Random House.

Bobko, P., Roth, P. L., & Potosky, D. (1999). Derivation and implication of a meta-analytic matrix incorporating cognitive ability, alternative predictors, and job performance. *Personnel Psychology, 52,* 561–590.

Callinan, M., & Robertson, I. T. (2000). Work sample testing. *International Journal of Selection and Assessment, 8,* 248–260.

Cleary, T. A. (1968). Test bias: Prediction of grades of negro and white students in integrated colleges. *Journal of Educational Measurement, 5,* 115–124.

Cortina, J. M., Goldstein, N. B., Payne, S. C., Davison, H. K., & Gilliland, S. W. (2000). The incremental validity of interview scores over and above cognitive ability and conscientiousness scores. *Personnel Psychology*, *53*, 326–351.

De Corte, W. (1999). Weighing job performance predictors to both maximize the quality of the selected workforce and control the level of adverse impact. *Journal of Applied Psychology*, *84*, 695–702.

Dewberry, C. (2001). Performance disparities between whites and ethnic minorities: Real differences or assessment bias? *Journal of Occupational and Organizational Psychology*, *74*, 659–673.

Dorans, N. J., Schmitt, A. P., & Bleistein, C. A. (1992). The standardization approach to assessing comprehensive differential item functioning. *Journal of Educational Measurement*, *29*, 309–319.

Dubin, J. A., Osburn, H., & Winick, D. M. (1969). Speed and practice: Effects on Negro and white test performances. *Journal of Applied Psychology*, *15*, 19–23.

DuBois, C. L. Z., Sackett, P. R., Zedeck, S., & Fogli, L. (1993). Further exploration of typical and maximum performance criteria: Definitional issues, prediction, and white–black differences. *Journal of Applied Psychology*, *78*, 205–211.

Durán, R. P. (1983). *Hispanics' education and background: Predictors of college achievement.* New York: College Entrance Examination Board.

Eitelberg, M. J., Laurence, J. H., Waters, B. K., & Perelman, L. S. (1984). *Screening for service: Aptitude and education criteria for military entry.* Alexandria, VA: Human Resources Research Organization.

Evans, F. R., & Reilly, R. R. (1973). A study of test speededness as a potential source of bias in the quantitative score of the Admissions Test for Graduate Study in Business. *Research in Higher Education*, *1*, 173–183.

Eysenck, H. J. (1959). *Manual for the Maudsley Personality Inventory.* London: University of London Press.

Ford, J. K., Kraiger, K., & Schechtman, S. (1986). Study of race effects in objective indices and subjective evaluations of performance: A meta-analysis of performance criteria. *Psychological Bulletin*, *99*, 330–337.

Galton, F. (1892). *Hereditary genius.* London: MacMillan.

Goldberg, L. R., Sweeney, D., Merenda, P. F., & Hughes, J. E., Jr. (1998). Demographic variables and personality: The effects of gender, age, education, and ethnic/racial status on self-descriptions of personality attributes. *Personality and Individual Differences*, *24*, 393–403.

Gottfredson, L. S. (1988). Reconsidering fairness: A matter of social and ethical priorities. *Journal of Vocational Behavior*, *33*, 293–319.

Gottfredson, L. S. (2002). Where and why *g* matters: Not a mystery. *Human Performance*, *15*, 25–46.

Gross, M. L. (1962). *The brain watcher.* New York: Random House.

Guion, R. M. (1965). *Personnel testing.* New York: McGraw-Hill.

Guion, R. M. (1998). *Assessment, measurement, and prediction for personnel decisions.* Mahwah, NJ: Lawrence Erlbaum.

Hartigan, J. A., & Wigdor, A. K. (Eds.). (1989). *Fairness in employment testing: Validity generalization, minority issues, and the General Aptitude Test Battery.* Washington, DC: National Academy Press.

Harville, D. L. (1996). Ability test equity in predicting job performance work samples. *Educational and Psychological Measurement*, *56*, 344–348.

Hernnstein, R. J., & Murray, C. (1994). *The bell curve: Intelligence and class structure in American life.* New York: Free Press.

Hough, L. M. (1992). The "big five" personality variables – construct confusion: Description versus prediction. *Human Performance*, *5*, 139–155.

Hough, L. M. (1997). The millennium for personality psychology: New horizons or good old daze. *Applied Psychology: An International Review*, *47*, 233–261.

Hough, L. M. (1998). Personality at work: Issues and evidence. In M. Hakel (Ed.), *Beyond multiple choice: Evaluating alternatives to traditional tests for selection* (pp. 131–159). Hillsdale, NJ: Erlbaum.

Hough, L. M., Oswald, F. L., & Ployhart, R. E. (2001). Determinants, detection, and amelioration of adverse impact in personnel selection procedures: Issues, evidence and lessons learned. *International Journal of Selection and Assessment, 9*, 152–194.

Houston, W. M., & Novick, M. R. (1987). Race-based differential prediction in air force technical training programs. *Journal of Educational Measurement, 24*, 309–320.

Huffcutt, A. I., & Arthur, W., Jr. (1994). Hunter and Hunter (1984) revisited: Interview validity for entry-level jobs. *Journal of Applied Psychology, 79*, 184–190.

Huffcutt, A. I., & Roth, P. L. (1998). Racial group differences in employment interview evaluations. *Journal of Applied Psychology, 83*, 179–189.

Huffcutt, A. I., Roth, P. L., & McDaniel, M. A. (1996). A meta-analytic investigation of cognitive ability in employment interview evaluations: Moderating characteristics and implications for incremental validity. *Journal of Applied Psychology, 81*, 459–473.

Hunter, J. E. (1983). *Fairness of the General Aptitude Test Battery: Ability differences and their impact on minority hiring rates* (USES Test Research Report No. 46). Washington, DC: US Employment Service, US Department of Labor.

Hunter, J. E., & Hunter, R. F. (1984). Validity and utility of alternative predictors of job performance. *Psychological Bulletin, 96*, 72–98.

Hunter, J. E., Schmidt, F. L., & Hunter, R. F. (1979). Differential validity of employment tests by race: A comprehensive review and analysis. *Psychological Bulletin, 87*, 721–735.

Hunter, J. E., Schmidt, F. L., & Judiesch, M. K. (1990). Individual differences in output variability as a function of job complexity. *Journal of Applied Psychology, 75*, 28–42.

Jensen, A. R. (1974). The effect of race of examiner on the mental test scores of white and black pupils. *Journal of Educational Measurement, 11*, 1–14.

Jensen, A. R. (1980). *Bias in mental testing*. London: Methuen.

Jensen, A. R. (1998). *The g factor: The science of mental ability*. London: Praeger.

Jones, P. R., & Stangor, C. (2004). *The effects of activated stereotypes on stigmatized and non-stigmatized individuals: A meta-analysis of the stereotype threat literature*. Unpublished manuscript.

Kehoe, J. F. (2002). General mental ability and selection in private sector organizations: A commentary. *Human Performance, 15*, 97–106.

Knapp, R. R. (1960). The effects of time limits on the intelligence test performance of Mexican and American subjects. *Journal of Educational Psychology, 51*, 14–20.

Kraiger, K., & Ford, J. K. (1990). The relation of job knowledge, job performance, and supervisory ratings as a function of ratee race. *Human Performance, 3*, 269–279.

Landy, F. J., Shankster, L. J., & Kohler, S. S. (1994). Personnel selection and placement. *Annual Review of Psychology, 45*, 261–296.

Linn, R. L. (1982). Ability testing: Individual differences, prediction, and differential prediction. In A. K. Wigdor & W. R. Gardner (Eds.), *Ability testing: Uses, consequences, and controversies* (pp. 335–388). Washington, DC: National Academy Press.

Llabre, M. M., & Froman, T. W. (1987). Allocation of time to test items: A study of ethnic differences. *Journal of Experimental Education, 55*, 137–140.

Llabre, M. M., & Froman, T. W. (1988*). Allocation of time and item performance in Hispanic and Anglo examinees* (Final report). Institute for Student Assessment and Evaluation, University of Florida.

Mayer, D. M., & Hanges, P. J. (2003). Understanding the stereotype threat effect with "culture-free" tests: An examination of its mediators and measurement. *Human Performance, 16*, 207–230.

McDaniel, M. A., Whetzel, D. L., Schmidt, F. L., & Maurer, S. D. (1994). The validity of employment interviews: A comprehensive review and meta-analysis. *Journal of Applied Psychology, 79*, 599–616.

McFarland, L. A., Lev-Arey, D. M., & Ziegert, J. C. (2003). An examination of stereotype threat in a motivational context. *Human Performance, 16*, 181–205.

Motowidlo, S. J., Dunnette, M. D., & Carter, G. W. (1990). An alternative selection procedure: The low-fidelity simulation. *Journal of Applied Psychology, 75,* 640–647.

Neisser, U., Boodoo, G., Bouchard, T. J., Jr., Boykin, A. W., Brody, N., Ceci, S. J., et al. (1996). Intelligence: Knowns and unknowns. *American Psychologist, 51,* 77–101.

Nguyen, H.-H. D., O'Neal, A., & Ryan, A. M. (2003). Relating test-taking attitudes and skills and stereotype threat effects to the racial gap in cognitive ability test performance. *Human Performance, 16,* 261–293.

O'Brien, L. T., & Crandall, C. S. (2003). Stereotype threat and arousal: Effects on women's math performance. *Personality and Social Psychology Bulletin, 29,* 782–789.

Ones, D. S., & Anderson, N. (2002). Gender and ethnic group differences on personality scales in selection: Some British data. *Journal of Occupational and Organizational Psychology, 75,* 255–276.

Ones, D. S., & Viswesvaran, C. (1998). Gender, age and race differences on overt integrity tests: Analyses across four large-scale applicant data sets. *Journal of Applied Psychology, 83,* 35–42.

Ones, D. S., Viswesvaran, C., & Schmidt, F. L. (1993). Comprehensive meta-analysis of integrity test validities: Findings and implications for personnel selection and theories of job performance. *Journal of Applied Psychology, 78,* 679–703.

Pearson, B. Z. (1993). Predictive validity of the Scholastic Aptitude Test (SAT) for Hispanic bilingual students. *Hispanic Journal of Behavioral Sciences, 15,* 342–356.

Pennock-Román, M. (1992). Interpreting test performance in selective admissions for Hispanic students. In K. F. Geisinger (Ed.), *Psychological testing of Hispanics.* Washington, DC: APA.

Peterson, N. G., Hough, L. M., Dunnette, M. D., Rosse, R. L., Houston, J. S., Toquam, J. L., et al. (1990). Project A: Specification of the predictor domain and development of new selection/classification tests. *Personnel Psychology, 43,* 247–276.

Phillips, L. H., & Rabbitt, P. M. A. (1995). Impulsivity and speed–accuracy strategies in intelligence test performance. *Intelligence, 21,* 13–29.

Ployhart, R. E., Ziegert, J. C., & McFarland, L. A. (2003). Understanding racial differences on cognitive ability tests in selection contexts: An integration of stereotype threat and applicant reactions research. *Human Performance, 16,* 231–259.

Pulakos, E. D., & Schmitt, N. (1996). An evaluation of two strategies for reducing adverse impact and their effects on criterion-related validity. *Human Performance, 9,* 241–258.

Ramos, R. A. (1981). Employment battery performance of Hispanic applicants as a function of English or Spanish test instructions. *Journal of Applied Psychology, 66,* 291–295.

Reynolds, C. R., & Kaiser, S. M. (1990). Bias in assessment of aptitude. In C. R. Reynolds & R. W. Kamphaus (Eds.), *Handbook of psychological and educational assessment of children: Intelligence and achievement* (pp. 611–653). New York: Guilford.

Robertson, I. T., & Kandola, R. S. (1982). Work sample tests: Validity, adverse impact and applicant reaction. *Journal of Occupational Psychology, 55,* 171–183.

Roth, P. L., Bevier, C. A., Bobko, P., Switzer, F. S., III, & Tyler, P. (2001). Ethnic group differences in cognitive ability in employment and educational settings: A meta-analysis. *Personnel Psychology, 54,* 297–330.

Roth, P. L., Huffcutt, A. I., & Bobko, P. (2003). Ethnic group differences in measures of group performance: A new meta-analysis. *Journal of Applied Psychology, 88,* 694–706.

Ryan, A. M., Ployhart, R. E., & Friedel, L. A. (1998). Using personality testing to reduce adverse impact: A cautionary note. *Journal of Applied Psychology, 83,* 298–307.

Saad, S., & Sackett, P. R. (2002). Investigating differential prediction by gender in employment-oriented personality measures. *Journal of Applied Psychology, 87,* 667–674.

Sackett, P. R. (2003). Stereotype threat in applied selection settings: A commentary. *Human Performance, 16,* 295–309.

Sackett, P. R., & DuBois, C. L. Z. (1991). Rater–ratee race effects on performance evaluation: Challenging meta-analytic conclusions. *Journal of Applied Psychology, 76*, 873–877.

Sackett, P. R., & Ellingson, J. E. (1997). The effects of forming multi-predictor composites on group differences and adverse impact. *Personnel Psychology, 50*, 707–721.

Sackett, P. R., Hardison, C. M., & Cullen, M. J. (in press). On interpreting stereotype threat as accounting for Black–White differences on cognitive tests. *Journal of Applied Psychology*.

Sackett, P. R., Laczo, R. M., & Lippe, Z. P. (2003). Differential prediction and the use of multiple predictors: The omitted variables problem. *Journal of Applied Psychology, 88*, 1046–1056.

Sackett, P. R., Schmitt, N., Ellingson, J. E., & Kabin, M. B. (2001). High-stakes testing in employment, credentialing, and higher education. *American Psychologist, 56*, 302–318.

Salgado, J. F. (1997). The Five Factor Model of Personality and Job Performance in the European Community. *Journal of Applied Psychology, 82*, 30–43.

Salgado, J. F., & Anderson, N. (2003). Validity generalization of GMA tests across countries in the European Community. *European Journal of Work and Organizational Psychology, 12*, 1–17.

Salgado, J. F., Anderson, N., Moscoso, S., Bertua, C., & De Fruyt, F. (2003). International validity generalization of GMA and cognitive abilities as predictors of work behaviours: A European contribution and comparison with American findings. *Personnel Psychology, 56*, 573–605.

Salgado, J. F., & Moscoso, S. (2002). Comprehensive meta-analysis of the construct validity of the selection interview. *European Journal of Work and Organizational Psychology, 11*, 299–324.

Schmidt, F. L. (1988). The problem of group differences in ability test scores in employment selection. *Journal of Vocational Behavior, 33*, 272–292.

Schmidt, F. L. (1992). What do data really mean? Research findings, meta-analysis, and cumulative knowledge in psychology. *American Psychologist, 47*, 1173–1181.

Schmidt, F. L. (2002). The role of general cognitive ability and job performance: Why there cannot be a debate. *Human Performance, 15*, 187–210.

Schmidt, F. L., & Hunter, J. E. (1998). The validity and utility of selection methods in personnel psychology: Practical and theoretical implications of 85 years of research findings. *Psychological Bulletin, 124*, 262–274.

Schmidt, F. L., & Hunter, J. E. (2004). General mental ability in the world of work: Occupational attainment and job performance. *Journal of Personality and Social Psychology, 86*, 162–173.

Schmidt, F. L., Pearlman, K., & Hunter, J. E. (1980). The validity and fairness of employment and educational tests for Hispanic Americans: A review and analysis. *Personnel Psychology, 33*, 705–724.

Schmitt, A. P., & Dorans, N. J. (1990). Differential Item Functioning for minority examinees on the SAT. *Journal of Educational Measurement, 27*, 67–81.

Schmitt, N., Clause, C. S., & Pulakos, E. D. (1996). Subgroup differences associated with different measures of some common job-relevant constructs. *International Review of Industrial and Organizational Psychology, 11*, 115–139.

Schmitt, N., Rogers, W., Chan, D., Sheppard, L., & Jennings, D. (1997). Adverse impact and predictive efficiency of various predictor combinations. *Journal of Applied Psychology, 82*, 719–730.

Scott, N., & Anderson, N. (2003, May). *Ethnic and gender differences in GMA test scores: Findings from the UK*. Paper presented at the EAWOP Conference, Lisbon.

Society for Industrial and Organizational Psychology. (1987). *Principles for the validation and use of personnel selection procedures*. College Park, MD: SIOP.

Steele, C. M. (1997). A threat in the air: How stereotypes shape intellectual identity and performance. *American Psychologist, 52*, 613–629.

Steele, C. M., & Aronson, J. (1995). Stereotype threat and the intellectual test performance of African Americans. *Journal of Personality and Social Psychology, 69*, 797–811.

Steele, C. M., Spencer, S. J., & Aronson, J. (2002). Contending with group image: The psychology of stereotype and social identity threat. *Advances in Experimental Social Psychology, 34*, 379–440.

Stricker, L. J. (1998). *Inquiring about examinees' ethnicity and sex: Effects on AP Calculus AB Examination performance* (College Board Rep. No. 98-1; ETS Research Rep. No. 98-5). New York: College Entrance Examination Board.

Stricker, L. J., & Ward, W. C. (1998). *Inquiring about examinees' ethnicity and sex: Effects on Computerized Placement Tests Performance* (College Board Rep. No. 98-2; ETS Research Rep. No. 98-9). New York: College Entrance Examination Board.

Tellegen, B. (1968). *Over rigiditeit* [On rigidity]. Zaltbommel, The Netherlands: Avanti.

te Nijenhuis, J., de Jong, M.-J., Evers, A., & van der Flier, H. (2004). Are cognitive differences between immigrant and majority groups diminishing? *European Journal of Personality, 18*, 405–434.

te Nijenhuis, J., Evers, A., & Mur, J. P. (2000). Validity of the Differential Aptitude Test for immigrant children. *Educational Psychology, 20*, 99–115.

te Nijenhuis, J., & van der Flier, H. (1999). Bias research in The Netherlands: Review and implications. *European Journal of Psychological Assessment, 15*, 165–175.

te Nijenhuis, J., & van der Flier, H. (2000). Differential prediction of immigrant versus majority group training performance using cognitive ability and personality measures? *International Journal of Selection and Assessment, 8*, 54–60.

te Nijenhuis, J., & van der Flier, H. (2003). Immigrant–majority group differences in cognitive performance: Jensen effects, cultural effects, or both. *Intelligence, 31*, 443–459.

te Nijenhuis, J., van der Flier, H., & van Leeuwen, L. (1997). Comparability of personality test scores for immigrants and majority group members: Some Dutch findings. *Personality and Individual Differences, 23*, 849–859.

te Nijenhuis, J., van der Flier, H., & van Leeuwen, L. (2003). The use of a test for neuroticism, extraversion, and rigidity for Dutch immigrant job-applicants. *Applied Psychology: An International Review, 52*, 630–647.

van den Berg, R. H. (2001). *Psychologisch onderzoek in een multiculturele samenleving: Psychologische tests, interview- en functioneringsbeoordelingen* [Psychological research in a multicultural society: Psychological tests, interview ratings and job proficiency assessment]. Amsterdam: NOA.

van der Flier, H., & Drenth, P. J. D. (1980). Fair selection and comparability of test scores. In L. J. Th. van der Kamp, W. F. Langerak & D. N. M. de Gruijter (Eds.), *Psychometrics for educational debates* (pp. 85–101). Chichester, UK: John Wiley & Sons.

van Leest, P. F. (1997). *Persoonlijkheidsmeting bij allochtonen* [Assessment of personality for ethnic minorities]. Lisse, The Netherlands: Swets & Zeitlinger.

Waldman, D. A., & Avolio, B. J. (1991). Race effects in performance evaluations: Controlling for ability, education, and experience. *Journal of Applied Psychology, 76*, 897–901.

Wiesner, W. H., & Cronshaw, S. F. (1988). A meta-analytic investigation of the impact of interview format and degree of structure on the validity of the employment interview. *Journal of Occupational Psychology, 61*, 275–290.

Wigdor, A. K., & Garner, W. R. (Eds.). (1982). *Ability testing: Uses, consequences, and controversies.* Washington, DC: National Academy Press.

Wild, C. L., Durso, R., & Rubin, D. B. (1982). Effect of increased test-taking time on test scores by ethnic group, years out of school, and sex. *Journal of Educational Measurement, 19*, 19–28.

Wilson, K. M. (1990). *Population differences in speed versus level of GRE reading comprehension: An exploratory study* (GRE Report No. 84-09). Princeton, NJ: Educational Testing Service.

Young, J. W. (1994). Differential prediction of college grades by gender and ethnicity: A replication study. *Educational and Psychological Measurement, 54*, 1022–1029.

Part IV

CRITERION MEASURES

15

The Prediction of Typical and Maximum Performance in Employee Selection

UTE-CHRISTINE KLEHE AND NEIL ANDERSON

In any selection process, organizations wish to distinguish between what applicants *can* (i.e., maximum performance) and what they *will* (i.e., typical performance) do in terms of their likely job performance. Our objectives for the current chapter are to outline the distinction between typical and maximum performance and to demonstrate how it can add valuable information for both practitioners and researchers in personnel selection, for while this distinction fits well with current models of job performance and has received considerable attention in theoretical accounts, it is frequently overlooked by both scientists and practitioners in personnel selection. Researchers run extensive validation studies while organizations make huge financial investments in the selection of new employees without knowing which of these two aspects of performance they are predicting, or even trying to predict (Guion, 1991). Finally, we will propose areas of future research, such as moderators and boundary conditions, and we will outline potential pitfalls in the study of typical and maximum performance.

DIFFERENCES BETWEEN TYPICAL VERSUS MAXIMUM PERFORMANCE

Cronbach (1960) used the distinction between typical and maximal performance to differentiate between measures of ability and measures of personality. This distinction is still used widely with regard to personnel selection procedures (e.g., Dennis, Sternberg, & Beatty, 2000). However, it can be equally applied to the criterion predicted: Sackett, Zedeck, and Fogli (1988) adopted the concept to describe variations in job performance. They argued that during typical performance, the day-to-day performance on the job, performers a) are relatively unaware that their performance may be observed or even evaluated, b) are not consciously trying to continually perform their "absolute best," and c) are working on their task over an extended period of time.

For many jobs, ranging from car-mechanics to researchers to chief executives, typical performance represents the broadest part of daily activities. In situations of maximum performance, however, such as when car-mechanics become aware of the boss watching over their shoulder or when researchers present their scientific reports at international conferences, performers a) are very well aware of being evaluated, b) are aware and accept implicit or explicit instructions to maximize their effort, and c) are observed for a short enough time-period to keep their attention focused on the task.

Whether a performance situation is either typical or maximum will have considerable impact on the role of motivation and ability in this situation. Job performance is generally conceptualized as a function of ability and motivation (Locke, Mento, & Katcher, 1978). Motivation is defined by three choices (Campbell, 1990): a) to expend effort (direction), b) which level of effort to expend (level), and c) whether to persist in the expenditure of that level of effort (persistence). Sackett et al. (1988) and DuBois, Sackett, Zedeck, and Fogli (1993) proposed a continuum ranging from typical performance on the one end to maximum performance on the other, with the defining difference being the role of motivation. During typical performance, each of these choices lies within the performers' own hands: a) Since their performance is not being evaluated, performers can choose to focus on the most relevant task or can equally choose to procrastinate; b) since performers have not received or accepted any instruction to do their very best, they can choose to invest their full level of effort in the task or just any proportion of it; and finally, c) as they may tire during the continuation of the task, performers can choose to persist in that level of effort or to reduce it.

However, each of these choices will be affected whenever a typical performance situation is turned into a maximum performance situation. DuBois et al. (1993) and Sackett et al. (1988) argued that during maximum performance, motivation is constrained to be high because a) the choice to perform is high due to the performers' knowledge of being monitored. DuBois et al. (1993) argued, "Unless one is inviting disciplinary action, one has little choice but to expend effort on the task in question" (p. 206). Furthermore, b) the level of effort expended is high, since the second characteristic of maximum performance situations demands that individuals are aware of and accept the instruction to expend effort, and c) persistence of effort is neither demanded nor measured in situations of maximum performance, since performance is only observed for a period brief enough for individuals to stay focused on the task. Of course, one cannot assume that performers are never motivated to perform at the best of their ability under typical performance conditions; however, in contrast to maximum performance conditions, one cannot expect it, either (P. R. Sackett, personal communication, January 6, 2004).

The change in motivation during maximum compared to typical performance will influence the relative impact of both ability and motivation on performance (see Figure 15.1). During typical performance ("what people will do," Sackett et al., 1988), both motivation and ability should be relevant predictors of performance. Given that in situations of maximum job performance motivation is constrained to be high, however, maximum performance should be limited primarily by performers' ability ("what people can do," Sackett et al., 1988). Janz (1989, p. 164) summarized the distinction as follows: "Maximum performance focuses on competencies, whereas typical performance focuses on choices."

Maybe the distinction between typical and maximum performance would not matter all that much, if a number of empirical studies had not revealed that the relationship between employees' typical and maximum performance on exactly the same task can be

Predictor   **Performance**

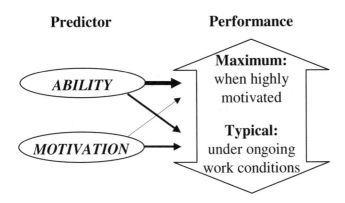

FIGURE 15.1   Prediction of typical and maximum performance through measures of ability and motivation

low. In a first study about this distinction, Sackett et al. (1988) compared the typical and maximum speed and accuracy with which 1,370 supermarket cashiers processed grocery items. Typical performance consisted of the mean number of items processed per minute over a four-week period on the job. Since data were obtained through electronic register systems, data collection was unobtrusive. During the same time-period, maximum performance was assessed on two or three occasions through the processing of two carts of grocery items each. This time, cashiers were told that the data collection served to assess their performance, and were asked to do their very best. Correlations between measures of employees' typical and maximum performance ranged from only .11 to .32, raising considerable doubt regarding the treatment of typical and maximum performance as interchangeable. Later studies by Ployhart, Lim, and Chan (2001), Klehe and Latham (2003), and Klehe and Anderson (2004a) replicated the distinction between typical and maximum performance for psychosocial and administrative tasks, assessed by soft as well as hard criterion measures, in both laboratory and field settings across North America, East Asia, and Europe.

A complete test of Sackett et al.'s assumptions regarding the role of motivation and ability has been accomplished by Klehe and Anderson (2004a): In a laboratory setting, 138 participants had to find hardware prices on the Internet and enter them into a program. While participants worked on this task for close to two hours, they were not obviously observed or evaluated during most of that time (typical performance). The computer unobtrusively recorded all of the participants' actions. Only for a five-minute interval in the midst of the experiment did the experimenter enter the room and look over participants' shoulder (maximum performance). While the experimenter had been instructed to remain as silent and to invite as little interaction as possible, the observatory nature of his intrusion was obvious. Results revealed that participants did not work significantly smarter during the assessment of maximum performance, but that they worked harder during this short period of experimenter attendance: they focused more on the task, measured in time working on the task. Their level of effort was higher, measured in task-related clicks undertaken per minute, and persistence appears to have been less of an issue during maximum performance, as indicated by the development of level over time. Consequently, their performance during the maximum performance period surpassed their performance during the rest of the experiment, a finding also reported by Klehe and Latham (2003) for the psychosocial criterion of team-playing.

In addition, Klehe and Anderson (2004a) found that Internet knowledge correlated significantly more ($r = .45$ versus .32 and .29), and Internet self-efficacy ($r = .18$ versus .37 and .33) as well as computer self-efficacy ($r = .31$ versus .45 and .44) correlated significantly less with maximum, compared to typical performance. These results present a first empirical test and confirmation of Sackett et al.'s (1988) propositions, at least within the realm of a controlled laboratory setting in which participants worked on a moderately difficult and primarily boring administrative task.

Fit with Earlier Theories of Job Performance

Given that the distinction between typical and maximum performance is real, the question arises how it may fit into existing theories of job performance. Campbell (1990) suggested that performance consists of eight facets, the core facets applicable across jobs being job-specific task proficiency, demonstrating effort, and maintaining personal discipline (resigning from counterproductive behavior). He further suggested that these factors could be used to distinguish maximum from typical performance: while task proficiency was closely related to maximum performance, demonstrating effort and maintaining personal discipline are especially relevant during typical performance. A similar approach could be taken by trying to explain the distinction between typical and maximum performance with the use of Viswesvaran, Ones, and Schmidt's (1996) model of ten interrelated factors, distinguishing typical and maximum performance primarily through the dimension "effort."

However, the continuum between typical and maximum performance may relate less to the different dimensions of performance than to the determinants of these dimensions. Campbell (1990) proposed that performance was determined by the three factors declarative knowledge, procedural knowledge and skills, and motivation. Following Sackett et al.'s arguments, the last of these factors, motivation, is likely to be constrained to be high during maximum performance, while it is likely to vary and predict performance during typical performance. Campbell (1990, p. 707) suggested motivation to be a function of "Whatever independent variables are stipulated by your favourite motivation theory." Expectancy theory (VIE; Vroom, 1964) postulates that people will be more motivated to work hard the more they believe that their effort will result in effective performance (expectancy), the more they believe that such performance will be rewarded (instrumentality), and the more they value those rewards (valence). Following DuBois et al.'s (1993) arguments, the variable most influenced through a change from a typical to a maximum performance situation is probably instrumentality, the belief that high performance will be rewarded, or, alternatively, that low performance will be punished: during typical performance situations, instrumentality is likely to be relatively weak. Since no external evaluation is present, the perceived link between good performance and reward primarily depends on the degree to which the task is intrinsically motivating, as well as on performers' ability to set goals and rewards contingent on the achievement of those goals (that is, to create the missing instrumentality themselves). During situations of maximum perform-ance, however, when performers are encouraged to invest their full effort and are evalu-ated on the basis of their performance, the link between performance and extrinsic rewards becomes highly apparent, leading performers to be highly motivated and the resulting performance to be a reflection of their ability.

THE DISTINCTION BETWEEN TYPICAL AND MAXIMUM PERFORMANCE IN PERSONNEL SELECTION

Sackett et al.'s (1988) assumptions regarding typical and maximum performance have gained considerable attention for their wide-reaching implications for industrial, work, and organizational (IWO) psychology in general (e.g., Viswesvaran, Sinangil, Ones, & Anderson, 2001), and personnel selection in particular (e.g., Ackerman & Humphreys, 1990; Arvey & Murphy, 1998; Borman, 1991; Herriot & Anderson, 1997). Through the distinction and the constrained role of motivation during maximum performance, Sackett et al. (1988) hoped to gain an estimate of the role of ability during typical performance. Chernyshenko, Stark, Chan, Drasgow, and Williams (2001) applied the distinction to item response theory (IRT) and argued that traditional IRT models may model well the con-strained responding to maximum performance situations, but not the complexity of responding to typical performance situations. Guion (1991) proposed that the low corre-lation between measures of typical and maximum performance may explain the low criterion-related validity found for numerous predictors of job performance. More specif-ically, Campbell (1990) argued that basing selection decisions on predictors of maximum performance could be one cause for the weak relationship often found between results of personnel selection procedures and typical performance on the job. Such a mismatch could also bear considerable financial consequences for the organization in question: Boudreau (1991) noted that results from utility analyses regarding a selection procedure's prediction of typical job performance are likely to be biased if the dollar value of performance is based on maximum performance criteria, and vice versa. Consequently, both researchers and practitioners need to know which of the two aspects of performance they aim to predict. While this may be especially true for validation studies, Guion (1991, 1998) empha-sized that researchers in general needed to decide which construct was more useful as a criterion in their specific research situation. Similarly, Sackett and Larson (1990) discussed threats to the generalizability of research findings, including the importance of not gen-eralizing empirical findings from typical performance situations to maximum performance situations and vice versa.

In the following section, we will discuss three studies outlining the relevance of typical versus maximum performance for the criterion-related validity and construct validity of diverse selection procedures, followed by considerations on further possible benefits for per-sonnel selection and how typical and maximum performance may relate to typical and maximal predictors or performance. Broadly, however, it can be argued that for jobs where critical-incident job analysis techniques are appropriate (see Voskuijl, Chapter 2, this volume), the prediction of maximum performance is also of crucial importance during employee selection.

Consequences for criterion-related validity

Because the determinants of typical and maximum performance criteria differ, Sackett et al. (1988) and DuBois et al. (1993) argued that the usefulness of any personnel selection procedure would vary, depending on whether it was used for predicting typical or maximum performance. Measures of ability should be better predictors of maximum performance, while measures of motivation should show increased validity for the prediction of typical performance (Klehe & Anderson, 2004a, 2004b). This proposition has stimulated most of the empirical attention paid to typical and maximum performance.

Given the argument that variations in maximum performance are not due to differences in individuals' motivation but primarily due to differences in individuals' abilities, DuBois et al. (1993) hypothesized that cognitive ability should show a stronger correlation with maximum performance than with typical performance. Using the same dataset examined by Sackett et al. (1988), DuBois et al. found support for this hypothesis. Supermarket employees' cognitive ability showed a stronger relationship with maximum than with typical speed of processing grocery items ($r = .34$ versus $.21$, $p < .05$).

Using the same argument, Klehe and Latham (2003) proposed that a test on team-playing knowledge, skills, and abilities (KSA test; Stevens & Campion, 1999) and practical intelligence should correlate higher with maximum than with typical team-playing performance among 167 MBA students. Predictors were assessed before students entered the MBA program; criteria were assessed at the end of students' first term. Peers in study groups assessed typical performance, and other peers in project groups assessed maximum performance at the end of a one-week class project. This project accounted for 25% of students' final grade in the class, 5% of which was determined by the peer assessments of team-playing performance. Again, typical and maximum performance were distinct but related constructs ($\rho = .30$). Practical intelligence correlated significantly higher with maximum ($r = .38$) than with typical performance ($r = .24$). While pointing in the same direction ($r = .40$ vs. $r = .32$), this distinction did not turn out to be significant for team-playing KSAs.

Ployhart et al. (2001) adopted a different approach. An earlier study had revealed that agreeableness, openness to experience, and extroversion were related to transformational leadership (Judge & Bono, 2000). Ployhart et al. argued that this relationship should be pronounced under maximum performance conditions, since transformational leadership might be especially relevant under those circumstances. In contrast, they argued that the situational constraints inherent in maximum performance situations should cause both the rather motivational personality dimensions of conscientiousness and neuroticism to be better predictors of typical than of maximum performance. They consequently collected peer and supervisory ratings for 1,259 Singaporean military recruits' transformational leadership during a two-day assessment center (which they labeled an assessment of maximum performance) and at the end of basic training (typical performance). After accounting for measurement effects, Ployhart et al. found maximum and typical transformational leadership performance to be related, but distinct, latent constructs ($\rho = .69$) that also differed in their relationship to the "Big Five" personality factors. Openness to experience was predictive of maximum ($\rho = .16$), and extroversion was predictive of both maximum ($\rho = .36$) and typical transformational leadership performance ($\rho = .25$). Ployhart et al.'s assumption that conscientiousness was a better predictor of typical than of maximum transformational leadership performance was not supported ($\rho = .05$). In addition, Ployhart et al.'s final model included a significant but weak path coefficient ($\rho = .08$) between neuroticism and typical performance but did not assume any path between neuroticism and maximum performance.

Consequences for construct validity

While the case may be relatively easy for predictors representing either clearly ability-related (e.g., cognitive ability) or motivational (e.g., neuroticism) measures, DuBois et al.'s (1993) assumptions have led to more heated debates regarding methods that may assess either motivation or ability, such as structured selection interviews: Latham (1989) argued that situational interviews (SI), which ask applicants what they would do in hypothetical job-related dilemmas, assess intentions, the direct motivational instigators of behavior (Fishbein & Ajzen, 1975; Locke & Latham, 1990). Janz (1989) disagreed, arguing that SIs measured verbal and inductive reasoning skills rather than actual intentions. He concluded that SIs should be worse predictors for typical than for maximum performance. At the same time he proposed that patterned behavior description interviews (PBDI), which ask applicants about past behavior, assess choices made in the past and should hence be valid predictors of typical performance. Taylor and Small (2002) made a similar argument. They proposed that SIs assess applicants' job knowledge and that PBDIs assess also applicants' motivation to apply such knowledge on the job. Consequently, PBDIs should be better predictors of typical performance than SIs. Other constructs proposed to be primarily assessed by either SI or PBDI include cognitive ability (e.g., Schmidt, 1988), practical intelligence (e.g., Conway & Peneno, 1999; Schuler & Moser, 1995), and job knowledge (Motowidlo, 1999).

Including both typical and maximum performance in a predictive validation study for an SI and a PBDI, Klehe and Latham (2003) were able to address this debate on a stronger empirical basis than is possible through the correlations between interview performance and proposed constructs alone. Both SI and PBDI predicted typical performance significantly better ($r = .41$ for SI; $r = .34$ for PBDI) than maximum performance ($r = .25$ for SI; $r = .11$ for PBDI). Team-playing KSAs and practical intelligence mediated the prediction of maximum but not of typical performance. Given that Sackett et al.'s (1988) assumptions regarding the role of motivation and ability during typical and maximum performance are correct (Klehe & Anderson, 2004a), these findings suggest that both the SI and the PBDI primarily assessed motivational constructs, such as intentions or choices. However, these motivational variables may still be informed and influenced by interviewees' practical intelligence and job knowledge (see also Anderson, 1992, 2003). While future research in this direction is clearly needed, this study outlines the possibility of using the continuum between typical and maximum performance to establish the construct validity of specific selection procedures.

Typical and maximum performance as criteria

Including measures of both extreme points as criteria in validation studies, as done by Ployhart et al. (2001) or Klehe and Latham (2003), presents an obvious benefit of the continuum between typical and maximum performance. Additionally, however, the distinction can be used to examine to which degree phenomena found during personnel selection also exist during typical and maximum job performance. For example: Past research has found that applicants engage in different impression management tactics not only during unstructured, but also during structured selection interviews (Stevens & Kristof, 1995), such as SIs and PBDIs (Ellis, West, Ryan, & DeShon, 2002). However, this research could not conclude whether the amount of impression management during those interviews exceeds that used on a day-to-day basis, and "(impression management) strategies, when true reflections of the applicant, are valuable input to the interviewer's decision" (Ellis et al., 2002, p. 206). An observation of the same impression management strategies under typical and maximum performance conditions could help clarify the degree to which the impression management found during structured interviews exceeds that found on a day-to-day basis.

The connection to maximal versus typical predictors of performance

While this chapter deals primarily with typical and maximum performance as criteria, the distinction between typical and maximal (not "maximum") performance on the predictor side has undergone further development as well. It will be interesting to note how typical and maximal predictors relate to typical and maximum criteria of performance. When comparing typical and maximal predictors, Fiske and Butler (1963, pp. 253, 258) argued that for maximal performance "We want a pure measure, one that is determined almost wholly by one thing, the subject's capacity, rather than a measure which is affected by several influences" – hence maximal tests should predominantly assess facets of ability. For personality testing, "We are ordinarily concerned with the typical strength of this tendency because this provides the best estimate of what a person is most likely to do. A straightforward conclusion of this statement would be to presume that maximal performance (ability) tests will primarily predict maximum job performance and that typical performance (personality) tests will primarily predict typical job performance. However, the findings outlined by Ployhart et al. (2001) indicate that some personality constructs, such as extroversion and openness to experience, may indeed be better predictors of maximum than of typical performance, at least for certain content domains (e.g., transformational leadership). Additionally, Ackerman and Heggestad (1997) meta-analytically found that the differentiation between ability, personality, and interests is not always clear cut.

Table 15.1 presents a number of predictors used in personnel selection and whether they are assumed to predict typical or maximum performance. This table suggests that tests of cognitive ability or general mental ability (GMA) would be most likely to predict maximum performance in particular (DuBois et al., 1993). GMA tests are given internationally in most cases under standardized conditions and with a strict time limit (with the only obvious exception being computer adaptive variants), so applicants are highly motivated to perform to their maximum level of ability over a relatively short test period. However, we would of course acknowledge that major meta-analyses conducted in both the USA (e.g., Hunter & Hunter, 1984; Schmidt & Hunter, 1998) and in Europe (e.g., Salgado & Anderson 2002; Salgado et al., 2003) have found that tests of GMA are highly robust predictors of typical performance also. However, it should be noted that these meta-

TABLE 15.1 Predictors used in personnel selection and their proposed relationships to typical and maximum performance

Measure	Predicts . . . performance		Reference
Declarative knowledge	Maximum		Klehe & Latham 2003
General mental ability (GMA)	Maximum		DuBois et al. 1993
Fluid intelligence/reasoning	Maximum		DuBois et al. 1993
Visual perception	Maximum		
Perceptual speed	Maximum		DuBois et al. 1993
Memory	Maximum		DuBois et al. 1993
Ideational fluency	Maximum		
Crystallized intelligence	Maximum		
Psychomotor skill	Maximum		
Physical skill	Maximum		
Interpersonal skill	Maximum		
Self-management skill	Maximum		
Practical intelligence	Maximum		Klehe & Latham 2003
Openness to experience	Maximum		Ployhart et al. 2001
Extroversion	Maximum	Typical	Ployhart et al. 2001
SI		Typical	Klehe & Latham 2003
	Maximum		
PBDI		Typical	Klehe & Latham 2003
	Maximum		
Assessment centers		Typical	
	Maximum		
Interest		Typical	
Conscientiousness		Typical	
Integrity		Typical	
Self-efficacy		Typical	

analyses have typically used supervisor ratings of job performance or training success as their criterion measures. As will be discussed below, the validity of both supervisory and training evaluations for assessing typical performance has been questioned (Dewberry, 2001; Klehe & Anderson, 2004a; Sackett et al., 1988; Thorsteinson & Balzer, 1999). These findings do not counter our proposals in Table 15.1, yet there has simply been a dearth of research into tests of GMA and specific abilities using measures of clearly maximum or of clearly typical performance as the criterion (see also Salgado & Anderson, 2003). We propose that such studies will most likely uncover stronger predictor-criterion relationships for maximum performance than even the existing meta-analyses suggest for tests of GMA and specific abilities against typical performance. As we indicate below, further research is needed to empirically verify or refute many of the relationships we suggest in Table 15.1. The propositions regarding predictors of primarily typical performance, of course, assume that test takers are not overly engaging in impression management (e.g., Ones & Viswesvaran, 1998).

Some predictors are included in the list, although they present methods rather than constructs since they are frequently used in personnel selection. Structured interviews and some assessment center exercises may primarily predict typical performance (Klehe & Latham, 2003). However, these methods could also predict primarily maximum performance if developed to assess abilities. For example, Campion, Campion, and Hudson (1994) developed an SI and a PBDI to measure cognitive ability. These specific interviews are likely to have been primarily predictors of maximum rather than of typical performance.

The last column of Table 15.1 indicates past research that has examined any of the proposed predictions. Apparently, many relations still need to be tested, and all of the presented results need to be replicated. Indeed, it is apparent that only a handful of studies have been published to date on the criterion-related validity of different selection methods as predictors of typical and maximum performance. This is a notable shortcoming in the selection literature, leaving open to question many issues concerning whether different predictors could most parsimoniously be used by organizations to predict typical, or alternatively, maximum performance.

Unfortunately, this dearth of consideration of the distinction between typical and maximum performance continues into current meta-analytic reviews of criterion-related validities of predictors of job performance. For example, at first glance, performance criteria such as "job proficiency" (Hough, 1992) appear to be presentations of maximum performance, until the reader realizes that researchers also included measures of "overall job performance" in such criteria. A clearer distinction between typical versus maximum performance criteria in meta-analytic reviews would be commendable. For job roles where employee behavior in critical situations (i.e., maximum performance) is vital, such research would obviously be of great pragmatic value.

Influences on the Relationship between Typical and Maximum Performance

To the authors' knowledge, no other published studies have included assessments of both typical and maximum performance. This is unfortunate, as the relationship between the two measures may not always be weak. Sackett (personal communication, January 6, 2004) noted that he never assumed that unless all maximum performance conditions are met, one cannot observe employees' top performance; only that one could oftentimes not be sure whether the presented performance was or was not maximum in nature. Given the importance of this distinction, it will be relevant to know the conditions under which it will be more pronounced and when it will be less pronounced. This section deals with a number of potential moderators for the relationship between typical and maximum performance, as well as with other psychological constructs that may influence the distinction.

Moderators

Task complexity. After finding very low correlations ($r = .11$ to $.32$) between supermarket cashiers' typical and maximum performance on a psychomotor task, Sackett et al. (1988)

proposed that the relationship between typical and maximum performance might vary depending on the type of job. The question of generalizability is important, as simple psychomotor tasks are becoming rare, while tasks involving psychosocial skills are growing in prevalence (Hesketh & Bochner, 1994).

The distinction between typical and maximum performance may be less vital in a dynamic setting requiring continuous learning and mutual adaptation than in a relatively static job. Sternberg (1999) conceptualized ability as developing expertise, and argued that the main constraint in achieving this expertise is not some fixed capacity, but deliberate practice. Thus, an individual's ability to perform a complex task may depend on that person's prior motivation to learn how to perform this task effectively. An extreme argument could be made for professions in which the typical day-to-day performance constitutes nothing but training for the moment of maximum performance, such as professional musicians or athletes – or students studying for their final exams. For complex tasks, typical performance may become a prerequisite for the development of maximum performance, and the distinction between the two may become less clear than is indicated by Sackett et al.'s (1988) results. The widely varying correlations found for high (Klehe & Latham, 2003; Ployhart et al., 2001) as well as low complexity tasks (Klehe & Anderson, 2004a; Sackett et al., 1988) counter this proposition, yet there are too few studies around to draw any definite conclusion on this proposition, and future research on this and related moderators is clearly needed.

Moderators found in the social loafing literature. Yet other potential moderators exist. The literature on social loafing, the tendency for individuals to expend less effort when working collectively than when working alone, shares major characteristics with the distinction between typical and maximum performance. Like typical and maximum performance, social loafing is dependent on the level of evaluation potential existent in the situation. Latané, Williams, and Harkins (1979, p. 830) proposed that people only engage in social loafing if they think that their performance is not identifiable because they believe that "they can receive neither precise credit nor appropriate blame for their performance." In a meta-analysis combining 163 effect sizes, Karau and Williams (1993) confirmed that people engage in social loafing if they feel unaccountable for the outcome, but not if they feel that they can be evaluated for their results. DuBois et al.'s (1993, p. 206) argument that "unless one is inviting disciplinary action [under maximum performance conditions], one has little choice but to expend effort on the task in question" follows the exact same train of thought. It can thus be proposed that the results obtained in studies on social loafing may also be applicable to typical and maximum performance.

Fortunately, the research on social loafing has accumulated a considerable body of knowledge, including meta-analytically confirmed findings regarding its moderators (Karau & Williams, 1993). It is likely that many of these variables will equally moderate the relationship between typical and maximum performance. The relationship between typical and maximum performance might increase if people a) work on tasks or b) in groups of high valence, c) are given a group-level comparison standard, d) expect their coworkers to perform poorly, e) perceive their individual input to be unique rather than redundant with the input of others, f) perform in small compared to large groups, g) are female, and h) come from an eastern cultural background.

Other relevant psychological constructs

Campbell (1990) questioned whether differences between maximum and typical performance were solely a function of motivation being variable in situations of typical performance but being constrained in situations of maximum performance. Kirk and Brown (2003) assessed the performance of 90 Australian blue-collar workers on a walk-through performance test. After receiving the testing material, participants could spend as long as they pleased in preparing for the actual test. After the test, participants indicated their proximal (work-domain self-efficacy) as well as distal (need for achievement) motivation. Findings revealed that both motivational variables were significantly related to performance in the walk-through performance test ($\beta = .46$).

Kirk and Brown's (2003) operationalization may not have completely complied with Sackett et al.'s (1988) statement that maximum performance situations should be short, so that persistence was not an issue. Since they allowed participants to prepare for the test as long as they wished, persistence probably became a relevant variable for predicting performance. Still, Kirk and Brown's (2003) findings are relevant in that they question the "held true" but never tested assumption that motivation is constrained to be high in maximum performance situations.

Achievement motivation. One could even propose that when comparing typical and maximum performance, achievement motivation may correlate more strongly with maximum than with typical performance. After all, unlike typical performance situations, maximum performance situations are likely to make it more salient, especially among performers scoring high on this motivational trait. Performers scoring low on achievement motivation, however, may be less likely to invest full effort even under maximum performance conditions, since they simply don't care. Yet, a comparison of the influence of achievement motivation (or related constructs) on typical versus maximum performance still needs to be undertaken.

Self-efficacy. Klehe and Anderson (2004a) also found that self-efficacy is a valid predictor of performance under maximum performance conditions, although it was a less robust predictor for maximum than for typical performance. Yet, the motivational variable self-efficacy may – under certain conditions – be even more important during maximum than during typical performance. Social loafing research suggests that self-efficacy is a strong moderator for the relationship between expectation of evaluation and performance: among performers with high self-efficacy, expectation of evaluation usually improves or has no effect on performance. Yet evaluation expectation can inhibit performance among performers with low self-efficacy (Bond, 1982; Sanna, 1992; Sanna & Shotland, 1990). Klehe, Hoefnagels, and Anderson (under review) found comparable effects for typical versus maximum performance. After manipulation of their self-efficacy through feedback on a multiple-choice test, 93 first year psychology students explained three topics from one of their lectures to a confederate (typical performance) and three related topics to the experimenter in the presence of a camera and a microphone (maximum performance). On both occasions performance was assessed in the form of the content and the communicative quality of the explanation. In line with above research on social loafing and inhibition, but contradicting the assertions made by Sackett et al. (1988), the performance of low self-efficacy participants in the maximum performance condition fell significantly short of their typical performance.

Mediators.   Klehe et al. (under review) also searched for potential cognitive and affective mediators of this effect by questioning participants about their cognitive interference and their state anxiety after both performance trials. They argued that self-efficacy has strong impacts on the focus of attention. People with low self-efficacy construe uncertain situations as risky and are likely to visualize failure scenarios (Kruger & Dickson, 1994). Research from social psychology (Alden, Teschuk, & Tee, 1992), feedback intervention theory (Kluger & DeNisi, 1996), and educational psychology (Eysenck, 1979; Wine, 1971) suggests that this mechanism may happen during maximum performance situations especially. Similarly, self-efficacy has strong effects on individuals' affective reactions (Alden, 1986; Bandura, 1997; Krampen, 1988; Leland, 1983). Maximum performance situations might trigger a higher rate of fear and of self-related meta-task processes. Evaluating the meaning of task-performance for the self while all cognitive resources would be needed to accomplish the task in question might inhibit performance. Klehe et al. found such a mediating effect on the impaired performance of low self-efficacy participants in the maximum performance condition for state anxiety. The effect for cognitive interference, however, did not turn out to be significant.

While Klehe et al. (under review) proposed that participants' high intrinsic motivation during typical performance and the fear-eliciting maximum performance setting would account for the effects found, further research is needed that outlines the conditions under which maximum performance conditions may harm rather than foster performance. Such research is important not only from a theoretical, but also from a humanitarian standpoint. It is likely that maximum performance situations not only trigger performers' high motivation to show themselves to the best of their ability, but that such situations can also induce fear, lowering the well-being as well as the performance of at least some individuals. Assuming that the resulting performance reflects these individuals' best ability may lead to wrong conclusions.

Creative tasks

Independently of the role of self-efficacy, Sackett et al.'s (1988) assumption may not be valid for all kinds of tasks. Researchers on creativity have long assumed that evaluation may actually do more harm than good by inhibiting the creative process (e.g., Amabile, 1983; Anderson, De Dreu, & Nijstad, 2004). Research on idea generation has found that although potential for evaluation can have positive effects on the number of ideas created, it often has negative effects on the quality of ideas (Bartis, Szmanski, & Harkins, 1988). Numerous studies have shown that expectation of evaluation- or performance-contingent rewards lowers performance on diverse creative tasks (see Amabile, 1996; West & Anderson, 1996). As Amabile (1996) noted, the negative effects of evaluation become especially likely when participants perceive the evaluation to be of a controlling (as is the case in maximum performance situations), rather than of an informative nature. Again, the explanation offered for this detrimental effect of evaluation on performance is decreased task-focused attention. A direct empirical examination of the effect of typical versus maximum performance conditions on creativity and work role innovation, however, still needs to be undertaken.

Choking under pressure

Performance evaluation, as during maximum performance situations, can also impair performance on well-learned sensorimotor skills (Baumeister, 1984; Masters, 1992). "Choking," or performing below one's level of skill, tends to occur in situations fraught with performance pressure, the anxious desire to perform especially well (Baumeister, 1984). Masters (1992) argued that well-learned complex skills were encoded in a procedural form that supports effective real-time performance without requiring step-by-step attentional control. Increased attention to the execution of such a skill, however, which is likely to be fostered during highly evaluative situations, may prompt attention to skill execution, which results in a breakdown of task components, which then must each be run separately and be coordinated with one another, leading to impaired performance.

Beilock and Carr (2001) found in two experiments that the performance of experienced golfers was guided by proceduralized knowledge. Two additional experiments revealed that practice in coping with self-consciousness-raising situations counteracted choking under pressure, but that mere practice of the task in the presence or absence of other distracting stimuli did not. Beilock and Carr (2001, p. 723) concluded that "The notion that performance pressure induces self-focused attention, which in turn may lead to decrements in skill execution, is now a reasonably well-supported concept for proceduralized skills." It has yet to be tested whether this conclusion also holds true for maximum versus typical performance.

METHODOLOGICAL ISSUES IN TYPICAL AND MAXIMUM PERFORMANCE

Given the above comments regarding the scarcity of research on typical and maximum performance and consequent research ideas, some methodological concerns should be added for researchers interested in studying typical and/or maximum performance. This section will outline considerations to be taken into account when designing studies that either compare typical or maximum performance or assume that the performance criterion measured will assess either of the two aspects of performance.

Comparing typical and maximum performance

Sackett et al. (1988) argued that when comparing typical and maximum performance, the measures should be comparable in a) the modality of measurement, b) the level of specificity, c) the time of assessment in an individual's job tenure, and should d) be reliable in order to ensure that results obtained are truly a function of participants' knowledge of being evaluated, their acceptance of instruction to invest effort, and the time duration. While these demands sound easy enough, P. R. Sackett (personal communication, June 2002) proposed that the difficulty of manipulating performance situations in a way that created truly parallel typical and maximum performance situations was likely to be a major cause of the scarcity of empirical research on this obviously important distinction. One could argue, for example, that Sackett et al.'s (1988) results are not a function of typical versus maximum performance per se, but of varying job demands during typical performance – e.g., during slow periods, speed of processing items might be less indicative of good cashier performance than, for example, establishing friendly interpersonal relationships with customers. Ployhart et al.'s results could be equally explained in that the assessments of typical performance (military training developed primarily to train recruits' physical fitness) and maximum performance (assessment center developed primarily to assess recruits' leadership skills) differed in more aspects than the three motivational conditions differentiating typical and maximum performance situations.

It is important to maintain clean distinctions between typical and maximum performance situations and keep them otherwise as parallel as possible to ensure that results are not caused by alternative possible explanations. Especially important, according to DuBois et al. (1993), is to distinguish maximum performance from what they label "typical performance in high-demand situations." They argued that motivation would not be automatically given in the face of high demands. The resulting performance was hence again rather a case of what employees "will do," compared to what they "can do."

Yet, we believe that many concerns regarding a comparison between typical and maximum performance can be handled by adequate research designs and measurement. The first step, of course, is to employ situations to assess typical and maximum performance that resemble each other as closely as possible, except for a) perceived evaluation and b) instruction to invest effort to be more and c) duration to be less a given during the maximum performance assessment, compared to the typical performance assessment. The second step is to test whether this attempt was sufficiently successful. That is, one should assess both the comparability of the two measurement settings as well as their difference. Post hoc data collected by Klehe and Latham (2003) suggest that MBA students evaluated the team-playing items used in that study as comparably important and observable in the typical as well as in the maximum performance condition.

As Sackett et al. (1988) noted, typical and maximum performance represent a continuum. Hence, every comparison between the two aspects of performance will be relative. Ultimately, the distinction will depend on participants' perception of the degree to which a) the situation was evaluative, b) they had to perform at their best, and c) the test period was short. The only way to ascertain these presumptions is to ask participants about their perceptions. Unfortunately, to our knowledge, only one of the studies on typical and maximum performance included a manipulation check (Klehe & Latham, 2003).

To facilitate future research and to allow researchers to draw their conclusions regarding typical and maximum performance with more certainty, we are currently developing a scale to distinguish the degree to which a situation is perceived as typical or maximum (Klehe & Anderson, 2004b). The current version of the Typical and Maximum Performance Scale (TMPS) uses the 20 self-report items presented in Table 15.2. Each item loads on one of the three situational factors a) knowledge of evaluation, b) receiving and

TABLE 15.2   Items of Typical and Maximum Performance Scale (TMPS; Klehe & Anderson, 2004b)

1	2	3	4	5	Factor
Strongly disagree				*Strongly agree*	

While working, I thought about other, work-unrelated, things. (*r*)	Direction
I took "mental breaks" during the work. (*r*)	Direction
I daydreamed while doing the work. (*r*)	Direction
I fully focused on the work at hand.	Level
I expended my maximum effort on the task.	Level
I was not consciously attempting to perform my best. (*r*)	Level
I worked as hard as I could.	Level
The work became tiresome after a while. (*r*)	Persistence
Remaining continually focused on the work became difficult. (*r*)	Persistence
I had no problem maintaining a high level of effort throughout the task.	Persistence
I lost interest in the work for short periods. (*r*)	Persistence
It was very obvious to me that my performance was being evaluated.	Evaluation
I didn't think that I was being evaluated. (*r*)	Evaluation
Doing well would have been rewarded.	Evaluation
I had been instructed to maximize my efforts.	Instruction
I was expected to focus my full attention on doing the work as well as possible.	Instruction
I had not received instructions to invest my full effort. (*r*)	Instruction
I understood and accepted that I should focus my full attention on the task.	Instruction
I only did this work under the given conditions for a short time-period.	Duration
I was working on this task under the given conditions for a long time. (*r*)	Duration

Note: (*r*) = reversed scoring. For permission to use this scale, please contact the first author.

acceptance of instructions to maximize effort, c) duration, or on one of the three motivational consequences d) direction, e) level, and f) persistence of effort. All subscales but the subscale "duration" have shown internal consistencies above .70 and have successfully distinguished between situations of clearly typical and clearly maximum performance, while being unaffected by gender, age, cognitive ability, and most facets of personality.

Establishing a situation as either typical or maximum

The use of a scale such as the TMPS may not only be helpful when comparing typical and maximum performance, but may also help to establish whether a situation itself could be categorized as typical or maximum. This might be helpful, as the current research indicates some confusion about the degree to which researchers categorize a situation to elicit either typical or maximum performance.

Smith-Jentsch, Jentsch, Payne, and Salas (1996), for example, assessed performance in a training flight-simulator. They labeled this a measure of maximum performance since participants were aware of the evaluative nature of the task, accepted the explicit instructions to maximize effort, and were observed only over a short time period (35 minutes). In another experiment, Smith-Jentsch, Salas, and Brannick (2001) used the same flight-simulator to assess both typical and maximum performance, but they did not vary the time-duration across conditions or the fact that participants knew about the performance evaluation. The only difference was that participants in the "maximum performance" condition were made aware of the skills to be assessed and the fact that their team-mates were confederates, whereas those in the "typical performance" condition were not given this information.

Sackett et al. (1988) and Dewberry (2001) argued that studies conducted in a professional training rather than a work context may assess maximum rather than typical performance. This is because the trainees are likely to give their best possible performance in order to enter their chosen profession. Their performance on the job, however, could be quite different. Ployhart et al. (2001), however, labeled their three-month military training an assessment of typical performance. As a comparison, Ployhart et al. employed a two-day assessment center to measure maximum performance. Yet, assessment centers were originally constructed to measure typical performance (Thornton & Byham, 1982), although this point is certainly debatable given their evaluative nature and the fact that they often serve to assess ability-related dimensions such as "leadership capabilities" or "social proficiency." Again, comparing such situations through a measure such as the TMPS may help to validate whether a situation reflects typical or maximum performance conditions.

Similar concerns have been voiced regarding laboratory studies. Sackett and Larson (1990) argued that laboratory studies were often assessments of maximum rather than of typical performance, and cautioned generalizing findings derived through laboratory studies to typical performance situations. At the same time, compared to field settings, laboratory settings may facilitate the establishment of truly parallel situations of typical and maximum performance while allowing for a relatively controlled research setting. Initial laboratory studies (e.g., Klehe & Anderson, 2004a) supporting Sackett et al.'s (1988) assumptions regarding the role of motivation and ability during typical and maximum performance situations suggest that the distinction between typical and maximum performance can, at least in parts, also be studied in the laboratory.

Finally, Thorsteinson and Balzer (1999) suggested that different raters may rate different aspects of employees' performance. While coworkers may observe daily information about individuals' typical level of motivation and performance, supervisors may only be allowed to observe individuals' maximum performance. As presented in our laboratory experiment, the mere presence of the experimenter motivated participants to work significantly harder than they did during the rest of the experiment. How much stronger might this effect be on tasks that people perform not just for two hours but for years, so that even the last novelty-effect has worn off? And how much stronger may it be in real-life settings, given that employees know that the impressions formed about them by a supervisor, unlike those formed by an experimenter in a psychology department, can have actual administrative consequences for their careers? Hence, it may not be a surprise that Sackett et al. (1988) found supervisory ratings of performance to be significantly more strongly related to the maximum than to the typical speed and accuracy with which supermarket cashiers processed grocery items.

CONCLUSIONS

After reading theoretical accounts (e.g., Arvey & Murphy, 1998), handbook chapters (e.g., Ackerman & Humphreys, 1990; Borman, 1991), and the discussions of research publications using the distinction between typical and maximum performance (e.g., Dewberry, 2001), one would believe this topic to be alive and fiercely studied. Unfortunately, this appears not to have been the case for most of the time since the distinction was officially introduced (Sackett et al., 1988). Given the amount of theoretical attention and lip service paid to the distinction between typical and maximum performance, this area still faces a severe lack of empirical testing. Fortunately, the empirical literature is slowly catching up. The fact that most of the studies cited in this chapter that deal with typical and maximum performance have been published or presented within the past five years is no recency effect, but reflects a rising empirical interest in the distinction.

As it is, one can conclude that current research found typical and maximum performance to be different though related constructs, and measures of ability to be better predictors for maximum than for typical performance. Apparently some predictors, such as structured interviews developed to assess intentions or past choices, may serve especially well to predict typical performance (Klehe & Latham, 2003), but replications of such findings are clearly needed. We also know that the assumptions issued by Sackett et al. (1988) regarding the role of motivation and ability during typical and maximum performance hold true under at least some conditions (Klehe & Anderson, 2004a). However, this does not exclude motivation from playing any role during maximum performance (Kirk & Brown, 2003; Klehe & Anderson, 2004a, under review). Equally, maximum performance situations may demand some additional skills needed to a lesser extent during typical performance, such as self-management skills in the sense of the ability to regulate one's thoughts and emotions when under pressure. As outlined in the above references to the literature on social facilitation (Sanna, 1992), pedagogical psychology (Wine, 1971), and feedback intervention theory (Kluger & DeNisi, 1996), maximum performance conditions may raise cognitive interference and anxiety, giving performers additional foes to battle against while they are asked to concentrate on the task.

As we noted earlier, the paucity of extant research into typical–maximum performance is a real gap in our understanding of the practical implications for using different selection methods to predict job performance outcome. The state of this research field at the present juncture is that of being able to make some sensible suggestions and assertions for practice. Yet, it is far from being the mature and developed sub-discipline described by Anderson, Herriot, and Hodgkinson (2001) as constituting "Pragmatic Science." Selection psychology throughout its history has been bedeviled by criterion measurement problems, and the case of typical–maximum performance is no exception. In terms of practical implications, perhaps the most pressing need for empirical research is in the use of predictors of maximum performance in job roles where highly consequential critical incidents occur. Earlier we gave some examples but others include health care and nursing, medical operations, commercial and military pilots, safety-critical operator roles, and creative performance occupations. Here, the potential importance of maximum performance, for however brief a period, outweighs that of typical performance of considerably longer periods and durations of tenure in the job role. To be able to base recommendations to organizations for the design of selection procedures purely for such maximum performance situations would be of immense value (Anderson et al., 2001). Yet, selection research is currently at the rather frustrating point of development of having insufficient empirical studies upon which to base such important recommendations. We therefore call for substantial additional research effort in this area and hope that this chapter will stimulate several potentially fruitful lines of initial enquiry.

NOTE

The authors wish to thank Paul R. Sackett, Arne Evers, and Olga Voskuijl for their valuable comments on an earlier version of this chapter. This research was funded by a DAAD grant (German Academic Exchange Service) to the first author during her Post-Doc studies at the University of Amsterdam.

REFERENCES

Ackerman, P. L., & Heggestad, E. D. (1997). Intelligence, personality, and interests: Evidence for overlapping traits. *Psychological Bulletin, 121*, 219–245.

Ackerman, P. L., & Humphreys, L. G. (1990). Individual differences theory in industrial and organizational psychology. In M. D. Dunnette & L. M. Hough (Eds.), *Handbook of industrial and organizational psychology* (2nd ed., Vol. 1, pp. 223–282). Palo Alto, CA: Consulting Psychologists Press.

Alden, L. (1986). Self-efficacy and causal attributions for social feedback. *Journal of Research in Personality, 20*, 460–473.

Alden, L., Teschuk, M., & Tee, K. (1992). Public self-awareness and withdrawal from social interactions. *Cognitive Therapy and Research, 16*, 249–267.

Amabile, T. M. (1983). *The social psychology of creativity*. New York: Springer-Verlag.

Amabile, T. M. (1996). *Creativity in context: Update to the social psychology of creativity*. Boulder, CO: Westview.

Anderson, N. (1992). Eight decades of employment interview research: A retrospective meta-review and prospective commentary. *The European Work and Organizational Psychologist, 2*, 1–32.

Anderson, N. (2003). Applicant and recruiter reactions to new technology in selection: A critical review and agenda for future research. *International Journal of Selection and Assessment, 11*, 121–136.

Anderson, N., DeDreu, C. K. W., & Nijstad, B. A. (2004). The routinization of innovation research: A constructively critical review of the state-of-the-science. *Journal of Organizational Behavior*, in press.

Anderson, N., Herriot, P., & Hodgkinson, G. P. (2001). The practitioner-researcher divide in industrial, work and organizational (IWO) psychology: Where we are and where we do we go from here. *Journal of Occupational and Organizational Psychology, 74*, 391–411.

Arvey, R. D., & Murphy, K. R. (1998). Performance evaluation in work settings. *Annual Review of Psychology, 49*, 141–168.

Bandura, A. (1997). Self efficacy: The exercise of control. New York: Freeman.

Bartis, S., Szmanski, K., & Harkins, S. G. (1988). Evaluation and performance: A two-edged knife. *Personality and Social Psychology Bulletin, 14*, 242–251.

Baumeister, R. F. (1984). Choking under pressure: Self-consciousness and paradoxical effects of incentives on skillful performance. *Journal of Personality and Social Psychology, 46*, 610–620.

Beilock, S. L., & Carr, T. H. (2001). On the fragility of skilled performance: What governs choking under pressure? *Journal of Experimental Psychology: General, 130*, 701–725.

Bond, C. F. (1982). Social facilitation: A self-presentational view. *Journal of Personality and Social Psychology, 42*, 1042–1050.

Borman, W. C. (1991). Job behavior, performance, and effectiveness. In M. D. Dunnette & L. M. Hough (Eds.), *Handbook of industrial and organizational psychology* (2nd ed., Vol. 2, pp. 271–326). Palo Alto, CA: Consulting Psychologists Press.

Boudreau, J. W. (1991). Utility analysis for decisions in human resource management. In M. D. Dunnette & L. M. Hough (Eds.), *Handbook of industrial and organizational psychology* (2nd ed., Vol. 2, pp. 621–745). Palo Alto, CA: Consulting Psychologists Press.

Campbell, J. P. (1990). Modeling the performance prediction problem in industrial and organizational psychology. In M. D. Dunnette & L. M. Hough (Eds.), *Handbook of industrial and organizational psychology* (2nd ed., Vol. 1, pp. 687–732). Palo Alto, CA: Consulting Psychologists Press.

Campion, M. A., Campion, J. E., & Hudson, J. P., Jr. (1994). Structured interviewing: A note on incremental validity and alternative question types. *Journal of Applied Psychology, 79*, 998–1002.

Chernyshenko, O. S., Stark, S., Chan, K. Y., Drasgow, F., & Williams, B. (2001). Fitting item response theory models to two personality inventories: Issues and insights. *Multivariate Behavioral Research, 36*, 523–562.

Conway, J. M., & Peneno, G. M. (1999). Comparing structured interview question types: Construct validity and applicant reactions. *Journal of Business and Psychology, 13*, 485–506.

Cronbach, L. J. (1960). *Essentials of psychological testing* (2nd ed.). New York: Harper & Row.

Dennis, M. J., Sternberg, R. J., & Beatty, P. (2000). The construction of "user-friendly" tests of cognitive functioning: A synthesis of maximal- and typical-performance measurement philosophies. *Intelligence, 28*, 193–211.

Dewberry, C. (2001). Performance disparities between whites and ethnic minorities: Real differences or assessment bias? *Journal of Occupational and Organizational Psychology, 74*, 659–673.

DuBois, C. L. Z., Sackett, P. R., Zedeck, S., & Fogli, L. (1993). Further exploration of typical and maximum performance criteria: Definitional issues, prediction, and White–Black differences. *Journal of Applied Psychology, 78*, 205–211.

Ellis, A. P. J., West, B. J., Ryan, A. M., & DeShon, R. P. (2002). The use of impression management tactics in structured interviews: A function of question type? *Journal of Applied Psychology, 87*, 1200–1208.

Eysenck, M. W. (1979). Anxiety learning and memory: A reconceptualization. *Journal or Research in Personality, 13*, 363–385.

Fishbein, M., & Ajzen, I. (1975). *Belief, attitude, intention and behavior: An introduction to theory and research.* Reading, MA: Addison-Wesley.

Fiske, D. W., & Butler, J. M. (1963). The experimental conditions for measuring individual differences. *Educational and Psychological Measurement, 23*, 249–266.

Guion, R. M. (1991). Personnel assessment, selection, and placement. In M. D. Dunnette & L. M. Hough (Eds.), *Handbook of industrial and organizational psychology* (2nd ed., Vol. 2, (pp. 327–397). Palo Alto, CA: Consulting Psychologists Press.

Guion, R. M. (1998). *Assessment, measurement, and prediction of personnel decisions.* Mahwah, NJ: Lawrence Erlbaum.

Herriot, P., & Anderson, N. (1997). Selecting for change: How will personnel and selection psychology survive? In N. Anderson & P. Herriot (Eds.), *International handbook of selection and assessment* (pp. 1–38), Chichester, UK: John Wiley & Sons.

Hesketh, B., & Bochner, S. (1994). Technological change in a multicultural context: Implications for training and career planning. In H. C. Triandis & M. D. Dunnette (Eds.), *Handbook of industrial and organizational psychology* (2nd ed., Vol. 4, pp. 191–240). Palo Alto, CA: Consulting Psychologists Press.

Hough, L. M. (1992). The "big five" personality variables – construct confusion: Description versus prediction. *Human Performance, 5*, 139–155.

Hunter, J. E., & Hunter, R. F. (1984). Validity and utility of alternative predictors of job performance. *Psychological Bulletin, 96*, 72–98.

Janz, T. (1989). The patterned behaviour description interview: The best prophet of the future is the past. In R. W. Eder & G. R. Ferris (Eds.), *The employment interview: Theory, research, and practice* (pp. 158–168). Newbury Park, CA: Sage.

Judge, T. A., & Bono, J. E. (2000). Five factor model of personality and transformational leadership. *Journal of Applied Psychology, 85*, 751–765.

Karau, S. J., & Williams, K. D. (1993). Social loafing: A meta-analytic review and theoretical integration. *Journal of Personality and Social Psychology, 65*, 681–706.

Kirk, A. K., & Brown, D. F. (2003). Latent constructs of proximal and distal motivation predicting performance under maximum test conditions. *Journal of Applied Psychology, 88*, 40–49.

Klehe, U. C., & Anderson, N. (2004a). *Working hard and smart during typical and maximum performance.* Paper presented at the 19th annual meeting of the Society of Industrial and Organizational Psychology, Chicago.

Klehe, U. C., & Anderson, N. (2004b). *TMPS: Typical and Maximum Performance Scale.* Paper presented at the 19th annual meeting of the Society of Industrial and Organizational Psychology, Chicago.

Klehe, U. C., Hoefnagels, E. A., & Anderson, N. (under review). *The effect of self-efficacy on maximum versus typical performance.* Paper submitted to the annual meeting of the Academy of Management, New Orleans, 2004.

Klehe, U. C., & Latham, G. P. (2003, April). *Towards an understanding of the constructs underlying the situational and patterned behavior description interview in predicting typical versus maximum performance.* Paper presented at the 18th annual meeting of the Society of Industrial and Organizational Psychology, Orlando, FL.

Kluger, A. N., & DeNisi, A. (1996). Effects of feedback intervention on performance: A historical review, a meta-analysis, and a preliminary feedback intervention theory. *Psychological Bulletin, 119*, 254–284.

Krampen, G. (1988). Competence and control orientations as predictors of test anxiety in students: Longitudinal results. *Anxiety Research, 1*, 185–197.

Kruger, N. F., Jr., & Dickson, P. R. (1994). How believing in ourselves increases risk taking: Perceived self-efficacy and opportunity recognition. *Decision Sciences, 25*, 385–400.

Latané, B., Williams, K., & Harkins, S. (1979). Many hands make light the work: The causes and consequences of social loafing. *Journal of Personality and Social Psychology, 37*, 822–832.

Latham, G. P. (1989). The reliability, validity, and practicality of the situational interview. In G. Ferris & R. Eder (Eds.), *The employment interview: Theory, research and practice.* Newbury Park, CA: Sage.

Leland, E. I. (1983). *Self-efficacy and other variables as they relate to precompetitive anxiety among male interscholastic basketball players.* Ph.D. diss., Stanford University. *Dissertation Abstracts International, 44*, 1376A.

Locke, E. A., & Latham, G. P. (1990). *A theory of goal setting and task performance.* Englewood Cliffs, NY: Prentice Hall.

Locke, E. A., Mento, A. J., & Katcher, B. L. (1978). The interaction of ability and motivation in performance: An exploration of the meaning of moderators. *Personnel Psychology, 31*, 269–280.

Masters, R. S. (1992). Knowledge, knerves, and know-how: The role of explicit versus implicit knowledge in the breakdown of a complex motor skill under pressure. *British Journal of Psychology, 83*, 343–358.

Motowidlo, S. J. (1999). Asking about past behaviour versus hypothetical behaviour. In R. W. Eder & M. H. Harris (Eds.), *The employment interview handbook* (pp. 179–190). Newbury Park, CA: Sage.

Ones, D. S., & Viswesvaran, C. (1998). The effects of social desirability and faking on personality and integrity assessment for personnel selection. *Human Performance, 11*, 245–269.

Ployhart, R. E., Lim, B.C., & Chan, K. Y. (2001). Exploring relations between typical and maximum performance ratings and the five factor model of personality. *Personnel Psychology, 54*, 809–843.

Sackett, P. R., & Larson, J. R. (1990). Research strategies and tactics in industrial and organizational psychology. In M. D. Dunnette & L. M. Hough (Eds.), *Handbook of industrial and organizational psychology* (2nd ed., Vol. 1, pp. 419–490). Palo Alto, CA: Consulting Psychologists Press.

Sackett, P. R., Zedeck, S., & Fogli, L. (1988). Relations between measures of typical and maximum job performance. *Journal of Applied Psychology, 73*, 482–486.

Salgado, J. F., & Anderson, N. (2002). Cognitive and GMA testing in the European Community: Issues and evidence. *Human Performance, 15*, 75–96.

Salgado, J. F., & Anderson, N. (2003). Validity generalization of GMA tests across countries in the European Community. *European Journal of Work and Organizational Psychology, 12*, 1–17.

Salgado, J. F., Anderson, N., Moscoso, S., Bertua, C., de Fruyt, F., & Rolland, J. P. (2003). A meta-analytic study of general mental ability validity for different occupations in the European Community. *Journal of Applied Psychology, 88*, 1068–1081.

Sanna, L. (1992). Self-efficacy theory: Implications for social facilitation and social loafing. *Journal of Personality and Social Psychology, 62*, 774–786.

Sanna, L., & Shotland, R. L. (1990). Valence of anticipated evaluation and social facilitation. *Journal of Experimental Social Psychology, 26*, 82–92.

Schmidt, F. L. (1988). The problem of group differences in ability test scores in employment selection. *Journal of Vocational Behavior, 33*, 272–292.

Schmidt, F.L., & Hunter, J. E. (1998). The validity and utility of selection methods in personnel psychology: Practical and theoretical implications of 85 years of research findings. *Psychological Bulletin, 124*, 262–274.

Schuler, H., & Moser, K. (1995). Die Validität des Multimodalen Interviews [The validity of the multimodal interview]. *Zeitschrift für Arbeits- und Organisationspsychologie, 39*, 2–12.

Smith-Jentsch, K. A., Jentsch, F. G., Payne, S. C., & Salas, E. (1996). Can pretraining experiences explain individual differences in learning? *Journal of Applied Psychology, 81*, 110–116.

Smith-Jentsch, K. A., Salas, E., & Brannick, M. T. (2001). To transfer or not to transfer? Investigating the combined effects of trainee characteristics, team leader support, and team climate. *Journal of Applied Psychology, 86*, 279–292.

Sternberg, R. J. (1999). Intelligence as developing expertise. *Contemporary Educational Psychology, 24*, 359–375.

Stevens, C. K., & Kristof, A. L. (1995). Making the right impression: A field study of applicant impression management during job interviews. *Journal of Applied Psychology, 80*, 587–606.

Stevens, M. J., & Campion, M. A. (1999). Staffing work teams: Development and validation of a selection test for teamwork settings. *Journal of Management, 25*, 207–228.

Taylor, P. J., & Small, B. (2002). Asking applicants what they would do versus what they did do: A meta-analytic comparison of situational and past behaviour employment interview questions. *Journal of Occupational and Organizational Psychology, 75*, 277–294.

Thornton, G. C., III, & Byham, W. C. (1982). *Assessment centers and managerial performance*. New York: Academic Press.

Thorsteinson, T. J., & Balzer, W. K. (1999). Effects of coworker information on perceptions and ratings of performance. *Journal of Organizational Behavior, 20*, 1157–1173.

Viswesvaran, C., Ones, D. S., & Schmidt, F. L. (1996). Comparative analysis of the reliability of job performance ratings. *Journal of Applied Psychology, 81,* 557–574.

Viswesvaran, C., Sinangil, H.K., Ones, D. S., & Anderson, N. (2001). Where we have been, where we are, (and where we could be). In N. Anderson, D. S. Ones, H. K. Sinangil, & C. Viswesvaran (Eds.), *Handbook of industrial, work and organizational psychology* (Vol. 1, pp. 1–9). London: Sage.

Vroom, V. H. (1964). *Work and motivation.* Oxford, UK: Wiley.

West, M. A., & Anderson, N. (1996). Innovation in top management teams. *Journal of Applied Psychology, 81,* 680–693.

Wine, J. (1971). Test anxiety and direction of attention. *Psychological Bulletin, 76,* 92–104.

16

Job Performance: Assessment Issues in Personnel Selection

CHOCKALINGAM VISWESVARAN AND DENIZ S. ONES

An important construct in Industrial, Work and Organizational (IWO) psychology, organizational behavior, and human resources management (personnel selection, training, and performance evaluation) in general, and personnel selection in particular, is the construct of job performance. Job performance is the most important dependent variable in IWO psychology (Schmidt & Hunter, 1992). A general definition of the construct of job performance reflects behaviors (both visually observable and non-observable) that can be evaluated (Viswesvaran, Ones, & Schmidt, 1996). In other words, job performance refers to scalable actions, behaviors, and outcomes that employees engage in or bring about that are linked with and contribute to organizational goals (Viswesvaran & Ones, 2000). To date, most researchers focusing on the construct of job performance have confined themselves to particular situations and settings with no attempt to generalize their findings. Also, there has been an emphasis on prediction and practical application rather than explanation and theory building. The consequence of these two trends has been a proliferation of the various measures of job performance in the extant literature. Virtually every measurable individual differences dimension thought to be relevant to the productivity, efficiency, or profitability of the unit or organization has been used as a measure of job performance. Absenteeism, productivity ratings, violence on the job, and teamwork ratings are some examples of the variety of measures used to measure job performance.

There are multiple uses for job performance data. In selection contexts, measures of job performance are used to validate predictors. Thus, the choice of the job performance measure has important substantive implications for our practice and science of personnel selection. Measures of individual job performance play a central role at each step of the personnel selection function. Consider the first step in selection: recruitment of qualified applicants. One question in recruitment is whether the different sources of recruitment result in attraction of individuals who differ in job performance levels (Barber, 1998). Following successful recruitment efforts, attempts are made to identify individual differences variables that are related to individual differences in job performance, and select individuals based on those characteristics (Guion, 1998). Individual differences in job performance are assessed and those assessments are used in placement and promotion decisions.

Individual job performance data can be used in numerous other ways that have relevance for personnel staffing. Cleveland, Murphy, and Williams (1989) identified several uses of individual job performance data. They classified these uses into four categories: 1) between-person decisions, 2) within-person decisions, 3) systems maintenance, and 4) documentation. The need for clear documentation of individual job performance is evident in several landmark legal decisions (Malos, 1998). Individual job performance assessment has been used for administrative purposes for many decades (Whisler & Harper, 1962). DeVries, Morrison, Shullman, and Gerlach (1986) report that surveys conducted in the 1970s in both the USA and the UK indicated the prevalence of individual job performance assessment for the purpose of making administrative decisions. Thus, understanding the issues in job performance assessment is critical in personnel selection.

Several issues have been raised in the assessment of job performance (Austin & Villanova, 1992; Campbell, 1990; Viswesvaran, Schmidt, & Ones, 2002). Although the literature on each of these issues can be expanded into a book-length exposition, in this chapter we will attempt to cover some of the major issues. First, we will briefly discuss the different measurement methods by which job performance could be measured. Second, we will provide an overview of different sources of ratings, the widespread use of multi-source feedback, and the claims made for the unique perspective of raters at different levels of an organization. Our review found scant empirical evidence that raters at different levels of an organization have different conceptualization of job performance dimensions. When ratings are provided on a job performance dimension, say interpersonal competence or teamwork, supervisors, peers, and subordinates of an employee provide equivalent construct-level ratings. Different manifestations of the construct could be the focus for different sources, but the underlying construct assessed remains the same.

Following this, we will discuss the content or dimensionality of job performance measures. The relative merits of using a broad or a narrow conceptualization for assessing job performance and the subsequent implications for issues such as differential validity of predictors are covered. Finally, we conclude this chapter with some emerging issues, both psychometric (e.g., appropriate reliability coefficient to use, role of halo) and substantive (e.g., assessing team performance).

MEASUREMENT METHODS

Individual job performance can be measured utilizing different methods. However, these methods can be classified into two broad categories: 1) organizational records, and 2) subjective evaluations. Organizational records are considered to be more "objective," in contrast to the subjective evaluations that depend on a human judgment. This distinction is parallel to what Smith (1976) described as hard criteria (i.e., organizational records) and soft criteria (i.e., subjective evaluations).

However, it is important to stress that even "objective" organizational records depend on human evaluation/judgment and recording of observed events. Furthermore, it is not necessarily the subjectivity that should be cause for concern. Measurements of job performance should be evaluated on psychometric properties such as criterion contamination, deficiency, relevance, reliability, appropriateness, etc. Blum and Naylor (1968) identify eleven dimensions or characteristics on which the different criteria can be evaluated, whereas Brogden (1946) identifies relevance, reliability, and practicality as the criteria for criteria. Relevance refers to the overlap between what is measured and what was intended to be measured. Thus, criterion relevance is similar to construct validity of measures. Criterion contamination is the inclusion of sources of variance in a measure that was not intended in the theoretical conceptualization. Criterion deficiency is the lack of relevant sources of variance in the measure employed but which was intended to be measured (i.e., the intended criterion). Practicality refers to the ease with which a measure could be administered. On all these criteria (e.g., contamination, deficiency, etc.) both organizational records and rater judgments and evaluations are affected to different degrees. As such, there is no basis for assuming that organizational records are more "objective" or "accurate" than ratings.

Methods of assessments should be distinguished from types of criteria. Different types of criteria have been formed based on either the time span of performance considered or what is included in the measure of performance. For example, Thorndike (1949) identifies three types of criteria: immediate, intermediate, and ultimate criteria. The ultimate criterion summarizes the total worth of the individual to the organization over the entire career span. The immediate criterion is a measure of individual job performance at that particular point in time. Intermediate criteria summarize performance over a period of time. Similarly, Mace (1935) argued that measures of individual job performance can stress either capacity or will to perform. This distinction is a forerunner to the distinction between maximal and typical performance measures (e.g., DuBois, Sackett, Zedeck, & Fogli, 1993; Klehe & Anderson, Chapter 15, this volume; Sackett, Zedeck, & Fogli, 1988). Maximal performance is what an individual can do if highly motivated, whereas typical performance is what an individual is likely to do in a typical day. The distinction between ultimate, intermediate, and immediate criteria or between maximal and typical performance refers to types of criteria. Both organizational records and subjective evaluations (methods) can be used to assess them.

Organizational records can be further classified into direct measures of productivity and personnel data (Schmidt, 1980). Direct measures of productivity stress the number of units produced. Also included are measures of quality such as the number of errors, scrap material produced, etc. Personnel data, on the other hand, do not directly measure productivity but inferences of productivity can be derived based on them. Lateness or tardiness, tenure, absences, accidents, promotion rates, and filing grievances can be considered as indirect measures of productivity – there is an inferential leap involved in using these personnel data as measures of individual job performance. Organizational records, by focusing on observable, countable, discrete outcomes, may overcome the biasing influences of subjective evaluations but may be affected by criterion contamination and criterion deficiency just like subjective evaluations. Contamination occurs in that outcomes could be due to factors beyond the control of the individuals; deficiency occurs because the outcomes assessed may not take into account important aspects of individual job performance.

Subjective evaluations can be either ratings or rankings of performance. Ratings are criterion-referenced judgments where an individual is evaluated without reference to other individuals. The Graphic Rating Scale (GRS) is commonly used and several different formats have been introduced. The formats differ in the number of scale points, the clarity or discreteness of the scale points, etc. Empirical research suggests that psychometric properties are not affected by issues such as the number of scale points (Austin & Villanova,

1992). However, providing a common frame of reference across raters as to what each scale point refers to (e.g., what does an evaluation of 2 on a scale of 1–5 mean in behavioral terms?) has been suggested as an aid to improving consistency across and within raters. In fact, the behaviorally anchored rating scales (BARS) were developed based on this logic. To address the concern that some raters will be more comfortable recording observed behavior rather recording their evaluations of them, procedures such as checklists, weighted checklists, and behavioral observation scales (BOS) have been introduced. However, in a seminal review, Landy and Farr (1980) found that the different rating-scale formats do not make a large difference in the quality of the ratings.

Some attempts have been made to address the problem that raters could intentionally distort their ratings (especially the issue of rater leniency), by designing scales where the raters are not sure of the scoring rules. Forced Choice Scales and Mixed Standard Scales (MSS) are two such attempts. In a Forced Choice assessment, raters are provided with two equally favorable statements, only one of which discriminates between good and poor performers. The idea is that the rater who wants to give lenient ratings may choose the favorable but nondiscriminating statement as descriptive of the ratee. The MSS comprises three statements for each dimension of performance rated, with the three statements depicting an excellent, average, and poor performance, respectively, on that dimension. The rater rates the performance of each ratee as better than, equal to, or worse than the performance depicted in that statement. Statements across dimensions are mixed. The objective is to check whether a rater who rates an employee behavior as better than an excellent statement also provides better-than ratings for statements depicting average or poor performance in that dimension (Blanz & Ghiselli, 1972). Although such scales could reduce leniency and identify careless or inconsistent raters, their acceptability by raters has been found to be low (Austin & Villanova, 1992; Landy & Farr, 1980).

In contrast to ratings which are criterion-referenced assessments, rankings are norm-referenced assessments. The simplest form of ranking is to rank all ratees from best to worst. The ranking will depend on the set of ratees and it is impossible to compare the rankings from two different sets of individuals. The worst in one set may be better than the best in the second set of ratees. A modified version, called alternate ranking, involves 1) picking the best and worst ratees in the set of ratees under consideration, 2) removing the two chosen ratees, 3) picking the next best and worst from the remaining ratees, and 4) repeating the process until all ratees are ranked. The advantage of the alternate ranking method is that it reduces the cognitive load on the raters. Yet another approach is to compare each ratee to every other ratee, a method of paired comparisons that becomes unwieldy when the number of ratees increases. Finally, forced distribution methods can be used where a fixed percentage of ratees are placed in each level. Forced distribution methods can be useful to generate the desired distribution (mostly normal) of assessed scores. However, it is an open question whether such distributions reflect reality.

Sources of Ratings

With subjective evaluations (ratings or rankings), the question of who should rate arises. Typically, in traditional organizations the supervisors of the employees provide the ratings. Recent years have seen an increase in the use of 360-degree feedback systems (Church &

Bracken, 1997) where rating assessments can be made by the ratee himself or herself (self), subordinates, peers, and customers or clients. However, when ratings are used for administrative and personnel-selection-related purposes, self-ratings are mostly inappropriate. Traditionally, supervisory ratings have been used for validating selection predictors, to make promotion and selection decisions, etc. For example, Lent, Aurbach, and Levin (1971) found in their review of 1,506 validation studies that 63% of the studies used ratings as the criterion measurement method. Of these studies, 93% used supervisory ratings. Bernardin and Beatty (1984) estimated that over 90% of the ratings used in the literature are supervisory evaluations.

In addition to the use of supervisory ratings, peer ratings are also used in validation research. Lent et al. (1971) reported that the remaining 7% (after the 93% that used supervisory ratings) of validation studies used peer ratings to measure the criterion. Given that the traditional hierarchical structure of organizations is being replaced by more team-based work (Norman & Zawacki, 1991), the use of peer ratings in personnel selection research and practice is likely to increase. Several researchers have argued that the validity of predictors may differ depending on the use of peer or supervisor ratings. For example, Conway and Huffcutt (1997) suggest that the validity of predictors differs based on the source of the ratings. This is basically a hypothesis of differential validity by job performance rating source.

Some boundary conditions on our discussion of differential validity here are to be noted. Differential validity has also been claimed based on the content of the criterion. For example, it has been argued that personality will better predict teamwork and ability will better predict productivity. We will take up this form of differential validity based on content in a subsequent section in this chapter. Further, the term differential validity has also been used to assess whether predictor–criterion combinations are the same for different groups of individuals (e.g., Whites, Blacks). In this chapter we do not discuss differential validity in terms of different validity coefficients for the same predictor–criterion combinations for different groups of individuals. In this section, we are referring only to differential validity based on peer versus supervisory ratings.

When we discuss the potential for differential validity based on source of ratings (peer or supervisors), we are essentially discussing the equivalence of the two sources of ratings. This equivalence can be assessed either by estimating their intercorrelation or by assessing the pattern of correlations the two sources of ratings have with external variables. The first line of evidence focuses on the internal structure of the construct assessed by the two sources, whereas the second line of evidence explores the cross-structure of measures of job performance with measures of other constructs (Nunnally & Bernstein, 1994).

Several theoretical mechanisms have been proposed as to why peers and supervisors should differ. Most prominently, opportunity to observe has been postulated to differ across the two sources. In addition, Borman (1974) suggests that the objectives may be different for peers and supervisors. However, empirical evidence is not especially supportive of these proposed mechanisms. For example, Albrecht, Glaser, and Marks (1964) found that the convergence between peer and supervisor ratings in rating sales ability was .74. Harris and Schaubroeck (1988) reported that the correlation between peer and supervisor ratings of overall job performance was .62. Such high values of overlap between the two sources of ratings suggest that the prospects of differential validity are remote. Further, it should be noted that the reported value of .74 is uncorrected for measurement error and the value of .62 was based on an attenuation correction value (reliability) of .60. Recent research (Rothstein, 1990; Salgado & Moscoso, 1996; Viswesvaran et al., 1996) suggests that inter-rater reliability of supervisory ratings is .52 and that of peer ratings is .42, values which suggest that the convergence is much higher than the reported values of .74 and .62.

An additional point needs to be taken into account in judging the convergence value of .74 as reported above. Viswesvaran et al. (2002) make a distinction between construct-level convergence and rating difficulty. Viswesvaran et al. (2002) state:

> Agreement between raters can be reduced by the absence of agreement on the nature of the construct to be rated or by difficulty of rating a particular agreed upon dimension, or by both. The correlation between peer and supervisory ratings may be reduced because peers and supervisors are rating different constructs or perceived dimensions of job performance (i.e., lack of construct-level convergence) because of differences in their understanding of the exact nature of the dimensions. That is, they are actually rating somewhat different performance dimensions. Conversely, even when peers and supervisors are rating the same performance dimension (or construct), the correlation between peer and supervisor ratings of a performance dimension may be lower for one dimension than another because it is difficult to rate reliably, leading to lower supervisor-peer correlations . . . In this paper we refer to this effect or process as "rating difficulty" for the sake of brevity. The two effects, lack of construct-level convergence and rating difficulty, are confounded in the observed correlation between peer and supervisor ratings. (p. 346)

In assessing differential validity, the focus should be on construct-level disagreements. Just because two measures differ in their reliabilities, their external correlates may be different. Such differences do not constitute evidence of differential validity. In fact, by introducing measurement error into measures one can generate evidence of differential validity. As such, in this section we will review the correlation between peer and supervisor ratings after correcting for rating difficulty and measurement error. We will not consider in this section evidence of differential validity of peer and supervisor ratings based on observed correlations with external variables.

A key question essentially then becomes whether, for any given dimension of job performance, peers and supervisors are rating the same construct or performance dimension. If the answer is in the affirmative, the true score correlation between peer and supervisor ratings is expected to be 1.00 (within sampling error). The observed peer–supervisor correlation can be corrected for measurement error to determine whether corrected values are within sampling error of 1.0. To this end, the confidence intervals around the observed correlation are corrected for measurement error. The end points of the confidence intervals can be corrected with the same attenuation formula as the observed correlation (Hunter & Schmidt, 1990). If inter-peer and inter-supervisor reliability values are used to make the attenuation corrections, then what is unique or idiosyncratic to a particular supervisor or peer (not shared with other supervisors or peers, respectively) is considered to be measurement error. That is, the construct underlying peer ratings is defined as what is common across peers, and the construct underlying supervisor ratings is defined as what is common across supervisors.

Viswesvaran et al. (2002) reported, in a meta-analytic cumulation of the existing literature reporting peer–supervisor ratings correlations, that the overlap between the two sources is substantial. For two-thirds of the dimensions they investigated there was construct-level convergence. Peers and supervisors were rating the same construct and observed correlations between the two sources of ratings were lowered primarily due to measurement error (i.e., disagreements and idiosyncrasies between peers or between supervisors). This conclusion that peers and supervisors are rating the same constructs is also borne out by several other large-scale studies.

Mount, Judge, Scullen, Sytsma, and Hezlett (1998) found in a large-scale study of performance ratings that a model which postulated separate latent factors for rater-level (supervisors, peers) did not do better than one where each rater was treated as an independent method. That is, there were more disagreements across raters belonging to the same level than there was shared variance across raters of the same level. A similar finding was reported by Facteau and Craig (2001) who used item response theory (IRT) and confirmatory factor analyses (CFA) to demonstrate the equivalence of peer and supervisor ratings. In short, ample evidence exists that peers and supervisors converge in their evaluations of the same job performance dimensions. In other words, they are simply different, randomly parallel methods for assessing the same sets of constructs.

How does this square with arguments that peers and supervisors emphasize, observe, and value different behaviors? A reference to the domain-sampling model of reliability (Nunnally & Bernstein, 1994) will be informative. In test construction, we have a domain of interest and there are several items that could be used to assess the construct defining that domain. Similarly, the different behaviors observed by peers and supervisors have specific variance associated with them (i.e., the item specific variance), but that specificity does not affect the construct of interest. Teamwork is teamwork is teamwork – whether measured by behaviors considered relevant by peers or by behaviors considered relevant by supervisors. This explanation is also compatible with the findings that the same individual differences variable (e.g., general mental ability, conscientiousness) is predictive of different workplace behaviors of interest. A conscientious individual who is likely to engage in behaviors that result in better ratings from peers is just as likely to engage in behaviors that will result in similar ratings from supervisors. Different behaviors and manifestations of underlying traits may be observed by peers and supervisors, but the construct domain sampled and assessed remains the same.

As a practical consequence, for assessment of job performance in personnel selection, we would recommend the collection of ratings from different sources (i.e., peers and supervisors), not because there is likelihood of differential validity but because of a more comprehensive sampling of the domain of performance. A composite based on both peer and supervisory ratings will result in a more reliable and valid assessment. Furthermore, user acceptability may be enhanced by using the multiple sources in validation.

The Construct Domain of Individual Job Performance

What is included in the construct domain of individual job performance? Essentially this question addresses what dimensions are part of the construct. There is no one correct set of dimensions, since just as a pie can be sliced in different ways, a construct can be sliced into different sub-dimensions and facets that vary in terms of behavioral specificity, depending on the objectives of the researcher/practitioner. The attempt here is more to review the different dimensions or aspects of performance so as to glean an idea of what the construct of job performance entails. Further, given the numerous dimensions of job performance postulated in the extant literature, it might be confusing for a practitioner to select a subset of dimensions to assess. Defining the job performance construct domain for any job can, to a large extent, be guided by job-analytic data. However, it is also useful to recognize that similar categories of behaviors span across jobs and a summary of these main dimensions would be useful. For this purpose, we provide in Table 16.1 a summary of major job performance dimensions that have been discussed and utilized in the extant job performance literature.

Several strategies can be used to assess the dimensionality of the job performance construct. These include rational, theoretical, and factor analytic approaches. First, researchers have reviewed job performance measures used in different contexts and attempted to synthesize what dimensions make the construct of job performance. This rational method of synthesizing and theory building is, however, affected by the personal biases of the individual researchers. It is true that the factor analytic approach reviewed below is also influenced by the personal biases of researchers in the interpretation of the ensuing factor analytic results. However, compared to rational synthesis, there is an additional safeguard in factor analytic approaches, in that personal biases are checked by the empirical data collected and analyzed. Further, the cognitive load in integrating the vast number of dimensions proposed in the literature results cannot be denied. The same label has been used to refer to different dimensions as well as different labels for the same dimension (teamwork, interpersonal facilitation may overlap in many studies). In job performance assessments this has resulted in what personality psychologists have described as a jingle-jangle fallacy in personality assessments.

Second, researchers (e.g., Welbourne, Johnson, & Erez, 1998) have invoked organizational theories to define what the content of the job performance construct should be. Welbourne et al. used role theory and identity theory to explicate the construct of job performance. Borman and Motowidlo (1993) used the literature on socio-technical systems to specify that job performance should have two components: task and contextual performance that parallels the social and technical systems that are postulated to make up the organization.

Rational synthesis and theory-based specifications have to be empirically tested and factor analysis has been used to study the construct domain of job performance. In such an empirical approach, several measures of job performance are obtained from a sample of employees and their interrelationships assessed (e.g., Rush, 1953). The use of confirmatory factor analysis has enabled researchers to combine rational synthesis and empirical partitioning of variance. In a typical factor analytic study, individuals are assessed on multiple indices of job performance. Correlations are obtained between the measures of job performance and factor analysis is used to identify the measures that cluster together. Based on the commonalties across the measures that cluster together, a dimension is defined. For example, when absence measures, lateness measures, and tenure cluster together, a dimension of withdrawal behaviors is hypothesized.

The literature on the number of dimensions necessary to represent the domain has been contradictory. Rush (1953) factor analyzed nine rating measures and three

TABLE 16.1 Common job performance dimensions

Job performance dimension	Description
Productivity or task performance	This dimension typically refers to the actual counts of the units produced or ratings of the same, as well as ratings of behaviors deemed to constitute the core tasks of jobs.
Interpersonal competence	This refers to how well an individual behaves interpersonally at work as well as builds and maintains relationships in the work environment; can variously include teamwork, facilitating peers performance, etc.
Leadership	Behaviors associated with inspiring others, taking charge of situations for groups, bringing out extra performance in others, motivating others to scale great heights. Sometimes specific components such as leadership judgment and decision making could be stressed.
Effort	The persistence and initiative shown by individuals in getting tasks done. Sometimes lack of effort is reflected in facets of the counterproductive behavior dimensions such as tardiness, absences.
Job knowledge	Declarative and procedural knowledge to perform the job, including explicit and implicit rules and procedures to follow.
Counterproductive behaviors	Negative behaviors that detract from the value of employees to the organization, that are disruptive as they disrupt work-related activities, that are antisocial as they violate social norms, and that are deviant as they diverge from organizationally desired behaviors. Includes withdrawal behaviors, rule breaking, theft, violence, substance abuse on the job, sabotage, etc. Originally conceptualized as the polar opposite of citizenship behavior, recent empirical findings indicate that this is a separate dimension from citizenship behaviors.
Citizenship behaviors	Also referred to as contextual performance, prosocial behavior, altruism, etc. Refers to the extent an individual contributes to the welfare of the organization in ways not formally stated in job descriptions.

organizational-records-based measures of job performance for 100 salespeople and identified four factors: objective achievement, learning aptitude, general reputation, and proficiency of sales techniques. Baier and Dugan (1957) obtained data on 346 sales agents on fifteen objective variables and two subjective ratings and factor analysis of the 17×17 intercorrelation matrix resulted in one general factor. In contrast, Prien and Kult (1968) factor analyzed a set of 23 job performance measures and found evidence for seven distinct dimensions. Roach and Wherry (1970), using a large sample of ($N = 900$) salespersons, found evidence for a general factor whereas Seashore, Indik, and Georgopolous (1960), using comparably large samples ($N = 975$), found no evidence for a general factor.

Ronan (1963) conducted a factor analysis of a set of eleven job performance measures and found evidence for four factors. Gunderson and Ryman (1971) examined the factor structure of individual job performance in extremely isolated groups and suggested three dimensions: task efficiency, emotional stability, and interpersonal relations. Klimoski and London (1974) used multi-source data and reported evidence for the presence of a general factor, a finding that is interesting when considered in the wake of arguments that raters at different levels of job performance construe the content domain of job performance differently. Factor analytic studies in the last two decades (1980–99) have used much larger samples and refined techniques of factor analysis. However, each of these studies, even when they postulate the same number of dimensions, comes up with different dimensions. The four dimensions identified by Rush (1953) are not the same four dimensions presented by Murphy (1989). Sometimes, different names are used to refer to the same dimension whereas at other times the same label is used to refer to different dimensions.

Viswesvaran and Ones (2000) developed a two-dimensional grid to group and provide a format structure to these different taxonomies. The first dimension is whether the taxonomy was developed for a single occupation or is applicable across occupations. For example, Hunt (1996) developed a model of generic work behavior applicable to entry-level jobs especially in the service industry. Using performance data from over 18,000 employees primarily from the retail sector, Hunt (1996) identified nine dimensions of job performance that do not depend on job-specific knowledge. The nine dimensions were: adherence to confrontational rules, industriousness, thoroughness, schedule flexibility, attendance, off-task behavior, unruliness, theft, and drug misuse. Alternately, taxonomies can be developed that will be applicable across occupations. One such example is the eight-dimensional taxonomy provided by Campbell (1990), who describes the latent structure of job performance in terms of eight dimensions: job-specific task proficiency, non-job-specific task proficiency, written and oral communication, demonstrating effort, maintaining personal discipline, facilitating peer and team performance, supervision, and management or administration. The description of these eight dimensions is further elaborated in Campbell (1990) and Campbell, McCloy, Oppler, and Sager (1993). Five of the eight dimensions were found in a sample of military jobs (Campbell, McHenry, & Wise, 1990).

The second dimension that Viswesvaran and Ones (2000) used to group the different taxonomies is the focus on specific performance aspects versus clusters of performance aspects. For example, Smith, Organ, and Near (1983) popularized the concept of "organizational citizenship behavior" (OCB) in the job performance literature. Recently, taxonomies of counterproductive behaviors have been proposed (Gruys & Sackett, 2003). Here the focus is on certain aspects of performance and not on the overall job performance construct. The goal is not to define the entire construct domain of job performance but to home in on specific sub-dimensions.

This empirical approach to specifying the construct of job performance is limited by the number and type of measures included in the data collection phase. Recently, the combination of meta-analysis and structural equations modeling (Viswesvaran & Ones, 1995) has greatly extended this approach. No longer are we limited to the number of measures that can be administered to one sample of employees. As long as we can estimate the correlation between different measures (even based on different samples), a structural equations modeling of the meta-analyzed correlation matrix can be employed to investigate the factor structure of job performance.

Viswesvaran (1993) combined meta-analyses and structural equations modeling to investigate the factor structure of job performance. A large general factor was found across the different measures. To avoid biases in judgmentally describing the construct domain of job performance, Viswesvaran (1993) invoked the lexical hypothesis from personality literature (Goldberg, 1995). The lexical hypothesis states that practically significant individual differences in personality are encoded in the language used, and therefore, a comprehensive description of personality can be obtained by collating all the adjectives found in the dictionary. Extending this principle to job performance assessment suggests that a comprehensive specification of the content domain of the job performance construct can be obtained by collating all the measures of job performance that have been used in the extant literature.

The model of job performance that emerges from the meta-analytic cumulation by Viswesvaran (1993) views the various measures of job performance, such as quality and quantity of work performance, absenteeism, turnover, violence on the job, and teamwork, as the manifestations of a general construct of job performance. This can be stated in factor analytic terms as follows. The standing of an individual on any specific performance measure (e.g., absenteeism) can be *hypothesized* to depend on the general factor (i.e., overall job performance), the group factor (e.g., the withdrawal behavior of the employee; absenteeism, tardiness, time theft, turnover all may belong to this group), the specific factor (i.e., absenteeism), and a random error component. There may or may not be group factors for a specific measure of job performance such that that measure of job performance correlates more with the measures of job performance in that group than with the measures of job performance in any other group. The existence of such clusters or groups of measures of job performance is an empirical question. Demonstrating the existence of such a hierarchy of performance measures is an empirical question that depends on an investigation of the true score intercorrelations between the different measures of job performance. Viswesvaran (1993), on meta-analyzing over 2,600 correlations, concluded that a general factor exists across all measures of job performance used in the extant literature over the past 100 years.

Recently, Viswesvaran, Schmidt, and Ones (in press) refined this analysis to disentangle the effects of idiosyncratic halo error from this general factor. Cumulating results across over 300 studies, Viswesvaran et al. (in press) estimated the true score correlations across different dimensions of job performance. Within-peer and within-supervisor correlations were analyzed separately from between-supervisor and -peer correlations. The within or intra-rater correlations (same peer or same supervisor rates both dimensions being correlated) are affected by halo and measurement error whereas the between-rater correlation (peers rating one dimension and supervisors rating the other in any inter-dimension correlation) is not affected by halo. Similarly, within-rater reliability (i.e., alphas) is inflated by halo but not interrater reliabilities (which are actually lowered by halo). Thus correcting within-rater correlations with within-rater reliabilities accounts for measurement error but not halo. Correcting interrater correlations (peer–supervisor) with interrater reliabilities corrects for both halo and measurement error. A comparison of these two sets of correlations estimates the inflationary effects of halo. Viswesvaran et al. (in press) present evidence to suggest the presence of a general factor (that explains 27% to 54% of variance) across job performance dimensions, even after accounting for rater idiosyncratic halo. Cumulative empirical evidence clearly supports the presence of a general factor and hence a hierarchical view where specific dimensions of job performance all load onto a higher-order factor in varying degrees.

The presence of a general factor raises the question of whether differential validities will be found in using the same predictor for different dimensions of performance. A job performance measure, when used as a criterion in a validation study, is a standard used for two purposes (Schmidt, 1980): a) to decide which selection procedures to use and which to reject (i.e., to determine the best test battery); and b) to weight the selection procedures selected for use. As such, any two job performance measures are equivalent if their use leads to the adoption of the same selection procedures and assignment to them of the same relative weights. Schmidt (1980) reports that in one large sample study done in the army it was found that a job sample criterion, supervisory ratings, and a job knowledge measure all resulted in the adoption of the same selection procedures and assignment of essentially identical relative weights. Oppler, Sager, McCloy, and Rosse (1993) found, using a sample of 3,086 soldiers, that prediction composites developed using job knowledge tests as the criterion compared favorably in validity to those developed using hands-on tests. Nathan and Alexander (1988) investigated whether or not job performance measurement method moderates validities of cognitive ability tests. They meta-analytically cumulated the validities reported for supervisory ratings, rankings, work samples, production quantity, and production quality. No evidence was found for differential validity.

Despite these results, researchers have continued to focus on the question of differential prediction. In examining differential prediction, it is essential to keep in mind the influence of sampling error, which greatly influences the results when multiple regression strategies are used to develop batteries that include correlated predictors (Hunter, Crosson, & Friedman, 1985). Multiple regression does not work very well (especially with correlated predictors, which inflate sampling error in the regression weight estimates) unless sample sizes are extremely large (Helme, Gibson, & Brogden, 1957).

Recent years have seen theoretically based tests of differential validity. Borman and Motowidlo (1993) postulated that ability will predict task performance more strongly than individual differences in personality. On the other hand, individual differences in personality were hypothesized to predict contextual performance better than ability. However, empirical evidence is not wholly supportive of this claim. Alonso (2001) cumulated the literature on a) personality predicting contextual and task performance, and b) ability predicting contextual and task performance. Across 512 validity coefficients, Alonso found that cognitive ability predicted both task and contextual performance. Some personality variables were found to be predictive of contextual performance. This lack of strong empirical support for differential validity based on the content of the criterion is perhaps due to the general factor in job performance assessment. Just as we did not find differential validity for source of ratings (peers and supervisors), there is no evidence of differential validity based on content of the criteria.

In personnel selection, writers interested in downplaying the importance of traits such as ability (where there are large ethnic group differences) have sometimes pinned their hopes on findings of differential validity by what is included in the content of the criterion. The hope was that individuals high on ability may score high on some dimensions of job performance but not on others. If true, every employee could be in the top 10%, albeit in different dimensions of performance (evaluated by different sources). Cumulative empirical evidence, however, is not supportive of this Polyanna-ish view of success. The prospects of differential validity in personnel selection based either on the dimensional content or on the source of assessment are improbable (see also Viswesvaran et al., in press).

Emerging Issues

In this section, we address four issues: 1) definitional issues surrounding the job performance construct, 2) issues in assessing the reliability of job performance assessment, 3) job performance assessment for personnel selection in a team context, and 4) job performance measurement in an international context for expatriate selection and assignment. We should note that for some of the topics to be discussed the empirical data is scant or virtually non-existent. When confronted with such situations, we raise the relevant issues for future research to consider.

Definitional issues

We noted that individual job performance refers to behaviors that can be evaluated. Although we used the term behaviors, we note that the difference between behaviors and outcomes is not clear cut in many instances. Some researchers (Campbell, 1990) insist on a clear demarcation between behaviors and outcomes. The main thrust of this argument is that individuals should be evaluated on what they can control. Other researchers (Austin & Villanova, 1992; Bernardin & Pence, 1980) de-emphasize this difference between behaviors and outcomes. However, in many instances it is not clear what is under the control of an employee. Consider the research productivity of a professor. A relevant behavior to evaluate in the context of this job is writing research papers. But what gives meaning to such a behavior are factors such as whether the papers written are published and, if so, the quality of the outlets. The number of papers published is certainly influenced by many factors beyond the control of the professor. Even the number of papers *written* is influenced by factors outside the control of a professor. Thus, this distinction between behaviors and outcomes is something to be evaluated in the choice of a measure for assessing job performance in personnel selection.

Second, researchers need to pay more attention to temporal relations between different dimensions of job performance. Is teamwork likely to increase productivity? That is, instead of studying predictor–criterion relationships of the type x → y, researchers need to investigate relationships of the type x → y1 → y2 (see Alonso, Viswesvaran, & Sanchez, 2001, for an illustrative example). To some extent this has been explored in team and group dynamics literature where some dimensions are construed as process variables. At this point we want to be clear that calling for an investigation of dynamic relations between job performance dimensions is different from the issue of criterion dynamicity. Criterion dynamicity refers to whether the measurement of a particular dimension changes over time. The changes could be either in the mean performance levels or in the relationships with other variables (of which test–retest reliability is a special case of relationship with same variable). Cumulative evidence (Barrett, Caldwell, & Alexander, 1989) indicates that job performance measures are stable over time.

Reliability issues in job performance assessment

The question of the appropriate reliability coefficient to use in personnel selection validation studies has also occupied IWO psychologists in recent years (Murphy & DeShon, 2000; Schmidt, Viswesvaran, & Ones, 2000). Of course, one has to answer a more fundamental question of whether any corrections are to be made to observed validity coefficients. Arguments have been made (Outtz, 2002) that corrections distort "what is" from "what could be" (see DeShon, 2002, for a harsh but misguided critique of reliability corrections). Another argument is that researchers should be conservative in their estimates – thus, although unreliability lowers the validity coefficients, practitioners should take the conservative value in evaluating the success and utility of their predictors.

It is the corrected correlations that reflect what is (Viswesvaran, 2003). The observed uncorrected (note, we are discussing criterion unreliability here) correlations reflect merely what researchers were able to do with their criterion measurement and the quality of their data collection and does not reflect the validity or utility of the selection tool (see Sackett, Schmidt, Tenopyr, & Kehoe, 1985; Schmidt, Hunter, Pearlman, & Rothstein, 1985). Finally, the objective in science should be to obtain precise estimates and not conservative estimates. Even in a practical application, the question of conservative in what direction arises – similar to the Type I and Type II errors in statistical tests. Thus, correcting for criterion unreliability in personnel selection validation studies is always an essential step (Viswesvaran et al., 1996).

Given that correcting for unreliability in the criterion is essential, the question becomes that of what reliability coefficient should be used. Different reliability coefficients treat different sources of variance as error (Guion, 1998; Schmidt & Hunter, 1996). Broadly speaking, there are three types of variance – transient error, rater idiosyncratic variance, item-specific variance when several items are used to measure a dimension, and random response error. All reliability coefficients take into account random response error. The coefficient alpha that is used in most studies (Cortina, 1993) treats item-specific variance and random response as errors.

However, in personnel selection validation research we want to generalize our findings across raters. There really is no logic in claiming that our predictor scores are likely to predict job performance as measured by one idiosyncratic rater. Rater idiosyncratic variance is a large component in the variance of job performance ratings; Viswesvaran et al. (in press) estimate this component to be as much as 30%. Only interrater reliability estimates this error component and, as such, interrater reliabilities are the only appropriate reliability coefficient (cf. Schmidt et al., 2000) in personnel selection validation research (and in research that attempts to generalize findings across raters).

Thus, the choice of reliability coefficient used to assess measurement error in criteria has enormous practical implications. The hallmark of a good predictor in personnel selection is its high criterion-related validity. Criterion-related validity is a correlation between predictor scores and criterion scores. Given that most of the criterion data are obtained from ratings (cf., Bernardin & Beatty, 1984; Viswesvaran et al., 1996), failure to account for the idiosyncrasies of an individual rater distorts our validation efforts. Pragmatic science (Anderson, Chapter 1, this volume; Anderson, Herriot, & Hodgkinson, 2001) requires the use of an appropriate reliability coefficient – in this instance, interrater reliability.

Of course, the realities of assessing interrater reliability should also be considered. In an organization, the same pair of supervisors does not assess all employees. Thus, different pairs of supervisors will be rating different individuals, and to estimate interrater reliability we will arbitrarily designate one rater as Rater 1 and the other as Rater 2. That is, Rater 1 and Rater 2 may be different raters for different individuals; the only restriction is that Rater 1 and Rater 2 should be different for the same individual employee. Some researchers (Murphy & DeShon, 2000) have focused on this fact to argue that interrater correlations do not estimate interrater reliability.

It is important to note that the realities of data collection outlined above merely include a new component into the reliability estimation. This is the rater main effect or leniency/harshness. While research must investigate factors that influence this variance component, in personnel selection practice it is important to correct for rater idiosyncrasies. We do not want to design a selection system to predict job performance as idiosyncratically defined by a single rater. Our predictors should predict performance as defined consensually. Legal and fairness concerns demand such professional practice. Perhaps recourse to the concept of "natural distance" that Anderson (this volume) advocates will be useful here. While the best practice of using interrater reliability is used, future research should empirically examine the influence of rater main effects on outcomes.

The issues involved can be further elucidated within the framework that Anderson (Chapter 1, this volume) advances. Anderson notes four scenarios of potential interaction between the science and practice of personnel selection. One of the scenarios involves unreliable findings influencing practice. In assessing the reliability of job performance measures, arguments were made that even if the same two supervisors rate all employees, intercorrelation does not estimate reliability because the two raters are not (strictly) parallel. For example, raters differ in leniency. However, later research showed that strict parallelism is not required and raters are randomly equivalent (the difference in reliability estimates between the assumption of random equivalence and strict parallelism was only .02). Thus, a lot of concern was expressed over a trivial issue. Consider another example. For a long time it was argued that raters at different levels (i.e., positions) observe different behaviors. Thus, even if the same two supervisors rate all employees, they will have different perspectives due to their different role relationships with the employee, and therefore, the intercorrelation between their ratings fails to assess reliability. However, as our review of peer–supervisor convergence showed, despite such widespread claims there was no construct-level disagreement between peers and supervisors. This is another example of unreliable findings influencing practice. To avoid similar mishaps in future, research should evaluate different assumptions and sources of variance in ratings at a safe distance (natural distance?) while practitioners obtain the best estimate possible for the criterion with interrater reliability.

A related issue has been raised by some researchers (e.g., Morris & Lobsenz, 2003; Murphy & DeShon, 2000). The argument is that classical measurement theory is limited and that generalizability coefficients are appropriate. This argument is logically flawed. Both classical measurement theory and generalizability theory can be used to assess the different sources of error **if the appropriate data are collected**. If researchers want to estimate the generalizability coefficient where rater idiosyncratic variance is construed as error, they have to collect ratings from two raters. Similarly, if researchers also want to generalize over time, the raters should provide ratings at two different points in time. But if such data are available, classical methods of reliability estimation can be profitably employed. Researchers merely need to correlate the ratings given by one rater at one time with the ratings given by the second rater at an alternate time. These issues are pertinent to the arguments presented by Murphy and DeShon (2000) and Murphy (2003). The authors argue initially about how classical reliability estimates are not appropriate for correcting validity coefficients and conclude their analyses by recommending the use of generalizability coefficients, although all the sins they visit on interrater correlation is also applicable to generalizability coefficients (and if different data are available in the generalizability assessments, the appropriate interrater correlations can be easily computed). Thus, it is erroneous to claim that generalizability coefficients provide more information than classical reliability estimates. Both can yield the same information, provided the appropriate data are collected and analyzed.

Assessment of team performance

Teams are widely used in organizations (Sundstrom, DeMeuse, & Futrell, 1990). The increasing complexities of work and technological advances have necessitated, and at times facilitated, the use of teams. The composition of individual performance to assess team and group performance is an important area. In fact, volumes have been written on assessment of team performance (cf., Swezey & Salas, 1992). Our purpose here is not to review issues in team performance assessments but to show how developments in that field influence job performance assessment in personnel selection settings.

Consider our delineation of what a criterion should do for personnel selection (see also Schmidt, 1980). In personnel selection, the job performance assessed is used to validate predictors. Once validated, the predictors are used to select employees from a pool of applicants. Viewed from this functional perspective, a large number of unanswered questions about assessments of team performance arise. We summarize some of the questions in Table 16.2.

First, consider the definition of a team. A broad definition suggests that teams involve two or more people who interact dynamically and share a common goal (Reilly &

TABLE 16.2   Team performance: issues to consider in personnel selection

Identifying level of team aggregation
Identifying dimensions of job performance that are common across levels of aggregation
Identifying dimensions of job performance that are unique to one level
Specifying composition models
Assessing equivalence of rater techniques and methods across levels
Assessing equivalence of rater cognitive processes/biases in individual and team evaluations
Distinguishing between assessing individual performance of employees in teams from team
    performance

McGourty, 1998; Salas, Dickinson, Converse, & Tannenbaum, 1992). However, by this definition an entire organization can be considered as a team. In fact, one can extend this to say that a particular industry is a team. Extended further, we can say that an entire economy is a team. For personnel selection purposes, we need to be more specific about the definition of our team. We have to specify whether we are interested in selecting individuals to work as a defined task group, or as an organizational member, or assessing candidates for their fit to occupations (e.g., vocational counseling). Stevens and Campion (1994) proposed a predictor to select individuals for work teams, although the discriminant validity of the knowledge measure from individual cognitive ability was not robust. Person–organization fit measures have been proposed, although not used much in selection. Interest inventories have been proposed to assess suitability for occupations (again not used widely in selection contexts).

Once we have decided whether we are selecting an individual or an individual for a team (level specified most likely to be groups), other questions arise. First, are the performance dimensions identified at the individual level applicable to the group level? Are there new dimensions that emerge at team level? What are the implications of some of these dimensions (e.g., cohesion) for selecting individuals? What are the individual differences variables that relate to these dimensions of team performance? Although the techniques used to assess individual performance (records, ratings, etc.) could be helpful in assessing team performance, sources of ratings may differ. In evaluating performance in teams, there could be a greater emphasis on peer assessments, for example.

Assessments of performance in international contexts

As noted earlier, increasing globalization is a fact of life (Anderson et al., 2001) and the science and practice of personnel selection have to accommodate this fact. There is a large literature (Sinangil & Ones, 2001) on expatriate selection, and assessment of individual job performance in international contexts is a critical issue. Some of the questions that arise in this context are summarized in Table 16.3.

First, are the existing dimensions (identified in Table 16.1) similar in international contexts? Are measurement techniques and rating scales comparable? In our review of rating scales used in personnel selection, we noted how graphic rating scales and behaviorally

TABLE 16.3   Issues in job performance assessment in international contexts

Are existing dimensions (cf., Table 16.1) the same in different cultures? Are there new dimensions
 of job performance when assessing performance in international contexts?
Are the behaviors associated with performance dimensions the same in different cultures?
Are measurement techniques/rating scales comparable across cultures?
Are the relative weights given to the different dimensions in assessing overall performance the
 same across cultures?
Which raters (i.e., rating sources) have face validity and are deemed acceptable in different
 cultures?
What dimensions should be used in validating predictors for expatriate selection?
What factors differentially influence the collection of performance appraisal data across cultures?

anchored rating scales are preferred by users more than mixed standard scales (where
it is not clear to the rater what rating is being given). Will this result translate to cultures
where users are more likely to accept larger power distances and in cultures that tolerate
uncertainty?

Are there new dimensions that need to be included when considering individual job
performance in a global context? Some research (e.g., Conner, 2000; Kanter, 1995) suggests that individuals should develop a global mindset to succeed in a globalized economy.
In the area of expatriate selection, research stresses the need to assess individual performance on dimensions that relate to cultural adjustment (Caligiuri, 2000; Deshpande &
Viswesvaran, 1992), although Ones and Viswesvaran (2001) have argued that adjustment
is best considered a determinant of expatriate performance rather than a sub-dimension.
The source of ratings deemed acceptable may differ based on organizational culture.

CONCLUSIONS

New dimensions of job performance are appearing. Given that the concept of job is changing, it is an open question whether we would be discussing task and work performance in
future. Technological assessments have provided new tools to obtain measurements and
sometimes provided new measures (electronic performance monitoring). In personnel
selection assessment issues in measuring job performance may change over the decades,
but the centrality of the construct of job performance is likely to remain undimmed. Scientists and practitioners should gain a comprehensive understanding of the issues in job
performance measurement and assessment to be effective in personnel selection. Hopefully, this chapter has summarized the important findings to date so as to give readers an
understanding of the importance of this construct to personnel selection.

NOTE

The order of authorship is arbitrary; both authors contributed equally.

REFERENCES

Albrecht, P. A., Glaser, E. M., & Marks, J. (1964). Validation of a multiple-assessment procedure for managerial personnel. *Journal of Applied Psychology*, *48*, 351–360.

Alonso, A. (2001). *The relationship between cognitive ability, big five, task and contextual performance: A meta-analysis.* Unpublished Master's Thesis, Florida International University, Miami, FL.

Alonso, A., Viswesvaran, C., & Sanchez, J. I. (2001, April). *Mediating roles of task and contextual performance on predictor validity: A meta-analysis.* Poster presented at the 16th annual meeting of the Society for Industrial and Organizational Psychology, San Diego, CA.

Anderson, N., Herriot, P., & Hodgkinson, G. P. (2001). The practitioner-researcher divide in Industrial, Work and Organizational (IWO) psychology: Where are we now, and where do we go from here? *Journal of Occupational and Organizational Psychology*, *74*, 391–411.

Austin, J. T., & Villanova, P. (1992). The criterion problem: 1917–1992. *Journal of Applied Psychology*, *77*, 836–874.

Baier, D. E., & Dugan, R. D. (1957). Factors in sales success. *Journal of Applied Psychology*, *41*, 37–40.

Barber, A. E. (1998). *Recruiting employees: Individual and organizational perspectives.* Thousand Oaks, CA: Sage.

Barrett, G. V., Caldwell, M. S., & Alexander, R. A. (1989). The predictive stability of ability requirements for task performance: A critical reanalysis. *Human Performance*, *2*, 167–181.

Bernardin, H. J., & Beatty, R. (1984). *Performance appraisal: Assessing human behavior at work.* Boston: Kent-PWS.

Bernardin, H. J., & Pence, E. C. (1980). Effects of rater training: Creating new response sets and decreasing accuracy. *Journal of Applied Psychology*, *65*, 60–66.

Blanz, F., & Ghiselli, E. E. (1972). The mixed standard scale: A new rating system. *Personnel Psychology*, *25*, 185–199.

Blum, M. L., & Naylor, J. C. (1968). *Industrial psychology: Its theoretical and social foundations.* New York: Harper & Row.

Borman, W. C. (1974). The rating of individuals in organizations: An alternate approach. *Organizational Behavior and Human Performance*, *12*, 105–124.

Borman, W. C., & Motowidlo, S. J. (1993). Expanding the criterion domain to include elements of contextual performance. In N. Schmitt & W. C. Borman (Eds.), *Personnel selection in organizations* (pp. 71–98). San Francisco, CA: Jossey Bass.

Brogden, H. E. (1946). An approach to the problem of differential prediction. *Psychometrika*, *11*, 139–154.

Caligiuri, P. M. (2000). The Big Five personality characteristics as predictors of expatriate desire to terminate the assignment and supervisor-rated performance. *Personnel Psychology*, *53*, 67–88.

Campbell, J. P. (1990). Modeling the performance prediction problem in industrial and organizational psychology. In M. Dunnette & L. M. Hough (Eds.), *Handbook of industrial and organizational psychology* (Vol. 1, 2nd ed., pp. 687–731). Palo Alto, CA: Consulting Psychologists Press.

Campbell, J. P., McCloy, R. A., Oppler, S. H., & Sager, C. E. (1993). A theory of performance. In N. Schmitt & W. C. Borman (Eds.), *Personnel selection in organizations* (pp. 35–70). San Francisco: Jossey-Bass.

Campbell, J. P., McHenry, J. J., & Wise, L. L. (1990). Modeling job performance in a population of jobs. *Personnel Psychology*, *43*, 313–333.

Church, A. H., & Bracken, D. W. (1997). Advancing the state of the art of 360 degree feedback. *Group and Organization Management*, *22*, 149–161.

Cleveland, J. N., Murphy, K. R., & Williams, R. E. (1989). Multiple uses of performance appraisal: Prevalence and correlates. *Journal of Applied Psychology*, *74*, 130–135.

Conner, J. (2000). Developing the global leaders of tomorrow. *Human Resource Management, 39* (2 & 3), 147–158.

Conway, J. M., & Huffcut, A. I. (1997). Psychometric properties of multisource performance ratings: A meta-analysis of subordinate, supervisor, peer, and self-ratings. *Human Performance, 10,* 331–360.

Cortina, J. M. (1993). What is coefficient alpha? An examination of theory and applications. *Journal of Applied Psychology, 78,* 98–104.

DeShon, R. (2002). Generalizability theory. In F. Drasgow & N. Schmitt (Eds.), *Measuring and analyzing behavior in organizations* (pp. 189–220). San Francisco: Jossey-Bass.

Deshpande, S. P., & Viswesvaran, C. (1992). Is cross-cultural training of expatriate managers effective? A meta-analysis. *International Journal of Intercultural Relations, 16,* 295–310.

DeVries, D. L., Morrison, A. M., Shullman, S. L., & Gerlach, M. L. (1986). *Performance appraisal on the line.* Greensboro, NC: Center for Creative Leadership.

DuBois, C. L. Z., Sackett, P. R., Zedeck, S., & Fogli, L. (1993). Further exploration of typical and maximum performance criteria: Definitional issues, prediction, and white–black differences. *Journal of Applied Psychology, 78,* 205–211.

Facteau, J. D., & Craig, S. B. (2001). Are performance appraisal ratings from different rating sources comparable? *Journal of Applied Psychology, 86,* 215–227.

Goldberg, L. R. (1995). What the hell took so long? Donald Fiske and the big-five factor structure. In P. E. Shrout & S. T. Fiske (Eds.), *Advances in personality research, methods, and theory: A festschrift honoring Donald W. Fiske.* New York: Erlbaum.

Gruys, M. L., & Sackett, P. L. (2003). Investigating the dimensionality of counterproductive work behavior. *International Journal of Selection and Assessment, 11,* 30–42.

Guion, R. M. (1998). *Assessment, measurement, and prediction for personnel selection.* Mahwah, NJ: Lawrence Erlbaum.

Gunderson, E. K. E., & Ryman, D. H. (1971). Convergent and discriminant validities of performance evaluations in extremely isolated groups. *Personnel Psychology, 24,* 715–724.

Harris, M. M., & Schaubroeck, J. (1988). A meta-analysis of self–supervisor, self–peer, and peer–supervisor ratings. *Personnel Psychology, 41,* 43–62.

Helme, W. E., Gibson, N. A., & Brogden, H. E. (1957). *An empirical test of shrinkage problems in personnel classification research.* Personnel Board, Technical Research Note 84.

Hunt, S. T. (1996). Generic work behavior: An investigation into the dimensions of entry-level, hourly job performance. *Personnel Psychology, 49,* 51–83.

Hunter, J. E., Crosson, J. J., & Friedman, D. H. (1985). *The validity of ASVAB for civilian and military job performance.* Technical Report.

Hunter, J. E., & Schmidt, F. L. (1990). *Methods of meta-analysis: Correcting for error and bias in research findings.* Newbury Park, CA: Sage.

Kanter, R. M. (1995). *World class: Thinking locally in a global economy.* New York: Simon & Schuster.

Klimoski, R. J., & London, M. (1974). Role of the rater in performance appraisal. *Journal of Applied Psychology, 59,* 445–451.

Landy, F. J., & Farr, J. L. (1980). Performance rating. *Psychological Bulletin, 87,* 72–107.

Lent, R. H., Aurbach, H. A., & Levin, L. S. (1971). Predictors, criteria, and significant results. *Personnel Psychology, 24,* 519–533.

Mace, C. A. (1935). *Incentives: Some experimental studies.* (Report 72). London: Industrial Health Research Board.

Malos, S. B. (1998). Current legal issues in performance appraisal. In J. W. Smither (Ed.), *Performance appraisal: State of the art in practice* (pp. 49–94). San Francisco: Jossey-Bass.

Morris, S. B., & Lobsenz, R. (2003). Evaluating personnel selection systems. In J. E. Edwards, J. C. Scott, & N. S. Raju (Eds.), *The human resources program-evaluation handbook* (pp. 109–129). Thousand Oaks, CA: Sage.

Mount, M. K., Judge, T. A., Scullen, S. E., Sytsma, M. R., & Hezlett, S. A. (1998). Trait, rater, and level effects in 360-degree performance ratings. *Personnel Psychology*, *51*, 557–576.

Murphy, K. R. (1989). Dimensions of job performance. In R. Dillon & J. Pelligrino (Eds.), *Testing: Applied and theoretical perspectives* (pp. 218–247). New York: Praeger.

Murphy, K. R. (Ed.). (2003). *Validity generalization: A critical review.* Mahwah, NJ: Erlbaum.

Murphy, K. R., & DeShon, R. (2000). Inter-rater correlations do not estimate the reliability of job performance ratings. *Personnel Psychology*, *53*, 873–900.

Nathan, B. R., & Alexander, R. A. (1988). A comparison of criteria for test validation: A meta-analytical investigation. *Personnel Psychology*, *41*, 517–535.

Norman, C. A., & Zawacki, R. A. (1991, December). Team appraisals – team approach. *Quality Digest*, *11*, 68–75.

Nunnally, J. C., & Bernstein, I. H. (1994). *Psychometric theory* (3rd ed.). New York: McGraw-Hill.

Ones, D. S., & Viswesvaran, C. (2001). Integrity tests and other Criterion-focused Occupational Personality Scales (COPS) used in personnel selection. *International Journal of Selection and Assessment*, *9*, 31–39.

Oppler, S. H., Sager, C. E., McCloy, R. A., & Rosse, R. L. (1993, May). The role of performance determinants in the development of prediction equations. In F. L. Schmidt (Chair), *Job performance: Theories of determinants and factor structure*. Symposium conducted at the eighth annual meeting of the Society of Industrial and Organizational Psychologists, San Francisco.

Outtz, J. L. (2002). The role of cognitive ability tests in employment selection. *Human Performance*, *15*, 161–171.

Prien, E. P., & Kult, M. (1968). Analysis of performance criteria and comparison of a priori and empirically-derived keys for a forced-choice scoring. *Personnel Psychology*, *21*, 505–513.

Reilly, R. R., & McGourty, J. (1998). Performance appraisal in team settings. In J. W. Smither (Ed.), *Performance appraisal: State of the art in practice* (pp. 244–277). San Francisco: Jossey-Bass.

Roach, D. E., & Wherry, R. J. (1970). Performance dimensions of multi-line insurance agents. *Personnel Psychology*, *23*, 239–250.

Ronan, W. W. (1963). A factor analysis of eleven job performance measures. *Personnel Psychology*, *16*, 255–267.

Rothstein, H. R. (1990). Interrater reliability of job performance ratings: Growth to asymptote level with increasing opportunity to observe. *Journal of Applied Psychology*, *75*, 322–327.

Rush, C. H. (1953). A factorial study of sales criteria. *Personnel Psychology*, *6*, 9–24.

Sackett, P. R., Schmitt, N., Tenopyr, M. L., & Kehoe, J. (1985). Commentary on forty questions about validity generalization and meta-analysis. *Personnel Psychology*, *38*, 697–798.

Sackett, P. R., Zedeck, S., & Fogli, L. (1988). Relations between measures of typical and maximum job performance. *Journal of Applied Psychology*, *73*, 482–486.

Salas, E., Dickinson, T. L., Converse, S. A., & Tannenbaum, S. I. (1992). Towards an understanding of team performance and training. In R. W. Swezey & E. Salas (Eds.), *Teams: Their training and performance* (pp. 3–29). Norwood, NJ: Ablex.

Salgado, J. F., & Moscoso, S. (1996). Meta-analysis of interrater reliability of job performance ratings in validity studies of personnel selection. *Perceptual and Motor Skills*, *83*, 1195–1201.

Schmidt, F. L. (1980). *The measurement of job performance.* Unpublished manuscript.

Schmidt, F. L., & Hunter, J. E. (1992). Causal modeling of processes determining job performance. *Current Directions in Psychological Science*, *1*, 89–92.

Schmidt, F. L., & Hunter, J. E. (1996). Measurement error in psychological research: Lessons from 26 research scenarios. *Psychological Methods*, *1*, 199–223.

Schmidt, F. L., Hunter, J. E., Pearlman, K., & Rothstein, H. R. (1985). Forty questions about validity generalization and meta-analysis. *Personnel Psychology*, *38*, 697–798.

Schmidt, F. L., Viswesvaran, C., & Ones, D. S. (2000). Reliability is not validity and validity is not reliability. *Personnel Psychology, 53*, 901–912.

Seashore, S. E., Indik, B. P., & Georgopoulos, B. S. (1960). Relationships among criteria of job performance. *Journal of Applied Psychology, 44*, 195–202.

Sinangil, H. K., & Ones, D. S. (2001). Expatriate management. In N. Anderson, D. Ones, H. Sinangil, & C. Viswesvaran (Eds.), *Handbook of industrial, work, & organizational psychology: Vol. 1, Personnel psychology* (pp. 424–443). London: Sage.

Smith, C. A., Organ, D. W., & Near, J. P. (1983). Organizational citizenship behavior: Its nature and antecedents. *Journal of Applied Psychology, 68*, 655–663.

Smith, P. C. (1976). Behavior, results, and organizational effectiveness: The problem of criteria. In M. D. Dunnette (Ed.), *Handbook of industrial and organizational psychology* (pp. 745–775). Chicago: Rand McNally.

Stevens, M. J., & Campion, M. A. (1994). The knowledge, skill, and ability requirements for teamwork: Implications for human resource management. *Journal of Management, 20*, 503–530.

Sundstrom, E., DeMeuse, K. P., & Futrell, D. (1990). Work teams: Applications and effectiveness. *American Psychologist, 45*, 120–133.

Swezey, R. W., & Salas, E. (Eds.). (1992). *Teams: Their training and performance*. Norwood, NJ: Ablex.

Thorndike, R. L. (1949). *Personnel selection: Test and measurement techniques*. New York: Wiley.

Viswesvaran, C. (1993). *Modeling job performance: Is there a general factor?* Unpublished doctoral dissertation, University of Iowa, Iowa City, IA.

Viswesvaran, C. (2003). [Review of *Measuring and analyzing behavior in organizations*. San Francisco: Jossey-Bass, 2002, 591 pages.]. *Personnel Psychology, 56*, 283–286.

Viswesvaran, C., & Ones, D. S. (1995). Theory testing: Combining psychometric meta-analysis and structural equations modeling. *Personnel Psychology, 48*, 865–885.

Viswesvaran, C., & Ones, D. S. (2000). Perspectives on models of job performance. *International Journal of Selection and Assessment, 8*, 216–227.

Viswesvaran, C., Ones, D. S., & Schmidt, F. L. (1996). Comparative analysis of the reliability of job performance ratings. *Journal of Applied Psychology, 81*, 557–574.

Viswesvaran, C., Schmidt, F. L., & Ones, D. S. (2002). The moderating influence of job performance dimensions on convergence of supervisory and peer ratings of job performance: Unconfounding construct-level convergence and rating difficulty. *Journal of Applied Psychology, 87*, 345–354.

Viswesvaran, C., Schmidt, F. L., & Ones, D. S. (in press). Is there a general factor in job performance ratings? A meta-analytic framework for disentangling substantive and error influences. *Journal of Applied Psychology*.

Welbourne, T. M., Johnson, D. E., & Erez, A. (1998). The role-based performance scale: Validity analysis of a theory-based measure. *Academy of Management Journal, 41*, 540–555.

Whisler, T. L., & Harper, S. F. (Eds.). (1962). *Performance appraisal: Research and practice*. New York: Holt.

17

The Prediction of Contextual Performance

Lisa M. Penney and Walter C. Borman

It is our belief that empirical test validation is highly important in selection research, and this type of validation requires that the criterion measures accurately depict the performance levels of organization members being assessed in the research. This is in part a measurement issue, with a focus on reliable and valid assessment of criteria. However, criterion measurement in test validation research is also a conceptual matter. It is critical to represent with the criterion measures all important performance requirements for the target job.

This is the central theme of the present chapter. Our and others' research has expanded the criterion domain to consider dimensions of performance outside of the technical proficiency or task performance elements of job performance. In particular, building on others' work (e.g., Barnard, 1938; Brief & Motowidlo, 1986; Katz & Kahn, 1966; Smith, Organ, & Near, 1983) we (Borman & Motowidlo, 1993, 1997; Borman, Motowidlo, & Hanser, 1983) have introduced the notion of contextual performance, defined as "activities (that) support the organizational, social, and psychological environment in which the technical core must function" (Borman & Motowidlo, 1993, p. 73). We distinguish contextual performance from task performance, defined as "the proficiency with which job incumbents perform activities that are formally recognized as part of their jobs, activities that contribute to the organization's technical core either directly by implementing a part of its technological process, or indirectly by providing it with needed materials or services" (Borman & Motowidlo, 1993, p. 73). Contextual performance includes such activities as volunteering for extra duties and assignments; persisting with extra enthusiasm and effort; helping and cooperating with others; following organizational rules and procedures; and supporting the organization. As we will see, including contextual performance as part of the criterion domain has important implications for personnel selection, and more broadly, for organizational effectiveness.

CONTEXTUAL PERFORMANCE DEFINED

As previously stated, contextual performance supports the larger environment in which task performance occurs. According to Borman and Motowidlo, contextual performance differs from task performance in three important ways. First, task behavior varies across jobs, whereas contextual behavior is fairly similar across jobs. For example, carpenters and accountants perform very different tasks, but both may volunteer to work late on projects or offer job-related assistance to coworkers in need. Second, task activities are more likely to be formally expected as a job requirement than contextual activities. That is, while an organization may appreciate or benefit from employees who put in extra effort to help others complete their work, those kinds of behaviors are generally considered above and beyond the call of duty. Finally, antecedents of task performance are more likely to involve cognitive ability, whereas antecedents of contextual performance are more likely to be dispositional or personality-related.

Organizational researchers have been investigating these types of behaviors for several decades. Although most researchers describe a similar set of overlapping behaviors and trace the roots of their constructs back to Katz's (1964) notion of "innovative and spontaneous behavior," each uses slightly different definitions to delineate the boundaries of their construct domain. The model of soldier effectiveness proposed by Borman et al. (1983) is one example of a related construct and a predecessor to the model of contextual performance. In their work to define the performance domain for first tour soldiers, Borman et al. (1983) recognized that an individual's "overall worth" to an organization encompasses more than technical proficiency to include commitment to the organization, socialization, and morale (p. 2). Their model of solider effectiveness focused on those three factors and how they combine to produce three performance dimensions. Commitment and socialization combine to form Allegiance (e.g., following orders, military bearing, following regulations, respect for authority). Socialization and morale merge to define Teamwork (e.g., cooperation, camaraderie, leadership, concern for and boosting unit morale). Finally, Morale and Commitment combine to form Determination (e.g., perseverance, endurance, initiative, discipline, conscientiousness).

Of all the constructs related to contextual performance, perhaps the most widely recognized is organizational citizenship behavior or OCB. Organ (1988) defined OCB as "individual behavior that is discretionary, not directly or explicitly recognized by the formal reward system, and that in the aggregate promotes the effective functioning of the organization" (p. 4). Organ's definition of OCB is very similar to Van Dyne, Cummings, and Parks' (1995) notion of extra-role behavior and George and Brief's (1992) concept of organizational spontaneity. All three constructs describe voluntary behavior that goes beyond formal organizational roles or requirements and contributes to organizational effectiveness. However, although OCB and extra-role behavior include actions that are not generally recognized by an organization's formal reward program, organizational spontaneity includes behavior that may be rewarded (George & Brief, 1992; George & Jones, 1997).

Another related construct is prosocial organizational behavior (Brief & Motowidlo, 1986). According to Brief and Motowidlo, prosocial organizational behavior is behavior directed toward other individuals or the organization that intends to promote the welfare of or benefit the individual or organization. Prosocial organizational behavior differs from the other constructs in that it introduces the notion of intention to help as the driving force behind these behaviors. The other constructs do not specify any particular motive and instead focus on the net effect of the behavior as beneficial to the organization. Brief and Motowidlo also rejected the in-role, extra-role distinction, thus prosocial organizational behavior may be either in-role or extra-role. Finally, unlike contextual performance and other related constructs, prosocial organizational behavior includes behavior that may benefit individuals while detracting from organizational functioning. An example is an employee who spends time at work helping a coworker with a personal problem, but at the expense of lost time to the organization. Because the main focus of contextual performance is that the behavior supports the organization's goals, these kinds of prosocial behaviors are not generally considered to be part of the construct domain.

With the exception of contextual performance and prosocial organizational behavior, most of the construct definitions include only extra-role behaviors as part of the domain. However, clearly distinguishing between behaviors that are formally prescribed by an organization versus those that are voluntary or discretionary has proven problematic. Research has demonstrated that organization members do not necessarily agree on whether behaviors fall within or outside of formal job boundaries. In a survey by Morrison (1994), 317 clerical workers classified 18 of 20 behaviors taken from existing measures of OCB as in-role, suggesting that individuals may consider OCB as part of their job. In addition, Lam, Hui, and Law (1999) found that supervisors were more likely to see extra-role behaviors as part of the formal job requirements (i.e., in-role) than were subordinates. Organ (1997) conceded that requiring this class of behaviors to be distinguished as extra-role is inherently "muddy," and instead argued in favor of Borman and Motowidlo's definition of contextual performance to describe citizenship behaviors. Therefore, for the remainder of the chapter, the term contextual performance will be used in lieu of OCB or alternative terms.

In addition to the numerous terms to describe contextual performance and related concepts, several different solutions describing the underlying dimensions of these behaviors have been derived. Borman and Motowidlo (1997) presented a five-dimension taxonomy of contextual performance: a) persisting with enthusiasm and extra effort to complete own task activities successfully; b) volunteering to carry out task activities that are not formally part of own job; c) helping and cooperating with others; d) following organizational rules and procedures; and e) endorsing, supporting, and defending organizational objectives. Their five factors encompasses the five dimensions of OCB, although the configuration is somewhat different (Organ & Konovsky, 1989; Organ & Ryan, 1995; Smith et al., 1983): a) altruism or behaviors directed toward individuals in the organization; b) generalized compliance which refers to "impersonal contributions to the organization in such forms as exemplary attendance, use of work time, respect for company property, and faithful adherence to rules" (Organ & Ryan, 1995; p. 782); c) courtesy or taking action to avoid potential problems; d) sportsmanship or good-naturedly tolerating minor inconveniences and impositions; and e) civic virtue, which involves being an active participant in organizational governance (Organ & Ryan 1995). Podsakoff, MacKenzie, Paine, and Bachrach (2000) reviewed the citizenship behavior/contextual performance literature, comparing the different models available. They noted that researchers have recognized nearly 30 potentially different dimensions of contextual performance and summarized these into seven themes: a) helping behavior; b) sportsmanship; c) organizational loyalty (e.g., promoting, protecting, and defending the organization); d) organizational compliance (e.g., following organizational rules and policies); e) individual initiative (e.g., "persisting with extra enthusiasm and effort, volunteering to take on extra responsibilities"); f) civic virtue (e.g., taking personal responsibility for the well-being of the organization); and g) self-development (e.g., volunteering for education or training to improve one's knowledge and/or skill set) (p. 516).

Clearly, many different possible solutions have been presented in the literature. Perhaps the most parsimonious is the two-factor model offered by Williams and Anderson (1991). They distinguished between behavior that is directed toward the organization (e.g., coming to work on time, following rules) and behavior that is directed toward individuals (e.g., supporting or helping other employees). This distinction was supported by Coleman and Borman (2000) who compiled a list of 27 contextual performance dimensions and their definitions based on the dimension sets available and asked 47 industrial-organizational psychologists to sort the list according to content. Their analyses resulted in two factors that mirror the organization versus individual targets proposed by Williams and Anderson, which they labeled Personal Support and Organizational Support, as well as a third dimension, Conscientious Initiative, to represent persistence, taking initiative to do everything necessary to meet objectives, and taking advantage of opportunities for self-development. This revised model of contextual performance is presented in Table 17.1.

SIGNIFICANCE OF CONTEXTUAL PERFORMANCE

Although not directly contributing to an organization's technical core, contextual performance supports the overall environment in which task performance occurs and therefore has important implications for organizational functioning. One way of determining whether contextual performance enhances organizational functioning is by examining the relationship between contextual performance and ratings of individual job performance. Supervisors are often required to provide performance ratings that should in essence capture employees' overall contribution to organizational functioning. Therefore, if contextual performance facilitates the accomplishment of an organization's goals or contributes to the overall functioning of an organization, it should be related to supervisors' ratings of job performance.

Research has shown that supervisors do consider contextual performance when making performance ratings. In an experiment to determine the kind of information supervisors seek out when making ratings, Werner (1994) found that supervisors attended to information on ratees' contextual performance and that contextual performance had a significant impact on overall performance ratings. In a related study, Johnson (2001) examined the relative weights of contextual and task performance to overall performance ratings and determined that, across eight job families, contextual performance contributed significant unique variance to overall ratings.

Moreover, results of a meta-analysis conducted by Podsakoff et al. (2000) found that the influence of contextual performance on overall performance ratings was at least as much as task performance. On average across eight studies, after controlling for common method variance, contextual performance accounted for approximately 12% of the variance in performance ratings, whereas task performance accounted for approximately 9.3%. This finding was extended to peer ratings by Borman, White, and Dorsey (1995). They found in a path analysis that the path coefficients linking overall performance ratings on the part of peers and, respectively, a technical proficiency performance score and an

TABLE 17.1   Revised taxonomy of contextual performance

Dimension	Sub-dimensions
A. Personal Support Helping others by offering suggestions, teaching them useful knowledge or skills, directly performing some of their tasks, and providing emotional support for their personal problems. Cooperating with others by accepting suggestions, informing them of events they should know about, and putting team objectives ahead of personal interests. Showing consideration, courtesy, and tact in relations with others as well as motivating and showing confidence in them.	Helping: Helping others by offering suggestions about their work, showing them how to accomplish difficult tasks, teaching them useful knowledge or skills, directly performing of their tasks, and providing emotional support for their personal problems. Cooperating: Cooperating with others by accepting their suggestions, following their lead, and putting team objectives over own personal interests; informing others of events or requirements that are likely to affect them. Motivating: Motivating others by applauding their achievements and successes, cheering them on in times of adversity, showing confidence in their ability to succeed, and helping them to overcome setbacks.
B. Organizational Support Representing the organization favorably by defending and promoting it, as well as expressing satisfaction and showing loyalty by staying with the organization despite temporary hardships. Supporting the organization's mission and objectives, complying with organizational rules and procedures, and suggesting improvements.	Representing: Representing this organization favorably to outsiders by defending it when others criticize it, promoting its achievements and positive attributes, and expressing own satisfaction with the organization. Loyalty: Showing loyalty by staying with the organization despite temporary hardships, tolerating occasional difficulties and adversity cheerfully and without complaining, and publicly endorsing and supporting the organization's mission and objectives. Compliance: Complying with organizational rules and procedures, encouraging others to comply with organizational rules and procedures, and suggesting procedural, administrative, or organizational improvements.
C. Conscientious Initiative Persisting with extra effort despite difficult conditions. Taking the initiative to do all that is necessary to accomplish objectives even if not normally a part of own duties, and finding additional productive work to perform when own duties are completed. Developing own knowledge and skills by taking advantage of opportunities within the organization and outside the organization using own time and resources.	Persistence: Persisting with extra effort to complete work tasks successfully despite difficult conditions and setbacks, accomplishing goals that are more difficult and challenging than normal, completing work on time despite unusually short deadlines, and performing at a level of excellence that is significantly beyond normal expectations. Initiative: Taking the initiative to do all that is necessary to accomplish team or organizational objectives even if not typically a part of own duties, correcting non-standard conditions whenever encountered, and finding additional work to perform when own duties are completed. Self-development: Developing own knowledge and skills by taking courses on own time, volunteering for training and development opportunities offered within the organization, and trying to learn new knowledge and skills on the job from others or through new job assignments.

Note: From Borman et al. (2001, p. 55). Copyright 2001 by Blackwell Publishers. Reprinted with permission.

independently derived rating on a contextual performance dimension were virtually equal. Taken together, these studies clearly demonstrate that contextual performance is something that supervisors and probably peers attend to and consider when evaluating overall job performance. Because supervisor ratings of job performance are frequently used to assess individual contributions to organizational functioning, these studies also demonstrate that contextual performance plays a significant role in the overall operation of an organization.

Research examining the relationship between contextual performance and job performance ratings demonstrates how contextual performance works on an individual level to enhance organizational functioning. Thus, it stands to reason that contextual performance in the aggregate should also improve an organization's effectiveness. According to Podsakoff et al. (2000), contextual performance should be related to the success of an organization because it: a) enhances employee and managerial productivity; b) frees up resources for more productive uses; c) facilitates work group functioning by improving coordination, communication, and relationships among group members; d) improves an organization's ability to recruit and retain better employees; e) creates a more stable work environment; and f) allows for smoother transitions in times of change (pp. 544–545). For example, employees that help one another enhance unit productivity and free up organizational resources such as managerial time for more productive tasks. Several studies have examined the effect that contextual performance by organization members has on organizational effectiveness in a variety of organizations, including textiles, sales, and food service (Podsakoff & MacKenzie, 1994; Podsakoff, Ahearne, & MacKenzie, 1997; MacKenzie, Podsakoff, & Ahearne, 1996; Walz & Niehoff, 1996). The studies used a number of effectiveness indicators, including sales volume, revenue, production quantity, production quality, and customer satisfaction. As Borman and Penner (2001) noted in their review, the median variance accounted for in the various effectiveness indicators by employee contextual performance was 17.5%.

As these studies illustrate, contextual performance plays an integral role in the overall effectiveness of organizations. Because all organizations strive to be successful, contextual performance is something that organizations should attend to and attempt to increase to improve their performance. To do so, it is important to understand what factors or conditions are necessary to enhance contextual performance. The remainder of this chapter is dedicated to reviewing the extant literature on antecedents of contextual performance.

ANTECEDENTS OF CONTEXTUAL PERFORMANCE

Research attempting to identify and understand conditions under which contextual performance occurs is perhaps the most widely explored in this area. Researchers have approached this issue from a number of different directions depending on their theoretical perspective. On the whole, the antecedents of contextual performance can be divided into four separate categories: situational antecedents; attitudinal/affective antecedents, dispositional antecedents, and motivational antecedents. The following sections examine the literature pertaining to each, and summarize the relevant findings.

Situational antecedents

Situational antecedents refer to conditions that are present in the environment of the organization, such as leader behaviors, task feedback, and organizational politics. Situational antecedents might in turn be subdivided into two categories. The interpersonal category includes factors related to the quality of the social environment of an organization, for example organizational justice, leader behaviors, and organizational politics. Job characteristics, on the other hand, refer to aspects of the job itself, including task characteristics (routinization, feedback, significance) and level of autonomy.

Interpersonal factors.   An important antecedent of contextual performance is organizational justice. Organizational justice refers to the perceived fairness of interactions between individuals and the organization. Researchers have discussed justice in terms of its three forms: distributive, procedural, and interactional justice. Distributive justice relates to the perceived fairness of the outcomes received from an employer, whereas procedural justice refers to the perceived fairness of the processes and decisions that determine organizational outcomes, independent of the fairness of the actual outcomes received (Thibaut & Walker, 1975). Interactional justice addresses the quality of interpersonal treatment received during the execution of organizational procedures (Bies & Moag, 1986).

There are two theories that explain why perceptions of justice should be related to contextual performance. Although each theory makes similar predictions regarding the relationship between justice and individual contextual performance, they provide different explanations for the underlying processes that motivate behavior. The first is equity theory. According to equity theory (Adams, 1965), individuals compare their ratio of organizational outcomes (e.g., pay, promotions) to inputs (e.g., effort, abilities) with the ratios of similar others in order to determine fairness. Equity theory predicts that when employees perceive their ratio to be relatively large (i.e., overpayment inequity), they will experience guilt or remorse and may increase inputs (such as contextual performance) to restore equity. When employees perceive their ratio to be smaller (i.e., underpayment inequity), they will become dissatisfied or resentful and attempt to restore equity by reducing inputs (again, such as contextual performance).

The second, social exchange theory (Blau, 1964) argues that employees define their relationship with their organization or supervisor in terms of social exchange. Thus, employees engage in contextual behaviors to reciprocate favorable treatment by the supervisor or organization. If employees believe the organization is looking out for their best interests (i.e., high justice), then they will respond in kind by performing more contextual behaviors. However, if employees do not believe the organization is providing just treatment, they will reciprocate by reducing actions that benefit the organization, including contextual performance.

Overall, research has been supportive of the relationship between organizational justice and contextual performance (LePine, Erez, & Johnson, 2002; McNeely & Meglino, 1994; Moorman, 1991; Moorman, Niehoff, & Organ, 1993; Organ & Konovsky, 1989; Skarlicki & Latham, 1996, 1997; Tansky, 1993). Tanksy (1993) reported that perceptions of overall fairness were related to supervisor ratings of altruism ($r = .26$) and conscientiousness ($r = .21$). Also, in their meta-analysis, LePine et al. (2002) reported a corrected correlation of

.23 between overall fairness and contextual performance. In each of these studies, the authors did not separate out the three justice factors, but instead examined overall fairness. This may result in the loss of valuable information because other studies have shown differences in relationships between the three forms of justice and contextual performance. For example, Moorman et al. (1993) found that procedural justice was related to the courtesy, sportsmanship, and conscientiousness dimensions of contextual performance, but not to altruism or civic virtue. Moorman (1991) also examined the differential effects of distributive, procedural, and interactional justice on contextual performance. Although the zero-order correlations between each of the three forms of justice and contextual performance were significant, only interactional justice had a significant direct path to contextual performance. This finding suggests that the quality of interpersonal treatment employees receive from supervisors is a particularly important determinant of contextual performance, perhaps more so than the fairness of reward distribution or the procedures that determine rewards.

In addition to these cross-sectional studies, a few researchers have examined the directionality of the relationship between justice and contextual performance using quasi-experimental designs. Skarlicki and Latham (1996) conducted a study wherein they trained leaders of a public service union to exhibit behaviors that demonstrated procedural and interactional justice. Compared to union leaders that did not receive the training, the work groups of the trained leaders exhibited significantly higher levels of contextual performance. These results were replicated in a second study (Skarlicki & Latham, 1997). In that study, researchers also examined the mediational effects of perceived fairness on contextual performance. Their results indicated that perceived fairness mediated the relationship between leader training and contextual performance directed at organizations, but not for contextual performance directed at individuals. In other words, employees engaged in contextual performance directed at the organization because they perceived their leader as being fair. In addition to demonstrating the causal direction of the relationship between justice and contextual performance, these studies also provide support for psychological processes suggested by social exchange theory.

A second interpersonal factor is leader behavior. One of the main findings to arise from the justice research is that leader behaviors, particularly those that indicate the quality of interpersonal treatment that employees receive, play an important role in employee contextual performance. As mentioned, in Skarlicki and Latham's studies, when leaders were trained to exhibit behaviors that demonstrated a concern for the fairness and quality of interactions with subordinates, employees engaged in more contextual performance. Although social exchange theory provides an underlying framework to explain this relationship, leader–member exchange theory also offers insight.

Leader–member exchange (LMX) theory (Dansereau, Graen, & Haga, 1975) focuses on the relationships that supervisors have with individual employees rather than with an entire work group. According to Dansereau et al., supervisors develop two different types of relationships with their subordinates: those related to in-group and out-group. Members of the in-group are generally perceived as reliable and hard-working, are trusted by the supervisor and allowed to participate in decision making. In contrast, supervisors are more directive with members of the out-group and give them little input into the decision-making process. Because in-group members are given more responsibilities and have fewer constraints on their behavior, they should have more opportunity to engage in contextual performance. In-group members may also have more reason to engage in contextual performance since they likely feel they are being treated fairly.

Research evidence indicates that leader behaviors are related to subordinate contextual performance. Tansky (1993) found that employee ratings of the quality of the relationship with their supervisor were significantly related to supervisor ratings of all five dimensions of contextual performance (altruism, conscientiousness, sportsmanship, courtesy, and civic virtue). In their meta-analysis, LePine et al. (2002) reported uncorrected validities of .25 for leader support (.32 corrected) against overall contextual performance. Similar findings were reported by Podsakoff, MacKenzie, and Bommer (1996) for leader support and sportsmanship, courtesy, and civic virtue.

Also, Tepper and Taylor (2003) looked at the relationship between supervisor contextual performance (mentoring), subordinate perceptions of justice, and subordinate contextual performance. They examined the relationship in terms of a trickle-down model and hypothesized that contextual performance by supervisors would be related to subordinate perceptions of procedural justice, which in turn would influence subordinate contextual performance. Their data were supportive of the trickle-down model and provide additional support that leader behaviors are an important predictor of employee contextual performance.

Another interpersonal factor that may be important for contextual performance is organizational culture, specifically as it relates to organizational politics. Witt, Kacmar, Carlson, and Zivnuska (2002) described a politically charged atmosphere as one wherein individuals engage in behaviors that violate norms regarding what is acceptable behavior in order to further their own self-interest, often doing so with little regard for the well-being of others and the organization. This kind of atmosphere may discourage contextual performance by affecting the balance of social exchange. In other words, it would create perceptions of unfair or inequitable treatment. A politically charged atmosphere might affect the development of social relationships by fostering a lack of trust among organization members. This in turn would make it less likely that individuals would go out of their way to help others, because they would be more preoccupied by protecting their own interests.

Although reasons why political behavior would affect contextual performance seem reasonable, few studies have examined the relationship between these variables. However, the Witt et al. paper, just mentioned, found that employee perceptions of the level of politics in the organization were negatively related to supervisor ratings of contextual performance. Thus, the more employees perceive their work environment as politically charged, the less likely they are to engage in contextual performance.

On a related note, it's plausible that a highly political organization might tend to discourage the cohesiveness of work groups. In politically charged organizations, self-interests may take precedence over group interests, in turn reducing group cohesion. Therefore, group cohesiveness may serve as an indirect indicator of the level of organizational politics. In their meta-analysis, Podsakoff et al. (1996) reported that group cohesiveness significantly predicted the contextual performance dimensions of sportsmanship, courtesy, and civic virtue. Taken together, these studies indicate that a politically charged atmosphere discourages employee contextual performance. However, this is a relatively new area within the contextual performance literature and more research is needed to explore this relationship further.

Job characteristics. The second type of environmental antecedent involves the characteristics of jobs themselves that may inhibit or encourage contextual performance. Research examining job characteristics in relation to contextual performance comes mainly from the substitutes-for-leadership literature. The previous section discussed the impact that leader behavior has on contextual performance. According to leader–member exchange theory, members of the in-group have more autonomy, are given more responsibility, and presumably, have more significant tasks to perform. However, these factors could also be conceptualized as being a part of the formal job requirements rather than distributed by a leader. Thus, within a social exchange framework, in exchange for receiving more responsibility, autonomy, and task significance from the organization, employees may tend to engage in more contextual performance.

Although only a few studies have examined specific job characteristics in relation to contextual performance, the research that is available is generally supportive. For example, Gellatly and Irving (2001) found that employee ratings of job autonomy were correlated with supervisor ratings of contextual performance ($r = .33$). Podsakoff et al. (1996) conducted a meta-analysis of leadership substitutes against performance measures including contextual performance. According to their review, task feedback was significantly related to altruism ($r = .15$), conscientiousness ($r = .23$), sportsmanship ($r = .15$), courtesy ($r = .19$), and civic virtue ($r = .31$). Task routinization was also significantly related to all five dimensions of contextual performance (βs $= -.23, -.24, -.10, -.20,$ and $-.38$, respectively). Thus, it appears that jobs providing greater autonomy, feedback, and task variety may encourage more employee contextual performance.

Attitudinal antecedents

Two job attitudes have been investigated as potential antecedents of contextual performance: organizational commitment and job satisfaction. Organizational commitment was described by Meyer, Allen, and Smith (1993) in terms of three components: affective, normative, and continuance. Affective commitment refers to the emotional attachment to their organization that employees may develop. Normative commitment occurs when employees feel obligated to the organization out of a sense of duty or what is right, and continuance commitment relates to employees remaining with an organization because of a lack of viable alternatives or because they need the rewards (e.g., money, benefits) provided by the organization. In general, research indicates that affective commitment is most strongly related to contextual performance ($\rho = .23$ for altruism and .30 for generalized compliance; Organ & Ryan, 1995).

The relationship between job satisfaction and contextual performance has been investigated in a number of studies (Kidwel, Mossholder, & Bennett; 1997; Le Pine et al., 2002; Miller, Griffin, & Hart 1999; Moorman, 1991; Moorman et al., 1993; Netemeyer, Boles, McKee, & McMurrian, 1997; Organ & Konovsky, 1989; Organ & Ryan, 1995; Tanksy, 1993; Williams & Anderson, 1991), and overall, results suggest that they are positively related. For example, Organ and Ryan (1995) reported sample-weighted mean estimates of .28 with altruism and .28 with generalized compliance in their meta-analysis.

Although the majority of the relevant job satisfaction literature has used measures of overall job satisfaction, in recent years researchers have approached job satisfaction as representing both a cognitive and an affective component. According to Lee and Allen (2002), cognitions are "employees' considered judgments about aspects of the work situation" (p. 131), in other words, the "cool" or unemotional appraisal of their job or some aspect of their working conditions (e.g., pay). Affect, on the other hand, refers to the actual feelings employees have about their work situation (Lee & Allen, 2002, p. 131).

Recent studies indicate that these two components may have different implications for contextual performance. For example, Organ and Konovsky (1989) reported that supervisor ratings of contextual performance were determined more by cognitions than affect. They suggested that acts of contextual performance may be more planned and purposeful rather than a means of expressing satisfaction. In a separate study, Lee and Allen (2002) found that affect was a stronger predictor of contextual performance directed at individuals, whereas cognitions were more strongly related to contextual performance directed at the organization. Thus, behavior such as helping coworkers finish tasks may be more of a natural expression of feelings toward others, whereas behaviors such as volunteering to serve on a committee may be more planful and deliberate.

Although the early thinking regarding job attitudes was that they are directly related to contextual performance, some researchers have suggested something different. Organ and his colleagues (Konovsky & Organ, 1996; Moorman et al., 1993; Organ & Konovsky, 1989) proposed that the relationship between job satisfaction and contextual performance may be due to the shared variance with organizational justice. Several studies have reported that the relationships between job satisfaction and contextual performance drop to near zero when the variance due to perceived justice is controlled (Moorman, 1991; Moorman et al., 1993). Thus, it is possible that satisfaction, like contextual performance, is a consequence of perceived fairness.

Dispositional antecedents

One of the main reasons for expanding the criterion domain to include contextual performance was the lack of significant research findings linking personality traits to job performance. The theory of individual differences and performance put forth by Motowidlo, Borman, and Schmit (1997) argues that task performance is largely determined by individual differences in knowledge, skills, and abilities. However, contextual performance is more likely to be predicted by individual differences in personality and motivation.

In general, the research findings for personality traits as predictors of contextual performance have been mixed. In their meta-analysis, Organ and Ryan (1995) reported weak relationships between personality (e.g., agreeableness, positive and negative affectivity) and generalized compliance and altruism. Only conscientiousness showed higher relationships, with reported corrected validities of .22 against altruism and .30 against generalized compliance. And, validities were lower when studies using self-ratings of contextual performance were excluded (.04 against altruism and .23 against generalized compliance).

In contrast, the results of a separate meta-analysis by Borman, Penner, Allen, and Motowidlo (2001) of 20 studies since Organ and Ryan's 1995 review were more promising. Results of their study are summarized in Table 17.2. Unlike Organ and Ryan, Borman et al. used an overall composite criterion (i.e., they did not separate contextual performance into different dimensions) and also included a larger sample of personality traits. Once again, conscientiousness was the single best predictor of contextual performance,

TABLE 17.2   Mean uncorrected correlations between personality and citizenship performance criteria

Personality construct	All criteria			Self-report criteria deleted		
	Number of studies	Total N	Weighted mean correlation	Number of studies	Total N	Weighted mean correlation
Conscientiousness	12	2378	.24	.10	1963	.19
Agreeableness	7	1554	.13	7	1554	.13
Positive affectivity	5	985	.18	5	970	.16
Extroversion	8	1832	.08	7	1728	.06
Negative affectivity	6	1151	−.14	5	1047	−.12
Locus of control	3	599	.16	3	599	.12
Collectivism	4	857	.15	1	132	.04
Other-oriented empathy	7	1343	.28	4	434	.17
Helpfulness	7	1343	.22	4	434	.15

Note: From Borman et al. (2001, p. 64). Copyright 2001 by Blackwell Publishers. Reprinted with permission.

with weighted mean validities of .24 (.19 if self-ratings of contextual performance were excluded). In addition, Borman et al. also reported significant validities with other personality traits, including agreeableness ($r = .13$), positive affectivity ($r = .18$), extroversion ($r = .08$), negative affectivity ($r = -.14$), locus of control ($r = .16$), and collectivism ($r = .15$).

Two other personality constructs that were included in the Borman et al. meta-analysis reflect a different approach to examining personality traits associated with contextual performance. Penner and his associates developed a measure of "prosocial personality orientation" to assess personality traits associated with prosocial thoughts, feelings, and behaviors (Midili & Penner, 1995; Penner & Fritzsche, 1993; Penner, Fritzsche, Craiger, & Freifeld, 1995; Penner & Finkelstein, 1997; Penner, Midili, & Kegelmeyer, 1997; Schroeder, Penner, Dovidio, & Piliavin, 1995). The Prosocial Personality Battery (PSB) developed by Penner et al. (1995) measures two factors: other-oriented empathy ("the tendency to experience empathy for, and to feel responsibility and concern about the well being of others") and helpfulness ("a self-reported history of engaging in helpful actions and an absence of egocentric physical reactions to others distress") (Penner et al., 1997, p. 122). The PSB has shown significant correlations with contextual performance measures across a number of studies. In Borman et al.'s meta-analysis, other-oriented empathy and helpfulness had weighted mean validities (uncorrected) of .28 and .22, respectively.

Although some personality traits, such as conscientiousness, other-oriented empathy, and helpfulness show definite promise as predictors of contextual performance, this line of research has been criticized because the evidence overall is not overwhelmingly positive. With the exception of Borman et al.'s meta-analysis, the validities have been fairly modest. Perhaps the relationship between personality and contextual performance is more complex than originally thought, and the reason that stronger relationships have not consistently been found is that the links depend on the organizational or occupational situation. Recently, a number of studies have examined the interactive effects of both person and situation factors on contextual performance, and their results are promising.

For example, Gellatly and Irving (2001) examined whether the degree of autonomy afforded by a job moderates the relationship between personality and contextual performance. They reasoned that greater autonomy would result in fewer constraints on behavior (a weaker situation according to Mischel (1977)), and therefore, greater opportunity for personality to influence behavior. Their results indicated that when autonomy was high, both extroversion and agreeableness had a positive relationship with supervisor ratings of contextual performance. When autonomy was low, however, extroversion was not related to contextual performance. Surprisingly, when autonomy was low, the relationship between agreeableness and contextual performance was negative, indicating that individuals high in agreeableness engaged in less contextual performance than individuals low in agreeableness. Gellatly and Irving suggested that highly agreeable people may have difficulty in low autonomy jobs wherein they are required to enforce rules, although the authors cautioned that further investigation is necessary.

Beaty, Cleveland, and Murphy (2001) examined the effect of strength of situation on the relationship between Big Five personality traits and contextual performance. In both a lab and a field study, they found that the relationships between personality and contextual performance were greatest when situational cues regarding job performance were weak. Similar to Gellatly and Irving's findings, these results suggest that a situation with weak demands allows for greater expression of personality through behavior.

Additionally, Witt et al. (2002) assessed the relationships between conscientiousness, agreeableness, extroversion, and contextual performance in highly political environments. They found that agreeableness moderated the relationship between politics and contextual performance (interpersonal facilitation). Although individuals engaged in less interpersonal facilitation overall when politics were high, individuals low in agreeableness engaged in substantially less interpersonal facilitation compared to individuals high on agreeableness. These results suggest that organizational politics have less of an effect on the contextual performance of individuals high on agreeableness than those low in agreeableness.

Similarly, Hogan, Rybicki, Motowidlo, and Borman (1998) conducted two studies to examine how personality is related to contextual performance under different environmental conditions. Hogan et al. reasoned that correlations between personality traits and contextual performance might differ based on the availability of opportunities for advancement. The hypothesis was largely confirmed. Results indicated that for jobs with few opportunities for advancement, the strongest predictor of contextual performance was conscientiousness as measured by the Hogan Personality Inventory (HPI) Prudence scale ($r = .20$ for Work Dedication and $r = .17$ for Interpersonal Facilitation). In contrast, for jobs with ample opportunities for advancement, the strongest predictor of contextual performance was the HPI Ambition scale. The correlation between contextual performance and Prudence in this sample was non-significant (near-zero). Their results, along with the studies by Gellatly and Irving (2001), Beaty et al. (2001), and Witt et al. (2002), suggest that whether personality is related to contextual performance, as well as the specific traits that are associated with contextual performance, depends to some extent on the characteristics of the organizational environment. Moreover, Hogan et al.'s study suggests that different environmental conditions will influence the kinds of motives individuals have for engaging in contextual performance. That theme is expanded upon in the next section.

Motivational antecedents

An alternative approach to predicting contextual performance lies in understanding and identifying individuals' motives for engaging in this behavior. Investigating motives of contextual performance is a fairly new direction, and a number of different motives for contextual performance have been suggested (Bolino, 1999; Ferris, Judge, Rowland, & Fitzgibbons, 1994). Penner and his colleagues (Connell, 2003; Penner et al., 1997; Rioux & Penner, 2001; Tillman, 1998) sought to identify motives for contextual performance using the functionalist approach (Snyder, 1993), which argues that human behavior is driven by a desire to meet certain needs or motives. In order to understand why people behave the way they do, it is necessary to understand what function the behavior serves, or what needs it meets for them.

According to the functionalist approach, two people may perform the same behavior, but do so for different reasons. For example, two employees may volunteer to chair an organization's fundraising committee; the first may volunteer to support the organization to enhance the image of the organization and to benefit the greater community. In this case, the employee's motives are altruistic. The second may volunteer in order to increase his/her visibility to executives and other influential individuals in the organization. In this case, the employee's motives are to create a positive image in order to further his/her career. Moreover, individual behavior may be influenced by more than one motive, and any single behavior may fulfill any number of needs or goals.

Rioux and Penner (2001) developed an instrument to assess people's motives for engaging in contextual performance called the Citizenship Motives Scale (CMS). Factor analyses of the CMS indicate that it measures three distinct motives for contextual performance: organizational concern (e.g., I care what happens to the company), prosocial values (e.g., I believe in being courteous to others; it is easy for me to be helpful), and impression management (e.g., to avoid looking bad in front of others; to look better than my coworkers). In a field study examining the relationship between the three CMS motives and ratings of contextual performance, two of the motives demonstrated differential relationships with dimensions of the predictors and the criteria. Specifically, the organizational concern motive was most highly correlated with conscientiousness whereas the prosocial values motive was most strongly correlated with altruism. And, concern for the organization was associated with contextual behavior directed toward the organization, while concern for other people was associated with contextual behavior directed at individuals.

Connell (2003) took the issue of motives a step further and proposed that motives play a mediational role in contextual performance. He found that the relationships between various antecedents and contextual performance were mediated by different motives. Specifically, the relationship between affective commitment, procedural justice, and the generalized compliance dimension of contextual performance were mediated by the organizational concern motive. Thus, the reason that commitment and procedural justice are related to contextual performance seems to be that they promote concern for the organization. Similarly, the relationship between conscientiousness and generalized compliance was mediated by the organizational concern motive. This finding suggests that conscientious individuals follow rules and support the organization because of concern for the welfare of the organization. In contrast, the prosocial values motive mediated the relationship between the personality trait, other-oriented empathy, and altruism. Thus, individuals high on empathy engage in behaviors such as helping their coworkers because they are concerned with developing positive relationships with others. Taken together, these results provide evidence that motives are important predictors of contextual performance and also provide a framework to describe the process by which antecedents influence contextual performance.

Although Rioux and Penner (2001) found evidence for a distinct impression management motive, they did not find any significant correlations between it and either dimension of contextual performance. However, the nature of impression management is such that it may impact contextual performance differently. In fact, Bolino (1999) presented a theoretical framework to explain how impression management concerns drive contextual performance. According to his model, individuals are motivated to use contextual performance for impression management purposes when: a) individuals see contextual performance as instrumental in achieving their goals; b) individuals value being seen as a "good organizational citizen"; and c) a discrepancy exists between individuals' desired image and their actual image. Bolino also proposed that impression management motives would moderate the relationship between contextual performance and work effectiveness such that the relationship will be weaker if employees engage in contextual performance to manage their work image. Typically, contextual performance should lead to an increase in organizational effectiveness because it creates a social environment that facilitates the accomplishment of tasks. However, when individuals are motivated by self-enhancement concerns, then those behaviors (contextual performance) are likely to be perceived as ingratiation, thereby mitigating the effects of those behaviors on organizational effectiveness.

At least one researcher (Eastman, 1994) examined how perceptions of the motive behind contextual performance affect supervisor reward distributions. In a lab study, Eastman found that managers gave the least rewards (e.g., lower performance ratings, smaller bonus) to employees whose behavior was attributed to ingratiation, and the highest rewards to employees whose behavior was attributed to prosocial values or organizational concern motives. If the rewards distributed are an indication of employees' contributions to organizational effectiveness, then these findings suggest that behavior perceived to be motivated by self-enhancement contributes less to an organization's effectiveness than behavior motivated by more altruistic concerns. However, because of the paucity of research in this area, more studies are clearly needed to fully understand how impression management motives affect contextual performance.

CONCLUSION

As the preceding sections have demonstrated, the antecedents of contextual performance are many and varied. From an organizational perspective, research has given us greater insight into how and why contextual performance occurs on the level of social exchange between an organization and its employees, as well as between managers and their subordinates. Moreover, research has identified how individual differences in personality can affect the propensity to engage in contextual performance. And recent studies indicate that some personality traits may be even better predictors of contextual performance under specific situations. Finally, individual differences in motivation for engaging in contextual performance may predict not only the type of contextual performance that individuals perform, but also how effective those behaviors are perceived to be.

In addition to informing science, the research findings presented also have important implications for practice. Few would disagree that contextual performance is an important way that employees contribute to organizational functioning. Research has shown that managers do consider contextual performance when rating employee job performance (Johnson, 2001; Werner, 1994) and that contextual performance does contribute to the overall effectiveness of organizations (Podsakoff & MacKenzie 1997). Therefore, it is in the best interest of organizations and organizational decision makers to attend to those factors that contribute to contextual performance.

Specifically, research suggests that organizations should take steps to ensure that employees are treated equitably or justly, especially in terms of the quality of interpersonal treatment they receive. These efforts should focus particularly on the treatment employees receive from their managers or immediate supervisors, as the quality of this relationship is an important predictor of contextual performance. Also, contextual performance can be encouraged by giving employees greater autonomy and control over the specific behaviors they perform while completing their work. Finally, organizations should take steps to curtail problematic organizational politics, as research suggests that organizations that are highly political discourage contextual performance.

The antecedents of contextual performance that are most relevant for selection are those that pertain to individual differences in the propensity to engage in contextual performance. Research has identified several personality traits associated with contextual performance, including conscientiousness, agreeableness, positive affectivity, extroversion, and prosocial personality orientation. Organizations should be able to increase the amount of contextual performance employees perform by using personality measures to select applicants high on these traits. It is also interesting to note that some of these personality traits (conscientiousness and agreeableness) are also associated with refraining from counterproductive work behavior such as coming to work late, wasting time, theft, sabotage, and interpersonal conflict (Ones, Viswesvaran, & Schmidt, 1993; Skarlicki, Folger, & Tesluk, 1999).

Although research has shown that personality is related to contextual performance in general, recent studies indicate that this relationship may be moderated by situational characteristics pertaining to the job and job environment. For example, Beaty et al. (2001) demonstrated greater validity of Big Five personality traits when situational cues for performance were weak as opposed to strong. Moreover, Hogan et al. (1998) found that ambition is a better predictor of contextual performance in jobs with opportunities for advancement, whereas conscientiousness is a better predictor for jobs with few opportunities for advancement. While these examples demonstrate how the job environment can affect the strength of the relationship, other characteristics, such as job autonomy, may affect the direction of the relationship. Gellatly and Irving (2001) reported significant positive validities for extroversion and agreeableness for positions with high autonomy. However, the validities were negative for jobs with low autonomy. Thus, practitioners should consider the overall work environment when deciding which traits to include as part of a selection system, as some traits may be valid in some situations and not in others.

Although much has been learned about the prediction of contextual performance, there are several areas that merit further study. First, the relationship between job characteristics and contextual performance has not been widely explored. As Podsakoff et al. (2000) point out, it may be useful to examine a wider range of job characteristics, including job scope, feedback, and skill variety (Hackman & Oldham, 1980) in relation to contextual performance. Furthermore, little is known about why job characteristics are related to contextual performance. They may operate through a social exchange process or through reciprocity between organizations and employees. Another possibility is that they work through their influence on employee attitudes such as job satisfaction and organizational commitment.

Regarding personality predictors of performance, most of the research to date has focused on the Big Five traits; thus it would be worth while to explore the validity of lower-order traits. Growth need strength, in particular, may be worthy of investigation as studies have shown it to moderate the relationship between job characteristics and job satisfaction (Loher, Noe, Moeller, & Fitzgerald, 1985). Moreover, because recent research suggests that the validity of personality as a predictor of contextual performance may depend on organizational or job characteristics, such as level of autonomy and promotional opportunities, additional research is needed to identify those factors that may have the greatest impact and how they interact with personality so as to better inform the choice of predictors.

Although studies suggest that motives may influence the type of contextual performance (i.e., whether it is directed at the organization or individuals), more research is needed to understand how individual motives operate to influence behavior. It would be especially interesting to investigate how the impression management motive affects not only the choice of contextual behaviors, that is whether it is directed towards the organization or individuals and which individuals (e.g., peers versus supervisors), but also whether they are perceived as being more effective when contextual performance is motivated by more altruistic concerns. Research on organizational politics suggests that contextual performance motivated by impression management may contribute less to individual and organizational effectiveness, but how accurately can supervisors and others recognize the difference between contextual behaviors motivated by different concerns?

Finally, more research is needed to understand how the various predictors interact with each other to influence contextual performance. For example, do job characteristics, leader behaviors, and organizational culture directly relate to contextual performance or do they operate through their influence on employee attitudes? It is also likely that the specific motives employees have to engage in contextual performance may be influenced by individual differences in personality, as well as by leader behavior and the broader organizational context. In fact, because contextual performance does not occur in a vacuum, employees' motives and behavior likely influence leader behavior and the organizational culture as well.

We have tried to make the case that contextual performance is important for contemporary organizations. There is evidence that contextual performance on the part of organization members is linked to individual and organizational effectiveness. In our judgment, attending to and researching contextual performance and *all* of its antecedents is likely to enhance even more levels of organizational effectiveness.

REFERENCES

Adams, J. S. (1965). Inequity in social exchange. In L. Berkowitz (Ed.), *Advances in experimental social psychology* (Vol. 2, pp. 267–299). New York: Academic Press.

Barnard, C. I. (1938). *The functions of the executive*. Cambridge, MA: Harvard University Press.

Beaty, J. C., Jr., Cleveland, J. N., & Murphy, K. R. (2001). The relation between personality and contextual performance in "strong" versus "weak" situations. *Human Performance, 14*, 125–148.

Bies, R. J., & Moag, J. S. (1986). Interactional justice: Communication criteria of fairness. *Research on Negotiation in Organizations, 1*, 43–55.

Blau, P. (1964). *Exchange and power in social life*. New York: Wiley.

Bolino, M. C. (1999). Citizenship and impression management: Good soldiers or good actors? *Academy of Management Review, 24*, 82–98.

Borman, W. C., & Motowidlo, S. J. (1993). Expanding the criterion domain to include elements of contextual performance. In N. Schmitt & W. C. Borman (Eds.), *Personnel selection in organizations* (pp. 71–98). San Francisco: Jossey-Bass.

Borman, W. C., & Motowidlo, S. J. (1997). Task performance and contextual performance: The meaning for personnel selection research. *Human Performance, 10*, 99–109.

Borman, W. C., Motowidlo, S. J., & Hanser, L. M. (1983, August). A model of individual performance effectiveness: Thoughts about expanding the criterion space. In *Integrated criterion measurement for large scale computerized selection and classification*, Symposium presented at the 91st Annual Convention of the American Psychological Association, Washington, DC.

Borman, W. C., & Penner, L. A. (2001). Citizenship performance: Its nature, antecedents, and motives. In B. W. Roberts & R. Hogan (Eds.), *Personality psychology in the workplace* (pp. 45–61). Washington, DC: American Psychological Association.

Borman, W. C., Penner, L. A., Allen, T. D., & Motowidlo, S. J. (2001). Personality predictors of citizenship performance. *International Journal of Selection and Assessment, 9*, 52–69.

Borman, W. C., White, L. A., & Dorsey, D. W. (1995). Effects of ratee task performance and interpersonal factors on supervisor and peer performance ratings. *Journal of Applied Psychology, 80*, 168–177.

Brief, A. P., & Motowidlo, S. J. (1986). Prosocial organizational behaviors. *Academy of Management Review, 11*, 710–725.

Coleman, V. I., & Borman, W. C. (2000). Investigating the underlying structure of the citizenship performance domain. *Human Resource Management Review, 10*, 25–44.

Connell, P. W. (2003). *The antecedents of OCB: Motives as mediators*. Unpublished master's thesis, University of South Florida, Tampa, FL.

Dansereau, F., Graen, G. B., & Haga, W. J. (1975). A vertical dyad linkage approach to leadership with formal organizations. *Organizational Behavior and Human Performance, 13*, 46–78.

Eastman, K. K. (1994). In the eyes of the beholder: An attributional approach to ingratiation and organizational citizenship behavior. *Academy of Management Journal, 37*, 1379–1391.

Ferris, G. R., Judge, T. A., Rowland, K. M., & Fitzgibbons, D. E. (1994). Subordinate influence and the performance evaluation process: Test of the model. *Organizational Behavior and the Human Decision Processes, 58*, 101–135.

Gellatly, I. R., & Irving, P. G. (2001). Personality, autonomy, and contextual performance of managers. *Human Performance, 14*, 231–245.

George, J. M., & Brief, A. P. (1992). Feeling good – doing good: A conceptual analysis of the mood at work–organizational spontaneity relationship. *Psychological Bulletin, 112*, 310–329.

George, J. M., & Jones, G. R. (1997). Organizational spontaneity in context. *Human Performance, 10*, 153–170.

Hackman, J. R., & Oldham, G. R. (1980). *Work redesign.* Reading, MA: Addison-Wesley.

Hogan, J., Rybicki, S. L., Motowidlo, S. J., & Borman, W. C. (1998). Relations between contextual performance, personality, and occupational advancement. *Human Performance, 11*, 189–207.

Johnson, J. W. (2001). The relative importance of task and contextual performance dimensions to supervisor judgments of overall performance. *Journal of Applied Psychology, 86*, 984–996.

Katz, D. (1964). The motivational basis of organizational behavior. *Behavioral Science, 9*, 131–143.

Katz, D., & Kahn, R. L. (1966). *The social psychology of organizations.* New York: Wiley.

Kidwell, R. E., Mossholder, K. W., & Bennett, N. (1997). Cohesiveness and organizational citizenship behavior: A multilevel analysis using work groups and individuals. *Journal of Management, 23*, 775–793.

Konovsky, M. A., & Organ, D. W. (1996). Dispositional and contextual determinants of organizational citizenship behavior. *Journal of Organizational Behavior, 17*, 253–266.

Lam, S. S. K., Hui, C., & Law, K. S. (1999). Organizational citizenship behavior: Comparing perspectives of supervisors and subordinates across four international samples. *Journal of Applied Psychology, 84*, 594–601.

Lee, K., & Allen, N. J. (2002). Organizational citizenship behavior and workplace deviance: The role of affect and cognitions. *Journal of Applied Psychology, 87*, 131–142.

LePine, J. A., Erez, A., & Johnson, D. E. (2002). The nature and dimensionality of organizational citizenship behavior: A critical review and meta-analysis. *Journal of Applied Psychology, 87*, 52–65.

Loher, B. T., Noe, R. A., Moeller, N. L., & Fitzgerald, M. P. (1985). A meta-analysis of the relation of job characteristics to job satisfaction. *Journal of Applied Psychology, 70*, 280–289.

MacKenzie, S. B., Podsakoff, P. M., & Ahearne, M. (1996). Unpublished data analysis. Indiana University, Bloomington.

McNeely, B. L., & Meglino, B. M. (1994). The role of dispositional and situational antecedents in prosocial organizational behavior: An examination of the intended beneficiaries of prosocial behavior. *Journal of Applied Psychology, 79*, 836–844.

Meyer, J. P., Allen, N. J., & Smith, C. A. (1993). Commitment to organizations and occupations: Extension and test of a three-component conceptualization. *Journal of Applied Psychology, 78*, 538–551.

Midili, A. R., & Penner, L. A. (1995, August). *Dispositional and environmental influences on Organizational Citizenship Behavior.* Annual meeting of the American Psychological Association, New York.

Miller, R. L., Griffin, M. A., & Hart, P. M. (1999). Personality and organizational health: The role of conscientiousness. *Work and Stress, 13*, 7–19.

Mischel, W. (1977). On the future of personality measurement. *American Psychologist, 32*, 246–254.

Moorman, R. H. (1991). Relationship between organizational justice and organizational citizenship behaviors: Do fairness perceptions influence employee citizenship? *Journal of Applied Psychology, 76*, 845–855.

Moorman, R. H., Niehoff, B. P., & Organ, D. W. (1993). Treating employees fairly and organizational citizenship behavior: Sorting the effects of job satisfaction, organizational commitment, and procedural justice. *Employee Responsibilities and Rights Journal, 6*, 209–225.

Morrison, E. W. (1994). Role definitions and organizational citizenship behavior: The importance of employee's perspective. *Academy of Management Journal, 37*, 1543–1567.

Motowidlo, S. J., Borman, W. C., & Schmit, M. J. (1997). A theory of individual differences in task and contextual performance. *Human Performance, 10*, 71–83.

Netemeyer, R. G., Boles, J. S., McKee, D. O., & McMurrian, R. (1997). An investigation into the antecedents of organizational citizenship behaviors in a personal selling context. *Journal of Marketing, 61*, 85–98.

Ones, D. S., Viswesvaran, C., & Schmidt, F. L. (1993). Comprehensive meta-analysis of integrity test validities: Findings and implications for personnel selection and theories of job performance. [Monograph]. *Journal of Applied Psychology, 78*, 679–703.

Organ, D. W. (1988). *Organizational citizenship behavior: The Good Soldier Syndrome.* Lexington, MA: Lexington.

Organ, D. W. (1997). Organizational citizenship behavior: It's construct clean-up time. *Human Performance, 10*, 85–97.

Organ, D. W., & Konovsky, M. A. (1989). Cognitive versus affective determinants of organizational citizenship behavior. *Journal of Applied Psychology, 74*, 157–164.

Organ, D. W., & Ryan, K. (1995). A meta-analytic review of attitudinal and dispositional predictors of organizational citizenship behavior. *Personnel Psychology, 48*, 775–802.

Penner, L. A., & Finkelstein, M. A. (1997). Dispositional and structural determinants of volunteerism. *Journal of Personality and Social Psychology, 74*, 525–537.

Penner, L. A., & Fritzsche, B. A. (1993). Magic Johnson and reactions to people with AIDS: A natural experiment. *Journal of Applied Social Psychology, 23*, 1035–1050.

Penner, L. A., Fritzsche, B. A., Craiger, J. P., & Freifeld, T. R. (1995). Measuring the prosocial personality. In J. Butcher & C. D. Spielberger (Eds.), *Advances in personality assessment* (Vol. 10, pp. 147–163). Hillsdale, NJ: LEA.

Penner, L. A., Midili, A. R., & Kegelmeyer, J. (1997). Beyond job attitudes: A personality and social psychology perspective on the causes of organizational citizenship behavior. *Human Performance, 10*, 111–131.

Podsakoff, P. M., Ahearne, M., & MacKenzie, S. B. (1997). Moderating effects of goal acceptance on the relationship between group cohesiveness and productivity. *Journal of Applied Psychology, 82*, 374–983.

Podsakoff, P. M., & MacKenzie, S. B. (1994). Organizational citizenship behavior and sales unit effectiveness. *Journal of Marketing Research, 31*, 351–363.

Podsakoff, P. M., & MacKenzie, S. B. (1997). Impact of organizational citizenship behavior: A review and suggestions for future research. *Human Performance, 10*, 133–151.

Podsakoff, P. M., MacKenzie, S. B., & Bommer, W. H. (1996). Meta-analysis of the relationships between Kerr and Jermier's substitutes for leadership and employee job attitudes, role perceptions, and performance. *Journal of Applied Psychology, 81*, 380–399.

Podsakoff, P. M., MacKenzie, S. B., Paine, J. B., & Bachrach, S. G. (2000). Organizational citizenship behaviors: A critical review of the theoretical and empirical literature and suggestions for future research. *Journal of Management, 26*, 513–563.

Rioux, S. M., & Penner, L. A. (2001). The causes of organizational citizenship behavior: A motivational analysis. *Journal of Applied Psychology, 86*, 1306–1314.

Schroeder, D. A., Penner, L. A., Dovidio, J. F., & Piliavin, J. A. (1995). *The psychology of helping and altruism.* New York: McGraw-Hill.

Skarlicki, D. P., Folger, R., & Tesluk, P. (1999). Personality as a moderator in the relationship between fairness and retaliation. *Academy of Management Journal, 42*, 100–108.

Skarlicki, D. P., & Latham, G. P. (1996). Increasing citizenship behavior within a labor union: A test of organizational justice theory. *Journal of Applied Psychology, 81*, 161–169.

Skarlicki, D. P., & Latham, G. P. (1997). Leadership training in organizational justice to increase citizenship behavior within a labor union: A replication. *Personnel Psychology, 50*, 617–633.

Smith, C. A., Organ, D. W., & Near, J. P. (1983). Organizational citizenship behavior: Its nature and antecedents. *Journal of Applied Psychology, 68*, 653–663.

Snyder, M. (1993). Basic research and practice problems: The promise of a "functional" personality and social psychology. *Personality and Social Psychology Bulletin, 19*, 251–264.

Tansky, J. W. (1993). Justice and organizational citizenship behavior: What is the relationship? *Employee Responsibilities and Rights, 6*, 195–207.

Tepper, B. J., & Taylor, E. C. (2003). Relationships among supervisors' and subordinates' procedural justice perceptions and organizational citizenship behaviors. *Academy of Management Journal, 46*, 97–105.

Thibaut, J., & Walker, L. (1975). *Procedural justice: A psychological analysis.* Hillsdale, NJ: Lawrence Erlbaum.

Tillman, P. (1998). *In search of moderators of the relationship between antecedents of organizational citizenship behavior and organizational citizenship behavior: The case of motives.* Unpublished master's thesis, University of South Florida, Tampa, FL.

Van Dyne, L., Cummings, L. L., & Parks, J. M. (1995). Extra role behaviors: In pursuit of construct and definitional clarity (a bridge over muddied waters). In L. L. Cummings & B. M. Shaw (Eds.), *Research in organizational behavior* (Vol. 17, pp. 215–285). Greenwich, CT: JAI Press.

Walz, S. M., & Niehoff, B. P. (1996). Organizational citizenship behaviors and their effect on organizational effectiveness in limited-menu restaurants. In J. B. Keys & L. N. Dosier (Eds.), *Academy of Management Best Papers Proceedings* (pp. 307–311). Briarcliff Manor, NY: Academy of Management.

Werner, J. M. (1994). Dimensions that make a difference: Examining the impact of in-role and extra-role behaviors on supervisory ratings. *Journal of Applied Psychology, 79*, 98–107.

Williams, L. J., & Anderson, S. E. (1991). Job satisfaction and organizational commitment as predictors of organizational citizenship and in-role behaviors. *Journal of Management, 17*, 601–617.

Witt, L. A., Kacmar, K. M., Carlson, D. S., & Zivnuska, S. (2002). Interactive effects of personality and organizational politics and contextual performance. *Journal of Organizational Behavior, 23*, 911–926.

Part V

Emerging Trends and Assessment for Change

18

Computer-Based Testing and the Internet

Dave Bartram

This chapter will outline the ways in which computer technology can be used in selection. In so doing, it will take a broad view of the literature and current practice to consider not just what is being done but also what could and, no doubt, will be done in the future. Thus we will also look at some work in areas outside of selection: for example, educational testing and assessment for licensing and certification, where these provide insights into how selection practices may change. It is not the intention of this chapter to provide an exhaustive review of the literature on computer-based testing (CBT) and the Internet; rather it will attempt to illustrate how these technologies are being used in selection and how they could be used. In particular, it will focus on practice issues arising from the application of these technologies.

A decade ago, Bartram (1994) introduced a review of CBT (at that time, the Internet did not even figure in the title), by pointing out that it was rather odd to base a review on a technology. Prior to the development of computers, we tended to talk about tests and selection without making explicit references to the strengths or limitations of paper or electro-mechanical technologies. The fact that we are now so concerned with the impact of technologies on assessment methodology is testament to the power of those technologies to affect what can be done and the impact it can have on people.

In reviews going back over two decades (Bartram & Bayliss, 1984; Bartram, 1994), the authors commented on the fact that while there was much research on CBT, there was relatively little evidence of it having had an impact in practice in areas such as selection. The reasons for this were clear. Computer technology was expensive, difficult to use, and unreliable. There was very little standardization – for example, every manufacturer tended to define their own format for recording information on disks. In addition, the capacity of computers was very limited. Early tests were developed on machines without hard drives, with no more than 16k of random access memory (RAM), and with processors that bore little resemblance to those of today.

The point at which computers started to be widely used in practice for selection corresponded to a number of changes in technology that had a major influence on practice during the early 1990s:

◆   the rapid increase in computing power, memory and the associated reduction in costs;
◆   the adoption of a standard software operating system (the ubiquitous Windows);
◆   the increasing availability of computer hardware within the workplace as it becomes
    a standard piece of office equipment.

However, probably the most significant impact came in the mid-1990s with the introduction of the World Wide Web (WWW). Though the Internet had been around for some
decades prior to that, it had been the province of the military and university communi-
ties. It was a very unfriendly environment within which to operate, and there was little of
interest or value to people who were not involved in IT. The introduction of an easy-to-
use hypertext-based system of interacting with the Internet changed all that, and in less
than a decade we have seen both computers and the Internet become a part of many
people's everyday life at home and at work. While, in financial terms, the dot-com bubble
may have burst, in practice access to and use of the Internet has continued to grow rapidly
over the past five years, and the rate of growth shows no sign of abating.

Bartram (1994) noted that it was disappointing to find that many issues emerging from
a review of the literature at that time were the same ones that people were concerned with
a decade earlier (as reviewed in Bartram & Bayliss, 1984). It is interesting to note that these
same issues continue to be the subject of research and debate:

◆   the equivalence of computer-based and paper-based versions of the same test;
◆   the use of computers to generate interpretive reports;
◆   the development and application of item response theory based tests and, in particu-
    lar, adaptive testing technologies.

However, to these issues can now be added two new ones:

◆   the impact of the Internet on testing;
◆   the reactions of applicants and other users to Internet-delivered tests.

In this chapter we will:

◆   review applications of CBT in the field of selection;
◆   consider the impact on selection of the Internet as an assessment medium;
◆   consider how things may change over the next ten years.

In relation to the Internet we will look particularly at:

◆   the role of unproctored testing in assessment for selection;
◆   research on applicant reactions.

The focus of this chapter will be on CBT in the context of selection, both delivered in
standalone mode on a PC and delivered across the Internet. There are a whole host of
related issues that could be discussed around this topic, which relate to the use of the Internet more broadly for recruitment (e.g., for job boards, candidate attraction, managing can-

didate application workflows, and so on). The interested reader is referred to Lievens and Harris (2003) and Bartram (2000) for relevant reviews.

Equivalence of Tests across Modes of Administration

For conventional tests, a major issue has been that of equivalence. The question raised is whether the results from a test delivered by computer can be regarded as being comparable to the results from the same test when administered in traditional paper form. Mead and Drasgow (1993) reported a meta-analysis of equivalence studies, King and Miles (1995) reviewed cross-mode equivalence of non-cognitive tests, and Bartram (1994) reviewed the literature in relation to ability tests and inventories, questionnaires, and survey instruments. The general consensus from all these reviews was that there was no problem associated with computerization of non-cognitive tests, so long as due care was taken in the process of designing the computerized delivery. The same was true for tests of ability that were not highly speeded. The only area where equivalence is an issue is where speeded ability tests are concerned. Mead and Drasgow reported mean disattenuated cross-mode correlations of .97 for power tests and .72 for speeded ones.

The main issue is one of ergonomics. Under time pressure, differences in mode of response may act to significantly change the nature of the task. Thus, speeded tests, like clerical checking tasks, may need to be carefully redesigned and renormed when computerized. For most other ability tests, whether timed or untimed, so long as the timing does not introduce a high degree of speededness, paper and computer versions can be treated as equivalent forms. An important caveat to this, however, is that the implementation of the test in computer form must have been carried out carefully with due regard to readability and legibility of content. Problems can arise for tests that rely on the test taker having to make use of various resource materials (charts, diagrams, reference materials, etc.). Where it is not possible to fit these onto the computer screen, the nature of the task may be adversely affected by computerization.

More recent studies have supported these general conclusions. Gibson and Weiner (1997) report an elegantly designed study in which two forms of each of a number of different ability tests are presented in both computer and paper modes with complete balancing of forms and orders of modes of administration. They found that the average disattenuated correlation between modes was .94, and was greater for un-speeded tests than for speeded tests. For the latter they found an average disattenuated correlation of .86. For un-speeded tests, the average disattenuated correlation was close to unity (.98).

Use of the Internet for Selection Testing

In relation to selection, the Internet has been used more for personality testing than for ability testing. Personality tests are relatively easy to implement on the web, as standard HTML can be used and there are no issues over timing. Ability test delivery tends to require the use of more sophisticated software to ensure control over timing and security of scoring.

While there appears to a be a broad consensus on the issue of equivalence across modes of administration for PC-based tests, the advent of Internet-based administration has renewed interest in this question. Despite this interest and the rapid and widespread use of online personality assessment, there is relatively little literature dealing with issues of equivalence or impact on the selection process. There is even less literature on the issue of online versus paper version equivalence for ability tests.

However, a number of studies (reviewed in Bartram, 2000, and Lievens & Harris, 2003) have been carried out. These include studies that look broadly at the use of the WWW for data collection (e.g., in surveys, for psychosocial experimentation, and for use in 360 degree feedback within organizations). These studies indicate little if any differences between Internet-based data collection and traditional paper-and-pencil methods. Other studies have focused specifically on selection instruments. Studies by Mead and Coussons-Read (2002) and Reynolds, Sinar, and McClough (2000) both find high congruence coefficients for the 16PF and a biodata instrument respectively. Salgado and Moscoso (2003) reported high levels of congruence between paper and Internet versions of a Big Five instrument, with coefficients ranging from .93 to .98 for the five scales.

Similar results are reported by Bartram and Brown (2003a) for the OPQ32i. Their study compared matched samples of data from paper and Internet administered versions of the instrument under real selection or assessment for development conditions. They found no differences in scale means, reliabilities, or scale intercorrelations. It should be noted that in addition to the groups in the Bartram and Brown study differing in terms of mode of administration, the web-based administration was unproctored while the paper-based one was proctored in traditional group sessions. This implies that neither mode of presentation nor the presence or absence of a proctor affected scores in a substantive fashion.

There is, however, some evidence that changing modes of administration can result in loss of equivalence. Ployhart, Weekley, Holtz, and Kemp (2003) examined incumbent and applicant samples with paper and web-based administration of personality, biodata, and situational judgment tests. Of interest here are the differences they report between modes of administration (there are also differences between incumbent and applicant groups). Web-based measures had more normal distributions than paper-based ones, and generally had lower means (between .3 and .5 SDs for the personality scales). The web-based data demonstrated higher reliability, but also demonstrated higher degrees of scale intercorrelation than the paper-based data. This study suggests the need for some caution in assuming equivalence. However, it must be noted that the various groups in the study were not randomly equivalent to each other, and some at least of the differences reported could be due to sampling biases.

A more controlled manipulation of variables is reported by Oswald, Carr, and Schmidt (2001). They used undergraduate students in a study that systematically varied mode of administration (paper versus web) in both supervised and unsupervised conditions for both personality and ability tests. Their results, surprisingly, tended to show some effects of supervision on measurement properties for personality measures but no effects on ability tests.

Preckel and Thiemann (2003) report a study comparing Internet and paper administration of a figural matrices test and report that reliable and valid data could be collected over the Internet and that both test versions were comparable with regard to the contribution of item design features to task difficulty.

Kurz and Evans (2004) report an interesting set of data comparing five equivalence studies that span a period of over twelve years. The studies compared a number of different computer-based versions and paper-and-pencil versions of the same numerical and verbal reasoning tests. One sample (1991) used a PC DOS-based version of the tests, three other samples from the mid-1990s used Windows-based versions of the tests, and the final sample, collected in 2002, was an online version. Correlations between computer and paper modes showed very little variation across studies, with a sample weighted average correlation between modes of administration of .75 for the verbal tests and .80 for the numerical tests. In both cases, these correlations are approximately equal to the reported reliabilities of the tests. All the data in these studies were collected under standardized proctored conditions.

Beaty, Fallon, and Shepard (2002) used real applicants and compared proctored and unproctored Internet testing conditions. Applicants first completed an unproctored test at home or at work. The best 76 of these were selected for retesting in a proctored environment. The average score for these candidates in the proctored session was 42.2 and in the unproctored session 44.1. Based on the applicant population SD, the difference is about one-third of an SD. This small increase in scores could be due to a number of factors. Retesting itself is known to lead to an increase in scores (Burke, 1997). There is no control in this study for people who do a proctored test first and then an unproctored version. The other explanations (cheating or collusion on the unproctored test) cannot be ruled out, but other research by the author and his colleagues suggests that this is not a substantive issue so long as applicants are aware that they will be reassessed if successful in the unproctored session.

Baron, Miles, and Bartram (2001) reported data from the use of a short online numerical reasoning test designed for use as an unproctored sift. This used test generation technology (see below) to ensure that every candidate received a different version of the test. Following the sift, short-listed candidates were retested under proctored conditions with a full-length numerical reasoning test. Prior to use of this sift, 880 applicants were short-listed for assessment centers. Of these, only 30% passed the numerical reasoning test given at the assessment center and 211 of these met the overall criterion for hiring. Following introduction of the screening test, the number going forward for assessment was reduced to 700, the pass rate on the proctored numerical reasoning test rose to 50%, and 280 of those people met the criterion for hiring. The estimated savings in recruitment costs were $1,000 per hire.

Examination of the distributions of scores on the screening test in the above study did not give any indication that cheating was a problem. If it has been, one would have expected to find a bias in the number of false positives on the screening. There was no indication of this. The fact that this did not occur was attributed to three factors:

1. The screening test software was designed to prohibit tampering.
2. The test items varied from person to person.
3. The test administration was embedded within a process involving an "honesty contract." This made clear at the beginning of the selection what the candidates would be expected to do if they passed the screen, and asked them to agree to take the screening test under appropriate conditions and without asking for assistance.

At present, there is insufficient data to draw firm conclusions about the impact of Internet administration on the psychometric properties of tests. What evidence there is suggests that, given due care has been exercised in the implementation to ensure that ergonomic factors do not cause differences, there is unlikely to be any major impact of web-delivery on equivalence. What effects do occur are more likely to be due to other potentially confounding factors (presence or absence of proctoring, group as opposed to individual sessions, and so on). Many of these variables have begun to be studied within the general field of applicant reactions. Future research needs to explore these in more detail.

USER AND APPLICANT REACTIONS

There has been a tendency to make use of the Internet's potential for remotely administered assessment to change the standard practice of giving tests to people in groups under the supervision of a proctor. One consequence of this has been an interest in user and applicant reactions to different forms of test delivery and administration. In order to clarify the range of administration options the Internet provides, Bartram (2001) has classified current usage in terms of four modes of test administration:

1. Open mode. These are conditions where there is no means of identifying the test taker and there is no direct human supervision. Examples of this include tests that can be accessed openly on the Internet without any requirement for test-taker registration. Such tests may sit on an organization's website as a "taster" for potential applicants. More commonly, practice tests are made available in an open mode. This mode provides no control over test security, nor does it provide any control over who does the test or the volume of test takers.

2. Controlled mode. This is similar to the open mode in that no human supervision of the test session is assumed. However, the test is only made available to known test takers. For the Internet this is controlled through the requirement for the test taker to be provided with a logon username and password. This is typically the mode used in the early stages of selection and for screening. It is typically also used for the administration of personality inventories in the final stages of selection. This both allows recruiters to reduce the time required for people to attend assessment centers and ensures that the test results are available prior to other final assessments.

3. Supervised mode. For this mode, a level of direct human supervision is required, whereby the identity of the test taker can be authenticated and test-taking conditions validated. This mode also provides a better level of control over dealing with unexpected problems or issues. For Internet testing, this mode is achieved by requiring the test administrator to login the candidate and to confirm that the testing was completed correctly at the end of the session. Typically, this mode would be used for Internet delivery of secure ability tests into an assessment center environment.

4. Managed mode. This is a mode where a high level of direct human supervision is assumed and where there is also the need for control over the test-taking environment. This is achieved through the use of dedicated testing centers. The organization managing the testing process can define and assure the performance and specification of

equipment in test centers. They can also generally exercise more control over the competence of the staff. In addition to standard "thin-client" Internet applications, managed mode also provides the opportunity for delivering "thick-client" applications under highly controlled conditions. Managed-mode assessment for selection tends to be the province of large organizations, such as the military, or those requiring the use of specialized tests, such as for the selection of trainee pilots by commercial airlines.

User and applicant reactions will tend to vary as a function of the mode of administration used and the function for which it is used – i.e., whether it seems appropriate. In practice, selection procedures involve a sequence of stages which transition applicants through these modes, from open to controlled, and from controlled to supervised or managed, as they move further down the selection funnel.

One concern about the use of computer-based testing, which applies equally to the Internet as to standalone testing, is that some applicants might be disadvantaged through their fear or phobia of computers. From the early days of computer-based testing, computer-phobia or anxiety about using computers has been noted as a potential barrier to computer-based testing. While this may have been a genuine concern in the 1980s and 1990s, is it still an issue? Arguably, computers are now as much a part of everyday life, at least in the developed world, as are paper and pencil. Indeed, many of us now feel more at home working on a word processor than writing on paper. Nevertheless, studies have found relationships between expressed computer anxiety and performance on computer-based tasks (e.g., Brosnan, 1998; Mahar, Henderson, & Deane, 1997). However, recent research by Frericks, Ehrhart, and O'Connell (2003) suggests that computer anxiety may be an expression of general trait anxiety. They found that people scoring high on a measure of computer anxiety performed less well on both computer and paper-and-pencil tests.

The impact of mode of presentation on socially desirable responding (SDR, or "faking good") is another area of interest. This issue may be confounded with differences in practice relating to supervision, as most Internet delivery of self-report inventories now occurs in unproctored modes. Wilkerson, Nagao, and Martin (2002) examined the impact of questionnaire purpose (job screening – high SDR demand, or consumer survey – low SDR demand) and mode of administration (paper versus computer) on SDR. They found no effect of mode of presentation, but did find the expected effect of purpose, with higher SDR in the job-screening situation. This is consistent with the earlier report by Richman, Kiesler, Weisband, and Drasgow (1999). They meta-analyzed the results of studies on the equivalence of non-cognitive measures and concluded that computerization had no overall effect on SDR. However, they did report that when people were completing questionnaires alone and had the opportunity to backtrack and to skip items, they were more likely to self-disclose and less prone to SDR than under other conditions. They also confirmed that there was less SDR when candidates were anonymous than when they were not (as would be the case in selection).

Mead (2001) reported a high degree of satisfaction with online administration of 16PF amongst users, owing to both the advantages of remote administration and the speed with which results were obtained. However, he also noted that users were concerned about the levels of technical difficulties. It was this factor that tended to differentiate between satisfied and dissatisfied users. Reynolds et al. (2000) also reported more positive attitudes by applicants toward Internet testing than traditional testing, and also noted that this preference did not vary as a function of ethnic group membership. Applicants considered that the most important issues in relation to Internet testing were speed and efficiency (a finding supported by a later study by Sinar & Reynolds, 2001): in particular, concern was expressed in situations where Internet speed was slow. Sinar and Reynolds (2001) conclude by noting that in addition to speed and efficiency, candidates commented on the need for systems to be user-friendly – easy to navigate and well explained – and stated a clear preference for working in non-proctored environments.

Bartram and Brown (2003b) describe the results from 54 feedback forms completed anonymously by applicants after they had completed the OPQ32i online. As noted by Sinar and Reynolds, technical problems were one of the main issues for test takers. However, the overall evaluations were very positive and there was a clear preference in the present study for computer-based administration over paper and pencil, with most people saying they would prefer to complete such inventories online despite some of the technical difficulties encountered with the Internet. There was also a clear preference for working remotely rather than at a supervised location. This latter finding is consistent with Sinar and Reynolds' (2001) finding. As they note, it is likely that such differences in preference will be affected by the function and context of testing: lack of personal contact may become an issue if the system is difficult to use or if other problems arise.

Although other research (Bartram & Brown, 2003a) had shown that score distributions were the same for both online unsupervised and offline supervised administrations of the OPQ32i, we were interested to gain applicant reactions to the lack of supervision. In the questionnaire we directly asked them if they have sought any assistance in completing the questionnaire. Only two out of the 54 said that they had asked their partners for an opinion as to which choice better suited them in some instances (one respondent said this only occurred for one question and the other respondent said that it had happened a number of times). All but two also said that they would not get someone else to help complete an online questionnaire in a selection situation in the future. However, while only 4% admitted to some degree of collusion in completing the inventory, 19% of respondents expressed concerns that other applicants might seek assistance in completing the questionnaire, 37% said that they were not concerned, and 43% said that this possibility had not even occurred to them. Respondents who had expressed concern said that experienced people might know how to answer questions to fit job requirements, which would put truthful applicants at a disadvantage. Given the conditions of anonymity under which this was conducted, we can be fairly confident that these are honest responses. They suggest that concerns about others cheating or colluding may exaggerate the actual extent to which people do this. However, one potential downside of unsupervised administration is that people may perceive it as being less fair – because they believe other people may take unfair advantage of it.

Wiechmann and Ryan (2003) examined applicant reactions to an in-basket test. This was administered in either paper or computerized form and varied in difficulty according to the technical level of the job. The outcome selection decision (accepted or rejected) was the third variable manipulated in this between-subjects design. Post-test perceptions did not differ as a function of mode of administration. However, computer anxiety and experience with computing were important factors in performing successfully on this task.

Wiechman and Ryan (2003) reported finding only one published study (Arvey, Strickland, Drauden, & Martin, 1990) that looked at applicant reactions to computerized testing within a genuine selection context. Unfortunately, Wiechman and Ryan themselves used student surrogates in their study.

Of particular importance in selection situations is the impact of outcomes on applicant reactions. Whether or not the applicant is hired is likely to have strong influence on their perception of the selection process (Gilliland, 1994). Other outcome variables which need to be considered are perceptions of fairness (Gilliland, 1994), perceptions of organizational attractiveness (Bauer, Maertz, Dolen, & Campion, 1998), and recommendation intentions (Ployhart & Ryan, 1997). Apart from Wiechman and Ryan's study, the impact of these variables on applicant reactions does not appear to have been systematically studied in the context of computerized assessment for selection.

A recent review of the research on applicant reactions is presented in Anderson (2003). This raises a number of issues for future research. In particular, the current literature suffers from an over-reliance on studies using student populations as surrogate applicants and a failure to disentangle the variables which may impact on applicants:

♦ anonymity;
♦ mode of administration;
♦ presence or absence of a proctor;
♦ administration in group versus individual settings;
♦ prior experience and familiarity with the medium;
♦ outcome measures – for example, whether the applicant was successful; applicant perceptions of equity and fairness; how the process affected applicant perceptions of the organization.

Novel Forms of Item and Test

Within the general field of CBT it is useful to distinguish between the use of computers to administer conventional tests and their use in innovative testing. By "conventional" we mean tests that either exist as paper-and-pencil versions or which could be delivered in paper format. Innovative tests are those that could only be delivered using the computer as a medium. Tests can be innovative in a number of different ways. The most obvious is where the actual test content is innovative. However, innovation can also occur in less obvious ways. The process used to construct the test may be innovative and rely on computer technology and the nature of the scoring of the items may be innovative. In practice, there is an interaction between these different aspects of innovation, in that some of the most interesting developments in test content also involve innovation in how that content is created.

Innovation in content

For computer-based testing, the most obvious examples of content innovation can be found where tests use sound or video to create multimedia items. Drasgow, Olson-Buchanan, and

Moberg (1999) describe a full-motion interactive video assessment, which uses video clips followed by multiple choice questions. Simulations can also be run on computer to provide realistic work-sample assessments. Hanson, Borman, Mogilka, Manning, and Hedge (1999), for example, describe the development of a computer-based performance measure for air traffic control selection.

Innovation in content also relates to the use of more dynamic item types, for example where drag-and-drop or other familiar Windows-based operations are used rather than the simple point-and-click simulation of paper-and-pencil multiple response. A review of this area of innovation in item types is presented by Drasgow and Mattern (in press).

Innovation in content, however, is often associated with novel methods of content generation. Item generation techniques have provided the potential for a whole host of new item types as well as more efficient production of conventional items. Bartram (2002a) and Goeters and Lorenz (2002) describe the use of generative techniques to develop a wide range of task-based and item-based tests for use in pilot selection. It is worth noting, however, that most of the developments in this area of innovation have occurred in areas where selection leads to very high-cost training or into high-risk occupations or both (as is the case for trainee military pilot selection). Innovation is expensive, and the sort of tests described in the papers referred to above have required extensive research and development programs. However, as in all areas of testing, the lessons learned from this work will result in benefits in due course for the general field of selection testing.

Novel ways of scoring tests

Computer software provides for the recording of very detailed information about a test taker's performance. In addition to the response given to an item, we can record how long the person took to respond. We can also record information about choices made and changed during the process of responding. For more complex item types we can track the performance of the person as they work their way through a task or series of subtasks.

Bartram (2002b) reported validation data from the use of a set of computer-based ability tests that were administered without any time limit. These were designed for use in a diagnostic mode for people entering further education training courses. Time to respond was normed independently for each item and response latency was scored together with accuracy to produce a measure of efficiency. This efficiency score had higher validity than the traditional number-correct score.

While there has been some experimentation in the use of response latency data for checking response stability (Fekken & Jackson, 1988) and socially desirable responding (Holden & Fekken, 1988; George & Skinner, 1990a, b), these approaches have not been developed into practical applications for general use in selection as yet.

New methods of test construction

Item response theory (IRT) has been with us for over two decades (Lord, 1980), but its application has tended to be confined to educational and some large-scale occupational uses. It has tended not to be applied in the area of general occupational selection testing until relatively recently. IRT has the considerable advantage of approaching test construction from the item level. Its application to routine occupational assessment has become possible with the advent of better data collection and data management procedures. IRT has many advantages over traditional methods; however, it also comes with some costs: the need for larger samples of data with which to determine the properties of items:

♦ IRT provides estimates of the psychometric properties of items (questions) that are independent of the properties of all other items. When traditional or classical psychometric models are used to create a test, the statistics associated with a question or item (e.g., how difficult it is and how well it discriminates between different levels of ability) are all relative to the particular test concerned. The item statistics provided by IRT models are independent of any particular "test" or combination of items. Because of this, items in a bank can be calibrated and, using relevant mathematical algorithms, can be combined to produce tests of known psychometric properties.

♦ IRT-based item banks enable tests to be created that are pre-normed. The norms for a new test can be derived from the data used to calibrate the items. In practice, test users will still require information on the relationship between an individual's test score and that of members of one or more reference groups. However, this process, which might be described as "benchmarking," is distinct from the use of norms in classical test theory for scale standardization.

♦ IRT models estimate the properties of items across the full theoretical range of ability. As well as providing item statistics that are independent of other items, IRT also provide estimates of ability that are independent of the sample the research is conducted on.

♦ Reliability is not a constant for a test; it actually varies depending on the pattern of responses a person gives. IRT provides the means of defining the reliability and hence the SEM uniquely for each individual who takes a test, based on their pattern of responses to the items.

(For a brief history of IRT, see Bock, 1997. For more detailed accounts of IRT, the interested reader is referred to Hambleton & Swaminathan, 1985; Hambleton, Swaminathan, & Rogers, 1991; Van der Linden & Hambleton, 1997; Wainer et al., 1990.)

The key advantage of using IRT is test efficiency. IRT provides a means of measuring how much information each item will provide about a person's ability; by choosing items which provide the most information, we can construct tests that are much shorter than those produced in the classical way, but which have the same reliability and construct validity.

Using IRT-calibrated item banks it is possible to generate tests to meet a variety of needs. There are a number of pressing needs in selection which traditional testing finds it difficult to meet:

♦ Tests need to be reusable but also secure.
♦ Testing time needs to be as short as possible, but the results need to be reliable.

Using IRT, tests can be generated that are optimized for use in particular situations and which tend to be about half the length of conventional tests with comparable levels of reliability. Item banking can also be used as the basis for generating large numbers of test variants to reduce the chances of test takers getting to know the items and the scoring key. This approach has been used very successfully by SHL in its development of online randomized ability tests for screening purposes. By ensuring that each applicant receives a different, but equivalent, test variant, it is possible to provide unproctored online screening. This is subsequently followed up with proctored testing of short-listed candidates. As described earlier, research (Baron et al., 2001) has shown that this process leads to substantial savings in recruitment costs, by significantly reducing the numbers that have to be assessed post-screening.

True adaptive testing, where item selection is managed on the fly, with the test being optimally tailored to each applicant, tends to have been confined to use in the military or large organizations. Two examples of the development of adaptive testing systems for use in selection are described by Zickar, Overton, Taylor, and Harms (1999) for the selection of computer programmers in a financial services company (State Farm Insurance Companies) and by Segall and Moreno (1999) for the computerized adaptive testing version of the Armed Services Vocational Aptitude Battery (ASVAB). Both these chapters make clear that the development of these systems is a major undertaking, not least for the work associated with the production of a well-calibrated and sufficiently large bank of items.

Internet testing has made it potentially easier to achieve this for "smaller" consumers, as it is possible through the Internet to pool data from different client organizations in order to calibrate items and develop banks for use in general-purpose ability testing. However, there are technical limitations on the use of the Internet for truly adaptive testing, as Internet browser technology relies on a dialog between a "thick server" and a "thin client." While there are techniques for reducing the impact of Internet speed and denials of service, it is likely to be some time before we find computer adaptive testing routinely used over the Internet. For the present it is likely to be confined to use in dedicated computer testing centers, where there is sufficient control over security to permit the downloading of significant quantities of item data.

Adaptive personality tests

The development of IRT to deal with graded response item formats (Samejima, 1972) as well as dichotomous ones introduced the potential for adaptive personality assessment. This was first explored in the late 1980s (Dodd, Koch, & de Ayala, 1989; Koch, Dodd, & Fitzpatrick, 1990; Waller & Reise, 1989; Singh, Howell, & Rhoads, 1990). Applications of adaptive testing to tailored interviewing and survey administration were described by Kamakura and Balasubramanian (1989).

However, it is only recently that we are beginning to see the application of this technology to selection testing. Schneider, Goff, Anderson, and Borman (2003) describe the development of computerized adaptive rating scales to measure task and contextual performance or organizational citizenship behavior. Based on earlier work by Borman et al. (2001), this uses a forced choice format where pairs of behavioral statements are chosen according to effectiveness levels and administered iteratively according to an IRT algorithm. Stark and Chernyshenko (2003) have also noted the potential value of using IRT methods to produce ipsative format personality instruments that are resistant to faking.

We are likely to see much more use made of this type of approach in the future, as it makes possible the tailoring of questionnaire items to cover just those characteristics that it is required to measure, and to do so to a defined level of precision.

Traditionally, personality assessment for selection has been exhaustive – and, for the applicant, exhausting: whatever the position a person is being assessed for, they are required to complete large multi-scale inventories. In practice, it may only be necessary to obtain half that information in order to provide accurate predictions of the essential competencies. While IRT provides one basis for adaptive instruments to better the assessment needs of a selection situation, there are also simpler techniques that can be used with computer-managed assessments. The construction of assessment instruments can, for example, be driven by a competency analysis of the job requirements, such that items (not scales) are selected which provide the most information about those competencies. This not only ensures that only relevant questions are asked during selection, but also that the number of questions asked is kept to a minimum.

CBT AND INTERNET SYSTEMS

CBT involves far more than just the delivery of a set of items or questions over the Internet or on a PC. In this section of the chapter we will examine some of the main components of computer-based testing systems. Luecht (in press) has outlined the conceptual architecture of a CBT enterprise in the context of licensing and certification. Much the same structure applies for systems used in selection. This architecture has five main components:

1. item development and banking;
2. test assembly;
3. candidate registration and assessment session scheduling;
4. test delivery;
5. post-test processing.

We will consider each of these in more detail as they pertain to selection testing.

Item development and banking

CBT systems require software to manage item databases and item banks and to manage the procedures of new item development, and prototyping. Traditionally, items were written by a team of item writers; these were then trialed and the data analyzed. The "good" items were then kept to form a test. The potential approach now is very different. Pools of items can be held in databases that reference them in terms of a wide number of content descriptors and psychometric parameters. These items are version controlled as they are adapted or modified, so that one can track their history of usage: which tests they have been included in, how often they have been exposed, and so on.

Increasingly, developers are making use of item generation and item morphing techniques (see Irvine & Kyllonen, 2002, for a recent set of papers covering this field). Item generation techniques use rules to create items with known properties. A very simple example would be a rule to create sums that are either correct or incorrect, and which all take the form $X = A + B$. The rules would specify the range of numbers that can be substituted for A and for B and the magnitude of the difference between X and A + B for those sums which are incorrect. The challenge in item generation is to define those rules that enable items of comparable levels of difficulty to be generated, and those rules than enable one to directly manipulate the difficulty of the items in a predictable fashion. Item morphing procedures are rather different. They work on a prototype item and act to change it in ways that should maintain its psychometric properties while altering its "surface" characteristics. Thus one might use morphing techniques to create multiple numerical reasoning items from a single prototype.

Depending upon the nature of the item generation process, generation may be used as a substitute for human item writers, but still require item trialing to take place, or it may be possible to create items with well-estimated parameters that are ready for executive use.

The old test development cycles can also be changed by the potential for computer-delivered tests to be rapidly reconfigured. Thus, every "executive" test can be configured to contain some trial items for calibration. In this way the item pool can be continually refreshed without the need for separate item trials. What is more, the new items are "tested" under realized conditions alongside the executive items, in real selection situations. As a result, we know the data is not biased by having been collected under surrogate rather than actual selection conditions.

Test assembly

Test assembly can now be highly automated. A test is essentially a set of items. The choice of which items go into a test can be driven by criteria in such a way that tests are optimally "tailored" to the selection situation. Test assembly can also be carried out in more conventional ways, by setting criteria such as the construct to be assessed, the target population, the length of the test, or required reliability level.

Candidate registration and assessment session scheduling

There is a whole set of functionality that has nothing directly to do with testing, but which is an essential part of the test administration workflow. Procedures need to be in place to check on the identity of the applicant taker and to ensure that they are able to take the test at the allocated time and place. For Internet-delivered tests, the time and place may be of the applicants' own choosing or can be placed under the control of the test administrator. In many cases, we require applicants to take more than one test, or for tests to be allocated to different stages in the selection process (e.g., some may be used as online screening tools while others are administered under proctored conditions in an assessment center). CBT and Internet systems need to provide the workflow control and management necessary for users to structure assessments appropriately for their selection needs.

Test delivery

Test delivery involves a number of components. First, one needs some software that is capable of taking the item content and presenting it to the applicants and controlling the workflow and data collection aspects of the test administration. This, in turn, will depend on a mechanism for transmitting the test from the supplier to the user. This may be over the Internet in real time, either to a wired PC, an interactive TV, or a wireless device (such as a 3G mobile phone), or by download from the Internet onto a PC or hand-held device for running offline, or by download of printable materials for paper-and-pencil administration. Test administration software can also, of course, be delivered on CD.

Depending on the nature of the test, it may be necessary to exercise control over the physical testing conditions and the nature of the delivery medium. For example, it may be practical to administer a personality inventory over a 3G phone, but not an ability test. Because of the considerable variety of potential delivery media, and the range of options that often arise within media (e.g., the range of different browsers running on the Internet), it is necessary for the provider to do more than specify the minimum requirements for hardware and software at the user end. It is increasingly necessary to actively manage the type of devices that can be used by the test taker.

Post-test processing

Post-assessment processing includes the scoring of the test results, data recording and archiving, data warehousing for future psychometric analyses, and score reporting. Good data warehousing is a vital part of ensuring that the item pool is kept refreshed and up to date. However, we will focus attention here on score reporting and interpretation.

The earliest use of computers in testing was not for test administration but for test interpretation and reporting. The most time-consuming part of testing and the process that involves the greatest expertise is the interpretation of scores. As a consequence, it is in this part of the process where the greatest costs arise and where the greatest savings can be made through automation.

In selection, computer-based testing systems provide a number of types of report. Some are quite straightforward and are, in effect, management information reports. Such reports might provide a "merit" list of applicants, ordered in terms of their scores on one or more screening tests, or a report describing the relative performance on certain selection measures of male and female applicants.

Of more interest, however, are what may be called "expert reports." These use expert systems technology to interpret results and provide users with reports similar to those that might be produced by a human expert test user. It is such reports that provide users with the real "added value" of using computers in assessment. Ideally, reports are designed to provide the user with the information they need to help them make selection decisions. Such reports may be in the form of short-lists with recommendations, or provide structured interview prompts tailored to individual applicant strengths and weaknesses.

There is not space to discuss the variety of reports here (see Bartram, 1995, for a taxonomy), but it is important to note that the validity and utility of computer-based reports can vary considerably and is not determined by the validity of the tests on which they are based. In practice, we can identify three steps in the process of obtaining a useful outcome from an assessment. First, the tests used need to produce valid data. This is the "validity" that tends to be addressed in the test user's technical manual and which is the subject of formal test reviews. Second, however, the report generated from the test needs to make appropriate use of that data and not distort or add to it in ways that are not supported by the validation evidence. Finally, the report needs to present this information in a manner that ensures the user takes the right messages away from it. As such, it is vital that reports are designed to suit particular categories of users, especially in terms of their knowledge and expertise with regard to tests and testing.

Conclusions

For a long time, the potential of computer-based testing has not been realized within the general occupational selection arena. The reason for this has been the ongoing predominance of paper-and-pencil testing. Computer-based testing has either been used in a novel way for highly specialized selection situations or it has had to mimic paper-and-pencil testing in more routine situations. The advent of the Internet and the resulting increase in availability of, and accessibility to, inexpensive, powerful, interconnected computing resources may change that. Despite the rapid growth of the use of the Internet for testing, especially in the recruitment and selection field, the volume of tests delivered in this way is still far less than that delivered through paper and pencil.

Until that balance changes significantly, it will be difficult for providers to justify the costs of developing new forms of testing. The costs of support and maintenance for traditional methods are considerable. At present, new technologies are simply adding more and more to the costs of being able to provide a range of different modes of test delivery, all of which are equivalent.

Technology, as described in this chapter, provides more than just a means of delivering novel types of test. Probably more important than that is the fact that it will provide the means of making better "conventional" tests, through the use of IRT, item banking, and data warehousing technologies. Item generation techniques will develop and become the standard methodology for creating new tests in the future. The costs associated with the "craft industry" of traditional test item writing are too high to sustain in an increasingly competitive marketplace, where the demand is for valid, reliable tests that are short and that do not keep reusing the same items.

The development of the Internet over the past ten years has revolutionized the testing industry. In the next ten years we are likely to see its impact increase and to see computer-based tests, rather than paper-and-pencil, becoming the default mode of assessment for selection. When that happens, we will be able to begin to realize the true potential of computer-based testing in all areas of selection rather than just confining it to one or two high-cost specialist areas like the selection of pilots or air traffic controllers.

REFERENCES

Anderson, N. (2003). Applicant and recruiter reactions to new technology in selection: A critical review and agenda for future research. *International Journal of Selection and Assessment, 11*, 121–136.

Arvey, R. D., Strickland, W., Drauden, G., & Martin, C. (1990). Motivational components of test taking. *Personnel Psychology, 43*, 695–716.

Baron, H., Miles, A., & Bartram D. (2001, April). *Using online testing to reduce time to hire.* Paper presented at the 16th annual conference of the Society for Industrial and Organizational Psychology, San Diego, CA.

Bartram, D. (1994). Computer based assessment. *International Review of Industrial and Organizational Psychology, 9*, 31–69.

Bartram, D. (1995). The role of computer-based test interpretation (CBTI) in occupational assessment. *International Journal of Selection and Assessment, 3*, 178–185.

Bartram, D. (2000). Internet recruitment and selection: Kissing frogs to find princes. *International Journal of Selection and Assessment, 8*, 261–274.

Bartram, D. (2001). *The impact of the Internet on testing for recruitment, selection and development.* Keynote paper presented at the Fourth Australian Industrial and Organizational Psychology Conference, Sydney.

Bartram, D. (2002a). The Micropat pilot selection battery: Applications of generative techniques for item-based and task-based tests. In S. H. Irvine & P. Kyllonen (Eds.), *Item generation for test development* (pp. 317–338). Mahwah, NJ: Lawrence Erlbaum.

Bartram, D. (2002b). Power and efficiency: Expanding the scope of ability measures. *Proceedings of the BPS Occupational Psychology Conference, Blackpool, England,* pp. 116–121.

Bartram, D., & Bayliss, R. (1984). Automated testing: Past, present and future. *Journal of Occupational Psychology, 57*, 221–237.

Bartram, D., & Brown, A. (2003a). Online testing: Mode of administration and the stability of OPQ32i. *BPS Occupational Psychology Conference, Bournemouth, England, Compendium of Abstracts,* p. 63.

Bartram, D., & Brown, A. (2003b). Test-taker reactions to online completion of the OPQ32i. *SHL Group Research Report, 13 January 2003.* Thames Ditton, UK: SHL Group.

Bauer, T. N., Maertz, C. P., Jr., Dolen, M. R., & Campion, M. A. (1998). Longitudinal assessment of applicant reactions to employment testing and test outcome feedback. *Journal of Applied Psychology, 83*, 892–903.

Beaty, J. C., Jr., Fallon, J. D., & Shepard, W. (2002, April). Proctored versus unproctored web-based administration of a cognitive ability test. In F. L. Oswald & J. M. Stanton (Chairs), *Being virtually hired: Implications of web testing for personnel selection.* Symposium conducted at the 17th Annual Conference of the Society for Industrial and Organizational Psychology, Toronto, Canada.

Bock, D. (1997). A brief history of item response theory. *Educational Measurement: Issues and Practice, 16* (4), 21–32.

Borman, W. C., Buck, D. E., Hanson, M. A., Motowidlo, S. J., Stark, S., & Drasgow, F. (2001). An examination of the comparative reliability, validity, and accuracy of performance ratings made using computerized adaptive rating scales. *Journal of Applied Psychology, 86*, 965–973.

Brosnan, M. J. (1998). The impact of computer anxiety and self-efficacy upon performance. *Journal of Computer Assisted Learning, 14*, 223–234.

Burke, E. (1997). A short note on the persistence of retest effects on aptitude scores. *Journal of Occupational and Organizational Psychology, 70*, 295–302.

Dodd, B. G., Koch, W. R., & Ayala, R. (1989). Operational characteristics of adaptive testing procedures using graded response model. *Applied Psychological Measurement, 13*, 129–143.

Drasgow, F., & Mattern, K. (in press). New tests and new items: Opportunities and issues. In D. Bartram & R. Hambleton (Eds.), *Computer-based testing and the Internet: Issues and advances*. London: John Wiley & Sons.

Drasgow, F., Olson-Buchanan, J. B., & Moberg, P. J. (1999). Development of an interactive video assessment: Trials and tribulations. In F. Drasgow & J. B. Olson-Buchanan (Eds.), *Innovations in computerized assessment* (pp. 177–196). Mahwah, NJ: Lawrence Erlbaum.

Fekken, G. C., & Jackson, D. N. (1988).Predicting consistent psychological test item responses: A comparison of models. *Personality and Individual Differences, 9*, 381–387.

Frericks, L., Ehrhart, K. H., & O'Connell, M. S. (2003, April). *Computer anxiety and test performance: Comparing selection test formats*. Paper presented at the 18th annual conference of the Society for Industrial and Organizational Psychology, Orlando, FL.

George, M. S., & Skinner, H. A. (1990a). Using response latency to detect inaccurate responses in a computerized lifestyle assessment. *Computers in Human Behavior, 6*, 167–175.

George, M. S., & Skinner, H. A. (1990b). Innovative uses of microcomputers for measuring the accuracy of assessment questionnaires. In R. West, M. Christie, & J. Weinman (Eds.), *Microcomputers, psychology and medicine* (pp. 251–262). Chichester, UK: John Wiley & Sons.

Gibson, W. M., & Weiner, J. A. (1997, April). *Equivalence of computer-based and paper–pencil cognitive ability tests*. Paper presented at the 12th annual conference of the Society for Industrial and Organizational Psychology, St Louis.

Gilliland, S. W. (1994). Effects of procedural and distributive justice on reactions to a selection system. *Journal of Applied Psychology, 79*, 691–701.

Goeters, K.-M., & Lorenz, B. (2002). On the implementation of item-generation principles for the design of aptitude testing in aviation. In S. H. Irvine & P. Kyllonen (Eds.), *Item generation for test development* (pp. 339–360). Mahwah, NJ: Lawrence Erlbaum.

Hambleton, R. K., & Swaminathan, H. (1985). *Item response theory: Principles and applications*. Boston, MA: Kluwer-Nijhoff.

Hambleton, R. K., Swaminathan, H., & Rogers, H. J. (1991). *Fundamentals of item response theory*. Newbury Park, CA: Sage.

Hanson, M. A., Borman, W. C., Mogilka, H. J., Manning, C., & Hedge, J. W. (1999). Computerized assessment of skill for a highly technical job. In F. Drasgow & J. B. Olson-Buchanan (Eds.), *Innovations in computerized assessment* (pp. 197–220). Mahwah, NJ: Lawrence Erlbaum.

Holden, R. R., & Fekken, G. C. (1988). *Using reaction time to detect faking on a computerized inventory of psychopathology*. Paper presented at the Canadian Psychological Association Annual Convention, Montreal, Canada.

Irvine, S. H., & Kyllonen, P. C. (Eds.). (2002). *Item generation for test development*. Mahwah, NJ: Lawrence Erlbaum.

Kamakura, W. A., & Balasubramanian, S. K. (1989). Tailored interviewing: An application of item response theory for personality measurement. *Journal of Personality Assessment, 53*, 502–519.

King, W. C., & Miles, E. W. (1995). A quasi-experimental assessment of the effects of computerized non cognitive paper-and-pencil measurements: A test of measurement equivalence. *Journal of Applied Psychology, 80*, 643–651.

Koch, W. R., Dodd, B. G., & Fitzpatrick, S. J. (1990). Computerized adaptive measurements of attitudes. *Measurement and Evaluation in Counseling and Development, 23*, 20–30.

Kurz, R., & Evans, T. (2004). Three generations of on-screen aptitude tests: Equivalence of superiority? *BPS Occupational Psychology Conference, Bournemouth, Compendium of Abstracts*, p. 202.

Lievens, F., & Harris, M. M. (2003). Research on Internet recruitment and testing: Current status and future directions. In C. L. Cooper & I. T. Robertson (Eds.), *International Review of Industrial and Organizational Psychology* (Vol. 18, pp. 131–165). Chichester, UK: John Wiley & Sons.

Lord, F. M. (1980). *Application of item response theory to practical testing problems.* Hillsdale, NJ: Lawrence Erlbaum.

Luecht, R. (in press). Operational Issues in Computer-Based Testing. In D. Bartram & R. Hambleton (Eds.), *Computer-based testing and the Internet: Issues and advances.* London: John Wiley & Sons.

Mahar, D., Henderson, R., & Deane, F. (1997). The effects of computer anxiety, state anxiety, and computer experience on users' performance of computer based tasks. *Journal of Personality and Individual Differences, 22,* 683–692.

Mead, A. D. (2001, April). How well does web-based testing work? Results of a survey of users of NetAssess. In F. L. Oswald (Chair), *Computers = good? How test-user and test-taker perceptions affect technology-based employment testing.* Symposium presented at the 16th Annual Conference of the Society for Industrial and Organizational Psychology, San Diego, CA.

Mead, A. D., & Coussons-Read, M. (2002, April). The equivalence of paper- and web-based versions of the 16PF questionnaire. In F. L. Oswald & J. M. Stanton (Chairs), *Being virtually hired: Implications of web testing for personnel selection.* Symposium presented at the 17th Annual Conference of the Society for Industrial and Organizational Psychology, Toronto, Canada.

Mead, A. D., & Drasgow, F. (1993). Equivalence of computerized and paper-and-pencil cognitive ability tests: A meta-analysis. *Psychological Bulletin, 114,* 449–458.

Oswald, F. L., Carr, J. Z., & Schmidt, A. M. (2001, April). The medium and the message: Dual effects of supervision and web-testing on measurement equivalence for ability and personality measures. In F. L. Oswald (Chair), *Computers = good? How test-user and test-taker perceptions affect technology-based employment testing.* Symposium presented at the 16th Annual Conference of the Society for Industrial and Organizational Psychology, San Diego, CA.

Ployhart, R. E., & Ryan, A. M. (1997). Applicants' reactions to the fairness of selection procedures: The effects of positive rule violations and time of measurement. *Journal of Applied Psychology, 83,* 3–16.

Ployhart, R. E., Weekley, J. A., Holtz, B. C., & Kemp, C. (2003). Web-based and paper-and-pencil testing of applicants in a proctored setting: Are personality, biodata and situational judgement tests comparable? *Personnel Psychology, 56,* 733–752.

Preckel, F., & Thiemann, H. (2003). Online- versus paper–pencil version of a high potential intelligence test. *Swiss Journal of Psychology, 62,* 131–138.

Reynolds, D. H., Sinar, E. F., & McClough, A. C. (2000, April). Evaluation of Internet-based selection procedure. In N. J. Mondragon (Chair), *Beyond the demo: The empirical nature of technology-based assessments.* Symposium presented at the 15th annual conference of the Society for Industrial and Organizational Psychology, New Orleans, LA.

Richman, W. L., Kiesler, S., Weisband, S., & Drasgow, F. (1999). A meta-analytic study of social desirability distortion in computer-administered questionnaires, traditional questionnaires and interviews. *Journal of Applied Psychology, 84,* 754–775.

Salgado, J. F., & Moscoso, S. (2003). Paper-and-pencil and Internet-based personality testing: Equivalence of measures. *International Journal of Selection and Assessment, 11,* 194–295.

Samejima, F. (1972). A general model for free-response data. *Psychometrika Monograph Supplement,* No. 18.

Schneider, R. J., Goff, M., Anderson, S., & Borman, W. C. (2003). Computerized adaptive rating scales for measuring managerial performance. *International Journal of Selection and Assessment, 11,* 237–246.

Segall, D. O., & Moreno, K. E. (1999). Development of the computerized adaptive testing version of the Armed Services Vocational Aptitude Battery. In F. Drasgow & J. B. Olson-Buchanan (Eds.), *Innovations in computerized assessment* (pp. 34–66). Mahwah, NJ: Lawrence Erlbaum.

Sinar, E. F., & Reynolds, D. H. (2001, April). *Applicant reactions to Internet-based selection techniques.* Paper presented at the 16th annual conference of the Society for Industrial and Organizational Psychology, San Diego, CA.

Singh, J., Howell, R. D., & Rhoads, G. K. (1990). Adaptive design for Likert-type data: An approach for implementing market surveys. *Journal of Marketing Research, 27*, 304–321.

Stark, S., & Chernyshenko, O. S. (2003, April). *Using IRT methods to construct and score personality measures that are fake resistant.* Paper presented at the 18th annual conference of the Society for Industrial and Organizational Psychology, Orlando, FL.

Van der Linden, W., & Hambleton, R. K. (Eds.). (1997). *Handbook of modern item response theory.* New York: Springer.

Wainer, H., Dorans, N. J., Flaughter, R., Green, B., Mislevy, R., Steinberg, L., et al. (1990). *Computerized adaptive testing: A primer.* Hillsdale, NJ: Lawrence Erlbaum.

Waller, N. G., & Reise, S. P. (1989). Computerized adaptive personality assessment: An illustration with the absorption scale. *Journal of Personality and Social Psychology, 57*, 1051–1058.

Wiechmann, D., & Ryan, A. M. (2003). Reactions to computerized testing in selection contexts. *International Journal of Selection and Assessment, 11*, 215–229.

Wilkerson, J. M., Nagao, D. H., & Martin, C. L. (2002). Socially desirable responding in computerized questionnaires: When questionnaire purpose matters more than the mode. *Journal of Applied Social Psychology, 32*, 544–559.

Zickar, M. J., Overton, R. C., Taylor, L. R., & Harms, H. J. (1999). The development of a computerized selection system for computer programmers in a financial services company. In F. Drasgow & J. B. Olson-Buchanan (Eds.), *Innovations in computerized assessment* (pp. 7–34). Mahwah, NJ: Lawrence Erlbaum.

19

A Review of Person–Environment Fit Research: Prospects for Personnel Selection

ANNELIES E. M. VAN VIANEN

Person–environment (P–E) fit, or the match between individuals and their environment, has been the focus of much research in the past thirty years. Few researchers have addressed the possible role of P–E fit in personnel selection. Recruiters aim to select those applicants who occupy the capacities that are necessary for the job and who fit with the organization (Rynes & Gerhart, 1990). The latter topic has received far less attention in the selection literature than the first one. To fill this void, I will discuss the outcomes of P–E fit research in the context of personnel selection. The aim of this chapter is to explore the possible utility of including P–E fit in selection procedures.

Person–environment (P–E) fit research has drawn heavily on interactionistic models of human behavior and on Lewin's (1935) notion that behavior (B) is a function of the person (P) and the environment (E), expressed as $B = f(P,E)$. Interactionist models assume that the *interaction* of the person and the environment influence human behavior (Endler & Magnusson, 1976; Lewin, 1935). Schneider (2001) rightly noticed that Lewin's claim that behavior is a function of person and environment allows for a larger variety of operationalizations than only an interactional one where $B = P \times E$. In this chapter I will use the original definition of person–environment fit (person and environment need to match) and I will argue that other operationalizations of P–E fit that have been used in the literature, such as the interactional one, should not be referred to as P–E fit.

Essentially, P–E fit theory posits that people will have positive experiences when their environment is compatible with their personal characteristics. Kristof (1996, p. 4) defined P–E fit as: "The compatibility between people and environment that occurs when: (a) at least one entity provides what the other needs, or (b) they share similar fundamental characteristics, or (c) both." Kristof referred to (a) as complementary fit, and to the (b)-part of this definition as supplementary fit. The distinction between these two types of fit seems somewhat artificial, for if an organization fulfills the needs of an employee both entities have the focal characteristic in common. For example, a person fits the organizational environment if she/he places *high* value on *peer support* and the organizational culture is assessed as *high* regarding *peer support*. Similarity of two entities is the basic premise of fit theory. Thus, if a team that can be characterized as "introverts" seek to energize (i.e., a need) their team by including new extrovert team members, these newcomers will not fit, although they complement the needs of the team. To overcome any misconceptions of what fit actually is, it would be helpful to describe the entities according to *what they value* or *what they have (to offer)*, and then to define fit exclusively as supplementary fit. As such, P–E fit can be mathematically expressed as: $B = (|P - E|)$, where B is any behavioral or attitudinal outcome that is most optimal when P and E are equal in size. Thus, discrepancies between persons and environments will result in lower outcomes such as organizational commitment, job satisfaction, and performance, and higher turnover intentions and strain.

In this chapter, I will present a review of the P–E literature. It will be shown that very few P–E fit studies have actually used the (right) P–E fit mathematical expression as the basis of their research. Rather they have employed a large variety of P and E constellations (see Schneider, 2001) that do not address the theoretical foundation of P–E fit. This brings me to the early conclusion that most P–E fit studies were not about fit, but about $B = f(P,E)$.

Environments: Levels of Fit

There are three domains of human characteristics that are important for personnel selection (Smith, 1994). The first domain concerns characteristics that are relevant to all work, such as cognitive ability and work motivation. The second domain concerns characteristics that are relevant to particular jobs or occupations, such as job-specific cognitive abilities, knowledge, and personality traits. The third domain involves characteristics that are relevant to the way a person relates to a particular work setting. The fit literature refers to the first and second domains as demands–abilities (D–A) or person–job (P–J) fit: Fit occurs when an individual has the skills and abilities that are highly valued for successful job performance. Instruments used in selection procedures mostly concern this type of fit. However, people's jobs encompass more than just task performance. Employees need to collaborate with other people, have to work in teams, and have to deal adequately with the organizational culture and its context. Thus, selection may include three levels of fit assessment: the individual, the team, and the organization.

Individual level: Person–job (P–J) fit

Traditionally, person–environment fit has been extensively studied in the vocational behavior literature. Holland's (1959) RIASEC theory has dominated person–job fit research in the past. In this chapter I will not discuss these types of studies because they were basically concerned with vocational and job *choice*, which is not the focus of this chapter.

Person–job fit refers not only to the match between an applicant and the requirements of a specific job (D–A fit), but also to the fit between the characteristics of the job and the needs of a person. Stress research has typically been focused on job characteristics such as demands and workload, job insecurity, the lack of promotion opportunities, role ambiguity, lack of supervisor support, and lack of autonomy. As opposed to the Job Characteristics model (Hackman & Oldham, 1980) and Karasek's (1979) Demands–Control model, which both emphasize universal needs of employees, P–J fit theory proposes that employees differ in their needs, abilities, and skills and that jobs should match these individual characteristics rather than to create jobs that are ideal for everyone.

Team level: Person-team (P–T) and person-person (P–P) fit

Person–team fit, defined as the match between the employee and the immediate workgroup, has mainly been studied through comparing the characteristics of each team member with those of other team members, actually a measure of P–P fit. P–P fit concerns homogeneity of characteristics of people, i.e., interpersonal similarity. Individual characteristics may include demographics, personality, attitudes, and values. P–P fit corresponds to the similarity-attraction hypothesis, which states that people are drawn to similar others. Both Festinger's theory of social comparison and Heider's "balanced state" theory (Byrne, 1971) suggest that people are looking for consensual validation of their opinions and abilities and seek to maximize consistency among the elements of their belief system. They therefore will be more attracted to people who are closer in their opinions.

Organizational level: Person–organization (P–O) fit

Organizational characteristics may involve aspects such as structures, tasks, technology, and organizational culture. Many P–O fit studies have examined the match between people's values and those of the organization, because values are conceived of as fundamental and relatively enduring. Values represent conscious desires held by the person and encompass preferences, interests, motives, and goals (Edwards, 1996). Value congruence and person–culture fit are often treated as equivalent terms (Kristof, 1996).

One of the P–O fit models that has initiated much empirical research in the past decade is Schneider's Attraction–Selection–Attrition (ASA) framework (Schneider, Goldstein, & Smith, 1995). This framework describes the mechanism of mutual adaptation between the person and the organization. People are not randomly assigned to organizations, but select themselves into and out of organizations. Schneider et al. (1995) emphasized that "persons make environments" (p. 751) and that situations should not be conceptualized as separate and distinct from the individuals behaving in them. The personality attributes and attitudes of people in a setting are considered to be the fundamental defining characteristics of that setting. If true, this implies that the organizational environment should be assessed in terms of characteristics of people in the setting and that fit measures should concern P–P fit and P–T fit. Although there is some evidence that people make the place (Schneider, Smith, Taylor, & Fleenor, 1998), there are organizational characteristics that go beyond the level of individuals, such as organizational structures and goals.

Research that combined different levels of fit showed that the fit measures were empirically distinct constructs and could explain unique variance in affective outcomes (Cable & DeRue, 2002; Kristof-Brown, Jansen, & Colbert, 2002). It has been suggested that person–job fit facilitates job proficiency, person–group fit enhances group cooperation, and person–organization fit positively affects work attitudes (Werbel & Johnson, 2001). If fit indeed affects work attitudes and behaviors beyond and above the cognitive abilities, knowledge, and personality traits that are found to be predictive of job functioning, personnel selection should include indicators of fit. The time has come to make up our minds about fit.

Effects of Fit: It Depends on Which Hammer Has Hit Which Nail

Very few fit studies have operationalized fit according to its theoretical origin, namely $B = (|P - E|)$. Instead, P–E fit studies have used a large variety of conceptualizations and operationalizations of fit, which should be discussed in a review of fit relationships. The current review concerns fit studies published in the main scientific journals from 1990.[1] Only fit studies involving employees' affective reactions to their jobs and performance (rather than organizational attractiveness), and where the fit measure was the independent variable, were included. Furthermore, studies concerning fit regarding demographics were not included in this review. This yielded a total number of 67 P–E fit publications, 18 studies concerned P–J fit, 15 studies concerned P–P or P–T fit, and 34 studies examined P–O fit. These fit studies differ regarding: a) the fit dimensions that were examined, b) the methods that were used to assess fit, c) the fit index that was employed, and d) the dependent variables that were involved. Before discussing the results of these fit studies, I will specify parts a) to c) because, as will be shown, fit effect sizes largely depend on the conceptualizations and operationalizations of the fit measure.

Dimensions of fit

The characteristics associated with fit encompass values, attitudes, goals, personality, cognitive abilities, or a combination of different aspects into a more general personal profile that is matched with a general environmental profile. Most researchers stress the use of commensurate measurement of the components of the fit measure. Measurement is commensurate when precisely the same dimensions are measured for P and E. However, others define relevant P (personal) factors and compare these with situational indicators that are logically linked with P but that are not described in similar wording. Gustafson and Mumford (1995) examined individuals' personal style, including job-related personality characteristics, with the environmental opportunities and constraints for promoting or thwarting individuals' goal attainments. Similarly, Quick, Nelson, Quick, and Orman (2001) suggested measuring individuals' internal locus of control, tolerance for ambiguity, and self-reliance, and matching these personality factors with organizational factors such as job decision latitude, environmental certainty, and social support. Finally, Stevens and Ash (2001) showed that individuals' agreeableness and openness to experience are related to preferences for a participative management style in the organization.

Schneider (2001, p. 146) rightly refers to the emphasis on commensurate measurement as being an "obsession," "because it asks us to anthropomorphize environments." Specifically in the context of personal selection it is not always feasible or even preferable to seek commensurate measures. Generally, personnel selection uses personality measures exclusively as indicators of applicants' suitability for the job (D–A fit). The literature as presented above illustrates that applicants' personality could also serve as a predictor of fit with the organization or the team. Recently, Hollenbeck and colleagues (2002) have successfully linked cognitive ability and personality to features of organizational structure and task environment.

Methods of fit assessment

A simple method to assess fit is asking respondents themselves to estimate the congruence between P and E, for example "My personal values match my organization's values and culture" (cf. Cable & DeRue, 2002). The problem with this measure is that it provides no information about the exact direction of misfit. If an individual responds negatively to this question, it may mean that the organization offers too much or too little compared to what the person needs. However, *direct* measures of fit are stronger predictors of people's affective reactions and choices than *indirect* measures of fit (Cable & Judge, 1997). In the case of *indirect* fit measures, the P and E components are assessed separately. This can be done through asking the focal person about both her/his own characteristics (P) and those of the environment (E) and then combining these components into a fit index. This index is based on the use of the *same source* for a *subjective* establishment of P and E. In the fit literature, most substantial relationships with outcomes were found when E was measured as perceived by the subject (Kristof-Brown & Stevens, 2001). There is overwhelming evidence for the importance of people's constructions of reality, where individuals' attitudes and behaviors are based on their perceptions rather than a more objective standard (Ferris & Judge, 1991). The main problem with this *subjective, same source* fit measure is the danger of common method variance. Moreover, the results of fit studies that used the *direct* or the *indirect, same source* methods are less easily applicable to the selection situation in which the applicant can only provide the P component of the fit measure. The E component can be established through involving organizational citizens, which produces a *subjective* measure of fit based on *different sources*, or through an *objective* assessment of environmental characteristics (e.g., organizational structure). Measures of organizational environment that are based on the shared perceptions of organizational members other than the focal person are used when objective measures are not available, which is often the case. The literature on organizational culture, however, shows that shared perceptions are not always found (West & Anderson, 1996). The level of agreement among organizational members depends on factors such as organizational structure (i.e., high task specialization will decrease the level of agreement), socialization practices, and the amount of social interactions (Lindell & Brandt, 2000). Furthermore, the literature recognizes the existence of subcultures rather than a single, unitary organizational culture, and the existence of strong and weak cultures (Lindell & Brandt, 2000). Assessing the E component in weak (sub)cultures will result in low valid fit measures. Thus, the utility of *subjective, different source* fit measures in selection will be particularly low for organizations with weak cultures.

Fit indices

P–E fit theory essentially refers to the absolute discrepancy between P and E, assuming that outcomes are optimal if P = E and that they will linearly decline with larger positive or negative discrepancies between P and E. Quadratic discrepancy scores $(P - E)^2$ also comply with fit theory but with the supposition that large discrepancies weight more heavily than small discrepancies. The use of congruence measures has been questioned because of concerns with conceptual ambiguity, discarded information, and unrealistic restrictive constraints (Edwards, 1993, 1994). In particular, discrepancy scores such as the algebraic, absolute, and quadratic differences conceal the unique contribution of each of the components to the overall fit score and information regarding the magnitude of the components is lost. Edwards advocated using polynomial regression analysis, incorporating separate person and environment ratings $(P, E, P^2, P \times E, E^2)$ and allowing for testing the different discrepancy models. Actually, he argued that researchers should validate P–E fit theory through the exclusion of all other hypothetical relationships between the P and E components, and specific combinations of P and E and outcomes, such that P–E fit proves to be the most powerful predictor after testing alternative models. These models are, for example, the ones that represent an asymptotic relationship between fit measure and outcomes. This relationship can be labeled in two ways: *deficiency* and *excess*. *Deficiency* represents a positive relationship with outcomes only when E is less than P. Increasing E enhances outcomes up to the point of satiation (P = E), but have little effect thereafter (for example, when environmental supplies are greater than individuals' preferences). *Excess* represents a negative relationship with outcomes only when E is greater than P.

Kalliath, Bluedorn, and Strube (1999) compared the fit results using polynomial regression with several discrepancy scores $(P - E, |P - E|, (P - E)^2)$. The polynomial regression analyses yielded higher levels of explained variance (nearly two to three times as much) as those yielded by the discrepancy measures. However, these larger effects for the polynomial regression analyses were mostly due to main (curvilinear) effects of P and O.

In case the fit measure comprises several dimensions on which P and E differences are assessed, researchers may take the sum of the separate discrepancy scores if they adhere to establishing the actual size of the differences between P and E as representing the basic principle of fit. Several researchers adopted a profile comparison approach for assessing fit, which is a holistic comparison of persons and situations across multiple dimensions rather than the comparison of persons and situations on specific dimensions. The scores of the P-dimensions are correlated with those of the (commensurate) O-dimensions. These researchers typically employ an ipsative (or Q-sort) technique through asking their respondents to rank-order the dimensions (e.g., O'Reilly, Chatman, & Caldwell, 1991). A correlation between profiles, however, utilizes only shape, i.e., the rank-ordering information of the P and E profile. As in discrepancy scores, correlation fit measures conceal the effects of P and E. Furthermore, Edwards (1993) noted that profile similarity indices discard information on direction of misfit and rely on the assumption that each dimension of fit contributes equally to outcome measures. As I will show later on in this chapter, this latter assumption cannot be maintained.

EFFECTS OF P–J, P–T, AND P–O FIT: A REVIEW OF RECENT B = f(P,E) FINDINGS

In the following paragraphs I will summarize the main results of P–J, P–T, and P–O fit studies, respectively, in view of their fit dimensions, fit assessment, and fit indices. The large variety of methods and approaches applied to fit studies makes it difficult to compare their findings. The existence of significant findings might be due to confounding and concealing measures, while the absence of significant findings might be due to the use of inappropriate dimensions and assessments rather than to the lack of real fit relationships.

Effects of person–job (P–J) fit

Person–job fit is the congruence between individuals and their job, operationalized as the abilities and skills required for the job. The literature does not always distinguish P–J fit clearly from P–O fit. Characteristics on which people need to fit with the job, such as autonomy, are sometimes perceived as not being a feature of the job, but of organizational climate. In a similar vein, usually people's values are matched with organizational values as a measure of P–O fit, but Rounds (1990) matched individuals' work values with values that are important for specific jobs as a measure of P–J fit. Indeed, characteristics of jobs may be a reflection of organizational climate rather than representing the core features of the jobs. Regarding P–J fit; the focus should be on those job demands and abilities that are exclusively linked to the specific job and the *work* context in which the job is performed and not necessarily to the organizational environment as a whole.

Eight of the 18 P–J fit studies have operationalized P–J fit as D–A fit. In one study, D–A fit was specified as the combination of traits that is most optimal for job performance (Girodo, 1991). The other D–A fit studies measured fit on a general level, without specifying the specific demands and abilities of the job. Job incumbents were asked if they experienced fit between their own skills and abilities and the demands of the job and this fit measure was particularly related to affective outcomes (job satisfaction, organizational commitment, and turnover intentions) but also to performance and actual turnover. With a few exceptions (see Werbel & Landau, 1996; Cable & DeRue, 2002), the results of these studies show that perceived D–A fit is related to affective outcomes; employees who experience job fit are satisfied with their job, show commitment to the organization, and intend to stay (e.g., Cable & Judge, 1996). Whether job-fitting employees actually stay with the organization is not convincingly shown yet, because different results were found in the two studies involving actual turnover (Riordan, Weatherly, Vandenberg, & Self, 2001; Werbel & Landau, 1996). Moreover, perceived fit is apparently not related to performance (Lauver & Kristof-Brown, 2001). These studies on direct D–A fit perceptions are somewhat problematic, because it remains unclear whether D–A fit affects individual outcomes or that job satisfaction and organizational commitment influence D–A fit perceptions. Employees who feel committed to the organization for other reasons than the content of their job may close their eyes to differences between job demands and their abilities. Saks and Ashforth (1997, 2002) examined the effects of pre-entry D–A fit perceptions on post-entry affective outcomes and found positive relationships, suggesting that D–A fit perceptions are important for affective outcomes.

Partial support for this contention is provided by studies that examined fit *perceptions* regarding specific job characteristics as measured *indirectly* (e.g., Caldwell & O'Reilly, 1990), and those that estimated fit effects by using polynomial regression (Edwards, 1994, 1996). These studies show fit relationships with individual outcomes (mostly job satisfaction) for some but not for all job characteristics. Fit relationships seem to be moderated by importance of the task. Employees' characteristics need to fit the demands of the job only if these demands are recognized as important for fulfilling the job (Edwards, 1996). Some demands are also dictated by the direct work context of the job. Chan (1996) showed that the cognitive style (adaptive or innovative) of new entry-level engineers needed to fit with the predominant style demands of an R&D engineering function or a staff engineering function. If both didn't fit, employees were more likely to leave their job.

Fit regarding creativity and innovativeness seems related to job satisfaction and commitment (Edwards, 1993; Livingstone, Nelson, & Barr, 1997). However, in most cases the functional forms of relationships between P, J, and outcomes do not reflect the strict assumptions of fit along the full range of possible P and J scores. Rather, deficiency and excess effects were found (Edwards & Van Harrison, 1993) or fit mainly concerned a combination of high P with high J. For example, job satisfaction is high when both employees' preferences for decision making, planning, and coordinating in the job (P) and the time spent on these activities (J) are high. All other P and J combinations resulted in lower outcomes (Edwards, 1994, 1996). In addition, autonomy and low work structure in the job are positively related to job satisfaction (Edwards & Rothbard, 1999; Roberts & Foti, 1998), but only if autonomy in the job does not exceed preferred autonomy to a large extent.

Traditionally, applicant selection begins with a job analysis which leads to a description of the skills and abilities that are needed for successfully performing the job. People are then selected for the job after an assessment of their skills and abilities. Hence, selection criteria are usually defined from the employer's perspective. Note that the P–J fit studies were all from the perspective of the employee. What can be learned from these studies for personnel selection? First, fit perceptions are important in that they affect individual outcomes, but they do not seem to be a direct predictor of performance. Secondly, applicants mainly need to fit those aspects of the job that jobholders perceive as crucial for functioning. Thirdly, applicants who rate high on specific job preferences are the ones who will be satisfied with their job if the job fulfills their needs. Those with lower preferences will be less satisfied, irrespective of their fit with the job. Finally, in the context of a P–J fit selection approach, job analysis could be more focused on the *opportunities* that jobs offer *to satisfy* specific individual *needs*. As an example, Medcof and Hausdorf (1995) developed an instrument to measure the opportunities specific jobs offer to satisfy needs, such as achievement, power, and affiliation. They did this by asking jobholders about the extent to which the job gave them opportunities, for example, to exert power over others. When opportunities profiles of jobs are known, applicants' needs could be matched with these profiles. In this way, personnel selection should aim to choose not only *the best* of the applicants but also those that are likely to be satisfied with their future job. The P–J fit approach seems to offer a suitable framework for predicting applicants' future affective outcomes rather than their future performances.

Effects of person–team (P–T) and person–person (P–P) fit

Environments can be defined as the collection of people in them (Schneider et al., 1995). From this perspective, person–environment fit can be conceived of as the match between the characteristics of people. The basic premise is that people will be more satisfied with their job and will perform better if they have to work together with others to whom they feel attracted due to the characteristics they share. Previous studies on the relationship between similarity and interpersonal attraction included similarity of attitudes (Tan & Singh, 1995), similarity of values (Johnson, 1989), and similarity of personality (Moskowitz & Coté, 1995). Studies on attitude and value similarity showed the most unequivocal results: people like those who hold similar attitudes and opinions more than those with dissimilar attitudes (Shaikh & Kanekar, 1994).

Personal liking and the *similar-to-me* effect have been conceived of as *bias* in the selection literature, although a *similar-to-ideal candidate* has been referred to as "a useful match to an ideal prototype, if the prototype is valid" (Guion, 1998, p. 623). Personal liking and similar-to-me are related to interviewers' impression of applicants' personality rather than their attitudes and values. Likewise, applicants are compared to the ideal candidate regarding their personality. Moreover, ideal candidates are described in terms of the ideal personality attributes for being successful in the job and not necessarily for matching with others in the company.

Fifteen of the studies included in this review have examined similarity in teams and/or similarity between employees and supervisors. Five of these studies investigated similarity in personality through calculating the absolute difference in personality ratings between persons (Bauer & Green, 1996; Day & Bedeian, 1995; Hui, Cheng, & Gan, 2003) or by estimating the variance of personality ratings (as an indicator of low similarity) in the team (Barrick, Stewart, Neubert, & Mount, 1998; Van Vianen & DeDreu, 2001). Two studies that employed an *absolute fit* index found that employees' similarity in agreeableness (Day & Bedeian, 1995) and positive affectivity, i.e., a disposition to feel enthusiastic, active, and alert (Bauer & Green, 1996), were related to performance as judged by their supervisors. Unfortunately, these studies did not inspect the direction of misfit. It is likely that particularly *low* (and not high) agreeableness and positive affectivity ratings of the focal persons as compared to those of their coworkers resulted in lower performance appraisals. Individuals' agreeableness and positive affectivity may affect liking on the part of the supervisor (Judge & Ferris, 1993), irrespective of their fit with others. The three studies that examined personality *variance* in teams found equivocal results. Conscientiousness fit related to higher performance (Barrick et al., 1998) and task cohesion (Van Vianen & DeDreu, 2001), but fit regarding general mental ability went together with more team conflict and less communication (Barrick et al., 1998). Moreover, strongest relationships with outcomes were found if mean personality ratings of team members were high, suggesting that a large proportion of conscientious, agreeable, and emotionally stable team members rather than their overall personality fit positively affects team outcomes (see also George, 1990).

Tett and Murphy (2002) showed that most people prefer working with others high on affiliation, in particular when they themselves rate high on affiliation. These researchers examined whether not similar but complementary personalities are preferred for some personality aspects. They found support for both the similarity and complementarity hypotheses: Similarity in dominance was preferred, but also dominant individuals showed a strong preference for non-defensive coworkers. The authors conclude that: "People prefer those who let them be themselves" (p. 238), thus autonomous individuals will avoid dominant coworkers because the latter will restrict their independence.

Regarding personality selection, recruiters rightly focus on the ideal personality attributes as predictors of success on the job. Applicants should have the desirable personality make-up for the specific job rather than fit with others with respect to their personality, as team members who are all low on conscientiousness do fit perfectly but their performances are likely to be below standard. Similarly, high dominance in the group will easily lead to conflicts, although group members may like and fit with each other.

Recruiters are concerned with applicants' personalities but they usually neglect their values and goals. Value congruence has been assumed to facilitate interaction among team members and the development of shared understanding (Meglino & Ravlin, 1998). Most studies on P–T and P–P fit investigated similarity in values, attitudes, and goals (e.g., Basu & Green, 1995; Engle & Lord, 1997; Harrison, Price, & Bell, 1998; Jehn, 1994; Meglino, Ravlin, & Adkins, 1992; Philips & Bedeian, 1994; Vancouver & Schmitt, 1991). These studies show that value fit is positively related to job attitudes, the quality of leader–member exchange, and group cohesion, and negatively to emotional and task conflict in the group. Adkins, Ravlin, and Meglino (1996) found that fit effects were most prominent in those employees who are relative newcomers. Moreover, similarity in job attitudes facilitates social integration (Van der Vegt, 2002). Adkins et al. (1996) also found relationships between value fit and performance, but only in case of high job interdependence between coworkers. When individuals are not dependent on one another for task performance, value congruence may even be detrimental for performance, because individuals socialize with their coworkers at the expense of their performance. All in all, value fit benefits group processes and communication and it facilitates performance in teams with highly interdependent jobs. In particular, value fit together with great skill diversity in the group (see Hollenbeck, Ilgen, LePine, Colquitt, & Hedlund, 1998) may facilitate group effectiveness.

Before drawing any firm conclusions for personnel selection, I should make a critical note about these studies. Most of them relied on constrained fit indices, neglected the main effects of the components, and ignored the contribution of specific value dimensions. Moreover, the contents of value dimensions were different among the studies. The latter could suggest that value fit affects individual outcomes irrespective of its content, but such a statement would come far too early given the insufficient fit analyses. On the contrary, studies that differentiated between value dimensions and employed a polynomial regression analysis suggest that some dimensions may be more important for fit effects than others (Kristof-Brown & Stevens, 2001; Van Vianen, 2000). Regarding P–T and P–P fit, it can be concluded that, in the context of personnel selection, it seems fruitful to take value fit into account, but what values should be included in the selection procedure needs further exploration.

Effects of person–organization (P–O) fit

The characteristics associated with P–O fit are personality traits and values. Only a few studies examined personality fit ($N = 4$), while most studies concerned values or a comparison between the person and the organization on a general level ($N = 30$). The personality studies showed main effects for personality and/or work environments rather than fit effects on individual outcomes (Day & Bedeian, 1991; Gustafson & Mumford, 1995). Camacho, Higgins, and Luger (2003) examined personality fit in an experimental setting. They examined the fit between individuals' regulatory orientation and the strategic manner of goal pursuit (*regulatory fit*). Individuals can pursue the same goal activity as the organization, but with a different regulatory orientation and in a different manner than is emphasized in the organization (for example, a nurturance and accomplishment orientation versus a safety and responsibility orientation). Camacho et al. (2003) showed that regulatory fit is associated with "feeling and being right" and that it influences people's moral evaluations. The lesson that can be learned for personnel selection is that recruiters should assess applicants' regulatory orientations, particularly when the organization's strategies for goal attainment can cause moral dilemmas for their employees. Note that regulatory orientation has been defined as a personality trait, while it also could have been conceived of as a value orientation.

Recently, Hollenbeck and colleagues (2002) examined personality–organization fit on a structural level and showed that divisional structures demand high levels of cognitive ability on the part of employees if there is a good fit between the structure and the environment. In case a divisional structure doesn't fit with its environment, team members' emotional stability becomes a critical factor for performance. Additionally, Greenberg (2002) found that individual performance improved when time urgency as an individual characteristic matched time urgency as a situational demand. These studies indicate that organizational design and culture make personality attributes that are generally viewed as relevant for the job even more salient in the context of personnel selection. Finally, personality traits seem to be related to performance, particularly under conditions of misfit. Simmering, Colquitt, Noe, and Porter (2003) examined the relationship between employees' conscientiousness and their development (i.e., self-directed improvement of their competencies and work environment) as moderated by their fit regarding autonomy. They found that autonomy fit moderated the relationship between conscientiousness and development, such that this relationship was strong under conditions of misfit but did not exist under conditions of fit. Thus, conscientious individuals, who are inherently more focused on development, suppress their developmental activities under conditions of optimal fit. For selection, this may imply that the predictive validity of personality factors is less under conditions of fit.

The studies into general or value fit were highly diverse regarding their operationalizations. In eight of these studies, individuals were asked directly about their fit perceptions. Overall, this fit measure was related to affective outcomes (Cable & Judge, 1996; Cable & DeRue, 2002; Lauver & Kristof-Brown, 2001; Lovelace & Rosen, 1996; Netemeyer, Boles, McKee, & McMurrian, 1997; Posner, 1992; Saks & Ashforth, 1997, 2002) and contextual performance (Cable & DeRue, 2002; Lauver & Kristof-Brown, 2001). As concluded earlier in this chapter, perceptions of fit are important for job attitudes. Comparable results are found in studies that employed a subjective fit measure with P and O assessed by the focal person (i.e., *same source*), particularly for those that used an algebraic difference score or a correlation between profiles as their fit index (Boxx, Odom, & Dunn, 1991; Bretz & Judge, 1994; O'Reilly et al., 1991; Vigoda, 2000; Vigoda & Cohen, 2002). However, studies that were based on *same source measures* and that examined the interaction of P and O or applied the polynomial regression technique were less supportive of clear fit effects. These researchers mostly found main effects of the O-component (i.e., supplies, organizational values), sometimes combined with weak interaction or curvilinear effects for specific values (Finegan, 2000; Goodman & Svyantek, 1999; Hesketh & Gardner, 1993; Kalliath et al., 1999; Livingstone et al., 1997; Robert & Wasti, 2002; Taris & Feij, 2001).

The studies that assessed fit objectively or through independently measuring P and O (i.e., *subjective, indirect, different sources*) are of most interest for personnel selection. This category of studies only showed consistent fit effects if the correlation between P and O profiles was used as a fit index. Profile similarity was related to affective outcomes (Chatman, 1991; Christiansen, Villanova, & Mikulay, 1997; Cooper-Thomas, van Vianen, & Anderson, in press; Ostroff, 1993; O'Reilly et al., 1991), performance and absenteeism (Ryan & Schmit, 1996), and actual turnover (Vandenberghe, 1999). P and O main effects rather than fit effects were found when interaction effects were examined or polynomial regression was applied (Nyambegera, Daniels, & Sparrow, 2001; Parkes, Bochner, & Schneider, 2001; Van Vianen, 2000). In these latter studies, and contrary to the studies that measured profile similarity, the finding of fit effects was highly dependent on the types of values that were involved.

Overall, P–O fit theory, conceptualized as the absolute (or quadratic) discrepancy between P and O, receives only marginal support. This doesn't imply, however, that the theory should be rejected, because the results, based on the profile similarity approach and on fit with respect to very specific values, suggest that a certain match between persons and environments is beneficial for individual outcomes. Rather, we should seek explanations for why the results of studies on fit are somewhat disappointing. A first explanation is that most P–O fit studies involved individuals who had already been in their company for a certain amount of time. Employees' organizational perceptions grow to be more realistic in the first period after socialization (Cooper-Thomas et al., in press). The ones that stayed in their company already fitted their company to a reasonable extent at entry or were able to improve their fit by increasing organizational supplies (Simmering et al., 2003). This restricts the possibility of finding large discrepancies between P and O. Secondly, individuals may enter organizations as less naïve than supposed by fit theory, for most employees probably do not expect to optimally match their work environment, particularly when they have few other options on the labor market. Thus, fit is not only restricted to the point of satiation (where P = O) but may refer to a broader area around this point: Employees are satisfied with their job as long as the discrepancy between their needs and organizational supplies doesn't exceed a specific threshold. This explanation corresponds to the findings of several fit studies using polynomial regression or testing interaction effects. These studies found main effects for organizational supplies and only weak interaction effects (Finegan, 2000; Hesketh & Gardner, 1993; Kalliath et al., 1999; Livingstone et al., 1997; Parkes et al., 2001, Taris & Feij, 2001).

A third explanation for the weak fit effects is low variance in P: Employees desire all positive things to a great extent (Ryan & Schmit, 1996). This was one of the reasons why researchers employed the profile similarity index, whereby individuals are forced to rank-order their preferences. If the variance of individual needs is low, the fit index may actually reflect the variance of organizational supplies, resulting in main effects of organizational supplies. Further research is needed to distinguish needs and values that are universally shared from those that clearly differ among people and that are relevant for the work context. Moreover, individuals differ in the extent to which some of their needs and values are vulnerable to perceptions of misfit. Lovelace and Rosen (1996) collected information about critical incidents that helped respondents to learn whether they fitted well or poorly with their organization. They found that individuals use many different organizational cues and events to assess their overall fit, ranging from ethical/value issues to how the organization does business. Maier and Brunstein (2001) asked individuals to generate long-term goals that they considered being most important for them in the following months. The findings of their study suggest that employees evaluate their work experiences with respect to these idiosyncratic goals they feel committed to pursue, and these evaluations affect their job attitudes. If they perceive the work environment to be supportive of the accomplishment of valued goals, they are satisfied with their job and committed to the organization.

Weak value fit effects might also be due to the moderating role of personality (Tinsley, 2000). Individuals differ in their flexibility, adaptability, emotional stability, and positive affectivity and these personality dimensions might moderate the relationship between fit and individual outcomes. This relationship will be attenuated under conditions of high scores on these personality dimensions, because individuals with positive attitudes may perceive misfit as a challenge in their job rather than something that is extremely negative. Personality has been most often studied as a predictor of job perceptions (e.g., Judge, Locke, Durham, & Kluger, 1998). Future studies should examine how personality affects fit perceptions and/or the relationship between fit and outcomes.

Finally, weak fit relationships are found in case of weak conceptual linkages between the characteristics on which fit is assessed and criterion measures. Fit research often treats discrepancies between the person and the environment as having the same weight for each characteristic. Research that employed the polynomial regression approach has convincingly shown that fit can explain variance in outcomes for a restricted number of fit characteristics and outcomes. For example, fit relationships are found for the human side (i.e., support, peer cohesion, participation) of organizational culture (Van Vianen, 2000) and for values such as development, initiative, creativity, and openness (Finegan, 2000). Typically, these are cultural dimensions that are not determined by the type of industry but vary within industries (Van Vianen & Kmieciak, 1998). Organizational newcomers may already fit with organizational characteristics that are linked to organizational goals, productivity, and efficiency, because they were attracted to and have applied for a specific type of industry. Fit is often related to specific facets of job satisfaction.

IMPLICATIONS FOR SELECTION

In this concluding section I will discuss the potential utility of establishing applicants' pre-entry fit in the selection procedure. First, I will summarize the effects of fit perceptions and actual fit. Secondly, I will elaborate on the question whether recruiters (are able to) select on fit. Finally, I will address some possibilities for assessing fit in selection procedures.

To date, few studies have examined *actual* pre-entry fit and its relationship with post-entry outcomes. Cooper-Thomas et al. (in press) found that actual fit at entry could predict organizational commitment after four months, but the results of their study were based

on a relatively small sample of newcomers. From this review of fit relationships conclusions can be drawn regarding the different levels of fit. Apart from the skills and capacities that are necessary to fulfill those job demands that are recognized as most important,
employees need to fit their job with respect to cognitive style, creativity, and innovativeness. Furthermore, those applicants with high preferences are particularly in need of a
good fit with their job. Employees do not necessarily need to match the people they work
with regarding their personality characteristics. Nevertheless, more attention could be paid
to the personality composition of teams and whether this composition facilitates or undermines team performance. If the latter is the case, newcomers' personalities should complement rather than supplement those of the other team members. If team members work
closely together it is important that they share some of their goals and values, since this
facilitates group processes. The studies on both P–T and P–O fit have shown that most
strong fit effects were found when P and E value profiles were compared and when values
were included that refer to the human side of organizations. The strong fit effects with the
profile comparisons are at least partly due to a statistical artifact since the larger variance
of the correlational index increases the correlation with outcomes. Yet, the profile similarity approach may be useful for personnel selection, particularly if combined with establishing discrepancies between those values that are perceived as important by applicants
on the one hand and/or the organization on the other. Primarily if the organization has
a strong climate, it seems useful to include value fit measures in personnel selection for predicting future individual affective outcomes and team processes.

Do recruiters select on fit?

Although it is common practice that recruiters are concerned with applicants' fit with the
organization, fit assessment is usually based on intuitive impressions of applicants' personality, knowledge, skills, and abilities (KSAs). Kristof-Brown (2000) examined the types
of characteristics that assessors spontaneously associated with P–J and P–O fit. The resulting 62 characteristics were placed into categories of KSAs, values, personality traits, or
other attributes. Most characteristics referred to personality ($n = 30$) and KSAs ($n = 25$),
respectively. Only five characteristics referred to values. Moreover, recruiters were less likely
to report values as indicative of P–J or P–O fit than KSAs and personality. Recruiters' perceptions were dominated by idiosyncratic ideas of what made an applicant a good P–J or
P–O fit and they seldom agreed on the specific indicators of good fit. Cable and Judge
(1997) found a relatively small relationship between applicants' actual values congruence
and perceived values congruence by recruiters. Applicants who were liked by their
recruiters were more likely to be perceived as having congruent values. Recently, Kristof-
Brown, Barrick, and Franke (2002) showed that interviewers' assessment of person–job fit
and similarity was influenced by applicants' self-promoting impression management tactics
and nonverbal behaviors such as smiling and making eye-contact. These results imply that
recruiters' inferences about applicants' value fit are likely to be inaccurate. There is,
however, some evidence that recruiters are more accurate in assessing applicants' values if
they are instructed to focus on applicants' values and if these values are important in their
organization (Parsons, Cable, & Wilkerson, 1999).

Possibilities for assessing fit

Judge, Higgins, and Cable (2000) have discussed the selection interview as an instrument for establishing person–environment fit. They called into question whether interviewers are able to assess applicants' values and goals with significant validity and they therefore suggested the use of structured or situational interviews regarding organizational values. However, other – more objective – measures might be needed. A first essential prerequisite for developing P–E fit selection instruments is the valid assessment of the job environment. Although organizational values and goals are often perceived differently by incumbents, particularly in weak cultures, these perceptions are useful in that they come from individuals who have stayed in the organization and apparently did fit. Furthermore, to minimize subjectivity in the assessment of the J, T, or O of the fit measure, more fact-based instruments should be developed. A good example of this is the Factual Autonomy Scale as developed by Spector and Fox (2003). Rather than asking respondents to rate the overall amount of autonomy they were allowed, items were designed that asked specific questions whereby subjectivity was removed as much as possible. One such item is "*How often does someone tell you what you are to do?*" instead of "*How much autonomy is there in your job?*" This fact-based scale was shown to have a better convergent and discriminant validity as compared to the Job Diagnostic Survey autonomy scale.

Another way to establish the environmental component of the fit measure, particularly T and O values, is to ask tenured incumbents or recruiters about their own values instead of those of the team or the organization as a whole. Again, these incumbents have been shown to fit and therefore may serve as valid referents for the future fit of applicants who have comparable value ratings (see Van Vianen, 2000).

The organizational environment has typically been conceptualized as organizational climate or culture, a molar concept that comprises a large variety of climate dimensions. Ostroff (1993) developed a taxonomy of organizational climate including 12 climate dimensions and three higher-order facets. The three higher-order facets are affective (participation, cooperation, warmth, and social rewards), cognitive (growth, innovation, autonomy, and intrinsic rewards), and instrumental (achievement, hierarchy, structure, extrinsic rewards) climate perceptions. Recent research has shown that affective climate perceptions in particular were related to job satisfaction and commitment (Carr, Schmidt, Ford, & DeShon, 2003). This is in line with the results of P–E fit studies that found fit relationships with respect to the human (affective) side of organizational climates. Future research should examine in a more systematic way whether P–E climate fit can explain additional variance in job attitudes beyond and above climate perceptions at the dimensional level and facet level. Dimensions or facets that are salient for applicants and/or organizations should be included as measures for establishing fit in selection procedures.

Surprisingly, little is known about what aspects of organizational environment trigger employees' perceptions of fit or misfit. More research is needed that examines dimensions of misfit that have played a major role in employees' decision to leave the organization. Additionally, Werbel and Landau (1996) asked current job incumbents what they found to be the three best and three worst attributes of their job. This type of information provides an opportunity to establish applicants' fit by measuring their reactions to these attributes.

P–E fit research has emphasized the match between what people value/prefer and what environments have to offer. Another option is to assess those aspects of the job or the work environment that applicants do *not* prefer. Applicants do not expect optimal environments and they will therefore accept deficiency to a certain extent. They may, however, less easily accept excess on aspects that they explicitly dislike. Future P–E fit research should focus not only on individuals' needs but also on their aversions.

People's values are conceived of as being relatively stable. Cable and Parsons (2001) indeed found a strong relationship between newcomers' pre-entry and post-entry values. Their study supports the notion that measuring values during selection will have predictive power for future fit with the organization. Selection procedures most often include the assessment of cognitive abilities and personality. The literature has evidenced the utility of cognitive abilities for predicting learning and task performance. Personality predictors have been found to be related to performance, particularly contextual performance (Borman, Hanson, & Hedge, 1997). The focus of selection was on the prediction of employees' performance rather than their job attitudes. Including value fit measures in selection procedures that can predict future job attitudes actually is an indirect way to predict future performance, since job attitudes and performance are related (Judge, Thorensen, Bono, & Patton, 2001).

NOTES

1. I used journal papers that could be identified with Psych-Info. Some of these papers were not available or were not published in English and could not therefore be included. However, based on the English abstracts of these missing papers, I believe that the results and conclusions are not affected by the exclusion of some P–E fit publications.

   I would like to refer to Meglino and Ravlin (1998) for an overview of studies before 1990.

REFERENCES

Adkins, C. L., Ravlin, E. C., & Meglino, B. M. (1996). Value congruence between co-workers and its relationship to work outcomes. *Group and Organization Management, 21*, 439–460.

Barrick, M. R., Stewart, G. L., Neubert, M. J., & Mount, M. K. (1998). Relating member ability and personality to work-team processes and team effectiveness. *Journal of Applied Psychology, 83*, 377–391.

Basu, R., & Green, S. G. (1995). Subordinate performance, leader–subordinate compatibility, and exchange quality in leader–member dyads: A field study. *Journal of Applied Social Psychology, 25*, 77–92.

Bauer, T. N., & Green, S. G. (1996). Development of leader–member exchange: A longitudinal test. *Academy of Management Journal, 39*, 1538–1567.

Borman, W. C., Hanson, M. A., & Hedge, J. W. (1997). Personnel selection. *Annual Review of Psychology, 48*, 299–337.

Boxx, W. R., Odom, R. Y., & Dunn, M. G. (1991). Organizational values and value congruency and their impact on satisfaction, commitment and cohesion. *Public Personnel Management, 20*, 195–205.

Bretz, R. D., Jr., & Judge, T. A. (1994). Person–organization fit and the Theory of Work Adjustment: Implications for satisfaction, tenure, and career success. *Journal of Vocational Behavior, 44*, 32–54.

Byrne, D. (1971). *The attraction paradigm.* New York: Academic Press.

Cable, D. M., & DeRue, D. S. (2002). The convergent and discriminant validity of subjective fit perceptions. *Journal of Applied Psychology, 87*, 875–884.

Cable, D. M., & Judge, T. A. (1996). Person–organization fit, job choice decisions, and organizational entry. *Organizational Behavior and Human Decision Processes, 67*, 294–311.

Cable, D. M., & Judge, T. A. (1997). Interviewers' perceptions of person–organization fit and organizational selection decisions. *Journal of Applied Psychology, 82*, 546–561.

Cable, D. M., & Parsons, C. K. (2001). Socialization tactics and person–organization fit. *Personnel Psychology, 54*, 1–23.

Caldwell, D. F., & O'Reilly, C. A., III. (1990). Measuring person–job fit with a profile comparison process. *Journal of Applied Psychology, 75*, 648–657.

Camacho, C. J., Higgins, E. T., & Luger, L. (2003). Moral value transfer from regulatory fit: What feels right is right and what feels wrong is wrong. *Journal of Personality and Social Psychology, 84*, 498–510.

Carr, J. Z., Schmidt, A. M., Ford, J. K., & DeShon, R. P. (2003). Climate perceptions matter: A meta analytic path analysis relating molar climate, cognitive and affective states, and individual level work outcomes. *Journal of Applied Psychology, 88*, 605–619.

Chan, D. (1996). Cognitive misfit of problem-solving style at work: A facet of person–organization fit. *Organizational Behavior and Human Decision Processes, 68*, 194–207.

Chatman, J. A. (1991). Matching people and organizations: Selection and socialization in public accounting firms. *Administrative Science Quarterly, 36*, 459–484.

Christiansen, N., Villanova, P., & Mikulay, S. (1997). Political influence compatibility: Fitting the person to the climate. *Journal of Organizational Behavior, 18*, 709–730.

Cooper-Thomas, H. D., Van Vianen, A. E. M., & Anderson, N. (in press). Changes in person–organization fit: The impact of socialization tactics on perceived and actual P–O fit. *European Journal of Work and Organizational Psychology.*

Day, D. V., & Bedeian, A. G. (1991). Work climate and Type A status as predictors of job satisfaction: A test of the interactional perspective. *Journal of Vocational Behavior, 38*, 39–52.

Day, D. V., & Bedeian, A. G. (1995). Personality similarity and work-related outcomes among African-American nursing personnel: A test of the supplementary model of person–environment congruence. *Journal of Vocational Behavior, 46*, 55–70.

Edwards, J. R. (1993). Problems with the use of profile similarity indices in the study of congruence in organizational research. *Personnel Psychology, 46*, 641–665.

Edwards, J. R. (1994). The study of congruence in organizational behavior research: Critique and a proposed alternative. *Organizational Behavior and Human Decision Processes, 58*, 51–100.

Edwards, J. R. (1996). An examination of competing versions of the person–environment fit approach to stress. *Academy of Management Journal, 39*, 292–339.

Edwards, J. R., & Rothbard, N. P. (1999). Work and family stress and well-being: An examination of person–environment fit in the work and family domains. *Organizational Behavior and Human Decision Processes, 77*, 85–129.

Edwards, J. R., & Van Harrison, R. (1993). Demands and worker health: Three-dimensional reexamination of the relationship between person–environment fit and strain. *Journal of Applied Psychology, 78*, 628–648.

Endler, N. S., & Magnussen, D. (1976). *Interactional psychology and personality.* Washington, DC: Hemisphere.

Engle, E. M., & Lord, R. G. (1997). Implicit theories, self-schemas, and leader–member exchange. *Academy of Management Journal, 40*, 988–1010.

Ferris, G. R., & Judge, T. A. (1991). Personnel/Human Resources Management: A political influence perspective. *Journal of Management, 17*, 447–488.

Finegan, J. E. (2000). The impact of person and organizational values on organizational commitment. *Journal of Occupational and Organizational Psychology, 73*, 149–169.

George, J. M. (1990). Personality, affect, and behavior in groups. *Journal of Applied Psychology, 75*, 107–116.

Girodo, M. (1991). Personality, job stress, and mental health in undercover agents: A structural equation analysis. *Journal of Social Behavior and Personality, 6*, 375–390.

Goodman, S. A., & Svyantek, D. J. (1999). Person–organization fit and contextual performance: Do shared values matter. *Journal of Vocational Behavior, 55*, 254–275.

Greenberg, J. (2002). Time urgency and job performance: Field evidence of an interactionist perspective. *Journal of Applied Social Psychology, 32*, 1964–1973.

Guion, R. M. (1998). *Assessment, measurement, and prediction for personnel decisions.* Mahwah, NJ: Lawrence Erlbaum.

Gustafson, S. B., & Mumford, M. D. (1995). Personal style and person–environment fit: A pattern approach. *Journal of Vocational Behavior, 46*, 163–188.

Hackman, J. R., & Oldham, G. (1980). *Work re-design.* Reading, MA: Addison-Wesley.

Harrison, D. A., Price, K. H., & Bell, M. P. (1998). Beyond relational demography: Time and the effects of surface- and deep-level diversity on work group cohesion. *Academy of Management Journal, 41*, 96–107.

Hesketh, B., & Gardner, D. (1993). Person–environment fit models: A reconceptualization and empirical test. *Journal of Vocational Behavior, 55*, 315–332.

Holland, J. L. (1959). A theory of vocational choice. *Journal of Counseling Psychology, 6*, 34–45.

Hollenbeck, J. R., Ilgen, D. R., LePine, J. A., Colquitt, J. A., & Hedlund, J. (1998). Extending the multi-level theory of team decision making: Effects of feedback and experience in hierarchical teams. *Academy of Management Journal, 41*, 269–282.

Hollenbeck, J. R., Moon, H., Ellis, A. P. J., West, B. J., Ilgen, D. R., Sheppard, L., et al. (2002). Structural contingency theory and individual differences: Examination of external and internal person–team fit. *Journal of Applied Psychology, 87*, 599–606.

Hui, C. H., Cheng, K., & Gan, Y. (2003). Psychological collectivism as a moderator of the impact of supervisor–subordinate personality similarity on employees' service quality. *Applied Psychology: An International Review, 52*, 175–192.

Jehn, K. A. (1994). Enhancing effectiveness: An investigation of advantages and disadvantages of value-based intragroup conflict. *The International Journal of Conflict Management, 5*, 223–238.

Johnson, M. A. (1989). Variables associated with friendship in an adult population. *Journal of Social Psychology, 129*, 379–390.

Judge, T. A., & Ferris, G. R. (1993). Social context of performance evaluation decisions. *Academy of Management Journal, 36*, 80–105.

Judge, T. A., Higgins, C. A., & Cable, D. M. (2000). The employment interview: A review of recent research and recommendations for future research. *Human Resource Management Review, 10*, 383–406.

Judge, T. A., Locke, E. A., Durham, C. C., & Kluger, A. N. (1998). Dispositional effects on job and life satisfaction: The role of core evaluations. *Journal of Applied Psychology, 83*, 17–34.

Judge, T. A., Thorensen, C. J., Bono, J. E., & Patton, G. K. (2001). The job satisfaction–job performance relationship: A qualitative and quantitative review. *Psychological Bulletin, 127*, 376–407.

Kalliath, T. J., Bluedorn, A. C., & Strube, M. J. (1999). A test of value congruence effects. *Journal of Organizational Behavior, 20*, 1175–1198.

Karasek, R. A. (1979). Job demands, job decision latitude, and mental strain: Implications for job redesign. *Administrative Science Quarterly, 24*, 285–311.

Kristof, A. L. (1996). Person–organization fit: An integrative review of its conceptualizations, measurement, and implications. *Personnel Psychology, 49,* 1–49.

Kristof-Brown, A. L. (2000). Perceived applicant fit: Distinguishing between recruiters' perceptions of person–job and person–organization fit. *Personnel Psychology, 53,* 643–671.

Kristof-Brown, A. L., Barrick, M. R., & Franke, M. (2002). Applicant impression management: Dispositional influences and consequences for recruiter perceptions of fit and similarity. *Journal of Management, 28,* 27–46.

Kristof-Brown, A. L., Jansen, K. J., & Colbert, A. E. (2002). A policy-capturing study of the simultaneous effects of fit with jobs, groups, and organizations. *Journal of Applied Psychology, 87,* 985–993.

Kristof-Brown, A. L., & Stevens, C. K. (2001). Goal Congruence in project teams: Does the fit between members' personal mastery and performance goals matter? *Journal of Applied Psychology, 86,* 1083–1095.

Lauver, K. J., & Kristof-Brown, A. L. (2001). Distinguishing between employees' perceptions of person–job and person–organization fit. *Journal of Vocational Behavior, 59,* 454–470.

Lewin, K. (1935). *Dynamic theory of personality.* New York: McGraw-Hill.

Lindell, M. K., & Brandt, C. J. (2000). Climate quality and climate consensus as mediators of the relationship between organizational antecedents and outcomes. *Journal of Applied Psychology, 85,* 331–348.

Livingstone, L. P., Nelson, D. L., & Barr, S. H. (1997). Person–environment fit and creativity: An examination of supply-value and demand–ability versions of fit. *Journal of Management, 23,* 119–146.

Lovelace, K., & Rosen, B. (1996). Differences in achieving person–organization fit among diverse groups of managers. *Journal of Management, 22,* 703–722.

Maier, G. W., & Brunstein, J. C. (2001). The role of personal work goals in newcomers' job satisfaction and organizational commitment: A longitudinal analysis. *Journal of Applied Psychology, 86,* 1034–1042.

Medcof, J. W., & Hausdorf, P. A. (1995). Instruments to measure opportunities to satisfy needs, and degree of satisfaction of needs, in the workplace. *Journal of Occupational and Organizational Psychology, 68,* 193–208.

Meglino, B. M., & Ravlin, E. C. (1998). Individual values in organizations: Concepts, controversies, and research. *Journal of Management, 24,* 351–389.

Meglino, B. M., Ravlin, E. C., & Adkins, C. L. (1992). The measurement of work value congruence: A field study comparison. *Journal of Management, 18,* 33–43.

Moskowitz, D. S., & Coté, S. (1995). Do interpersonal traits predict affect? A comparison of three models. *Journal of Personality and Social Psychology, 69,* 915–924.

Netemeyer, R. G., Boles, J. S., McKee, D. O., & McMurrian, R. (1997). An investigation into the antecedents of organizational citizenship behaviors in a personal selling context. *Journal of Marketing, 61,* 85–98.

Nyambegera, S. M., Daniels, K., & Sparrow, P. (2001). Why fit doesn't always matter: The impact of HRM and cultural fit on job involvement of Kenyan employees. *Applied Psychology: An International Review, 50,* 109–140.

O'Reilly, C. A., III, Chatman, J., & Caldwell, D. F. (1991). People and organizational culture: A profile comparison approach to assessing person–organization fit. *Academy of Management Journal, 34,* 487–516.

Ostroff, C. (1993). Relationships between person–environment congruence and organizational effectiveness. *Group and Organization Management, 18,* 103–122.

Parkes, L. P., Bochner, S., & Schneider, S. K. (2001). Person–organization fit across cultures: An empirical investigation of individualism and collectivism. *Applied Psychology: An International Review, 50,* 81–108.

Parsons, C. K., Cable, D., & Wilkerson, J. M. (1999). Assessment of applicant work values through interviews: The impact of focus and functional relevance. *Journal of Occupational and Organizational Psychology, 72*, 561–566.

Philips, A. S., & Bedeian, A. G. (1994). Leader–follower exchange quality: The role of personal and interpersonal attributes. *Academy of Management Journal, 37*, 990–1001.

Posner, B. Z. (1992). Person–organization value congruence: No support for individual differences as a moderating influence. *Human Relations, 45*, 351–361.

Quick, J. C., Nelson, D. L., Quick, J. D., & Orman, D. K. (2001). An isomorphic theory of stress: The dynamics of person–environment fit. *Stress and Health, 17*, 147–157.

Riordan, C. M., Weatherly, E. W., Vandenberg, R. J., & Self, R. M. (2001). The effects of pre-entry experiences and socialization tactics on newcomer attitudes and turnover. *Journal of Managerial Issues, 13*, 159–177.

Robert, C., & Wasti, S. A. (2002). Organizational individualism and collectivism: Theoretical development and an empirical test of a measure. *Journal of Management, 28*, 544–566.

Roberts, H. E., & Foti, R. J. (1998). Evaluating the interaction between self-leadership and work structure predicting job satisfaction. *Journal of Business and Psychology, 12*, 257–267.

Rounds, J. B. (1990). The comparative and combined utility of work value and interest data in career counseling with adults. *Journal of Vocational Behavior, 37*, 32–45.

Ryan, A. M., & Schmit, M. J. (1996). An assessment of organizational climate and P–E fit: A tool for organizational change. *International Journal of Organizational Analysis, 4*, 75–95.

Rynes, S. L., & Gerhart, B. (1990). Interviewer assessments of applicant "fit": An exploratory investigation. *Personnel Psychology, 43*, 13–35.

Saks, A. M., & Ashforth, B. E. (1997). A longitudinal investigation of the relationships between job information sources, applicant perceptions of fit, and work outcomes. *Personnel Psychology, 50*, 395–426.

Saks, A. M., & Ashforth, B. E. (2002). Is job search related to employment quality? It all depends on the fit. *Journal of Applied Psychology, 87*, 646–654.

Schneider, B. (2001). Fits about fit. *Applied Psychology: An International Review, 50*, 141–152.

Schneider, B., Goldstein, H. W., & Smith, D. B. (1995). The ASA framework: An update. *Personnel Psychology, 48*, 747–773.

Schneider, B., Smith, D. B., Taylor, S., & Fleenor, J. (1998). Personality and organizations: A test of the homogeneity of personality hypothesis. *Journal of Applied Psychology, 83*, 462–470.

Shaikh, T., & Kanekar, S. (1994). Attitudinal similarity and affiliation need as determinants of interpersonal attraction. *Journal of Social Psychology, 134*, 257–259.

Simmering, M. J., Colquitt, J. A., Noe, R. A., & Porter, C. O. L. H. (2003). Conscientiousness, autonomy fit, and development: A longitudinal study. *Journal of Applied Psychology, 88*, 954–963.

Smith, M. (1994). A theory of the validity of predictors in selection. *Journal of Occupational and Organizational Psychology, 67*, 13–31.

Spector, P. E., & Fox, S. (2003). Reducing subjectivity in the assessment of the job environment: Development of the Factual Autonomy Scale (FAS). *Journal of Organizational Behavior, 24*, 417–432.

Stevens, C. D., & Ash, R. A. (2001). Selecting employees for fit: Personality and preferred managerial style. *Journal of Managerial Issues, 8*, 500–517.

Tan, D. T. Y., & Singh, R. (1995). Attitudes and attraction: A developmental study of the similarity-attraction and dissimilarity-repulsion hypotheses. *Personality and Social Psychology Bulletin, 21*, 975–986.

Taris, R., & Feij, J. A. (2001). Longitudinal examination of the relationship between supplies-values fit and work outcomes. *Applied Psychology An International Review, 50*, 52–80.

Tett, R. P., & Murphy, P. J. (2002). Personality and situations in co-worker preference: Similarity and complementarity in worker compatibility. *Journal of Business and Psychology, 17*, 223–243.

Tinsley, H. E. A. (2000). The congruence myth: An analysis of the efficacy of the person–environment fit model. *Journal of Vocational Behavior, 56,* 147–179.

Vancouver, J. B., & Schmitt, N. W. (1991). An exploratory examination of person–organization fit: Organizational goal congruence. *Personnel Psychology, 44,* 333–352.

Vandenberghe, C. (1999). Organizational culture, person–culture fit, and turnover: A replication in the health care industry. *Journal of Organizational Behavior, 20,* 175–184.

Van der Vegt, G. S. (2002). Effects of attitude dissimilarity and time on social integration: A longitudinal panel study. *Journal of Occupational and Organizational Psychology, 75,* 439–452.

Van Vianen, A. E. M. (2000). Person–organization fit: The match between newcomers' and recruiters' preferences for organizational cultures. *Personnel Psychology, 53,* 113–149.

Van Vianen, A. E. M, & DeDreu, C. K. W. (2001). Personality in teams: Its relationship to social cohesion, task cohesion, and team performance. *European Journal of Work and Organizational Psychology, 10,* 97–120.

Van Vianen, A. E. M., & Kmieciak, Y. E. (1998). The match between recruiters' perceptions of organizational climate and personality of the ideal applicant for a management position. *International Journal of Selection and Assessment, 6,* 153–163.

Vigoda, E. (2000). Internal politics in public administration systems. An empirical examination of its relationship with job congruence, organizational citizenship behavior, and in-role performance. *Public Personnel Management, 29,* 185–210.

Vigoda, E., & Cohen, A. (2002). Influence tactics and perceptions of organizational politics. A longitudinal study. *Journal of Business Research, 55,* 311–324.

Werbel, J. D., & Johnson, D. J. (2001). The use of person–group fit for employment selection: A missing link in person–environment fit. *Human Resource Management, 40,* 227–240.

Werbel, J. D., & Landau, J. (1996). The effectiveness of different recruitment sources: A mediating variable analysis. *Journal of Applied Social Psychology, 26,* 1337–1350.

West, M. A., & Anderson, N. R. (1996). Innovation in top management teams. *Journal of Applied Psychology, 81,* 680–693.

20

Selection of Leaders in Global Organizations

Nicole Cunningham-Snell and David Wigfield

To operate successfully, global organizations must recruit, develop, and retain high-performing leaders who work across cultural boundaries. Without these global leaders, organizations risk missing opportunities to gain entry into different parts of the world and losing stakeholders who seek a global service offering. Yet the selection of leaders for global roles is complex: the fundamental demands of the role are different as virtual management and working, for example, become critical; candidates may come from anywhere in the world; multiple legal jurisdictions need to be considered; and candidates from different cultural backgrounds may not share the same view on how they expect to be selected. Organizations need assessment criteria and selection methodologies that are valid, fair, positively regarded, and legally robust for global selection. We review the empirical research around leadership, cross-cultural values, and personnel selection to discuss the behaviors associated with leadership in global organizations and the selection of leaders for global roles. We use the term "global leader" to refer to leaders – both expatriates and those based in their home country – who have responsibilities that cover two or more nations.

To guide the chapter we explore two fundamental questions:

1. Some researchers argue that they can define the "full range" of leadership behavior (e.g., Bass, 1996) whereas others argue that leadership behavior varies across situation and culture (e.g., Smith & Peterson, 1988; Yukl, 2002). Our first question asks: Is it possible to identify leadership behaviors for selection criteria that apply universally to global leaders?
2. Research over the past 90 years has provided insight into which selection methods provide the most valid predictions (e.g., Salgado, Anderson, Moscoso, Bertua, & De Fruyt, 2003; Schmidt & Hunter, 1998) and yet research indicates cross-national differences in preferred selection techniques (e.g., Lévy-Leboyer, 1994; Shackleton & Newell, 1994). Our second question asks: Are there selection techniques that can be used across nations and cultures for the selection of global leaders?

We draw on the literature to address these two questions and refer to our own work in a cross-national organization to give practical examples of how global leaders can be selected. We conclude with seven recommendations about the selection of leaders in global organizations.

QUESTION ONE: IS IT POSSIBLE TO IDENTIFY LEADERSHIP BEHAVIORS FOR USE AS SELECTION CRITERIA THAT APPLY UNIVERSALLY TO GLOBAL LEADERS?

Although there are several thousand published empirical studies on leadership (Bass, 1990), many are unsuitable for global generalization due to one or several of the following reasons: sample bias (domination by US populations); research is based on assumptions that are excessively Westernized; insufficient attention is given to the situation (e.g., culture) in which leaders operate; insufficient attention is given to persons other than the leader involved in the process (see critiques by Smith & Peterson, 1988, and Yukl, 1999, 2002). There are of course a number of vitally important studies, too, several of which we cite in this chapter. However, in our view the most compelling empirical evidence concerning global leader behaviors for selection comes from the recently conducted studies in cross-cultural psychology.

Cross-cultural leadership studies have shown that what is viewed as effective leadership behaviors within organizations often varies substantially between nations; indeed employees' whole system of thinking about work events and leadership is seen to be culturally programmed (Hofstede, 1980; Smith, Dugan, & Trompenaars, 1996; Smith, 1997). In his groundbreaking study on cross-cultural differences Hofstede (1980) showed that the fundamental beliefs and values of individuals expressed in the workplace can be organized according to variables that operate at the cultural level. Hofstede initially identified four dimensions, labeled *power distance*, *uncertainty avoidance*, *individualism*, and *masculinity/femininity*; these are frequently used to guide cross-national research on differences at the country level in attitudes, values, and behaviors. Hofstede (1994) later added a fifth dimension, which concerns the extent to which people in a country prefer to focus on time with a short-term versus long-term perspective. Two other models of cultural orientations have emerged from research involving substantial population sizes (Schwartz, 1994; Trompenaars & Hampden-Turner, 1998). Substantial convergent validity between the three models emerged from empirical study on cultural values involving 47 countries conducted by Smith et al. (2002).

Research into these models shows that, for example, Australians are more masculine than the Dutch, Greeks prefer a greater level of situational structure than the British, and Americans share similar views to Italians about the distribution of power within society. Since values affect behavior (Smith et al., 2002), research on cultural values suggests that the task confronting global leaders is a complex one; what is seen as appropriate behavior for a leader will vary between national cultures. Empirical support for this view comes from several sources, including an international study of leadership, the Global Leadership and Organizational Behavior Effectiveness (GLOBE) Research Programme. The findings have revealed important patterns of similarity and differences in cross-cultural conceptions of leadership. Throughout Europe, national concepts of leadership match national cultural values. As part of the GLOBE study, 6,052 mid-level leaders from 22 European countries rated an outstanding business leader using a leadership questionnaire. Brodbeck and associates (2000) clustered countries according to previous research on cultural values and found that leadership prototypes were strongly associated with cultural values. Outside the GLOBE study, other cross-cultural psychologists have also found differences in how leadership is conceptualized at the country level. In a study involving 17 European nations, Smith (1997) found that leaders from different nations handle routine work events in different ways.

Given these findings, is it possible to identify stable characteristics of leaders that cross boundaries? We believe the answer is *yes* but it is a complex skill set. Global leadership involves additional complexities beyond leading people in a single nation. Global leaders need to achieve goals through people in a way that is acceptable to both the organization and the representatives of national cultures with whom they interact. This can require leaders to adapt their own cultural programmed preferences in favor of behaviors that are more suitable to the particular set of circumstances at hand.

The GLOBE findings show differences between cultures with respect to perceptions of leadership, but they also show that leaders are able to act in certain ways that are universally deemed as appropriate. Drawing on GLOBE data from 62 countries, Den Hartog and colleagues (Den Hartog et al., 1999) identified that 30 leadership traits are universally seen as positive or negative. In Table 20.1 we have grouped these traits as five sets of behavior and added an additional three behaviors that we believe from our experience are critical for leaders working in global organizations. We now review support for this proposition with evidence from a range of empirical research studies.

We begin with *communication* as a vital leader behavior as it is the medium through which social exchange occurs. All theories and models of leadership involve communication between the leader and other people (e.g., Fiedler & Garcia, 1987; Fleishman, 1953; House & Mitchell, 1974; Mintzberg, 1973; Yukl, Wall, & Lepsinger, 1990). A variety of empirical studies indicate that leader effectiveness is linked to the demonstration of effective communication skills (e.g., Kanter, 1983; Kim & Yukl, 1995; Peters & Austin, 1985). We believe that the ability to communicate effectively with a diverse range of stakeholders becomes critical for the global leader.

Secondly, we see *motivating and building high-performing teams* as universally applicable to global leaders. Several major theories of leadership (Bass, 1996; House, 1977; Conger & Kanungo, 1987) have at their heart a leader's ability to inspire and motivate people. Motivational behavior typically emerges as important in opinion surveys of leader behaviors (e.g., Rajan & Van Eupen, 1997; Tampoe, 1998). Praise and contingent reward (see Podsakoff, Todor, Grover, & Huber (1984) for a review) and team-building (Bennis & Nanus, 1985; Peters & Austin, 1985; see also West, 2003) have been shown to have a motivational effect on employees. With increasing demands placed upon leaders operating in a global and virtual context, there is a clear need to build motivated teams with a shared understanding and to empower others to take the lead themselves (Avolio & Kahai, 2003; Kreitner, Kinicki, & Buelens, 2002; Zigurs, 2003).

The third important behavior for global leaders is *building and sustaining trust.* The complexity and importance of this behavior also increases as the leader is often geographically separated from his or her team (Yukl, 2002). Several studies have confirmed that trust and integrity are important qualities in leaders (e.g., Kouzes & Posner, 1987; Rajan & Van

TABLE 20.1 Taxonomy of global leader behaviors and attributes

Behavioral heading	Universally endorsed leader attributes (Den Hartog et al., 1999)	
	Positive	Negative
Communicating and working collaboratively	Communicative Coordinator Effective bargainer Win–win problem solver	Asocial Dictatorial Egocentric Loner Non-cooperative Non-explicit Ruthless
Motivating and building high-performance teams	Confidence builder Dynamic Encouraging Excellence oriented Team builder Motivational Motive arouser Positive	Irritable
Building and sustaining trust	Dependable Honest Just Trustworthy	
Planning and monitoring	Administratively skilled Foresight Plans ahead	
Analyzing and decision making	Decisive Informed Intelligent	
Self-awareness and situational effectiveness	–	–
Achieving goals	–	–
Cultural adaptability	–	–

Eupen, 1997; Tampoe, 1998). Trust is the defining quality of effective leader–subordinate relationships in leader–member exchange (LMX) theory (Graen & Scandura, 1987; Graen & Uhl-Bien, 1995). There is evidence from several empirical research studies that high LMX relationships are associated with positive outcomes, including greater commitment to the organization (Deluga, 1994), reduced turnover, greater performance and productivity, and faster career advancement (Bauer & Green, 1996; Steiner, 1997).

The fourth critical behavior for global leaders is *planning and monitoring*. To achieve results, leaders need to prioritize tasks and coordinate restricted resources (staff, time, budget, equipment, etc.). Monitoring is a key activity since it provides feedback to the leader enabling him/her to compare intended and actual performance, and to regulate the process. Mintzberg (1973) observed that the allocation of resources was an important role for leaders. Survey studies have shown a positive relationship between planning and an independent measure of leader effectiveness (Carroll & Gillen, 1987; Morse & Wagner, 1978). Observational studies of leaders have also revealed that time spent monitoring subordinates' work related to measures of leader effectiveness (e.g., Komaki, 1986; Komaki, Desselles, & Bowman, 1989).

The fifth behavioral theme that applies to all global leaders is *analyzing and decision making*. Whether the task at hand is managing an interpersonal interaction or managing information, the ability to analyze complex inputs and make decisions is a fundamental activity at all stages of the process. In a study involving 4,492 leaders from the USA and 4,784 leaders from seven European countries, Robie, Johnson, Nilsen, and Fisher Hazucha (2001) found that the ability to analyze issues is a critical leadership skill. The quality of decision making and a readiness to make decisions have also both been related to evaluations of leader effectiveness (e.g., Connelly et al., 2000; Morse & Wagner, 1978; Peters & Austin, 1985). As leaders enter the global arena, the complexity and ambiguity of information increase and so the ability to analyze this data and make decisions is critical.

The next behavior that we believe is important for global leaders is *self-awareness and situational effectiveness*. This behavior was not associated with the GLOBE findings but is suggested by the criticism that leadership research and theory have frequently failed to take the situation into account. Several theorists (e.g., Hersey & Blanchard, 1982; Zaccaro, Gilbert, Thor, & Mumford, 1991) have suggested that effective leaders use self-awareness as a device to read situational and social cues, and to adapt their behaviors accordingly. This ability is sometimes referred to as self-regulation (e.g., Tsui & Ashford, 1994). Advocates of emotional intelligence (e.g., Goleman, 1998; Mayer & Salovey, 1997; see also Clark, 2004) support the view that effective leaders have high self-awareness and are attuned and respond appropriately to social information. There is also some empirical evidence that feedback-seeking (a component of self-regulation) is linked to leader effectiveness ratings. Receiving 360-degree feedback (time one) has been associated with enhanced leader effectiveness (time one versus time two) in several studies (e.g., Baldry & Fletcher, 2002; Hazucha, Hezlett, & Schneider, 1993; London & Wohlers, 1991).

The seventh behavior that applies to all leaders is *achieving goals*. All theories of leadership state or imply that leadership concerns getting people to work toward the achievement of particular goals. Achievement-oriented behaviors repeatedly appear in competency definitions used to define successful leaders in a wide range of organizations (Dulewicz, 1989; Matthewman, 1999). Empirical support for the importance of goal-oriented behaviors in leaders comes from observational studies (e.g., Mintzberg, 1973) and survey studies (e.g., Lowe, Kroeck, & Sivasubramaniam, 1996; Yukl, 2002). Some cross-cultural studies have shown that leaders in many different nations are all concerned with driving for results or handling work events to achieve goals (e.g., Robie et al., 2001; Smith et al., 1996, 2002). Sinangil and Ones (2001) also note that expatriate leaders are typically chosen for an assignment abroad in order to achieve a work-related goal.

Finally, we provide an eighth leadership behavior that is of particular importance to global leadership roles: *cultural adaptability*. This is conceptually linked to situational effectiveness, since both behaviors involve scanning the social environment for cues and making modifications in one's own behavior. Cultural adaptation, however, involves a mindset that welcomes new cultural experiences and sees the benefits that diversity in social membership can bring. Knowledge of expected patterns of behavior in different cultures is also a component of this skill. In a review of research on expatriates, Sinangil and Ones (2001) identify cultural openness and sensitivity as one of the key predictors of expatriate success. Further support for the importance of cultural adaptability in global leaders comes from research on global executive derailment. Derailment is the term used to describe the failure of executives recognized as high potential (McCall, 1998). Drawing on their own and other research, McCall and Hollenbeck (2002) state that a number of factors contribute to executive derailment, including individual characteristics, contextual factors, and organizational mistakes. The contextual factors include a failure to adapt to differences in values, norms, beliefs, religions, and economic systems as well as group and community identities that impact how business is conducted. Clearly, selecting for the cultural adaptability is critical as for global leaders.

In summary, the following eight sets of behaviors are important to global leaders:

♦ communicating and working collaboratively;
♦ motivating and building high-performing teams;
♦ building and sustaining trust;
♦ planning and monitoring;
♦ analyzing and decision making;
♦ self-awareness and situational effectiveness;
♦ achieving goals;
♦ cultural adaptability.

In addition to leadership research and theory that support this model, confirmatory support comes from job performance research: Campbell's (Campbell, 1990; Campbell, Gasser, & Oswald, 1996) eight-factor model and Viswesvaran's (Viswesvaran & Ones, 2000; Viswesvaran, Ones, & Schmidt, 1996) hierarchical model of cross-situational job performance both refer to behaviors that are similar to the eight listed above. We make no claim that this list covers the full range of leadership behaviors; additional behaviors may be added, for instance, when the current paucity of research on leadership in virtual organizations (Yukl, 2002; Zimmerman, 2004) is addressed. The list is not rank-ordered in any way; the level of importance of each behavior is likely to vary with the unique set of circumstances surrounding a leader. Further, the way that these behaviors are demonstrated is likely to vary between countries. Smith, Peterson, and associates (e.g., Smith, Misumi, Tayeb, Peterson, & Bond, 1989) present evidence that suggests that while high-level behavioral descriptions of leadership are endorsed by countries that are culturally dissimilar, the way that leaders behave at the more specific level varies between cultures. In this case, for example, it would mean that there is universal agreement that leaders need to build and sustain trust, but the way of doing this can look very different in, say, the USA compared to Greece or Thailand.

Definitions of global leader behaviors in a multinational oil company

One of the weaknesses of previous research is that respondents from various nations are often working for different organizations. As such, research findings that are attributed to culture could in fact represent organizational effects. When research is conducted within a single organization we can control for the effects of organizational culture. Shell is a natural research environment for cross-cultural work because of its scale and scope; it has over 110,000 staff, has global reach through operations in over 140 countries, and has more expatriates than any other organization in the world. Shell's goal of sustainable global profitability has led to thorough research to produce selection systems for the global leaders of today and the future. In this section we present our research into designing a competency model for this purpose. The model provides further evidence of the eight sets of global leadership behaviors described above.

In 2002 the authors conducted research with 185 leaders in Africa, Asia, Europe, Latin America, the Middle East, and the USA to design a globally valid leadership competency model for recruiting experienced hires (professionals with five+ years' experience) into Shell. Our approach involved a series of job analysis techniques and was based on the integration of the following activities:

1. identification of the appropriate content and business relevance for the model through gathering critical incidents and statements about the global strategy and future challenges for leaders;
2. differentiation of effectiveness at different job grades through analysis of repertory grid data and focus group outcomes;
3. identification of the cultural appropriateness of behavioral descriptions via literature searches, discussions with experts and focus groups with participants from culturally diverse backgrounds;
4. cross-validation of the initial model with independent and diverse samples.

The model that emerged from our work is summarized in the first column of Table 20.2. The more detailed version of the model shows a series of specific behavioral indicators that sit beneath the eleven titles that describe how global leaders in Shell behave when they are performing at an optimal level. The second column of Table 20.2 links Shell's eleven competencies to our proposed model of eight global leader behaviors. Each model represents a different grouping of the same core behaviors; since the relationships between these behavioral clusters are not orthogonal, this different categorization is inevitable. Our sampling of jobs and attitudes in Shell across six major geographical regions supports our view i) that global leader behaviors exist, and ii) that these represent the eight behaviors outlined above.

The eleven selection competencies are also aligned to a leadership framework used by Shell for internal leadership development initiatives at management and executive levels in the organization. More than 1,500 leaders representing more than 50 nationalities have completed a Development Center where this leadership framework has been rigorously assessed. The data indicate no significant variation across nations and a high level of consistency in the profile of our leaders across the globe. This research provides further support for the appropriateness of using a global model of leadership behaviors.

We have referred to similarities between cultures, but we also found some differences between national cultures in terms of leader behaviors. For example, in parts of Asia the importance of building *informal* and personal relationships with stakeholders was

TABLE 20.2 Links between Shell's competencies for global leaders and global leader behaviors

Shell's competencies for global leader selection	Global leader behaviors
Builds shared vision: *Understands and contributes to the business vision and strategy. Aligns work to broader organizational goals and shares the vision with others.*	Communicating and working collaboratively Achieving goals
Maximizes business opportunities: *Creates and pursues opportunities to enhance business results. Prepared to take calculated risks and conducts business with integrity.*	Planning and monitoring Achieving goals
Champions customer focus – customer and stakeholder relationships: *Develops mutually beneficial, trusting long-term relationships with customers and stakeholders*	Building and sustaining trust Cultural responsiveness
Demonstrates professional mastery: *Demonstrates and shares professional expertise.* *Understands own strengths and development areas, and seeks learning opportunities.*	
Displays personal effectiveness – builds relationships: *Builds and maintains strong team relationships and wider networks. Knows how to make use of networks and demonstrates communication and influencing skills.*	Self-regulation
Displays personal effectiveness – analyzing and decision making: *Makes good decisions based on sound analysis despite incomplete or conflicting data. Involves people appropriately in decision making and communicates the rationale for decisions.*	Analyzing and decision making
Motivates, coaches and develops: *Motivates individuals and enables them to improve their performance. Places a high value on supporting staff in their learning and development.*	Motivating people and building teams
Demonstrates courage – manages conflict: *Manages conflict in a constructive and culturally appropriate way. Has the courage to assert own view and challenge appropriately.*	Cultural responsiveness
Demonstrates courage – manages change: *Makes improvements through introducing and managing change. Anticipates consequences, gains acceptance for change and measures the resulting impact.*	Cultural responsiveness
Values difference: *Appreciates the value of capitalizing on differences between people. Seeks out alternative perspectives and consistently incorporates others' views and approaches.*	Cultural responsiveness
Delivers results: *Consistently achieves results by setting challenging targets, organizing work effectively and overcoming obstacles. Where appropriate, delivers results through others, creating an environment that supports achievement.*	Planning and monitoring Achieving goals

emphasized, whereas in Eastern Europe the emphasis was on building *formal* stakeholder relationships. The same outcome was universally supported – to build and sustain relationships – but the process by which this was achieved varied, a finding that is consistent with some of Smith and Peterson's results (e.g., Smith et al., 1989) described earlier. We believe that leadership factors generalize across countries, but the specific behaviors do not always translate. To this extent, the cultural adaptability criterion is critical, as effective global leaders must adapt their behavior to the local environment. For this reason we have worded our behavioral indicators so that they provide less information about *how* the behavior is demonstrated and focus more on *what* the behavior needs to achieve.

Our findings are influenced by the fact that our respondents were all working in the same multinational organization. It is probable that Shell's selection and socialization processes have resulted in our sample being more homogeneous in values and behaviors than would be seen through sampling across organizations. Further work in other global organizations in different industry sectors is now required to test the model of eight competencies for global leaders.

QUESTION TWO: ARE THERE UNIVERSAL SELECTION TECHNIQUES FOR THE IDENTIFICATION OF GLOBAL LEADERS?

We have argued that global leader behaviors exist that can be presented as a set of universal descriptions for leaders. Our second question concerns whether or not it is possible to find a universal selection methodology for global leaders. In this section we report the findings of surveys exploring the different use of selection methods across nations and research on differential reactions to selection procedures. Research themes associated with this question concern, firstly, how nations vary in the use of selection methods; and secondly, whether there are cross-national differences in candidate reactions to selection methods. The findings enable us to draw conclusions about the particular methods that can be used equitably across cultures.

International usage of selection methods

There are cross-national differences in the use of different selection methods, and this has been the focus of a number of research studies (e.g., Krause & Gebert, 2003; Lévy-Leboyer, 1994; Salgado & Anderson, 2002; Shackleton & Newell, 1994). Much of this research has compared Western European nations. A notable exception is a study by Ryan, McFarland, Baron, and Page (1999) in which 959 organizations were surveyed from 20 countries. Ryan et al. found that some selection methods did not vary across nations (e.g., use of educational qualifications) while there was considerable variation in the use of other methods. In particular, they found greater use of structured interviews with fixed sets of questions in Australia, Canada, New Zealand, and South Africa than in Italy, the Netherlands, and Sweden. Situational judgment tests were used with moderate frequency in Hong Kong, but almost never in Australia, France, Greece, and Italy; personality tests tended to be used in Spain, South Africa, and Sweden, but were almost never used in Italy and Germany.

These findings suggest that selection methods found to be generally more valid than others (e.g., Barrick & Mount, 1991; McDaniel, Finnegan, Morgeson, Campion, & Braverman, 2001) are among those that are particularly subject to cross-national variability in use. Research also suggests that the predictive validities for at least some selection methods generalize across countries (Salgado et al., 2003).

Differences in selection method usage across countries may be explained by a number of factors, including: technology lags, ideological factors, legislative differences, and cultural differences. Firstly, in terms of technology lags, empirical data on the validity of more structured interview techniques is slowly diffusing across the world, which may explain why some countries have not yet adopted these practices (Ryan et al., 1999). Furthermore, in some countries there are ideologically rooted reservations about using certain selection methods (see Krause & Gebert, 2003). Differences in legislation result in different selection practices; for example, worker rights laws in Italy limit selection test use (Lévy-Leboyer, 1994). A fourth explanation concerns cultural values; for instance, in a review of survey studies across the European Community, Salgado and Anderson (2002) found that individualistic cultures (e.g., Britain, the Netherlands, Germany) report greater use of cognitive ability tests than collectivist cultures (e.g., Italy, Greece). It is most likely that a combination of these and other factors contribute to the variability in selection method practice.

Factors such as cultural beliefs and legal systems are deeply embedded and may inhibit the successful implementation of global selection methodologies. However, we believe it is possible to identify certain selection methods that are universally applicable for the selection of global leaders. While these methods are currently more familiar in some nations than others, the available research on candidate reactions suggests that these methods can be deployed internationally without negative consequences. We now review this evidence.

Candidate reactions to selection methods

Following a key paper by Gilliland (1993), research has systematically employed an organizational justice framework to explore candidates' reactions to selection. This framework provides two main types of justice that can impact candidates' reactions: firstly, procedural justice which concerns perceived fairness of the selection process; and secondly, distributive justice which concerns perceptions of hiring decision fairness (Gilliland, 1993). Procedural justice is determined by a series of procedural justice rules, including those relating to the formal characteristics of the process, information sharing, and interpersonal treatment. In terms of distributive justice, the focus in selection research is usually given to one distributive justice rule – equity – whereby decisions are made based on a person's inputs and past experiences.

Research using the organizational justice framework has explored candidates' reactions to various selection methods and examined the determinants of different procedural justice reactions (e.g., Gilliland, 1994, 1995; Steiner & Gilliland, 2001). There are only a small number of studies that have directly compared reactions across nations, for instance the UK and the Netherlands (Cunningham-Snell, 1999), Singapore and the USA (Phillips & Gully, 2002), France and the USA (Steiner & Gilliland, 1996). Overall, this research indicates that across nations, candidate reactions to different selection methods are highly similar: interview, resumés, and work samples consistently receive favorable ratings; personal references tests tend to have moderate reactions; and personal contacts and graphology are perceived poorly. National differences have been found for reactions to personality tests, ability tests, honesty tests, and biodata. Further research on a more diverse set of countries is required. Nevertheless, the existing evidence on cross-cultural preferences for selection methods is encouraging for multinational organizations wishing to operate global selection systems. Interviews, resumés, and work samples are each likely to be viewed as acceptable in different countries.

Paying attention to several features of design can strengthen the likelihood of these selection methods being found acceptable across cultures. Through identifying universal factors that underlie procedural justice reactions, we can develop selection methods that appeal to candidates globally. Empirical studies have linked each of the following outcomes to procedural justice: candidates' test performance (e.g., Chan, 1997; Chan & Schmitt, 1997); candidates' self-efficacy (e.g., Gilliland, 1994; Ployhart & Ryan, 1997); their attitudes toward the organization (e.g., Bauer et al., 2001); their job acceptance intentions (e.g., Ployhart & Ryan, 1997, 1998); and their withdrawal from the selection process (Schmit & Ryan, 1997). The design of selection methods and the way in which a recruitment campaign is run, then, affect the success of the campaign. Let us now consider which design features will enhance success.

Candidates in France (Steiner & Gilliland 1996), Singapore (Phillips & Gully, 2002), South Africa (De Jong & Visser, 2001, cited in Steiner & Gilliland, 2001), and the USA (Phillips & Gully, 2002; Steiner & Gilliland, 1996) endorse both *job relatedness* and *opportunity to perform* as being procedurally just, and employers' perceived rights to solicit information also emerged as an important factor. Interpersonal considerations, such as warmth and respect for privacy, tend to be moderate or weaker predictors of procedural fairness evaluations. Cross-cultural differences in the magnitude of relationships between these dimensions and overall favorability are likely to exist and may be rooted in cultural values. Phillips and Gully (2002), for example, found that interpersonal sensitivity and respect for privacy were more salient for the Americans as determinants of overall favorability than for Singaporeans. These effects may be associated with Singaporeans having higher *power distance* than Americans (Hofstede, 1980), meaning that Americans are more sensitive to abuses of power and violations of law. Each of the four nations studied is of course Westernized and, once again, further research is required to permit global generalizations. Based on the available evidence, we submit that global selection practice will be enhanced if selection methods are designed to maximize i) job relatedness and ii) candidates' opportunity to perform.

Use of selection methods in a multinational oil company

The design of global selection methods in Shell reflects some of the research findings on procedural justice. We designed a selection system for the global recruitment of experienced leaders and professionals into Shell. These recruits have gained significant work experience in other organizations and some join Shell to become part of the talent pool with longer-term promotion potential. Our task was to design a system to enable line managers and local HR practitioners to assess candidates in any country against the eleven selection competencies (Table 20.2) in a way that was efficient, accurate, and would be seen as procedurally just around the world. We reviewed data from a range of sources, including candidate and recruitment manager feedback on existing approaches, benchmark data against recruitment practice in other multinationals, stakeholders' perceptions, and external experts' opinions on world-class selection. Several features were included or rejected due to procedural justice concerns. We rejected the idea of a full assessment center (AC) since feedback indicated that this would be unpopular with many candidates with significant work experience. As an alternative we produced a system consisting of a technical interview, a behavioral interview, and an individual presentation/discussion exercise where candidates present an example of some of their best work and then engage in a discussion with assessors. Each assessment activity was designed to elicit several of the competencies. To encourage objectivity and consistency we provide recommended questions and a universal rating scale for the competencies with behavioral anchors; users are required to attend a rigorous training program. We found that candidates from different countries positively regarded the combination of exercises. To enable candidates to perform optimally, clear instructions are sent in advance so that they can prepare, and the timetable allows them "breathing space" between assessments to maximize their opportunity to perform.

Given the range of target-level jobs this system was being designed for, we decided that users would reject a "one size fits all" selection system. In loose terms the system is globally standardized – the competencies and selection methods are universal – but the system permits local decisions about its application. For instance, local managers are allowed to choose which of the competencies to assess and which combination of methods to use (the guidelines recommend all three). This choice of competencies is informed by use of a simple job analysis questionnaire that rank-orders the competencies by relevance to the job. This flexibility enables managers to make decisions about how the selection system can best be adapted to the specific job vacancy in local job market conditions.

A contrasting global selection process is Shell's AC for the recruitment of high-potential graduates or campus recruits from university. Shell aims to hold constant its selection standards for its graduate recruits around the world to build confidence in its graduate talent pool. The assessment process is highly standardized and is centrally controlled by HR. Typically the same assessment process is used from one country to the next, although there have been some local modifications; for instance, the group discussion did not produce useful assessment data in the Middle East due to prevailing norms concerning social roles and gender, so the exercise was excluded in this region. Generally, however, as we have implemented the AC methodology around the world we have found few cases where tailoring has been required.

Conclusions

In this chapter we have reviewed the literature to argue that it is possible to implement a global standardized approach for selecting leaders in global organizations. Drawing on a range of research studies, including cross-cultural work, we have argued that effective global leaders in any organization demonstrate certain universal behaviors, which enable them to build effective and trusting relationships and teams, motivate team members, plan work and make decisions, achieve goals, and improve their effectiveness through adapting their own behavior to different individuals and cultures. These behaviors *inter alia* can form the basis of selection criteria. The behavioral descriptors of these criteria need to be kept open enough to allow for cultural diversity in approach. Cross-cultural differences exist with respect to selection method usage, and some of these differences are probably driven by cultural values. The limited research does indicate that resumés, interviews, and work samples have cross-national appeal, particularly when candidates can see that these methods are overtly job related and are presented in a way that enables candidates to perform at their optimal level.

When making decisions about how to select global leaders, organizations can view the range of options concerning standardization as a continuum: at one extreme an organization may decide to localize all recruitment practices and give a high level of freedom around how recruitment happens; and at the other extreme they may decide to run global systems that are totally standardized and without local variation. The advantages of the former are to avoid the myriad of complexities of designing and managing selection systems that work across cultures, including differences in legal frameworks around selection, possible differences in expected leadership behaviors, and differences in candidate familiarity with selection methods and contextual differences. However, the advantages of running global selection systems include an ability to directly compare candidates for one vacancy from different countries, efficiencies from designing and maintaining one selection system, the opportunity to present one organizational image to an increasingly global marketplace, and opportunities to integrate selection and recruitment more broadly within the HR strategy of the organization (e.g., the creation of a shared understanding across the organization of expected leadership behaviors).

Ultimately the organization's mission must drive where it chooses to place its selection approach on the continuum. In our experience we have found that the added complexities of initially designing a global approach can be outweighed by these strategic benefits. We have found that some local flexibility is desirable to meet the needs of the local recruitment market and to enable local managers to have some control over the process, which results in recruitment decisions that they can trust.

For those who must recruit global leaders through standardized recruitment processes, we would make the following recommendations:

1. Identify the selection criteria through job analysis conducted on a global basis. Review the criteria to see whether adequate coverage is given to the eight global leader behaviors proposed in this chapter.
2. Make decisions about the extent of global standardization required in the system. Consider the strategic purpose of the system and which stakeholders need to feel empowered though the system.
3. Choose objective selection methods that are suitable in all recruitment locations and that meet procedural justice needs. Give sufficient attention to stakeholder consultation around these methods.
4. Ensure that the methods are developed carefully through expert design and piloting in representative locations with diverse populations. Consider the appropriateness of local variations.

5. Research the legal requirements of the system in the locations where it will be used. Keep a proper audit trail of design concerns in case of challenge.
6. Implement the system via a proper strategy that engages with end-users; involve them in the design and pilot of the system so that they feel ownership for it.
7. Monitor and review the system. Track candidate performance with respect to diversity and subsequent job performance. Make periodic process improvements to reduce adverse impact and enhance predictive validity.

We acknowledge that much of the research on leadership and selection that we have drawn upon throughout this chapter is inevitably based on Western populations, and this weakens our ability to make cross-cultural generalizations. Research is required at a cross-cultural level on the scale of the GLOBE project and attention needs to be given to the virtual context in which leaders increasingly operate. We, the authors of this chapter, are products of British educational and social systems and work in a multinational organization whose Anglo-Dutch history continues to permeate its culture. You, the reader, must decide whether we have been able to escape our own culture in making the case for a set of behaviors and an assessment system for leaders that transcends culture.

ACKNOWLEDGMENTS

We would like to thank Dennis Baltzley, Leah Podratz, and Julie Regan for their comments on an earlier draft of this chapter.

REFERENCES

Avolio, B. J., & Kahai, S. R. (2003). Adding the "E" to E-leadership: How it may impact your leadership. *Organizational Dynamics, 31*, 325–338.

Baldry, C., & Fletcher, C. (2002). The impact of multiple source feedback on management development: Findings from a longitudinal study. *Journal of Organizational Behaviour, 23*, 853–867.

Barrick, M. R., & Mount, M. K. (1991). The Big Five personality dimensions and job performance: A meta analysis. *Personnel Psychology, 44*, 1–26.

Bass, B. M. (1990). *Bass & Stogdill's handbook of leadership: Theory, research and managerial applications* (3rd ed.). New York: Free Press.

Bass, B. M. (1996). *A new paradigm of leadership: An inquiry into transformational leadership.* VA: US Army Research Institute for the Behavioral and Social Sciences.

Bauer, T. N., & Green, S. G. (1996). Development of leader–member exchange: A longitudinal test. *Academy of Management Journal, 39*, 1538–1567.

Bauer, T. N., Truxillo, D. M., Sanchez, R. J., Craig, J., Ferrara, P., & Campion, M. A. (2001). Applicants' reactions to selection: Development of the Selection Procedural Justice Scale (SPJS). *Personnel Psychology, 54*, 387–419.

Bennis, W. G., & Nanus, B. (1985). *Leaders: The strategies for taking charge.* New York: Harper & Row.

Brodbeck, F. C., Frese, M., Akerblom, S., Audia, G., Bakacsi, G., Bendova, H., et al. (2000). Cultural variation of leadership prototypes across 22 European Countries. *Journal of Occupational and Organizational Psychology, 71*, 1–29.

Campbell, J. P. (1990). Modeling the performance prediction problem in Industrial and Organizational Psychology. In M. D. Dunnette & L. M. Hough (Eds.), *Handbook of industrial and organizational psychology* (2nd ed., Vol. 1, pp. 687–732). Palo Alto, CA: Consulting Psychologists Press.

Campbell, J. P., Gasser, M. B., & Oswald, F. L. (1996). The substantive nature of job performance variability. In K. R. Murphy (Ed.), *Individual differences and behavior in organizations* (pp. 258–299). San Francisco: Jossey-Bass.

Carroll, S. J., Jr., & Gillen, D. J. (1987). Are the classical management functions useful in describing managerial work? *Academy of Management Review, 12*, 38–51.

Chan, D. (1997). Racial subgroup differences in predictive validity perceptions on personality and cognitive ability tests. *Journal of Applied Psychology, 82*, 311–320.

Chan, D., & Schmitt, N. (1997). Video-based versus paper-and-pencil method of assessment in situational judgement tests: Subgroup differences in test performance and face validity perceptions. *Journal of Applied Psychology, 82*, 143–159.

Clark, S. (2004). Leading by feel. *Harvard Business Review,* January, pp. 27–37.

Conger, J. A., & Kanungo, R. N. (1987). Toward a behavioral theory of charismatic leadership in organizational settings. *Academy of Management Review, 12*, 637–647.

Connelly, M. S., Gilbert, J. A., Zaccaro, S. J., Threlfall, K. V., Marks, M. A., & Mumford, M. D. (2000). Exploring the relationship of leadership skills and knowledge to leader performance. *Leadership Quarterly, 11*, 65–86.

Cunningham-Snell, N. (1999). *Alternative perspectives on selection: Social impact and validation of graduate selection within a multinational oil company.* Unpublished PhD thesis, University of London, UK.

Deluga, R. J. (1994). Supervision trust building, leader–member exchange and organizational citizenship behavior. *Journal of Occupational and Organizational Psychology, 67*, 315–326.

Den Hartog, D., House, R. J., Hanges, P. J., Ruiz-Quintanilla, S. A., Dorfman, P. W., Abdalla, I. A., et al. (1999). Culture specific and cross culturally generalizable implicit leadership theories: Are attributes of charismatic/transformational leadership universally endorsed? *Leadership Quarterly, 10*, 219–256.

Dulewicz, V. (1989). Assessment centres as the route to competence. *Personnel Management, 21* (11), 56–59.

Fiedler, F. E., & Garcia, J. E. (1987). *New approaches to effective leadership: Cognitive resources and organizational performance.* New York: John Wiley & Sons.

Fleishman, E. A. (1953). The description of supervisory behavior. *Personnel Psychology, 37*, 1–6.

Gilliland, S. W. (1993). The perceived fairness of selection systems: An organizational justice perspective. *Academy of Management Review, 18*, 696–734.

Gilliland, S. W. (1994). Effects of procedural and distributive justice on reactions to a selection system. *Journal of Applied Psychology, 79*, 691–701.

Gilliland, S. W. (1995). Fairness from the applicant's perspective: Reactions to employee selection procedures. *International Journal of Selection and Assessment, 3*, 11–19.

Goleman, D. (1998). *Working with emotional intelligence.* London: Bloomsbury.

Graen, G. B., & Scandura, T. A. (1987). Toward a psychology of dyadic organizing. In L. L. Cummings & B. M. Staw (Eds.), *Research in Organizational Behavior* (Vol. 9, pp. 175–208). Greenwich, CT: JAI Press.

Graen, G. B., & Uhl-Bien, M. (1995). Development of LMX theory of leadership over 25 years: Applying a multi-level-multi-domain perspective. *Leadership Quarterly, 6*, 210–247.

Hazucha, J. F., Hezlett, S. A., & Schneider, R. J. (1993). The impact of 360-degree feedback on management skills development. *Human Resource Management, 32*, 325–351.

Hersey, P., & Blanchard, K. H. (1982). *Management of organizational behavior: Utilizing human resources.* Englewood Cliffs, NJ: Prentice-Hall.

Hofstede, G. (1980). *Culture's consequences: International differences in work-related values*. Beverly Hills, CA: Sage.

Hofstede, G. (1994). Management scientists are human. *Management Science, 40*, 4–13.

House, R. J. (1977). A 1976 theory of charismatic leadership. In J. G. Hunt & L. L. Larson (Eds.), *Leadership: The cutting edge* (pp. 189–207). Carbondale, IL: Southern Illinois University Press.

House, R. J., & Mitchell, T. R. (1974). Path–goal theory of leadership. *Journal of Contemporary Business, 3*, 81–97.

Kanter, R. M. (1983). *The change masters*. New York: Simon & Schuster.

Kim, H., & Yukl, G. (1995). Relationships of managerial effectiveness and advancement to self-reported and subordinate-reported leadership behaviors from the multiple-linkage model. *Leadership Quarterly, 6*, 361–377.

Krause, D. E., & Gebert, D. (2003). A comparison of assessment centre practices in organizations in German-speaking regions and the United States. *International Journal of Selection and Assessment, 11*, 297–312.

Kreitner, R., Kinicki, A., & Buelens, M. (2002). *Organizational behavior* (2nd European ed.). New York: McGraw-Hill.

Komaki, J. L. (1986). Toward effective supervision: An operant analysis and comparison of managers at work. *Journal of Applied Psychology, 71*, 270–279.

Komaki, J. L., Desselles, M. L., & Bowman, E. D. (1989). Definitely not a breeze: Extending an operant model of effective supervision to teams. *Journal of Applied Psychology, 74*, 522–529.

Kouzes, J. M., & Posner, B. Z. (1987). *The leadership challenge: How to get things done in organizations*. San Francisco: Jossey-Bass.

Lévy-Leboyer, C. (1994). Selection and assessment in Europe. In H. C. Triandis, M. D. Dunnette, & L. M. Hough (Eds.), *Handbook of industrial and organizational psychology* (2nd ed., Vol. 4, pp. 173–190). Palo Alto, CA: Consulting Psychologists Press.

London, M., & Wohlers, A. J. (1991). Agreement between subordinate and self-ratings in upward feedback. *Personnel Psychology, 44*, 375–390.

Lowe, K. B., Kroeck, K. G., & Sivasubramaniam, N. (1996). Effectiveness correlates of transformational and transactional leadership: A meta-analytic review of the MLQ literature. *Leadership Quarterly, 7*, 385–425.

Matthewman, J. (1999). The sixth HR-BC/IRS annual competency survey. *Competency: The Annual Benchmarking Survey, 1998/99*, 2–11.

Mayer, J. D., & Salovey, P. (1997). What is emotional intelligence? In P. Salovey & D. J. Sluyter (Eds.), *Emotional development and emotional intelligence: Educational implications* (pp. 3–31). New York: Basic Books.

McCall, M. W., Jr. (1998). *High flyers: Developing the next generation of leaders*. Boston: Harvard Business School Press.

McCall, M. W., Jr., & Hollenbeck, G. P. (2002). *Developing global executives: The lessons of international experience*. Boston: Harvard Business School Press.

McDaniel, M. A., Finnegan, E. B., Morgeson, F. P., Campion, M. A., & Braverman, E. P. (2001). Use of situational judgement tests to predict job perforce: A clarification of the literature. *Journal of Applied Psychology, 86*, 730–740.

Mintzberg, H. (1973). *The nature of managerial work*. New York: Harper & Row.

Morse, J. J., & Wagner, F. R. (1978). Measuring the process of managerial effectiveness. *Academy of Management Journal, 21*, 23–35.

Peters, T. J., & Austin, N. (1985). *A passion for excellence: The leadership difference*. New York: Random House.

Phillips, J. M., & Gully, S. M. (2002). Fairness reactions to personnel selection techniques in Singapore and the United States. *International Journal of Human Resource Management, 13*, 1186–1205.

Ployhart, R. E., & Ryan, A. M. (1997). Toward an explanation of applicant reactions: An examination of organizational justice and attribution frameworks. *Organizational Behavior and Human Decision Processes, 72*, 308–335.

Ployhart, R. E., & Ryan, A. M. (1998). Applicants' reactions to the fairness of selection procedures: The effects of positive rule violation and time of measurement. *Journal of Applied Psychology, 83*, 3–16.

Podsakoff, P. M., Todor, W. D., Grover, R. A., & Huber, V. L. (1984). Situational moderators of leader reward and punishment behavior: Fact of fiction? *Organizational Behavior and Human Performance, 34*, 21–63.

Rajan, A., & Van Eupen, P. (1997). Take it from the top. *People Management, 23*, October, 26–32.

Robie, C., Johnson, K. M., Nilsen, D., & Fisher Hazucha, J. (2001). The right stuff: Understanding cultural differences in leadership performance. *Journal of Management Development, 20*, 639–649.

Ryan, A. M., McFarland, L., Baron, H., & Page, R. (1999). An international look at selection practices: Nation and culture as explanations for variability in practice. *Personnel Psychology, 52*, 359–391.

Salgado, J. F., & Anderson, N. R. (2002). Cognitive and GMA testing in the European Community: Issues and evidence. *Human Performance, 15*, 75–96.

Salgado, J. F., Anderson, N., Moscoso, S., Bertua, C., & De Fruyt, F. (2003). International validity generalization of GMA & cognitive abilities: A European Community meta-analysis. *Personnel Psychology, 56*, 573–605.

Schmidt, F. L., & Hunter, J. E. (1998). The validity and utility of selection methods in personnel psychology: Practical and theoretical implications of 85 years of research findings. *Psychological Bulletin, 124*, 262–274.

Schmit, M. J., & Ryan, A. M. (1997). Applicant withdrawal. The role of test-taking attitudes and racial differences. *Personnel Psychology, 50*, 855–876.

Schwartz, S. H. (1994). Beyond individualism-collectivism: New cultural dimensions of values. In U. Kim, H. C. Triandis, C. Kagitcibasi, S. C. Choi, & G. Yoon (Eds.), *Individualism and collectivism: Theory, method and applications* (pp. 85–119). Newbury Park, CA: Sage.

Shackleton, V. J., & Newell, S. (1994). European management selection methods: A comparison of 5 countries. *International Journal of Selection and Assessment, 2*, 91–102.

Sinangil, H. K., & Ones, D. S. (2001). Expatriate management. In N. Anderson, D. S. Ones, H. K. Sinangil, & C. Viswesvaran (Eds.), *Handbook of industrial, work and organizational psychology* (Vol. 1, pp. 424–465). London: Sage.

Smith, P. B. (1997). Leadership in Europe: Euro-management or the footprint of history? *European Journal of Work and Organizational Psychology, 6*, 375–386.

Smith, P. B., Dugan, S., & Trompenaars, F. (1996). National culture and the values of organizational employees. *Journal of Cross-Cultural Psychology, 27*, 231–264.

Smith, P. B., Misumi, J., Tayeb, M., Peterson, M., & Bond, M. (1989). On the generality of leadership style measures across cultures. *Journal of Occupational Psychology, 62*, 97–109.

Smith, P. B., & Peterson, M. (1988). *Leadership, organizations and culture: An event management model.* London: Sage Publications.

Smith, P. B., Peterson, M. F., Schwartz, S. H., Ahmad, A. H., Akande, D., Anderson, J. A., et al. (2002). Cultural values, sources of guidance, and their relevance to managerial behavior: A 47 nation study. *Journal of Cross-Cultural Psychology, 33*, 188–208.

Steiner, D. D. (1997). Attributions of leader–member exchanges: Implications for practice. *European Journal of Work and Organizational Psychology, 6*, 59–71.

Steiner, D. D., & Gilliland, S. W. (1996). Fairness reactions to personnel selection techniques in France and the United States. *Journal of Applied Psychology, 81*, 134–141.

Steiner, D. D., & Gilliland, S. W. (2001). Procedural justice in personnel selection: International and cross-cultural perspectives. *International Journal of Selection and Assessment, 9*, 124–137.

Tampoe, M. (1998). *Liberating leadership: Releasing leadership potential throughout the organization*. London: Industrial Society.

Trompenaars, F., & Hampden-Turner, C. (1998). *Riding the waves of culture: Understanding diversity in global* business (2nd ed.). New York: McGraw Hill.

Tsui, A. S., & Ashford, S. J. (1994). Adaptive self-regulation: A process view of managerial effectiveness. *Journal of Management, 20*, 93–121.

Viswesvaran, C., & Ones, D. S. (2000). Perspectives on models of job performance. *International Journal of Selection and Assessment, 8*, 216–226.

Viswesvaran, C., Ones, D. S., & Schmidt, F. L. (1996). A comparative analysis of the reliability of job performance ratings. *Journal of Applied Psychology, 81*, 557–594.

West, M. A. (2003). *Effective teamwork: Practical lessons from organizational research* (2nd ed.). Oxford, UK: Blackwell.

Yukl, G. (1999). An evaluative essay on current conceptions of effective leadership. *European Journal of Work and Organizational Psychology, 8*, 33–48.

Yukl, G. (2002). *Leadership in organizations* (5th ed.). Upper Saddle River, NJ: Prentice-Hall.

Yukl, G., Wall, S., & Lepsinger, R. (1990). Preliminary report on validation of the Managerial Practices Survey. In K. E. Clark & M. B. Clark (Eds.), *Measures of leadership* (pp. 223–238). West Orange, NJ: Leadership Library of America.

Zaccaro, S. J., Gilbert, J. A., Thor, K. K., & Mumford, M. D. (1991). Leadership and social intelligence: Linking social perspectiveness and behavioral flexibility to leader effectiveness. *Leadership Quarterly, 2*, 317–342.

Zigurs, I. (2003). Leadership in virtual teams: Oxymoron or opportunity? *Organizational Dynamics, 31*, 328–338.

Zimmerman, P. (2004). *Desired leadership behaviors in global virtual organizations: Positioning, scoping and justification of the research project*. Unpublished paper, University of Strathclyde, Glasgow, Scotland.

21

Expatriate Selection: A Process Approach

ANNELIES E. M. VAN VIANEN, IRENE E. DE PATER, AND PAULA M. CALIGIURI

Private and public organizations have been sending members of their organizations to other parts of the world for centuries (Ones & Viswesvaran, 1997). During the past decades, global economic integration, the evolution of information and telecommunication technologies, and political development have led to the rapid globalization of the world economy. The increasing international activity and global competition resulted in an increase in the number of firms that are conducting business globally (Harvey & Novicevic, 2002) as they explore opportunities worldwide (Mervosh & McClenahen, 1997). As a consequence, the number of employees embarking on international assignments has increased significantly during the past decades (Forster, 1997; Gupta & Govindarajan, 2000). Despite a growing body of research focusing on international assignments, there are no precise estimates of the number of expatriates working for multinational companies (Oddou, Derr, & Black, 1995). The US government calculated that 4.1 million US citizens live overseas (Olsen, 2004). Others estimated that the number of expatriates and third-country nationals is around 30 million worldwide (Allianz Worldwide Care, 2004).

International assignees or expatriates can be defined as "employees of business or government organizations who are sent by their organization to a related unit in a country which is different from their own, to accomplish a job or organization-related goal for a pre-designated temporary time period of usually more than six month and less than five years in one term" (Aycan & Kanungo, 1997, p. 250). Global assignments are considered highly developmental for employees, and are frequently used as part of a leadership development strategy within international firms. It is even suggested that international assignment experience has become "a ticket to the top" (Lublin, 1996, in Carpenter, Sanders, & Gregersen, 2000), and executives reported their international assignments as the single most influential leadership development experience (Gregersen, Morrison, & Black, 1998). Furthermore, international assignment experience should result in higher levels of pay, increased probability of promotion, and stronger external mobility, because the value of international assignment experience is only partly firm specific (Carpenter et al., 2000).

International assignment experience not only benefits the individual expatriates, but the organizations they represent as well. For many organizations, sending expatriates abroad to develop global competencies is part of their overall strategic human resource plan (Caligiuri, 1997; Caligiuri & Lazarova, 2001). Expatriate assignments can develop significant global competence which adds to employees' human capital and strategic value to a transnational organization. It has been argued that expatriate experiences may be related to a firm's business opportunities abroad (Carpenter et al., 2000) and international success (Gregersen et al., 1998). "International assignment experience lets executives develop the tools necessary to profit consistently from global uncertainty regarding exchange rates, government policy, and competitors' moves" (Carpenter et al., 2000, p. 278). The so-called "global leader" is characterized as a very important resource for organizations that want to compete on the international market (Aycan, 1997b; Gregersen et al., 1998). Internationally experienced managers are better able to manage the complexity associated with the internationality of an organization and add to an organization's global knowledge and competence (Caligiuri & Lazarova, 2001).

Clearly, the potential benefits of expatriate assignments for both companies and individuals are tremendous. However, companies and individuals only benefit from these expatriate assignments when the assignments are, in fact, successful. Therefore, it is critical for global organizations to attract, select, develop, and retain employees who possess the necessary knowledge, skills, and abilities required for international jobs. Given the important role successful expatriates will play, determining who will be most successful on an expatriate assignment also becomes critical. Thus, rigorous selection for international assignments is likewise critical. Proper expatriate selection will help reinforce corporate integrity, values, and culture (with the right corporate representatives in place), improve the multinational's return on investment (of the expensive human capital investment), and avoid assignment failure (GMAC Global Relocation Services, 2003).

Criteria of Expatriate Success

Although expatriate failure rates may not be as high as previously expected (Harzing, 1995; Takeuchi, Yun, & Russell, 2002), recent research reported an attrition rate of 17% during international assignments (GMAC Global Relocation Services, 2003), and 32% of the respondents rated their company's expatriate assignments as fair or poor in terms of return on investment (i.e., accomplishing assignment objectives at the expected cost). Considering the strategic importance of international assignments, failure of the assignment (i.e., premature termination of the assignment or sub-optimal performance) can have negative consequences for the future of the multinational organization in the host country.

The effect of a less successful assignment can be detrimental for many reasons. For multinational organizations, unsuccessful international assignees are associated with significant direct costs in terms of finances (e.g., Copeland & Griggs, 1985; Mervosh & McClenahen, 1997), and indirect costs, such as damaged organization reputation, lost business opportunities, and lost market or competitive share (Black & Gregersen, 1991; Naumann, 1992). In addition, an unsuccessful international assignment might have a negative impact on one's subsequent commitment to the parent organization (Naumann,

1993), one's motivation (Takeuchi et al., 2002), and one's performance after repatriation. An unsuccessful international assignment might have an adverse impact on the decision of other qualified candidates to accept an international assignment. This is especially problematic now that organizations are confronted with a decrease in the pool of employees willing to accept an international assignment (Harzing, 1995).

For years, research on expatriate success has been plagued by a lack of consensus about the criteria of expatriate success (Aycan, 1997a, 1997b; Caligiuri, 1997; Ones & Viswesvaran, 1997). Aycan and Kanungo argued (1997) that characteristics that are considered important in the domestic context should also be considered desirable in the international context. Employee management in the domestic context is concerned with job attendance, job performance, and employee well-being. The most successful domestic employees are those "who are present in their jobs, perform well, and feel satisfied with their work content and context" (Aycan & Kanungo, 1997, p. 252). Therefore, "expatriates who remain in their assignments until the end of the term (attendance), meet the performance standards, and adjust to the new culture (satisfaction, well-being) are considered as the most successful ones" (p. 252). Developing selection instruments to predict these important criteria have been challenging given that an expatriate assignment is a job context, rather than a job description. Also, selection instruments with predictive validity in the domestic context may have less predictive power in international selection procedures due to the very specific requirements of an international job, such as language proficiency, adaptability, and cross-cultural awareness (Lievens, Harris, Van Keer, & Bisqueret, 2003). Thus, employees' competencies as shown in their home organization are not a guarantee for employees' cross-cultural effectiveness during their global assignments. In most firms, the selection of expatriates is mainly based on job knowledge and technical competence (Aryee, 1997; Harvey & Novicevic, 2002). In this chapter we will discuss which specific abilities might be crucial for successful expatriation. This chapter will analyze the international assignment by describing the factors with which international employees are confronted beyond those of their domestic counterparts. We use a model that encompasses several steps that have to be taken in the process toward successful expatriation, and selection criteria and possible predictors are linked to this process. This chapter also reviews existing literature on predictors for expatriate selection, and we conclude by proposing a process approach for selecting global assignees.

What Is So Special About Expatriation?

Unlike relocation for work in the domestic context, expatriates who relocate to another country must adjust to the host culture, with different living conditions and interactions (language and communication style). Berry (1997) outlined a conceptual framework of factors influencing the process of acculturation and adjustment. This framework is mainly focused on the adaptation strategies of minority groups in case of immigration, but it can easily be applied to expatriation. Berry (1997) described five phenomena included in the process of psychological adaptation. The first is the experience of being confronted with another culture, which tends to be more dramatic when the new culture highly differs from the individuals' own culture. The second is the way in which individuals perceive the meaning of these cultural experiences, either in a positive or negative way. The third is the way in which individuals engage in coping strategies in order to deal with strange (and potentially problematic) situations. When individuals do not adequately cope with the stressors they face, they will experience the fourth phenomenon – high stress levels and the associated anxiety and depression. Finally, a level of psychological adjustment is achieved by each individual experience of this global relocation, ranging from poorly adjusted (or maladjusted) to highly adjusted (psychological well-being) to the host culture. Black (1988) identified three types of adjustment: general adjustment to non-work activities, interaction adjustment with host country nationals (HCNs), and work adjustment to work-related roles. Shaffer and Harrison (1998) showed that cross-cultural adjustment both directly and indirectly, through its influence on expatriates' commitment and satisfaction, affected expatriates' withdrawal cognitions. Hence, expatriate selection measures should not exclusively be focused on predicting expatriates' performance in their international job but also on predicting their cross-cultural adjustment. In order to establish selection measures that might be suitable in the context of expatriation it is useful to address the different phases in the adjustment process in more detail, as will be done in the following sections.

Cultural experiences

Cultural novelty.   Expatriate employees must acculturate enough to live and work effectively in their host country. Van Vianen, De Pater, Kristof-Brown, and Johnson (in press) distinguished between the experience of surface and deep-level cultural differences. Characteristics of the host country's culture such as food, housing conditions, or climate, which are easily observable by the expatriate, can be considered surface-level differences. Other characteristics of the host country's culture, such as beliefs and values, are not immediately visible and must be indirectly inferred. These deep-level differences may only be revealed to expatriates after extended interactions with residents of the host country. Van Vianen et al. (in press) found that surface-level differences were related to general adjustment even after controlling for expatriates' family situation (i.e., accompanied by a spouse), tenure in the host country, and previous assignments. Similarly, Birdseye and Hill (1995) showed that material satisfaction with daily life circumstances was a prominent predictor of turnover intentions for American expatriates. These results suggest that for some expatriates surface-level differences are difficult to overcome and that organizations should include "dealing with new, ambiguous, and/or uncomfortable daily living situations" as a possible characteristic in the job description of an international assignment. The inclusion of this dimension would reinforce the need for cultural adaptation for many expatriate assignments (Caligiuri & Lazarova, 2001).

Role ambiguity.   Many international employees struggle with experiencing role ambiguity in the host organization, because of insecurity about the appropriate actions, behaviors, and codes of conduct (Shaffer, Harrison, & Gilley, 1999; Takeuchi et al., 2002). Their perceptions of leadership and its related behaviors may not hold in the new situation. Cultural values predict the typical sources of guidance (e.g., rules, social sources, expertise, beliefs) on which managers rely in handling work events (Smith et al., 2002). Guidance sources referring to coworker participation are typically employed in Western Europe (individualistic, egalitarian, harmony); reliance on superiors and rules are more associated with the nations of Africa; and management in countries such as Israel, Korea, and the Philippines more frequently relies on unwritten rules. Similarly, influence tactics that have shown to be effective in the home organization often do not have the same impact in the host organization. For example, more Western task-oriented tactics that involve direct confrontation are less likely to be effective in Asian cultures where personal relationships or indirect approaches are preferred as a tactic to resolve a disagreement (Yukl, Fu, & McDonald, 2003). Furthermore, different culture groups have different conceptions of what 'good' leadership should involve (see Den Hartog et al., 1999). Thus, if Western companies use their own criteria standards for selecting their (international) executives, these managers may have skills that do not meet the culturally contingent criteria for outstanding leadership in host country cultures. Den Hartog et al. (1999) found several attributes to be culturally contingent, such as sensitive, ambitious, status conscious, and cunning, with some countries rating high and others rating low on the contribution of these attributes to outstanding leadership. Other leadership attributes are universally endorsed (particularly charismatic or transformational ones, integrity) as contributors to outstanding leadership or universally disapproved of (e.g., ruthless, asocial, dictatorial) as impediments to outstanding leadership. However, Den Hartog et al. (1999) noted that a universally shared preference for leadership attributes does not mean that these attributes are enacted in exactly the same way across countries or that similar meaning is attached to these behaviors. This brings us to the conclusion that international executives should be able to adapt or, if necessary, even drastically change their "normal" management style to the new situation.

Value differences. After being exposed to the new culture, expatriates become aware of deep-level cultural differences in values. For example, as expatriates become engaged in work activities, they are required to interact frequently with host nationals on complex issues. By observing their overt behaviors, and possibly even through the explicit discussion of assumptions and values, expatriates gain insight into the deep-level differences between themselves and their coworkers. Van Vianen et al. (in press) argued that generally people are attracted to others who share their values and who therefore perceive events and behave in similar ways. The importance of perceived value similarity was also shown in the context of international cooperation. Similarity in cultures was found to be associated with successful cooperation (Van Oudenhoven & Van der Zee, 2002b).

Expatriate employees, however, often accept an international assignment knowing that they will be confronted with local residents who may have values that differ from their own. Nevertheless, the study of Van Vianen et al. (in press) showed that some value differences are more difficult to deal with than others. In particular, when people in the host national culture endorse values such as helpfulness, protection, loyalty, equality, and social justice (self-transcendence basic values; Schwartz, 1999) less than the expatriate does, work and interactional adjustment are likely to be hampered. Thus, international applicants whose core identity is mainly based on values such as equality and social justice risk harm to their self-identities when confronted with host cultures that adhere less to these values. International employees are expected to conform to values of their host country that may conflict with their own cultural values. Leong and Ward (2000) showed that individuals with a higher tolerance for ambiguity experienced less identity conflict.

To summarize, cultural experiences are essential ingredients of an expatriate's job. A job analysis should include specific job characteristics associated with the cultural context of the job. In particular, selection of expatriates should be focused on measuring 1) flexibility regarding uncomfortable daily living situations, 2) flexibility regarding leadership styles and the use of influence tactics and/or specific leadership abilities that fit the host culture perceptions of leadership, and 3) applicants' basic values and their tolerance for ambiguity.

Appraisal of and coping with cultural experiences

International employees may differ in the way they consider the meaning of their cultural experiences. First, although the new culture is dissimilar from expatriates' own culture, as objectively established, expatriates may still encounter different experiences of dissimilarity, for example through processes of categorization and stereotyping the new culture and its members. Thus, cultural distances can be made smaller or larger in the expatriates' minds. For an expatriate, the ability to correctly assess the social environment is more complicated given that the host country may provide ambiguous social cues (Caligiuri & Day, 2000). Secondly, expatriates' appraisal reactions will depend on their pre-departure expectations and motivations. Relevant pre-departure training facilitates generating accurate expectations about the international assignment (Caligiuri, Phillips, Lazarova, Tarique, & Bürgi, 2001). It has been suggested that modest expectations about what the expatriate will encounter in the new culture may mitigate the experience of the so-called "culture shock" (Aycan, 1997a; Caligiuri & Phillips, 2003). In addition, if an international assignment was accepted based on pull rather than push intentions, expatriates will appraise their cultural experiences more positively. Pull factors refer to intrinsic and extrinsic advantages that are to be gained from the international assignment (personal growth, better career opportunities, curiosity to other cultures), while push factors refer to conditions and situations that the individual wants to escape from (unpleasant work and/or non-work circumstances).

Furthermore, individuals have a dispositional tendency to evaluate unknown situations or tasks as a threat or to welcome them as a challenge. A threat is something one wants to avoid while a challenge is something that one wants to master. The first evokes avoidance behavioral predispositions while the latter induces approach behavioral predispositions (Elliot & McGregor, 2001). Expatriates who are predisposed to avoid making mistakes or doing anything incorrectly may react in a more horrified way to the new culture than those who value strange situations as an opportunity to show one's competency in mastering the situation successfully.

In the stress literature, there is a large body of research about coping strategies people use in stressful situations. In general, there are two types of coping: problem-focused and emotion-focused coping (Folkman & Lazarus, 1985). Problem-focused coping includes taking constructive and direct approaches to solving stressful events. Emotion-focused coping concentrates on the regulation of emotional responses to problems. Endler and Parker (1990) have identified a third strategy, namely, avoidance. Avoidance-oriented coping can include either emotion- or problem-focused strategies. "An individual can avoid a particular stressful situation by seeking out other people (seeking social support), or by engaging in another task than the task at hand" (Endler & Parker, 1990, p. 846).

Stress research has highlighted the role of social support in helping individuals reduce uncertainty (Aycan, 1997b; Berry, 1997). Selmer (2001a) found that expatriates who were unwilling or unable to adjust made little use of strategies such as showing tolerance and patience, feeling responsible for the situation, and seeking contact with HCNs. Recently, Johnson and colleagues (Johnson, Kristof-Brown, Van Vianen, De Pater, & Klein, 2003) investigated the number and quality of social relationships of expatriates with host country nationals and with other expatriates in their host country. Social ties can relieve stress and anxiety, but they also provide expatriates with information about the host country, and improve communication with, and understanding of, HCNs. The researchers distinguished between the total number of relationships with other expatriates and HCNs and the breadth and depth of these relationships. Breadth was operationalized as the variety of resources provided by others, namely the extent to which expatriates obtained non-work information, business information, and social support from their network members. Depth of relationships referred to the quality of relationships, such as their closeness to other people, the length of time they had known them, and how frequently they interacted with them. It was shown that social ties did play a role in general, interaction, and work adjustment. However, the content of various social ties was differentially associated with cross-cultural adjustment. Expatriates benefit from deep relationships with other expatriates through which they receive social support, while it is advantageous to have a large rather than deep-level network with HCNs who provide them with information about norms and behaviors in the host country organization. The number of social ties was related to personality: individuals with high core self-evaluations, which include self-esteem, generalized self-efficacy, internal locus of control, and emotional stability (see Judge, Van Vianen, & De Pater, in press), formed a greater number of social relationships than did their counterparts with low core self-evaluations.

To summarize, appraisal of and coping with culture experiences affect cross-cultural adaptation. Appraisal of cultural experiences is influenced by the extent to which expatriates use categorizations and stereotypes. Research has shown that categorization is related to individual differences in personal need for structure (PNS) that is conceptually similar to intolerance of ambiguity. Individuals who score high on personal need for structure create simple stereotypes of new groups. Low tolerance of ambiguity has been found to be associated with ethnocentrism and prejudice (Hall & Carter, 1999; Moskowitz, 1993). Additionally, expatriates' motivation for an international assignment and their dispositional tendency to approach or avoid unknown situations affect their evaluation of cultural experiences. Finally, expatriates' coping styles, particularly those that are focused on seeking social support, are directly related to their psychological cross-cultural adjustment. Consequently, selection of expatriates should include measures that refer to 1) tolerance of ambiguity, 2) pull and push motivations and expectations, 3) dispositional mastery-avoidance goals (see Elliot & McGregor, 2001), and 4) personality predictors of seeking social ties and support, such as core self-evaluations.

In the next section we review the personality measures that were included in studies examining possible predictors for expatriate success.

PERSONALITY FACTORS AND EXPATRIATE SUCCESS

Personality characteristics predispose humans to behave in certain ways, given particular situations, to accomplish certain goals, etc. (e.g., Costa & McCrae, 1992). While many personality characteristics exist, research has found that five factors provide a useful typology or taxonomy for classifying them (Digman, 1990; Goldberg, 1992; McCrae & John, 1992). These five factors, including extroversion, agreeableness, conscientiousness, emotional stability, and openness or intellect, have been found repeatedly through factor analyses and confirmatory factor analyses across, time, contexts, and cultures (Digman, 1990; Goldberg, 1992; McCrae & John, 1992).

Ones and Viswesvaran (1999) examined the importance that managers attach to personality for personnel decisions in an international context. Managers gave most weight to conscientiousness. This indicates that international recruiters apply their domestic selection model, in which conscientiousness dominates, to expatriate selection. In the domestic context, employees who are perceived to be conscientious are more trusted in their respective organizations. These trusted employees are more likely to become leaders, gain status, get promoted, earn higher salaries, etc. Employees who are conscientious are not only *perceived* to be better, but their objective work performance is also better (e.g., Barrick & Mount, 1991; Day & Silverman, 1989). The positive relationship between conscientiousness and performance has also been established in the international context. Expatriates with greater conscientiousness are rated as better performers (Caligiuri, 2000a; Ones & Viswesvaran, 1997).

Researchers have proposed that other Big Five personality characteristics also have some relationship to expatriate success and should be considered in expatriate selection systems (Ones & Viswesvaran, 1997; Caligiuri, 2000a, 2000b).

Extroversion seems important, because expatriates who are assertive enough to establish some interpersonal relationships with both host nationals and other expatriates are able to learn the work and non-work social culture of the host country more effectively (Black, 1990; Caligiuri, 2000a, 2000b; Dinges, 1983; Johnson et al., 2003; Searle & Ward, 1990). A shy, timid, and introverted person may feel isolated and may have a far more difficult time adjusting to the host country (Caligiuri, 2000b).

In addition to extroversion, the ability to form reciprocal social alliances is achieved through the personality characteristic of *agreeableness* (Buss, 1991). Expatriates who are more agreeable (i.e., deal with conflict collaboratively, strive for mutual understanding, and are less competitive) report greater cross-cultural adjustment and greater success on the assignment (Caligiuri, 2000a, 2000b; Ones & Viswesvaran, 1997; Black, 1990; Tung, 1981). We would like to note that the role of agreeableness is still indefinite. Research has shown significant linkages between individuals' agreeableness and their scores on basic values that belong to the self-transcendence value dimension (Roccas, Sagiv, & Knafo,

2002). Earlier in this chapter we have argued that individuals adhering strongly to these values are also the ones that are vulnerable to cultural misfit with HCNs.

Emotional stability is a universal adaptive mechanism enabling humans to cope with stress in their environment (Buss, 1991). Given that stress is often associated with living and working in an ambiguous and unfamiliar environment (Richards, 1996), emotional stability was found to be an important personality characteristic for expatriates' adjustment to the host country (Black, 1988; Gudykunst, 1988; Mendenhall & Oddou, 1985) and completion of an expatriate assignment (Ones & Viswesvaran, 1997).

Successful expatriates must possess cognitive complexity, openness, and intuitive perceptual acuity to perceive and interpret the host culture accurately (Caligiuri, Jacobs, & Farr, 2000; Dinges, 1983; Finney & Von Glinow, 1988; Ones & Viswesvaran, 1997). *Openness to experience* is related to expatriate success because individuals higher in this personality characteristic have fewer rigid views of right and wrong, appropriate and inappropriate, etc., and are more likely to be accepting of the host culture (e.g., Black, 1990; Cui & van den Berg, 1991; Hammer, Gudykunst, & Wiseman, 1978).

Criterion-related validity studies indicated that, in particular, openness to experience seems predictive for expatriate performance. Recently, Lievens et al. (2003) examined the validity of a broad set of predictors for selecting European managers for a cross-cultural training program in Japan. They argued that the process of selecting people for cross-cultural training, receiving actual training, and then being sent abroad after successful training rather than directly selecting people for an international assignment may reduce costs (of failure) and may shape realistic perceptions about the foreign culture. Moreover, abilities and traits may not only predict expatriate performance directly, but are also essential for the development of other more dynamic cross-cultural competencies such as knowledge and skills that can be acquired through training. Included in the training selection were cognitive ability, Big Five measures, assessment center exercises, and behavior description interviews. Cognitive ability was significantly related to language proficiency after training and the Big Five personality dimension of openness was positively related to cross-cultural training performance. Moreover, scores regarding communication, adaptability, and teamwork in a group discussion exercise was shown to add incremental validity over and beyond personality and cognitive ability measures.

Several researchers have examined other personality traits as possible predictors for successful international assignments. Harrison, Chadwick, and Scales (1996) found significant positive relationships between self-monitoring, self-efficacy, and general and interaction adjustment. Caligiuri and Day (2000) investigated the relationship between self-monitoring and performance ratings of global assignees. Positive relationships were found only between self-monitoring and assignment-specific performance (e.g., the transfer of information and language and cultural proficiency), while relationships with other performance dimensions were negative or did not exist. The authors suggest that it could be useful to use self-monitoring as a predictor for expatriate success if the international position concerns high levels of intercultural interaction.

Harvey and Novicevic (2002) proposed that intuition and creativity should be added to the list of (Big Five) selection criteria. Intuition refers to the part of intelligence that concentrates on the possibilities rather than details and on finding solutions directly without necessarily basing decisions on facts. Creativity in this context refers to being able to develop business ideas that have not been considered by others and to recognize patterns in events, environments, and people. Both intuition and creativity accelerate decision making in competitive situations through the use of tacit knowledge of the environment and through improvisation and taking risks (Andersen, 2000).

As an alternative to the general personality questionnaires based on the Big Five, several researchers developed measurement tools that are more tailored to predictions regarding multicultural effectiveness. Van Oudenhoven and Van der Zee (2002a) developed the Multicultural Personality Questionnaire (MPQ) comprising cultural empathy, open-mindedness, emotional stability, social initiative, and flexibility. The MPQ appeared to be predictive of the adjustment of international students beyond and above self-efficacy, which warrants further validity testing with international employees. Spreitzer, McCall, and Mahony (1997) created the Prospector, including 14 dimensions: sensitive to cultural differences, business knowledge, courage, bringing out the best in people, integrity, insightful, committed, taking risks, seeking feedback, using feedback, culturally adventurousness, seeking learning opportunities, openness to criticism, and flexibility. This instrument was partly successful in identifying competencies for international executives, whether they were in an expatriate assignment or in a job dealing with international issues more generally. Caligiuri (1996) developed The Self-Assessment for Global Endeavors (The SAGE), which includes Big-Five-based dimensions, such as openness to people, intellectual curiosity, flexibility, and the like. The SAGE has demonstrated predictive validity with criteria such as intention to remain on the assignment, supervisor-rated performance, and adjustment.

While the scientific literature has suggested relevant personality factors, dimensions, and even provided tools for predicting cross-cultural adaptation, firms have been slow to adopt them in their expatriate management programs, albeit this is changing as leading firms adopt a more strategic approach to managing their important international talent. The factors influencing a firm's use of selection and the best practices used by leading firms will be described in the following sections.

SELECTION PRACTICES

In the past, practical insights and management perceptions, rather than the theoretical frameworks described in the previous section, have driven the selection of international employees. Hechanova, Beehr, and Christiansen (2003) report that a large number of multinational companies do not have structured procedures for selecting expatriates, but rely on manager recommendations. Recruiters identify adaptability of spouse and family and spouse's willingness to live abroad as one of the most important factors contributing to success in an international assignment (Arthur & Bennet, 1995). Indeed, spouse–family cross-cultural adjustment positively influences expatriates' cross-cultural adjustment and vice versa (Caligiuri, Hyland, Joshi, & Bross, 1998; Takeuchi, Yun, & Tesluk, 2002). Thus, expatriates' family members should be treated as part of the expatriate team. To date, little is known about whether (and how) spouses are actually involved in the selection process. Some authors even argue that finding valid selection instruments for expatriate selection becomes less relevant for international companies now that they struggle with the recruitment of potential expatriates (see Selmer, 2001b). Problems with recruitment are due to the growing number of dual-career couples, mismanagement of expatriates' repatriation, and deteriorating expatriate compensation packages because more companies view international experience as a standard career route for their employees.

Despite these skeptical views, the literature as presented above suggests that international companies could benefit from using valid instruments for selecting their international employees. The implementation of these instruments might be hindered because multinational organizations recruit their international managers from different countries and therefore each may have developed their own selection criteria and employ unique selection practices. Recently, Huo, Huang, and Napier (2002) made a cross-national comparison of personnel selection practices in ten countries. Although a personal interview and establishing a person's ability to perform the technical requirements of the job were mentioned as selection practices in most countries, differences between groups of countries did exist. Existing similarities in practices between some countries could be attributed to their common cultural roots, such as among Asian nations which assign more value to criteria such as: "A person's potential to do a good job, even if the person is not that good when he/she first starts" and "A person's ability to get along well with others already working here."

Ryan and colleagues (Ryan, McFarland, Baron, & Page, 1999) found similar results when examining variability in selection practices across 20 countries. National differences particularly concerned the use of fixed interview questions and multiple methods of verification. The researchers concluded that adopting a worldwide standardized selection battery "is likely to encounter objections on different bases in different cultures" (p. 386). Cross-cultural differences exist not only regarding selection criteria (see our discussion of differences in ideal leadership perceptions) but also regarding valuable and acceptable selection methods. Moreover, if selection procedures require subjective judgments of assessors (based on interviews and assessment center exercises), selection decisions may be culturally biased since assessors qualify applicants' performances based on behavioral norms in the context of their own culture. In this latter case, global organizations could involve recruiters and assessors from their foreign units to select international employees for these units rather than conducting the selection in the home country. Another and more money-saving option is the use of standardized tests, if these tests are accepted across the foreign units and show similar construct and criterion-related validities across cultures, and use local selection criteria and norms if necessary. Evidence exists regarding comparable criterion-related validities of general mental ability tests in European countries and the USA (Salgado, Anderson, Moscoso, Bertua, & De Fruyt, 2003). Moreover, personality inventories based on the Five Factor Model have been shown to be comparable across cultures (Salgado, Moscoso, & Lado, 2003).

STEPS IN DEVELOPING AN EXPATRIATE SELECTION SYSTEM

As this chapter suggests, it takes a special person to thrive personally and professionally outside his or her home country. A global assignment is not right for everyone. Given the high personal and professional risk associated with expatriate assignments, understanding and predicting who will be most successful on an expatriate assignment is important for firms to consider. Selection systems for global assignments should include an assessment of skills and personality very early in the selection process. Organizations will get the best possible global assignees when they consider many possible candidates and engage the candidates' decision-making processes long before a position becomes available. This decision-making process will help them decide whether the assignment is really right for them. That is, the selection decision needs to be acceptable to the employee, his or her organization, and his or her family.

It has only been recently that some global companies have begun to implement a *strategic process* for selecting global assignees. Outlined below we propose a "best practice process" that is already starting to be used by some multinational organizations for selecting their global assignees. This process for selecting global assignees has four phases: 1) decision making or self-selection, 2) creating a candidate pool, 3) technical and managerial skills assessment, and 4) making a mutual decision.

Phase one: Allow for self-selection

When practical, the potential candidate pool should be identified. It is most important at this phase to contact any employee who may have the requisite technical knowledge, skills, and abilities for a given assignment. Companies at this phase are casting a wide net to assess interest in the possibility of a global assignment. To help facilitate this, self-selection instruments are available, such as The Self-Assessment for Global Endeavors, The SAGE™ (Caligiuri, 1996). The goal of a self-selection instrument is to help employees make a thoroughly informed and realistic decision about a global assignment. This will encourage employees to critically evaluate three significant dimensions: 1) personality and individual characteristics, 2) career issues, and 3) family issues. *Personality characteristics* that we have proposed in this chapter as being particularly relevant for cross-cultural adjustment are: openness, emotional stability, core self-evaluations, flexibility, tolerance of ambiguity, avoidance-approach behavioral dispositions, values, and tolerance of uncomfortable daily life conditions. *Career issues* should include expectations and (push and pull) motives regarding expatriation. *Family issues* are crucial at this stage and spouses and children need to be involved. International organizations might even consider spouses' voluntary evaluation of personality and career issues.

Several organizations, such as Procter & Gamble and EDS, have made a self-selection instrument available on their company's intranet to encourage self-assessment among those who may not have previously considered a global assignment. Organizations such as FedEx give a self-selection instrument to a targeted group of employees. Regardless of the method, a decision counselor should be available to talk with employees who have taken the instrument. In this phase, HR should provide the best possible information that will assist the employee in the decision-making process. For this phase to be successful, the focus should be on self-selection and decision making, and not evaluation (Caligiuri & Phillips, 2003).

Phase two: Create a pool of candidates

From the self-selection phase, the candidate pool is created. HR will give interested employees the opportunity to place themselves in the candidate pool database. This candidate pool can be organized quite differently, depending on the staffing needs of the organization. The database may include the following pieces of information: availability, languages the employee speaks, countries preferred, technical knowledge, skills, abilities, etc. For this phase to be successful, all interested employees should be in the candidate pool database.

Phase three: Assess candidates' technical and managerial skills

Next, the available global assignments are analyzed in terms of their technical and logistical requirements. HR then scans the database for all possible candidates that match the requirements and this list is forwarded to the business unit making the request. In the business unit, each candidate's technical and managerial readiness will be assessed, relative to the needs of the assignment. Depending on the specific assignment, candidates' cross-cultural leadership skills and their flexibility in leadership style should be assessed together with their cognitive abilities, conscientiousness, intuition, and creativity as relevant predictors of performance.

Phase four: Make a mutual decision

In this last phase, it is often the case that only one or two people, at most, are identified as acceptable candidates. An assignee, at this phase, has been tentatively "selected." Given the high stakes often associated with a global assignment, organizations may still want to consider offering additional opportunities for self-selection (de-selection) or assessment (selection) at this phase.

There are three common elements in all successful global assignee selection programs. The first is that they *start early* by engaging employees to consider a global assignment. The best candidates are found when individuals' decision-making processes are engaged long before a position becomes available. The second element is to *involve the family* as early as possible in the process. Research has concluded that each family member will influence the assignment positively or negatively. The third element is to maintain enough flexibility in the system to *allow for deselection* at every phase. The best selection decision will be acceptable to the employee, his or her organization, and his or her family.

CONCLUSION

Given the extraordinarily high financial, relational, and personal costs for expatriates, their families, and their organizations, understanding who will benefit most from being on an international assignment is important. In a practical sense, research has done much to encourage the use of appropriate selection and self-assessment tools, especially in positions where the expatriates will be interacting more extensively with host nationals. As this chapter suggests, organizations should convey to its employees that a global assignment *is not right for everyone*. Organizations will get the best possible global assignees when they consider many possible candidates and engage the candidates' decision-making processes before a position becomes available. Given the effects beyond the expatriate alone, the selection decision needs to be acceptable to the employee, his or her organization, and his or her family. These best practices should improve multinational firms' chances of having well-adjusted expatriates and successful expatriates in their critical international assignments. In turn, improved expatriate success should lead to enhanced global competence and better firm performance in the global arena.

Overall, international companies are somewhat reluctant to provide information about their international assignments that failed. However, such information, which can be collected through in-depth interviews with expatriates, is needed to disclose the crucial factors that affect cross-cultural adjustment and performance. Moreover, such data should not only be gathered after the international assignment has been completed (successfully or not) but particularly during each of the different stages of cross-cultural adjustment as described in this chapter. For example, little is known about the effects of categorization and stereotyping in the first stage of the adjustment process. Categorization may prevent people from deepening their understanding of the foreign culture, but it may also help them to cope emotionally with the cultural shock. Finally, more research is needed on the predictive validity of selection procedures of expatriate selection and whether or not these procedures should include additional predictors beyond and above those that have already been found useful for predicting success in complex management jobs in a domestic context.

References

Allianz Worldwide Care. (2004). Retrieved February 10, 2004, from http://company.monster.ie/allianzie/.

Andersen, J. A. (2000). Intuition in managers. Are intuitive managers more effective? *Journal of Managerial Psychology, 15*, 46–67.

Arthur, W., Jr., & Bennet, W. (1995). The international assignee: The relative importance of factors perceived to contribute to success. *Personnel Psychology, 48*, 99–114.

Aryee, S. (1997). Selection and training of expatriate employees. In N. Anderson & P. Herriot (Eds.), *International handbook of selection and assessment* (pp. 147–160). Chichester, UK: Wiley.

Aycan, Z. (1997a). Acculturation of expatriate managers: A process model of adjustment and performance. In D. M. Saunders (Series Ed.) & Z. Aycan (Vol. Ed.), *New approaches to employee management: Vol. 4. Expatriate management: Theory and research* (pp. 1–40). Greenwich, CT: JAI Press.

Aycan, Z. (1997b). Expatriate adjustment as a multifaceted phenomenon: Individual and organizational level predictors. *International Journal of Human Resource Management, 8*, 434–456.

Aycan, Z., & Kanungo, R. N. (1997). Current issues and future challenges in expatriation research. In D. M. Saunders (Series Ed.) & Z. Aycan (Vol. Ed.), *New approaches to employee management: Vol. 4. Expatriate management: Theory and research* (pp. 245–260). Greenwich, CT: JAI Press.

Barrick, M. R., & Mount, M. K. (1991). The Big Five personality dimensions and job performance. *Personnel Psychology, 44*, 1–26.

Berry, J. W. (1997). Immigration, acculturation, and adaptation. *Applied Psychology: An International Review, 46*, 5–68.

Birdseye, M. G., & Hill, J. S. (1995). Individual, organizational/work and environmental influences on expatriate turnover tendencies: An empirical study. *Journal of International Business Studies, 26*, 787–813.

Black, J. S. (1988). Work role transitions: A study of American expatriate managers in Japan. *Journal of International Business Studies, 19*, 277–294.

Black, J. S. (1990). The relationship of personal characteristics with adjustment of Japanese expatriate managers. *Management International Review, 30*, 119–134.

Black, J. S., & Gregersen, H. B. (1991). Antecedents to cross-cultural adjustment for expatriates in Pacific Rim assignments. *Human Relations, 44*, 497–515.

Buss, D. M. (1991). Evolutionary personality psychology. In M. R. Rosenzweig & L. W. Porter (Eds.), *Annual Review of Psychology* (Vol. 42, pp. 459–492). Palo Alto, CA: Annual Reviews Inc.

Caligiuri, P. M. (1996). *Technical manual: Reliability and validity of The SAGE.* New Brunswick, NJ: Caligiuri & Associates.

Caligiuri, P. M. (1997). Assessing expatriate success: Beyond just "being there." In D. M. Saunders (Series Ed.) & Z. Aycan (Vol. Ed.), *New approaches to employee management: Vol. 4. Expatriate management: Theory and research* (pp. 117–140). Greenwich, CT: JAI Press.

Caligiuri, P. M. (2000a). The Big Five personality characteristics as predictors of expatriate success. *Personnel Psychology, 53*, 67–88.

Caligiuri, P. M. (2000b). Selecting expatriates for personality characteristics: A moderating effect of personality on the relationship between host national contact and cross-cultural adjustment. *Management International Review, 40*, 61–80.

Caligiuri, P. M., & Day, D. V. (2000). Effects of self-monitoring on technical, contextual, and assignment-specific performance: A study of cross-national work performance ratings. *Group and Organization Management, 25*, 154–175.

Caligiuri, P. M., Hyland, M., Joshi, A., & Bross, A. (1998). A theoretical framework for examining the relationship between family adjustment and expatriate adjustment to working in the host country. *Journal of Applied Psychology, 83*, 598–614.

Caligiuri, P. M., Jacobs, R. J., & Farr, J. L. (2000). The attitudinal and behavioral openness scale: Scale development and construct validation. *International Journal of Intercultural Relations, 24*, 27–46.

Caligiuri, P. M., & Lazarova, M. (2001). Strategic repatriation policies to enhance global leadership development. In M. Mendenhall, T. Kuehlmann, & G. Stahl (Eds.), *Developing global business leaders: Policies, processes, and innovations* (pp. 243–256). Westport, CT: Quorum Books.

Caligiuri, P., & Phillips, J. (2003). An application of self-assessment realistic job previews to expatriate assignments. *International Journal of Human Resource Management, 14*, 1102–1116.

Caligiuri, P. M., Phillips, J., Lazarova, M., Tarique, I., & Bürgi, P. (2001). The theory of met expectations applied to expatriate adjustment: The role of cross-cultural training. *International Journal of Human Resource Management, 12*, 357–372.

Carpenter, M. A., Sanders, W. G., & Gregersen, H. B. (2000). International assignment experience at the top can make a bottom-line difference. *Human Resource Management, 39*, 277–285.

Copeland, L., & Griggs, L. (1985). *Going international.* New York: Random House.

Costa, P. T., Jr., & McCrae, R. R. (1992). Four ways five factors are basic. *Personality and Individual Differences, 13*, 653–665.

Cui, G., & Van den Berg, S. (1991). Testing the construct validity of intercultural effectiveness. *International Journal of Intercultural Relations, 15*, 227–241.

Day, D. V., & Silverman, S. B. (1989). Personality and job performance: Evidence of incremental validity. *Personnel Psychology, 42*, 25–36.

Den Hartog, D. N., House, R. J., Hanges, P. J., Ruiz-Quintanilla, S. A., Dorfman, P. W., Abdalla, I. A., et al. (1999). Culture specific and cross-culturally generalizable implicit leadership theories:

Are attributes of charismatic/transformational leadership universally endorsed? *Leadership Quarterly, 10,* 219–256.

Digman, J. M. (1990). Personality structure: The emergence of the five factor model. *Annual Review of Psychology, 41,* 417–440.

Dinges, N. (1983). Intercultural competence. In D. Landis & R. W. Brislin (Eds.), *Handbook of intercultural training: Issues in theory and design* (Vol. 1, pp. 176–202). New York: Pergamon Press.

Elliot, A. J., & McGregor, H. A. (2001). A 2 × 2 achievement goal framework. *Journal of Personality and Social Psychology, 80,* 501–519.

Endler, N. S., & Parker, J. D. A. (1990). Multidimensional assessment of coping. *Journal of Personality and Social Psychology, 58,* 844–854.

Finney, M., & Von Glinow, M. A. (1988). Integrating academic and organizational approaches to developing the international manager. *Journal of Management Development, 7,* 16–27.

Folkman, S., & Lazarus, R. S. (1985). If it changes it must be a process: A study of emotion and coping during three stages of a college examination. *Journal of Personality and Social Psychology, 48,* 150–170.

Forster, N. (1997). 'The persistent myth of high expatriate failure rates': A reappraisal. *International Journal of Human Resource Management, 8,* 414–433.

GMAC Global Relocation Services. (2003, March). *Global relocation trends 2002 survey report.* Retrieved February 11, 2004, from http://www.gmacglobalrelocation.com/Surveys.html

Goldberg, L. R. (1992). The development of markers for the Big-Five factor structure. *Psychological Assessment, 4,* 26–42.

Gregersen, H. B., Morrison, A. J., & Black, J. S. (1998). Developing leaders for the global frontier. *Sloan Management Review, 40,* 21–32.

Gudykunst, W. B. (1988). Uncertainty and anxiety. In Y. Kim & W. B. Gudykunst (Eds.), *Theories in intercultural communication* (pp. 123–156). Newbury Park, CA: Sage.

Gupta, A. K., & Govindarajan, V. (2000). Managing global expansion: A conceptual framework. *Business Horizons, 43,* 45–54.

Hall, J. A., & Carter, J. D. (1999). Gender-stereotype accuracy as an individual difference. *Personality Processes and Individual Differences, 77,* 350–359.

Hammer, M. R., Gudykunst, W. B., & Wiseman, R. L. (1978). Dimensions of intercultural effectiveness: An exploratory study. *International Journal of Intercultural Relations, 2,* 382–393.

Harrison, J. K., Chadwick, M., & Scales, M. (1996). The relationship between cross-cultural adjustment and the personality variables of self-efficacy and self-monitoring. *International Journal of Intercultural Relationships, 20,* 167–188.

Harvey, M., & Novicevic, M. M. (2002). The hypercompetitive global marketplace: The importance of intuition and creativity in expatriate managers. *Journal of World Business, 37,* 127–138.

Harzing, A. W. (1995). The persistence myth of high expatriate failure rates. *International Journal of Human Resource Management, 6,* 457–474.

Hechanova, R., Beehr, T. A., & Christiansen, N. D. (2003). Antecedents and consequences of employees' adjustment to overseas assignment: A meta-analytic review. *Applied Psychology: An International Review, 52,* 213–236.

Huo, Y. P., Huang, H. J., & Napier, N. K. (2002). Divergence or convergence: A cross-national comparison of personnel selection practices. *Human Resource Management, 41,* 31–44.

Johnson, E. C., Kristof-Brown, A. L., Van Vianen, A. E. M., De Pater, I. E., & Klein, M. R. (2003). Expatriate social ties: Personality antecedents and consequences for adjustment. *International Journal of Selection and Assessment, 11,* 277–288.

Judge, T. A., Van Vianen, A. E. M., & De Pater, I. E. (in press). Emotional stability, core self-evaluations, and job outcomes: A review of the evidence and an agenda for future research. *Human Performance.*

Leong, C. H., & Ward, C. (2000). Identity conflict in sojourners. *International Journal of Intercultural Relations, 24*, 763–776.

Lievens, F., Harris, M. M., Van Keer, E., & Bisqueret, C. (2003). Predicting cross-cultural training performance: The validity of personality, cognitive ability, and dimensions measured by an assessment center and a behavior description interview. *Journal of Applied Psychology, 88*, 476–489.

McCrae, R. R., & John, O. P. (1992). An introduction to the five factor model and its applications. *Journal of Personality, 60*, 175–216.

Mendenhall, M., & Oddou, G. (1985). The dimensions of expatriate acculturation: A review. *Academy of Management Review, 10*, 39–48.

Mervosh, E. M., & McClenahen, J. S. (1997). The care and feeding of expats. *Industry Week, 246*, 68–72.

Moskowitz, G. B. (1993). Individual differences in social categorization: The influence of personal need for structure on spontaneous trait inferences. *Journal of Personality and Social Psychology, 65*, 132–142.

Naumann, E. (1992). A conceptual model of expatriate turnover. *Journal of International Business Studies, 23*, 499–531.

Naumann, E. (1993). Antecedents and consequences of satisfaction and commitment among expatriate managers. *Group and Organization Management, 18*, 153–187.

Oddou, G., Derr, C. B., & Black, J. S. (1995). Internationalizing managers: Expatriation and other strategies. In J. Selmer (Ed.), *Expatriate management: New ideas for international business* (pp. 3–16). Westport, CT: Quorum Books.

Olsen, E. (2004, February 2). U.S. try a census of expatriates. *International Herald Tribune*. Retrieved February 9, 2004, from http://www.iht.com/articles/127547.html.

Ones, D. S., & Viswesvaran, C. (1997). Personality determinants in the prediction of aspects of expatriate job success. In D. M. Saunders (Series Ed.) & Z. Aycan (Vol. Ed.), *New approaches to employee management: Vol. 4. Expatriate management: Theory and research* (pp. 63–92). Greenwich, CT: JAI Press.

Ones, D. S., & Viswesvaran, C. (1999), Relative importance of personality dimensions for expatriate selection: A policy capturing study. *Human Performance, 12*, 275–294.

Richards, D. (1996). Strangers in a strange land: Expatriate paranoia and the dynamics of exclusion. *International Journal of Human Resource Management, 7*, 553–571.

Roccas, S., Sagiv, L., & Knafo, A. (2002). The Big Five personality factors and personal values. *Personality and Social Psychology Bulletin, 28*, 789–801.

Ryan, A. M., McFarland, L., Baron, H., & Page, R. (1999). An international look at selection practices: Nation and culture as explanations for variability in practice. *Personnel Psychology, 52*, 359–391.

Salgado, J. F., Moscoso, S, & Lado, M. (2003). Evidence of cross-cultural invariance of the Big Five personality dimensions in work settings. *European Journal of Personality, 17*, S67–S76.

Salgado, J. F., Anderson, N., Moscoso, S., Bertua, C., & De Fruyt, F. (2003). International validity generalization of GMA and cognitive abilities: A European community meta-analysis. *Personnel Psychology, 56*, 573–605.

Schwartz, S. H. (1999). A theory of cultural values and some implications for work. *Applied Psychology: An International Review, 48*, 23–47.

Searle, W., & Ward, C. (1990). The prediction of psychological and sociocultural adjustment during cross-cultural transitions. *International Journal of Intercultural Relations, 14*, 449–464.

Selmer, J. (2001a). Psychological barriers to adjustment and how they affect coping strategies: Western business expatriates in China. *International Journal of Human Resource Management, 12*, 151–165.

Selmer, J. (2001b). Expatriate selection: Back to basics? *International Journal of Human Resource Management, 12*, 1219–1233.

Shaffer, M. A., & Harrison, D. A. (1998). Expatiates' psychological withdrawal from international assignments: Work, nonwork, and family influences. *Personnel Psychology, 51,* 87–117.

Shaffer, M. A., Harrison, D. A., & Gilley, K. M. (1999). Dimensions, determinants, and differences in the expatriate adjustment process. *Journal of International Business Studies, 30,* 557–582.

Smith, P. B., Peterson, M. F., Schwartz, S. H., Ahmad, A. H., Akande, D., Anderson, J. A., et al. (2002). Cultural values, sources of guidance, and their relevance to managerial behavior. A 47-nation study. *Journal of Cross-Cultural Psychology, 33,* 188–208.

Spreitzer, G. M., McCall, M. W., Jr., & Mahony, J. D. (1997). Early identification of international executive potential. *Journal of Applied Psychology, 82,* 6–29.

Takeuchi, R., Yun, S., & Russell, J. E. A. (2002). Antecedents and consequences of the perceived adjustment of Japanese expatriates in the USA. *International Journal of Human Resource Management, 13,* 1224–1244.

Takeuchi, R., Yun, S., & Tesluk, P. E. (2002). An examination of crossover and spillover effects of spousal and expatriate cross-cultural adjustment on expatriate outcomes. *Journal of Applied Psychology, 87,* 655–666.

Tung, R. L. (1981). Selection and training of personnel for overseas assignments. *Columbia Journal of World Business, 16,* 21–25.

Van Oudenhoven, J. P., & Van der Zee, K. I. (2002a). Predicting multicultural effectiveness of international students: The Multicultural Personality Questionnaire. *International Journal of Intercultural Relations, 26,* 679–694.

Van Oudenhoven, J. P., & Van der Zee, K. I. (2002b). Successful international cooperation: The influence of cultural similarity, strategic differences, and international experience. *Applied Psychology: An International Review, 51,* 633–653.

Van Vianen, A. E. M., De Pater, I. E., Kristof-Brown, A. L., & Johnson, E. C. (in press). Fitting in: Surface- and deep-level cultural differences and expatriates' adjustment. *Academy of Management Journal.*

Yukl, G., Fu, P. P., & McDonald, R. (2003). Cross-cultural differences in perceived effectiveness of influence tactics for initiating or resisting change. *Applied Psychology: An International Review, 52,* 68–82.

22

Selection for Teams

Natalie J. Allen and Michael A. West

Over the past twenty years, organizations and their employees have experienced many changes in the way work gets done. Prominent among these, particularly in the Western industrialized world, is the increased use of teams or work groups (e.g., Mohrman, Cohen, & Mohrman, 1995; Orsburn & Moran, 2000; Osterman, 1994, 2000; West 2003).

There are numerous reasons for the extensive use of teams. In many work situations, tasks have simply become so complicated that their performance requires a combination of knowledge, skills, and abilities that one person rarely possesses. Consequently, completing such tasks effectively requires that several people work in an interdependent fashion. Further, many organizations have become so much larger and/or more complex in their structures that activities must be closely coordinated, via teamwork, if organizational objectives are to be achieved (West & Markiewicz, 2003; West, Tjosvold, & Smith, 2003). Others argue that, in some situations, organizations have adopted teams because of their popularity elsewhere (e.g., Staw & Epstein, 2000), while others point to the psychological benefits (e.g., Allen & Hecht, in press) and to the fiscal and human resource advantages (Applebaum & Batt, 1994; Macy & Izumi, 1993) that can be associated with teamwork.

Despite the prevalence of teams in organizational settings, however, only a modest amount of research attention has been devoted to the issue of how best to select people for team-based work. Indeed, in contrast to research on the relationship between selection devices and individual job performance, research on predicting performance in teams is very much in the early stages. This likely reflects, at least in part, the complexities associated with this particular selection challenge.

The overall purpose of this chapter is to provide a research-focused overview of this challenge. First, though, it is important to describe what we mean by "teams" and to outline some organizational, team, and role characteristics that have been associated with optimized team functioning.

Conceptualizing and Designing Workplace Teams

Throughout the chapter, and consistent with others (e.g., Guzzo, 1996), the terms work group, group, work team, and team are used interchangeably. We use them to refer to two or more employees who are characterized by the following:

1. Team members have shared objectives in relation to their work.
2. Team members interact with each other in order to achieve those shared objectives.
3. Team members have more or less well-defined roles, some of which are differentiated from one another (for example, in a health care team, there are nurses, receptionists, and doctors).
4. Teams have an organizational identity – that is, they have a defined organizational function and see themselves as a group within the larger organization (e.g., the Research and Development department for a medium-sized manufacturing company).
5. Teams are not so large that they would be better defined as an organization. In practice this means that few are likely to exceed 20 members.

Long before selecting for a particular team, of course, it is critical that attention should be given to the design or structure of the work that team members will do and the roles they will occupy. Although several models of group effectiveness have been proposed, most represent variations of the Input–Process–Outcome (IPO) framework forwarded by Hackman (1987). Much of the specific research examining how to maximize team effectiveness has focused on input variables (e.g., see Campion, Medsker, & Higgs, 1993; Guzzo & Shea, 1992; West, 1996). Taken together, this work suggests that attention must be paid to several key team design principles, each of which has downstream implications for the design and implementation of team selection systems:

1. Individual roles within the teams should be necessary to the team. Prior to selection it is important to determine each team member's role and identify team and individual objectives in order that team members can see and demonstrate the value of their work to team success.
2. Individual roles should be meaningful and intrinsically rewarding. If individuals are to be selected who are committed and creative, then their team tasks must be rewarding, engaging, and challenging.
3. Individual contributions to the team should be identifiable and subject to evaluation. Those selected to work in teams not only have to feel that their work is important, but also that their performance will be visible to other team members.
4. The team should have an intrinsically motivating and interesting set of tasks to perform. Selecting motivated people to work in teams requires that team tasks are intrinsically engaging and challenging.
5. Perhaps of greatest importance, there should be clear team goals with clear team performance feedback.
6. The team should have a just sufficient number of members to successfully complete its task, but should not be so big that participation becomes difficult (Hackman, 1990; West, 2004).
7. The organization should provide adequate (though not necessarily abundant) resources to enable the team to achieve its targets or objectives (Payne, 1990). Resources include: having the right number and skill mix of people; adequate financial resources to enable effective functioning; necessary secretarial or administrative support; adequate accommodation; adequate technical assistance and support.

Selecting for Teams: An Overview of the Issues

Selecting the right individual for any job is a complex endeavor. Arguably, this is made even more complex when that individual is expected to work as part of a team. To further set the stage for our discussion of the relevant research literature, we outline some of the more specific issues that should be considered when evaluating strategies to select work team members. We raise these not because we can supply complete answers to the challenges they pose but, rather, to provide the reader with what we hope will be useful background to use when considering the existing research evidence.

Predictors of teamwork: Generic and specific considerations

In jobs that are not team-based, the selection challenge essentially involves determining what set of individual characteristics best predict how well candidates will perform the tasks involved in a particular job. Although most of these jobs and, hence, the selected individual's job performance, will likely involve activities that are influenced by other people within the work unit and/or organization, employee interdependence is less pronounced than it is in explicitly team-based work. Thus, in addition to selecting the person who will perform his/her job duties best, selecting for teams involves determining who will do so in a way that successfully takes account of this interdependence. It is not surprising, therefore, that one approach to team selection involves the search for generic characteristics that may make a person particularly "team-worthy." The basic premise underlying this approach, of course, is that some people are simply better suited to teamwork than are others and that this suitability generalizes across various types of teams and organizational settings. Is this generic suitability for teamwork considered a set of skills that can be developed? Or is it seen as more dispositional in nature? As we will see, the "team player" notion has been examined from both perspectives.

Another, perhaps complementary, approach that could be taken focuses on the characteristics that are specific to particular teams or types of teams. Needless to say, teams can vary enormously and on several dimensions and these variations can have important implications for selecting team members. Prominent among these are the types of task the team performs (e.g., Klimoski & Jones, 1995), although other team structure, design, contextual, and process characteristics are critically important as well (e.g., Paris, Salas, & Cannon-Bowers, 2000). All of these factors strongly suggest the need to begin the development of selection systems by conducting a *team-level* job/task analysis, something for which there has been repeated calls in the literature (e.g., Paris et al., 2000) but correspondingly little progress to date.

Validation at the individual, and group level

Against what criteria should strategies for team member selection be assessed? Some approaches to selecting for teamwork focus specifically on individual-level criteria such as peer or supervisor ratings of "teamwork" or individual job performance ratings. Validation at this level is relatively straightforward, with individual predictors examined in relation to whatever individual performance rating is used. It is clear, however, that selection for teamwork must also consider outcome measures that represent the collective activity of the team's members. Thus, team-level criteria can include such things as team innovation (e.g., West & Anderson, 1996), team viability (e.g., Barrick, Stewart, Neubert, & Mount, 1998), and team task performance. The case can certainly be made for examining both individual and group-level outcomes and for validating at both levels. After all, even when the job is team based, each "act of selection" involves the choice of an individual employee. Thus, it is reasonable to evaluate that person's work performance and to validate selection strategies at that level. Evaluation of team performance in the context of validation is also entirely reasonable.

It is important to note that, to date, relatively few validation efforts have considered both levels. Nor are such efforts without their complications. First, similar patterns of findings may not occur across the levels and there may be numerous trade-offs between predictor–criterion relations at different levels of analysis (for a more thorough discussion of selection from a multilevel perspective, see Ostroff, 2002; Ployhart & Schneider, 2002a, 2002b; Schmitt, 2002). The particular individual performance outcome that gets assessed may, or may not, represent a construct that overlaps sufficiently with that captured by the team-level outcome. And, even if this construct overlap is substantial, processes within the team (or factors external to the team) may well impede the straightforward "translation" of individual efforts/performance into team accomplishment.

A second complication involves the derivation of (group-level) team composition with respect to the predictor in question. That is, in most situations, the assessment of predictor–criterion relations at the group level first requires a strategy for combining the relevant characteristic, across team members, to produce a team-level measure of composition (e.g., "team extraversion"; "team KSAs"). As we will see, there are numerous strategies for doing so, each with its own logic. Typically, team-level "predictors" have been derived by averaging the individual scores across the team. Team composition has also been operationalized, however, in terms of the team's lowest scorer, the team's highest scorer, and the variability across within-team scores.

Team history, time and change

A further complication is that some situations involve several personnel who are being selected to form newly created teams while, in others, a single individual is being selected to fill a spot in an already existing team. If one takes the perspective that there are generic characteristics that will serve an individual well regardless of the teams he or she is being selected for, this issue has little relevance. Nor is it relevant in the case of characteristics that have been validated in particular types of teams and are being applied to those types of teams. Selection based on such characteristics would proceed in a traditional, top-down fashion regardless of the team's history or its existing composition. This issue *is* relevant, however, if one takes the perspective that *variability* in the to-be-selected-for characteristic enhances team performance. Knowing that existing team members are "high to moderate" on the characteristic, for example, would mean that a "low" scoring candidate would be the most appropriate choice. It will also be relevant if one takes the perspective that team performance is optimized by having a particular blend of members who represent different personal styles or personality types. Team composition theories of this sort argue that a team needs types A, B, C, and D. Knowing that existing members represent A, B, and D types makes it clear that a "Type C" candidate would be the most appropriate choice.

A related issue, under this general banner of team history/time, has to do with "maturity" or "life cycle" of the team. Quite possibly this has implications for the kind of validation studies researchers design. Would we be wiser, for example, to validate potential selection techniques against the "early stage" performance of teams (and their members) or to wait until the team is more established and, hence, its members have had a chance to go through whatever developmental stages are needed to arrive at their "typical" performance? To our knowledge, this validation issue has received no research attention. In a related vein, however, LePine (2003) recently examined relations between team composition and team adaptation to unforeseen change. His results suggest the intriguing possibility that the team member characteristics that predict performance in routine situations may not be useful in predicting performance in changing situations.

Selecting for Teams: Some Relevant Research

Despite all these complications, and the limitations in the selection literature, the psychological literature on groups is extensive and contains much relevant information. In what follows, we provide an overview of research that specifically focuses on selecting for teams and, in addition, we draw together relevant information from other areas of research within the groups literature. In doing so, we address two distinct, but related questions: 1) What characterizes the "team-worthy" individual? and 2) What do we know about the composition of groups and teams that may be relevant to the issue of selection?

Selecting "team-worthy" employees

Typically, individuals are recruited and selected to work as part of a group because they have the particular set of knowledge, skills, and abilities deemed necessary for particular aspects of the job. This is, of course, entirely reasonable and such "individual-task KSAs" (Klimoski & Jones, 1995, p. 308) must be given serious attention. Also reasonable, however, would be an examination of the degree to which candidates have the personal characteristics necessary to work effectively as part of a team. Indeed, since it is unlikely that people are equally well suited to, or interested in, group-based work, characteristics of this sort may well play an important role in the recruiting and selection of group members.

This approach, then, is based on the premise that some people are simply psychologically better suited to team-based work than are others. Note, this approach does not typically involve a consideration of the nature of the team, the particular tasks the team does, or who else is (or may become) part of the team. Rather the approach takes a generic look for "team-worthy" characteristics. Research to date is suggestive, though limited and hardly conclusive, that such characteristics might exist. Some researchers who take this approach focus on inclinations toward, or preference for, group-based activity; others emphasize teamwork skills.

Orientations toward groups. It seems clear that people differ somewhat in their interest in, or orientation toward, working in groups – a difference that is most strongly reflected in their choice of group activity over solo activity (Kelly & Allen, 2002) and their satisfaction with group activity (e.g., Campion et al., 1993). Both theoretical and empirical work, however, have also suggested a link between orientation toward group-based activity and behavior/performance in groups. In an early study, Davis (1969) asked participants whether they preferred working individually or in groups. When groups were given a task that was both divisible and benefited from interaction among members, those that were composed of people with a preference for group work performed better than did groups whose members preferred to work alone. More recently, Shaw, Duffy, and Stark (2000) reported that preference for work groups interacted with task interdependence in the prediction of performance. Specifically, individuals with a strong preference for group work performed better in groups than their low preference counterparts when they perceived that the task required interdependent activity. Under conditions perceived to be low in task interdependence, a reverse pattern was observed. Although more research examining this interaction is needed, these results suggest that managers who base team member selection on preference for group work should do only if the team's activities are truly interdependent. Some would suggest, however, that the point is moot – arguing that because task interdependence represents a defining feature of work groups, the only "true groups" *are* those with task interdependence.

Although it sets the stage for thinking about team selection based on group preference, little of the above research was designed with this particular issue in mind. Indeed, Kline (1999a) describes the Team Player Inventory as the "only measure that is specifically designed to assess predisposition of individuals toward working in teams" (p. 108). She provides evidence of the reliability of this ten-item measure, and using personality scales, evidence of its convergent and discriminant validity, but notes that, of the three samples used in the development of the measure, two were student samples. Further, criterion-related validity information is limited to date. The measure has been shown to correlate with the number of team or group activities in which respondents have participated, but its direct relation to performance in teams has not been established (Kline, 1999a, 1999b).

Teamwork skills. Another approach to "team worthiness" focuses on skills or competencies that may be needed when working in a team. Several years ago, Cannon-Bowers, Tannenbaum, Salas, and Volpe (1995) distinguished between team-specific and team-generic competencies. The latter include individually held communication skills, leadership skills, and interpersonal skills and are hypothesized to influence team performance directly and to do so regardless of the characteristics of other team members. To date, this distinction has been used more to inform the training, than the selection, of team members (Cannon-Bowers et al., 1995). Given that this training research has demonstrated the value of the general competencies framework, however, it seems reasonable to suggest that the assessment of generic team skills might be implemented into a system aimed at selecting the most team worthy.

Stevens and Campion (1994) also emphasize generic teamwork skills. In taking this approach, they argued that because knowledge, skills, and abilities (KSAs) are better predictors of individual job performance than are personality attributes, this is also likely to be the case for teamwork. Based on the literature on team functioning, they identified two broad skill areas (interpersonal KSAs and self-management KSAs) consisting of a total of 14 specific KSA requirements for effective teamwork. From this taxonomy, Stevens and Campion (1999) developed the 35-item multiple choice Teamwork KSA Test in which respondents are presented with challenges they may face in the workplace and asked to identify the strategy they would most likely follow. Using both supervisor and peer ratings of individual job performance, Stevens and Campion report substantial criterion-related validities, some in excess of .50. Given its very substantial correlations with employment aptitude test (.91–.99), however, it seems clear that the test has a significant cognitive ability component, an issue that Stevens and Campion acknowledge. They report, however, that this measure added, albeit quite modestly, to the prediction of individual performance, over and above that contributed by such employment tests.

Since its development, the Teamwork KSA Test has been used in at least three other published studies. In their study of ad hoc student teams, McClough and Rogelberg (2003) reported that test scores predicted individual team performance as assessed by both peers (team mates) and observers who were external to the team, thus contributing further validity information. Chen, Donahue, and Klimoski (2004) reported two findings of some relevance to validity: 1) that students given a team training course subsequently scored higher on the test than control group students and 2) that relations between cognitive ability and test scores ($r = .40$, $.42$, pre- and post-training, respectively) were weaker, although still significant, than those reported in Stevens and Campion's (1999) work. Expressing concerns that the Teamwork KSA Test had only been validated at the individual level, however, Miller (2001) examined the relations between test scores and performance at the team level of analysis. In this study, which also used student teams, there was no significant relation between mean Teamwork KSA Test scores and team performance. Based on this finding and the test's strong relation with cognitive ability, Miller suggests that the test "may actually be measuring individual rather than team potential" (p. 760) and questions its value as a tool to select members for high-performance teams. To date, then, available evidence regarding this test paints a fairly mixed picture. First, it seems clear that the test has a strong cognitive ability component – not surprising, perhaps, in a paper-and-pencil "knowledge based" test. With respect to this, Miller makes the cogent point that, although cognitively able individuals have knowledge about the skills needed for teamwork, they may not necessarily have acquired and/or mastered these skills. Further, although there is some evidence that the test contributes incremental validity, this increment may not be enough to warrant its inclusion in selection systems that already incorporate cognitive ability. For those that do not, the Teamwork KSAs Test may be more appropriate. Second, the evidence strongly suggests that the test predicts individual performance in teams. At the team level, results are less promising although, clearly, further research of this sort is needed.

Overall, then, there is some evidence to suggest that the generic teamwork approach may have merit in predicting individual performance in, and adjustment to, teams. People who seem more oriented toward teams – in terms of preferences, personal styles, and KSAs – are seen as better "team players" by their team mates and perform their jobs better. Of some promise, although requiring additional investigation, are two self-report measures designed for the selection context: the Team Player Inventory (Kline, 1999a) and the Team-work Test (Stevens & Campion, 1999).

As we noted at the beginning of this section, this approach has focused on the problem of selecting individuals who are best suited to work in teams. Not unreasonably, then, atten-tion has focused on the individual and the individual's behavior/performance outcomes, rather than the member composition of the individual's team and/or the team's collective performance. How these generic "team-worthy" characteristics – or indeed, other relevant characteristics – play themselves in terms of producing *combinations* of people who, as a group, perform better has yet to be clearly established. Thus, for example, we know little about the impact of introducing a strong team player into any of the various "combina-tions" that existing teams could represent (e.g., a group of all weak, or all strong, team players; a group with some weak, some strong). We turn now to an examination of group-level research that focuses – from varying perspectives – on the membership composition of teams.

Team composition research

Team composition – used here to refer to the "mix" of members making up a team – has been examined in various ways. Although these have not yet been applied explicitly to the problem of team selection, each has considerable relevance for it. The reader will note some overlap between the lines of team composition research that we identify here. Both for simplicity and in order to reflect the traditions from which they originate, however, we have organized our discussion as follows. "Diversity research" conceptualizes team com-position in terms of the variability of one (or more) team member characteristics. As its not-very-catchy name implies, "Research using other team composition measures" goes beyond this and considers alternate ways of operationalizing team composition (i.e., group means; lowest, and highest, scores in the group). Finally, in the "Teams as jigsaw puzzles" section we describe research in which team composition is viewed as being specific blends of various personal characteristics.

Diversity research.   In this line of research, the basic strategy is to assess team members with respect to particular characteristics and ask the very general question of whether hetero-geneity (or diversity) is advantageous or disadvantageous to groups and their members. Is it "better" to put together a group whose members are quite different from each other? Or is group functioning disadvantaged by such diversity? Both arguments have been made. Theoretically, it has been argued that heterogeneity will serve the group by providing a wide range of perspectives and, hence, performance enhancement. On the other hand, it seems possible that heterogeneity can increase team process difficulties (less clear commu-nication, interpersonal challenges) and, hence, diminish performance.

Clearly, group members can differ from each other in a wide variety of ways and, hence, diversity research has had many guises (see Williams & O'Reilly, 1998, for a review). Research in this area has tended to focus on heterogeneity in terms of demographic variables, skills, attitudes, cognitive ability, and, more recently, personality traits. Although much of the early research on group heterogeneity examined experimental laboratory-based groups, focus on "real-world" groups has typified more recent research in this area; it is on this latter work that we focus most attention here. In our discussion of the team heterogeneity research, however, we leave aside those findings that involve demographic variables. To be sure, this line of research provides intriguing insights into issues such as the recruitment, socialization, and retention of team members as well as the management of diversity more generally. In the absence of bona fide requirements that employees be members of particular demographic groups, however, it seems neither wise, nor likely, that demographic variables would be used to inform selection decisions.

Some studies suggest facilitative effects of heterogeneity on team performance. This pattern is most likely when the characteristics in question are skills or educational specialization. Wiersema and Bantel (1992), for example, reported that strategic management initiatives were more likely to be made by groups that were heterogeneous with respect to educational specialization, while Bantel (1993) reported that banks whose teams were heterogeneous with respect to education and functional background developed clearer corporate strategies (see also Bantel & Jackson, 1989). More recently, in a study of primary health care teams, Borrill, West, Shapiro, and Rees (2000) found that the greater the number of professional groups represented in the team, the higher the levels of innovation in patient care. It might be that skill heterogeneity means that each group member is more likely to have non-redundant – and, presumably, relevant – expertise to contribute to the team activities. In one sense, then, these sorts of results may simply reflect appropriate staffing: individuals have been chosen who have the necessary skills and job experience to carry out their particular duties within the team. Interestingly, however, Dunbar (1997) noted that groups that include both diverse *and* overlapping knowledge domains and skills are particularly creative.

Some debate has surrounded the question of whether it is advantageous to have groups that are homogeneous or heterogeneous with respect to cognitive ability and, indeed, results of two recent meta-analyses suggest that the relation between ability heterogeneity and performance may be somewhat complex. Based on their analysis, Bowers, Pharmer, and Salas (2000) concluded that, in general, ability heterogeneity and performance are unrelated. Although they examined potential moderators, their analysis simultaneously examined other forms of heterogeneity (e.g., personality, gender); thus, it is not possible to isolate the moderators of particular relevance to ability. More recently, however, Devine and Philips (2001) focused exclusively on team composition based on ability and came to a somewhat similar conclusion about the link between cognitive ability heterogeneity and group performance. Thus, there would seem little justification to select team members with a view to dispersing their cognitive ability levels. Devine and Philips also examined alternate ways of operationalizing team-level cognitive ability; these findings are addressed in the following section.

Finally, the Bowers et al. (2000) meta-analysis also examined heterogeneity with respect to personality and found little relation between it and team performance. On the basis of this at least, there seems no evidence to support selecting for trait diversity (or homogeneity) within a team. Unfortunately, for those seeking information about the value of doing so with respect to specific traits or personality dimension, the Bowers et al. (2000) study provides relatively little guidance. Although studies included in the meta-analysis covered a wide range of traits, effects due to particular traits were not isolated; that is, only trait homogeneity (and not trait type) was accounted for in the meta-analysis. Fortunately, over the past few years, attention has been paid to the relations between heterogeneity on *specific* traits and team outcomes. Because this same research also examines other ways of operationalizing team-level "personality," we summarize these findings together in the next section.

Research using other team composition measures
Cognitive ability. In the review mentioned above, Devine and Philips (2001) meta-analytically addressed the question posed in the title of their article, "Do smarter teams do better?". In addition to team heterogeneity (see above), they operationalized team cognitive ability (CA) in terms of the mean, lowest scorer, and highest scorer. Each had a modest, positive relation to team performance (ranging from .21 to .29). Although this suggests, at first blush, that teams might be well served by selection strategies that take CA into account, it appeared that these relations were likely moderated by other variables. Only the relation involving mean CA was amenable to this analysis and, of the various moderator possibilities, Devine and Philips were only able to code for one: study setting. Interestingly, they found that the CA–performance relation was much stronger in laboratory-based studies than in those conducted in organizational settings and that, within the organizational sub-sample, substantial variation in the magnitude of the effects was observed across studies. What is not yet clear from this, then, is which features of teams make CA more or less relevant to staffing. Based on this finding, as well as findings in the individual-level CA literature and theorizing about teams and their tasks, Devine and Philips (2001) quite reasonably suggest that task complexity is a possibility – and one that requires further research attention.

Personality. Over the past few years, several team composition researchers have also focused on relations between team performance (and team viability) and the personality characteristics of team members, in particular as conceptualized using the five-factor (Big Five) model. As mentioned above, researchers have operationalized "team personality" in several ways. Typically, this is done using mean, variability, maximum scorer, minimum scorer approaches, although researchers have also used other approaches that rely on normative levels of the trait in question (Barry & Stewart, 1997). Two general comments can be made with respect to the observed pattern of results. First, while they do not *defy* succinct summary, they certainly challenge it. Second, and likely related to the first, they point – once again! – to the importance of carefully considering the team's task and its design/structure.

Of the Big Five traits, team-level conscientiousness has received the most research attention. In at least three studies (Barrick et al., 1998; Neuman, Wagner, & Christiansen, 1999; Neuman & Wright, 1999) the mean conscientiousness of the team predicted team performance. In contrast, Barry and Stewart (1997) reported no relation between team-level conscientiousness and performance on student teams conducting academically oriented problem-solving tasks. They suggested that the nature of the tasks might have accounted for this. LePine (2003) examined the two aspects of conscientiousness (achievement and dependability) separately using the mean approach; neither predicted routine task performance but, interestingly, both predicted performance when the team was faced with an unforeseen change. High-achievement teams adapted particularly well to a change; the reverse was found for high-dependability teams. Although neither the "highest scorer" nor "variability" forms of team-level conscientiousness have fared all that well as predictors of team performance, the "lowest scorer" form has done so (Barrick et al., 1998; Neuman & Wright, 1999). The idea here is that, particularly in highly interdependent tasks, the lowest scorer will behave as a true "weakest link," constraining performance by his/her degree of conscientiousness. There are, however, team factors that will moderate this effect. Consider, for example, teams with formal, high-status leaders. Those in which the leaders themselves have low conscientiousness show no team member conscientiousness effect on performance; in essence, such leaders serve to "neutralize the effect of good staff" (LePine, Hollenbeck, Ilgen, & Hedlund, 1997, p. 807).

Turning to the trait of extraversion, Barry and Stewart (1997) reported that although, at the individual level, extraverts were viewed by their team mates as having greater impact on the team's performance, overall performance was higher among teams that had only a *moderate* proportion of high-extraversion members. Mean extraversion, however, was correlated with team viability (but not performance) in the Barrick et al. (1998) study of manufacturing teams and the "lowest scorer" operationalization of team extraversion was correlated with both team viability and team performance. In order words, at least for additive tasks, teams do better if none of their members is particularly introverted, but neither do they require high levels of extraversion across the entire team. This latter point is consistent with Neuman et al. (1999)'s finding that, although mean extraversion was unrelated to team performance, variability in extraversion was related. Of the remaining Big Five traits, only agreeableness has received sufficient attention to warrant discussion here. Overall, the evidence suggests that team agreeableness, operationalized in terms of both the mean (Barrick et al., 1998; Neuman et al., 1999) and lowest score (Barrick et al., 1998; Neuman & Wright, 1999), is related to team performance, but that agreeableness based on the highest score measure is unrelated to performance (Neuman & Wright, 1999). As with extraversion, and perhaps not surprisingly, having a very disagreeable team member may not serve teams well.

So where does all this leave us from a selection perspective? In general, it seems that, as in individual performance literature, conscientiousness plays a particularly important role. Diversity is not helpful on this trait. And, in general, the more conscientiousness, the better. Further, particularly for some types of tasks, having even one member who is low in conscientiousness may jeopardize performance. Team member conscientiousness, however, cannot carry all the freight here. If the group has a leader with formal status, his/her conscientiousness will moderate any of these effects; thus it is critical that this person be strongly conscientious (LePine et al., 1997). Overall, it seems reasonable to suggest that selecting those with high levels of trait conscientiousness will serve most teams well. It is important to recognize, however, that recent work using this construct (e.g.,

LePine, Colquitt, & Erez, 2000) suggests that it may have two facets: achievement and dependability, and that, for some kinds of tasks/environments, these may have differential predictions for performance (LePine, 2003). For extraversion and agreeableness, how high the overall "level" in the group is may not matter as much as the level of its lowest member. Thus, the message for selection is that, all else being equal, "aberrant" introverts and disagreeable candidates might be avoided when composing a team.

Teams as jigsaw puzzles: achieving the "right mix." It could be argued that jigsaw puzzles represent a reasonable team metaphor. As in such puzzles, the differently shaped "pieces" (people) must "fit together" or complement each other in a particular fashion. The underlying premise of this approach is that team heterogeneity – on key personal characteristics – is critical for team success, but that this variation must occur in a specific form or pattern. Obviously, work that takes this perspective could conceptualize these "people/pieces" in terms of numerous personal characteristics. For the most part, however, the focus has been on skills and on personality or personal style.

Skill mix. Obviously, team performance depends on the competencies of team members. Taking this theme further, a currently popular notion, particularly within teams in health service settings (NHSME, 1992), is that of skill mix. Skill mix is defined as "the balance between trained and untrained, qualified and unqualified, and supervisory and operative staff within a service area as well as between different staff groups . . . Optimum skill mix is achieved when the desired standard of service is provided, at the minimum cost, which is consistent with the efficient deployment of trained, qualified and supervisory personnel and the maximization of contributions from all staff members. It will ensure the best possible use of scarce professional skills to maximize the service to clients." A skill mix review involves discovering what activities need to be carried out within the team; who is currently doing them; the skill level of people doing them; the minimum level of skill required to do them; and the potential for combining tasks in new ways to create in some case new roles and staff groupings. This orientation to selecting for teams therefore focuses on the identification of particular technical skills required by the team that are not already supplied, or are supplied at higher cost, by others in the team. Finally, in thinking about this issue, it is important to note that the skill mix required by some teams may well fluctuate over time as they undergo changes in focus, technology, or positioning within the organization.

Personality and personal styles. Given that team members must frequently interact with each other, the extent of their personal compatibility would seem to play an important part in team effectiveness. What personality types work best together? What mix of personalities is needed for a team to be effective? In what ways must group members be compatible in order to work together effectively? For the most part, personal compatibility approaches have not fared well in the research literature.

Several years ago, Schutz (1955, 1958, 1967) proposed the theory of fundamental interpersonal relations orientations (FIRO) to explain that how people express their basic needs for inclusion, control, and affection influences interaction in groups. In essence, he described compatible groups as those in which the initiation and receipt of the needs were balanced. For example, a group would be balanced, with respect to the affection dimension, if the overall desire to receive affection among group members was similar to the amount given within the group. When compared to incompatible groups, where such a balance does not exist, compatible groups are expected to perform particularly well. Although there some research evidence in support of this general prediction, overall, it is neither strong nor consistent across studies (e.g., Moos & Speisman, 1962; Reddy & Byrnes, 1972; Shaw & Webb, 1982). Unfortunately, it is not clear whether this is due to theoretical misinterpretation (see Schutz, 1992) or to psychometric inadequacies of the FIRO-B, the measure that Schutz originally developed to assess inclusion, control, and affection (e.g., Hurley, 1989, 1990, 1991, 1992; Salminen, 1988, 1991).

Another popular approach to team personality issues, particularly in the UK, is Belbin's Team Roles Model (Belbin, 1981, 1993). Belbin suggests that there are nine team personality types and that a balance of these team personality types is required within teams. These include the coordinator – a person-oriented leader; the shaper – a task-focused leader; the plant – the creative person within the group; the resource investigator – who explores opportunities and develops contacts; the implementer – who works for the team in a practical and realistic way; the monitor evaluator – who prudently judges quality of decisions; the team worker – who makes helpful interventions to avert potential friction and maintain team spirit; the completer finisher – who aims to complete and to do so thoroughly; and the specialist – who provides knowledge and technical skills within the team. Belbin argues that a balance of all nine team roles is required for a team to perform effectively. Individuals usually incorporate several of these team role types in their personality profiles and so, within teams of only three or four individuals, there may nevertheless be primary and secondary team role types which cover the nine areas of team role functioning. However, there is little evidence to support these predictions. Further, although there is some disagreement on this point (e.g., Swailes & McIntyre-Bhatty, 2002), the instruments developed to measure the team role types do not appear to have good psychometric properties (Anderson & Sleap, in press; Broucek & Randell, 1996; Furnham, Steele, & Pendleton, 1993). In light of this, the widespread use of the Belbin model in organizational settings is curious.

IMPLICATIONS FOR RESEARCH AND PRACTICE

In this chapter, we have taken a broad look at issues involving team selection and composition. The existing research in these areas can serve as a guide, we feel, for both researchers and practitioners. Though it is certainly premature to make definitive statements about how best to select for, and structure, work teams, much of practical use has been learned. In addition, the existing research highlights some directions in which future research could profitably head.

What are the implications of this research? Of some promise, we feel, is work on the development of selection instruments assessing the generic suitability of individuals for teamwork (e.g., Kline, 1999a; Stevens & Campion, 1999). At the practical level, this research reminds us that there is indeed individual variation in team-worthiness and that, though some might prefer to believe otherwise, teamwork may not be for everyone. Clearly, however, there is not yet consensus as to whether individual suitability for teams is best thought of in terms of personality, knowledge, skills, or abilities. Moreover, much validation work is needed, in particular at the group level of analysis. While individual performance criteria are important, and possibly critical, in order to defend the use of such predictors in selection, team-level performance criteria must also be incorporated into further validation studies. Though this will add considerable complexity to validation efforts, failing to do so is to ignore the fact that, ultimately, the products or services provided by team members are the result of their collective efforts. The critical need for job/task analysis done at the team level is also made evident, we would argue, by the complex pattern of findings emerging from recent research that examines personality at the team level (e.g., Barrick et al., 1998; LePine, 2003; Neuman et al., 1999) in which observed relations between team composition and performance vary considerably as a function of team tasks and team design factors.

In general, the notion that particular combinations of personal styles or personalities are needed to produce particularly successful teams has received very little support. At this point it is not entirely clear why this is the case, leaving us somewhat reluctant to abandon the general idea completely. Unquestionably, adequate tests of this idea are cumbersome and difficult to conduct as they require multiple groups and, across these groups, multiple representations of the various "people combinations" outlined in the theory in question. Further, it may well be that this approach has merit, but that existing theories about "what goes with what" are off the mark – perhaps because we have spent too little time examining and describing how effective and ineffective teams differ. To return to the jigsaw puzzle analogy used earlier, in order to know which pieces of the puzzle to choose and where to place them, one needs to know what the puzzle ought to look like. Once again, team-level job (or task) analyses, augmented with good descriptive studies of team behavior (e.g., Ancona, 1990; Gersick & Hackman, 1990), could provide this sort of information.

Turning to another of our streams of team composition research, it is clear that differences between team members do have implications. Groups do seem to be advantaged, for example, by heterogeneity with respect to types of expertise or skills. Increasingly, organizations will want to examine heterogeneity of expertise to find not only a skill mix that will work, but one that will do so in the most cost-effective manner. We suggest that such efforts should go beyond traditional performance variables and consider skill/expertise mixes that will enhance such things as group and individual innovation (West, 2004), boundary-spanning (Ancona, 1990), the ability of the group to modify its habits when necessary (Gersick & Hackman, 1990), and team viability (e.g., Barrick et al., 1998). Each of these has been identified as important outcomes yet they have received less formal attention than they deserve.

In addition, we recommend that team leaders be selected, not only for their cognitive ability and conscientiousness (LePine et al., 1997), but also for their ability to deal with team composition effects. At its core, this may require the ability to mobilize team members under a common banner. Strategies may include: the articulation by the leader of clear team-based goals, the use of socialization tactics that focus on what team members have in common rather than how they differ, and the development of mentoring relationships that capitalize on mentor/mentoree similarity (Anderson & Thomas, 1996). Team leaders will need to be able to do all this while, at the same time, maintaining the differentiation among roles that provide team members with a sense of their unique contribution to the team. Above all, they need to facilitate the exploration and integration of diverse, and often conflicting, viewpoints and to do so in ways that enable teams to derive benefits from the variety therein. These benefits could include enhanced creativity and innovation, as well as skill sharing and team member development.

Finally, as with other team/group issues, those interested in staffing cannot ignore the growing consensus among researchers that the effectiveness of teams is strongly dependent upon supports supplied by the organizational context within which the team is located (Guzzo & Shea, 1992; Hackman, 1990). By organizational supports we are referring to technical and training assistance available to the group, information systems enabling the group to set goals and plan performance, resources available to the group (staff, equipment, money), constraints in the work technology, and the structure of the reward systems within the organization. If team members are encouraged to work interdependently, for example, yet are rewarded only in terms of individual performance, what message is the organization sending about the value of teamwork (Allen, 1996)? Other elements of the organizational context include the structure of, and climate within, the organization. If the organizational structure is hierarchical and the climate authoritarian, for example, the effectiveness of teamwork may be limited, since team members will be unlikely to have the autonomy and control needed to maximize the benefits accruing from team performance. In short, the organization must provide a context that reinforces the notion that teamwork is valuable and valued. Taken together, the research and practitioner literature suggests that organizational support for teams may be the exception rather than the rule. From a staffing perspective, this is of considerable concern. Indeed, we would argue that, in the long run, any payoffs associated with selecting the best person for the team will be severely limited if organizational supports for teamwork are not in place.

In a recent review of personnel selection conducted during the final years of the 20th century, Hough and Oswald (2000) referred to team member selection as an emerging topic. In order to make the necessary advances on this emerging topic, we need research that develops our understanding of relations – at multiple levels – among team member characteristics, structure, processes, contexts, and outcomes. To be sure, some of this groundwork has been laid, but a great deal more is needed.

References

Allen, N. J. (1996). Affective reactions to the group and the organization. In M. A. West (Ed.), *Handbook of work group psychology* (pp. 371–396). Chichester, UK: John Wiley & Sons.

Allen, N. J., & Hecht, T. D. (in press). The "romance of teams": Toward an understanding of its psychological underpinnings and implications. *Journal of Occupational and Organizational Psychology.*

Ancona, D. G. (1990). Outward bound: Strategies for team survival in an organization. *Academy of Management Journal, 33,* 334–365.

Anderson, N. R., & Sleap, S. (in press). An evaluation of gender differences on the Belbin team role self-perception inventory. *Journal of Organizational Behavior.*

Anderson, N. R., & Thomas, H. D. C. (1996). Work group socialization. In M. A. West (Ed.). *The handbook of work group psychology* (pp. 423–450). Chichester, UK: John Wiley & Sons.

Applebaum, E., & Batt, R. (1994). *The new American workplace*. Ithaca, NY: ILR Press.

Bantel, K. A. (1993). Strategic clarity in banking: Role of top management team demography. *Psychological Reports, 73*, 1187–1201.

Bantel, K. A., & Jackson, S. E. (1989). Top management and innovations in banking: Does the composition of the top team make a difference? *Strategic Management Journal, 10*, 107–124.

Barrick, M. R., Stewart, G. L., Neubert, M. J., & Mount, M. K. (1998). Relating member ability and personality to work-team processes and team effectiveness. *Journal of Applied Psychology, 83*, 377–391.

Barry, B., & Stewart, G. L. (1997). Composition, process, and performance in self-managed groups: The role of personality. *Journal of Applied Psychology, 82*, 62–78.

Belbin, R. M. (1981). *Management teams: Why they succeed or fail*. London: Heinemann.

Belbin, R. M. (1993). *Team roles at work: A strategy for human resource management*. Oxford, UK: Butterworth, Heinemann.

Borrill, C., West, M. A., Shapiro, D., & Rees, A. (2000). Team working and effectiveness in health care. *British Journal of Health Care, 6*, 364–371.

Bowers, C. A., Pharmer, J. A., & Salas, E. (2000). When member homogeneity is needed in work groups: A meta-analysis. *Small Group Research, 31*, 305–327.

Broucek, W. G., & Randell, G. (1996). An assessment of the construct validity of the Belbin Self-Perception Inventory and Observer's Assessment from the perspective of the five-factor model. *Journal of Occupational and Organizational Psychology, 69*, 389–405.

Campion, M. A., Medsker, G. J., & Higgs, A. C. (1993). Relations between work group characteristics and effectiveness: Implications for designing effective work groups. *Personnel Psychology, 46*, 823–850.

Cannon-Bowers, J. A., Tannenbaum, S. I., Salas, E., & Volpe, C. E. (1995). Defining competencies and establishing team training requirements. In R. Guzzo & E. Salas (Eds.), *Team effectiveness and decision-making in organizations* (pp. 333–380). San Francisco: Jossey-Bass.

Chen, G., Donahue, L. M., & Klimoski, R. J. (2004). Training undergraduates to work in organizational teams. *Academy of Management: Learning and Education, 3*, 27–40.

Davis, J. H. (1969). Individual-group problem solving, subject preference, and problem type. *Journal of Personality and Social Psychology, 13*, 362–374.

Devine, D. J., & Philips, J. L. (2001). Do smarter teams do better?: A meta-analysis of cognitive ability and team performance. *Small Group Research, 32*, 507–532.

Dunbar, K. (1997). How scientists think: On-line creativity and conceptual change in science. In T. B. Ward, S. M. Smith, & J. Vaid (Eds.), *Creative thought: An investigation of conceptual structures and processes* (pp. 461–493). Washington, DC: American Psychological Association.

Furnham, A., Steele, H., & Pendleton, D. (1993). A psychometric assessment of the Belbin Team-Role Self-Perception Inventory. *Journal of Occupational and Organizational Psychology, 66*, 245–257.

Gersick, C. J., & Hackman, J. R. (1990). Habitual routines in task-performing groups. *Organizational Behavior and Human Decision Processes, 47*, 65–97.

Guzzo, R. A. (1996). Fundamental considerations about work groups. In M. A. West (Ed.), *The handbook of work group psychology* (pp. 3–23). Chichester, UK: John Wiley & Sons.

Guzzo, R. A., & Shea, G. P. (1992). Group performance and inter group relations in organizations. In M. D. Dunnette & L. M. Hough (Eds.), *Handbook of industrial and organizational psychology* (Vol. 3, pp. 269–313). Palo Alto, CA: Consulting Psychologists Press.

Hackman, J. R. (1987). The design of work teams. In J. Lorsch (Ed.), *Handbook of organizational behavior* (pp. 315–342). Englewood Cliffs, NJ: Prentice-Hall.

Hackman, J. R. (Ed.). (1990). *Groups that work (and those that don't): Creating conditions for effective teamwork.* San Francisco: Jossey-Bass.

Hough, L. M., & Oswald, F. L. (2000). Personnel selection: Looking toward the future – remembering the past. *Annual Review of Psychology, 51,* 631–664.

Hurley, J. R. (1989). Dubious support for FIRO-B's validity. *Psychological Reports, 65,* 929–930.

Hurley, J. R. (1990). Does FIRO-B relate better to interpersonal or intrapersonal behavior? *Journal of Clinical Psychology, 46,* 454–460.

Hurley, J. R. (1991). FIRO-B's dissociation from two central dimensions of interpersonal behavior. *Psychological Reports, 68,* 243–254.

Hurley, J. R. (1992). Further evidence against the construct validity of the FIRO-B scales. *Psychological Reports, 70,* 639–640.

Kelly, E. C., & Allen, N. J. (2002, May). *Choosing group versus individual work.* Paper presented at the meeting of the Canadian Psychological Association, Vancouver, BC.

Klimoski, R., & Jones, R. G. (1995). Staffing for effective group decision making: Key issues in matching people and teams. In R. A. Guzzo & E. Salas (Eds.), *Team effectiveness and decision making in organizations* (pp. 291–332). San Francisco: Jossey-Bass.

Kline, T. J. B. (1999a). The Team Player Inventory: Reliability and validity of a measure of predisposition towards organizational team working environments. *Journal for Specialists in Group Work, 24,* 102–112.

Kline, T. J. B. (1999b). *Remaking teams: The revolutionary research-based guide that puts theory into practice.* San Francisco: Jossey-Bass/Pfeiffer.

LePine, J. A. (2003). Team member adaptation and postchange performance: Effects of team composition in terms of members' cognitive ability and personality. *Journal of Applied Psychology, 88,* 27–39.

LePine, J. A., Colquitt, J. A., & Erez, A. (2000). Adaptability to changing task contexts: Effects of general cognitive ability, conscientiousness, and openness to experience. *Personnel Psychology, 53,* 563–593.

LePine, J. A., Hollenbeck, J. R., Ilgen, D. R., & Hedlund, J. (1997). Effects of individual differences on the performance of hierarchical decision-making teams: Much more than g. *Journal of Applied Psychology, 82,* 803–811.

Macy, B. A., & Izumi, H. (1993). Organizational change, design, and work innovation: A meta-analysis of 131 North American field studies – 1961–1991. *Research in Organizational Change and Development, 7,* 235–313.

McClough, A. C., & Rogelberg, S. G. (2003). Selection in teams: An exploration of the Teamwork Knowledge, Skills, and Ability Test. *International Journal of Selection and Assessment, 11,* 53–64.

Miller, D. L. (2001). Reexamining teamwork KSAs and team performance. *Small Group Research, 32,* 745–766.

Mohrman, S. A., Cohen, S. G., & Mohrman, A. M. (1995). *Designing team-based organizations: New forms for knowledge work.* San Francisco: Jossey-Bass.

Moos, R. H., & Speisman, J. C. (1962). Group compatibility and productivity. *Journal of Abnormal and Social Psychology, 65,* 190–196.

NHSME. (1992). *The nursing skill mix in district nursing.* London: HMSO.

Neuman, G. A., Wagner, S. H., & Christiansen, N. D. (1999). The relationship between work-team personality composition and the job performance of teams. *Group and Organization Management, 24,* 28–45.

Neuman, G. A., & Wright, J. (1999). Team effectiveness: Beyond skills and cognitive ability. *Journal of Applied Psychology, 84,* 376–389.

Orsburn, J. D., & Moran, L. (2000). *The new self-directed work teams: Mastering the challenge* (2nd ed.). New York: McGraw Hill.

Osterman, P. (1994). How common is workplace transformation and who adopts it? *Industrial and Labor Relations Review, 47*, 173–188.

Osterman, P. (2000). Work reorganization in an era of restructuring: Trends in diffusion and effects on employee welfare. *Industrial and Labor Relations Review, 53*, 179–196.

Ostroff, C. (2002). Levelling the selection field. In F. J. Yammarino & F. Dansereau (Eds.), *The many faces of multi-level issues* (pp. 141–154). New York: Elsevier Science/JAI Press.

Paris, C. R., Salas, E., & Cannon-Bowers, J. A. (2000). Teamwork in multi-systems: A review and analysis. *Ergonomics, 43*, 1052–1075.

Payne, R. L. (1990). The effectiveness of research teams: A review. In M. A. West & J. L. Farr (Eds.), *Innovation and creativity at work: Psychological and organizational strategies* (pp. 101–122). Chichester, UK: John Wiley & Sons.

Ployhart, R. E., & Schneider, B. (2002a). A multi-level perspective on personnel selection research and practice: Implications for selection system design, assessment, and construct validation. In F. J. Yammarino & F. Dansereau (Eds.), *The many faces of multi-level issues* (pp. 95–140). New York: Elsevier Science/JAI Press.

Ployhart, R. E., & Schneider, B. (2002b). A multi-level perspective on personnel selection: When will practice catch up? In F. J. Yammarino & F. Dansereau (Eds.), *The many faces of multi-level issues* (pp. 165–175). New York: Elsevier Science/JAI Press.

Reddy, W. B., & Byrnes, A. (1972). Effects of interpersonal group composition in the problem-solving behavior of middle managers. *Journal of Applied Psychology, 56*, 516–517.

Salminen, S. (1988). Two psychometric problems of the FIRO-B questionnaire. *Psychological Reports, 63*, 423–426.

Salminen, S. (1991). Convergent and discriminant validity of the FIRO-B questionnaire. *Psychological Reports, 69*, 787–790.

Schmitt, N. (2002). A multi-level perspective on personnel selection: Are we ready? In F. J. Yammarino & F. Dansereau (Eds.), *The many faces of multi-level issues* (pp. 155–164). New York: Elsevier Science/JAI Press.

Schutz, W. C. (1955). What makes groups productive? *Human Relations, 8*, 429–465.

Schutz, W. C. (1958). *FIRO: A three dimensional theory of interpersonal behavior.* New York: Holt Rinehart.

Schutz, W. C. (1967). *JOY: Expanding human awareness.* New York: Grove Press.

Schutz, W. C. (1992). Beyond FIRO-B – Three new theory-derived measures – Element B: Behavior, Element F: Feelings, Element S: Self. *Psychological Reports, 70*, 915–937.

Shaw, J. D., Duffy, M. K., & Stark, E. M. (2000). Interdependence and preference for group work: Main and congruence effects on the satisfaction and performance of group members. *Journal of Management, 26*, 259–279.

Shaw, M. E., & Webb, J. N. (1982). When compatibility interferes with group effectiveness. *Small Group Behavior, 13*, 555–564.

Staw, B. M., & Epstein, L. D. (2000). What bandwagons bring: Effects of popular management techniques on corporate performance, reputation, and CEO pay. *Administrative Science Quarterly, 4*, 523–559.

Stevens, M. J., & Campion, M. A. (1994). The knowledge, skill, and ability requirements for teamwork: Implications for human resource management. *Journal of Management, 20*, 503–530.

Stevens, M. J., & Campion, M. A. (1999). Staffing teams: Development and validation of a selection test for teamwork settings. *Journal of Management, 25*, 207–228.

Swailes, S., & McIntyre-Batty, T. (2002). The "Belbin" team role inventory: Reinterpreting reliability estimates. *Journal of Managerial Psychology, 17*, 529–536.

West, M. A. (Ed.). (1996). *The handbook of work group psychology.* Chichester, UK: John Wiley & Sons.

West, M. A. (2003). *Effective teamwork. Practical lessons from organizational research* (2nd ed.). Oxford, UK: Blackwell Publishing.

West, M. A. (2004). *The secrets of successful team management. How to lead a team to innovation, creativity and success.* London: Duncan Baird Publishers.

West, M. A., & Anderson, N. (1996). Innovation in top management teams. *Journal of Applied Psychology, 81,* 680–693.

West, M. A., & Markiewicz, L. (2003). *Building team-based working: A practical guide to organizational transformation.* Oxford: Blackwell Publishing Inc.

West, M. A., Tjosvold, D., & Smith, K. G. (Eds.). (2003). *International handbook of organizational teamwork and cooperative working.* Chichester, UK: John Wiley & Sons.

Wiersema, M. F., & Bantel, K. A. (1992). Top management team demography and corporate strategic change. *Academy of Management Journal, 35,* 91–121.

Williams, K. Y., & O'Reilly, C. A. (1998). Demography and diversity in organizations: A review of 40 years of research. *Research in Organizational Behavior, 20,* 77–140.

23

Multilevel Selection and Prediction: Theories, Methods, and Models

Robert E. Ployhart and Benjamin Schneider

If personnel selection is to remain a vibrant and important discipline of organizational science, it must adopt multilevel theories, methods, and models. To believe that effective selection procedures contribute to organizational effectiveness is to believe that the implications of personnel selection extend across levels of analysis. And yet other than research on utility theory (which only estimates such cross-level relationships), the vast majority of selection research has not examined this belief. What this means is that selection research may not be capable of answering many of the questions that extend beyond the individual level:

♦ We generally do not know whether knowledge, skill, ability, and other (KSAO)-criterion relationships established at the individual level generalize to higher levels. Do KSAOs cluster within units (e.g., groups, organizations)? Are units comprised of employees with more cognitive ability and higher levels of conscientiousness better performing units? Preliminary research finds both similar and different predictive relationships across levels (Chen & Bliese, 2002; Chen et al., 2002).

♦ Focusing validation efforts at the individual level may not identify important KSAO predictors of performance at higher levels. For example, the personality trait openness to experience shows little criterion-related validity at the individual level (Barrick, Mount, & Judge, 2001), but in aggregate predicts group-level performance (LePine, 2003).

♦ There is practically no information about whether and how individual performance aggregates to unit levels. For example, do supervisory ratings of individual job performance cluster within unit, and as a result explain unit-level differences in effectiveness (e.g., sales)? As Goodman (2000) has so eloquently shown, it is very difficult to make generalizations across levels anywhere, much less in personnel selection.

♦ Individual-level selection cannot model and explain higher-level constructs, processes, and contexts (e.g., diversity, unit effectiveness). Attempts to disaggregate these constructs into an individual-level model result in misspecification, cross-level, and contextual fallacies (see Ployhart, in press; Rousseau, 1985). Likewise, selection practitioners are often held accountable for unit-level results, but how are such cross-level relationships established?

♦ We know relatively little about the effects of culture on individual selection practices. If people within a culture share more similarities than those from different cultures, then to what extent will selection findings generalize across cultures (Herriot & Anderson, 1997)? Or for that matter, what level of cultural generalizability is possible (Anderson, 2003)? Research has shown organizational/cultural differences in selection practices (Ryan, McFarland, Baron, & Page, 1999; Terpstra & Rozell, 1993; Wilk & Capelli, 2003), but has not incorporated a multilevel perspective into design and analysis and may have little to say about *how* individual-level selection results generalize across cultures.

Reflecting on nearly a century of personnel selection research, it is quite troubling to us that we have no solid answers to these very basic questions, and approaches to answering the questions remain outside of traditional personnel selection research. We may be able to show how hiring better people contributes to better individual job performance, but we have hardly examined whether this contributes to be better unit-level performance. The major reason is because the selection discipline defines itself within a single, individual level of analysis. That is, selection research has focused primarily on an individual-level model where all of the key constructs, processes, and measures occur within this level (Binning & Barrett, 1989; Motowidlo, Borman, & Schmit, 1997; Schmitt, Cortina, Ingerick, & Wiechmann, 2003). Yet the unfortunate consequence is that we could be winning the battle (being successful at predicting individual-level performance) but losing the war (an inability to demonstrate our value to organizational effectiveness in a compelling manner). We appear to be mired in what Viteles (1932, p. 58) considered the epitome of industrial psychology 70 years ago: "The science of industrial psychology is largely the study of the ways in which individuals differ . . . In the selection of workers, for example, the chief consideration is the variation among applicants in the capacity for performing the work for which the choice is made."

We believe selection research and practice must become multilevel in theory and method. Indeed, multilevel theories, methods, and models help address many of the limitations of a single-level system, yet the amount of truly multilevel, empirical selection research is nearly non-existent. In this chapter we outline why and how a multilevel selection research study should be conducted. We first review theoretical arguments articulating the importance of a multilevel perspective, discuss the methods used to conduct and analyze such a study, and conclude with a vision of what selection research and practice might look like if it adopts these multilevel selection models.

Prior to visiting the models and methods available for cross-level selection theory and research, it is important to note that we are not revisiting the literature that has emerged on strategic human resources management (SHRM). The SHRM literature is not cross-level; it is unit level, with a focus on what organizations do in the way of HRM practices and how what organizations do relates to organizational effectiveness (cf., Huselid, 1995; Wright, Dunford, & Snell, 2001). Our concern here is with a continuation of a focus on individual differences with an extension to exploring alternative models that simultaneously incorporate multiple levels on the predictor and/or the criterion side of the equation.

CONCEPTUALIZING MULTILEVEL SELECTION

It is obvious that individual behavior is nested within, and affected by, influences from multiple levels: workgroup (e.g., coworkers), department (e.g., work schedules), organization (e.g., HR practices), region (e.g., labor pool), nation (e.g., laws), and culture (e.g., individualism–collectivism), among others. These levels exist in a hierarchy such that lower levels (groups) are nested within higher levels (organizations). Because organizations are inherently multilevel and hierarchical, they must conform to the same laws that govern all multilevel systems (see Kozlowski & Klein, 2000). To acknowledge that selection occurs within organizations is to acknowledge that selection must also be part of this multilevel system and adhere to these rules. As Leonardo DaVinci is claimed to have said, "Nature must obey her own laws." So must selection.

In brief, here are the reasons why selection research and practice must be multilevel. First, much of the basis for why we select individuals is to ensure organizational effectiveness and findings at a single level may not generalize to higher levels. Second, because selection regulates organizational entry, hiring people with particular combinations of KSAOs determines unit composition. According to the attraction–selection–attrition model (Schneider, 1987), such selection will contribute to within-unit homogeneity on those KSAOs and therefore between-unit KSAO differences. We should know how the consequences of this homogeneity cascade throughout the organization. Third, the determinants of performance may change across levels and focusing on the individual level may miss KSAOs important for performance at higher levels of analysis. Finally, when work is performed in interactive social contexts, such as team-based structures or service contexts, the performance (and thus determinants of performance) for an individual may be affected by one's coworkers and social context.

Therefore, the laws of multilevel systems affect selection even when hiring decisions are made for individual persons. Ployhart, Schneider, and colleagues (Ployhart, in press; Ployhart & Schneider, 2002; Schneider, Smith, & Sipe, 2000) have integrated levels of analysis theory and research with the research on organizational staffing to identify how selection fits within a multilevel system. They have presented a number of conceptual issues that we do not detail here. Rather, Figure 23.1 presents a very simple multilevel selection model useful for illustrating the key principles. The figure shows two levels, the individual level and the unit level (two levels are sufficient for illustrating the basic points, but more levels may obviously be added). The unit level may refer to a group or team, department, organization, country, and so on. Boxes in the figure represent manifest measures of either predictors or criteria. Individual-level predictors might involve tests of cognitive ability, personality, situational judgment, and so on, while individual-level criteria might involve supervisory ratings. At the unit level, predictor measures are often the aggregate of individual-level KSAOs, and criteria are often indices of aggregate performance or effectiveness.

As noted in Ployhart (in press), it is critical to recognize mediating processes in multilevel staffing research. We recognize such mediating processes at both levels and place all predictor measures on a distal-proximal continuum. Proximal constructs (e.g., motivation, goals, effort) are more highly related to job performance but are also more variable and

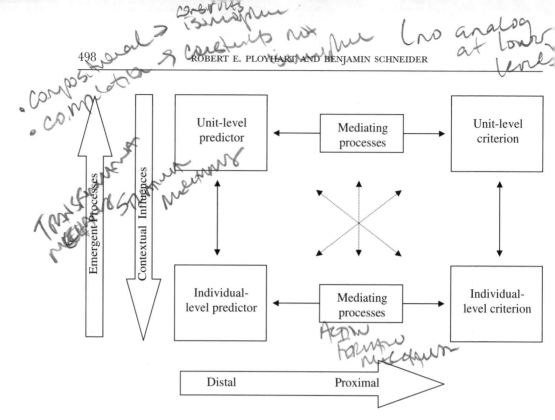

FIGURE 23.1   Sample multilevel selection framework. Note: dashed lines indicate weaker or less-examined relationships
Source: Adapted from Ployhart (in press); Ployhart & Schneider (2002).

state-like, compared to distal constructs (e.g., cognitive ability, personality) which are more stable and trait-like (George, 1992). At the individual level the emphasis is usually on assessing distal constructs because they are so stable, although it is critical to note that they are expected to operate through mediating processes such as motivation, choice, and knowledge (Campbell, 1990; Motowidlo et al., 1997; Schmitt et al., 2003). Thus, as one moves up levels, the direct effects of distal KSAOs become weaker because of the number of proximal mediating processes. For example, group research has shown that mediating processes such as group cohesion, coordination processes, and collective efficacy are critical proximal mediating processes through which aggregate KSAOs influence group performance (e.g., Marks, Mathieu, & Zaccaro, 2001). It follows that a very important implication of this distal-proximal distinction is that as one moves up levels, the direct effects of KSAOs – the variables on which selection research and practice has overwhelmingly focused – become continually weaker and mediated (Ployhart, in press). We note this important fact by symbolizing mediating processes in Figure 23.1.

The double-headed arrows in Figure 23.1 represent different forms of relationships within (horizontal) and across (vertical) levels. These arrows are double sided to recognize that "causal" direction may move in both directions. Horizontal arrows represent within-level relationships to indicate that causality may move from predictors to criteria or vice versa at higher levels of analysis (March & Sutton, 1997). For example, Schneider, Hanges,

Smith, and Salvaggio (2003) found that performance influenced aggregate attitudes, rather than the more typically theorized "attitudes influencing performance" sequence. These within-level relationships are estimated with traditional correlation coefficients, regression coefficients, or structural parameters. What is probably not understood is the meaning of the vertical arrows (we discuss diagonal arrows shortly). Here we must invoke multilevel principles because the nature of such cross-level relationships needs to be carefully articulated. We draw heavily from and summarize the terminology and models discussed in Kozlowski and Klein (2000). The cross-level relationships may take two general forms: contextual or emergence.

Contextual relationships. Contextual relationships are cross-level, top-down effects. Group cohesion, service climate, and culture are examples of psychological contextual effects because they are higher-level factors influencing an individual's behavior. For example, a retail employee may want to provide good service, but his/her service behavior is enhanced or constrained by the service climate within the store. Notice that in contextual models, the actions within the lower level of analysis are nested within the actions of the higher level. A consequence of this nesting is that individuals within a unit may share more similarities than individuals between units (it may also be said that individuals show more agreement with their own unit members than with members from other units). In statistical terms this is referred to as "non-independence of observations." To the extent non-independence is present, such as when group members share more similar values to each other than they do to other group members, standard errors are reduced and statistical significance tests tend to suffer from more Type I errors. The practical consequence is that when data are nested, it becomes difficult to place much faith in statistical significance tests and quite possibly the parameter estimates themselves. Bliese (2000) provides a clear summary of the statistical consequences of ignoring contextual effects, and we return to the statistical analysis of such data in a later section.

Emergent relationships. Emergent relationships are cross-level, bottom-up effects. For example, if we aggregate all individual KSAO scores within a group and create a group average KSAO score, we are modeling an emergent process. Emergence is therefore about how lower-level constructs and processes combine and aggregate to form higher-level constructs and processes. Notice a critical feature of emergent processes is that we may measure a construct at the individual level, but the level at which the construct is theorized to exist is at the unit level. If we obtain the KSAO scores of individuals within a team and relate these scores to individual indices of performance, both the measure and theory exist at the individual level. However, when we take those individual-level KSAO scores and aggregate them to create a single group-level KSAO composite, the level of measurement is at the individual level but the level of theory is at the group level.

How to best conceptualize and model emergent processes has been a longstanding problem in the organizational sciences. For example, to create the unit-level score, does one merely take the mean or variance of individuals' scores within a group? Should one focus on the score of the worst-performing member (conjunctive) or the highest-performing member (disjunctive)? Each of these ways of conceptualizing the unit-level score has a different substantive meaning and may show different relations to both individual and unit-level criteria (Barrick, Stewart, Neubert, & Mount, 1998). Klimoski and Jones (1995) and LePine, Hanson, Borman, and Motowidlo (2000) describe these various types of conceptualizations in some detail; the important point is that there are multiple ways of conceptualizing and operationalizing the unit-level score.

Fortunately, there have been several recent advances to aid in conceptualizing emergent processes. Kozlowski and Klein (2000) provide a thorough discussion of these issues and present a typology of various emergent models that lie on a continuum from *composition* to *compilation* (although Bliese, 2000, notes how the distinctions between such models are rarely clear, a term he calls "fuzzy composition models"). *Composition* models are models where the unit-level construct is isomorphic to the lower-level construct. Composition models therefore tend to be based on within-unit consensus or agreement, such as when the similarity of within-unit personality is used to justify a group average personality. There are multiple variations of composition models (see Chan, 1998; Kozlowski & Klein, 2000), but their primary common feature is a focus on the need for similarity of lower-level scores as a precondition for the aggregation of those scores to create unit-level scores. This means that the empirical justification supporting aggregation in composition models is an index of agreement or consensus (i.e., r_{wg}, intraclass correlations), and the typical unit-level score is the mean of the individual-level scores.

On the other hand, *compilation* models exist when the lower- and higher-level units represent conceptually different constructs. Diversity is an example of a compilation model because such a construct can only exist at the unit level; it has no corresponding analog at the lower level (Blau, 1977). Compilation models are assessed via indices of unit variance, dissensus, dissimilarity, or dispersion. It is not necessary to show agreement with compilation models because the concept of agreement has no meaning in this instance (Bliese, 2000). Rather, researchers would show the variability of unit members' scores, use the highest or lowest unit member score, or some other index of dispersion.

We conclude by noting a few additional characteristics of multilevel systems (see Kozlowski & Klein, 2000). There is a time asymmetry across levels, such that lower-level processes operate more quickly than higher-level processes. However, contextual effects tend to be stronger and operate more quickly than emergent effects. Because processes within the same level operate on the same time metric, within-level processes and relationships are stronger than cross-level processes and relationships. Finally, the larger the number of intermediate levels in a cross-level model, the weaker the direct effects from the lowest level to the highest level (or vice versa). So for example, the effect of a group on an individual should be stronger than the effect of an organization on an individual and the relationship of individual-level data to organizational performance would be expected to be weaker than the relationship between individual differences and individual performance (for exception, see Goodman, 2000).

CONDUCTING THE MULTILEVEL SELECTION STUDY

Table 23.1 provides an overview of the basic steps required to conduct a multilevel study. In deriving these steps, we have followed the advice of many excellent sources (Bliese, 2000; Chen, Bliese, & Mathieu, 2003; Chen, Mathieu, & Bliese, in press; Kozlowski & Klein, 2000). There are minimally ten steps required.

TABLE 23.1   Steps for conducting a multilevel selection study

Step	Procedures
1. Articulate the theory.	Describe the theoretical relationships within and across levels (single-level, cross-level, homologous multilevel). Determine appropriate forms of emergence (if relevant), such as type of composition or compilation model.
2. At what levels of theory and measurement are the criteria, and what is the nature of their relationship?	Articulate the level at which the criteria are expected to exist and the level at which they will be measured. Determine how to justify aggregation (e.g., type of composition or compilation model).
3. At what levels of theory and measurement are the predictors, and what is the nature of their relationship?	Articulate the level at which the predictors are expected to exist and the level at which they will be measured. Determine how to justify aggregation (e.g., type of composition or compilation model).
4. Specify the nature of within-level relationships.	Determine direction and strength of KSAO-performance relationships at each level.
5. Specify the nature of cross-level relationships (if appropriate).	Determine the types of contextual effects hypothesized (e.g., contextual influences moderating individual-level relationships; direct contextual effects on the criterion, etc.). In some instances, one might also hypothesize effects of individual predictors onto unit-level processes and criteria.
6. Sample the appropriate number of units at each level, over the appropriate time periods.	Ensures design will allow adequate test of within- and cross-level relationships.
7. Use appropriate measures.	For example, should individual-level measures of unit-level constructs contain a referent to oneself or the unit?
8. Test inferences of aggregation. Demonstrate sufficient within- and between-unit variability. Support inferences of aggregation (if necessary). Assess reliability of individual-level and unit-level variables.	Use ICC(1) to determine magnitude of unit-level variance. Assess whether aggregation is supported (e.g., estimate within-group consensus (r_{wg}) or dissensus). Determine reliability of individual-level variables and unit-level variables (using ICC(2)).
9. Analyze the data correctly.	Random coefficient modeling, growth modeling or lagged analyses, WABA, etc.
10. Interpret results.	Interpret results with careful consideration of generalizations across levels.

Step 1: Articulate the theory.   Like any sound research, multilevel selection research begins with a solid grounding in theory. Issues with levels are ultimately theories describing how constructs and processes interrelate within and across levels. There is a small but growing literature describing general conceptualizations of multilevel staffing. For example, at the team level there are several good sources for understanding the theoretical issues with selection into team settings (Klimoski & Jones, 1995; LePine et al., 2000). Schneider et al. (2000) and Ployhart and Schneider (2002) discuss a variety of cross-level issues with staffing, and these have been formally integrated and extended in a complete multilevel model of staffing by Ployhart (in press). This model formally integrates research on levels of analysis with the research on staffing across micro (selection), meso (group/team/department), and macro (HR practices and strategy) levels. The model proposes several "rules" that dictate how selection constructs and practices operate within and across levels, and provides a framework for conceptualizing selection within a multilevel system.

It is instructive to consider the various multilevel models that can assist in conceptualizing multilevel staffing theory. Kozlowski and Klein (2000) propose three classes of models, summarized in Figure 23.2. *Single-level models* are models where the constructs and processes are contained entirely within one level. The typical individual-level selection study is one example, but so is a study where the focus is only on group KSAO composition and group performance (in this case, individual-level measures of KSAOs may be assessed, but there is no interest in them other than to aggregate to the group level). *Cross-level models* are models where the constructs and processes cross at least two levels. For example, an examination of contextual factors, such as how group KSAO composition can influence individual-level validity and performance, would illustrate a cross-level model. Notice in Figure 23.2 that there are two types of cross-level effects. Effect 1 is a contextual moderator of a lower-level predictive relationship and effect 2 is a contextual main effect directly onto the lower-level criterion. Finally, *homologous multilevel models* are models where the same set of predictive relationships are present at each level. For example, we may expect the relationship between individual-level personality and individual-level performance to be the same or similar to group aggregate personality and group aggregate performance. Note that there are many variations within these three classes of models; readers should consult Kozlowski and Klein (2000) to consider other forms and Ployhart (in press) for selection examples.

Steps 2 & 3: Determine the level of theory and the level of measurement for the criteria (Step 2) and predictors (Step 3).   The fundamental concerns here involve determining the theory at which criterion and predictor constructs are hypothesized to exist, how lower-level and higher-level constructs will be measured, and how these constructs might be related to each other across the levels.

For example, one might have a theory arguing that aggregate store-level cognitive ability contributes to store-level sales. However, before aggregating the individual-level cognitive ability scores to the store level, one must first determine whether such a unit-level construct makes conceptual sense. What kinds of processes might contribute to homogenization of cognitive ability within stores? One possibility is through attraction–selection –attrition processes (Schneider, 1987). Notice that this is fundamentally a question about the emergent properties of cognitive ability. The answer to this question determines which

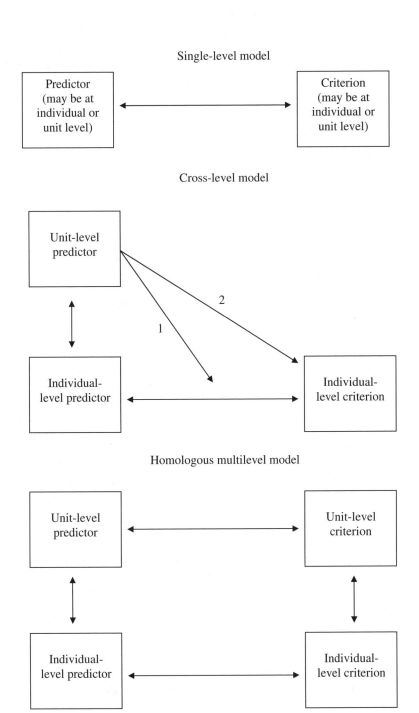

FIGURE 23.2   Different types of multilevel models (note: mediating processes have been excluded from the figure)

form of composition should take place (note – it is not compilation because the meaning of store-level cognitive ability is relatively isomorphic to individual-level cognitive ability). So for example, one may draw from Kozlowski and Klein (2000) and refer to this as a "convergent" composition model because the nature of the construct is isomorphic across levels and the emphasis is on sharedness. A consequence of choosing this type of composition model is that the unit-level predictor construct will be represented by the mean of the within-store cognitive ability scores, and empirical justification for aggregation will occur through the use of within-group agreement indices like ICC(1) and r_{wg}.

This thought process must take place for the criteria and predictor separately because different forms of aggregation may be appropriate on different sides of the equation. For example, we may use unit average cognitive ability as our predictor in a manner noted above, but use average store monthly sales as the criterion which exists only at the store level (i.e., the level of theory and measurement are at the same level). Alternatively, we may ask store managers to provide a rating of the store's cohesiveness, and in this instance the level of measurement is at the store level because the manager's responses are operating as "indicators" of the store-level construct. This last point brings attention to an important issue in multilevel research – the level of analysis that is the referent for the items. We return to this issue in Step 7.

Step 4: Specify the nature of within-level relationships. This is an extension of the individual-level predictive hypothesis, but the focus is now on determining whether such effects will occur in similar forms across levels. Perhaps the class of multilevel models that best speaks to this issue is the homologous multilevel model in Figure 23.1. Suppose we want to know whether store-level cognitive ability predicts store-level effectiveness on a magnitude similar to criterion-related validities found for cognitive ability at the individual level. One cannot simply assume that such relationships exist at the same magnitude because this violates numerous multilevel principles (Rousseau, 1985), and the sparse empirical literature available argues against this possibility (Bliese, 2000). Further, the multilevel selection model of Ployhart (in press) suggests that the presence of mediators will increase, and direct effects of KSAOs will decrease, as one moves up levels of analysis. So this seemingly innocent step actually represents a rather difficult problem for researchers.

An added complication to estimating effect sizes across levels is that the size of the higher-level unit influences the magnitude of the observed within-level correlations (Bliese, 1998). All else being equal, units with more members produce larger correlations because the aggregate unit-level variables are measured more reliably. Thus, there is a positive relationship between unit size and reliability, and the magnitude of the correlations observed. Bliese (2000) describes a simple procedure for correcting differences in unit size that should be considered when formulating and testing homologous models. Chen, Bliese, and Mathieu (Chen et al., 2003, in press) have described a number of steps and analytic methods for hypothesizing and detecting such homologous multilevel models. Chen et al. (2003) present a typology of homologous models helpful for answering many multilevel selection questions.

Step 5: Specify the nature of cross-level relationships. While the previous step focused only on within-level (horizontal) relationships, this step focuses on cross-level (vertical or diagonal) relationships. For example, those vertical and diagonal dashed arrows drawn in the middle of Figure 23.1 illustrate potential cross-level relationships. However, here we are not interested in forms of composition or compilation, but rather theoretical "causal" relationships between predictors and criteria across levels. Most often the emphasis will be on contextual influences. For example, we might attempt to test whether local economic conditions (a contextual influence) influence the relationship between individual perceptions of fit and individual perceptions of organizational attractiveness. The economic condition is a contextual effect because applicants are nested within their local economies. One might find that when the local economy is strong, there is a strong relationship between fit and attractiveness, but when the economy is weak fit is unrelated to attractiveness. We might further find that economic conditions produce a direct effect on attractiveness, such that poor economies make all jobs more attractive.

Notice in this last hypothesis the importance of studying the direct effect of contextual factors on lower-level criteria. This point has implications for validity generalization research and has been well described by Schneider et al. (2000). They argue that validity generalization (and meta-analysis) is essentially a cross-level moderator model, where variability in individual-level predictive relationships is examined across multiple units. This is shown by effect 1 in the cross-level model in Figure 23.2. However, they suggest that it is worth while also to examine whether unit differences exist on the criterion itself – a unit-level main effect. This is shown as effect 2 in Figure 23.2. Whether the effect exists for the moderator or main effect, both are examples of cross-level linkages, but validity generalization research examines only the moderator effect.

Step 6: Sample the appropriate number of observations over the appropriate number of time periods. This step is absolutely critical to ensure any possibility of detecting higher-level and cross-level effects. It also poses the greatest difficulty connected with conducting multilevel selection research in practice. As we noted earlier, the effect sizes for unit-level correlations are highly affected by the number of members within each unit (Bliese, 1998), and it is vital that sufficient numbers of units and individuals within each unit are present. But note an important point – it is the number of units *and* individuals within each unit that is critical. To study contextual effects with just two organizations will be difficult unless there are large numbers of people nested within each organization. So with fewer numbers of higher-level units we need more people nested within each unit; with larger numbers of higher-level units we need fewer people nested within each unit.

One sampling issue that becomes even more important in multilevel research is sampling across reasonable numbers of time periods. The reason is that different levels operate on different time scales (higher levels move more slowly), and there is a time asymmetry such that contextual effects happen more quickly than emergent effects. When one studies single-level relationships, time is obviously important but at least all of the processes are operating within a similar timeframe (and thus the consequences of doing cross-sectional research may be "more forgiving"). But in the multilevel study, cross-sectional research may very well underestimate effect sizes for contextual and emergent influences. For example, we may need to conduct studies where the unit-level contextual factor is measured months or years before the lower-level constructs to allow adequate time for the contextual factor to influence lower-level processes. Similarly, the more a composition model is based on consensus, the more time may need to elapse before the consensus composition model is present.

Schneider and colleagues have given many reasons for thinking about time in selection research. The ASA model (Schneider, 1987) predicts that, through the processes of attraction, selection, and attrition, organizations become increasingly homogeneous. This clearly occurs over time, and one could further predict that all else being equal, homogeneity is positively related to time. Similarly, Schneider et al. (2003) conducted a multiyear organizational-level study and demonstrated that in contrast to prevailing theory, it appears that unit-level performance exerts a stronger influence on unit-level attitudes than the reverse. Yet even more compelling in their work is the demonstration that the relationships between employee attitudes and organizational performance in any one-year period supported the opposite, that attitudes drive performance. This study highlights the importance of modeling processes over the relevant periods of time if causal ordering is of interest.

As organizational researchers, we often must live with the data that are available. It is oftentimes difficult to collect multilevel or multi-wave data. However, thanks to computers and database software, organizations are increasingly collecting massive amounts of data that span multiple levels and time periods. Indeed, nearly all studies linking unit-level perceptions to unit-level outcomes are based on archival databases. Like astronomers looking to the stars and testing their theories with strong models, so too can the selection scholar look to the digital twilight within the organizational database and test theories with strong multilevel, multi-wave models.

Step 7: Use appropriate measures.   Here, if the use of individual perception data is required, all the usual suggestions for item writing apply, but with one additional consideration – the item may reference either the individual or the unit. For example, if we intend to assess a unit-level construct like group collective efficacy, we might change an individual efficacy item such as "I believe *I* can effectively perform the task" to "I believe *my group* can effectively perform the task" or, perhaps even more appropriately, "My *group* believes it can effectively perform the task." This shift in referent is likely to enhance the within-unit agreement and between-unit differences for an aggregate score (Klein, Conn, Smith, & Sorra, 2001). The nature of the construct and form of composition model dictate whether such an approach is appropriate (Chan, 1998). However, as Kozlowski and Klein (2000) note, even in the absence of such unit-level referents, composition and within-unit agreement may still occur. When there are higher-level contextual factors that produce a within-unit nesting or clustering of observations, homogeneity may be found regardless of the item referent.

A different issue with multilevel measurement is whether one assesses higher-level constructs through the use of aggregation, or through the use of informants operating at the level of the construct. For example, SHRM studies often survey HR managers and ask them about their HR practices (e.g., use of selection, training, etc.). These "informant" scores are used to characterize the organizational-level "HR practice" construct. Thus, an individual may provide the response, but s/he is representing the organization as a whole. The key is to ensure that the informant actually answers the question from the appropriate perspective (using the appropriate referent in the items), and that the informant truly has knowledge of the constructs at the higher level. Using informants is not without potential limitations, however, and issues such as rater reliability and validity are still relevant (Gerhart, Wright, McMahan, & Snell, 2000).

Finally, it is obvious that some measures useful in selection studies may neither require nor permit aggregation. Suppose, for example, that like Schneider et al. (2003), the criterion of interest is ROA (return on assets) or EPS (earnings per share) and the predictor data concern aggregate cognitive test scores for organizations. ROA and EPS are organizational phenomena so the issue of aggregation is not relevant, though if the project is multi-wave the stability of ROA and EPS over time may be relevant.

Step 8: Test inferences of aggregation (if relevant).   So far we have described the theory and methods for conducting the multilevel study; the remaining steps focus on statistical inferences. There is a great deal of confusion regarding different multilevel statistical concepts (e.g., types of intraclass correlations, reliability versus agreement, etc.). Many advances have been made in recent years to help resolve these issues and provide a more coherent set of recommendations (in particular, Bliese, 1998, 2000, 2002; Klein & Kozlowski, 2000). In Step 8 we address the issue of empirically testing the amount of agreement/consensus, and hence supporting inferences of aggregation. Here we draw heavily from Bliese's suggestions and our own experiences for what types of indices support aggregation. Specifically, there are multiple indices that should routinely be reported: within-group agreement (r_{wg}), within-group variance, and the intraclass correlations – ICC(1) and ICC(2).

This first index we consider is r_{wg}. It is a useful estimate of within-group agreement or consensus (James, Demaree, & Wolf, 1984); it is a measure of absolute agreement. There are multiple variations of this basic index representing either single-item indices (r_{wg}) or multi-item indices ($r_{wg(j)}$), but for our purposes we refer to them similarly. As a measure of within-unit absolute agreement, this index is calculated for each unit and hence it will be possible to estimate absolute agreement for each unit (as well as the variability in agreement across units). The values range from zero to one, with higher numbers indicating more agreement. Many researchers use a .70 cutoff as a justification for aggregation (Klein et al., 2000), but this is merely a rule of thumb. Note that if this minimum threshold is reached, aggregation in terms of taking the within-unit average of scores is warranted. Thus, r_{wg} indices help determine whether it is appropriate to average (aggregate) within-unit scores to a unit-level score.

R_{wg} essentially compares the variance of within-unit scores to some hypothesized "null" variance estimate; the latter is typically based on a uniform distribution as would occur when there is no agreement. This null distribution is actually chosen by the researcher, but other distributions may be used (e.g., skewed distributions) depending on the substantive nature of the question. The ability of the researcher to choose these null distributions is both a blessing and a curse. It is a blessing because it allows the researcher to think about the nature of within-unit variance; it is a curse because it forces the researcher to think and thus requires more effort to implement! Bliese (2000) provides some useful suggestions for choosing the appropriate null distribution (e.g., modeling different types of null distributions, use of "pseudogroups" through random group resampling procedures; see also James et al., 1984; Kozlowski & Hults, 1987). Lindell and colleagues (Lindell & Brant, 1997; Lindell, Brandt, & Whitney, 1999) report a number of additional considerations when choosing a null distribution.

The second index examines variability or disagreement within units. Such variability may be important in the development and justification of compilation models (Kozlowski & Klein, 2000). In situations where dissensus or dispersion are of interest, one might use estimates of within-group average deviation indices (Burke & Dunlap, 2002) or the within-group standard deviation (Klein et al., 2001). These indices are simply estimates of the amount of within-unit variability expressed in variance or standard deviation units. One benefit of this approach is that no assumptions for a null distribution are necessary; one simply calculates the within-unit variability. Dispersion indices are calculated for each unit and will be negatively related to r_{wg}. Although these indices are related, they do not represent the same construct and it may be instructive to examine both within-unit agreement and variability. For example, within-unit agreement results in aggregating scores to a unit-level mean, while disagreement indices result in aggregating scores to a unit-level variance. One can find instances where the unit-level variance predicts performance beyond the unit-level mean (Bliese & Halverson, 1998) or moderates the relationship between the unit-level mean and unit-level performance (Schneider, Salvaggio, & Subirats, 2002).

The final indices are different versions of the intraclass correlation coefficient (ICC). Both the ICC(1) and the ICC(2) provide an overall single index – there is no ICC value specific to each unit. That is, ICCs are estimates for variables (e.g., a predictor or criterion measure) but not units. When calculated on the *criterion*, the ICC(1) examines the extent to which there is a contextual effect in the criterion scores, or stated differently, the extent to which there is a clustering or non-independence in the data. ICC(1) values can range from different numbers depending on whether one uses a one-way random effects analysis of variance procedure (range -1 to $+1$) or a random coefficient model (range 0 to 1). We focus on the latter because modeling such data with random coefficient models (RCM) leads naturally to the assessment of contextual effects and modeling non-independence. When modeled using RCM, the ICC(1) is a ratio of the between-group variance over the sum of within- and between-group variance.

Therefore, ICC(1) values closer to 1 indicate a stronger contextual effect for the individual-level criterion, i.e., criterion values tend to have lower within-group variance and higher between-group variance. An equal but alternative interpretation is that the ICC(1) estimates how much variance in the lower-level criterion construct can be explained by higher-level factors. Suppose we conduct an ICC(1) analysis on the lower-level criterion score and obtain a value of .15. This means that some of the variance in the individual-level criterion is "explained" by contextual factors, and up to 15% of the variance in this individual-level criterion may be accounted for by such factors. Bliese (2000) notes that it is rare to find ICC(1) values greater than .30, and one may test the statistical significance of the ICC(1).

Note that so far we have only discussed calculating ICC(1) values on the criterion. Bliese (2000) notes that the interpretation of the ICC(1) is different when it is performed on *predictor* scores. Even though the analytic procedure is the same, the ICC(1) for predictors is typically used to assess reliability of the predictor scores to determine whether one can reliably aggregate the score to the unit level. So when the ICC(1) is calculated on predictor scores, it determines whether aggregation is warranted. Because the calculation of

ICC(1) is the same regardless of whether or not it has been accomplished on the predictor or the criterion, it can also be used on the predictor side to explore contextual effects. For example, in Schneider, Smith, Taylor, and Fleenor (1998) it was shown that personality data for individuals yielded a significant ICC(1), suggesting a contextual effect for how individuals cluster into organizations à la the ASA framework.

The ICC(2) is a direct estimate of the reliability of the unit-level mean; it describes the reliability of the aggregate unit-level score (not whether aggregation is warranted). Because it represents reliability, traditional cutoffs (e.g., .70) seem a reasonable place to start. Note that the ICC(2) has the same interpretation for both predictors and criteria. See Bliese (2000, 2002) for how to calculate these indices.

To summarize, we have multiple indices to help us determine whether aggregation is justified, and to test whether our hypothesized model of emergence is correct. At the risk of oversimplifying:

- Use r_{wg} to estimate within-unit absolute agreement. This determines whether there is sufficient agreement to use a unit mean representing within-unit scores, as prescribed by a composition model. Values greater than .70 indicate that aggregation is warranted.
- Use within-unit variance to estimate within-unit dispersion. This determines whether there is sufficient variability to use the unit variance as a unit-level construct, as prescribed by compilation models.
- Use ICC(1) to estimate the extent to which there is non-independence in the criterion, and the extent to which the predictor scores can be reliably aggregated. Statistical significance of ICC(1) values support inferences of non-independence/reliability.
- Use ICC(2) to estimate the extent to which the unit-level mean is reliable. Values greater than .70 are minimal.
- Always report ICC(1) and ICC(2), and either r_{wg} (if proposing composition) or within-unit variance (if proposing compilation).

Step 9: Analyze the data correctly. Step 8 helps support various forms of aggregation, but Step 9 involves the tests of within- and cross-level effects. The Klein and Kozlowski (2000) book on levels of analysis describes in detail several statistical methods, including random coefficient models (RCM), within and between analysis (WABA), and the cross-level operator (CLOP). The appropriate uses and implementation issues with each are well described in that volume. Here we focus on what in our experience has been the most relevant statistical models – the familiar correlation and the RCM.

It may be surprising that after all of the "complexity" of multilevel modeling, the traditional correlation (or regression) coefficient remains remarkably useful. It is, and in fact it has the same interpretation regardless of the level at which it is calculated. Therefore, studies that attempt to show how organizational attitudes are related to organizational outcomes use the same correlation coefficient as studies that link individual KSAOs to individual performance. As such, the correlation can be used to estimate "validity" at each level, and this is a powerful idea because it allows the assessment of criterion-related validity at different levels. But recognize that our indicator of criterion-related validity – the correlation coefficient – can be computed only within a single level of analysis. This is an important point; the correlation does not allow us to make inferences to higher levels (and also creates an inherent limitation for utility analysis).

More advanced statistical techniques are necessary if the theoretical model proposes cross-level effects (moderators or direct effects). Here is where the RCM becomes so important. It is perfectly suited for testing contextual factors that may influence the individual-level predictive relationship. RCM is a fairly elaborate statistical technique, but it is still based on regression principles and should be quite accessible to most selection researchers. There are many excellent introductions to RCM that provide the technical details (Bliese, 2002; Bryk & Raudenbush, 1992); here we consider only the main features of the model (note: we use the term RCM, rather than hierarchical linear modeling, HLM, because HLM is a software package while RCM is the term that refers to a general class of random effects models).

The benefits of RCM are that it can model non-independence and provide the correct parameter estimates and significance tests, estimate and test within- and between-unit variability in lower-level relationships, and handle both missing data and units of varying sizes. Let us illustrate the approach with a simple example. Suppose we want to determine whether the validity of individual personality with individual performance differs across countries (where country is either a moderator or direct effect). This model would appear as the cross-level model in Figure 23.2. If we ignore the presence of country variables in the data, we essentially combine all data into a single analysis and regress performance onto personality (this would test a single-level model). But if we know there is a clustering or degree of non-independence of personality within countries (whether due to shared culture, language, laws, etc.), individual predictor and/or criterion scores within country will not be independent and thus effect sizes and significance tests may be affected. Therefore, we can test whether there are between-country differences in the intercept (a direct effect, effect 2 in Figure 23.2) and slope (a moderator, effect 1 in Figure 23.2) of the RCM. This is the equivalent of running a separate regression in each country and recording the intercept and slope parameters in each country. The means for the intercept and slope parameters represent the overall average intercept and validity, and the variance in these parameters represents the amount of variability across countries. To the extent that there are between-country differences in intercepts and/or slopes, we can attempt to explain them. For example, individualism–collectivism may explain these between-country differences such that there is no between-country variability once we control for culture.

When the research question specifies a homologous multilevel model, the RCM approach will not be appropriate. There are some reasonably well-established multilevel structural equation modeling approaches capable of handling the homologous multilevel modes, but a procedure proposed by Chen et al. (2003; in press) provides a more straight-forward alternative.

Beyond models that accommodate non-independence and cross-level effects, it is also important that the analytic method be able to model time. Linkage research has tended to use cross-lagged models (Schneider et al., 2003). Another alternative is to use the RCM growth model (Sacco & Schmitt, 2003). Bliese and Ployhart (2002) and Ployhart, Holtz, and Bliese (2002) provide non-technical introductions to RCM growth models.

Step 10: Present and interpret results. The final step in the multilevel study is the write-up and interpretation of the results. Here we wish to emphasize the importance of clearly articulating what levels of generalization are possible. For example, if one conducts a single-level study, it is inappropriate to claim that the results will generalize across levels (it is acceptable to speculate, of course). Likewise, if modeling a cross-level effect, it is important to remember that the effect could itself be influenced by a higher-level contextual factor, and the effect sizes may be affected by the number of units and individual-level observations. Finally, it is paramount to report summary statistics and results in the appropriate manner. In terms of summary statistics, report the sample size, means, standard deviations, and correlations *within* each level. In terms of results from a multilevel study that involves aggregation, minimally report agreement (r_{wg}) or dispersion (within-group variability) indices, and always the ICC(1) and ICC(2).

UPWARDS AND ONWARDS: A GLIMPSE INTO THE MULTILEVEL SELECTION FUTURE

The incorporation of a multilevel orientation into personnel selection offers the opportunity to examine a number of questions previously considered "unreachable." We leave readers with a set of questions we believe are the most pressing needs for multilevel selection research.

What are the primary KSAO determinants of performance across levels? Recent research on team KSAO composition and performance is suggesting that some predictors of performance are only apparent at the unit level. In particular, agreeableness and openness to experiences appear to show stronger (but mediated) effects at the team level (relative to the individual level) because they relate to the kinds of social and interpersonal mediating processes important for team performance (LePine, 2003; Neuman & Wright, 1999). Yet little support exists for using these predictors at the individual level (Barrick et al., 2001). To determine whether the individual-level selection model has missed important KSAOs such as openness to experiences, we can conduct a homologous multilevel study (Chen et al., 2003, in press; Sacco, 2003), but notice that we will need to include measures of personality (agreeableness and openness) even though they appear to have no relationship to performance at the individual level!

Do KSAOs aggregate to higher levels, and what are the consequences of such KSAO composition? The ASA model predicts within-unit personality homogeneity (Schneider, 1987), and while the consequences of such homogeneity have been hypothesized to exist at the unit level, there might be individual-level consequences as well. Note that the homogeneity hypothesis is essentially a composition model of emergence. Using a large sample of managers, Schneider et al. (1998) demonstrated that personality is indeed homogeneous within organizations and industries (as evidenced by ICC(1)). But we need to determine the nature of this composition. Might different SHRM practices create different types of composition?

Of course, in the arena of various fit models, Holland (1997) has shown for years that a) people with similar vocational interests tend to join vocations with others who share their interests, b) shared interests in vocations create career environments, and c) individuals who fit those environments best are more satisfied in them. It seems time to extend this line of inquiry to other KSAOs such as cognitive ability and personality.

How are meta-analysis and RCM related?   Notice an important implication of the cross-level model in Figure 23.2 – there may be a direct contextual effect on the criterion. This is Schneider et al.'s (2000) contention that contextual effects may still be present even when there is no contextual moderator and "validity generalizes." Such an effect would not be found in a traditional validity generalization study because of its focus only on slope differences. This leads one to wonder how meta-analysis and validity generalization might be conceptualized within a multilevel modeling framework. What if we conceptualize meta-analysis as a contextual cross-level model (e.g., RCM)? Notwithstanding the various artifact corrections, meta-analysis is essentially an RCM moderator model (effect 1 in Figure 23.2). Would an RCM result in the same point estimates and conclusions as derived from meta-analysis? Is the search for a cross-level interaction the same as the search for moderators in meta-analysis? How is nesting related to sampling variability? Many questions to keep researchers out of trouble for years!

Would modeling cross-cultural data with RCM better estimate the effects of culture?   An important question facing modern organizations is the extent to which selection practices transport across cultures (Herriot & Anderson, 1997). But beyond general issues of national culture, Anderson (2003) notes five different degrees of cultural generalizability (e.g., organization specific, country specific). Following from the previous points, might a better way to determine the cross-cultural generalizability of selection findings be to model the data with RCM, such that individuals are nested within organizations, which are nested within countries, which are nested within levels of culture? Such a model would allow one to separate the effects of organizations from culture, and model the effects of context on individual-level measures. For example, the RCM approach would allow one to test whether culture has a moderating effect on criterion-related validity, a direct effect on performance, or both.

How does one model diversity in a selection model?   Diversity is inherently a unit-level construct; it has no isomorphic representation at the individual level. This means that to examine diversity in selection, one needs to consider diversity and selection from a multilevel perspective: KSAOs and performance criteria may exist at the individual level, but diversity and its consequences exist at the unit level (although diversity may also influence individual-level criteria; Ployhart & Schneider, 2002; Ployhart, in press). A recent study by Sacco and Schmitt (2003) provides support for this perspective. Using a compilation model of diversity, they found that store-level racial diversity was negatively related to store-level indices of profitability, due in part to the greater turnover present in the more diverse locations. Further, they found that the match of store diversity to local customer diversity was unrelated to profitability. Clearly more research of this kind is necessary, but the results point to a number of innovative findings that could only have been discovered with multilevel theorizing (see also Sacco, Scheu, Ryan, & Schmitt, 2003).

Should the RCM replace the familiar regression model as our preferred analytical system?   The typical regression model is just one specific type of RCM, but as we have noted, RCM can handle a variety of nested and multilevel data structures that violate the usual regression assumptions. As a result, there may be a variety of selection problems for which RCM is better suited than fixed effects regression. For example, there has been so much research conducted on using regression to estimate differential prediction (effects of heterogeneity, power, etc.); might research start to compare RCM to regression to see if RCM is more useful? It may very well be a more powerful method for identifying group differences when the individuals within those groups are nested, non-independent, or have different variances. As another example, can RCM estimate objective fit better than existing approaches? Edwards (2002) has noted many limitations with assessing fit using difference scores and has proposed an alternative polynomial approach. But might the RCM be an even better alternative? For example, use an informant or internal organizational data to provide an estimate of the organization's values. Assess applicants' perceptions of their personal values. Because applicants are nested within the organization, organizational values can be modeled as a contextual variable and we can determine through the cross-level moderator whether fit has an effect. We can also determine whether the organizational context has a direct effect on the dependent variable (e.g., attraction, job choice).

Conclusion

To ignore the nested nature of selection within a multilevel system is to ignore the very basis of organizational science. We might select individuals, but who we select and how we select and how they will actually perform on the job are based on processes that evolve within a multilevel organizational system. The reason selection must become multilevel is apparent in the very reason organizations use selection procedures: we hire better employees with the expectation that doing so contributes to group and organizational behavior and effectiveness. This leaves nearly the entire selection profession in the undesirable position of having to assume that these relationships exist. Do organizations that hire superior candidates perform in superior ways? We do not know the answer. Do superior candidates or superior management and organizational practices produce superior organizational performance? We do not know the answer. This state of affairs cannot continue and it need not continue because we have the conceptual and statistical models and methods to do better.

References

Anderson, N. (2003). *The future of selection and assessment: Toward a globalized science and practice.* Keynote Address to the 5th Australian Industrial and Organizational Psychology Conference, Melbourne Australia.

Barrick, M. R., Mount, M. K., & Judge, T. A. (2001). Personality and performance at the beginning of the new millennium: What do we know and where do we go next? *International Journal of Selection and Assessment, 9,* 9–30.

Barrick, M. R., Stewart, G. L., Neubert, M. J., & Mount, M. K. (1998). Relating member ability and personality to work-team processes and team effectiveness. *Journal of Applied Psychology*, *83*, 377–391.

Binning, J. F., & Barrett, G. V. (1989). Validity of personnel decisions: A conceptual analysis of the inferential and evidential bases. *Journal of Applied Psychology*, *74*, 478–494.

Blau, P. (1977). *Inequality and heterogeneity*. New York: Free Press.

Bliese, P. D. (1998). Group size, ICC values, and group-level correlations: A simulation. *Organizational Research Methods*, *1*, 355–373.

Bliese, P. D. (2000). Within-group agreement, non-independence, and reliability: Implications for data aggregation and analysis. In K. Klein & S. W. J. Kozlowski (Eds.), *Multilevel theory, research, and methods in organizations: Foundations, extensions, and new directions* (pp. 349–381). San Francisco: Jossey-Bass.

Bliese, P. D. (2002). Multilevel random coefficient modeling in organizational research: Examples using SAS and S-PLUS. In F. Drasgow & N. Schmitt (Eds.), *Measuring and analyzing behavior in organizations: Advances in measurement and data analysis* (pp. 401–445). San Francisco: Jossey-Bass.

Bliese, P. D., & Halverson, R. R. (1998). Group consensus and psychological well-being: A large field study. *Journal of Applied Social Psychology*, *28*, 563–580.

Bliese, P. D., & Ployhart, R. E. (2002). Growth modeling using random coefficient models: Model building, testing, and illustration. *Organizational Research Methods*, *5*, 362–387.

Bryk, A. S., & Raudenbush, S. W. (1992). *Hierarchical linear models: Applications and data analysis methods*. Newbury Park, CA: Sage.

Burke, M. J., & Dunlap, W. P. (2002). Estimating interrater agreement with the average deviation index: A user's guide. *Organizational Research Methods*, *5*, 159–172.

Campbell, J. P. (1990). Modeling the performance prediction problem in industrial and organizational psychology. In M. Dunnette & L. M. Hough (Eds.), *Handbook of industrial and organizational psychology* (2nd ed., Vol. 1, pp. 687–732*)*. Palo Alto, CA: Consulting Psychologists Press.

Chan, D. (1998). Functional relations among constructs in the same content domain at different levels of analysis: A typology of composition models. *Journal of Applied Psychology*, *83*, 234–246.

Chen, G., & Bliese, P. D. (2002). The role of different levels of leadership in predicting self- and collective efficacy: Evidence for discontinuity. *Journal of Applied Psychology*, *87*, 549–556.

Chen, G., Bliese, P. D., & Mathieu, J. E. (2003). *Conceptual framework and statistical procedures for delineating and testing multilevel theories of homology*. Paper presented at the Academy of Management, Seattle, WA.

Chen, G., Mathieu, J. E., & Bliese, P. D. (in press). A framework for conducting multilevel construct validation. In F. Dansereau & F. J. Yammarino (Eds.), *Research in multi-level issues: The many faces of multi-level issues* (Vol. 3). Oxford, UK: Elsevier Science.

Chen, G., Webber, S. S., Bliese, P. D., Mathieu, J. E., Payne, S. C., Born, D. H., et al. (2002). Simultaneous examination of the antecedents and consequences of efficacy beliefs at multiple levels of analysis. *Human Performance*, *15*, 381–410.

Edwards, J. R. (2002). Alternatives to difference scores: Polynomial regression analysis and response surface methodology. In F. Drasgow & N. Schmitt (Eds.), *Measuring and analyzing behavior in organizations: Advances in measurement and data analysis* (pp. 350–400). San Francisco: Jossey-Bass.

George, J. M. (1992). The role of personality in organizational life: Issues and evidence. *Journal of Management*, *18*, 185–213.

Gerhart, B., Wright, P. M., McMahan, G. C., & Snell, S. A. (2000). Measurement error in research on human resources and firm performance: How much error is there and how does it influence effect size estimates? *Personnel Psychology*, *53*, 803–834.

Goodman, P. S. (2000). *Missing organizational linkages: Tools for cross-level research*. Thousand Oaks, CA: Sage.

Herriot, P., & Anderson, N. (1997). Selecting for change: How will personnel and selection psychology survive? In N. R. Anderson & P. Herriot (Eds.), *International handbook of selection and assessment.* London: Wiley.

Holland, J. L. (1997). *Making vocational choices: A theory of vocational personalities and work environments* (3rd ed.). Odessa, FL: PAR.

Huselid, M. A. (1995). The impact of human resource management practices on turnover, productivity, and corporate financial performance. *Academy of Management Journal, 38,* 635–672.

James, L. R., Demaree, R. J., & Wolf, G. (1984). Estimating within-group interrater reliability with and without response bias. *Journal of Applied Psychology, 69,* 85–98.

Klein, K. J., Bliese, P. D., Kozlowski, S. W. J., Dansereau, F., Gavin, M. B., Griffin, M. A., et al. (2000). Multilevel analytical techniques: Commonalities, differences, and continuing questions. In K. J. Klein & S. W. J. Kozlowski (Eds.), *Multilevel theory, research, and methods in organizations: Foundations, extensions, and new directions* (pp. 512–553). San Francisco: Jossey-Bass.

Klein, K. J., Conn, A. B., Smith, D. B., Sorra, J. S. (2001). Is everyone in agreement? An exploration of within-group agreement in survey responses. *Journal of Applied Psychology, 86,* 3–16.

Klein, K. J., & Kozlowski, S.W.J. (2000). *Multilevel theory, research, and methods in organizations: Foundations, extensions, and new directions.* San Francisco: Jossey-Bass.

Klimoski, R. J., & Jones, R. G. (1995). Staffing for effective group decision making: Key issues in matching people to teams. In R. Guzzo, E. Salas, & Associates (Eds.), *Team effectiveness and decision making in organizations* (pp. 291–332). San Francisco: Jossey-Bass.

Kozlowski, S. W. J., & Hults, B. M. (1987). An exploration of climates for technical updating and performance. *Personnel Psychology, 40,* 539–569.

Kozlowski, S. W. J., & Klein, K. J. (2000). A multilevel approach to theory and research in organizations: Contextual, temporal, and emergent processes. In K. J. Klein & S. W. J. Kozlowski (Eds.), *Multilevel theory, research, and methods in organizations: Foundations, extensions, and new directions* (pp. 3–90). San Francisco: Jossey-Bass.

LePine, J. A. (2003). Team adaptation and postchange performance: Effects of team composition in terms of members' cognitive ability and personality. *Journal of Applied Psychology, 88,* 27–39.

LePine, J. A., Hanson, M. A., Borman, W. C., & Motowidlo, S. J. (2000). Contextual performance and teamwork: Implications for staffing. In G. Ferris (Ed.), *Research in Personnel and Human Resources Management* (Vol. 19, pp. 53–90). Oxford, UK: Elsevier.

Lindell, M. K., & Brandt, C. J. (1997). Measuring interrater agreement for ratings of a single target. *Applied Psychological Measurement, 21,* 271–278.

Lindell, M. K., Brandt, C. J., & Whitney, D. J. (1999). A revised index of interrater agreement for multi-item ratings of a single target. *Applied Psychological Measurement, 23,* 127–135.

March, J. G., & Sutton, R. I. (1997). Organizational performance as a dependent variable. *Organization Science, 8,* 698–706.

Marks, M. A., Mathieu, J. E., & Zaccaro, S. J. (2001). A temporally based framework and taxonomy of team processes. *Academy of Management Review, 26,* 356–376.

Motowidlo, S. J., Borman, W. C., & Schmit, M. J. (1997). A theory of individual differences in task and contextual performance. *Human Performance, 10,* 71–83.

Neuman, G. A., & Wright, J. (1999). Team effectiveness: Beyond skills and cognitive ability. *Journal of Applied Psychology, 84,* 376–389.

Ployhart, R. E. (in press). Organizational staffing: A multilevel review, synthesis, and model. In G. R. Ferris & J. Martocchio (Eds.), *Research in personnel and human resource management* (Vol. 23). Oxford, UK: Elsevier.

Ployhart, R. E., Holtz, B. C., & Bliese, P. D. (2002). Longitudinal data analysis: Applications of random coefficient modeling to leadership research. *Leadership Quarterly, 13,* 455–486.

Ployhart, R. E., & Schneider, B. (2002). A multi-level perspective on personnel selection research and practice: Implications for selection system design, assessment, and construct validation. In F. J. Yammarino & F. Dansereau (Eds.), *The many faces of multi-level issues: Research in multi-level issues* (Vol. 1, pp. 95–140). Oxford, UK: Elsevier.

Rousseau, D. M. (1985). Issues of level in organizational research: Multi-level and cross-level perspectives. In L. L. Cummings & B. Staw (Eds.), *Research in organizational behavior* (Vol. 7, pp. 1–37). Greenwich, CT: JAI Press.

Ryan, A. M., McFarland, L., Baron, H., & Page, R. (1999). An international look at selection practices: Nation and culture as explanations for variability in practice. *Personnel Psychology, 52,* 359–391.

Sacco, J. M. (2003). *Validating personality and ability tests in customer service jobs at the business unit level.* Unpublished manuscript.

Sacco, J. M., Scheu, C. R., Ryan, A. M., & Schmitt, N. (2003). An investigation of race and sex similarity effects in interviews: A multilevel approach to relational demography. *Journal of Applied Psychology, 88,* 852–865.

Sacco, J. M., & Schmitt, N. (2003). *The relationship between demographic diversity and profitability: A longitudinal study.* Paper presented at the 18th annual conference of the Society for Industrial and Organizational Psychology, Orlando, FL.

Schmitt, N., Cortina, J. M., Ingerick, M. J., & Wiechmann, D. (2003). Personnel selection and employee performance. In W. C. Borman, D. R. Ilgen, & R. J. Klimoski (Eds.), *Handbook of psychology: Industrial and organizational psychology* (Vol. 12, pp. 77–105). New York: John Wiley & Sons.

Schneider, B. (1987). The people make the place. *Personnel Psychology, 40,* 437–453.

Schneider, B., Hanges, P. J., Smith, D.B., & Salvaggio, A. N. (2003). Which comes first: Employee attitudes or organizational financial and market performance? *Journal of Applied Psychology, 88,* 836–851.

Schneider, B., Salvaggio, A. N., & Subirats, M. (2002). Climate strength: A new direction for climate research. *Journal of Applied Psychology, 87,* 220–229.

Schneider, B., Smith, D.B., & Sipe, W. P. (2000). Personnel selection psychology: Multilevel considerations. In K. J. Klein & S. W. J. Kozlowski (Eds.), *Multilevel theory, research, and methods in organizations: Foundations, extensions, and new directions* (pp. 3–90). San Francisco: Jossey-Bass.

Schneider, B., Smith, D.B., Taylor, S., & Fleenor, J. (1998). Personality and organizations: A test of the homogeneity of personality hypothesis. *Journal of Applied Psychology, 83,* 462–470.

Terpstra, D. E., & Rozell, E. J. (1993). The relationship of staffing practices to organizational level measures of performance. *Personnel Psychology, 46,* 27–48.

Viteles, M. S. (1932). *Industrial psychology.* New York: Norton.

Wilk, S. L., & Capelli, P. (2003). Understanding the determinants of employer use of selection methods. *Personnel Psychology, 56,* 103–1242.

Wright, P. M., Dunford, B. B., & Snell, S. A. (2001). Human resources and the resource based view of the firm. *Journal of Management, 27,* 701–721.

Author Index

Numbers in *italics* indicate pages in reference lists.

Subject Index